English History

An Enthralling Story of England, from Ancient Times through the Medieval Period and the Tudors to the Dawn of the Modern Age

© Copyright 2024 - All rights reserved.

The content contained within this book may not be reproduced, duplicated, or transmitted without direct written permission from the author or the publisher.

Under no circumstances will any blame or legal responsibility be held against the publisher, or author, for any damages, reparation, or monetary loss due to the information contained within this book, either directly or indirectly.

Legal Notice:

This book is copyright protected. It is only for personal use. You cannot amend, distribute, sell, use, quote, or paraphrase any part, or the content within this book, without the consent of the author or publisher.

Disclaimer Notice:

Please note the information contained within this document is for educational and entertainment purposes only. All effort has been executed to present accurate, up-to-date, reliable, and complete information. No warranties of any kind are declared or implied. Readers acknowledge that the author is not engaging in the rendering of legal, financial, medical, or professional advice. The content within this book has been derived from various sources. Please consult a licensed professional before attempting any techniques outlined in this book.

By reading this document, the reader agrees that under no circumstances is the author responsible for any losses, direct or indirect, that are incurred as a result of the use of the information contained within this document, including, but not limited to, errors, omissions, or inaccuracies.

Free limited time bonus

Stop for a moment. We have a free bonus set up for you. The problem is this: we forget 90% of everything that we read after 7 days. Crazy fact, right? Here's the solution: we've created a printable, 1-page pdf summary for this book that you're reading now. All you have to do to get your free pdf summary is to go to the following website: https://livetolearn.lpages.co/enthrallinghistory/

Or, Scan the QR code!

Once you do, it will be intuitive. Enjoy, and thank you!

Table of Contents

PART 1: THE HISTORY OF ENGLAND 1
   INTRODUCTION 2
   CHAPTER 1: PREHISTORY AND THE BRONZE AGE 3
   CHAPTER 2: THE CELTS 11
   CHAPTER 3: ROMAN BRITAIN 19
   CHAPTER 4: THE ANGLO-SAXONS 28
   CHAPTER 5: THE VIKING RAIDS AND THE FORMATION OF ENGLAND 36
   CHAPTER 6: THE NORMAN CONQUEST 45
   CHAPTER 7: THE PLANTAGENETS 52
   CHAPTER 8: THE HUNDRED YEARS' WAR AND THE BLACK DEATH 62
   CHAPTER 9: THE WARS OF THE ROSES 70
   CHAPTER 10: THE TUDORS AND THE ENGLISH REFORMATION 79
   CHAPTER 11: ELIZABETH I 87
   CHAPTER 12: THE STUARTS 95
   CHAPTER 13: THE CIVIL WARS AND THE PROTECTORATE 103
   CHAPTER 14: RESTORATION AND THE UNION WITH SCOTLAND 110

CHAPTER 15: EIGHTEENTH-CENTURY BRITAIN: EXPANSION, WARS, AND REVOLUTIONS 119

CHAPTER 16: THE UNION WITH IRELAND 127

CHAPTER 17: THE VICTORIAN ERA 136

CHAPTER 18: WORLD WAR I AND II 143

CONCLUSION 151

PART 2: MEDIEVAL ENGLAND 153

INTRODUCTION 154

CHAPTER 1: EARLY MIDDLE AGES (600-1066) 156

CHAPTER 2: HIGH MIDDLE AGES (1066-1272) 167

CHAPTER 3: LATE MIDDLE AGES (1272-1485) 176

CHAPTER 4: THE ANGLO-WHO? 187

CHAPTER 5: SOCIETAL STRUCTURE 195

CHAPTER 6: STATUS OF WOMEN 202

CHAPTER 7: FOOD, CLOTHES, WORK, AND ENTERTAINMENT 209

CHAPTER 8: ART AND ARCHITECTURE 218

CHAPTER 9: ROYALTY THROUGHOUT THE MIDDLE AGES 228

CHAPTER 10: LAW AND ORDER 236

CHAPTER 11: FAITH AND RELIGIOUS IDENTITY 244

CHAPTER 12: ROLE OF THE CHURCH: CHURCH AND STATE 252

CHAPTER 13: KEY BATTLES THAT SHAPED MEDIEVAL HISTORY 260

CHAPTER 14: MEDIEVAL MYTH 268

CHAPTER 15: MEDIEVAL MEDICINE 277

CHAPTER 16: THE BLACK DEATH 286

CONCLUSION 295

PART 3: THE HOUSE OF TUDOR 297

INTRODUCTION 298

SECTION ONE: ENGLAND BEFORE THE HOUSE OF TUDOR 301

CHAPTER 1: ENGLAND BEFORE THE TUDORS 302

CHAPTER 2: THE ORIGINS OF THE HOUSE OF TUDOR 312

CHAPTER 3: THE TUDORS' RISE TO POWER 323
SECTION TWO: MONARCHS AND ROYALTY (1485-1603) 334
CHAPTER 4: HENRY VII (R. 1485-1509) 335
CHAPTER 5: HENRY VIII (R. 1509-1547) 345
CHAPTER 6: EDWARD VI (R. 1547-1553) 358
CHAPTER 7: MARY I (R. 1553-1558) 370
CHAPTER 8: ELIZABETH I (R. 1558-1603) 380
SECTION THREE: MILITARY AND WARFARE 390
CHAPTER 9: WARS AND BATTLES 391
CHAPTER 10: THE MILITARY AND THE ROYAL NAVY 401
CHAPTER 11: TUDOR WEAPONS 412
SECTION FOUR: LIFE IN TUDOR ENGLAND 424
CHAPTER 12: POLITICS AND ECONOMY 425
CHAPTER 13: SOCIETY AND EDUCATION IN TUDOR ENGLAND ... 433
CHAPTER 14: RELIGION AND THE CHURCH 442
CHAPTER 15: CULTURE AND ART 451
CHAPTER 16: DAILY LIFE IN TUDOR ENGLAND 461
CONCLUSION 470
PART 4: EARLY MODERN ENGLAND 473
  INTRODUCTION 474
  CHAPTER 1: WHO WERE THE TUDORS? 477
  CHAPTER 2: WHO WERE THE STUARTS? 485
  CHAPTER 3: THE MONARCHY IN EARLY MODERN ENGLAND 493
  CHAPTER 4: KEY ENGLISH FIGURES FROM 1485 TO 1714 510
  CHAPTER 5: THE RENAISSANCE 520
  CHAPTER 6: THE REFORMATION AND HENRY VIII 530
  CHAPTER 7: EXPLORATION AND TRADE 540
  CHAPTER 8: PROTESTANTISM AND ITS GROWTH 547
  CHAPTER 9: LAW(S) AND ORDER 555
  CHAPTER 10: REVOLUTION AND REBELLION 563

CHAPTER 11: SOCIETAL STRUCTURE 573
CHAPTER 12: BATTLES AND WARS ABROAD 581
CHAPTER 13: SCOTLAND AND WALES 589
CHAPTER 14: THE IRISH QUESTION 598
CHAPTER 15: CONQUEST AND COLONIZATION 608
CHAPTER 16: THE CONTINUATION OF THE EMPIRE 616
CONCLUSION 625
HERE'S ANOTHER BOOK BY ENTHRALLING HISTORY THAT YOU MIGHT LIKE 629
FREE LIMITED TIME BONUS 630
BIBLIOGRAPHY 631

Part 1: The History of England

An Enthralling Overview of English History

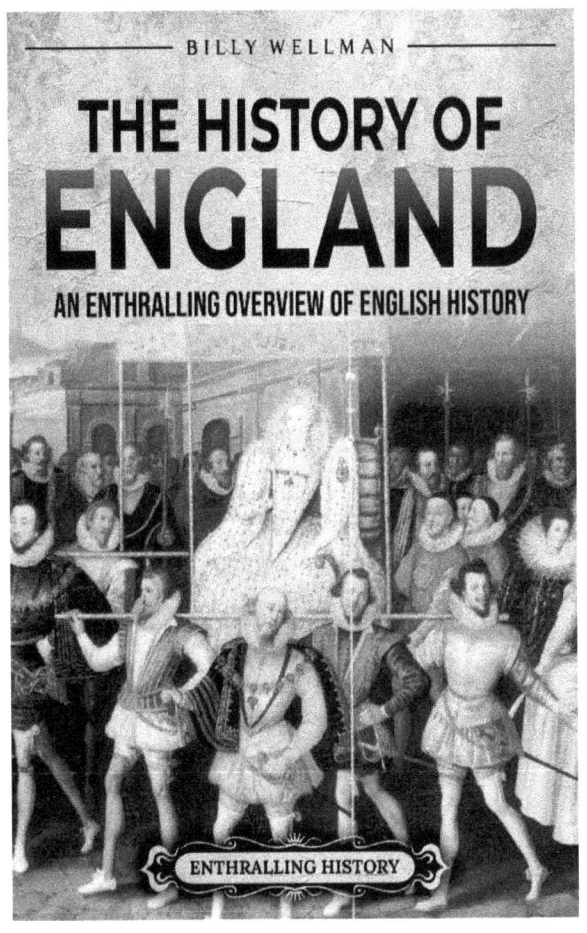

Introduction

The history of England is an enormous topic that we will discover has neither a set beginning nor end. From its origins as a nation to its presence in the modern day, enough has happened in England's history to fill countless volumes.

To discuss all those events is not possible, nor is it the goal of this book. The process of writing any history, and most especially the history of an entire country, inevitably requires that some things fall by the wayside. Therefore, this book seeks to give an overall picture of the major events that shaped the emergence of England as a nation and its growth and development. In these pages, you will learn things like who lived in England before the English, how England was formed, how its government developed, how the British Empire formed, and more.

What you won't find here are extensive biographies of every monarch or a detailed explanation of every major battle. While there will be plenty of interesting facts and fascinating details throughout, this book aims to be comprehensive rather than all-encompassing. It's an easy-to-understand guide to a long and complex topic. By the time you finish, you will have a working knowledge of the entire history of England!

Whether you are interested in the Roman Empire, Vikings, warfare, politics, kings and queens, exploration, or something else entirely, there's something in England's storied history for you. So, let's dive into the story of a nation that started on a small island and went on to profoundly impact the entire globe.

Chapter 1: Prehistory and the Bronze Age

Where does history start? If we are setting out on a tour of the history of England, where should we begin? The question of where to start history may sound philosophical, but it tends to be answered practically. We may believe that the history of England began with the beginning of time itself, but we will find ourselves extremely limited in our ability to discuss this because of a lack of information. For the historian, then, history begins with information—but what information, exactly? Information comes in many different forms, but the type of information we specifically use to define history is the written record. When written records begin, so does history.

Of course, there are problems with this approach. For one, records came into existence at vastly different times in various parts of the world. This means history starts at different times depending on where you are. The other problem is larger. Civilization doesn't necessarily start with writing. Many groups developed sophisticated cultures based on oral traditions.

If we begin history with the written record, what do we do with all the people and things that happened before written records appeared in a particular area? The answer is deceptively simple. We just don't call it history. Prehistory is the study of the past before written records. It does not mean the people living in this time were primitive or that not much was happening. It does mean we don't know as much about this time and are often forced to speculate about what we know.

Historians like written records because they are clear. Even when they are biased and misleading, written records offer clarity that makes piecing together the story of the past plausible. When looking at prehistory, we are forced to rely on very different sources. Archaeologists are the experts of prehistory. The burial sites, monuments, and relics of the past are all we have to complete the puzzle of what was happening before anyone started writing things down.

As we mentioned earlier, various cultures started using writing at different times. So, looking specifically at the history of England, when was that? For England, history starts in 43 CE with the Roman conquest, which brought the Latin language and writing. Technically, you could push this date back about a century to 55 BCE with Julius Caesar's *Commentaries on the Gallic Wars*. This is the first written description we have of Britain.

Even if we start with 55 BCE, that still leaves a lot of English prehistory to cover. Who did the Romans conquer? Who was living in England (otherwise known as Britain) before 43 CE, and what were they like? In the first two chapters of this book, we will cover the enormous time span that makes up Britain's prehistory before the Roman invasion.

Prehistory is typically divided into three main eras: the Stone Age, Bronze Age, and Iron Age, named for the materials that humans at that time used to fashion tools, weapons, and other objects. In this chapter, we will be taking a tour of the Stone and Bronze Ages.

The Stone Age

History begins with information, and prehistory is the same way, so what information do we have about the very beginnings of Britain? As you might suspect, the answer is not much. We know very little about the period referred to as the Stone Age, which covers roughly 800,000 BCE to 2000 BCE. Since it covers such a massive amount of time, the Stone Age is further subdivided into the Paleolithic, Mesolithic, and Neolithic eras, which mean Old, Middle, and New Stone Ages, respectively.

The Paleolithic era was not a happening time in Britain. It lasted from around 800,000 BCE to 10,000 BCE. This was the time of the Ice Age, and Britain's northern location meant that for large chunks of time, the island was uninhabitable for humans. However, "island" is not the right word to use, as it is believed that Britain was a peninsula connected to mainland Europe. Britain's connection to Europe is what allowed humans to travel there in the first place, but the extreme cold of the Ice Age prevented Britain from becoming a major hub of human activity in this period.

By the Mesolithic era, which lasted from around 10,000 BCE to 4000 BCE, things had started to warm up—so much so that sea levels rose and Britain began its existence as an island. With warmer temperatures, the island could sustain far more life. The humans who lived in Britain in the Mesolithic era were hunter-gatherers. They often moved with the seasons, following their food sources, but there is also evidence of small settlements.

Around 4000 BCE, farming came to the shores of England, and the Neolithic era began. The Neolithic era lasted from about 4000 BCE to 2000 BCE. It is thought that farming came to Britain through people migrating from the continent.

Farming had a profound impact on Britain and its people because it allowed a settled lifestyle that was impossible when people had to follow their food sources around. In the Neolithic era, we thus see an increase in the number of settlements.

Farming also causes humans to interact differently with their environment. Forests were cleared to make room for fields and pastures. The more permanent nature of farming communities also led to the construction of barrows and other monuments. With farming, humans were, for the first time, bending their environment to their will. They were still at the mercy of Mother Nature, but now that they were settling in one place, they had time to build. The Neolithic era witnessed the construction of stone circles, henges, mounds, and more. Stonehenge was built toward the end of the Neolithic age. We will discuss these mysterious monuments in more detail later in the chapter.

That's the gist of the Stone Age. England moved from being a frozen chunk connected to mainland Europe to an island with hunter-gatherers and then farmers.

The Bronze Age

In roughly 2000 BCE, metalworking arrived in Britain and began the period known as the Bronze Age. Metalworking began with copper and gold, but bronze (an alloy of copper and tin) is harder. By 2200 BCE, it was the metal of choice for making tools and weapons.

What we know about the Bronze Age is based on what managed to survive long enough for us to find it. This means we know a lot about burial practices because many graves from this era remained undisturbed. In the early Bronze Age, people in Britain buried their dead under barrows (shaped mounds of earth). These barrows and the graves they covered were often placed near other constructions like Stonehenge, creating large areas that appear to have been for solely ceremonial purposes.

A photograph of Stonehenge, Wiltshire, England in 2011.
Tristan J. Wilson, CC0, via Wikimedia Commons:
https://commons.wikimedia.org/wiki/File:TJDW_Stonehenge_20111107.tif

Another interesting thing to note about the barrows is that this is the first time we see large individual graves in Britain. The dead in these barrows were often buried with grave goods, as well. The fact that Bronze Age people took the time to build elaborate constructions for certain graves shows that some people were viewed as more important than others, indicating the establishment of a social hierarchy. Later in the period, cremation became more common, and our knowledge of burial practices dwindles through the remainder of the Bronze Age.

Other information we have gleaned about the Bronze Age through archaeological findings relates to the living rather than the dead. We know that roundhouses, which were round, single-room dwellings with a thatched roof, appeared in this era. We also see small groupings of houses, indicating the establishment of communities, and the earliest construction of hillforts, which suggests that warfare between rival communities had also begun. During this period, there was even trade with the continent, especially in metal.

With communities came other aspects of human society, such as hierarchies, warfare, and trade. Once humans in Britain began to settle down, they quickly began to acquire land and goods, and with this came the basic problem of economics: scarcity. There are not infinite resources, so inevitably some people have more than others. This results in social elites—those who have more—and warfare, as groups resort to taking what they don't have. Trade also emerges as a way of gaining resources that are not easily accessible.

Trade, hierarchy, and warfare existed in the Stone Age, but they began to increase in the Bronze Age as farming increased populations and created a surplus of time and resources. When the Bronze Age ended and the Iron Age began around 800 BCE, the importance of these aspects of human society in Britain only increased.

Stonehenge and Other Constructions

One of the most fascinating aspects of Britain's prehistory is easily the mysterious stone circles built during the period, many of which remain standing to this day. How and why did prehistoric peoples construct these massive monuments?

Stonehenge, located in southwest England, is by far the most famous of Britain's remaining stone circles. Before we go any further, let's answer the pressing question and admit that we don't know why Stonehenge was built. There are myriads of theories. Some say Stonehenge was part of druid rituals (although this is highly unlikely because Stonehenge predates the druids). Others believe it to be an ancient calendar since it is perfectly aligned with the movement of the sun. It could also be a monument to the dead, a gathering place, or a place of healing. In short, we don't know.

There's more to the mystery of Stonehenge besides its purpose, though. Another pressing question is just how prehistoric peoples managed to build it. Stonehenge was constructed over hundreds of years beginning in the Neolithic era around 3000 BCE and ending in the Bronze Age around 1500 BCE. The monument includes far more than just the central stone circle. It is surrounded by a circular earthwork henge, including two round barrows to the north and south and many others nearby. A series of holes surround the monument, and a few solitary stones are carefully positioned in relation to the movement of the sun. The Stonehenge area thus appears to be a sacred site rather than just a singular monument.

The idea that there is something special about the location of Stonehenge is furthered by the effort it undoubtedly took to get the stones to that location. Stonehenge consists of two types of stones: sarsen stones and bluestones. The sarsen stones are the large, shaped stones that make the post-and-lintel (two stones forming pillars with a stone on top) parts of the monument, and the bluestones are the smaller stones. Bluestones are only found in South Wales, which is over a hundred miles away from Stonehenge. Something was special enough about that location to make prehistoric people find a way to lug those enormous stones hundreds of miles.

There's a lot we don't know about Stonehenge, and the mystery is part of the fun. However, Stonehenge is also important for what it tells us about the people of prehistoric Britain. We know that they were capable of planning and executing projects that took many generations and a lot of manpower. We know they must have had some engineering knowledge because they could raise and place the stones. We know they had advanced astronomical knowledge because it is aligned with the movement of the sun. What Stonehenge tells us is that Britain's prehistoric people were far more advanced than the stereotypical cavemen we might be tempted to picture.

Of course, while it is the most famous, Stonehenge is far from the only stone circle or monument dating to Britain's prehistoric era. There are many stone circles scattered around Britain. This seems to indicate a large degree of shared culture across the island. But, since we don't know what the stone circles were used for, it is difficult to draw many conclusions about what the culture was like.

Stone circles are not the only large building projects from this period. Large tombs, hillforts, and earthwork henges and barrows are all evidence of this society's construction capabilities. These extensive building projects show us that by 3000 BCE and beyond, humans in Britain had figured out how to survive well enough to have time for building things for ceremonial and sacred importance. Even from our earliest history, humans have felt a drive to go beyond survival.

Piecing Together Prehistory

As mentioned and observed, what we know about prehistory comes from what people left behind. This means that while we know a lot about what prehistoric people had, trying to figure out why they had it and how they used it is a trickier task. How do we piece together the puzzle of prehistory from the remnants that remain today?

Butser Ancient Farm is a place in present-day England that is trying new ways to answer this question. The farm is an experimental archaeological site and open-air museum where reconstructions of ancient-style houses and farms are created. The researchers at Butser Ancient Farm recreated these buildings using the same tools prehistoric peoples had access to. They also make weapons, plant crops, take care of animals, and more, all using only the tools ancient people would have had.

Besides giving visitors a chance to see what prehistoric life might have looked like, the research at Butser Ancient Farm is crucial to examining how prehistoric peoples might have lived. By doing the same tasks with the same tools, researchers can at least begin to answer the question of how people lived. For example, researchers have established that it was possible to pull plows from the era using cows and produce enough grain to have a surplus for export using the agricultural techniques of the day. Of course, all these experiments can establish is plausibility, but plausibility gives us a much clearer picture of prehistoric life than we previously had.

What remains elusive about the prehistoric age is religion and culture. This was a period of oral traditions, which unfortunately means we know virtually nothing about what these people believed. We don't know why they built Stonehenge and other stone circles, what stories they told each other, what gods they believed in, or how they worshiped. Technically, we don't even know if they had gods or a form of worship.

Not knowing things for sure does not mean we cannot speculate based on archaeological findings, however. The discovery of a mummified body in the bogs of northwest England led to such speculation. Lindow Man, as the body was dubbed, was found in 1984. The body was that of a young man, and all that was left was a head, torso, and foot. He died sometime near the end of the Iron Age.

Lindow Man is puzzling because of the excessive violence that apparently caused his death. A garrote was around his neck, he had suffered blows to the head, and he had been stabbed. Any one of these three things would have killed him, so the multiple causes of death have led many to speculate that there was something more ritualistic about Lindow Man's death than plain murder. Some believe this was part of an elaborate execution. Others think Lindow Man may have been a religious sacrifice, perhaps even a willing one as his remains show no signs of a struggle.

Lindow Man and Butser Ancient Farm are both examples of how our knowledge of British prehistory continues to grow. Discoveries are still being made, and as we gather new information, we are forced to reevaluate our assumptions, leading to new speculations and conclusions about this era. The far reaches of Britain's past remain mysterious, but continuous research has allowed us to have a general idea of Britain's human beginnings.

Chapter 2: The Celts

Who were the first Britons? So far, we have simply referred to the people living on the island as the people in Britain, but who were they? The very first Britons don't have a name. We know they came from the continent, but the part of the continent they came from and who exactly they were remains a mystery. In the Stone and Bronze Ages, large tribes had yet to form. The people who migrated from the mainland of Europe to the British Isles were a disparate group we cannot lump together into a single identity.

The first group to settle in Britain that we assign a name to are the Celts. Celtic people and Celtic culture dominated Britain through the Iron Age and the arrival of the Romans, and their impact in the region can still be seen today, particularly in Cornwall, Scotland, and Wales, where Celtic languages are still spoken. But who exactly were the Celts? Where did they come from, and what were they like?

Who Were the Celts?

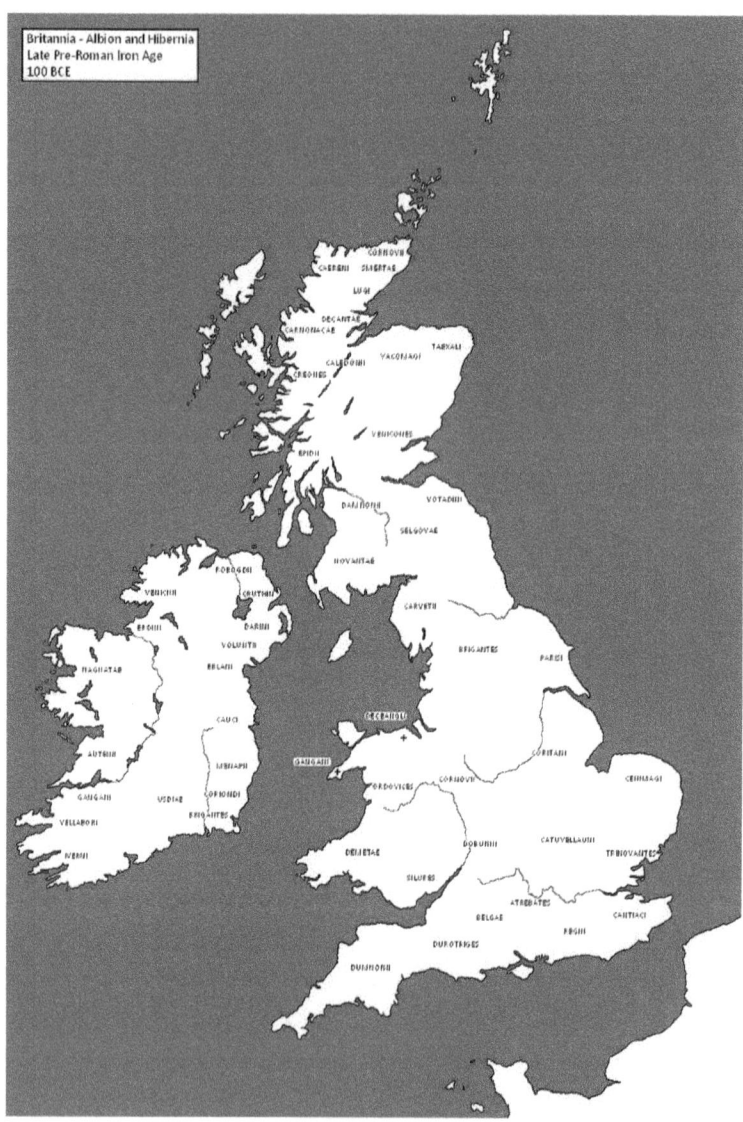

Map of Iron Age Britain.
Ulysses1975, CC BY-SA 3.0 <https://creativecommons.org/licenses/by-sa/3.0>, via Wikimedia Commons:https://commons.wikimedia.org/wiki/File:Map_-_Peoples_of_Britain_and_Ireland_100BCE.JPG

The Celts are a somewhat difficult group to define, largely because they are not a single group. The first archaeological evidence of the Celts' existence appears in central Europe, where they traded with the Greeks.

In fact, the word "Celt" comes from the Greek word *Keltoi*, which means "barbarian."

The Greeks believed that they were the only civilized culture. Since they tended to view all foreigners as barbarians, the word "Celt" is a rather broad term that refers to the entire group of varying tribes and clans of central Europe. The Celts likely saw themselves as disparate groups, but in the eyes of outsiders, like the Greeks, the culture and appearance of the tribes were close enough to lump them all together.

From central Europe, the Celts spread westward and eastward, eventually reaching as far west as Spain and the British Isles. As the Celts spread to different areas and were made up of different tribes, they acquired different names. The Celts who settled in the area that became modern-day France were known as the Gauls. Those who settled in Ireland and Scotland were the Gaels (from which the Gaelic languages are derived), and the Celts who settled in what would become modern-day England and Wales were the Britons.

Like the name "Celt," the subdivisions "Gauls," "Gaels," and "Britons" were assigned to the Celtic tribes by outsiders. The Britons, for instance, consisted of several different Celtic tribes, such as the Iceni and the Belgae. The name "Briton" is derived from the name the Greek explorer Pytheas gave the islands. Pytheas called the islands "Pretannike," from the Celtic word *Pretani*, which means "painted people." It is unclear if this is what the Celts called themselves, it was a name for a particular group, or something else. The *p* eventually changed to a *b*, and by the time of the Roman conquests, the Romans were calling the island "Britannia." The tribes living there were dubbed "Britons."

What does all this information about names have to do with understanding who the Celts were, though? For one, it is helpful to clarify that the term "Celtic" refers to many different groups (Britons, Gauls, Gaels, and more). Secondly, these groups were named by outsiders and did not see themselves as a single entity. The various tribes fought each other. The Celts spread and dominated Europe in the Iron Age, but they were not an empire in the sense that Rome would soon become. Finally, knowing the origin of some of these names teaches us the surprising fact that the Britons were not the original inhabitants of Britain. They were the Celtic tribes that migrated to the island of Britain in the Iron Age. They were technically invaders just like the Romans, Anglo-Saxons, Vikings, and Normans that would come after them.

England is, if nothing else, a land settled by outsiders.

You may be wondering, then, if the Celts were made up of different tribes, why we bother talking about them as a group. The Celts shared several commonalities in their culture that make it worth discussing them collectively.

Celtic Culture

Despite being made up of many warring tribes, the Celts shared a language, religious practices, art style, and other things that make a discussion of Celtic culture both possible and informative.

Perhaps the largest factor uniting the various tribes that made up the Celts was language. This does not mean that all the Celtic tribes across Europe in the Iron Age spoke the same language. Rather, their languages are all derived from a common source (Celtic). All the groups likely began speaking a common version of Celtic, but as they migrated and spread, the language evolved into different languages with a shared root.

The Celtic languages can be divided into two major groups: those spoken on the continent and those spoken on the British Isles. Unfortunately, we know little about the continental Celtic languages as these languages became extinct and we have few, if any, surviving examples of them. Perhaps because of their isolation, the Celtic languages of the British Isles survived far better. These languages include the British Celtic languages (derived from the Brittonic language used in the Iron Age and Roman period) of Welsh, Cornish, and Breton, and the Goidelic languages of Irish, Scottish Gaelic, and Manx. In the continued existence of these Celtic languages, we can see the perseverance of Celtic culture. This was the first group to inhabit Britain that would become an essential part of England's cultural heritage.

Another shared aspect of Celtic culture was religious beliefs. The Celts did not regularly build temples or statues of their gods, but they showed a belief in the sacred and the afterlife. Celts gave offerings and sacrifices to gods and believed that certain spaces, such as particular groves and springs, were sacred. They also buried their dead with objects, which is typical of cultures that believe in some sort of afterlife.

Besides these general characteristics, we don't know much about Celtic religious practices and beliefs because this aspect of Celtic life was overseen by the druids. Druids were the priest class of Celtic society who played a large role in life beyond religion. They were the tribe historians who acted as ambassadors, judges, and more. However, unfortunately for modern historians, the druids guarded their knowledge and secrets carefully. What they did pass on was through oral tradition. This means we now have essentially nothing left to tell us more about the druids and Celtic religious practices. We do know that the druids were quite the headache for the Romans later, and it is presumed that as leaders of their people, the druids were often behind uprisings against Roman rule.

What else do we know about Celtic culture? Although the Romans and Greeks viewed the Celts as barbarians, they had a sophisticated culture. While Greco-Roman artwork of the period was focused on clean lines and realism, Celtic art was more abstract and flowing. The Celts focused heavily on animal figures, and much of their art is decorating practical objects such as shields, pottery, and brooches.

One object peculiar to this period that Celts often wore and could make quite ornate was the torc. Torcs were rigid, metal necklaces that typically opened in the front. Torcs were not unique to the Celts. They were worn by other groups at this time, but they appear to have been particularly important to the Celts. Celtic torcs were often made of gold and appear to have been a sign of wealth and status. They may also have been connected with the spiritual realm, as Celtic gods were often depicted wearing torcs. Their importance to Celtic culture means that torcs are commonly associated with the Celts.

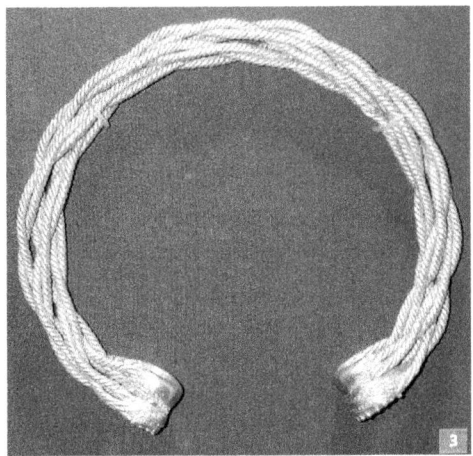

Iron Age Torc from the British Museum.
https://commons.wikimedia.org/wiki/File:IronAgeTorcBritishMuseum.JPG

So, even though the Celts were far from being a unified nation, they had many similarities that make it possible for us to discuss Celtic culture. Although they did not have a written tradition, the Celts had a sophisticated culture with their own art style, religion, and language. Unfortunately, because of the lack of written records, we do not know as much as we would like about Celtic culture, particularly the druids.

Celtic Society

Culture is not the only thing that makes the Celts unique. There are other aspects of Celtic society to consider, such as structure and economics. Celtic society, like most societies, was hierarchical. At the top of the hierarchy were the warriors. If you could protect your people and successfully take stuff from your neighbor, you got to be in charge. The religious leaders, druids, were also in the top echelon of society. Under the warrior aristocracy and druids were those with specialized skills and jobs such as poets, craftsmen, and traders. Beneath this group were the farmers and the enslaved. Most of the population would have been at the bottom of the hierarchy. However, it appears that movement between social classes (except for the enslaved) was possible if one acquired enough wealth.

Shockingly, gender does not appear to have been a major factor in the hierarchy of Celtic society. Women could own property and choose their husbands, and they could even rule, as evidenced by the famous queen of the Iceni, Boudicca. There is also evidence that Celtic women fought alongside the men.

This hierarchical society was broken into tribes, which might have been led by a monarch or an elected chief. Kinship was important for the ruling elite of Celtic society. It was crucial to maintaining control because the Celts lacked writing in the Iron Age. A single king could not effectively rule a large area because there was no way to issue laws, make decrees, and ensure uniformity across his realm. However, a king could give control of land to his brother or cousin. One way these alliances were formed was by fostering children with other families. The result of all this was that the elites of Celtic society were a web of extended families using kinship to consolidate control.

So, that's how Celtic society was organized, but what did the Celts do in their society? To outsiders, the Celts were seen as fierce warriors.

They were known for charging into battle naked and covered in paint, which was terrifying for their enemies. They might also wear helmets that looked like animals. To add to the terror Celtic warriors inspired, they also often wore the heads of enemies they had killed into battle. Besides being scary enough to make anyone think twice about going head-to-head with them, the Celts wore their enemies' heads because they believed the seat of the soul was in the head. To steal your enemy's head was to steal his essence and his power.

The Celts also favored the use of chariots in battle. They rode on light chariots that allowed them to strike their enemies fast and hard, causing the maximum amount of chaos. Imagine screaming, naked, paint-covered warriors hurtling forward on chariots, and you will begin to see why Celtic warriors were so feared in the ancient world. It is no wonder the Romans had so much trouble subduing the Celtic tribes in their quest to conquer Europe. Eventually, superior organization and resources would allow the Romans to triumph, but the Celts were a thorn in the empire's side for quite a while.

Although they were known for their skill in warfare, the Celts were ultimately farmers, not mercenaries. Farming was how they made their living, and the average Celt spent far more of his time plowing than fighting. It was the Celts who brought the iron plow to Britain, which helped increase agricultural productivity and cultivate more of the island.

While farming was their main occupation, the Celts were not purely subsistence farmers. Their economy thrived enough for them to engage in trade with other cultures. The Celts traded things like enslaved people, furs, and iron for things they could not make themselves, such as wine, silver, and luxury goods like fine pottery.

So, the Celts were farmers who charged into battle naked but also peacefully engaged with other civilizations of the ancient world through trade. This is true of the Celts in general, but what about the Celts specifically living in Britain?

Britain in the Iron Age

The Iron Age lasted from around 800 BCE to the end of British prehistory, which ended with the Roman occupation in 43 CE. This last age of prehistory was dominated by the Celts, who arrived in Britain around 750 BCE at the beginning of the Iron Age. It was the Celts who were responsible for bringing the Iron Age to Britain.

Archaeological evidence shows that the Celts had an advanced knowledge of iron making. Their iron weapons and plows gave them an advantage in warfare and farming. Still, while the Celts in Britain may have been living there during the Iron Age, they did not work exclusively in iron. Iron was the metal of choice for tools and weapons, but the Celts still used bronze and gold to make more decorative items such as torcs.

Like elsewhere, Celtic society in Britain was broken up into tribes, and those tribes often lived in hillforts. While hillforts first appeared in the Bronze Age in Britain, the arrival of the Celts and the Iron Age greatly increased their importance in prehistoric Britain. Hillforts were, as the name suggests, forts built on top of hills. Hillforts were easily defensible because of their high position and additional defensive measures such as ditches and walls. They also tended to be located near essentials like fresh water and to have storage areas within their walls. All of this indicates that these constructions were used as forts for warfare in Celtic society.

The use of hillforts may have extended beyond that, though. Many hillforts contained organized settlements within their walls, and the water sources tended to be located nearby rather than within the walls of the fort. This suggests the hillforts may have been defensible homesteads rather than constructions used solely for warfare.

The extensive number of hillforts in Iron Age Britain tells us quite clearly that the Celts of Britain were not unified. Today, we view Iron Age Britain as a Celtic land, but at the time, it was the home of many different tribes that did not consider themselves Celtic. There were multiple warring tribes, such as the Iceni, the Belgae, the Atrebates, the Brigante, the Catuvellauni, the Parisii, and many more. While they may have been fierce warriors, the Celtic tribes of Britain could not stop fighting among themselves long enough to stand against a bigger threat: the Romans. Although the Celts fought back against Roman rule, they could never gather into a unified front to push the Romans out. By 43 CE, Britain was a Roman province.

Chapter 3: Roman Britain

For Britain, prehistory ends with the Romans. This is not because the Romans were necessarily a more advanced civilization than the Celts but simply because the Romans wrote things down. The first Roman to write about Britain was one of the most famous figures in history, Julius Caesar.

Arrival of the Romans and Conquest

Julius Caesar invaded Britain twice in 55 and 54 BCE. He wrote about the island and his invasions in his book, *The Gallic Wars*. This is the first written record of Britain we still have.

So, why exactly did Julius Caesar invade Britain in the first place? For the Romans, Britain was the island at the edge of the world, at least the edge of the Roman world. It was a remote territory, and the Romans seemed comfortable leaving this island alone until Caesar decided to land there with some legions and cause trouble. Caesar's motivations were likely threefold. One was curiosity. The Romans knew little about Britain. Another reason was closely tied to curiosity, and that was prestige. Because the Romans knew so little about Britain, Caesar being the first to go there and gather information would bolster his reputation. The final reason was more strategic and the actual reason Caesar gives in *The Gallic Wars*.

Starting around 58 BCE, Julius Caesar had been engaged in warfare with the Gauls on the continent. Caesar claimed the Britons were sending aid to the Gauls, so an invasion of the island was necessary to cut off his enemies from their allies. His first invasion in 55 BCE was more of a reconnaissance mission, but in the second invasion in 54 BCE, Caesar's forces engaged with the Britons, led by Cassivellaunus.

Although Caesar's legions ultimately defeated the forces of Cassivellaunus, this was not a conquest. Caesar simply required that Cassivellaunus leave the more pro-Roman king of the Trinovantes, Mandubracius, alone. He then took his legions and went home. This shows that Caesar was not interested in truly conquering Britain. He simply hoped to boost his reputation as a military commander and establish Roman relations with the island. It wasn't until close to 100 years later that Rome would truly conquer Britain.

Rome's conquest of Britain occurred during the reign of Emperor Claudius. Command of the British invasion was given to Aulus Plautius, who was promised governorship of the island if he could successfully conquer Britain for Rome.

Tradition says that the army Plautius gathered for his invasion was none too eager to set sail for Britain. The invasion was held up for months on the Norman coast, and it's easy to see why they were apprehensive. Crossing the English Channel was not easy, and the Roman legions were anything but experienced sailors. Britain was also an entirely unknown land, and the great Julius Caesar had failed to conquer it. No one was pushing to be the first ones to set sail, attempt a rough passage, and land on a hostile shore.

To get his legions moving, Emperor Claudius sent a former slave named Narcissus to take command and represent the emperor. The legions were so offended and shamed at being addressed by a freedman that their fears were replaced by anger, and the invasion finally began in 43 CE.

While the invasion had not gotten off to a promising start, once they landed in Britain, the forces of Aulus Plautius were quite successful. The Roman legions rolled through southeastern Britain with relative ease, annexing territory and setting up client kingdoms wherein Rome controlled external affairs but allowed internal autonomy.

Still, conquering Britain was not an overnight affair for the Romans. Caratacus, chieftain of the Catuvellauni, led resistance to the Romans until his defeat in 51 CE. Southwest England, present-day Wales, was a hotbed of resistance for several decades after the Roman arrival.

To maintain control over the regions they conquered, the Romans established small forts at key positions. While this strategy allowed them to maintain control over a larger area, it left the Roman legions spread too thin to utterly eradicate British resistance. Fighting between the Celtic tribes on the island and the Romans continued for years after Rome's initial conquest in 43 CE. The most famous rebellion to come out of this time was led by the warrior queen of the Iceni, Boudicca.

Boudicca's Rebellion

By 60 CE, the Romans considered the lowlands (south) of Britain conquered. They were pushing north when the seemingly subdued people of the lowlands suddenly erupted in rebellion, led by Boudicca.

Boudicca was the wife of Prasutagus, king of the Iceni. During Prasutagus' lifetime, the Iceni were a client kingdom to Rome. When Prasutagus died, he did not have a male heir, so he left his wealth to his two daughters and Emperor Nero in the hopes that this show of favor would cause Rome to treat his family well. His hopes were in vain. Tradition says that the Romans not only took Boudicca's land but also raped her daughters. Boudicca had had enough. She raised a rebellious army that included not just the Iceni but other tribes in the area that later became East Anglia (southeast Britain).

Boudicca's rebellion was at first very successful, largely because she struck at a time when the current Roman governor, Suetonius Paulinus, was gone. Boudicca's rebel army burned three cities, Londinium (London), Camulodunum (Colchester), and Verulamium (St. Albans), to the ground and destroyed the Ninth Legion. According to the Romans, the rebellious army also massacred thousands of civilians, although we can't be sure of the numbers because the Roman sources are clearly biased in this situation.

The rebellion was not destined to last, though. Suetonius Paulinus and his army returned from quelling unrest led by the druids in Wales. Boudicca's forces were annihilated, and Boudicca died shortly after. Many believe she poisoned herself after seeing the destruction of her army and the ruin of her rebellion.

Although Boudicca's rebellion was not successful, it demonstrated that there was much unrest with Roman rule. Roman control was still tenuous, but over time its rule became much more firmly established. One of the people most responsible for that was General Agricola.

Agricola and the Expansion of Roman Control

Gnaeus Julius Agricola is most famous for his conquest of the Caledonian tribes. Caledonia was a name used by the Romans to describe the area north of their control, a territory corresponding roughly to modern-day Scotland.

Beginning in the late 70s CE, Agricola expanded Roman control west and north. He firmly subdued the area that would become modern-day Wales and began pushing farther north than any Roman general before him. He had forts and roads built, providing the Romans with important infrastructure to help them maintain control of the territory they conquered.

The northern tribes did not take this Roman expansion lying down. The tribes in the Caledonia territory united under the leadership of Calgacus and faced off against Agricola's forces at the battle of Mons Graupius in 83 CE. We aren't entirely sure where this battle took place, but it was somewhere in northeast Scotland and was a resounding success for Agricola's forces.

Agricola not only conquered the north but also implemented policies designed to Romanize the inhabitants of Britain. These policies included the building of temples, Roman public buildings, and Roman-style houses. The goal was to make the Britons culturally Roman, which would more effectively fold them into the empire and lessen British resistance to Roman rule. Thanks to Agricola, by the end of the 80s CE, Rome's control over Britain was much firmer. Agricola's efforts to bring Roman culture to the Britons had improved Roman control in the south, and his military prowess had allowed the Romans to conquer the north. For the first and only time, Rome had control over most of the island. This control, however, was destined to be short-lived.

The Retreat of Rome and Hadrian's Wall

Shortly after Agricola conquered Scotland, the Romans left this hard-won land. Threats in other parts of the empire forced the emperor to remove legions from Britain. With less personnel, the Romans simply could not hold all the land Agricola had conquered. This began a gradual southward retreat for the Romans. The north had essentially been abandoned, but the Romans stationed there continued to be harassed by local tribes. The border between Roman-controlled territory and the area controlled by the Caledonian tribes (or Picts, as they are also known) continued to move south and was a constant source of skirmishes and conflict.

In 122 CE, the current emperor, Hadrian, decided to personally address the British situation. After traveling to Britain and assessing the situation with his own eyes, Hadrian ordered a wall to be built along the border between Roman-controlled Britain and the wild north.

Hadrian's Wall, as it was aptly named, stretched for seventy-three miles. Spaced along the wall periodically were towers, small forts called fortlets, and forts. There was also a large ditch, called the vallum, dug behind the wall and the forts.

Hadrian's Wall West of Housesteads.
https://commons.wikimedia.org/wiki/File:Hadrian%27s_Wall_west_of_Housesteads_4.jpg

Although this description certainly makes Hadrian's Wall sound like a defensive fortification, it acted more like a border. The towers and forts along the wall were far too spaced out to form a unified front against any invasion. Besides, the Romans manning the walls were trained to meet their opponents in the open rather than defend from the top of a wall. What good was the wall, then? Hadrian's Wall was essentially a buffer. Its physical presence alone was enough to hold off minor threats from the northern tribes, and it also restricted travel, allowing the Romans to better control the border.

Despite taking six years to complete, Hadrian's wall was outdated soon after its completion. Hadrian's successor as emperor, Antoninus Pius, decided to try to extend Roman control northward once again. The result was the Antonine Wall. At thirty-seven miles, it stretched across a narrower part of the island farther north than Hadrian's Wall.

The Antonine Wall, however, did not last. The territory between Hadrian's Wall and the Antonine Wall proved too difficult for the Romans to hold. The Antonine Wall was abandoned, and Hadrian's Wall remained the northern border of Roman-controlled Britain until the end of the Roman occupation. Rome had given up on the north.

Romanization

Rome's efforts to conquer the area that would become Scotland were effectively over well before 200 CE. In the south, however, Roman rule would continue until about 410 CE. Such a long period of occupation was bound to leave its mark on the Britons.

Romanization had begun before the conquest in 43 CE. There was contact between the British Isles and the continent after Julius Caesar's invasion in 54 BCE. Trade took place between Rome and the British tribes, especially the tribes in southeast Britain. Romanization after the conquest began largely with towns. There were two types of Roman settlements in Britain: the *colonia* and the *municipium*. *Coloniae* were settlements founded and populated by Romans. In Britain, the Romans living in *coloniae* were typically ex-legionaries who were given land as payment upon retiring from their legion. Several of Britain's modern cities, such as Colchester, got their start this way.

So, *coloniae* were Roman from the start, but *municipia* were native settlements that were Romanized enough to be recognized by the Roman government as towns. St. Albans is an example of one such town. Despite being originally a British city, St. Albans was burned to the ground during Boudicca's rebellion, indicating that by 60 or 61 CE, it was considered Roman.

The establishment of both *coloniae* and *municipia* was the core of the process of Romanization. Each town managed its own affairs as well as those of the surrounding territory. Thus, when towns became Roman, their influence spread Romanization throughout the countryside.

But how exactly were the towns Roman? In layout, British towns of this era began to resemble their Roman counterparts on the continent. The streets crossed at perpendicular angles, dividing the towns into neat blocks. At the center of each town was the forum, which was a market and gathering place, and the basilica, a building used for public affairs.

Architecturally, the buildings within this Roman design did not resemble what one would find in Italy. Whether as a matter of style or practicality, the architecture of Rome did not catch on in Britain to a large extent. However, if one were to enter these British homes, one would quickly find Roman influence. Features like hypocausts (spaces below a floor used for heating) and mosaics were Roman inventions common in British homes. Archeology has also found further evidence of Romanization in British towns by the Roman coins, pottery, and decorative objects discovered.

Roman coins from the Hoxne Hoard.
https://commons.wikimedia.org/wiki/File:Hoxne_Hoard_coins_5.JPG

Romanization did not stop at the towns, however. Wealthy tribesmen soon began copying Roman influences in country life, as well. Villas (country estates) were built with Roman features. Over time, Latin spread as a common language, and the Britons embraced Roman entertainment and comforts, like amphitheaters and public baths, and even Roman fashions like the toga.

All this created a Britain that was a Roman territory rather than a conquered land. At some point, the people began to consider themselves Romans who lived in Britain rather than Britons.

That is not to say that Britain became a mini-Rome. While the Britons embraced many aspects of Roman life, Britain never achieved the pure scale of Rome. The towns were not as large, and the villas were not as grand as they were in Italy. Once the Romans left, little of Britain's Roman era survived. There were no grand Roman structures like the Colosseum that would stand for the next several hundred years. Britain's prehistoric monuments like Stonehenge proved to be more lasting than its Roman constructions.

Another aspect of Roman life that did not take hold in Britain was religion. Shrines to native gods remained throughout the Roman period, indicating the high persistence of the Briton religious beliefs. While Rome could not replace the native religion, it nevertheless had an impact. Celtic gods were given Roman form, the most famous example being the Celtic goddess of springs, Sulis, who at Bath was combined with the Roman goddess Minerva.

The Roman pantheon may not have replaced the native gods of the Britons, but the Romans introduced another religion that would prove to have an enormous impact on Britain: Christianity. How exactly Christianity came to the shores of Britain remains a topic of legend and debate, but we know for sure that by 314 CE, Britain had at least three Christian bishops who attended the Council of Arles. Christianity would have an immense impact on the Anglo-Saxons and the nation of England, making its introduction to the island in the Roman era one of the most impactful and lasting effects of the Roman occupation.

For more than three centuries, Britain was a Roman province, and this time transformed the culture and people of the island. By 400 CE, the Britons were speaking Latin, living in Roman towns, governing with Roman systems, and using Roman goods. If Britain was so thoroughly

Romanized, what was going to happen when the Romans left?

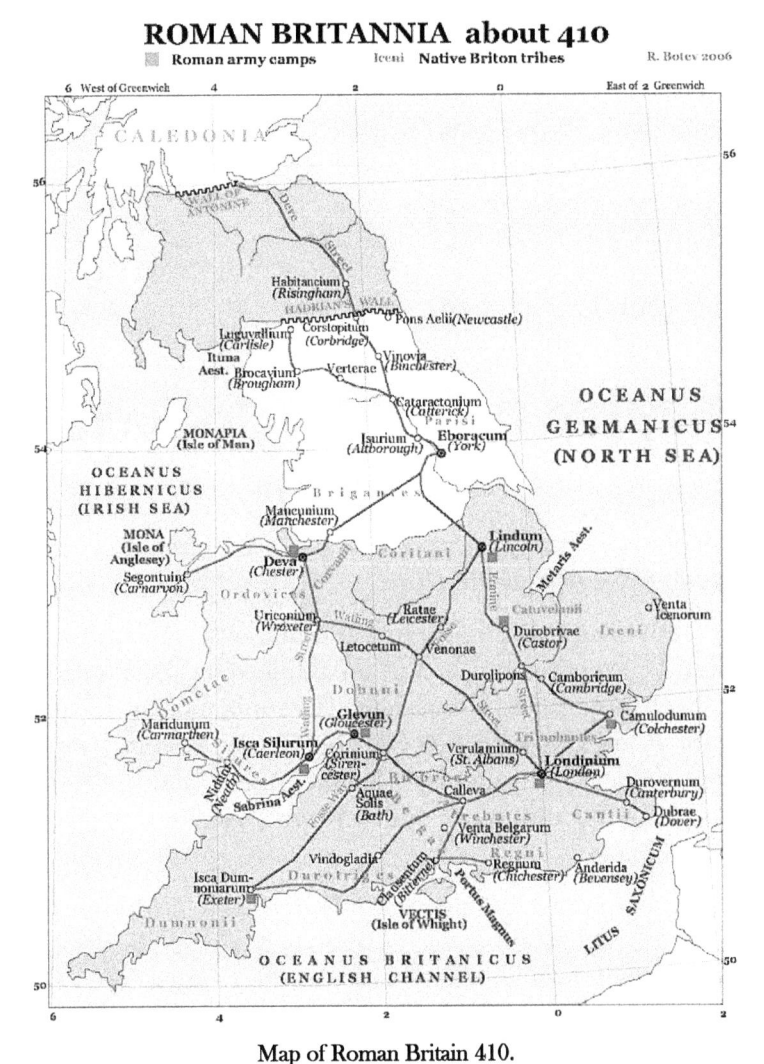

ROMAN BRITANNIA about 410

Map of Roman Britain 410.
https://commons.wikimedia.org/wiki/File:Roman_Britain_410_provinces.jpg

Chapter 4: The Anglo-Saxons

History is often repetitive, and one historical drama that has been played out repeatedly in human history is the fall of empires. Rome, for all its might, was no exception to this trope.

By the fifth century, the Roman Empire was collapsing due to a combination of external threats and infighting. As things went from bad to worse, the remote island province of Britannia was far down the list of priorities for Rome. Around 410 CE, the Roman legions were removed from Britain to deal with threats on the continent, and the legions never returned. Britain did not break out of Roman rule; it was thrown to the side by the Romans.

Having a conquering empire set you free with no bloodshed might sound great, but, as we discussed in the last chapter, the Celtic Britons had become rather Romanized. What's more, being a Roman province came with a crucial benefit—Roman legions. Without the legions to protect them, the Celtic Britons were left to defend themselves against all sorts of invaders.

Three main groups took advantage of a Britain without Roman legions: the Picts of Scotland, the Scotti of Ireland, and the Anglo-Saxons from the continent. Eventually, the Anglo-Saxons moved past raiding to settling until the land of Britain became England, the land of the Angles.

The Arrival of the Anglo-Saxons

With the arrival of the Anglo-Saxons, we are finally getting to the English part of English history. But who exactly were the Anglo-Saxons? According to early sources, the Anglo-Saxons were a group consisting of three different tribes of settlers from the continent: the Angles, the Saxons, and the Jutes. The Angles and Saxons were Germanic tribes, and the Jutes were a Norse tribe. These tribes came from northern Europe and settled in southeastern and southern Britain in the fifth and sixth centuries.

We do not have exact dates for the arrival of the Anglo-Saxons. Like the Celtic tribes, the Anglo-Saxons did not have a written language for some time, and as we discussed earlier, the lack of written records leaves historians with a harder job. We know very little about what happened in Britain from around 400 CE, when the Romans departed, to around 600 CE. By this time, seven Anglo-Saxon kingdoms (known as the Heptarchy) had emerged.

This means that the sources we have about the Anglo-Saxon settlement were written long after the events. These traditional sources, such as the Venerable Bede's *Ecclesiastical History of the English People* written in the eighth century, say that the Anglo-Saxons conquered southern Britain in a reign of terror between 400 and 600, annihilating the Celtic tribes and forcing the survivors to flee to what would become the Celtic nations of Wales, Cornwall, and Brittany.

While it is certain the Anglo-Saxons were not nice to the Celtic Britons (they stole their land), it is less certain whether the Anglo-Saxons committed genocide on the scale we originally thought. Another more likely possibility is forced assimilation. The Anglo-Saxons looked down on the Celtic Britons, forcing them into the lowest tier of society as they conquered their land. As a result, the Celtic Britons likely merged into Anglo-Saxon society to avoid social isolation and discrimination.

So, through a mixture of forced migration, assimilation, and murder, the Celtic Britons were replaced by these invaders from northern Europe. By the seventh century, the Anglo-Saxons had consolidated into seven main kingdoms: Mercia, Northumberland, Wessex, Essex, Kent, Sussex, and East Anglia.

Anglo-Saxon Culture

The Anglo-Saxons were here to stay, but what were they like? Writing did not come to the Anglo-Saxons until their conversion to Christianity, so we have no written records of the early Anglo-Saxon period. Later, after writing was introduced, there was still relatively little reliable information about these people. Many of the writings from the time have clear biases and inaccuracies that make them difficult to take completely at face value. This lack of information has caused the Anglo-Saxon period in English history to be known as the Dark Ages, but this is a misleading name based on a biased view.

The term "Dark Ages" is meant to describe a regression of human civilization. A dark age is a time of ignorance and barbarity. But assigning the name Dark Ages to the Anglo-Saxon period has far more to do with the Romans than the Anglo-Saxons. During the Renaissance, the period immediately following the Middle Ages, society saw a renewed interest and veneration for classical Greek and Roman culture. Rome was seen as the birthplace of Western civilization. With such a high view of Rome, it was only natural to assume that their departure from the island of Britain would set its society back. The fact that there were no written historical records to contradict this view did not help matters. The Anglo-Saxons were viewed as a brutish people by historians for a long time.

However, as research on this era has continued and we have learned more about the Anglo-Saxons, we now know that such a view is not only biased but also not true. As with Britain's prehistory, archeology has taught us much of what we know about the Anglo-Saxons. Burial sites like Sutton Hoo show that the Anglo-Saxons had a rich and sophisticated culture. They buried some of their dead with many grave goods, indicating both a social hierarchy and a large amount of wealth. Subsistence farmers barely scraping by could not afford to bury their dead with gold, jewelry, weapons, and more.

Helmet from Sutton Hoo Burial site.
https://commons.wikimedia.org/wiki/File:Sutton.hoo.helmet.jpg

Therefore, we now know that the Anglo-Saxons were a successful and complex society. That being said, Anglo-Saxon life could also be brutal. Anglo-Saxons lived in tribal societies that placed great emphasis on kinship and honor. These values translated into a culture where killing to avenge family members was quite common. The Anglo-Saxons developed *wergild,* a system that set a price on a person's life so that monetary compensation could be made for murder. This was necessary to stop the endless cycle of murders caused by a society that demanded honor and revenge.

Warfare was also a common part of Anglo-Saxon life. Remember that the Anglo-Saxons were technically invaders from the continent. To establish their kingdoms, they had to seize land from the Celtic Britons. Tradition says that the Celtic forces that resisted the Anglo-Saxon invasions were led by the legendary King Arthur, although we don't have any evidence that such a person existed. Regardless, the Anglo-Saxons certainly used military might to seize control of the island, and even after they had gained control, warfare continued.

By the seventh century, seven major Anglo-Saxon kingdoms shared the southeastern region of a small island. There were also Welsh kingdoms to the west and Scottish kingdoms to the north. With so many competing groups crammed into a small geographical area, competition for resources like land often became violent. Warfare was also tempting simply because it led to great gains. Stronger kingdoms could demand tribute from their weaker neighbors, people captured in conflicts could be used or sold as slaves, and treasure and resources could be seized from defeated opponents. In the Anglo-Saxon world, warfare was economics.

Map of the Anglo-Saxon kingdoms.
https://commons.wikimedia.org/wiki/File:Wiglaf_locations_incl._Offa%27s_Dyke.gif

That doesn't mean the Anglo-Saxons spent all their time fighting. This was still the era of human history where, if human society was to survive, most people needed to be farmers. So, daily life for most Anglo-Saxons would have involved working the land.

Life wasn't all working and fighting for the Anglo-Saxons, though. They also had entertainment. For instance, poetry was a large part of Anglo-Saxon culture. Because of its rhythm, poetry is easier to memorize and listen to, making it excellent entertainment for people without television or easy access to books.

The most famous Anglo-Saxon poem is the epic, *Beowulf*, which follows the titular hero through his adventures slaying monsters. Other examples of Anglo-Saxon poetry include *Caedmon's Hymn*, *The Seafarer*, and *The Battle of Maldon*.

These poems tell us a lot about what Anglo-Saxon culture valued. Poems like *Beowulf* and *The Battle of Maldon* both tell the tales of heroes who ultimately fall in battle. This tells us that the Anglo-Saxons viewed warfare as more than economic gain. There was a perceived honor in being a warrior and falling in battle. On the other hand, the Anglo-Saxons also wrote poems like *Caedmon's Hymn* and *The Seafarer*. *Caedmon's Hymn* is, as the name implies, a hymn praising God. *The Seafarer* is from a genre called wisdom poetry that describes the ups and downs of life. *The Seafarer* tells the tale of an exile at sea who must wait for the glory of heaven to find his redemption.

As you can tell from these last two poems, Christian values were a part of Anglo-Saxon culture. The Anglo-Saxons' conversion to Christianity is a key factor in understanding who they were and how they impacted England.

Conversion to Christianity

Christianity brought writing to the Anglo-Saxons and allowed the Anglo-Saxon kingdoms to claim a place in the grand scheme of European politics. Christian tradition says that Joseph of Arimathea, whose tomb Jesus was laid in after his crucifixion, brought Christianity to Britain during the time of the Romans, but there is no historical evidence to support this claim. A later legend says that Pope Gregory I sent Augustine in 597 to convert the Anglo-Saxons after remarking on the beauty of Angle boys in the slave market at Rome. While Augustine may have acted as a missionary to the English, we can hardly give him sole credit for bringing Christianity to England, as it was already on the island in the Roman age. Irish missionaries likely also played an important role in converting the Anglo-Saxons.

However it arrived, Christianity spread gradually over the island and had a huge influence on the Anglo-Saxons. It changed their holidays, rituals, and even their values. The church would soon be involved in a person's life from birth to marriage to death.

For an entire society to change its religious convictions, the ruling class must change, as well. As we will see much later in English history, it is very difficult to maintain a functioning government system when a ruler and the people are of different religions. Part of the reason Christianity took such a hold on the Anglo-Saxons may therefore be because their rulers were converted.

Many Anglo-Saxon kings converted to Christianity because of the benefits it offered them. One of these benefits sounds relatively simple but has far-reaching implications, and that is writing. Christian monks and missionaries were a literate group in a largely illiterate time. Their ability to write allowed the Anglo-Saxon kings they served to make laws and send orders across larger areas. Writing made the transmission of information far easier and more accurate, letting kings effectively rule much larger areas.

There were many other benefits that the rulers of Anglo-Saxon society gained from Christianity. Rituals like assigning godparents let rulers easily connect themselves with other ruling families. The church and other religious institutions like monasteries also gave rulers another place to appoint people loyal to themselves. Having bishops and monks loyal to the king scattered throughout a kingdom was another way that Christianity helped Anglo-Saxon kings consolidate and grow their power.

To understand why Christianity could offer Anglo-Saxon kings so much power, we need to consider that, previously, there were few public institutions involved in a person's daily life. Anglo-Saxons were concerned with their kin, but beyond the ties of blood, there was little connecting them to their neighbors or rulers. Christianity brought a uniform institution to the Anglo-Saxons. With Christianity, everyone across a kingdom was worshiping at the same time and in the same way. Churches also became important community centers for events like baptisms, marriages, and burials. Monasteries began to function as centers of charity in communities. Thus, Christianity provided institutions that united the Anglo-Saxons more firmly. The more firmly the people were united, the easier it was for the ruling class to expand its power.

However, it was ultimately not Christianity but something else entirely that at last united the seven Anglo-Saxon kingdoms into a single kingdom known as England.

Chapter 5: The Viking Raids and the Formation of England

In the last chapter, we talked about the Anglo-Saxons, but discussing the people who had settled in the area that would eventually become England as though they were one group can be misleading. The term Anglo-Saxons did not exist at the time. In the seventh and eighth centuries, the people living in England, although they did share many cultural similarities, would not have thought of themselves as one people group.

The seven kingdoms of the Anglo-Saxons were constantly vying for power. At times, one kingdom (particularly Northumbria, Mercia, and Wessex) emerged as the most powerful and required tribute from the others, but there was no consolidation or unity between the kingdoms. It would take a significant external threat to turn the Anglo-Saxon kingdoms into England.

Enter the Vikings

At the very end of the eighth century, the British Isles faced a new threat. Invaders from Scandinavia, known collectively as Vikings, began raiding. The earliest raids date to the 790s but only increased over the next hundred years, and it's not hard to see why. A growing population in Scandinavia was looking for resources, and Britain was a prime target. The now-Christian Anglo-Saxons had built many monasteries furnished with much wealth and inhabited by monks and nuns who would not fight back. They were easy and profitable targets for the Vikings, who held no religious qualms that would keep them from preying on these religious centers.

You can imagine how much (or rather, how little) resistance a group of armed Viking warriors met with from monks. There was nothing to discourage the raids from continuing, and the fact that many of the monks persistently rebuilt after each devastating raid only meant that the Vikings never seemed to run out of targets.

Of course, the great devastation caused by the Vikings was not simply because they picked easy targets. Even when attacking settlements with inhabitants who fought back, the Vikings were a deadly force. Their longboats were narrow and had shallow draughts, which allowed them to land directly on the beach near settlements. The Vikings could strike quickly before a village knew what was upon them and then be back out to sea again before the victims knew what had happened.

As devastating as these raids were, especially for those living on the coast, we probably wouldn't be discussing them here if the Vikings had stopped at raiding. There must've been something appealing about the British Isles because the Viking raiders turned into something far scarier: Viking settlers.

Much like the Anglo-Saxons before them, around the middle of the ninth century, the Vikings began extending their time in England beyond the raiding season. They started to overwinter (spend the season when the seas were too rough for travel) on the isles, establishing settlements. With the establishment of settlements came larger conflicts with the Anglo-Saxons. Now it was not only coastal towns that had to fear the invaders.

In 865 CE, things went from bad to worse for the Anglo-Saxons. A large army of Vikings landed and soon began to conquer the Anglo-Saxon kingdoms. This huge force was aptly known as The Great Heathen Army. The name, which we get from the Anglo-Saxon Chronicle, reveals a bias toward the invaders, so some historians refer to this force simply as the Great Army or Great Viking Army instead. All three names refer to the same group.

Regardless of what you call it, the Great Army was undoubtedly effective. The Vikings conquered East Anglia, Mercia, and Northumbria with little trouble. Their influence and increasing power in Britain went relatively unchecked for the next decade.

Alfred the Great and the Rise of Wessex

After the initial success of the Great Army's invasion, the Vikings, having conquered three kingdoms with relative ease, had one last major Anglo-Saxon territory to defy them: Wessex.

Wessex had faced Viking onslaughts during the early years after the landing of the Great Army. Their king was even killed in the fighting in 871 CE, leaving his brother Alfred, who was the fifth of five sons, as the new king of Wessex. For a while, there was a reprieve in the fighting, but in 876 CE, the Vikings renewed their efforts to conquer Wessex. In 878 CE, the Vikings looked very close to victory. Their surprise attack on the Wessex fortress at Chippenham forced King Alfred to flee into the marshes of Somerset with only a few of his men. Wessex was all but conquered.

Letting King Alfred escape turned out to be a big mistake. While hiding in the marshes, Alfred and his men conducted a type of guerrilla warfare against the Vikings. Perhaps more importantly, though, Alfred was also able to rebuild his forces. With his new army, Alfred marched against the Vikings later that year. The clash between the two forces took place at Edington, outside the fortress of Chippenham, which the Vikings had occupied after forcing Alfred to flee.

Alfred's forces beat the Vikings, led by Jarl Guthrum, at Edington, forcing the Vikings to flee back to Chippenham, where they surrendered to Alfred after a short siege. The terms of the treaty that followed were relatively simple: Guthrum must be baptized as a Christian, and the Vikings must leave Wessex.

Let's dive into both aspects further because they tell us much about this time and what comes after in English history. First, why would Alfred require Guthrum to be baptized?

In our modern world, it is hard for us to truly grasp how embedded religion was in every aspect of life in the Middle Ages. In fact, there are two mistakes we can make when thinking about religion in this day. One would be to assume that no one took their religion seriously. Religion, Christianity especially, was a huge part of medieval life because so many people believed. It would also be a mistake to think that religion never became a tool of politics or power. When an institution or belief system is so widespread that it melds into every aspect of life, people will try to use it to their own ends.

With these two things in mind, we can perhaps better understand why Alfred would require Guthrum to be baptized, which was a clear sign of conversion to Christianity. To undergo baptism was a sign of political allegiance and a serious commitment. This does not mean that Guthrum necessarily had a change of heart and truly converted religions but that he was at least committed to a public show of peace and, on some level, submission to Alfred. It was not an act that could be conveniently forgotten later. As a religious act, it was a more effective way of binding the peace agreement than a simple shaking of hands.

When we consider the other part of the peace agreement between Alfred and Guthrum, the baptism requirement only makes more sense. Alfred wanted the invading Vikings to leave Wessex, and he did not want them to return. The Vikings had been trying to conquer Wessex for around a decade, and a more permanent treaty was required for a more permanent peace.

For Alfred, achieving that peace meant letting the Vikings have what they had already conquered. Alfred and Guthrum agreed to divide southeastern Britain. Alfred maintained control of Wessex and the smaller Anglo-Saxon kingdoms it dominated (including Kent), and Guthrum and his followers were given the area of East Anglia and parts of Mercia and Northumbria. To agree to let pagans have land conquered by Christians would have been a very unsavory, if prudent, decision, but by having Guthrum baptized, Alfred was in effect negotiating with a fellow Christian ruler.

The area settled by Guthrum and his Vikings became known as the Danelaw because it was under a Danish-style legal system. Since you may be confused at this point, let's take a quick moment to clarify some things. Although we refer to the great invading force that conquered the Anglo-Saxon kingdoms and fought with Alfred as the Vikings, Alfred and his contemporaries referred to these people as the Danes. That's because the Vikings that invaded southern Britain were Danes. However, for the sake of correctness, we should also point out that not all Vikings are Danish. The Viking raiders that attacked other parts of the British Isles such as Ireland and Scotland were Norse. "Vikings" is a general term that refers to the raiders from the Scandinavian countries of this period.

Thanks to the Vikings, Wessex was now the dominant Anglo-Saxon kingdom on the island, and Alfred was the premier ruler, but England still did not exist. The Vikings still controlled huge chunks of what had been Anglo-Saxon land.

Lasting Peace?

If the peace arrangement created by Guthrum and Alfred had lasted, England might not have been formed. However, based on what happened next, we can assume neither party took the peace established after the battle of Edington seriously despite the baptism and setting of boundaries.

By 885 CE, seven years after the Battle of Edington, Alfred was again repelling Danes/Vikings from Kent. This invasion was supported by the Danes of East Anglia (Guthrum's people) and was a breach of the peace that had been established. Still, Alfred was not simply a victim of Viking war lust. The following year, Alfred captured London, an important strategic position between the Anglo-Saxon-controlled area and the land controlled by the Danes.

England at the time of the Danelaw.
https://commons.wikimedia.org/wiki/File:Britain_886.jpg

According to John Asser, a contemporary biographer who knew Alfred personally, this act of retaking London earned Alfred the acceptance of the other Anglo-Saxons as their king. However, we do not consider this the start of the Kingdom of England, for much of Anglo-Saxon territory remained under Danish rule.

With the possession of London, Alfred may have intended to launch new assaults to drive the Danes from the island, but he never got the chance. He was forced to go on the defensive again in 892 CE against Danish forces from the continent. By the time he died in 899 CE, Alfred had made no more progress toward retaking the rest of the Anglo-Saxon kingdoms. That was a task left up to Alfred's children.

But before we move on to Alfred's children, we should spend more time talking about Alfred because he is one of the few kings in history to have received the moniker "the Great."

Alfred the Great from the Brief Abridgement of the Chronicles of England.
https://commons.wikimedia.org/wiki/File:Alfred_the_Great_in_the_Brief_Abridgement_of_the_Chronicles_of_England.jpg

As he is better known to history, Alfred the Great did far more than save the Anglo-Saxons from the Vikings. He was also a scholar and skilled administrator. Alfred worked to improve literacy rates in his kingdom and translated several prominent works into English to make their knowledge available to those who did not know Latin. He translated several works himself and had others translated in his name. This promotion of the English language also helped create a greater sense of a single English identity.

As a ruler, Alfred was judicious. He was responsible for the creation of a law code that gave the Anglo-Saxons, who previously had many different laws and legal systems, a more united legal structure. While this might seem like a boring fact, the establishment of a single law code is vastly important. There could be no unified kingdom and thus no England without a single legal system. A king could not effectively rule an area with a dozen different sets of laws. Thus, although Alfred himself did not unite the Anglo-Saxons into the nation we now know as England, the work he did in stopping the advance of the Danes and beginning to unify the Anglo-Saxons made the formation of England possible.

The Start of England

If Alfred the Great did not form England, who was the first king of England? It took the military and diplomatic work of Alfred's son and grandson to put the Danelaw back under Anglo-Saxon control. In 927, Alfred's grandson Athelstan became the first king to effectively rule all the Anglo-Saxon lands. This, however, was not the beginning of a long line of English kings passing the throne from father to son. While that might be how a monarchy ideally functions, in the tumultuous Middle Ages, it rarely went that smoothly. When Athelstan died in 939, he did not have a son, so the throne went to his half-brother, Edmund I.

Then, shockingly, the Vikings invaded again. This time, it was Norse Vikings (not the Danes) based in Dublin who attacked and seized control of Northumbria and raided the Midlands. Just like that, the unification of Anglo-Saxons that Athelstan had achieved was over.

But this situation also did not last long. By 944, Edmund I had regained control of the Midlands and Northumbria. A united Anglo-Saxon kingdom was restored, but things still weren't over. When Edmund I was killed by an outlaw in 949, his brother Eadred took the throne, as Edmund's children were still too young to rule. Eadred's reign witnessed rebellion from Northumbria, but he had firmly consolidated his control over the region before he died in 955. His successor was his nephew, Eadwig, who became king at just fifteen years old.

Eadwig was not a popular king. His poor handling of the church and other powerful members in his court led to both Mercia and Northumbria pledging their allegiance to his fourteen-year-old younger brother, Edgar, in 957. Eadwig's support was so low that this arrangement was accepted, and the kingdom was effectively split, with Edgar ruling Mercia and Northumbria and Eadwig ruling Wessex and Kent. Once again, the unity of the Anglo-Saxons had been destroyed.

This, too, only lasted a short while. King Eadwig died two years later in 959, and Edgar became the sole ruler of the Anglo-Saxons. With his reign, England began to see a more stable existence as a single kingdom. Edgar was the first king to officially be crowned in a coronation ceremony as the King of England. His coronation took place late in his reign in 973 as a celebration of the stability England had experienced under him. It was not until later that coronations began to take place at the beginning of the monarch's rule.

Stained glass window depicting King Edgar at All Souls Chapel.
https://commons.wikimedia.org/wiki/File:King_Edgar_from_All_Souls_College_Chapel.png

A United Kingdom

Thus, thanks largely to the Vikings, England came into existence. The external threat the Vikings presented forced England to unify in a way that nothing else could. And, although it had a bit of a rocky start, the unification of the English that Alfred the Great started was well established by the time of Edgar's coronation in 973. Over the next century, this sense of collective identity grew stronger as the Wessex dynasty continued to rule. Common language, common laws, a common king, and even common local administration all worked together to create a common people. However, England would not always remain exclusively the land of the English. In 1066, another group arrived and brought some big changes.

Chapter 6: The Norman Conquest

The Wessex dynasty included the first kings of England, but they were not destined to rule the country forever. Keeping the throne in a single dynasty is a lot harder than you might think. Two major issues stop dynasties from continuing. One is a lack of heirs. If a family can't produce the next generation, it will ultimately lose the throne. The other problem that can interrupt a dynasty is a hostile takeover. To a certain degree, it took might to keep a throne in the Middle Ages.

In 1066, one of the most famous years in English history, England found itself facing both problems simultaneously. Their king had died without an heir, and not one but several invaders landed in the hopes of seizing the throne and the kingdom by force. This is the story of the Norman Conquest.

Background

With an interruption from 1016-1042 when England was again invaded and temporarily ruled by the Danes, the Wessex dynasty ruled from the time of Athelstan to Edward the Confessor.

Edward the Confessor ruled from 1042 to 1066, directly following the Danish interruption. He was called "the Confessor" for his piety, which included a supposed vow to celibacy that extended even into his marriage. Whether or not Edward was celibate remains a point of contention, but regardless, when he died in 1066, he did not have any heirs. He therefore named his most powerful advisor as his heir: Harold

Godwinson.

Harold would have to fight, however, if he wanted to keep the throne. The death of a childless king was just too much of an opportunity for many. The first threat Harold faced was not the Normans, though. Harold's brother, Tostig, and the King of Norway, Harald Hardrada, joined forces and attacked York. Harold hurried north to meet them.

Harold's first attempt to beat off rival claimants to the throne was a resounding success. At the Battle of Stamford Bridge on September 25, 1066, Harold's forces were victorious, and both of his rivals were killed in the fighting. Harold had proven he could defend his right to the throne, but he wasn't done. There was another person who felt he had a claim to the English throne: William of Normandy.

Now why in the world would the Duke of Normandy think he had a right to the English crown? In short, William claimed that Edward had named him as his successor and, what's more, that Harold Godwinson had promised to support William's claim. How much truth there is to William's claims remains debatable. Edward indeed had ties to Normandy due to his time spent in exile there. Edward even caused tension as king when he began appointing too many Normans to positions in his government. It is therefore not impossible that Edward would name William as his successor.

The other part about Harold promising to honor William's claim seems less likely. It was a rather convenient excuse for William because it gave him justification with the pope for invading England to push his claim. Such a claim may even have been forced from Harold during a diplomatic mission gone wrong a few years prior, but it is highly doubtful that Harold felt such an oath binding. Regardless of whether Harold had sworn an oath or not, he was not going to hand the throne over to William without a fight. William thus gathered an army and sailed across the channel.

The Battle of Hastings

On September 28, only three days after the Battle of Stamford Bridge and while Harold and his forces were still far in the north, William and his men landed in southern England. Instead of marching inland from this point, William made Hastings his base and waited for Harold to come to him, burning the surrounding countryside to entice Harold to come to the rescue.

And Harold did exactly that, rushing his army southward to face the Norman forces. Although we cannot be sure of Harold's reasons for rushing to engage William, there can be no doubt it was a military blunder. By trying to move his forces so quickly, Harold lost parts of his army and did not have time to gather any more men before confronting William on October 14, 1066.

Despite these disadvantages, the Battle of Hastings was far from a Norman rout. The English formed a shield wall on top of an incline to withstand the charges from the Norman cavalry. The battle raged for most of the day, with each side unable to break the other. Ultimately, the English forces, which were comprised entirely of foot soldiers, could not break the Normans. The shield wall was a strong defensive formation, but it lacked the offensive surge needed to scatter and destroy the Normans. The Norman cavalry, on the other hand, eventually broke through the shield wall, killing the English leaders—including Harold. Thus ended the brief reign of Harold Godwinson.

Part of the Bayeux Tapestry showing Harold's death.
https://commons.wikimedia.org/wiki/File:Bayeux_Tapestry_scene57_Harold_death.jpg

Having defeated Harold, William made his way slowly toward London. With no one of real power to resist him, the leading men of England accepted the inevitable and submitted to William before he arrived in London. He was crowned king on Christmas Day in Westminster Abbey. The Normans had conquered England.

England under the Conqueror

The Norman Conquest did far more than give England a new king. The new regime implemented quite a few changes. One of the first things a conquering king must worry about is staying in control. To cement his hold on the country, William went on a castle-building spree, erecting the first at Hastings before he had even conquered England. Surprisingly, before 1066, England had relatively few castles. The houses of the elites in Anglo-Saxon England were not built with extreme defense in mind, and the towns were too big to be defended well.

Building a network of castles allowed William to keep a firm grip on his new country. Castles were defensible places from which power could be wielded since they held garrisons that could be used to deal with any rebellions. William's castle-building thus gave him strong footholds all over the country.

Castles were not enough to stop a rebellion, however. In the first five years of his reign, William faced several rebellions as the English chafed at the new rule. A major uprising in the north in 1069 made William so enraged that he commanded his army to raze the area, burning food supplies and causing devastation that lasted for years.

Still, by 1071, William's rule was fairly secure, and there were more changes to come. The Conqueror brought several ideas from the continent that he implemented in England, feudalism being perhaps the most influential.

Although we may think feudalism applies to all the Middle Ages, England before 1066 did not have a feudal system. Feudalism refers to when a tenant is granted land (called a fief) from a lord, swearing allegiance to the lord for the right to work the land. Although people in Anglo-Saxon England swore allegiance to the lords and king, they did not receive their land from lords (they were not tenants), which is the key component of feudalism.

While feudalism as an idea came from the continent, in England, William introduced a feudal system that existed nowhere else. As a conqueror, William felt that all of England belonged to him. He could thus parcel out the land however he saw fit, giving large chunks of the land to his Norman supporters. William even considered land held by the church to be under his control, with bishops and abbots also his tenants. This meant that all of England was held by the king, and every landowner in England received his land from the king. These "tenants-in-chief" who were granted land directly from the king then parceled out the land to their supporters, who swore similar oaths to them. Thus, the feudal chain was created. Nowhere else in Europe did feudalism exist in such a perfect hierarchy, with the king ultimately owning all the land. This was only made possible by the circumstances of the Norman Conquest.

As the person who owned the land, the king had several important privileges in the feudal system. Everyone who held land had to supply knights for the king's army. Fees must be paid to the king upon the death of the tenant if the land was to pass to the heir. If there was no heir, the land returned to the king, and if the heir was a minor, the land returned to the king until the minor came of age. Meanwhile, they were a ward of the king. As the ultimate landowner, the king also had control over the marriage of widows who controlled land and heiresses set to inherit land.

What all these privileges amount to is a lot of political control. The hand of a wealthy heiress can be quite the political bargaining tool. This system also meant the king had direct control over more land than anyone else, which starkly contrasted with the previous Anglo-Saxon system. By the time of Edward the Confessor, several nobles had more land and wealth than the king. Under feudalism, the king was undoubtedly the most powerful man in the kingdom.

The Normans brought other changes, as well. Because William rewarded his followers with land, most of England soon lay in Norman hands. However, many of these Normans had no interest in moving to England. They simply wanted the wealth that could be gained from their new property. They were far more interested in receiving money than goods from the land. This desire led to a decrease in slavery, as the Normans preferred tenants who paid rather than slaves who produced goods. This doesn't necessarily mean people became freer, though. Under feudalism, a farmer who rented land from a lord could not leave the land and had to pay fees to his lord for actions such as having a daughter marry.

The emphasis on land that the feudal system relied on brought another change to England. In Anglo-Saxon England, a family was a large group that consisted of many extended relatives. Wealth and power came largely from who your family was, and land was often distributed among several relatives upon the death of the landowner, the overall goal being to keep the family strong. However, with the Normans came a narrowing of the sense of family. The Normans used the practice of primogeniture, which is when the entire estate passes intact to the eldest son. Primogeniture kept land together, which allowed the wealthy to consolidate larger holdings. This practice of passing everything to one person resulted in a greater focus on the immediate family and a narrowing of the sense of family duty and responsibility toward extended family. It was a cultural shift that would echo down into the Victorian age.

These changes highlight only some of the major impacts the Norman Conquest had on England. It was an event that shook and changed the kingdom to its core. But if it was such a dramatic change, why is England still English? What ultimately happened to the Normans?

The End of Norman Rule

The end of Norman rule was shockingly similar to the beginning. It all started with a king who did not have an heir. Henry I, the fourth son of William the Conqueror and the third Norman king to rule England, had children. His son William was set to become the next king but died unexpectedly during the sinking of the *White Ship* (an infamous incident in 1120 where a ship carrying many elite members of English society sank in the channel).

The sinking of the *White Ship* left Henry I with only one living child, his daughter Matilda, who had been married to the Holy Roman Emperor and later married the Count of Anjou. Henry I proclaimed his daughter his heir, but his Anglo-Norman court did not like it. When Henry died in 1135, the court put his nephew, Stephen of Blois, on the throne instead, and Matilda was none too happy about it.

Thus began a nearly two-decade-long civil war known as The Anarchy. While the name is a bit dramatic, it gives us a good idea of just how chaotic this time was for England. The war between Stephen and Empress Matilda proved to be largely a stalemate, with neither side gaining a decisive victory to end the war. This created a situation where the country was broken up into smaller units, each ruled by different powerful people, including more than just Stephen and Matilda. Their allies, such as Earl Robert, Empress Matilda's half-brother, ruled over their own sections of England at one point. The Scottish king, David, took advantage of the situation to seize control of land in the north. All these different rulers meant that everything from coins to laws differed throughout the country. And if that wasn't chaotic enough, there was a complete breakdown of law and order in the borderlands between these competing sections. England had broken into pieces.

Strangely enough, it was not a battle that ended this time in English history but an agreement. Having lost his heir, Stephen agreed to make Empress Matilda's son, Henry, his new heir. All parties were satisfied by this, and in 1153, eighteen years after it had started, The Anarchy ended. Only a year later, Stephen died, and Matilda's son became Henry II, starting a new dynasty.

Although Henry II was the son of Matilda and thus the great-grandson of William the Conqueror, he is not considered a member of the Norman line since lineage was traced through the father during this period. Instead, Henry II's dynasty is known by the last name of his father, Geoffrey Plantagenet.

Chapter 7: The Plantagenets

The Plantagenets ruled England from 1154 to 1485. While previous dynasties that ruled England had struggled due to a lack of legitimate heirs, the Plantagenets did not have that problem. The first Plantagenet king, Henry II, had five sons. The succession was certainly secure, but Henry II would eventually learn that too many heirs could also be a problem.

Henry II

Before getting to Henry II's family problems, though, let's take a moment to understand just who Henry II was. During The Anarchy, the English king had not managed to successfully rule over all of England, but when Henry II took the English throne, the opposite became true: Henry II's realm extended far beyond England. Henry's father was the Count of Anjou, which gave Henry control of the territories of Anjou and Maine upon his father's death. He was granted the title Duke of Normandy by the King of France, and when he married Eleanor of Aquitaine, he became Duke of Aquitaine and Gascony. Thus, when Henry Plantagenet became Henry II in 1154, he had quite the empire.

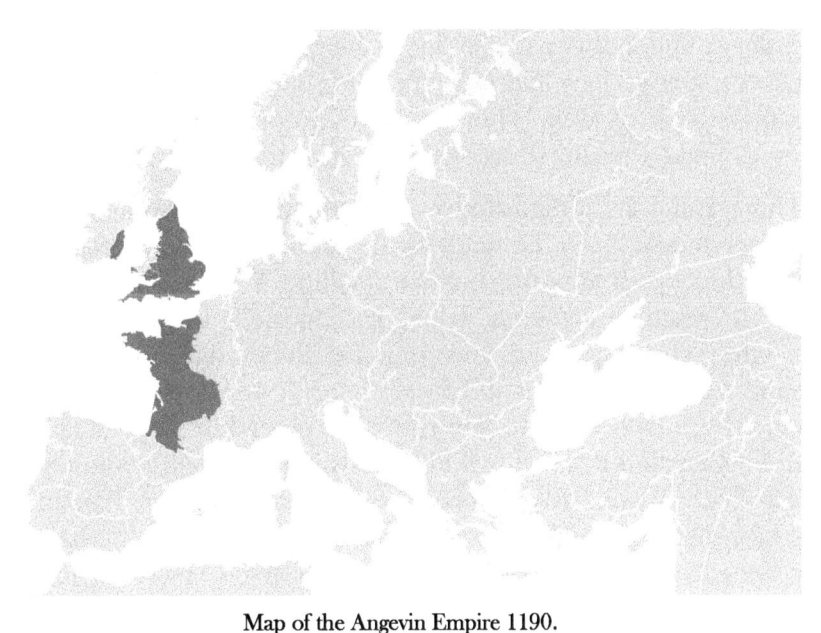

Map of the Angevin Empire 1190.
Blank map of Europe.svg: maixderivative work: Alphathon, CC BY-SA 4.0
<https://creativecommons.org/licenses/by-sa/4.0>, *via Wikimedia Commons:*
https://commons.wikimedia.org/wiki/File:Angevin_Empire_1190.svg

Now, although Henry Plantagenet was the king of England, the Angevin Empire was not necessarily an English empire. Henry II never consolidated his lands into a single territory. England remained separate from Anjou, Aquitaine, Normandy, etc. They simply had the same ruler. In fact, in his status as a Duke of Normandy, for instance, Henry Plantagenet's overlord was technically the King of France. The impact of the English king having so much land in France would ultimately have quite a few repercussions, but we will examine that more closely in the next chapter.

Henry II had so much land in France that he was the greatest landholder in France (holding more land than the King of France), and he spent most of his time on the continent and not in England. Because of this, Henry II worked to create a more effective administrative and bureaucratic system to run the country in his absence. For instance, his legal reforms established better central authority where judges were appointed by the king, and all justice came from the king's law.

These legal reforms attempted to correct a situation that had arisen under the feudal system started by William the Conqueror. In feudalism, barons were the king's tenants but could exercise similar feudal powers over those under them in the social hierarchy. Just as the king could demand marriage fees and give out land, barons could do these things with their land, as well. They could hold court, appoint officials, and generally make working decisions for all land they controlled.

This created an administrative problem. Because the king was at the top of the feudal chain, he rarely made practical decisions that impacted people directly. It was the barons deciding if someone was guilty or innocent, whether someone could get married, collecting taxes, and doing the other legal and governmental things that kept the country running. However, barons did these things however they saw fit, which made for a lot of different governmental procedures operating side by side. This created a situation where, despite not being at the top of the feudal chain, barons could wield more practical power than the king. The king's power was largely abstract, but the power of the barons was very concrete. By centralizing the legal system, Henry II took legal authority away from the barons and gave it back to the king.

The barons were not the only ones who became targets of Henry II's legal reforms. Inevitably, Henry II came into conflict with the church. At this point, when clerics were accused of a secular crime like rape, murder, theft, etc., they were tried and sentenced in church courts—a situation which almost always resulted in light sentencing, such as fasting or doing penance. Henry II saw this as a miscarriage of justice and, in 1164, created the Constitutions of Clarendon to rectify it. The constitutions simply stated that, while clerics were to be tried in church courts, they would be sentenced in the king's courts. The church did not like Henry II trying to step into their affairs one bit. It was an inevitable clash between church and state, and it led to one of the most infamous events in English history.

One of the most violent protesters to Henry II's Constitutions of Clarendon was the Archbishop of Canterbury, Thomas Becket. Becket had been a friend to Henry II before being appointed archbishop, and it is perhaps for this reason that Henry II did not take his protest well. Becket was forced into exile in France in 1165, spending five years there before finally returning to England in 1170. Upon his return, Becket promptly got the Archbishop of York suspended by the pope and excommunicated two other English bishops for their role in crowning Henry's son as heir (a ritual normally performed by the Archbishop of Canterbury).

As you can imagine, Henry II was not amused, and what happened next is slightly unclear. The story goes that when Henry II received word of Becket's actions toward the other English clergy, he burst out angrily, exclaiming, "Will no one rid me of this troublesome priest!" Four knights who were present took his exclamation seriously and decided to rid the king of this pest. Riding to Canterbury, they accosted Becket, murdering him at the altar.

Thomas Becket is murdered by Reginald Fitzurse, Hugh de Morville, William de Tracy, and Richard le Breton.
https://commons.wikimedia.org/wiki/File:Murder_of_Thomas_Becket.jpg

We do not know if this was Henry II's intention or how involved in the murder he was. However, once the deed was done, it quickly became clear that murdering a priest in a church was not a good look. Becket became a saint and martyr, and Canterbury turned into a pilgrimage site. Henry II even had to travel there to offer penance for his role in the murder, whether intentional or not.

The story of Thomas Becket is illustrative of not only the conflict between church and state but also the character of Henry II. He was an extremely competent administrator with a good head for government, but he did not always handle people effectively, and this would prove problematic, especially with his family.

The Sons of Henry II

Henry II had four adult sons: Henry, Geoffrey, Richard, and John. Henry II attempted to keep his sons happy by dividing his realm among them. But this strategy only frustrated his sons because, despite their titles, Henry did not allow them any real authority. For instance, he made his oldest son, Henry the Younger, his co-regent, but this amounted to little more than a fancy title.

The brothers also spent a lot of time quarreling over who got what. In 1173, Henry and Richard rebelled against their father for trying to give John more land. Their mother Eleanor supported the rebellion and spent the rest of Henry II's life in house arrest for it. After squashing the rebellion they had started, Henry II forgave his sons, but they had not learned their lesson. In 1181, Richard and Henry came to blows over Aquitaine. In 1183, Henry died, followed three years later by Geoffrey. This left only two sons to squabble, but that was enough. Richard joined forces with Philip II of France to fight against his father, and when John joined sides with his brother, it was all the king could take. Henry II was defeated and died in 1189, with many believing that the rebellion of his sons had hastened his end.

Richard was now king of England, but more attractive to Richard were all the French lands he had also inherited. Richard ruled for about ten years, but he only spent six months in England, preferring his continental holdings or to be on a Crusade. Indeed, Richard I is more often known as Richard the Lionheart for his crusading and military prowess.

Richard I the Lionheart, King of England by Merry-Joseph Blondel.
https://commons.wikimedia.org/wiki/File:Richard_coeur_de_lion.jpg

Considering that he spent less than a year in England, Richard's reputation as a fantastic king is largely undeserved. The popular view of him today has been largely skewed by the story of Robin Hood, which portrays Richard as a beloved and noble king. In reality, Richard seems to have cared little for England or administration. His capture during the Crusades by Muslims and subsequent ransom put a great financial burden on his people, and his military victories in the Crusades did not benefit England. As a king, Richard preferred warfare to law writing, and after a decade of leaving England to rule itself, he died during a siege in France in 1199.

Richard the Lionheart did not have an heir, so his brother John became king after him. Like Richard, the story of Robin Hood, which portrays John as a despicable tyrant, has also influenced how King John is viewed today. However, in John's case, the reality is a lot more complicated.

While his brother was known as "the Lionheart," John ended up with a much less flattering nickname: John Lackland. The nickname came from the fact that John, as the youngest son of Henry II, could not expect to inherit any significant land. This name turned out to be ironic for two reasons. John went on to inherit his father's holdings but then lost them. Thus, the nickname proved true but in an unexpected way.

John's inheritance of all his brother's land was a bit rocky, with Philip II, the King of France, initially recognizing his nephew, Arthur, as the inheritor of Anjou and Maine. However, John made concessions, and a year later had control over all of Richard's lands. The Angevin Empire was intact but not for long.

While we can sometimes be too harsh on King John, it's hard to argue that what happened next was not at least partially his fault. John had his marriage with his first wife dissolved to marry Isabella, the heiress to Angoulême, in 1200. Now, in some ways, this was a politically savvy marriage. It helped John to better secure his land in the south. But what was not politically savvy was failing to make things right with Hugh de Lusignan, the man Isabella had been betrothed to.

Lusignan complained about John to Philip II, which was all the excuse the ambitious French king needed. When John refused to appear before Philip II, war broke out, and King John did not make a good showing. While he had some initial success at the start of the war, his suspicious nature and poor decisions drove away his allies and lost battles. By 1206, he had lost Normandy, Anjou, and Maine. The loss cannot be placed entirely at John's feet. At this point, it would've been very hard for England to beat France even with a more competent leader. England had been strained funding Richard's military campaigns, and the French had more resources.

John was forced back to England, but he only had one goal: recovering the lands he had lost, which required a lot of funding. War is expensive, after all. John used every trick he could think of to gather more money from his people, including exploiting his feudal rights over his barons. This, along with instances of arbitrary justice where King John decided cases based on his whims rather than the law, sowed growing discontent among the barons of England. In 1215, a civil war known as the First Barons' War broke out.

Just like in France, John did not have much military success and soon found himself negotiating with the barons. On June 19, 1215, King John signed the Magna Carta, a document protecting the rights of the barons against the king and insisting that the king had to uphold the common law. The document is often seen as an important milestone in the protection of human rights.

It is possible to both over and understate the importance of the Magna Carta. It provided protection from tyranny, but only for the barons, not for everyday people. Still, the ideas and language of the Magna Carta found their way into later movements, such as the American and French revolutions of the eighteenth century. The Magna Carta was an important document for what it later came to represent but not for the impact it had at the time. It was overturned by the pope shortly after it was signed, and the civil war continued, ending when John died and his nine-year-old son became Henry III in 1216.

The Rise of Parliament

Henry III ruled from 1216 to 1272. During that time, he, like his more infamous father, also had conflicts with the barons, inciting the Second Barons' War from 1264 to 1267. It was during this conflict that Henry III's son, Edward, began to show a martial prowess that would have drastic consequences for not only England but the entire island of Great Britain.

When Henry III died in 1272, his son became Edward I. Edward the Confessor from centuries earlier was known primarily as the Confessor, so even though Edward I is technically the second English King Edward, he is still known as Edward I. Edward I inherited a throne that was in many ways a mess. The royal coffers were, if not empty, at least severely strained, and after two civil wars, the relationship between the king and the barons was still tense.

Correcting both issues required Edward I to learn how to work with a new institution: Parliament. The earliest idea for Parliament appears to have been the 1215 Magna Carta, which said that barons had the right to advise the king. At this point, this group of advisors was referred to as the Great Council, but eventually, it became known as Parliament. By Edward I's reign, it was clear that Parliament was there to stay. While it did not yet have all the powers it has today, Parliament had one very important right: to approve taxation.

This one power gave Parliament the ear of the king. If the king wanted revenue, he needed taxes, and if he wanted taxes, he needed Parliament's approval, and if he wanted their approval, he had to listen to them. This does not mean Parliament could bully the king. He still had ultimate power, but now there was a platform for grievances and opinions to be aired and an incentive for the king to take them seriously.

Edward I was greatly interested in replenishing the royal finances, especially to wage his wars, which we will discuss in more detail in a moment. Thus, he learned how to work with Parliament, not only enduring it but using Parliament as a tool to govern the realm. It was the start of a different type of kingship. With the rise of Parliament, Edward I's England was gaining a greater national sense of identity. The government was no longer just the king but the bureaucracy that surrounded him, particularly his council, which made up the core of Parliament. This was a transformation from the more feudal style of kingship where all power rested in and came from the king.

Wales and Scotland

With his predecessors having lost most their lands in France, Edward I set out to expand his kingdom, but he aimed closer to home.

Edward I.
Firkin, CC0, via Wikimedia Commons:
https://commons.wikimedia.org/wiki/File:King_Edward_I.png

Edward I conquered Wales with a brutally simple but effective strategy. Invading for the first time in 1277, Edward I fielded an enormous army against which the Welsh stood virtually no chance. Then, after overwhelming them with the initial strike, Edward I built many castles to cement his control—a tactic that William the Conqueror had employed after conquering England back in 1066. Although there were revolts, from this point, Wales was under the control of the English (though it would be a long time before the two nations were officially joined).

Edward I did not stop at Wales, though. He also had plans to conquer Scotland, an ambition which earned him the nickname "Hammer of the Scots." He invaded his northern neighbor in 1296, but he did not have the funds needed to repeat what he had done in Wales. The conquest of Scotland was therefore much slower, and despite stiff resistance from the Scots, it appeared that eventually Edward I would conquer Scotland, too. However, Edward I died in 1307 before the campaign was finished, leaving the conquest of Scotland to his son, Edward II.

Fortunately for Scotland, Edward II was not his father. The Scots, led by Robert the Bruce, defeated the English and Edward II at the Battle of Bannockburn in 1314, securing Scottish independence for the next four hundred years.

Edward II also failed to mimic his father in another way: keeping his barons happy. With a reputation for blatant favoritism and incompetent government, Edward II was not well-liked. He was ultimately deposed by a plot hatched by his wife and her lover, becoming the first English king to be forced off the throne while still alive. His son, Edward III, was put on the throne in his place in 1327 at the age of fourteen.

These were the first six kings of the Plantagenet dynasty and the England they ruled. The kingdom that Edward III took over in 1327 was much smaller than that ruled by Henry II, but it was also a bit more English. By 1327, years of discontented barons had forced the English king to give more consideration to the people he ruled. However, English kings had still not lost all interest in France.

Chapter 8: The Hundred Years' War and the Black Death

The fourteenth century was one of the most turbulent times in English history. Despite various wars, the general population of England had been increasing steadily over the twelfth and thirteenth centuries. But, by the end of the fourteenth century, around a third to a half of the English population was dead.

Not only would the fourteenth century see death on an enormous scale, but there was political turmoil. By the end of the century, England had entered a war that would last over a hundred years and seen its first popular uprising. It was enough to make many people think the world was ending, and in some ways, they were right. By the time the 1300s ended, medieval society was starting to crumble and transform.

So, what exactly happened? Let's back up a bit and start with 1315, the year of the famine.

The Great Famine

As we just noted, until the fourteenth century the English population had been steadily increasing. Agricultural production was improving, and with the ability to feed more mouths, population growth was inevitable. This situation made the entire population of Europe highly susceptible to food shortages, which is exactly what happened in 1315.

Periods of heavy rain and cooler temperatures rotted the crops and made it impossible to even make hay for the livestock. Farmers, unable to get food from their land, sold it and moved to large population centers in the hopes of buying food. But the extreme demand and low supply made prices skyrocket. There simply wasn't enough to go around. Farming conditions did not recover until 1322, and by then, about 15 percent of the English population had died of starvation.

Despite its great devastation, England recovered from The Great Famine relatively quickly. The population and economy were back to normal by 1330. Still, the event impacted all of Europe and left a traumatic memory with all those who survived. Medieval society had been completely unable to handle the crisis caused by the weather, and eventually, changes were made to government structure to better handle such wide-scale events. However, the fourteenth century still had a lot more to throw at England.

The Hundred Years' War

As we discussed in the previous chapter, English kings had held land in France since the time of Henry II. They had lost most of that land during the reign of King John, but the connections between France and England were still there. In 1337, Edward III decided it was time to push those ties, declaring his right to the French throne.

Now, this claim wasn't completely crazy. Edward III and the current French king, Philip the Fair, both shared a great-grandfather who had been king of France. When the direct line of the French monarchy failed, Philip the Fair ended up on the throne, but technically Edward III had just as much of a blood claim to the throne.

Still, becoming king of France was probably not Edward III's plan. What brought France and England to war in 1337 was not the French throne but French land, specifically Aquitaine. France claimed that Aquitaine was a French duchy subject to the French king. England believed that Aquitaine was part of its feudal territory since the time of Henry II. Under the systems of the day, both sides had a point, and Aquitaine was a rich enough holding for both to be prepared to fight over it. Thus, the Hundred Years' War began.

The name of this war in slightly misleading for two reasons. First, it lasted longer than a hundred years, from 1337 to 1453. It was also less an ongoing war and more a series of campaigns with frequent temporary truces and interruptions. France and England were at war for over a hundred years, but they were not actively fighting for a hundred years.

There are too many major battles for us to delve into here. Names like Crecy, Poitiers, Agincourt, Orleans, and Castilian would become forever seared in English memory. Some, like Agincourt, were great victories that would become almost mythic in the English psyche. Others, like Castilian, the last major battle of the war, were crushing defeats. While the English were initially very successful in the war, winning early battles like Crecy, the English had lost all land in France by the end of the war in 1453 (except for Calais, which the French would not recover until 1558).

King Henry V of England at the Battle of Agincourt, France, October 25, 1415. Line engraving, 19th century.
https://commons.wikimedia.org/wiki/File:King_Henry_V_of_England_at_the_Battle_of_Agincourt,_1415.jpg

War against France was ultimately an extremely costly endeavor that gained England very little. It caused periods of severe taxation on the English people, resulting in a popular uprising. The constant campaigning also created a nobility with high levels of military drive and know-how, which would prove disastrous during the internal conflicts of the fifteenth century, which we will discuss in the following chapter. Finally, a hundred years of war utterly destroyed relations between the two countries. England and France would remain fierce rivals until

World War I. But not even the outbreak of this conflict was the most disruptive event of the fourteenth century.

The Black Death

In 1347, the Black Death struck Europe, and nothing would ever be the same. But before we get into precisely what happened, what exactly is the Black Death? The Black Death refers to the specific outbreak of plague that hit Europe from 1347 to 1351. "Plague" in this sense does not refer to the outbreak of any disease. It is a term that refers to a specific disease caused by the bacterium *Yersinia pestis*. Plague still exists today, but thanks to antibiotics, it is no longer the threat it was in 1347.

The Black Death was also not the first time that plague had affected human populations. There had been outbreaks before, but nothing of the scale and devastation of the Black Death. Estimates state that the disease killed between a third and a half of the entire population of Europe (the disease also spread to Asia and Africa, where it caused similar levels of devastation). Entire villages were wiped out.

To put it in perspective, the second deadliest pandemic in history was the outbreak of Spanish influenza in 1918, which killed 3 percent of the world's population. The Black Death killed around 50 percent of people in Africa, Asia, and Europe. Almost no other event in history comes close to that level of destruction. How then did it all start, and how did it get so bad?

The Black Death began in Asia, and the story goes that it came to Europe through Italian ports. The town of Kaffa in Crimea was under siege by Mongols infected with the plague. The army spread the disease to the besieged city, and Kaffa was devastated. (Some argue that this was done purposely as the first act of biological warfare.) Ships fled the dying city, landing in Italian ports, and by the time the Italians realized what those ships carried, it was too late. The plague had arrived, and from Italy, it spread across Europe, rapidly reaching all the way to Scotland by 1350.

Just why was it so hard to stop the spread of plague, though? Plague is a disease originally carried by rats and passed to humans through flea bites. In the 1300s, lack of public and private hygiene meant there were plenty of rats and fleas to be had. It is also quite possible that the disease spread from human to human as well, making it even more difficult to stop. Add in the fact that people in this period had no idea what was causing the disease, and you can begin to see why the Black Death marched through Europe unhindered.

If you contracted the plague, your odds were not good. Most people who got the plague were dead within a week. There was no cure and not even an effective treatment to quell the symptoms—and the symptoms were quite horrible. Bubonic plague gave its victims high fever, nausea, and aches. On top of that, it caused extreme swelling of the lymph nodes, giving a person large, oozing bulges called buboes.

Bubonic was not the only form the plague took, though it was by far the most common. Pneumatic (plague that attacked the lungs) and septicemic (plague that got into the bloodstream) were the two other strains. The survival rate for both these types was almost completely nonexistent. Septicemic plague in particular was a death sentence and could cause a person's skin to turn black (due to tissue death) and body parts (like fingers and toes) to fall off.

The plague eventually ran its course, abating by around 1351, but the damage was irrevocable. Survivors were left in a very different world. For the first time, the demand for workers was higher than the supply, and workers had bargaining power. The plague also eliminated the strict differences between the rich and poor in brutal fashion. The plague was an indiscriminate killer, and it revealed that there was little difference between those at the top and bottom of society. With so many deaths, there was also a surplus of goods, causing prices to plummet. The standard of living for survivors went up because of these things.

It would take time, but the feudal system began to collapse in on itself because of these changes. This was the beginning of the end for the Middle Ages.

The Peasants' Revolt

Change, however, is rarely welcomed by all. As you can imagine, the elites were not too happy about many of the changes brought about by the Black Death. They did not want to pay their workers more, so a law was passed to create a wage ceiling. It did not make the people happy, and their discontent grew.

With the Black Death having run its course, England and France got back to the important business of fighting each other. Richard II took over the conflict from his grandfather, Edward III, when he became king in 1377. While Edward III and his son (Richard II's father, Edward the Black Prince) had done exceedingly well in the conflict with France, Richard II did not. The war was going poorly, and this created two problems. It made waging war even more expensive, and it made the people more unhappy with the war.

Losing a war was a guaranteed way to make your subjects very upset with you, and this was because of the way taxation worked. The king collected annual revenue through several streams, but that normal revenue did not include money directly from the people. A king could only tax the people directly in dire circumstances, which included war. What the king thus had were people unaccustomed to paying taxes every year who knew that their taxes were going to fund a war that England was losing. These people were also discontent because their wages had been fixed. These were all the ingredients needed for England's first popular uprising.

The final straw that started the revolt was the third poll tax issued by Richard II. Richard II had already used this tax to squeeze extra funds out of his people twice, and this came on top of four years of direct taxation in a row. Richard II was squeezing every last coin from his people, and in 1381, tensions exploded.

The revolt broke out in the southeast, led by a man named Wat Tyler. At first, the peasants were off to a great start. They marched toward London and were enough of a threat to secure a meeting with the mayor and king to voice their demands for reform. Their mistake, however, was in thinking that the elites would treat them as equals. Around thirty years had passed since the Black Death began the process of tearing down the feudal system, but not that much had changed. Wat Tyler was killed by the mayor of London at the meeting.

The painting depicts the end of the 1381 Peasants' Revolt. The image shows London's mayor, Walworth, killing Wat Tyler. There are two images of Richard II. One looks on at the killing while the other is talking to the peasants.
https://commons.wikimedia.org/wiki/File:Assassinat_de_Wat_Tyler_par_Walworth_sous_l%27%C5%93il_de_Richard_II.png

You would think that having its leader murdered would have caused the angry mob to erupt and attack the city, but that's not what happened. Somehow Richard II, who in all other areas had proved himself a very incompetent and cruel king, managed to talk down the rebels and get them all to go home, promising to implement some reform.

That reform never happened. Once the rebels were dispersed and no longer an active threat, they were rounded up and punished. England's first popular uprising had accomplished absolutely nothing. It was a grim reminder that society still had a very strict social hierarchy. The breakdown of feudalism was not going to result in a society where everyone was equal.

Despite not accomplishing anything, the Peasants' Revolt of 1381 is still an extremely important event. It showed that England's lower classes were beginning to have a sense of their rights and power. True rights for the people were still a long way off, but 1381 was the first time the people had even tried to demand it. Times were changing.

Medieval society was not going to go down without a fight, though. While the Black Death was the catalyst for much of the societal change that began around this time, it would take another type of catastrophe of the man-made variety to get England's nobles to accept such change: The Wars of the Roses.

Chapter 9: The Wars of the Roses

The Wars of the Roses is one of the most famous events in English history, even inspiring writers. George R.R. Martin's Game of Thrones series is based on this event, and Shakespeare wrote a trilogy of plays covering it. However, all this attention also means that the history and later legends and stories about the wars have blurred until it's sometimes hard to tell fact from fiction. Our aim in this chapter is to separate history from mythology and learn just what happened in this turbulent period of English history. Like many historical events, we need to start far earlier than the first battle date to do that. It all began with the death of a king.

Setting the Scene

Henry V took the throne in 1413 following the death of his father, Henry IV. Henry V jumped wholeheartedly into the conflict with France started by Edward III, and unlike Richard II, Henry V's military ambitions made him a popular king. The key difference was that Henry V was winning. Henry V's most famous victory was Agincourt, but he enjoyed other successes as well, earning a reputation as a military genius and turning England into a superpower. Henry V even got himself declared heir to the French throne and married the French princess.

All seemed set for England to rise to an unprecedented height when Henry V developed camp fever during a siege. He died suddenly in 1422, and this was very bad indeed for England. Kings die all the time, of course, but what made Henry V's death so untimely was that his son and heir, Henry VI, wasn't even a year old yet. To make matters even more interesting, Charles VI of France died only about a month after Henry V. Because Henry V had been named the French king's heir, this meant that Henry VI was now king of France, as well.

What do you do when the king isn't old enough to rule? In short, someone rules for him, making decisions on the king's behalf. But then, how do you decide who gets to do that? That's a difficult question, which is why Henry V tried to settle matters on his deathbed. He appointed his uncle (Henry VI's great uncle), Thomas Beaufort, to care for the royal person (although Henry VI's mother Catherine also had a very large role in raising her son). Henry V instructed that his brother, John of Bedford, be put in charge of France and named his other brother, Humphrey, Duke of Gloucester, as *tutela* while Henry VI remained a minor. This title could have meant that Gloucester was simply responsible for Henry VI's education, or it could have given Gloucester the effective regency until Henry VI came of age.

That, however, is not what happened after Henry V died. Gloucester was relatively well-liked, but he did not inspire the confidence necessary to give him sole effective reign over England. Instead, he was given a fancy title with strict powers and limitations. He was still a prime player in the English government, but he would not be handed the reins.

So, who was in charge, then? Strangely enough, legally and technically Henry VI was ruling the country. Instead of naming a regent, the elite of English society (Henry VI's uncles, mother, and others) worked together to run the country in Henry VI's name. Documents were worded as though they had been written by Henry VI, and the king was brought to open Parliament in 1423 when he wasn't even two yet. Thus, England operated under a political fiction in which a council of powerful people ran the country while pretending that Henry VI was making decisions.

While that might seem incredibly weird, it shows that the English were very aware of two facts. One was that for kingship and monarchical government to work, the person of the king had to be respected. England's entire governmental system was designed around the central figure of the king, so to throw that out entirely would have caused the system to collapse. Two, England was in a dangerous position. Henry V's military successes had put England in a very powerful position, but his death left the country vulnerable. To be weak and at the top makes you a prime target. The fiction that Henry VI was ruling in his own name was thus an obvious effort to maintain a strong front and keep the nation together. The fact that no one immediately tried to oust the infant king shows just how committed most of the English nobles were to this front.

Thus was the start of a very precarious situation. When a group of people share ultimate power, eventually someone is going to want more. While the conciliar government was in many ways necessary, it created a situation where many different people were commanding power. It would take a strong king to reign in such a group, and that is not what Henry VI turned out to be.

The Kingship of Henry VI

It's hard to be fair to Henry VI. Becoming king before the age of one is bound to give anyone a very strange childhood. There was immense pressure for Henry VI to take over the reins of government as soon as possible, which undoubtedly resulted in him being pushed into situations he was not ready for, such as his coronation at the age of seven. He was also the first English king to be crowned King of France, and his father, Henry V, was a legend to which Henry VI would inevitably be compared. In hindsight, the burden was so large that there was no way Henry VI could live up to expectations, especially as he had no example, having ascended to the throne without ever seeing his father's rule.

Illuminated miniature of Henry VI of England.
https://commons.wikimedia.org/wiki/File:Henry_VI_of_England,_Shrewsbury_book.jpg

However, there is also little doubt that Henry VI did not appear that interested in ruling. By 1437, he was old enough to rule in his own right, and it was soon clear that Henry VI was not his father. Henry VI was a pious and kind man who preferred to spend his time studying scripture and disliked war and government business. This was not what England needed, though. Since Henry V's death, the country had faced setbacks in France and was losing a grip on its conquered territory. John of Bedford was dead, and the English desperately needed their young king to take charge if they wished to keep France.

That, however, appeared to be something Henry VI could not do. Not only did he show little interest, even being described as vacant, but the decisions he made showed incompetence. He was simply not an effective ruler, nor did he have much of a spine, and that left room for other men to try to rule through him. The Duke of Somerset emerged as the victor in this political squabbling and shuffling, achieving a place as Henry VI's chief minister and thus the effective ruler of England. Richard, Duke of York, was quite unhappy with this, believing that he should hold that position. It was the conflict between these two and their allies that would eventually lead to war.

Seizing Power

By 1453, England had lost all its land in France, culminating in a final defeat at Castillon. The grand achievement of Henry V had been undone, and his son did not take the news well, falling into a stupor, or waking coma. The weak king became completely catatonic and would remain so for over a year. He was as effective a ruler as he had been when he had first taken the throne as an infant. Once again, England needed to work out some form of government that could operate without the king.

A council was summoned, and Richard of York did not waste his opportunity. He seized power, arresting his rival Somerset and making himself effective ruler of England during Henry VI's illness. For a year, York ruled the country. But then, suddenly, Henry VI got better. Just as quickly as he had seized power, York was thrown from grace as Henry VI backed Somerset over him. It became quite clear to York that he would never have power so long as Somerset stood in the way, and there was only one way to get around this. York raised an army. The wars were about to begin.

Early Stages of the Conflict

Initially, York did not intend to overthrow the king. He intended to remove the "traitors" around the king, the chief of which was Somerset. Although the two sides made attempts to negotiate, violence broke out at St. Albans on May 22, 1455.

That first battle went quite well for the Yorkists, who overran their opponents and captured the king. Taking the king back to London, York seized control of the country. Somerset had been killed in the fighting, and it appeared that York had successfully pulled off a coup. It is unlikely anyone at this stage could have guessed just how long the conflict would continue.

It was Henry VI's wife, Margaret of Anjou, who proved to be York's greatest opponent. She was not prepared to accept York's rule, and she had possession of one very important aspect of power: the heir. Prince Edward had been born in 1453, and Margaret believed she could wield power through him, especially since her husband Henry VI certainly did not seem prepared to defend his throne. When York lost the support of Parliament in 1456, Margaret acted quickly to increase her power, amassing wealth and appointing people she trusted to government positions, including people like Henry VI's half-brothers Jasper and Edmund Tudor, figures we will return to later.

With York out and Margaret consolidating power, there was a possibility that things might still end peacefully. Arrangements were made for talks in 1458. Although these were completed without the eruption of conflict, there was simply too much bad blood between the two sides for things to end well. Margaret and the Duke of York appeared to truly dislike each other, and many people on the royalist or Lancastrian side (so named because Henry VI was part of the House of Lancaster) had lost loved ones in the battle of St. Albans. The country was crackling with tension, and in late 1459, violence began again.

Again, the Yorkists won the initial battle, but this time they could not take advantage of their initial victory. Their second resort to arms had made it clear to many that they were opposed to the royal government, and Margaret, at least, was not prepared to negotiate. Royal forces, which greatly outnumbered the Yorkists, prepared to engage at Ludlow, and the Yorkist leaders, sensing inevitable defeat, fled to save their own lives, leaving their army to surrender and hope to be spared. Four years after York had so successfully seized power at St. Albans, he was on the run.

However, the Yorkists did not intend to stay in exile. Before the end of the next year, they returned, beat the royalist forces, and entered London. This time, though, York was done fighting to be the king's right-hand man. Now York was declaring himself king.

This was a shock to both his allies and enemies. Since the death of Henry V in 1422, every effort has been made to maintain the position and authority of the monarch, but York had had enough. With Queen Margaret opposed to him and in control of the heir to the throne, York had no chance of holding power as long as the future king was against him. The only way around this was to do the unthinkable and overthrow the king. But, although the king himself made no indication that he cared whether he was overthrown, his wife and her allies were not prepared to give in so easily. It would be a long struggle.

The Wars Drag On

These first years show quite neatly what would continue in England for the next three decades. Each side enjoyed victories and defeats, with periods of triumph and exile. As those first four years show, it was not a period of continuous fighting, which is why it is called the Wars of the Roses rather than a singular war. However, violence always seemed to erupt again, partially because the great amount of blood being spilled left little room for forgiveness. No one wanted to come to peaceful terms with the people responsible for the death of their brother or father. England was trapped in a cycle of violence and hate.

The people who started the conflict were not protected from that cycle, either. York died in the fighting in 1460, and his son Edward, who was now the Duke of York, took up his father's cause quite successfully. Edward defeated the Lancastrian forces and was crowned Edward IV in 1461.

That was far from the end of things, though. Edward IV owed his crown to his uncle, Richard Neville, the Earl of Warwick, who had been York's staunch supporter and the military might behind the Yorkist victory. Warwick expected this to mean that he could effectively rule through his nephew, but Edward IV wanted independence. He began making political moves against Warwick, who after being forced to leave the country, teamed up with old enemies, the Lancastrians, who had been biding their time in France.

Edward IV was now in real trouble, and the Wars of the Roses, which had been "off" for around nine years, were on again. Edward IV fled the country to regroup, and Henry VI, who had been in confinement in the Tower of London since 1465, was put back on the throne. This stage of the wars came to a head at the Battle of Tewkesbury where Edward IV thoroughly defeated his opponents, killing almost all the Lancastrian leaders. He even had Henry VI murdered because, despite his incompetence as a leader, his mere existence was proving too dangerous for the Yorkist king.

To many, the long conflict thus seemed to be over in 1471. Edward IV had two sons, securing his line, before his death in 1483. With twelve years of peace and most of the Lancastrians dead, the conflict should have been over. But the showdown between the House of York and Lancaster had one final act, and it would prove to be something no one expected.

Richard III and Henry Tudor

When Edward IV died in 1483, the throne passed to his eldest son Edward V, except Edward V never got a chance to claim it. His uncle, Richard, Duke of York, had the young king and his brother sent to the Tower of London. They were declared illegitimate, and Edward V was deposed. Their uncle became Richard III, and the boys were never heard from again.

Portrait of Richard III of England, painted by Barthel II (approximate date from tree-rings on panel). The blackletter text on the frame reads: "Richard(us) Rex terti(us)."
https://commons.wikimedia.org/wiki/File:Richard_III_earliest_surviving_portrait.jpg

Of course, the assumption is that Richard III had his nephews murdered, and it is a plausible assumption. Even though he would later face heavy criticism for these alleged murders, Richard III was never able to produce his nephews again after they disappeared into the Tower of London. If they had been alive, he could have saved himself a lot of grief by producing them; if they had escaped, we would expect them to appear in public to contest their uncle's claims to the throne. The bodies of two young boys were found hundreds of years later under some steps in the tower, and many believe that these were the young princes, though there is no proof that this is the case.

Although Richard III took the throne under suspicious circumstances, his reign nevertheless seemed fairly sure. Thanks to the Wars of the Roses, there simply wasn't anyone left to oppose him. At least there almost wasn't anyone.

One Lancastrian claimant to the English throne was left standing: Henry Tudor. You would be forgiven for wondering who this was, for Henry Tudor had little claim to fame. His father, Edmund Tudor, had been the half-brother of Henry VI (Edmund's father, Owen Tudor, a Welshman, had married Henry V's widow). Henry Tudor's mother, Margaret Beaufort, was the great-granddaughter of John of Gaunt, Duke of Lancaster, one of the sons of King Edward III. He thus had a claim to the throne by blood, but it was dubious at best. Dubious, however, proved to be enough. In 1485, Henry Tudor landed in England with an army prepared to push his claim to the throne, and Richard III prepared to meet him.

The two rivals clashed at Bosworth Field. Richard III had superior military experience and seemed confident of a victory over the young would-be king. The battle was decided by the men, not their leaders, though, and in this Henry Tudor proved superior. His forces won the day, and Richard III was killed in the fighting. Thus died the last Yorkist claimant to the throne.

With his victory, Henry Tudor became Henry VII, starting not only a new dynasty but a new era in English history. To cement his rule, he married Edward IV's daughter, Elizabeth of York, finally uniting the two warring houses. The Wars of the Roses were finally over, but there would be lasting changes. The English nobility had been largely wiped out in the decades of infighting, and with them went the last of the old feudal structure. The Middle Ages were ending, and the early modern period had begun.

Chapter 10: The Tudors and the English Reformation

The Battle of Bosworth began a new stage in English history. The Plantagenets, who had ruled England for 331 years, were all dead. All the land in France had now officially been lost (except for Calais). The old feudal system was collapsing. Henry Tudor was taking over a country that had been a mess for the past three decades. Would he be able to restore England to its former glory?

Henry VII

Henry VII has the unfortunate legacy of having been a very effective and capable ruler who was nonetheless not well-liked. His decision to marry Elizabeth of York to combine the houses of York and Lancaster shows some of his political acumen, but his skills were much greater than that. A very hands-on ruler, Henry VII managed his kingdom himself, doing everything from creating policies to managing funds. The consensus is that he did a pretty good job. From the time Henry VII took the throne in 1485 to his death in 1509, he managed to correct quite a few problems the previous English kings had faced.

Likely because of the Wars of the Roses, Henry VII carefully avoided making extremely powerful nobles. He handed out lands and titles sparingly, and while he listened to counsel, he did not rely on only a few powerful men. This refusal to play or promote favorites did not earn

Henry VII many friends, but it prevented the creation of super-powerful and competing nobles that could start another conflict like the Wars of the Roses.

However, this did not mean Henry VII had no uprisings or rebellions to worry about. Having been acquired on the field of battle, Henry VII's position, especially at the start of his reign, was precarious. A king who earns his kingdom through conquest can easily be overthrown by the same means, and there were several attempts. Twice, Henry VII would find himself dealing with imposters claiming to be either Edward V or his brother Richard (the princes who were likely killed in the Tower of London). There were other Yorkist rebellions as well, but Henry VII managed to quell them all. He was not the pushover that Henry VI had been. Henry VII meant to reestablish the strength of the Crown.

Another way Henry VII strengthened royal authority was by getting the royal finances in order. Unlike many kings before and after him, Henry VII lived strictly within his means, relying on the money generated by his lands to run the government and his household. While this was theoretically how kingship was supposed to work, the constant warfare of the past 200 years had caused many English kings to need far more revenue than they were producing, which led them to greatly tax their people. By not going to war, Henry VII saved a good deal of money. He also found ways to acquire more land, which increased his personal revenue. The result was a full treasury.

While Henry VII's policies were no doubt efficient, as we have already mentioned, they did not make him well-liked. Turning the royal revenue around required being extremely strict about collecting fees and stripping lands from some. The constant rebellions also made Henry VII an extremely suspicious and hard man. It can easily be argued that this is what was required of anyone hoping to be a successful king in the wake of the Wars of the Roses, but the difficulties of his situation did not make Henry VII's exacting and distrustful nature easier to bear. Thus, while he was extremely capable, England did not grieve much when he died in 1509. The nation and nobles looked forward to the reign of his more genial son, Henry VIII.

Henry VIII

Henry VIII was the second son of Henry VII and thus did not expect to be king until his elder brother Arthur died unexpectedly in 1502. To secure an alliance with Spain, Henry VIII then married his older brother's betrothed, Catherine of Aragon, an incident that would become extremely important later in his reign.

Portrait of Henry VIII (after 1537). Oil on canvas. Walker Art Gallery, Liverpool by Hans Holbein the Younger.
https://commons.wikimedia.org/wiki/File:After_Hans_Holbein_the_Younger_-_Portrait_of_Henry_VIII_-_Google_Art_Project.jpg

Before we dive into the numerous wives for which Henry VIII is most famous, let's take a moment to understand a bit more about what Henry VIII was like as a king. While his father had been cold and calculating and deeply involved in carrying out government, Henry VIII struck a very different chord as a king. Instead of running things himself, Henry VIII relied more on great men he appointed to run the country for him. That did not, however, mean that Henry VIII was a weak king. He could be incredibly tempestuous, and his councilors, while holding considerable power, only did so at the king's consent. They were often removed almost as quickly as they had risen to power.

One thing that both father and son had in common was an appreciation for the pageantry of royalty. Both Henry VII and Henry VIII knew that looking like a king was an important part of royal authority. They invested in the pomp and circumstance of monarchy, and that investment gave the Tudors an air of legitimacy that helped to cement their rule.

Of course, these traits are not what Henry VIII is remembered for, though. Henry VIII will forever be the king with six wives—and with good reason. Henry VIII's marital troubles would forever change England.

The Wives of Henry VIII and the Reformation

While by his death Henry VIII had been married to six wives, it was the second that caused the stir and changed England. Henry VIII had been married to Catherine of Aragon for two decades when the trouble started, and that trouble was named Anne Boleyn.

This was not the first time Henry VIII had sought a woman other than his wife. His extramarital affairs were well established, but two things made this time very different. First, Anne Boleyn would not become the king's mistress. She wanted to be queen, and she was not going to have sex with Henry VIII unless that happened. Secondly, Catherine of Aragon was now in her forties, which was well past childbearing age for a woman at this time, and she had no son. The only child of Henry VIII and Catherine of Aragon was a daughter named Mary. Even though it was legally allowable, no woman had ever successfully inherited the English throne. The last time one had tried, the result had been a fifteen-year civil war (The Anarchy). These two factors combined made Henry decide to throw off Catherine and marry Anne.

But this was the 1500s, and that was not a simple matter. Divorce was not allowed. Henry VIII needed to have his marriage annulled (to be declared null and void, as though it had never happened), and the only person who could do that was the pope. Except, the pope did not want to help Henry VIII. Rome but the forces of the Holy Roman Emperor, who just so happened to be Catherine of Aragon's nephew, and he did not like the idea of seeing his aunt tossed aside. Catherine was also not prepared to simply step aside. A stalemate ensued that lasted for years, and the entire affair became known as the "King's Great Matter."

If it had been any earlier in history, what happened next would not have been possible, but it just so happened that this occurred in the late 1520s and early 1530s. About a decade had passed since Luther had nailed his Ninety-Five Theses to the church in Wittenberg, sparking the religious tidal wave known as the Reformation. For the first time in Christendom, if Henry VIII didn't like what the pope had to say, he had other options.

That's how, in 1533, the Archbishop of Canterbury, the highest church official in England, annulled the marriage between Catherine and Henry. He then declared the secret vows that Anne and Henry had exchanged a year prior were valid and that the couple was married. This was all done without the pope's approval, sending a clear signal that the English king had turned his back on the Roman Catholic Church, specifically the pope. A year later, in 1534, this was confirmed when the English Parliament passed the Act of Supremacy, which made the king "the Supreme Head of the Church of England." England had officially broken with Rome.

Protestant England?

Since England was no longer Roman Catholic, you might think that made England Protestant by default. While this might be technically true, Henry VIII's Protestant England was a far cry from what was happening in Germany and other hotbeds of the Reformation.

Henry VIII had decided he no longer wanted to listen to the pope, but he still held largely Catholic religious opinions. Although there were ministers in his government who pushed for greater religious changes, Henry VIII kept most things the same. The bishops and archbishops remained but now answered to the king rather than the pope. Catholic doctrinal beliefs also remained intact. For the average person, religious practice in England did not differ much from what it had been before 1534.

Henry VIII made two important changes, however. Henry VIII allowed the Bible to be made available in English and systematically dissolved the entire monastic system in England. It was this second action that caused a bit of an uproar.

At the time of the break with Rome, England had around eight hundred monasteries. Something had to be done with all those Catholic institutions. The immediate response was to attempt to fold them into the new Church of England, but Henry VIII soon saw a more profitable use for the monasteries. The act of supremacy had made the king the Supreme Head of the Church of England, so technically all the monasteries belonged to Henry VIII now. Considering that monasteries owned a quarter of all the used land in England, that was no small gain, and Henry VIII decided to take advantage of it.

In 1536, the first Act of Suppression was passed, which dissolved monasteries with an income less than a certain amount. Dissolving a monastery meant that its land and possessions were taken by the Crown. For the most part, the elite of English society did not bat an eye at this drastic measure. After all, they stood to gain, as much of the monasteries' land would be redistributed among them. The common people, however, took great issue with this step. Monasteries were places of education and relief for the sick and poor. They often played a key role in their communities, so this particular step of Henry VIII's English Reformation was the first to disrupt local life. An uprising called the Pilgrimage of Grace broke out in the north in protest.

Henry VIII was not amused or sympathetic. The Pilgrimage of Grace was crushed swiftly and thoroughly, and the dissolution of the monasteries continued. By 1541, all the monasteries in England had been dissolved. Although it didn't get anywhere, the Pilgrimage of Grace does show that the English people reacted negatively to the sudden religious change forced on them by their king. Changes in the religious beliefs of the whole country take time. It would be many decades after 1534 before England was truly Protestant.

The Other Wives

While none of his other marriages would have quite the impact of Henry VIII's second marriage, it is worth mentioning what happened between Henry and Anne Boleyn and with the rest of his wives to get a better understanding of Henry and his children, who would all rule England.

Despite a successful pregnancy (which could be a rare thing in those days) early in their marriage, Anne did not deliver the much-wanted son and heir, instead only giving birth to a daughter named Elizabeth. Thus, three years after her marriage to the king, she was accused of infidelity, and the marriage was annulled. Two days later, Anne was beheaded, leaving the king to marry his newest infatuation, Jane Seymour. Although we don't know for sure, Anne was likely innocent, and the charges against her were fabricated to get rid of her and leave the king free to marry Jane. It is even more unclear if the scheme was Henry VIII's idea or if he truly believed Anne had been unfaithful thanks to the whispers of members of his court.

It was Jane who finally had the son Henry VIII so craved, giving birth in 1537 to Edward, but childbirth at this time was dangerous. She died twelve days later from complications.

Shockingly, Henry VIII stayed single for three years after Jane's death. His single status represented a great political and diplomatic tool, and his next wife was chosen very carefully. A German princess, Anne of Cleves, was the ideal choice because she was the sister of the Duke of Cleves, who happened to be Catholic but also anti-papal (against the pope). It was a smart alliance for an England that was trying to remain somewhat neutral in the great religious tension of the day.

The marriage was arranged diplomatically, and Anne of Cleves sailed off to marry Henry VIII, who found her repulsive. He went through with the marriage, but when it became clear that he would not start a war by getting rid of her, he had the marriage annulled on the grounds of non-consummation. Although he thought her ugly, Henry VIII did give Anne of Cleves lands and money as a settlement, and she escaped the marriage unscathed, which is more than can be said of his next wife.

The next woman to have the hand of Henry VIII was the Catholic Catherine Howard, an English noblewoman. Her time as queen from 1540 to 1542 saw a brief resurgence of Catholic power at the English court, but Henry VIII soon grew suspicious after having to put down several Catholic plots in the north. Catherine Howard was found guilty of adultery and, like Anne Boleyn before her, beheaded.

In 1543, Henry VIII married his last wife, Catherine Parr, a widow with Protestant sympathies. She outlived her husband and was by all accounts a good wife, good queen, and even a good stepmother to Henry VIII's three children: Mary, Edward, and Elizabeth. While Catherine Parr might not have had as exciting a story as Henry VIII's other wives, she was the only one who kept her marriage to the king intact.

By the time of his death, Henry VIII had accomplished something rather unique. He had had twice as many wives as children (not counting illegitimate children), and all three of his children would eventually reign over England. The children of Henry VIII turned out to be the last of the Tudor dynasty. With the break with Rome still fresh, England was on a journey of religious transformation, and each of Henry VIII's children's reigns would be shaped profoundly by their attempts to direct that religious change.

Chapter 11: Elizabeth I

When Henry VIII died in 1547, his son, Edward, succeeded him despite being the youngest of the children. Edward VI was only nine when he became king, but his health was poor, and his reign ended with his premature death in 1553.

Without another obvious male heir, Henry VIII's eldest child, Mary, managed something that no woman before her had ever done: she became Queen of England. Mary was the first queen to rule England in her own right. She was queen because she ruled England, not because she was married to a king. While that alone is an impressive feat, it can hardly be said that Mary's reign was a success. By the time she died in 1558, Mary had earned the immortal nickname "Bloody Mary." History would not remember her fondly.

Henry VIII's middle child, who came to the throne last, ruled the longest. Elizabeth succeeded her sister in 1558 and ruled until her death in 1603. As Elizabeth's reign was seven to eight times longer than those of her siblings, we will devote most of this chapter to England under Elizabeth I. But before we dive into what many considered to be a golden age for England, let's look more closely at the reigns of Edward VI and Mary.

Religious Settlement and the Children of Henry VIII

Both Edward VI and Mary's legacies revolved largely around how they handled England's religion. Although Edward VI was young, he held much deeper Protestant convictions than his father, Henry VIII. Under Edward VI, England began taking much larger strides toward Protestantism. With changes to things like the prayer book used in worship service, England experienced religious change that could be felt by the common people daily, and this did cause some backlash, such as the Prayer Book Rebellion in 1549.

Despite the resistance of some of the common people, Protestantism pushed forward resiliently under Edward VI, thanks largely to his ministers. Men like John Dudley, Earl of Northumberland, carried out the young king's wishes with what many would call severity. It seemed like a good policy. Edward VI was young, so a man who could please him could expect a long and powerful political career. Only, when the young king died in 1553, the fortunes of individuals and the country radically changed.

Edward VI had no male heirs, which meant the obvious person next in line for the throne was his older sister Mary, but Edward VI's ministers attempted to stop Mary from taking the throne. Mary was firmly Catholic, which did not look good to the people who had just helped Edward VI push England toward Protestantism. They attempted to install Lady Jane Grey on the throne instead. However, Mary acted quickly to gather support, and it soon became clear that the country preferred her to Jane. Mary became queen.

Mary may have secured her throne neatly, but the rest of her reign did not follow that promising beginning. She was determined to see her country return to what she considered the true faith—Roman Catholicism—and to accomplish that, she made a few errors in dealing with her people. Mary, ignoring the warnings of her counselors, married Philip of Spain, a Roman Catholic monarch who insisted on being a co-monarch rather than a consort. The English people did not like having a Catholic foreigner ruling them, and the marriage sparked a brief rebellion. Mary, still determined to return her people to Catholicism, then made herself even more hated by burning many Protestants at the stake as heretics. It was this action that immortalized her as Bloody Mary.

Queen Mary Tudor by Antonis Mor.
https://commons.wikimedia.org/wiki/File:Maria_Tudor1.jpg

Ultimately, though, burning people at the stake was a pretty normal practice in this time of religious upheaval. Elizabeth I would even be guilty of the same (burning Catholics, in her case), so why does Mary have such a bad reputation? History is written by the victors, and if you didn't know already, Mary failed to restore England to Catholicism. She died in 1558, and her Protestant sister Elizabeth took the throne, sealing England's religious future. The now Protestant nation would not fondly remember the queen who tried to return them to Catholicism, and Mary's image was certainly not helped by the immensely popular book by John Foxe, the *Book of Martyrs*, which detailed the deaths of Protestants under Mary, forever making her a villain.

Thus, when Elizabeth I took the throne, she was dealing with a country that had experienced quite a bit of religious whiplash in the last few decades, and her solution to the problem reflected her political acumen. Elizabeth I's religious settlement was decidedly moderate. While she returned England to Protestantism, she also firmly resisted the efforts of the more radical Protestants, namely the Puritans, to instill larger religious changes. For the Puritans, the Church of England far too greatly resembled the Catholic Church, but that did not bother Elizabeth I. Her church struck a middle ground that, although it certainly didn't make everyone happy, seemed to please enough people to stop any violent conflict from breaking out, which was more than could be said for the rest of Europe in the sixteenth and seventeenth centuries.

Elizabeth I - The Pelican Portrait by Nicholas Hilliard.
https://commons.wikimedia.org/wiki/File:Nicholas_Hilliard_Elizabeth_I_The_Pelican_Portrait.jpg

England and Spain

Religious problems were not the only thing that Elizabeth I had to contend with in her forty-four-year reign though. This was the time of both the Renaissance and the Age of Exploration. Writers like Shakespeare were penning plays that would become some of the bests known works of English literature, and explorers like Francis Drake were sailing unknown waters. England vied with other countries to take its place in a rapidly expanding world.

One of England's greatest triumphs in that contest was undoubtedly the defeat of the Spanish Armada in 1588. Although her sister had married Philip II of Spain, Elizabeth did not have a good relationship with the Spanish monarch. Besides the tensions caused by their differing religions (Spain was Roman Catholic), English privateers (pirates) often attacked Spanish ships to steal gold. While the queen did not officially support such illegal actions, she privately encouraged it. Tensions were high, and when England sided with the Protestant Netherlands in their rebellion against Philip II, who had inherited the crown, Spain considered it an act of war and made plans to destroy England.

At the time, Spain was undoubtedly a more powerful nation than England. It had been one of the first to take advantage of the discovery of the New World and had become wealthy from the resources found there. Thus, Spain had the resources to crush England, and Philip II seemed determined to do that, spending the years from 1585 to 1588 preparing an invasion fleet that consisted of 130 ships and 30,000 troops. There was little doubt that if the Spanish force managed to make landfall, England's army, which was poorly trained, did not stand a chance. However, as any basic map reveals, England is an island, so if the Spanish wanted to conquer it, they first had to land.

The Royal Navy was England's only chance, and even though they were outnumbered by Spanish ships, England's navy was not necessarily outgunned. The English ships were smaller and more maneuverable. When the Royal Navy successfully set fire to the Spanish fleet while it was docked at Calais, it managed to scatter the larger force and use more maneuverable ships to pick off targets. Bad weather made the journey home even worse for the defeated Spanish fleet. The whole thing was a disaster for the Spanish.

Defeat of the Spanish Armada, 8 August 1588 by Philip James de Loutherbourg.
https://commons.wikimedia.org/wiki/File:Defeat_of_the_Spanish_Armada,_8_August_1588_RMG_BHC0264.tiff

As bad as it was for the Spanish, the defeat of the Armada was almost equally as good for the English. They had defeated the sixteenth-century equivalent of a world superpower. England was now confident that it could hold its own in the empire-building game that was developing in Western Europe. The dominance of the seas that England established by defeating the Spanish Armada also proved to be a vital factor in England's dominance and colonization over the next few centuries.

England under Elizabeth I was thus a kingdom growing in strength. Coming off the turmoil of the Wars of the Roses and the great religious change caused by the previous monarchs, Elizabethan England began to establish a firmer place in both Europe and the world. We can assume from this alone that Elizabeth I must have been at least a competent ruler as few countries ruled by an absolute monarch can flourish with an inept ruler on the throne. But what was Elizabeth I really like as queen?

Elizabeth I and Mary Queen of Scots

Perhaps one of the best incidents that highlights what Elizabeth I was like as a queen was how she dealt with Mary Queen of Scots. Mary

Queen of Scots (called so partially to distinguish her from the numerous other royal Marys of the time) was Elizabeth I's cousin and, as long as Elizabeth I remained childless, next in line for the throne of England.

Monarchs tend to have interesting relationships with the people in line to replace them, and Mary Queen of Scots certainly made things more interesting for Elizabeth I. The Scottish Queen was a Catholic raised in France and ruling over a very Protestant nation. Her poor choice of husbands (the first of whom was blown up in a scheme that rumors said Mary had a hand in) made her subjects distrust and dislike her even more, forcing her to abdicate and flee Scotland in favor of her son, James VI, in 1567.

Mary fled to England, where her cousin, Elizabeth I, was not exactly happy to see her. Because she was Catholic and next in line to the throne of England, Mary was a natural beacon for discontented Catholics under Elizabeth's rule. Having been in a similar position herself while her sister Mary I ruled England, Elizabeth I was all too aware of what sort of plots and conspiracies could be produced by having her rival so close at hand.

Even with these tensions, Mary Queen of Scots lived in England under the watchful eye of Elizabeth I for eighteen years before things imploded. In 1586, a plot to assassinate Elizabeth I and replace her with Mary was discovered. Elizabeth I had had enough, but she did not want to be known for the murder of her cousin. Even with undeniable proof that Mary had been involved in the plot (a letter was found in which Mary agreed to the plan to kill her cousin), Elizabeth I appeared hesitant. She signed an execution warrant but did not give orders for it to be delivered and carried out. Her secretary of state, William Davison, delivered it for her anyway, and Mary was beheaded.

Elizabeth I was furious, claiming it had not been what she wished, and had Davison thrown into the Tower of London. However, he was later quietly released and even given land and a pension, which suggests that Elizabeth I's hesitancy in killing her cousin was feigned to redirect blame away from herself. If so, it was the move of a politically savvy monarch who understood the importance of reputation. Elizabeth I chose the way she presented herself, a skill that often left both her advisers and rivals guessing and allowed her to maintain firm control of her government.

The Virgin Queen

A final aspect to note about Elizabeth I is that her approach to marriage was the opposite of Henry VIII's. She remained unmarried throughout her long reign. It was an unusual move for a monarch but one that seems to match Elizabeth I's personality and ruling style.

As a queen, marrying would have meant sharing some of her royal power, and, as seen from her conflict with Mary Queen of Scots, that was not something Elizabeth I wanted to do. Her virginity also became part of the reputation Elizabeth I carefully crafted and used to inspire devotion to herself. Like her grandfather and father before her, Elizabeth I manipulated the royal image to consolidate her power and authority.

Her singleness also proved to be a constant political bargaining chip. Elizabeth I might have intended from the beginning to never marry, but she did not present herself as completely against the idea. English elites and foreign notables tried to gain the queen's hand, and Elizabeth I had no problem using those attempts for her own ends. For example, her negotiations with Francois, Duke of Alencon and Anjou, as well as a Catholic, may have delayed war with Spain, giving the Royal Navy more time to prepare for the conflict. Still, the older the queen became, the more worried her advisers became, not about her lack of a husband but about the lack of an heir.

Although there was a succession order based on blood, it was traditional for monarchs to officially name an heir to legitimize that person's claim. For all her good qualities, this was one area in which Elizabeth I could not be moved. She refused to name an heir no matter how much her council begged. Her reluctance may have been due to not wanting to repeat her tangles with Mary Queen of Scots, but it also created a tense situation for her kingdom. Changing monarchs leaves a nation vulnerable to external threats and internal fighting. Not having someone lined up to take the throne only greatly intensifies these problems. By not naming an heir, Elizabeth I was securing her power, but she was also leaving her country open to the possibility of a lot of strife when she died. Since she was not immortal, that day did come. Elizabeth I died in 1603. Who would rule England now?

Chapter 12: The Stuarts

The person next in line to the throne by blood was the son of Mary Queen of Scots, James VI of Scotland (also known as James Stuart). When Elizabeth I's approaching death became obvious, her council decided to back James' claim to the throne.

The transfer from the Tudors to the Stuarts could have gone extremely poorly. James was the King of Scotland, which England had a tense history with, and Elizabeth I had had his mother executed. It was very unclear if England would accept him as their new king, but somehow, the succession went smoothly. In 1603, following Elizabeth I's death, James VI of Scotland became James I of England.

This did not mean that the countries were now united. Scotland and England were still two separate kingdoms with different Parliaments and governments. They just happened to share a king. It was a strange arrangement, and James tried to combine his kingdoms to make ruling easier, but neither side was interested. It would be another century before Scotland and England were unified.

Monarchy in the Early Modern Era

To understand everything that unfolded during the reign of the Stuarts, we must pause a moment and consider the concept of monarchy in this period. A lot had changed since the Middle Ages. Early modern England had a very different understanding of who the monarch was and where their authority came from.

The Renaissance brought a revival of interest in classical ideas, including philosophy. Part of that revival was an interest in the Neoplatonist idea of the Great Chain of Being. There's a lot that could be said about this philosophy, but what you need to know is that this philosophy said that the universe consisted of a natural hierarchy. This meant that social hierarchies were part of the very order of the universe. This idea extended to the monarchy and developed into a belief in the divine right of kings, which suggested that monarchs were divinely appointed by God and therefore answerable only to him. This understanding of monarchy thus represented absolute sovereignty. Monarchs were at the top of the Great Chain and answerable only to God for their actions.

This was an idea many monarchs in Europe bought into during this time, but in England, monarchs were answerable in some ways to another governmental body: Parliament. By the era of the Stuarts, it had become incredibly difficult to run the country without Parliament's approval because Parliament controlled the purse strings. The Tudors had managed this by working with Parliament, using tact and political maneuvering to get what they wanted. The Stuarts, especially James I and his son Charles I, would instead try to bully the group into submission, causing tension that eventually erupted into civil war.

That was where things were headed when James I took the throne in 1603, but it would take several decades for things to get there, and a lot happened in between.

The Gunpowder Plot

Two years after James I took the throne, England experienced a conspiracy that lives on in infamy. The Gunpowder Plot was a conspiracy by a group of Roman Catholics to blow up Parliament using barrels of gunpowder. The plan was to kill not only the king but other English leaders in Parliament that day as well, which would hopefully cause enough confusion for the Catholics to seize the government.

The plot was set to take place on November 5, 1605, but the conspirators were found out, and one of them, Guy Fawkes, was arrested while guarding the very barrels of gunpowder. He was subsequently tortured for information about his fellow conspirators and then executed. Although he was not the leader of the plot, Guy Fawkes became so infamous that the English still burn effigies of him on November 5 every year.

Despite failing, the Gunpowder Plot seared itself into England's culture and conscience. Fear of popery (Catholicism) became rampant, a problem the Protestant government saw no reason to curb. Catholics would be discriminated against for generations. All the Gunpowder Plot had achieved was to turn the country even more against Catholicism and even more Protestant.

James I

James I had been king of Scotland since he was one, and he ascended to the throne of England at the age of thirty-six. He thus had something that almost no monarch has when they take the throne: experience. Unfortunately, that experience did not make James I a good king of England.

James I had several problems as a ruler, and some of them were only partially his fault. He ruled during a time of rapid inflation, and, unlike Elizabeth I, his royal household included his wife and children, who each required their own court. Still, his spending habits only made things worse, and he regularly spent more than the royal assets were bringing in. This contributed to one of his other weaknesses as a ruler: his inability to deal with the English Parliament.

While Scotland had a Parliament, it was a relatively weak body that did not leave James I well-equipped to deal with the more headstrong and powerful English Parliament. As a strong believer in the divine right of kings, James I had no idea how to manage a group that thought it had the right to tell him what to do. Even if the Tudors had also believed in their divine right to rule (and they probably did), they were far more tactful than James in how they addressed Parliament. James' solution was generally to avoid dealing with them (going as long as ten years without a full meeting) and find other ways to raise money. Trying to rule without Parliament was a practice his son would also take up with disastrous consequences.

James I did not just clash with Parliament, though. He angered the members of his court by blatantly playing favorites. His attitude and treatment of several young men at court sparked controversy, and the debate about whether these relationships were sexual continues today.

However, even if the relationships were sexual, this was not why many disapproved of James I's companions. The king tended to give these men money and power even when they displayed complete incompetence.

For instance, one of James' favorites, George Villiers, the Duke of Buckingham, was allowed to negotiate a marriage between the Spanish princess and James I's son, Charles. Not only did most of the English object to this because they hated Spain and did not want a Spanish princess who would eventually become queen, but Villiers' negotiation strategy also involved sneaking off to Spain with Prince Charles and trying to infiltrate the palace to see the princess. While it may have seemed romantic, the trip accomplished nothing, and the marriage did not happen, much to the relief of the English people.

Thus, James I's reign could hardly be called a great success. He had managed to greatly increase royal spending and tension with Parliament. Still, he made it to the end of his reign without that tension exploding, dying in 1625. His son would not be so lucky.

A Bad Start

Charles I by Anthony Van Dyck.
https://commons.wikimedia.org/wiki/File:Van_Dyck,_Sir_Anthony_-_Charles_I_-_Google_Art_Project.jpg

When Charles I took the throne, he had a problem similar to his father's—namely, the Duke of Buckingham. On their escapade to Spain, Villiers had managed to gain influence over Charles, and it wasn't long into his reign before this had consequences. Since he had been unable to arrange a marriage with Spain, Villiers was now convinced that England needed to go to war with the Catholic nation, a sentiment that already existed in Parliament. Just before James I died, Parliament voted to give the Crown funds to conduct the war. When the king died shortly after, Charles I was left to run the war with Buckingham by his side, of course.

The war was a complete disaster. Taxes spiked to pay for it, putting great strain on the English people. Martial law was implemented in some places, and people had to feed and house soldiers. Even with these extreme measures, there were no military successes.

Someone had to take the blame for all of it. Parliament tried to impeach Buckingham, but Charles I, instead of letting his favorite take the fall, as kings had always done, tried to take the blame himself. While that might seem noble, it was an extremely poor choice. The government and the country rested on the king's shoulders. By admitting to making mistakes, he was destabilizing everything on which the government rested and opening the door to the idea that the king could be blamed for things and held accountable. If that wasn't drastic enough, Charles I then dissolved Parliament to stop it from impeaching Buckingham.

This couldn't last, however. Parliament had to be called again when Buckingham managed to start another war with France (while the war with Spain was still going on). This time Parliament would not vote to give the king more money to fund his wars until he agreed to the Petition of Right, which guaranteed certain protections like not being able to implement martial law on civilians. The fact that Parliament demanded the king sign such a document shows how much trust had been lost between the monarch and his people. Charles I was being asked to sign this document because he had (in the eyes of many) abused his authority. This happened in 1627, only two years after he had become king. It was not a good start.

Ultimately it was not Parliament but a lone assassin that rid the country of Buckingham. He was stabbed to death by a disgruntled officer. Unfortunately, Charles I's rule did not improve with the death of Buckingham.

Worsening Tensions

By 1629, Charles I and Parliament were once again at odds. On March 2, in a rather dramatic scene, the speaker was forcibly held in his chair by some members of Parliament so that the House could pass three resolutions before the king dissolved Parliament. (Sessions of Parliament end when the speaker rises from his chair.) These resolutions were that anyone who paid impositions (import duties paid to the monarch), advised their collection, or pushed religious changes was an enemy of England.

Why were those three things such a big deal? Why would members of the House have held down the speaker to pass these resolutions? These three things were a direct attack on Charles I. It was he who had started impositions to generate money for his wars. To be fair, Charles I did not invent impositions. Other monarchs, including the much beloved Elizabeth I, had implemented them. But Charles I raised them to the point that merchants felt the financial demand was unjust, and Parliament sided with the merchants. Charles I had also married a Catholic wife (albeit for good political reasons) and was cracking down on Puritans (a Protestant sect with a voice in Parliament), whom he believed to be revolutionary and dangerous. Thus, in passing these resolutions, Parliament was saying outright that the king had done wrong. This was a step beyond even the Petition of Right because Parliament had not forced Charles I to agree to the resolutions. Parliament, through its own power, had condemned the king.

Needless to say, Charles I was not happy with this turn of events, and his counter to Parliament's condemnation showed a stubbornness that would ultimately become his fatal flaw. Charles I did not call another meeting of Parliament for the next eleven years. Whether he intended to do this from the start in 1629 or a resolution to not call Parliament happened gradually, Charles I ruled England from 1629 to 1640 without Parliament, a period that became known as the Personal Rule.

Before we get into how people reacted to this, how was it even possible for Charles I to rule without Parliament? Parliament approved new taxes, and it's extremely difficult to run a government without taxes. If Charles I wanted to get away with not calling Parliament, he had to find a way to finance his government without them. In the face of his strained finances, Charles I made some serious changes. He ended the wars with

France and Spain and let his treasurer reform his court and government to cut costs. Both methods proved quite effective in reducing government expenditure. However, cutting costs alone was never going to be enough to solve Charles I's financial issues. He still needed money, but without Parliament, where was he to get it?

The first thing Charles I did to raise money was to completely ignore Parliament's resolutions of 1629. The impositions that Parliament had so thoroughly condemned were raised again. That alone was nowhere near enough to get him the kind of revenue he needed. Other measures soon followed. He sold government offices and monopolies. He had his officials search the law books for any fees and fines technically still on the books that he could use to get money from his subjects without new taxation. Fees for things like hunting in royal forests and enclosing land were revived. Old taxes, such as the ship money tax paid by some coastal towns, were extended to the entire kingdom.

As you can imagine, these methods did not make Charles I very popular, but they turned out to be fairly effective. Charles I had enough money to run the country without Parliament, but it was never a situation that could last. Tax strikes soon began, and the local gentry Charles I had to rely on to collect these taxes often participated in the strikes themselves. England simply did not have a governmental bureaucracy that could operate without the consent of the upper tiers of society. Barons and earls effectively ran the government in their local areas, so without their help, Charles I could not make his people pay up. Thus, by 1640, his government was barely financially afloat.

The Tipping Point

As much trouble as Charles I had with the English Parliament, it was not England that caused the Personal Rule to eventually erupt. Like his father before him, Charles I was king of both England and Scotland. Ruling two distinct kingdoms as a single monarch was undoubtedly tricky, but in trying to make his kingdoms more similar, Charles I vastly underestimated the religious devotion of the Scots. In 1637, when Charles I tried to impose the Anglican English Book of Common Prayer on the Presbyterian Scots, the northern country, which was notoriously divided, united against the king. By 1638, the Scots had signed the National Covenant declaring their opposition to the king's religious policies and stating that only the Scottish Parliament and Presbyterian

General Assembly could make religious policy for Scotland. They were telling the king in no uncertain terms to stay out of their business.

Charles I could not ignore such an act of rebellion, not if he wished to maintain his authority. He raised an army to combat the rebellious Scots in the First Bishops' War. However, without money from Parliament, his army was poorly funded. Even worse, the English did not appear to care about helping Charles I crack down on his northern kingdom. Not only did they hate the Personal Rule, but many Englishmen (especially Puritans) sympathized with the Scots and their resistance to Charles I's religious policies. Charles I could not trust such a reluctant army. He instead made a truce with the Scots to buy time until he could raise money to fund a better army.

After eleven years, the king finally called Parliament again, but it was short-lived. The body had no intention of giving the king money for an army till he listened to their demands, and he, having no intention of listening to their demands, dissolved Parliament quickly, having accomplished nothing.

War with the Scots broke out again (the Second Bishops' War), and Charles I's forces were beaten and dispersed, allowing the Scots to occupy the north. Once again, Charles I was forced to sign a treaty, but it was only a temporary truce. He had to pay the Scots a large sum each day to maintain the peace (money he did not have). Unless Charles I found money to pay off the Scots and raise another army to deal with them, the Scots could simply march into London whenever they chose. Whether he liked it or not, Charles I had to talk to Parliament.

Chapter 13: The Civil Wars and the Protectorate

Things were only going from bad to worse in Charles I's reign, but the boiling point had not yet been reached. With the Scots on his doorstep, Charles I again called Parliament late in 1640. This time, Parliament would not be dismissed or disregarded so easily.

A Country Divided

In 1640, Charles I's popularity hit its lowest point. Almost all of Parliament was against the king, and now that Charles I had called Parliament, thanks to the impending threat of the Scots, the body quickly began passing legislation to show its displeasure. The passed acts said Parliament could not be dissolved without its consent, the king must call Parliament every three years at the least, and that taxation not approved by Parliament was illegal. None of these things could become law without Charles I's signature, but, desperate for money, he agreed to everything.

Why would such a stubborn king agree to sign acts that were intended to strip him of power? It's pretty simple. He never intended to let Parliament get away with it. All Charles I needed was the money to deal with the rebellious Scots, and then he could set about undoing everything Parliament had done to limit his sovereignty. In his mind, Charles I was completely justified in such a plan. Because he believed in the Great Chain of Being (discussed in the previous chapter) and the divine right of monarchs to rule, he viewed Parliament's attempts to restrict him as against the natural order and inherently wrong. To overturn all they had done would simply be to set things right.

Unfortunately for Charles I, the members of Parliament knew their king. They did not trust Charles I to keep his promises, so they continued to postpone giving him the money for his army. They were afraid that after Charles I dealt with the Scots, he would then turn that army on Parliament. Ironically, this delay benefited Charles I. As the Parliament wore on, Parliamentary leaders began passing more and more radical acts to check royal power. There were still many in Parliament with moderate and conservative tendencies, and they began to shy away from the direction the group was heading. When, in 1641, leaders on the radical side tried to pass the Grand Remonstrance, a long list of grievances against the king, Parliament split almost fifty-fifty. It was now clear that, two years after being almost universally condemned, the king still had many supporters.

In this divided atmosphere, the final straw came not from Scotland but from Ireland, which had been under English control since the twelfth century. Rebellion broke out in Ireland, and the native devotion to Catholicism quickly led to violence toward Protestant settlers. Ireland was in an uproar, and the English needed a military to stop it.

But Parliament was still not prepared to hand control of an army to the king and instead tried to appoint its own general. Charles I was furious and tried to arrest five key Members of Parliament, but the House of Commons would not give them up, humiliating the king. Lines had been drawn, and there was no turning back.

Soon after this incident, the king left Parliament and London for York. Two centers of English government now existed, and inevitably they must clash. Both Parliament and Charles I raised forces and armed themselves, not to deal with the Irish rebellion but in preparation for a conflict with each other. When Charles I raised his standard on August 22, 1642, this conflict officially began.

The Civil War

The English Civil War, as the clash came to be known, began very well for the Royalists (supporters of King Charles I, also known as Cavaliers). Parliament, although used to funding wars, simply did not have any experience running the military side of things. It was no match for the king's forces, who had most of the country's military talent on their side.

However, the Parliamentarians (also called Roundheads) did have advantages. They had seized control of London before the war officially began, and with that, they controlled southeast England, which happened to be the wealthiest part of the country and the closest to Europe. The navy had also sided with the Parliamentarians, giving them control of the ports. The Roundheads thus had superior resources and the ability to cut off the Royalists from outside help. If the Royalists wanted to win, they needed to do so quickly.

The first battles looked promising for the Royalists. However, they could not completely overwhelm their opponents, and this proved disastrous. The Royalists failed to take London, which was their best option for putting a quick end to the war. As the war dragged on, the Parliamentarians gained the military experience they had lacked at the outset, and one man in particular began to stand out.

Oliver Cromwell first became a notable figure in the English Civil War in 1644 at the Battle of Marston Moor, where he led a cavalry charge that scattered the Royalist flank. However, the Parliamentarian leadership failed to pursue the losing royal army, so the victory did little toward ending the war. The two sides had both had success at this point, but neither seemed able to push its advantage.

After about three years of indecisive battles, Parliament decided to make some major changes to its military structure, creating the New Model Army, a more centrally structured force with promotion by merit as opposed to the previous local militia-style force with ranking based on blood. Most of the Parliamentarian command was thus replaced, but not the successful Oliver Cromwell, who became the General of the Horse in the New Model Army.

It did not take long for the New Model Army to prove effective. On June 14, 1645, it beat the Royalist forces at the Battle of Naseby in the decisive victory that Parliament had been looking for. A large portion of the Royalist forces surrendered, and the war ended a few months later. The fighting was over, but the peace would prove just as trying.

Cromwell at the Battle of Naseby by Charles Landseer.
https://commons.wikimedia.org/wiki/File:Charles_Landseer_Cromwell_Battle_of_Naseby.JPG

Negotiating with the King

What happens after you beat a king? Parliament had won on the field of battle, but Charles I was still king. The war had not been to overthrow the king but to force him back to the negotiating table. Charles I had lost, and now he would be forced to make some concessions and agree to the winning side's demands. That was what everyone expected to happen—everyone, that is, except for Charles I.

Charles I may have lost the battle of the armies, but he still considered himself the moral victor. He did not believe Parliament had any right to restrict him and adamantly refused to negotiate with them. Not only would the king not reach an agreement with Parliament, but he attempted to negotiate with other groups that had an interest in the conflict, such as the Scottish and Irish, hoping to eventually raise another army and reverse his plight. An agreement between Charles I and Scottish Covenanters caused a brief renewal of violence in 1647 (two years after the Battle of Naseby had ended the war). Negotiations with the king were going nowhere, but many members of Parliament still would not give up on reaching an agreement.

Eventually, it was the New Model Army that decided to end things. It seized control of Parliament and would not allow members who had voted to continue negotiations with Charles I to enter. In these circumstances, many members simply chose to stay home. Thus, of the roughly 200-member body, only about seventy (known as the Rump Parliament) decided to put the king on trial for treason.

In some ways, this was ridiculous. Treason in a monarchy is betraying the monarch. How could Charles I be guilty of betraying himself? Legally, the Rump Parliament was never going to win a trial based on this kind of reasoning, which is why it instead argued that Charles I was guilty of treason against the English people.

Charles I did not think this was a reasonable argument. He did not even believe that he could be tried for a crime because he was the one who made the laws, and (as the head of the government) all the courts were technically his courts. In his mind, the whole trial was illegal and invalid, so he refused to defend himself during it. It was not a good attitude to take during a trial to determine whether he was guilty of a capital crime. On January 27, 1649, the king was found guilty and sentenced to beheading. On January 30, he was executed.

England had done the unthinkable. In a world where monarchy was the only major form of government in Europe and the right of the king to rule was seen as a divine prerogative, England had cast off its king. What were the English going to do now?

A Commonwealth

Killing the king was a radical step that went beyond simply getting rid of Charles I. To try and execute the king for treason was to attack the office itself. So, it should come as no surprise that by May 19, Parliament had abolished both the monarchy and the House of Lords and named England a commonwealth (a republic).

While this might seem like a natural progression to us today, the fact that it took four months between the death of the king and the establishment of the Commonwealth shows that this was not natural at the time. This was well over 100 years before the American Revolution, and there was hesitancy about trying such a radical government change. Could a commonwealth bring stability when it was throwing off so much?

The concern about stability was far more than political opponents trying to disregard the new republic style of government. It had been seven years since the Civil War started, and the country had descended into quite a bit of chaos during this time. The chaos of civil war only became worse when the war ended, and many common people who had helped Parliament achieve victory began to wonder why they must stay at the bottom of the social hierarchy. If the king could be toppled, why not the whole structure?

This sentiment led to the formation of many groups with radical ideologies (both political and religious), such as the Levellers (who wanted radical government reforms, such as universal suffrage for males), Baptists (who believed in adult baptism, a radical idea at the time), Diggers (who did not believe in private property), Ranters (who believed everyone could decide right and wrong for themselves), and the Quakers (who believed each person held an inner light, the Holy Spirit, which was to be obeyed above all else). From a twenty-first-century perspective, some of these groups appear more radical than others. Regardless, you can imagine the chaos of so many different ideologies springing up at once and trying to exercise their systems all over a war-torn country. While we might embrace this level of diversity today, in the 1600s, it was the definition of anarchy.

So, what was Parliament, which still consisted only of the people who had executed the king (the Rump), going to do about it? How would Parliament bring stability back to the nation? The Rump ultimately tried to walk a middle ground between radical change and the status quo that left no one happy, and the lack of supporters soon led to the Commonwealth's downfall. This downfall came in the form of the army. The New Model Army had won Parliament its power, but Parliament was eager to disband it. Getting rid of the army would have lowered taxes which is always a good way to win popular support. Unfortunately, the army could not be disbanded because Parliament still owed the men their pay, and the only way to raise the money to pay the army would have been to raise taxes. It was a paradox the Commonwealth couldn't solve.

The Commonwealth tried to prolong dealing with the army by sending it out to pacify Scotland and Ireland, which had chosen to support Charles I's son Charles II's claim. Here the New Model Army was greatly successful, which helped the Commonwealth gain some prestige, but Parliament could not seize advantage of the situation as it had hoped. It was still disliked by most, and when it tried to cut the army's pay, that was the end. On April 20, 1653, Oliver Cromwell entered the Commons Chamber with soldiers and dissolved Parliament. The Commonwealth had promised much but done little. It was time to try something else.

The Protectorate

There was another brief attempt at having another Parliament run the country, but this, too, proved ineffective. In December of 1653, a new government was created with Cromwell, who was by far the most powerful man in the country, as the executive. Avoiding the title of king, he was named Lord Protector, but in power and practice, he was running the country just as a monarch would.

Cromwell's government was in some ways a vast improvement over the other options of the past century. It was efficient and carried out reforms. Even though Cromwell was a Puritan, his government was largely religiously tolerant, leaving many (but not all) of the new religious sects in peace. The Protectorate was far from perfect, though. That effective and large government required substantial funds, so tax rates remained high. Also, during the Protectorate, many Puritans held positions of power and tried to enforce moral reform through legal means, combating everything from gambling to drinking. This was naturally not a popular move with the common people and led to a longstanding and often inaccurate understanding and dislike of Puritans in the English mind.

Whatever his government's flaws, Cromwell showed that he was a capable leader. He ruled England uncontested and managed to bring stability after many years of fighting and political chaos. However, while Cromwell's strong leadership made the Protectorate a viable government, it came with one glaring flaw. How would the government he had established survive without him?

Chapter 14: Restoration and the Union with Scotland

When Cromwell died suddenly of sickness in 1658, his son Richard Cromwell became Lord Protector in his place. This succession made it abundantly clear that the Protectorate functioned like a monarchy in all but name. But if that was so, why have the Protectorate in the first place?

The Restoration and Reign of Charles II

No one seemed able to answer that question because the Protectorate didn't last long without Oliver Cromwell. From the time of Cromwell's death to early 1660, chaos returned, with several failed governments. England, particularly the ruling elite, longed for an end to the constantly changing governments, and there seemed only one way to do that. After eleven years without one, England wanted its king back.

The king in question was Charles I's son, Charles II, who was living in exile on the continent. Calling him back to take the throne was no simple matter, though. England, Parliament particularly, had executed his father. How would Charles II feel about returning? Would he seek revenge on the men and families of those who had killed his father? Powerful people in England had no interest in inviting a king back who would immediately try to chop off their heads.

The situation was tense, but thanks to the advice of a man named Edward Hyde, Charles II managed to create a smooth restoration with a single masterstroke: the Declaration of Breda. This was a public announcement by Charles II that declared a general amnesty, some freedom of religion, the recognition of land settlements that had occurred during the Protectorate, and payment of arrears to the army. More basically, Charles II promised not to chop off the heads of anyone involved with the death of his father and not to take back any land people had gained. He was also offering to do what all the previous government had failed to do and pay the army. The Declaration of Breda offered the nervous Parliament a clear olive branch, and Parliament jumped to take it. Charles II entered London on May 29, 1660. England once again had a king.

But what exactly had changed? England was so eager to restore order that it accepted Charles II back without making any provisions to prevent what had happened with Charles I. After fighting a civil war and functioning without a king for eleven years, England appeared to have nothing to show for it.

While the changes might not have been immediately obvious, the turmoil of the past decades had changed a lot. The English government needed both Parliament and king, as attempts to rule without both had resulted in tyranny and chaos. Still, it was unclear which of these had the ultimate sovereignty. The king's powers were largely restored to what had been before the Civil War, but he did have to agree to the reforms that the Long Parliament had made in 1641 (such as calling Parliament at least every three years). Parliament also voted Charles II a much larger annual income than they had given his father, recognizing the king's need for adequate funds to run his government. Compromises had been made, and a settlement had been reached. Unfortunately, it didn't last.

At first Charles II seemed like exactly what England needed. He was charming, intelligent, and, unlike his father, flexible and willing to compromise. However, it eventually became clear that, like his father and grandfather, Charles II believed in the absolute authority of the monarch. Over his reign, he worked to whittle back the restrictions placed on him by the settlement. However, the new king was also rather lazy. He did not have the drive to seize absolute control from a resistant Parliament.

That wasn't the only problem, though. Charles II fought several expensive and largely unsuccessful wars against the Dutch. His need for money to fight these wars drove him to ally with France, which frightened the English people because France was a Catholic superpower. When, in 1672, Charles II tried to do the unthinkable and grant toleration to Catholics with the Declaration of Indulgence, the English had had enough. An angry Parliament refused the Declaration of Indulgence and instead passed the Test Acts, which required all officers to deny transubstantiation (a key Catholic doctrine) and take Anglican communion. The king had tried to open things up for Catholics but ultimately caused the door to be shut even more firmly against them.

The fear of Catholicism reached a new height in 1678 when a rumored plot to kill Charles II and restore England to Catholicism became widespread, despite being false. The Popish Plot, as it came to be known, caused the English to revert to an almost hysteric hatred and mistrust of Catholics and popery.

It was this hysteria that led to an event known as the Exclusion Crisis. The Whigs (an emerging political party with its origins in the Parliamentarian side of the Civil War) attempted to have Charles II's brother, James (who was next in line for the throne since Charles II had no legitimate heirs), excluded from the succession. Their reasoning was quite simple: James was Roman Catholic.

To exclude James from the succession, the Whigs needed to gain a Parliamentary majority and then pass legislation. With the English population almost rabid with its fear of popery, the Whigs won this majority quite easily in two elections. But, both times, Charles II managed to protect his brother by dissolving Parliament before it could pass the bill. This led to many protests and petitions, but Charles II did not back down, dissolving a third Parliament before it could exclude his brother.

Surprisingly, this delay tactic worked. The Whigs slowly lost their momentum, becoming more desperate and radical. In 1683, a plot was discovered (it is unclear how serious the plot was) to kidnap and kill both Charles II and his brother. This was all the ammunition the royal government needed. Radical Whigs were suppressed, and the Exclusion Crisis was over. In this last great test, Charles II had proved triumphant. When he died two years later in 1685, he left his brother a crown that was in an extremely strong position politically and financially. However, James II was still a Roman Catholic.

The Glorious Revolution

It had been over 100 years since England's last Catholic monarch (Mary Tudor, nicknamed Bloody Mary). Since then, England had become Protestant in more than name, and its dislike of anything stinking of popery had grown to levels of intense hatred and fear. In some ways, James II didn't stand a chance.

James II by Godfrey Kneller.
https://commons.wikimedia.org/wiki/File:King_James_II.jpg

Besides his religious convictions, was there anything wrong with James II as a king? During the reign of his brother, James II had served in the military and was a capable soldier. He was orderly, bringing an efficiency to the royal government that his pleasure-loving brother had lacked. While he was Roman Catholic and believed that England should return to what he considered the true faith, he pursued policies of religious toleration rather than trying to persecute Protestants.

However, James II had several flaws. His love of order made him a strong proponent of strict hierarchy. Like his beheaded father, James II did not like to be questioned. This attitude, combined with a strong sense of conviction, led to a monarch who doggedly pursued removing restrictions against Catholics even though most of his people were against such steps. The anti-Catholic sentiment ran so deep in England that James II faced a rebellion against his rule the same year he took the throne (1685). He put down the rebels without any difficulty, but it was not an auspicious start to his reign.

It did not take long for things to unravel, and the issue ultimately came down to a matter of heirs. When he took the throne in 1685, James II already had two daughters: Mary and Anne. They were both Protestant. As long as one of them was the heir, the throne would pass safely back into Protestant hands, and James II's reform attempts would come to nothing.

James II's first wife, Anne Hyde, had died in 1671, and he had remarried a Roman Catholic, Mary of Modena. Thus, when Mary of Modena became pregnant in late 1687, Protestant England became very nervous. If she gave birth to a boy, the Protestant eldest daughter Mary would be skipped in succession, and the throne would pass to a boy who was almost certain to be raised Roman Catholic.

In the summer of 1688, the worst happened. A prince was born. The issue of a Catholic heir was so controversial that James II invited a myriad of witnesses to be present for the birth to confirm its legitimacy. Many of the Protestant witnesses, however, found reasons to look away, and for many years there were rumors that the prince had been smuggled up in a warming pan after the queen gave birth to a stillborn child. This rumor was unfair and no doubt disheartening to the proud parents, but its persistence shows just how loathsome many in England found the idea of a Catholic heir. A Catholic king they could maybe endure. A Catholic dynasty, though, was unbearable.

It was thus the birth of the prince, named James after his father, that sparked one of the most unusual revolutions in history. Three days before the birth, the situation had become so tense that seven of the most powerful men in England wrote a letter to William of Orange, inviting him to invade.

Just who was William of Orange, though, and what stake did he have in England? William of Orange was the leader of the Dutch Republic and a major Protestant leader in the religious wars of this time. (He greatly opposed the expansion of the French Catholic empire.) He was also married to James II's eldest daughter, Mary, the heir to the throne of England until the birth of the prince. For England, William was the only way they could ensure the throne passed to Mary and out of Catholic hands. For William, England was a much-needed resource and ally in his fight against France. He accepted the invitation to invade, landing in England on November 5, 1688.

James II did not acquit himself well in what followed. Essentially, he panicked and hesitated when he needed to act decisively. He had the resources to beat back the invasion, but he lacked the confidence. Maybe he didn't trust his people, who so clearly disliked him, or maybe he couldn't forget the fate of his father, Charles I. Whatever the reason, the more James II hesitated the more supporters he lost. When even his daughter, Princess Anne, left the court, it became clear James II was on his own. Without even meeting William in battle, James II fled the country, and William and Mary became King and Queen of England.

William of Orange Landing in England by Hoynck van Papendrecht.
https://commons.wikimedia.org/wiki/File:William_of_Orange_III_and_his_Dutch_army_land_in_Brixham,_1688.jpg)

The fact that James II fled the country rather than be officially beaten became a point of contention in future days. There were those (known as

Jacobites) who thought James II and his descendants were the rightful holders of the English throne. These sentiments proved particularly strong in Scotland and Ireland and would lead to conflict later.

However, the revolution that replaced James II with William and Mary was itself relatively bloodless. The very bloody Civil War had occurred less than five decades before, making this revolution seem almost easy. It became known as the Glorious Revolution, and it was the last time an English monarch would lose the throne.

Union with Scotland

As kings, the Stuarts didn't have a great track record, but the dynasty still had a few monarchs left. Mary, the daughter of James II, was now queen, but it was her husband William's influence that shaped England more directly in the years following the Glorious Revolution.

William's goal, as mentioned earlier, was to stop France from turning Europe into a Catholic empire, and now that he was King of England, he expected the English to do their part in this very expensive conflict. He saw England as a major power that was crucial to the fight.

The English did not see it that way. What happened on the continent seemed remote to their island, but William was nothing if not determined. England found itself involved first in the Nine Years' War, which ended in 1697. Shortly after the conclusion of this war, France violated the treaty that had ended the war by trying to unite Spain and France into a single empire. War broke out again in 1701, and while William was ready to once again lead the charge against France, he never got the chance, dying following an accident on horseback in 1702. The throne passed to the only remaining Protestant Stuart: James II's youngest daughter, Anne.

England was at war with France, and Anne was the last Stuart. While these facts might seem wholly unconnected with Scotland, they would lead to a union that James I had failed to achieve when he became king of England. To understand just how, we need to establish the context.

Although Anne was married, she had numerous failed pregnancies and no surviving children. That meant when she died there would be no direct heir, and her closest living relative was Prince James, the Catholic son of James II. After everything they had gone through to get rid of James II and his Catholic heir, England was not simply going to accept

Prince James. Parliament passed the Act of Settlement, which settled the succession on Anne's nearest Protestant relatives, the descendants of James I's daughter Elizabeth, who would become the Hanover dynasty.

The solution seemed simple enough, but there was a problem. The Act of Settlement was legislation passed by the English Parliament, and although Scotland had the same queen, it had a separate Parliament. Scotland did not approve of the Act of Settlement and instead passed the Act of Security, which stated that after Anne's death, the Scottish Parliament would elect her successor in Scotland. There was little doubt as to whom they would choose: Prince James.

England did not like this. Not only would they have a northern neighbor with a king who thought he was the rightful heir to the English throne, but it was also likely this would result in Scotland reviving its old alliance (known as the Auld Alliance) with France, with whom England was currently at war. There was only one clear way to stop this from happening. The two kingdoms had to be united.

How would this happen, though? James I had tried, but both the English and the Scottish were against it. There was still much tension and resentment between the two countries in Queen Anne's Day. The English thought poorly of the Scots, and the Scots did not want to be absorbed by their southern neighbor. Because of things like the Act of Security and a fear of a resurgence of the Auld Alliance, England was prepared to overlook these tensions to secure Scotland before it could cause trouble. But how were the Scots to be convinced?

Ultimately, money was the motivating factor that made the union happen. By becoming part of the British nation, the Scots would gain access to the English trade empire, which could do much for the northern nation, which was struggling economically. Money also became a factor in less subtle ways. England paid Scotland a flat sum to unite the nations. It is also highly likely members of the Scottish Parliament received personal bribes, as well. England did have to make some concessions to seal the deal, such as agreeing to let Scotland maintain its religious practices (Presbyterianism) and laws. Thus, in 1707, the Act of Union was passed, creating Great Britain.

Union Jack.
https://commons.wikimedia.org/wiki/File:Flag_of_the_United_Kingdom_(3-5).svg

All the Stuarts had been monarchs of both England and Scotland, but it wasn't until the last ruler of the dynasty that the two countries became one. The Stuarts had at one point fractured the nation, but in the end, they managed to make it larger before passing the torch to the Hanovers. In 1714, Queen Anne died. She was succeeded by George of Hanover, the son of Sophia, who was the granddaughter of James VI. A new dynasty had begun.

Chapter 15: Eighteenth-Century Britain: Expansion, Wars, and Revolutions

English history until this point has been focused largely on the monarchs because, as a monarchy, England's course was shaped by the decisions and personality of its ruler. However, as we saw in the last several chapters, the power of Parliament had been steadily rising. England remained a monarchy and technically remains one today, but the monarch would come to have less and less real power as the Hanover dynasty progressed.

Instead, Parliament and political parties gained greater and greater influence on the direction of the country. By this time, two parties had emerged, the Whigs and the Tories. These parties had emerged after the English Civil War, with the Whigs coming from the Parliamentarian view and the Tories the Royalist side. The ideas of the two parties changed greatly over time, but it was still these two parties dominating Parliament as the eighteenth century began.

It isn't just monarchs and political parties that shape a nation, though. Larger forces and movements cause events and impact a country and its people. Eighteenth-century England was home to one of the most significant movements in history, an event that would forever change how people lived in England, Europe, and the entire world. This is the time of the Industrial Revolution.

The Industrial Revolution

In truth, to call the Industrial Revolution an event is not historically accurate. The Industrial Revolution refers to the process in which a country's economy becomes focused on factory rather than domestic production. It happened gradually over time, and in England, the time frame of that change was around the eighteenth century, particularly the second half.

Why the eighteenth century, and what caused the Industrial Revolution now in England's history? The simple answer is technological advancements. Many industries were impacted by new technology that made the production of goods faster and possible on a mass scale. The textile industry provides a great example. Inventions like the spinning jenny (a machine that could spin multiple threads at once) and the water frame (a spinning machine powered by a water wheel), both from the 1760s, made it possible to spin thread at a rate and scale completely unmatched by hand laborers.

Spinning Jenny from Museum of Industry.
https://commons.wikimedia.org/wiki/File:Mule_Jenny_Industriemuseum_Gent.jpg

The machines were one thing, but another important advancement that made the Industrial Revolution possible was the discovery of different sources to power those machines. With steam and coal powering their machines, factories could produce goods nonstop and at a constant rate.

There were other factors at play besides technology, though. A growing population created a workforce that could meet the high demand for labor required by the massive increase in business. This increase in population also came at a time when agricultural production had increased due to technological advancements, so fewer workers were needed for food production. For the first time in human history, most of the population did not need to be farmers, opening the possibility of an economy centered on the production of factory goods.

The mass production of goods during the Industrial Revolution made the economy boom, but it also drastically altered the structure of society. The machines that made such mass production possible were expensive and big, requiring someone with the initial capital to build a factory and start a business. The production of goods thus moved out of the homes of skilled laborers and into factories owned by manufacturers. As the number of factories grew, laborers who produced things by hand were forced out of business and moved to urban areas to get jobs in the factories. The demand for labor was so high that those who did not traditionally earn a wage, such as women and children, found themselves at work in the growing number of factories. Thus, from about 1750 to 1880, England went from being a primarily agricultural society with a spread-out population to an industrialized society with an increasingly urban-centered population.

New layers were added to society, as well. As industry increased, wealth became less tied to land. A new class of industrialists emerged who held great wealth without being members of the traditional landed gentry. The wealthy were not the only ones affected, though. The growing urban population and large number of factory workers created a more politically conscious people, leading to things like unions and eras of reform. Of course, much of the reform that was demanded was due to the terrible working conditions that the Industrial Revolution also produced.

The Industrial Revolution didn't just impact people in England. It also impacted England's place in the world. The wealth that industry brought would prove instrumental in allowing England to dominate the globe over the next 200 years. Economics alone, however, were not enough to turn England into a global superpower. In the eighteenth century, a country's fate was closely tied to its military might.

Establishing Dominance

During the eighteenth century, England was involved in several armed conflicts, including the War of Spanish Succession, the War of Austrian Succession, the Carnatic Wars, the Seven Years' War, and the American Revolution, and this list is far from exhaustive. Not only was England involved in other conflicts in this century, but most of the wars listed were made up of many separate conflicts. For instance, during the American Revolution, England was at war with the American colonists, but Spain, France, and the Netherlands all took the opportunity to take a shot at England as well.

But why are the wars of this century so complicated? The eighteenth century was a time of intense competition between the European powers. Spain, France, the Netherlands, and England were all competing to build overseas empires connected through trade. War broke out frequently around the globe as different countries vied for control of new areas, trade routes, and more. Alliances were forged and then broken. Many groups besides the four nations mentioned above became steeped in various conflicts. It was a high-stakes and complex game of colonization and conquest, and England (Great Britain by this point because England, Wales, and Scotland had been united) would come out as a pretty clear winner by the end of the century. There is no room to even begin to discuss all these conflicts here, but we can at least get a brief understanding of some of the major ones and their consequences for England.

The War of Spanish Succession (1701-1714)

After fighting the Nine Years' War to prevent the growth of the French empire, one of William of Orange's last acts as the King of England was to bring the nation into another war to prevent French imperial ambitions. Although William died shortly after, England stayed in the war, fighting alongside many allies to prevent France from uniting the Spanish and French empires.

England did very well militarily in this conflict, largely thanks to the military mind of John Churchill (a distant ancestor of Winston Churchill). However, despite the victories, the war dragged on until

Parliament had grown sick of fighting and sought a peace settlement. The war was ended by the Treaty of Utrecht, which gave Great Britain new territories, a monopoly on the slave trade, and more. While some saw this as a small victory, these strategic gains would prove crucial for England's empire-building.

The War of Jenkins' Ear (1739-1748)

This strangely-named conflict began when a ship captain named Jenkins presented Parliament with his ear, which had allegedly been cut off by the Spanish after they boarded and pillaged his ship. The incident took place in the West Indies (modern-day Caribbean), which the English and Spanish had been fighting over since the days of Queen Elizabeth. England was already unhappy with the Spanish over this area, so the incident of Jenkins' ear was enough to spark a war.

The War of Jenkins' Ear soon became part of the larger conflict of the War of Austrian Succession. Because of its absorption into the larger war, which involved many more countries, there was no clear ending to the conflict between Spain and Britain. The War of Austrian Succession was ended by the Treaty of Aix-la-Chapelle, which was negotiated largely by France and Britain. Although the treaty settled a lot of things, it notably did nothing to settle the colonial disputes between France and Britain, which had become the two superpowers. The failure to address these disputes led directly to the next war on our list.

The Seven Years' War (1756-1763)

Trouble was brewing between France and England, as they both sought to become the dominant colonizing power, and it finally broke out in the American colonies, of all places. A dispute over possession of the Ohio Valley, a border area between French and British-controlled areas, led to bloodshed in 1754, and by 1756, the dispute had escalated into a truly global conflict, with fighting in the Americas, India, and Europe and many other nations becoming involved.

With several different fronts and seven years of fighting, there is no space here to dive into the military history of this war. What you should know is that by the end of the war, Britain had come out on top. The war was ended by the Treaty of Paris in 1763, which gave Britain most of France's holdings in North America and India. Britain also gained Florida from the Spanish. With this victory, the British Empire was secure and expanding.

The Carnatic Wars

The Carnatic Wars were a series of conflicts throughout the eighteenth century in India. These wars were fought over control of the coastal Carnatic region of India. Both France and Britain were involved, seeking to support different claimants to the area. Britain ultimately won control of the area through the Treaty of Paris that ended the Seven Years' War.

What is interesting about these wars and revealing about this period is that, at times, the wars were fought by a company. The forces of the English East India Company wanted to ensure that they had a monopoly on the region's resources and trade. Colonization and trade had brought so much wealth to Europe that companies were able to act with powers normally restricted to governments. This would not last as, in the nineteenth century, the English government stepped in, breaking the company's monopoly and taking political control of India.

The American Revolution (1775-1783)

While it may come as a shock to many Americans, the American Revolution was not one of the key conflicts of the century for Britain. However, it is one of the few that Britain lost, and that does make it an interesting case study.

While the conflict was mainly over the American colonies' desire for independence, like other wars in this century, the American Revolution became more complicated. Spain and France, seeing an opportunity to hurt their rival, joined the colonists against Britain. At the same time, Britain was fighting a separate war with the Netherlands, which was also supporting the colonists. In this time of competition, no conflict was off limits as a chance to weaken rivals for imperial power.

Thanks largely to the help of France, as well as the colonists' perseverance and what can only be called military errors by the British, the colonists won their independence from Great Britain. The unstoppable juggernaut had been defeated, but how big of a deal was this for the British Empire?

While Britain had tried to prevent the loss of the American colonies and the loss was devastating, it was not to be a crippling blow to the empire. The wealth and power that Britain had built up over the century could not be overthrown with a single loss. Furthermore, trade between the new United States and Britain resumed shockingly fast, allowing Britain to continue to reap economic benefits from its former colonies. The American Revolution showed simultaneously that Britain was not unstoppable and that its status as a world power could be shaken but not undone. However, the American Revolution did not leave Britain unscathed, and perhaps the worst blow was dealt to King George III and the monarchy.

Internal Changes

For a long time, King George III has taken the brunt of the blame for the loss of the American colonies. The popular narrative of American independence claims that George III was a tyrant whose lust for power pushed the Americans to revolution. As with many simple explanations of history, this understanding fails to capture the nuance of what exactly went wrong in George III's reign. The king was less a tyrant and more sadly incapable of handling the complex political problems that arose during his reign. George III was king during a time of emerging popular politics when the opinions of the people were beginning to be manipulated as a political tool. It was also a time of political instability when control of Parliament was uncertain.

King George III proved unable to manage these problems. He picked his ministers poorly, leading to accusations of favoritism and a desire to restore royal prerogative. He supported Parliament and his ministers even as they made decisions that pushed the American colonies closer and closer to revolution. Once the war had begun, the king made things worse when he stubbornly insisted on continuing the fight to retain the colonies even after it became apparent that Britain was losing. Although many historians now believe, based on the evidence, that these actions were made by a king who believed strongly in his duty to guide the nation rather than a tyrant, it does not change the fact that George III often made poor decisions. By the time the American colonies had been lost, Parliament and England had little faith in its king.

George III did gain some competence as he gained experience. He successfully engineered the emergence of the government of William Pitt the Younger, but in doing so, he ensured his own increasing irrelevancy. Although the king had helped Pitt the Younger rise, both knew George III could not manage his political opponents without Pitt. This left most of the power in Pitt's hands. The prime minister was the real force of the

English government.

This change in the power of the monarch only became more entrenched when George III became mentally ill. It is now believed by many that the king had porphyria, a condition that caused the excessive production of certain compounds in the blood, poisoning the entire nervous system. While this exact diagnosis cannot be confirmed, it remains undoubtedly true that George III suffered from mental illness. In the late eighteenth century, he suffered only a bout of insanity, but in the last decade of his life (from 1811 to 1820), he was mentally unsound with only brief times of lucidity. Although his son, George IV, was named as regent during this decade, the king's mental illness left the government of England almost entirely in the hands of the ministers and Parliament.

Something had changed in the English government. The monarch, who for so long had been the government itself, could for the first time be seen as a figurehead. George III wielded real power (even late in his reign before the mental illness overcame him permanently), but he was the last English monarch to do so. From then on, England was ruled more by its prime minster than its monarch.

Chapter 16: The Union with Ireland

England had grown quite a lot since emerging as a nation back in the tenth century, and part of that growth was its union with Wales (made official under Henry VIII in 1536) and Scotland (achieved in 1707). These three together formed the country known as Great Britain, but there was another part of the British Isles that had yet to be officially incorporated: Ireland.

Thus far in this book we have not explored what was happening between England and Ireland. So, to understand how union with Ireland happened in 1801, we must go back in time and learn a bit more about the relationship between the two countries.

Kings of Ireland?

Wales was conquered by Edward I and then officially united with England under Henry VIII. Scotland became connected to England when James I became king of both nations, with the Stuarts ruling both as separate countries until the union under Queen Anne. Ireland's story is not so straightforward.

England first laid claim to Ireland in the Middle Ages under Henry II. As with Wales, England hoped to gain territory through conquest, but the conquest of Ireland was far from complete. England had secured a foothold in the country but only held control in one area, which became known as the Pale, leaving most of the island under the control of various Irish clans.

The Tudors tried to establish firmer control, but Ireland was too independently minded. Even the Anglo-Irish nobles (English settlers who arrived during the Middle Ages and intermarried with the Irish) who lived within the Pale did not always respect the English Crown. The Reformation then made the situation far worse. Whatever the English may have thought or tried, the Irish had no intention of becoming Protestant. Attempts to convert them only increased Irish nationalism and weakened England's hold.

With conversion making no progress, Elizabeth I tried another method to subdue the stubborn Irish: plantations. By taking lands from Irish Catholics and redistributing it to Protestant English settlers, the queen may have hoped to change the landowning class in Ireland into a group that was more sympathetic and willing to be ruled by England. These Protestant English settlers became known as the New English.

This plan, too, did not work. Giving away their land only made the Irish more resentful. A rebellion broke out in the Northern Ireland region of Ulster in 1594 under the leadership of the Earl of Tyrone. Hence, it became known as Tyrone's Rebellion. Tyrone picked his moment well because the English were engaged in other military conflicts on the continent and unable to devote their full attention to the Irish rebellion. The rebellion dragged on for nine years. A lot of land and property were destroyed, and many civilians died.

Ultimately, the English put the rebellion down, but the scars it caused were deep and bitter, only worsening the relationship between Ireland and England. Many of the Irish nobility fled to the continent in the aftermath, leaving Ulster without a ruling class. England acted quickly, giving the land to Protestant New English settlers. This was the origin of the region that would become Northern Ireland.

Ireland again tried to rebel during the English Civil War. For a while, the Civil War was so hectic that Ireland was left alone, but once Cromwell was in charge, Ireland was brutally brought to heel. The destruction was so great that many who escaped violent deaths later died of starvation.

Decades later, the Irish again saw an opportunity to throw off the English yoke. Unlike the rest of James II's kingdoms, Ireland was rather happy that he was a Catholic. After James II fled England during the Glorious Revolution, he garnered the support of Irish Catholics to reclaim his kingdoms. He had regained control of almost all of Ireland except for the Protestant-dominated Ulster when William of Orange met him at the Battle of Boyne (1690), where James II and the Irish Catholics were defeated. Once again, Ireland had failed in its rebellion.

William III at the Battle of the Boyne by Jan Wyck.
https://commons.wikimedia.org/wiki/File:King_William_III_at_the_battle_of_the_Boyne,_1690.jpg

The failure of this very Catholic uprising left the Protestant landowners with even more power. They controlled the Irish Parliament and soon passed laws restricting Catholics from doing everything from voting to buying land. Thus, while most of Ireland was Catholic, it was a terrible place to be a Catholic.

Although England had put down rebellion after rebellion, its control of Ireland was still unstable. The repeated subduing of Ireland made its people more and more resentful. England held on to Ireland only through might, and there was very little practical union between the two. How did a political union happen, then?

Ireland in the Eighteenth Century

Ireland going into the 1700s was a split nation. Most of the population was Catholic, but since Catholics were severely restricted, most of the land was owned by Protestants. This meant that the Protestants controlled the Irish Parliament and were making decisions for the Irish.

There was naturally a lot of tension between the two groups. The Protestant landowners rented land to Catholic tenants, but the lack of understanding and cooperation between the groups hindered any economic growth. Protestant landlords tended to spend most of their time in London instead of on their land. This meant that they were more interested in the rental income they could earn than investing in the land itself. To earn as much rent as possible, land was subdivided among as many tenants as possible, often leaving Irish peasants with too little land to make a living with. This problem of subdivision was only worsened by the Irish tendency to divide holdings among sons instead of passing them intact to the eldest as the English did.

All these problems were made even worse by the fact that there was little to do in Ireland other than farm. With no other industries to turn to, the problem of small land holdings increased as the population grew. Agricultural technology did not advance quickly in Ireland either, so the growing population put a great strain on the country. In short, Ireland in the eighteenth century was poor and divided sharply between the ruling elite and the peasant class.

However, a political nationalism that sought greater Irish independence was rising, and the source of that nationalism was shockingly the Protestant landlords. While this powerful ruling minority might not have cared about the rights of Irish Catholics, they cared about themselves and were becoming increasingly annoyed at the direct interference of the British Parliament in Irish affairs. Even though Ireland had a Parliament, the British Parliament often legislated directly for Ireland and made decisions that hurt the Irish. While Ireland saw itself as a separate kingdom with the same king (much as Scotland had been before the union), it was clear that England saw Ireland more like a colonial holding.

Thus, the Protestant Irish began to long for more autonomy, particularly the right of the Irish Parliament to legislate exclusively for

Ireland. Late in the eighteenth century, the Irish achieved this for a time. In 1780, taking advantage of the precarious imperial situation Britain found itself in due to the American Revolution, Ireland demanded free trade and got it (a major achievement considering that Scotland had had to unify with England to get the same). Then in 1782, the Irish Parliament was granted autonomy in Irish affairs. It was ironically a demand similar to what the American revolutionaries had made. However, the Irish made it when England was trying to hold its empire together and was in no mood to fight a repeat of the American Revolution in Ireland.

The elite class of Irish Protestants had what they wanted, but all was still not well. Although Ireland prospered now that it had free trade and the ability to make decisions for itself, most of the nation was still oppressed and unheard. There had been some loosening of the penal laws that restricted Catholics, but they still held no political power. Agricultural development also still lagged, and poverty was rampant in rural areas, where there were eruptions of violence against landowners and their policies. The country was divided not only along religious but also class lines.

These tensions were particularly bad in Armagh, a county in Ulster, where in the 1780s and 1790s, sectarian violence between a Protestant group called the Peep o' Day Boys and a Catholic group known as the Defenders was intense. A major confrontation between the two groups in 1795, called the Battle of the Diamond, caused the formation of a secret Protestant society known as the Orange Society. The Orange Society's goal was to maintain Protestant power in the face of growing demands for greater rights for Catholics.

The Orange Society was not the only society formed in the 1790s in Ireland. There was also the Society of United Irishmen, which was formed in 1791 and inspired by the French and American Revolution. This group was unique in that it did not have a religious affiliation. Its goal was Irish independence and greater voting rights. Over the decade, the group became more radicalized, entering into full rebellion against British rule in 1798. Like the many Irish rebellions before, the 1798 rebellion did not go well for the United Irishmen. It was snuffed out under the military might of England, and the consequences were severe.

To get Ireland under control, a new Act of Union was passed in 1801 that eliminated the Irish Parliament, instead giving Ireland seats in the

British Parliament. The stated goal was to strengthen the connection between the two nations, but it was clear that Ireland had been strong-armed and bribed into the union. The Irish Parliament had only had control of Ireland for eighteen years, and now Ireland was more firmly under British control than ever.

The Irish Question

If the British thought a political union would solve their troubles with Ireland, they had sorely underestimated just how deep the divide between the two kingdoms ran. The "Irish question," as the problem came to be known, was a frustratingly unsolvable and constant problem for Britain over the nineteenth century. But what exactly was the question? What were the problems that plagued the Anglo-Irish relationship after the union?

Despite now being a part of the wealthy British Empire, Ireland remained a poor nation with a stagnant economy. There was still much violence between landlords and tenants, and religious tensions, as always, remained high. The union brought added political tensions, as most of Ireland had no say in British (and hence their own) government since Catholics were excluded from Parliament. Ireland remained a poor and violent place, and England had no idea what to do with it.

In the first half of the nineteenth century, a political movement to emancipate Irish Catholics reached the British Parliament. Thanks largely to the work of a man named Daniel O'Connell, Parliament passed the Catholic Emancipation Act of 1829, which allowed Catholics to sit in Parliament and hold government positions. But there was a price to pay to get the British Parliament to pass such an act. Voting rights in Ireland were heavily reduced so that, even though Catholics could now sit in Parliament, few Irish Catholics could vote.

Catholic emancipation was not the only major thing the Irish wanted, though. Repeal of the Act of Union was the next goal, but on this one, Britain was not prepared to give in to pressure. To reverse the union with Ireland would have been for Britain to take a step backward in its empire building, and England saw this as a step toward destroying its position as a world power. No matter how difficult Ireland proved to be, England was not going to let it go without a fight.

The political unrest in Ireland took a major backseat in the middle of the nineteenth century with the outbreak of the Great Famine (also called the Irish Potato Famine). By the 1840s, much of the Irish population, particularly the vast number of poor farmers, had come to rely heavily on the potato as their food source. For some, potatoes were their sole food. Thus, when a blight devastated the potato crops across the country, the results were catastrophic. Around a million people died either from starvation or diseases caused by malnutrition. Over another million people moved to other countries to find work and food. So devastating was the famine that the Irish population has never recovered. Ireland is the only country in the world that has fewer people today than it did in the early 1800s before the famine.

The famine also worsened tensions between Britain and Ireland. The response of the British government to the disaster was inadequate, to say the least. Programs were started to feed the starving populace and then shut down while many were still starving. The fact that Britain was one of the wealthiest nations on earth at the time made the Irish extremely bitter over the lack of aid.

One group that became radicalized by the Great Famine was a movement called Young Ireland. Young Ireland was a group of young journalists who wanted to renew a sense of Irish culture and identity and repeal the union with Britain. The bitterness caused by the Great Famine turned the group revolutionary, and it tried to start an armed revolution in 1848. However, most of the population was still suffering too greatly from the famine to take up arms. It was a short-lived rising, but it would inspire later Irish nationalism and pushes for Irish independence.

Irish Independence

Irish flag.
https://commons.wikimedia.org/wiki/File:Flag_of_Ireland.svg

Over the next several decades, Ireland continued to simmer. IN the time between the Great Famine and World War I, several new political parties and groups with different ideas for Ireland emerged. The Home Rule movement sought to get the British Parliament to pass a Home Rule act that would give Ireland its own Parliament that would be subordinate to the British Parliament. In response to the Home Rule movement arose Unionism, an opposing movement focused in the Ulster area. The Unionists were against Home Rule. Many of them were Protestants who believed that Home Rule would result in a Catholic rule that destroyed the elite position Protestants had enjoyed for so long, especially in the north. There was also a third group: Sinn Féin. Sinn Féin was more closely aligned with the sentiments expressed by Young Ireland. It wanted independence for Ireland, although by 1905, it was operating as a political party within the British system.

The conflict between these different visions for Ireland reached a head during World War I. Militant Irish nationalists seized what they saw as an opportunity to rebel against British rule, declaring the independent Irish Republic on Easter of 1916, but the rebels had picked a bad time. They received no support from the Irish people or the political parties. However, once again Britain responded harshly, further alienating Ireland. The rebellion was put down, but the swift execution of its leaders by the British turned them into martyrs. The British response to the Easter Rebellion pushed the Irish people away from the Home Rule movement and into the arms of Sinn Féin.

Violence again erupted in 1919 after members of Sinn Féin legally elected to the British Parliament refused to go to London, instead sitting in their own Irish Parliament in Dublin. The ensuing Anglo-Irish War was a guerrilla-style war between the British forces and Irish nationalists. By 1921, both sides were sick of fighting. Britain, whose public had grown sick of the violence and atrocities committed in Ireland, finally agreed to let Ireland go. However, the terms were not to everyone's liking.

Through the terms of the 1921 treaty, Ireland became a dominion of the Commonwealth with an independent Parliament that swore allegiance to the British Crown (much like Australia and Canada). To the more radical members of Sinn Féin, who hated England, this was not good enough. They wanted the Irish Republic that had been declared on Easter of 1916. There was even a brief civil war in Ireland over this point immediately following the 1921 treaty, but the dominion status remained. (Ireland ultimately became a republic in 1949.)

The other point of contention was Northern Ireland. Six counties in Ulster (where Unionism was strongest) were left out of the dominion of Ireland, with the idea that they might be added later (something that has still not happened over a century later). Ireland was finally independent but no longer whole, and the impact of this rupture is still felt today. Northern Ireland has been a hotbed of violence and terrorism between Catholics and Protestants. The wounds of centuries of tension and strife have proven very hard to heal.

Chapter 17: The Victorian Era

As we saw in Chapter 15, by the close of the eighteenth century and the end of George III's reign, Britain had become a nation ruled primarily by Parliament and its ministers. The monarchs tried to hold onto political power, but by the end of the nineteenth century, their role became largely social and ceremonial.

Nevertheless, the monarch who ruled during this final waning of the British monarch's power has become one of the most famous in British history, with a reign long enough to have an entire age named after her. The Victorian age or era, named after Queen Victoria, who ruled from 1837 to 1901, is one of the most iconic periods of British history for its culture and the political and social changes that helped shape a more modern Britain. (Historians generally give the Victorian era broader dates, starting it in 1820 with the death of George III and ending it in 1914 with the outbreak of World War 1.)

Portrait of Queen Victoria of England, Empress Victoria of India
https://commons.wikimedia.org/wiki/File:Queen_Victoria_-Golden_Jubilee_-3a_cropped.JPG

Social Changes

By the Victorian age, the Industrial Revolution had changed the social makeup of Britain. Throughout the Victorian age, England would become the first nation to industrialize and urbanize. By World War 1, most of England's population lived in urban areas. This population movement had a profound impact on the social structure of the country.

Urbanization could have spelled serious trouble for the aristocratic or noble class in England. The peers and landed gentlemen that made up the top echelon of society originally had power because of the large amounts of land they owned. In an agricultural society, those who own the land own everything, so as cities became the new centers of wealth and power, what would happen to noblemen and their large country estates?

The boring answer is not much. Many of the landed elite were smart enough to invest in industry, and for a long time, the process of urbanization only increased the value of their land. These landowners also held many of the government positions, so even as the rest of society moved to cities and weren't tenant farmers anymore, the landed class still retained much power. Many of the landed elite also retained a sense of responsibility toward the rest of the society. These paternalistic feelings led many aristocrats to join the conservative political party known as the Tories, who believed that maintaining the social hierarchy in society was for the ultimate good of everyone.

Despite this, the Victorian era was the age of the middle class. The middle class included a large variety of occupations and incomes, from industrialists and bankers to clerks and shopkeepers. The middle class included those who worked for a living but not with their hands. This contrasted with the nobility, who prided themselves on the fact that they did not have to work but inherited their living, and the working class, made up of those who worked with their hands.

The Victorian middle class held to an ideology of hard work and the self-made man. They tended to be individualistic and moralistic, believing that people ought to help themselves and that they had earned their relatively good economic position in life. The Victorian middle class also valued a strict separation of public and private life, leading to the idea that women should be confined to homemaking. Since part of middle-class lifestyle was also having servants, this meant that the middle-class women's role in life was to have children.

These values created the society that we now think of as Victorian. Just as the landed class's attitudes lent themselves naturally to a conservative (Tory) political agenda, the middle class's strong sense of individualism led to the emergence of another powerful political movement: liberalism. Unlike the Tories, who wanted to keep things as they were, the liberals (known as the Whigs) wanted reform. With many of them middle-class men who believed strongly in the value of getting things done, the liberals achieved many reforms during the Victorian era.

Before we dive into some of those reforms and how they changed English society, let's discuss the working class. This was by far the largest segment of the population, but as a group, the working class, as we have dubbed them, did not have a sense of class consciousness like the landed elite and middle class. An aristocrat knew and thought of himself as an aristocrat. A middle-class man was middle class and proud of it. A working-class man, however, was more likely to consider himself a miner, an agricultural laborer, or a domestic servant rather than a member of the working class.

Because of this lack of class consciousness and the fact that they couldn't vote, the working class did not have the political presence of the other classes in this era. Some occupations formed trade unions that sought to protect the workers' rights, but these were technically illegal until 1871 and therefore had little political impact. It was the landed Tories and middle-class liberals who were determining the fate of the nation in Parliament.

The Reform Act of 1832

One of the most significant political acts of the Victorian era came in 1832 when the liberal Whigs were in power. Although members of Parliament were technically elected, the system could hardly be called democratic. Very few men could vote (to speak nothing of women). Parliamentary districts had not been reworked along the lines of the great population shifts caused by the Industrial Revolution, so some large industrial towns had no representatives in Parliament while other dying villages had two members in the House. Then there was the outright corruption. Without a secret ballot, it was easy for landlords to dictate votes to their tenants. In some boroughs (parliamentary districts), the member of the House was effectively appointed by the major landlord. Thus, while Parliament called itself a representative body, it was quite clear it did not accurately mirror the nation.

Now, Parliament had existed this way for quite some time, but what changed in the Victorian era was the rising political consciousness of the people, particularly the middle class. The middle class wanted a say in their government, and thanks to a fear of rebellion spawned by events like the American and French revolutions, the ruling class caved into their demands. The Great Reform Act became law in 1832 and represented the first step toward a more truly representative House of Commons.

By modern standards of democratic representation, the Reform Act of 1832 was a small step indeed. It widened the franchise (nationalizing the voting requirements that had previously varied from borough to borough), but voting was still restricted to men and property owners with a certain amount of wealth. There was still no secret ballot. However, the boroughs were reworked so that the growing towns now had representation, and there was no more outright appointment of members by landlords. In this way, the Reform Act of 1832 accomplished what it set out to do, which was to pacify an increasingly agitated and politically aware middle class. Revolution had been avoided, and the door had been opened for a series of continuing reforms that would eventually change the British system without extreme bloodshed.

The Advent of Darwinism

Political changes were not the only forces moving in Victorian Britain. There were also shifts in the scientific community that would have widespread impacts on the rest of society.

In 1831, a young man named Charles Darwin set sail on the HMS *Beagle*. His five-year journey on that ship would prove to be one of vast scientific impact. It was during this trip that Darwin developed his theory of evolution, publishing his famous book *On the Origin of Species* in 1859.

Darwin's theory initially rocked the intensely religious Victorian society, causing much debate. Strangely enough, though, by the end of the century, many people did not see evolutionary theory as a contradiction to Christianity. Theologians argued that natural selection showed the providence of God in all things and so made peace (at least temporarily) with the scientific theory.

Once religious leaders had found a way to work Darwinism into Christianity, many middle-class Victorians were quick to embrace the theory. The idea of natural selection and the survival of the fittest provided evidence for what many of the middle class already believed: the best will rise to the top. Inequality was not bad. It was simply the result of natural selection in human society. In the British Isles, such an attitude made relief to the poor, such as during the Irish Potato Famine, limited. Across the world, this social Darwinism provided scientific justification for Britain's growing empire.

Imperial Britain

With the rise of the middle class, clamor for political reform, and scientific discoveries, a lot was going on domestically in the Victorian era. However, this was also the era when Britain ruled a global empire. Imperialism became a large part of the British identity for the Victorians.

While imperialism normally brings to mind images of conquering armies (which was certainly part of it), Britain's power was largely economic in the Victorian age. Having directly conquered and established many colonies in the eighteenth century, Britain in the nineteenth century established such economic dominance that strict control was no longer necessary. Britain instead pursued a policy of free trade, allowing its colonies to trade with other nations.

Britain also found that establishing commercial dominance in an area did not require a formal takeover. It was cheaper to open trade routes and allow areas to become economically dependent on Britain without formally annexing the territory. Because of this, Britain's global dominance extended well beyond the boundaries of its formal empire.

Still, the colonies that were officially part of the empire remained important for many reasons beyond economics. Places like Canada proved to be ideal destinations for British emigrants. Australia became a convenient way to get rid of convicts. Some colonies served as important ports for British trade routes, and others acted as military outposts to protect the empire. Britain had thus come to rely on its imperial holdings in many ways, and one colony in particular became central to British success: India.

In the Victorian age, the British situation in India could hardly have been better. Trade with India was a source of economic prosperity, and the Indian army made Britain an Asian power. The Indian army was made up mostly of Indians and paid for by Indian taxes, but it was controlled by the British. Britain thus had enormous power for practically nothing. This strange situation was the result of the actions of the East India Company, which had gradually established dominance in India during the last century. That utter dominance passed to the English government when it took control of India in 1858.

The government was concerned with more than making money, however. The East India Company had cared little for changing Indian culture or social structure, but with the morally staunch middle-class Victorians now calling the shots, efforts soon began to civilize India. This push from Victorian society began even before the government took over. Christian missionaries were allowed into the country in 1813, and certain cultural practices were outlawed, such as *sati*, which was the practice of a widow burning herself on her husband's funeral pyre.

As to be expected, this push to change Indian culture did not sit well with the Indians. There was a mutiny of the Indian army that spread into a more general rebellion in 1847. There was great bloodshed on both sides, and the relationship between Britain and India was permanently soured. Racism and elitism on the British side increased, and dissatisfaction with British rule grew on the Indian side. Things were not resolved finally until Indian independence in 1947.

British India shows both the allure of the British Empire and its problems. The empire at once possessed both a self-bolstering efficacy, where more territory brought greater prosperity and power, and a self-destructive tendency, where more territory caused greater tension and required more management. By the end of the Victorian era, these two poles were fueling an imperialist snowball that would eventually lead to extreme nationalism and the outbreak of World War I.

Between 1870 and 1914, the territory that formally belonged to the British Empire grew rapidly. As other European nations expanded their colonial holdings, Britain felt pressured to expand even more to maintain global dominance. The increasing size of these empires only worsened tensions, as the colonizing powers began to bump into each other around the globe. At the same time, these worsening tensions made many feel that continuing to expand the empire was the only way Britain could have security. With the rivalry between European powers at an all-time high and the imperial presence of these countries across the globe, in some ways the coming of a global war was inevitable.

British Empire at its peak in 1921.
https://commons.wikimedia.org/wiki/File:British_Empire_1921.png

Chapter 18: World War I and II

As discussed in the previous chapter, there was a growing rivalry in empire-building among the European powers by the turn of the twentieth century. In this tense atmosphere, many alliances were formed. During the first decade of the 1900s, Britain made agreements with France and Russia. Although the written agreements between these three were technically a recognition of the other powers' colonial holdings, they signified an informal pledge to mutual aid, and the three countries became known as the Triple Entente.

But just what was the Triple Entente united against? Germany was the chief concern. Its rising dominance threatened Britain's position as a world power. The rapidly growing German navy added much to this distrust. Britain had been the dominant naval power in the world since the defeat of the Spanish Armada in 1588, and as an island nation, it could not but help see Germany's fleet as a direct threat.

Germany was not alone, though. As a member of the Triple Alliance, Germany had allied with Austria-Hungary and Italy. Although Italy would ultimately not honor this alliance, Germany's support of Austria-Hungary was crucial in turning an event in the Balkans into a world war.

When a Serbian nationalist assassinated the Austrian Archduke Franz Ferdinand on June 28, 1914, the dominoes began falling. A month later, Austria declared war on Serbia, perceiving the assassination of the archduke as a threat from that nation. Germany backed Austria in this, but Serbia was backed by Russia. Thus, when Austria and Serbia went to war, so did Germany and Russia. However, Russia had an alliance with France. If Germany wanted to stand a chance in this war, it needed to knock France out of the fight quickly so it could turn its full attention to Russia, and the fastest way to conquer France was to go through Belgium.

It was the German invasion of Belgium that finally crossed the line for Britain. This was too clear a sign of what Germany intended for Europe, and British public opinion and Parliament quickly united in favor of war. Britain declared war on Germany on August 4, 1914. It was believed then that the war would be quick. No one had any idea just how long and terrible this war would become.

Britain in World War 1

For the British and many others, World War I proved the cruelest form of whiplash. Men who marched off to war full of patriotic zeal and confidence found themselves fighting in muddy trenches and dying by the thousands. Instead of decisive offensives and open combat, this war (especially on the Western Front where Britain was most heavily involved) was a tedious and gruesome stalemate.

The First Battle of the Somme has become a bleak representation of just how terrible the war was. To drive the Germans out of France and thus win the war, Britain and France knew they had to be aggressive. In the Battle of the Somme, they tried to do this. After heavily bombarding the German lines with artillery, British troops attacked on July 1, 1916. They were to cross no-man's-land (the open land between the trenches) and seize the German position. It seemed simple enough, but new military technology like the machine gun made attacking an entrenched position all but impossible. The British troops that tried to cross no-man's-land were gunned down in waves, with 20,000 dying on the first day. The Somme offensive lasted several more months, ending on November 13 after 420,000 British casualties. It had achieved almost nothing and has garnered a lasting reputation as the epitome of the futileness and devastation of trench warfare.

By this point, it had become clear that World War I was not going to be like other wars. This was total war, and it would take the efforts of the entire nation for Britain to wage war. Not only were conscription acts passed to bolster the army, but the government also seized control of industries, distributing resources and the labor supply. There was rationing and even the restriction of holidays. The war was felt by all, especially as the horrendous casualty rates began to impact almost every family in England.

If things were so bleak, how did Britain and its allies win the war? Change began in 1916 after two years of stalemate. The British government changed hands from the leadership of H.H. Asquith to that of David Lloyd George. This change in leadership showed just how dissatisfied the country was with the progress of the war. Lloyd George's government would prove somewhat more effective than that of Asquith's. Lloyd George immediately drastically reduced the size of the war cabinet, which allowed decisions to be made quicker and more effectively. He also managed to solve the food crisis caused by German submarines through a convoy system and food rationing.

Lloyd George's success in these areas was the result of traits that also proved harmful in other areas. Lloyd George had a strong personality, and he was determined to end the stalemate and the war. This action-oriented attitude allowed him to make decisions decisively and pursue a course without getting bogged down in the administrative bureaucracy of government. However, his strong personality was not appreciated by the British military command. There was much distrust between Lloyd George and his generals, and their inability to work together hindered the progress of the war on the active front.

Ultimately it would take something outside of Britain to break the long and tedious stalemate. In April 1917, the United States of America declared war on Germany. With fresh resources and men to bring to the fight, the entry of the United States into the war was what the Allies needed. By November 11, 1918, the war was finally over. But what exactly would peace look like?

The Paris Peace Conference

The peace made after World War 1 has since become infamous. Many would argue that the failures of the peace created after World War 1 led directly to the outbreak of another world war less than three decades later. So, what exactly went wrong with the peace negotiations, and what was Britain's role in it?

The fighting of World War I ended with the armistice in 1918, but it would take a year to negotiate the official peace treaty, and "negotiate" is a generous term for what happened. The Paris Peace Conference involved negotiations and arrangements made between many countries, but only four countries had a say: Britain, America, France, and Italy (although the first three ended up making most of the decisions). Britain's representative was Lloyd George, who found himself caught between France's Prime Minister Clemenceau's desire for revenge on Germany and American President Woodrow Wilson's hopes for a more united and stable world. The other Allies were heeded little and the defeated nations not at all. The resulting treaties were thus destined to do little to achieve any lasting goodwill between the countries.

The most infamous example of this is the Treaty of Versailles, which officially ended hostilities between the Allies and Germany. Not only did the treaty force Germany to give up territory (a normal consequence of losing a war), but Germany also had to admit guilt for the war and agreed to pay reparations to the Allied countries. To the Germans, this added a grievous insult to an already bad enough wound. It was not the grounds for a lasting peace.

Appeasement and the Start of World War II

With the benefit of hindsight, it's easy to see now that the Treaty of Versailles was never going to keep the peace with Germany. It's crucial to remember as we move forward in British history that the people living in the time between the two world wars did not have this benefit. No one knew for certain that another world war was coming, and many people were prepared to do a lot to avoid it.

The trauma of World War I left many nations struggling to right themselves again, and a worldwide economic downturn in the 1930s did not help matters. Germany, suffering under the weight of heavy reparations, felt these difficulties most keenly, leaving the country vulnerable to the influence of someone like Adolf Hitler. Hitler promised the Germans restoration of their former greatness, and with his charismatic speaking ability, Hitler soon had control of Germany.

It became clear throughout the 1930s that Hitler did not intend to abide by the Treaty of Versailles. Germany began the construction of an air force in 1935 and re-militarized the Rhineland in 1936. These were steps that could only be regarded as hostile, but the rest of Europe and Britain were weary of war and unsure of how to respond to Hitler's actions.

In the 1930s, Britain ultimately decided to go with a strategy of appeasement, letting Hitler have his way in the hopes that this would prevent war. The most famous proponent of appeasement was Neville Chamberlain, British Prime Minister from 1937 to 1940. For much of the 1930s, appeasement took the form of simply ignoring Hitler's actions even when he went so far as to annex Austria in 1938. However, appeasement reached a new height (or rather low) when Chamberlain, along with representatives from France and Italy, negotiated the Munich Agreement with Hitler in 1939, handing over part of Czechoslovakia to the Germans. The Czechoslovakian government was not part of the negotiations at all. Appeasement had become more than a matter of ignoring Germany's violations of the treaty and was now a policy of even assisting Hitler to stave off war.

War had been avoided, but Chamberlain and his appeasement policies had opponents. One of the most vocal was Winston Churchill, who called the Munich Agreement "a total and unmitigated defeat." It did not take long for Churchill to be proved right. Hitler soon invaded other parts of Czechoslovakia, blatantly ignoring the Munich Agreement. When the Germans invaded Poland on September 1, 1939, Britain could no longer ignore Germany's obvious intentions. Britain declared war on Germany two days later. France did the same, and World War II had officially begun.

Winston Churchill

Although it might seem strange now, it was not obvious at the start of World War II that Winston Churchill was the man to lead Britain through this crisis. Churchill began his career as a soldier and reporter, making a living from his writings. He entered the political arena in 1900 as a conservative member of Parliament.

Winston Churchill.
https://commons.wikimedia.org/wiki/File:Sir_Winston_Churchill_-_19086236948.jpg

However, Churchill did not stay long with the conservatives. In 1904, he split with his party over a disagreement on free trade and joined the liberals. From there, Churchill's rise in politics was steady. He was a close ally and colleague of David Lloyd George, and by World War 1 had earned himself a position as First Lord of the Admiralty (the government minister in charge of the British navy). That, however, was an uncomfortable place to be. When the Gallipoli Campaign of World War 1 failed utterly, Churchill took the blame. He was left out of the coalition government headed by Lloyd George and, in 1915, left politics to become a soldier again.

But Churchill could not stay away long. He was back in government business by 1917, and from then to 1939, his political career was one of ups and downs with little overall progress. He was a constant but often ignored voice until he turned his attention to Germany. Churchill's constant warnings about Hitler and German aggression only became more accurate throughout the 1930s. By the time war broke out, Churchill looked like one of the only government figures who had seen things clearly. Neville Chamberlain thus appointed him to his old position as First Lord of the Admiralty.

By 1940, the war was swinging in Germany's favor, and Chamberlain, acknowledging his failures, resigned his position as prime minister. A coalition government with members of all parties was formed, and none other than Winston Churchill was at its head. Despite his failures in the past, Churchill seemed to be the man with the energy and drive needed to run a war, and no one doubted his unswerving commitment to defeat Germany. Churchill's wartime leadership of Britain would make him a famous historical figure not only in Britain but across the world.

Britain and World War II

Churchill's commitment to resisting Germany soon showed itself sorely needed as the war did not initially go well for Britain and her allies. The Germans' blitzkrieg strategy, which focused on fast offensives to overwhelm and quickly subdue their enemies, was extremely effective. By late June 1940, Germany had conquered the Netherlands, Belgium, and even France. Britain alone remained to defy the German conquest.

The struggle for Britain was fought largely in the air over two months (August and September) in 1940 known as the Battle of Britain. Germany knew that Britain needed to be subdued, but an invading force would never be successful until Germany controlled the skies. The German Luftwaffe thus set out to gain aerial supremacy over the British Royal Air Force (RAF). The air forces were fairly evenly matched; however, the RAF succeeded in beating off German assaults, and the German plan for a full-scale invasion of Britain was abandoned.

This did not mean that Germany had given up forcing Britain to surrender. The Luftwaffe turned its attention to bombing British cities, particularly London, in the hopes of destroying Britain's morale and forcing a surrender. This period of intense bombing was called the Blitz. Despite the onslaught, Britain held firm for an entire year against Germany. Then, in late June 1941, Hitler's forces invaded the Soviet Union, giving Britain an unlikely ally. Later that year when Japan bombed Pearl Harbor, the United States also entered the war. Britain now had two powerful allies and, with them, real hope of victory.

Victory did indeed come, though it would take four long years of fighting to get there. Throughout the war, Churchill met with US President Franklin Roosevelt and Soviet leader Joseph Stalin to discuss war operations and, as the war ended, the postwar situation. Although Britain continued to play an important role throughout the war in defeating Germany, to Churchill's dismay, his and Britain's position increasingly diminished in the face of the two larger powers. The world wars had so overturned the previous world order that Britain, for the first time in several centuries, found itself removed from the top tier of world power. The United States and the Soviet Union were the new superpowers.

Thus, while World War II was in many ways a triumph for Britain, it also spelled the end of British world supremacy. The total warfare had devastated Britain economically, and its wealth had been at the core of Britain's world dominance. After the war, Britain no longer had the resources or the interest to maintain its empire and lost the remainder of its colonial holdings. India gained independence just two years after World War II ended, and other colonies followed until Hong Kong was returned to Chinese sovereignty in 1997.

Churchill was also shockingly ousted as prime minister after the war. Despite his wartime triumph and personal victory in the election, Churchill's party lost its majority to the Labour Party immediately after the war. The decline of the empire and the success of the Labour Party showed how the era of world wars had changed Britain's attitude. In the postwar world, Britain was a country focused more internally on issues like social reform and economic recovery. Imperial Britain was gone, and from its ashes, the modern United Kingdom would emerge.

Conclusion

While much could be said of English history after World War II, we will end our tour of English history there. From a collection of rival Anglo-Saxon kingdoms occupying just a part of the British Isle to the largest empire in history and the United Kingdom, England's story is one of a slow, great rise and a rapid and inevitable decline.

In its beginnings, England was an unstable land. Constantly invaded by outsiders, no centralized sense of nation or government could develop. It was not until the Anglo-Saxons united against the Vikings that any nation that could be called England emerged. However, that was not the end of foreign invasions. The Norman Conquest of 1066 was the last time England would be successfully invaded and conquered. From that time forward, England was free to develop as its own nation without being ripped apart by external powers. But for many centuries, internal conflicts prevented any lasting stability. The Anarchy, Wars of the Roses, Civil War, and Glorious Revolution all highlight the difficulty in achieving a sense of national unity.

Eventually, though, England had settled much of its domestic strife and began to turn its attention ever more outward in the age of exploration and colonization. Thanks to its naval supremacy and the wealth generated by the Industrial Revolution, England beat out its rivals in the imperial game until it had gained an empire and undisputed world dominance.

Such an empire, however, could never last. The more territory England gained, the more resources it needed to maintain it, and the larger the empire, the more prone it was to internal strife. Weakened by back-to-back world wars, England's economy was no longer a world powerhouse, and its empire soon dissolved. Still, compared to those of other empires, England's fall was relatively mild. While its territory has been drastically reduced, England maintains its position as a stable and influential nation. The existence of the United Kingdom today speaks volumes about England's ability to persevere through the many changes its history has seen.

And even if England no longer dominates the world as it once did, its influence remains felt by people around the globe in many ways. English is the most spoken language in the world today. Trials by jury, which originated in England, spread during the period of colonization and continues in some form in many countries. And, although England can hardly take credit for the invention of democracy, the Magna Carta and the American Revolution are events deeply embedded in the development of democratic governments.

England's impact has also had many less favorable consequences. British imperialism and interference in other regions of the world created tensions that can still be felt to this day. Colonization may have created great wealth for Britain, but it was at the cost of the colonized and has left a legacy of prejudice and exploitation around the world. The great strife with Ireland outlined in Chapter 16 is only one story of many showcasing the extremely tense and complicated relationship former parts of the British Empire have with England.

Whether it is for good or ill, the one thing that cannot be denied is that England has had an impact. The history of this small nation has lessons of relevance for everyone.

Part 2: Medieval England

An Enthralling Overview of the English Middle Ages

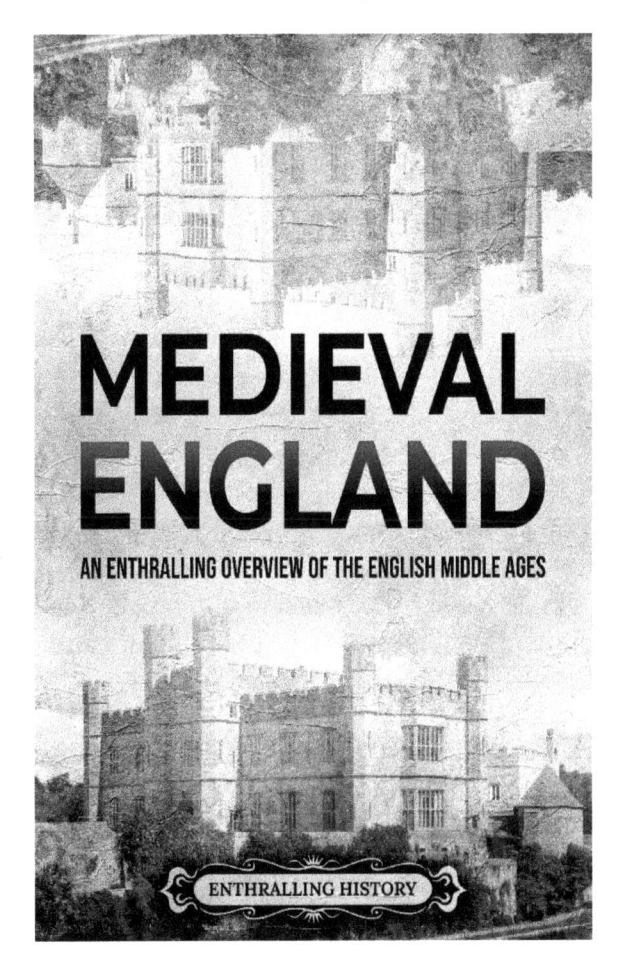

Introduction

When you hear the phrase medieval England, what do you think about? Knights in armor charging into battle on horseback? Kings with golden crowns sitting in castles? Maybe you even picture small towns with thatched roofs, a muddy road, and a pig ambling through the streets?

The time period known as the medieval period, also called the Middle Ages, has been incredibly romanticized in books, movies, and ultimately in our memories since it ended some six hundred years ago. Some people picture it as a grand time full of noble deeds, exciting battles, and simple living. Others refer to this period as the Dark Ages, indicating a time of filth, poverty, and general ignorance. The truth, as it often is, lies somewhere in the middle of these two extremes. Medieval England was neither as glamorous nor as horrendous as we often paint it; it was a lot more varied than those simple images we usually picture.

The medieval period in England covers roughly six hundred to eight hundred years. That's a whole lot of time for things to happen. To put it in perspective, six hundred years ago from today would be in the early 15th century. Shakespeare wasn't alive yet. Columbus hadn't yet sailed the ocean blue. The United States of America wouldn't become a country until over three hundred years later. In six hundred years, humans have gone from walking and riding as the main means of transportation to airplanes and cars. Six hundred years ago, most people still believed that the earth was at the center of the universe, and now, we have sent men to the moon.

The point is that a lot can happen in six hundred years. Medieval England in the year 600 looked quite different from medieval England in 1485. During this time, England saw the rise and fall of several royal dynasties. It saw barons repeatedly rebel against the king's authority and even England's first popular uprising. There were both foreign wars and civil wars. It was a period that saw the conversion to Christianity and the church becoming the most powerful institution in the Western world. The law system contained both the infamous and cruel trials by ordeal and the origins of the trial by jury. It was a time of knights and monks and peasants and lords. Over these six hundred years, England and its people went through a lot of changes, ordeals, and developments. There was a lot more to these six hundred years than castles and knights.

This book hopes to cut through those stereotypes to take a realistic look at the Middle Ages. We will talk about the armored knights charging into battle, but we look at why the use of armored knights in military strategy declined throughout the period. We will learn about some of the cruel and gruesome punishments used in the justice system, but we will also examine why the system was designed that way. We will talk about the corruption and immense power of the medieval church, but we will also see the role the church played in local life.

This book is about the real medieval England. Some of it may be similar to what you have always thought about the Middle Ages, but a lot of it may surprise you. For example, did you know that the famous Christian martyr Thomas Becket began as a politician, not a priest? Did you know that the infantry was strategically better than the cavalry? Did you know that women in the Middle Ages could work the same jobs as men? Did you know that King Arthur isn't English, that the Vikings are kind of responsible for the start of England, and that the Black Death might be the result of one of the first acts of biological warfare?

There are a lot of fascinating things to learn about the medieval era, and this book will walk you through them while also giving you a comprehensive understanding of the entire period. Whether you already know the basics or have no idea what years medieval England even covers, you'll be able to follow along and learn something new as this book takes you on a tour of one of the most interesting periods in English history.

Chapter 1: Early Middle Ages (600–1066)

In the year 600, England didn't exist, but by 1066, the English people had been united under a single king for close to a century.

The story of the Early Middle Ages in England is thus the story of how a nation came to be. Over these five hundred years, the disparate groups that inhabited the area joined into a nation with a single king and a distinct culture. There was a lot going on in England during this time. From the development of towns to Viking raids, this is how the nation we call England got its start.

Setting the Scene: England before 600

If we want to understand England in the medieval period, it helps to know a little bit about what was going on before that. The English were not actually the original inhabitants of Britain, so how did they get there, and who was living there first?

Prior to the Middle Ages, England, or rather Britain, was part of the Roman Empire as the province of Britannia. Emperor Claudius had his generals conquer the island in 43 CE, although it took much longer than this for the Romans to actually subdue all of the southern tribes living on the island at the time. These original tribes were the Celtic Britons (they weren't the native inhabitants of the island either; like the Romans and the Anglo-Saxons, they came over from the continent). Rome was never able to fully conquer and hold the northern part of the island (Scotland), but the south (England and Wales) was under firm Roman control, despite numerous rebellions, for around four hundred years.

During this time, the Celtic Britons inevitably became Romanized. They lived in Roman-style houses, wore Roman-style clothing, and even spoke a type of British Latin. Britain was covered in Roman roads and Roman settlements. By the 4th century, the people living there were fully Romano-Britons.

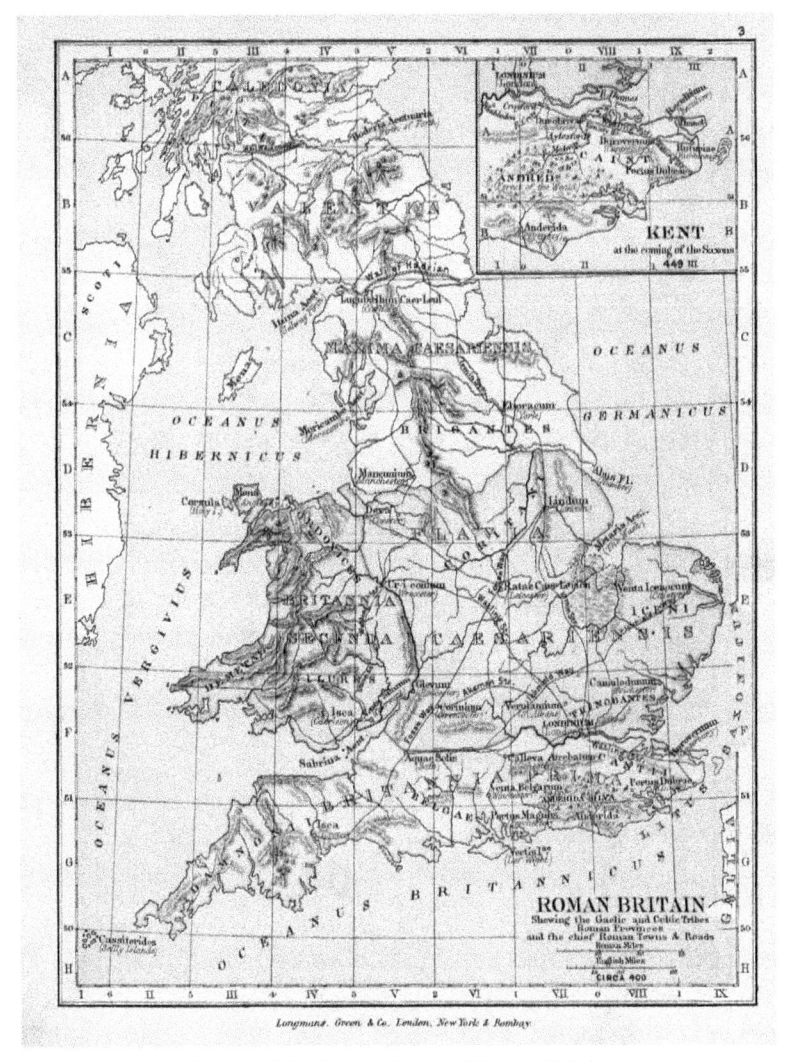

A map of the five provinces of Roman Britain
https://commons.wikimedia.org/wiki/File:Roman_britain_400.jpg

You might be surprised to learn that Britain was a Roman province for so long. We typically don't think of Britain as being Roman. Today, there are very few traces remaining of Roman Britannia, and while other previous Roman provinces speak Romance languages (like French and Spanish), which have their roots in Latin, the British speak English, which is a Germanic language. If the British people were fully Romanized by the 4th century, what happened?

In short, Rome fell. It was sacked by the Visigoths in 410, but by that time, things had been going downhill for a while anyway. We often think of the sack of Rome as the beginning of the end for the Roman Empire, but by this time, things were pretty much already over for the province of Britannia. The empire was already collapsing due to a combination of external threats and infighting. One of the various emperors vying for control during the period removed the Roman legions from Britain to fight elsewhere, and they simply never returned to the remote island province. Britannia was left high and dry without a Roman military presence.

While that might sound great, what it meant was that the inhabitants no longer had imperial protection. No Roman legions were protecting them, and unfortunately, there were a lot of groups who were happy to take advantage of that.

So, life suddenly got very hard for the Romano-Britons. They found themselves attacked by numerous barbarian groups: the Picts of Scotland, the Scotti of Ireland, the Angles and Saxons (both Germanic tribes), and the Jutes, who were a Norse tribe. The Angles, Saxons, and Jutes eventually moved past raiding Britain to settling there, and for the sake of convenience, we typically refer to them collectively as the Anglo-Saxons.

By the time we pick up with England two hundred years later, in 600 CE, at the start of the Middle Ages, the land was divided into several competing Anglo-Saxon kingdoms. The English nation eventually formed out of these nations.

But what happened to the Celtic Britons? Not only did they no longer have Roman military protection, but without Rome, the economic system that had been sustaining the province also collapsed, along with functions and services related to the imperial government. Roman towns with their now useless public buildings and marketplaces were abandoned, and then the Anglo-Saxons arrived.

We will talk more about this in Chapter 4, but tradition tells us that the Celtic Britons were pushed out of the area that would become England by Anglo-Saxon conquerors. Some chose to migrate to Brittany, an area in what is now northwestern France, and they did not completely disappear from the isle of Britain. Wales is a Celtic nation, as is Cornwall.

While the Britons maintained the area that became Wales, within a generation or two after the Romans departed, Roman Britannia had been fully replaced by *Angleland*, the land of the Angles.

Anglo-Saxon England

Thus, at the beginning of the Middle Ages, the area that would become England was effectively Anglo-Saxon, but it was not yet England. At the beginning of the 7th century, this area was divided into the Anglo-Saxon Heptarchy, which consisted of seven competing kingdoms: Northumbria, Mercia, Wessex, East Anglia, Sussex, Essex, and Kent.

The kingdoms of the Anglo-Saxon Heptarchy, along with the Welsh and Pict kingdoms
https://commons.wikimedia.org/wiki/File:British_kingdoms_c_800.svg

We'll get into greater detail about who exactly the Anglo-Saxons were and what they were like in Chapter 4, but for now, let's talk about how England, or rather the area that would become England, developed during the period when the Anglo-Saxons were in charge.

As we already discussed, when the Romans left, the towns they had built were completely abandoned. So, in the 5th and 6th centuries, there were no towns in England. The Anglo-Saxons at this time lived in a tribal and rural society. There was pretty much only one way to get rich in this world, and that was to take things from your neighbors. Warfare was a profitable business, and the elites of this society gained power and wealth by making war on and conquering their neighbors. There were many more than seven Anglo-Saxon kingdoms, but the seven of the Heptarchy were the ones that came to dominate as the different groups vied for power during the 5th, 6th, and 7th centuries.

While warfare can be highly profitable in the short term, it is also not the most viable long-term economic plan. The more territory you conquer, the more funds you need to rule that area. If your funds are coming solely from campaigns, that means you now have to conquer even more territory. Eventually, a kingdom simply gets too big to run off the spoils of war alone.

Now, warfare also provides one with a surplus of various goods (the things you take from the people you conquer). These surpluses can be used to develop a much less risky and more tenable economic plan: trade.

In 7th-century England, towns again began to appear. Trade flourished, and permanent settlements again became viable. As the economy continued to develop, communities developed around the production of certain key goods. There were settlements that focused on producing salt, mining iron, and harvesting timber.

So, over the first two centuries of the Middle Ages, Anglo-Saxon society grew and prospered. It remained a time full of war and other hardships that one would expect to find in the 6th and 7th centuries, but it was not the dark ages some have made it out to be.

The Viking Age

By the late 8th century, the Anglo-Saxon kingdoms were flourishing, but they were still very much competing kingdoms. It would take a significant outside threat to unite these kingdoms, and that threat was the Vikings.

The first Viking raids on England began in the 790s. These raids, though relatively small in scale, were devastating for the coastal settlements. The Vikings were Norse raiders who came from several different areas, such as Denmark, Sweden, and Norway. Although they had many differences, the Vikings all shared at least one crucial skill. They were excellent shipbuilders.

Vikings made many different kinds of ships, but the ones typically used in raids were called longboats. As the name suggests, these ships were long and narrow and, importantly, had shallow draughts. This meant that they could travel easily in shallow water. In these ships, the Vikings were able to land right on the beaches of settlements near the water and then swiftly push their boats out to sea again. They were also able to navigate rivers, extending the reach of their raids.

These fast and deadly raids were bad enough for the Anglo-Saxons, but things got much worse in the 9th century. The Vikings began to make more substantial attacks on the Anglo-Saxon kingdoms. They did not stop at burning and looting but began to conquer territory. Some even chose to settle on the island. In 865, the Viking threat became an all-out invasion with the arrival of the *mycel hæpen here*, or Great Heathen Army.

The Great Army was a Norse or Viking force that quickly set out to conquer the Anglo-Saxon kingdoms. In truth, the army was a more disparate group than the name suggests. It was not one large unified force but was rather made up of many distinct groups. Remember that although the Vikings were all Norse, they came from many different areas. The Great Heathen Army reflected this.

Of course, this variance among its members did not make the Great Heathen Army any less devastating for the Anglo-Saxons. The Great Army conquered Northumbria and installed a puppet king. East Anglia soon followed. Mercia held out longer, but it, too, fell to the Norse. Wessex was the last to submit, but eventually, the king of Wessex, King Alfred, was driven from his kingdom by the Vikings in 878.

At this point, it certainly looked like Angleland had become the land of the Norse instead, but if that had stayed true, England would probably look very different today. What happened?

King Alfred of Wessex had been driven from his kingdom, but he was not dead. In the same year, 878, King Alfred fought a battle against the Norse, and he won a decisive victory. From the brink of defeat, Alfred managed to push the Norse out and reclaim Wessex. This incredible victory and his subsequent reign earned Alfred a name that few monarchs managed to pull off: Alfred the Great.

The Rise of the Wessex Dynasty

Alfred's victory in 878 was crucial, but it was not the end of things. In 878, Alfred made a deal with the Norse Guthrum that required Guthrum to convert to Christianity and leave Wessex. Guthrum then established a kingdom in East Anglia, so while Wessex was recovering, the Norse still held sway over a large part of England. The boundaries negotiated by Alfred and Guthrum were made official around 886. The area controlled by the Norse would later come to be called the Danelaw, and it included the Anglo-Saxon kingdoms of Northumbria, East Anglia, Essex, and parts of the original Mercia.

The kingdoms of England in 886
https://commons.wikimedia.org/wiki/File:Britain_886.jpg

When Alfred died in 899, his children continued the fight against the Danes. Alfred's son, Edward the Elder, became the king of the Anglo-Saxons, a title his father had created. This means the House of Wessex continued to be in charge. Alfred's daughter, Æthelflæd, had married the king of the Mercians and was known as the "Lady of the Mercians."

With Alfred's death, the Danes again tried to conquer Mercia and Wessex, but both Edward and Æthelflæd built a ring of forts to protect their kingdoms. In 910, Edward won a decisive victory against the Danes at Tettenhall, ending their plans of reconquering Wessex.

Starting in 912, Edward was able to go on the offensive. Step by step, he regained the Anglo-Saxon kingdoms of Essex and East Anglia. His sister Æthelflæd again mirrored Edward's moves and also went on the offensive. She began to retake the Danish Five Boroughs, which were part of the area that had originally been part of Mercia. Æthelflæd had made enough progress with her campaign to receive a promise of submission from the Danes in Northumbria when she died in 918.

Upon hearing of his sister's death, Edward halted his campaign against the Danes to go to Tamworth, where he was able to get the Mercians to accept him as king, making an even larger Anglo-Saxon kingdom. Edward then succeeded in gaining back the rest of Mercia from the Danes. When Edward died in 924, the House of Wessex now had control of most of England, with the expectation of Northumbria, where a Norse king sat at York.

Edward was succeeded by his son, Æthelstan. Æthelstan was able to finish what his father started but with surprisingly less violent means. Æthelstan had his sister marry the Norse king in York, a man by the name of Sihtric. When Sihtric died in 927, Æthelstan gained control of Northumbria and became the first king to rule all of the English people. The year 927 is thus the start of England as a nation, and Æthelstan is widely considered to be the first king of England.

Taking a step back from the details that led to Æthelstan becoming the first king of England, there are two ways you can read the events that led to the domination of Wessex in the Anglo-Saxon kingdoms. You could argue that the Wessex dynasty, beginning with Alfred the Great, was the savior of the Anglo-Saxons. They drove the Danish invaders back and united the Angles into a more powerful kingdom that would be better equipped to defend itself.

However, you could also argue that the rise of the Wessex dynasty and the unification of the Anglo-Saxons under them was the simple product of opportunism. Alfred the Great and his descendants took advantage of the Danes weakening their Anglo-Saxon rivals. As they worked to push the Danes out, Wessex was able to easily consolidate the conquered Anglo-Saxon nations under their control. In a way, the Wessex kings were simply a different conqueror.

There is likely some truth to both interpretations. There can be no doubt that without Alfred the Great, the Danes would have most likely conquered the Anglo-Saxons, and England might have never come to exist. However, it is equally true that Wessex was not the only Anglo-Saxon kingdom and that the ultimate dominance of its rulers was largely due to their ability to take advantage of the opportunity created by the Norse takeover. So, ultimately, the Vikings are kind of responsible for the unification of England.

England under the Wessex Dynasty

We will talk more about this era in our discussion of the Anglo-Saxons, but for the sake of chronology, there are a few things you need to know about England under the Wessex dynasty. England was now under the rule of a single king, but it was not united in the way we think of nations today.

When Æthelstan became the king of the English in 927, he was ruling over several rather disparate areas. Things that are vital to government, such as currency, measuring systems for land ownership, and laws, differed greatly across England. Depending on where you were, you could be under a Mercian, West Saxon, or Danish style law system.

This might sound like an absolute logistical nightmare today, but in the 10th century, English kings were far less concerned with having everything in their administration the same. For the most part, local areas continued using their own systems, especially those that were using the Danish law, although a few changes were instituted. The kingdom began to use the same type of currency, and the Wessex system of dividing the kingdom into shires and those into even smaller units called "hundreds" was expanded. Eventually, there were national rules about how often the courts that presided over these localities had to meet.

Although these changes may seem insignificant, they were the beginning of the creation of an English nation that was unified in practice as well as in name. Living under the same king was one thing, but using the same coins and the same systems created much more commonality between the Anglo-Saxons in Wessex, Mercia, and elsewhere in England.

This process of practical unification would continue into the 11th century, only not under the Anglo-Saxon kings. In 1013, the Danes returned.

The Return of the Danes

To understand how the Danes managed to invade England again, we first need to talk about the Anglo-Saxon king at the time: King Æthelred. When Æthelred's father, King Edgar, died in 975, there was a dispute about whether the throne should pass to Æthelred or his older stepbrother, Edward. Both brothers had supporters, and although Edward initially seized the throne, he held it for less than three years. Edward was murdered, and Æthelred took the throne in 978 at the age of twelve.

Taking the throne after the assassination of the previous king and doing so as a child set the mood for most of Æthelred's reign. In short, he was not a good king. In fact, history has dubbed him Æthelred the Unready, and it was during the reign of Æthelred the Unready that the Vikings again began to raid England.

Æthelred was unable to deal with the Viking problem. He only succeeded in making it much worse by massacring Danes on St. Brice's Day in 1002. Æthelred was unable to fend the Danes off, so he paid them continuously higher tributes to buy peace. However, the raids only continued to get worse. In 1013, the English people had had enough. They accepted Sweyn, King of Denmark, as their king. Æthelred was forced to flee the country, seeking asylum with his family.

King Sweyn did not rule England long, however. He died in 1014, and the English invited Æthelred to return on the condition that he would be a better king, which he happily agreed to, again becoming the king of the English in 1014.

Sweyn's son, Cnut, however, was not happy with this arrangement. In 1016, Cnut led another Danish invasion of England. Æthelred died during the conflict, and his son Edmund Ironside was eventually defeated by Cnut. Cnut allowed Edmund to maintain control over Wessex, which proved to be an inconsequential arrangement because Edmund died within a few months, leaving Cnut ruler of all of England. For the next twenty-five years, England had a Danish king.

For nineteen of those years, Cnut ruled England, doing so from 1016 to 1035. There can be no argument that Cnut was an effective king. During his reign, he managed to conquer Norway, so he was the king of England, Denmark, and Norway. Cnut gained great popularity with the English people through his conversion to Christianity and dedication to maintaining the law. Under Cnut, England saw almost two decades of security and relative peace.

Despite his successes, Cnut's death again left England with a problem of succession. Cnut had two wives, one of whom was Æthelred's widow, Emma, and he had sons by both her and his other wife. Both his sons naturally felt that they had a claim to the throne. Harold, Cnut's son with his first wife, seized the throne of England first, holding it for five years before he suddenly died in 1040. Harold's early death gave his brother, Harthacnut, the son of Cnut and Emma, the chance to seize the English throne. Harthacnut ruled for only two years before he died suddenly. Neither of Cnut's sons was well-liked by the English people.

It was surprisingly one of Æthelred's sons who next took the throne after the death of both of Cnut's sons. Edward the Confessor was the last of the Wessex dynasty to rule England. He reigned from 1042 to 1066. Although Edward had a fairly successful reign, he and his wife Queen Edith failed to have any children. When he died childless in 1066, England was again thrown into confusion over the succession. This time, an outside threat decided to take advantage of that confusion. It would soon be the end of Anglo-Saxon England.

England from 600 to 1066 was an emerging nation. Although there was much progress in terms of economic growth and political unity, there was also an almost constant state of warfare due to both foreign invaders and infighting over succession issues. The monarchy had proved to be both a powerful consolidating force and the source of many issues. Starting with Æthelstan in 927, the kings and queens of England would continue to have an enormous impact on the country for the next eight hundred years, through the Middle Ages and beyond.

Chapter 2: High Middle Ages (1066–1272)

David Carpenter's book on this period of English history bears the title *The Struggle for Mastery*, and it certainly is an apt description. Beginning with the Norman Conquest in 1066, moving through the eighteen-year civil war known as the Anarchy, and ending in the 13th century with the conflicts between the barons and kings, the High Middle Ages in England was dominated by struggles for power. While the Early Middle Ages saw the establishment of the king and his government, the High Middle Ages would test that government and the extent of the king's power.

The Norman Conquest

In 1066, Edward the Confessor died childless, and, as usually happens with monarchies, the lack of a direct heir led to problems. Immediately after Edward's death, Harold Godwinson, an earl, was named the king. The quick appointment of Harold suggests that the powerful men of England were at least in partial agreement about Harold's appointment, and their quick action may also have been an attempt to preempt the rival claimants to the throne. However, Harold's appointment did not stop his rivals. If Harold wanted to keep the throne, he would have to fight for it.

The first trouble was not William of Normandy (later known as William the Conqueror) but someone far closer to home. Harold's brother, Tostig, joined forces with the king of Norway, Harald Hardrada, and attacked York. King Harold rode north with his army and engaged the forces of Tostig and Harald at Stamford Bridge on September 25th, 1066.

The Battle of Stamford Bridge was a decisive and total victory for King Harold. Both Tostig and Harald were killed in the battle, and the remains of their forces fled in ships. Harold had successfully defended his right to be the king of England, but unfortunately, there was still another rival. Three days after Harold's victory at Stamford Bridge, William, Duke of Normandy, landed in the south of England with an invading force.

Why did the duke of Normandy feel he had a right to the English throne in the first place? King Edward's childlessness was not just a subject of discussion on his deathbed. William of Normandy claimed that Edward had named him as his heir. It is possible that Edward might have made such a promise to William sometime around 1051 in an effort to maintain peaceful relations with Normandy, but it would not have been a serious promise since King Edward was still healthy and might even have had children at that time.

Norman narratives would later state that in 1064/1065, while acting as Edward's ambassador to Normandy, Harold Godwinson had confirmed William's appointment as heir and even swore an oath to William. It seems highly unlikely that this story is entirely true considering its source, but in 1066, Harold was condemned for breaking his oath. Since he never got the chance to defend himself, we will never know what exactly happened. What we do know is that William used this story to justify his invasion.

King Harold's army met William's at the Battle of Hastings on October 14th. Some consider Harold's move to confront William so soon after the Battle of Stamford Bridge as reckless, but it is always difficult to judge with the gaze of hindsight. The Battle of Hastings did not go well for King Harold, so it is easy to say that his decision to confront William at that time was unwise.

We'll get more into the details of the battle in our later chapter on battles, but needless to say, the Normans won the Battle of Hastings. The

English force was almost entirely annihilated, including King Harold and his brothers. William was the only rival to the throne left standing, and it did not take him long to claim his place. William was crowned king of England in London on December 25th, 1066.

Just as Anglo-Saxon and then Danish rule had brought changes to England, the rule of the Normans would have a great impact on the English nation. The first change was in the ruling elite. After putting down several rebellions in the first five years of his reign (1066-1070), William I had had enough of the remaining English aristocracy. They were removed from power and replaced with William's Norman appointees.

William didn't just stop at changing the faces in power, though. He also made some changes to the system. Although we often think of the feudal system as being a staple of the entire medieval period, it was only under Norman rule that England adopted a true feudal system, although the system that was in place before the conquest was feudal-like. We will discuss this system in greater detail in Chapter 5.

The Anarchy

As with both the Anglo-Saxon dynasty and the Danes, the Norman rule of England was also destined not to last, and it, too, ended due to problems with succession.

After William I, his son, William II, ruled England. When William II died without children, his brother Henry I took the throne. Things seemed set since Henry I had a son, William, who would become king after him. However, in 1120, William died when the *White Ship* sank in the English Channel. His death led to a period of English history that would become known as the Anarchy.

After William's death, King Henry I named Matilda, his daughter, as heir to the throne. However, when Henry died, the barons did not support Matilda's claim. She was married to Geoffrey Plantagenet, Count of Anjou, whom the Anglo-Norman barons disliked. Henry's nephew, Stephen of Blois, seized the throne.

Because Matilda was in Normandy at the time of Henry I's death, Stephen arrived in England first and was able to seize the throne with relatively little difficulty. However, his reign did not follow the pattern of this promising start.

The majority of Stephen's reign, in fact, all but one year of it, took place during the Anarchy, an English civil war that lasted from 1135 to 1153. This eighteen-year war was essentially a fight between Stephen and Empress Matilda (empress because her first husband was Holy Roman Emperor Henry V) for the English throne.

We do not have the space here to dive into a detailed account of the Anarchy. As the name suggests, it was a complex and chaotic time in English history. Stephen's problems extended beyond Empress Matilda's claim to the throne. In the west, the Welsh managed to raid and eventually seize control of some areas, and in the north, King David of Scotland invaded and conquered substantial areas of English land.

During this period, both Stephen and Empress Matilda granted lands and favors to try to win support. Various people switched sides throughout the war, and many took advantage of the chaos to try to gain more power. Earls waged war on other counties, and castellans and the garrisons stationed at the various castles across England terrorized the local populations. The national currency, which had been established by the Anglo-Saxon kings, fractured, with Stephen, Empress Matilda, and even some barons all issuing coins in their own name.

This did not mean that all of England was burning constantly, as the name "Anarchy" might suggest, but the constant warfare meant that at times in certain places, anarchy became very real. This was especially true in the border areas between the area controlled by Stephen and that controlled by Empress Matilda. Even as England was broken into multiple pieces, law and order still reigned within these smaller pieces controlled by people like King David, King Stephen, and Earl Robert (Empress Matilda's brother and supporter in the conflict).

So, what brought an end to the chaos? The war had proven to be a firm stalemate. While Matilda had returned to Normandy in 1148, her son Henry continued the fight in England in 1153. The powerful men of England were reluctant to enter into a final decisive battle since they did not want to give up their local power again to a powerful king. The church also refused to take sides, refusing to recognize Stephen's son Eustace as heir. Everyone appeared to be waiting for something to break the stalemate so that they could side with the victor.

The thing that broke the stalemate was ironically the same thing that had caused the civil war in the first place: the death of the male heir to the throne. In 1153, Eustace died, and Stephen was left without an heir. His other son, William, showed no desire to ascend the throne, so, in 1153, Stephen made Henry, Empress Matilda's son, his heir, effectively ending the Anarchy.

As it turned out, Henry did not have to wait long for his throne. Stephen died a little less than a year later in 1154, and Henry became Henry II.

The Angevin

Henry II marked the beginning of a new ruling dynasty in England, one which was to last for the remainder of the medieval period: the Plantagenets.

Henry II was the son of Empress Matilda and Geoffrey Plantagenet, making him the first English king in the Plantagenet line. However, historians often refer to Henry II and the two kings following him (Richard the Lionheart and King John) as the Angevins.

The Angevins were English kings with an empire. In fact, as a whole, they spent more time on the continent than they did in England. The Angevin Empire stretched from northern England to the Pyrenees Mountains, including part of Ireland and large areas of France (Anjou, Normandy, Aquitaine, Maine, and Brittany).

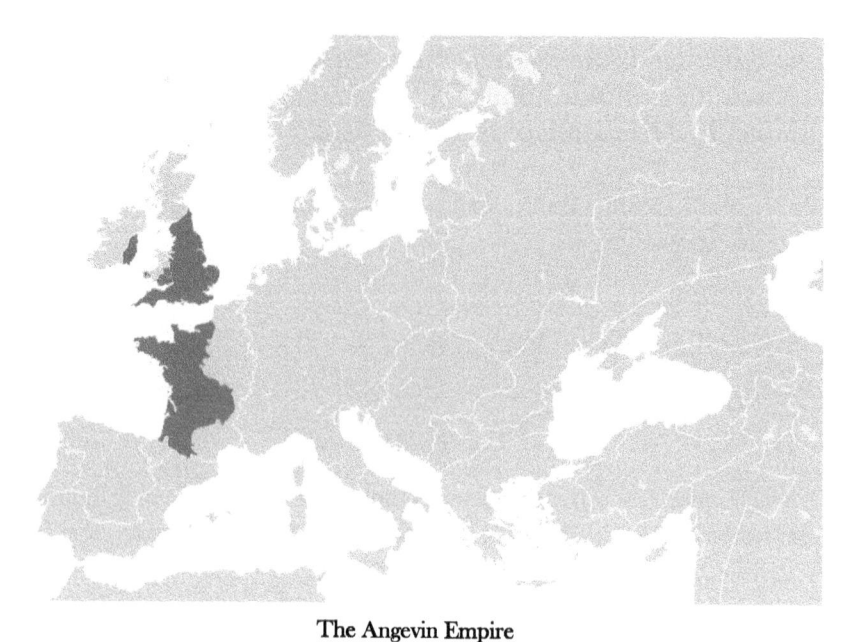

The Angevin Empire
*Blank map of Europe.svg: maixderivative work: Alphathon, CC BY-SA 4.0
<https://creativecommons.org/licenses/by-sa/4.0>, via Wikimedia Commons
https://commons.wikimedia.org/wiki/File:Angevin_Empire_1190.svg*

This large empire was not the result of conquest but rather of Henry II's position when he became the king of England. He inherited the title of count of Anjou and Maine from his father and was made duke of Normandy by the king of France in 1150. Perhaps his most successful maneuver was marrying Eleanor of Aquitaine in 1152. This marriage made him duke of Aquitaine. So, by the time Henry II became the king of England in 1154, he already held vast areas of land in western France.

Unfortunately, besides lots of land, Henry II also had lots of sons—five to be exact. He soon ran into problems with trying to find places for all of them to rule. His sons rebelled against him several times. Eventually, his son Richard allied with King Philip II of France and forced his father into a settlement. King Henry II died shortly after.

Despite his family issues, Henry II had an enormous lasting impact on England, and his reign was indeed a critical one in English history, largely because of the changes he made to the judicial system.

In brief, Henry II wanted greater control over local matters, and after the Anarchy, there was a greater push to develop a system that could more effectively keep the peace. Henry II's changes were complex, but they created a system with distinct procedures. Decisions were now made by juries and heard by the king's judges rather than local courts.

The new system was voluntary, so the amount of people who took their cases to it indicates that it had appeal. This was the start of a system that would last until the 1970s in England. We'll discuss law and order in the medieval period in greater detail in a later chapter, but this was one of the lasting impacts that Henry II had on England. His empire would not be as lucky.

Henry's youngest son John became the king in 1199 following the death of his brother, Richard the Lionheart. Although Richard spent only around six months of his reign in England, his military and diplomatic skills had kept the Angevin Empire together throughout his ten-year reign. King John was less skilled in these arts.

King Philip II of France took advantage of the opportunity and began seeking to drive King John out of France. Through both ill luck and bad decisions, John lost the Angevin Empire's continental holdings little by little. By 1204, he was effectively only the king of England, but King John's troubles did not stop with his continental failures. The rest of his reign would cement his place as one of England's worst kings.

The Magna Carta and the Barons' Wars

Fighting wars takes money, so to continue his military expeditions in France and win back Normandy, King John needed funds. He thus spent a good deal of time after 1204 finding ways to gain wealth, a task that was only heightened by the inflation during this period.

Squeezing every coin you can get from your subjects does not make for a popular king, and John did not stop there. The popular new judicial system developed by his father, Henry II, might have been a way for John to gain some popularity, but he failed to use it. Justice became a farce under King John, further antagonizing his subjects.

The barons became increasingly hostile to King John, and in 1212, the king discovered a plot to kill him. While he managed to gain control of the situation that time, three years later, tensions exploded again. This time, instead of trying to kill him, the barons sought to make John agree to a list of demands. These demands were the Magna Carta (the Great Charter), and it was one of the most significant moments in English history.

The Magna Carta was a document of sixty-two chapters that put a limit on the king's power. Specifically, it sought to do things like restrict the king's ability to raise funds and stop him from treating individuals however he pleased. The Magna Carta was the first time that restrictions were placed on an English king. It was a landmark moment in that it subjected the king to the law. Before this, the king had always been above the law since he was the one who made the laws. Now, there was something higher than the king.

The Magna Carta was a document prepared by the barons, so its concerns were mostly baronial. It did little to protect the common people, but the general idea and parts of the Magna Carta would become precedents for later democratic hallmarks like the American Bill of Rights. Some chapters of the Magna Carta, such as "To no one will we sell, to no one will we deny or delay right or justice," are still in force today.

Of course, King John did not want to agree to these demands, but the barons went to arms, and he was forced to seal the charter at Runnymede, a meadow near the Thames.

Unfortunately, the peace the Magna Carta seemed to ensure did not last long. King John asked the pope to condemn the Magna Carta, which he did, meaning that King John did not have to follow it. The barons instead went to war, rebelling against King John and offering the throne to Louis, the son of the king of France. Thus began the First Barons' War in 1215.

Louis might have succeeded in becoming the king of England were it not for King John's death. With King John dead, most of the barons switched their support from Louis to John's son, Henry, who was nine years old at the time. Without the support of the rebellious barons, Louis was defeated in 1217.

Although Henry III ruled for far longer, he ended up facing similar problems as his father. Henry III's expensive foreign campaigns were unpopular for the same reason King John's had been, and the local officials he appointed were detested. His half-brothers, the Lusignans, were also unpopular and helped fuel a growing English dislike of foreigners. Again, there was trouble with the barons, and in 1258, Henry III agreed to reforms. But like with his father, the paper reforms proved ineffective. In 1263, the Second Barons' War broke out, with the rebelling barons being led by Simon de Montfort.

During the conflict, both Henry III and his son and heir, Edward, were captured. It seemed as if Simon de Montfort and the barons would win, but Edward escaped capture and defeated Montfort at the Battle of Evesham. The war continued for two years after this. It finally ended in 1267, and Henry III was restored to the throne.

Henry III's victory did not come with the total restoration of royal power. During the later years of his reign, after the war, he was forced to agree to some of the barons' requests, such as restricting the king's local officials to prevent abuses and confirming the Magna Carta. He negotiated with Parliament to secure funds for his son's crusade, marking an important transition in English history. The king was now looking to Parliament for the approval of taxation, something that would become a staple of the English system. King Henry III died in 1272, and the reign of his son Edward would mark the beginning of the last medieval period: the Late Middle Ages.

The years 1066 to 1272 saw massive changes in the monarchy and powers that governed the English nation. In 1066, William I established himself as a strong conquering king. He was able to introduce a feudal system that theoretically placed a lot of power in the hands of the monarchy. However, by 1272, Henry III had accepted the fact that if he wanted to remain the king of England, he would need to please the barons.

While we often think of the medieval period as a time in which monarchs ruled with absolute sovereignty, this period in English history shows us that that was not always the case. Limits could be placed on a king's power. However, those limits often had to be confirmed with the sword rather than the pen.

Chapter 3: Late Middle Ages (1272–1485)

You might think that this last period of the Middle Ages would be a time of prosperity that ushered England into the Renaissance age. However, for the most part, the opposite is true of the Late Middle Ages. This was a time of great hardship and ruin for England. From the devastation of natural events like the Great Famine and the Black Death to the strain brought about by conflicts like the Hundred Years' War, the Peasants' Revolt, and that famous civil war now known as the Wars of the Roses, England from 1272 to 1485 was anything but boring, no matter one's station.

So, how did England make it through these two hundred years and into the Renaissance age? The many hardships would ultimately force a change in the attitude of England's rulers and people. The end of the Middle Ages would be brought about less by the events themselves and more by the changes in people's mindsets that these events produced.

Unity through War

Edward I took the throne in 1272 after over fifty years of fighting between the barons and the king. Edward himself had even participated in these conflicts, as he had beaten Simon de Montfort's forces at the Battle of Evesham and restored his father, Henry III, to the throne during the Second Barons' War.

It thus might have initially seemed that Edward I would experience similar infighting with the barons that had plagued both his father (King Henry III) and grandfather (King John). However, by the end of his reign, Edward I would be one of the most successful kings in English history. How did he transform his predecessors' legacy?

Both King John and Henry III had struggled with internal conflicts, and Edward I, whether he meant to or not, essentially put an end to this by introducing a different kind of conflict. During his reign, Edward I would conquer Wales and nearly conquer Scotland as well. His military prowess saw England's focus shift from infighting to external wars.

Edward I's conquest of Wales was both brutal and effective. He fielded an enormous force in 1277 for his first invasion and then further subdued the Welsh by crushing their revolt in 1282, during which the members of the Welsh ruling family were killed. By 1283, Wales was effectively under English control. Edward I's conquest and subsequent control over Wales was so successful because of the massive amounts of capital Edward poured into the campaign. Not only was Edward I's invading army big enough that the Welsh had virtually little hope of resistance, but he also built a series of castles in the conquered territory to cement his control over the area. It was expensive but highly effective.

Wales was not the only place to keenly feel the strong military aptitude of Edward I. Edward I was also known as the Hammer of the Scots. The exact reason for Edward I's invasion of Scotland is tied to a succession dispute that we will not get into here, but suffice it to say, in 1296, Edward I invaded Scotland.

Edward Longshanks—Hammer of the Scots
Firkin, CC0, via Wikimedia Commons
https://commons.wikimedia.org/wiki/File:King_Edward_I.png

Edward I's Scottish campaign was not nearly as successful as his conquest of Wales, largely because of the problem administrators to this day struggle with—lack of funds. The expense of Edward's Welsh conquest had not left him with enough money to repeat the same strategy in Scotland. Edward I also faced stern resistance in Scotland from figures such as William Wallace and Robert the Bruce.

While Edward I defeated Wallace in 1298, he marched again on Scotland in 1306 when Robert the Bruce was declared the king of Scotland. Edward I was able to best Robert the Bruce at the Battle of Methven in 1306, but he died in 1307 before he could finish his Scottish conquest. The campaign was left to his son, Edward II.

Edward II did not have the same military ability that his father possessed. In 1314, Robert the Bruce's forces defeated those of Edward II at the Battle of Bannockburn, effectively ending the English hopes of conquering Scotland, though a treaty was not signed until 1329.

Edward II's defeat at Bannockburn marked the sharp difference between him and his father. While Edward I had been able to effectively rule England, bringing national unity through foreign campaigns, Edward II was not a great military mind. He would soon find himself suffering from the same problem that his grandfather (Henry III) and great-grandfather (King John) had faced: discontent barons.

Edward II's reign can be described as little more than a disaster. The brazen promotion of his personal favorites, such as Piers Gaveston and the Despensers, led to poor governmental choices. It also greatly angered the ruling elites, who were being overlooked. The barons put pressure on Edward II to make changes in the Parliament in both 1311 and 1327, but they failed to make substantial and lasting reforms.

In the end, Edward II was deposed by his own family. His wife, Queen Isabella, and her lover, Roger Mortimer, invaded England in 1326. Edward II was captured shortly after, and his son Edward III was made king in his place in 1327.

Edward I's campaigns against Wales and Scotland had briefly united the king and barons under a common goal, but Edward II's military failures and poor kingship had again introduced the problem of baronial discontent. It was becoming more and more clear that England could only be governed effectively when the king had the support of his barons.

The Great Famine

Let's take a break from kings and barons to discuss what life was like for the everyday person in the Late Middle Ages. At the beginning of the 14th century, England, like the rest of Europe, was doing rather well economically. Agricultural productivity was at a high with more land in use than ever before, and the population had grown over the last two centuries as a result. This was not simply an era of subsistence farming. Surpluses allowed for trade to flourish, and towns offered places for peasants to both sell and buy various goods.

However, the society was still based on agriculture, and this left it vulnerable to agricultural disasters. The Great Famine, which began in 1315, was devastating to such a society. Although famines are often caused by drought, the Great Famine was the result of a very different weather problem: heavy rainfall. The Great Famine was caused by a period of heavy rainfall and cool temperatures. Not only did this lead to crop failures, but the wet conditions also meant that hay could not be made to feed the livestock.

The recent population growth made the famine all the more devastating. Before the famine, many peasants had finally been able to acquire their own land, and there were many farming communities developing in fringe locations with land that was harder to cultivate. These settlements were in their earlier precarious stages when the famine struck. The people sold land in droves and moved toward larger population centers in the hopes of being able to buy food. However, food prices quickly skyrocketed. People began to eat their livestock, and cooperation in small farming communities collapsed. By 1322, between 10 and 15 percent of the English population had died of starvation. Despite this devastation, the populace recovered relatively quickly once the weather began cooperating in 1322. By 1330, both the population and commerce had recovered.

Even though it had relatively few long-term effects on English history, the Great Famine shows us just how uncertain life in the Middle Ages could be, especially for the lower classes. Not just England but all of Europe faced huge losses of life because of the weather. While it was in some ways unavoidable, it also demonstrates the inability of medieval governments to deal with such crises effectively. This was a time of instability, where people were moved and torn by the whims of nature as well as the whims of kings.

The Hundred Years' War

In 1340, King Edward III made a decision that would greatly affect all of the English people for a long time to come. He declared himself the king of France. Edward III was not the first English king to make this claim, but he was the first one prepared to push his point. France and England had begun a period of conflict that would last for over one hundred years.

It can be easy to assume that the Hundred Years' War was the result of nothing more than Edward III's vaulted ambitions, but that far oversimplifies the matter. The French monarchy was also showing signs of great ambition, and Edward III needed to protect English trade in Flanders. Furthermore, Edward III seemed to have understood what made his grandfather Edward I so successful. Edward III's fight against France gave unity to his reign. Instead of arguing with their king, the French wars gave the English elite a place to cooperate and attain their own ambitions. After all, warfare is a very profitable business. Much like his grandfather, Edward III quelled infighting with an external conflict.

The actual fighting of the Hundred Years' War was not one hundred years of constant fighting but rather one hundred years of various campaigns in France (it also lasted longer than a hundred years, with most historians saying it began in 1337 and ended in 1453). There is not enough room to even begin to discuss the progress of the war here, but some notable battles include Crécy (1346), Poitiers (1356), Agincourt (1415), the Siege of Orléans (1429), and Castillon (1453).

The war was started by Edward III, and it would not end until the reign of Henry VI. Five English kings would continue this conflict with France, with some being more successful than others. Henry V became a national hero thanks to his victories, such as the one at Agincourt, and the military failures during Richard II's reign led to the first popular uprising in English history.

The Peasants' Revolt

To understand what led to the Peasants' Revolt in 1381, we must first understand how closely war and taxes were tied together in the medieval period. In the Middle Ages, taxes were the direct result of war. A king could only directly tax his subjects when there was an express need, i.e., the defense of the realm. This principle had also been used to justify taxation for aggressive wars, such as the French campaigns.

By this point in English history, taxation was also no longer solely in control of the king. Parliament had to approve taxes. Therefore, if kings wanted to continue their wars, they often had to agree to certain demands to get Parliament to approve their taxation plans. This check on a king's power was the result of over a century of baronial discontent and pressure on various kings.

What all this means is that in the eyes of the majority of the English population, defeat in warfare was the direct result of poorly managed funds from taxation and that taxation was the result of both Parliament and the king. To pay taxes for successful military campaigns was one thing, but to be forced to pay for losses was grating.

Unfortunately, the logic of war only exacerbates this issue. Whether you are winning or losing, wars are expensive. However, when you are winning, you can at least partially offset that expense with the spoils you gain. Thus, a war that is going poorly inevitably ends up costing more than a war that is going well.

In the late 1370s, the war was not going well for the English, and the English were being taxed heavily. From 1357 to 1371, there had been no direct taxation of the English people at all, but with Richard II's ascension to the throne in 1377, there was direct taxation every single year for four years. Despite this, there were still no great military triumphs. In 1381, when a third poll tax was issued, a popular revolt erupted.

This time of heavy taxation might not have resulted in an uprising were it not for the fact that the people were already resentful. The Black Death (which we will discuss in detail in a later chapter) had reached England around 1348, killing enough of the population to cause a labor shortage. The labor shortage meant that workers suddenly had the leverage to demand better wages and working conditions. However, the government, which was comprised of people who had to pay these workers, passed a maximum wage law, limiting the amount workers could demand. Such treatment naturally bred resentment, which boiled over under the heavy taxation from 1377 to 1381.

The revolt was concentrated in southeast England, and it was initially quite successful. Led by Wat Tyler, the rebels successfully marched into London. Tyler was even able to gain a meeting with the king and the mayor of London.

However, at the meeting, things quickly went south for the rebels. The mayor of London killed Tyler, and the king somehow managed to convince the rebels to go home by making promises of reform, promises that were not carried out. After dispersing, the rebels found themselves on the wrong end of the law, and many were punished. The revolt had come to nothing.

The death of Wat Tyler (the image shows King Richard twice, both talking to the peasants and watching Tyler's murder)
https://commons.wikimedia.org/wiki/File:DeathWatTylerFull.jpg

Despite its failure, the Peasants' Revolt of 1381 is a crucial event in English history. While the barons had issued the Magna Carta over a century earlier, this was the first time that the masses had defied the king's government. It was a landmark moment for this alone, but it also showed signs of something that would become a national sentiment by the end of the Middle Ages: weariness of war.

In the medieval period, war was the thing that made and broke kingdoms. As we have seen thus far in this chapter, war was often the sustaining factor that kept kings in power and governments stabilized, but it could also turn and become the thing that brought those very governments down. War was a unifying factor, but it was a volatile one. It would take one more brutal internal conflict before England would begin seeking a different path.

The Wars of the Roses

The Wars of the Roses is one of the most famous conflicts in English history. Even the incredibly popular *Game of Thrones* series is based on this particular event. Its lasting impact on the popular imagination is due in no small part to Shakespeare, who wrote a multi-play series about the event. Many of the things that come to mind when you hear the Wars of the Roses is likely because of Shakespeare. The idea that supporters of the different factions picked either a white or a red rose to show their support? Shakespeare. Richard III was an evil, ugly hunchback who murdered his nephews? Shakespeare. While the Bard didn't get everything wrong about the Wars of the Roses, we must remember that Shakespeare wrote his plays over a century after the events and that he was writing to entertain, not for accuracy.

So, what really happened during this conflict that would only later come to be called the Wars of the Roses? It was a chaotic time that saw two noble houses completely annihilated in their contest for the throne. We cannot hope to cover all the messy details here, but we will explore a basic overview of this war that brought an end to the Middle Ages in England.

Although the bloodshed officially began in 1455 at the First Battle of St. Albans, the problems that led to the war started long before then. Henry VI, who ascended to the throne as an infant after the untimely death of Henry V in 1422, was a weak king. Even when he had reached the age to govern in his own right, Henry VI was not a capable ruler. As this fact became more and more obvious, other men were eager to step into the role of being England's practical ruler while Henry VI continued to wear the crown.

One man who sought this role was Richard, Duke of York. By 1450, Richard saw himself as the best man to become the right hand of the king (which, in the case of Henry VI, meant ruling England). However, Richard did not anticipate that Henry VI would view Richard's offer of assistance as a threat. Matters were only made worse by the fact that Richard strongly disliked the man Henry VI had picked instead: Edmund Beaufort, Duke of Somerset.

Richard of York vied for power for five years without bloodshed before things reached a boiling point in 1455 at St. Albans. There, the Yorkist faction defeated the Lancastrian force (Henry VI was of the House of Lancaster) and captured Henry VI, marching him back to London. Henry VI remained the king, with York as his chief counselor and the de facto ruler of England.

Unfortunately, this would turn out to be only the beginning of a series of battles and conflicts between the Houses of Lancaster and York that would last for a little over thirty years, with the final claimant to the throne defeated in 1487. The advantage swung between either side like a pendulum. Below is a short list of how the battles went:

- 1455: First Battle of St. Albans – Yorkists win
- 1459: Battle of Ludford Bridge – Lancastrian win; Richard of York flees the country
- 1460: Battle of Wakefield – Lancastrian win; Richard of York killed.
- February 1461: Battle of Mortimer's Cross – Yorkist win led by Edward, Richard's son
- February 1461: Second Battle of St. Albans – Lancastrian win
- March 1461: Edward of York declared King Edward IV
- 1470: Henry VI restored to the throne
- 1471: Battle of Tewkesbury – Yorkist victory; Henry VI is killed in the Tower of London; Edward IV is the undisputed king

These dates give some idea of the absolute chaos of the time, but they only scratch the surface. Law and order suffered, as men seized power and then were ousted by rival forces. The fighting was brutal and left many people on both sides of the conflict seeking revenge for lost loved ones. It seemed like Edward IV was sitting victorious on the throne in 1471, but that was not the end to this drama.

When Edward IV died in 1483, his son became Edward V. However, only a few months later, both of Edward IV's sons were declared illegitimate. Edward IV's brother Richard was declared king. He became Richard III. It is widely believed that Richard III then had his nephews killed to secure his claim.

History does not remember Richard III fondly, but it might have seen his actions differently were it not for what would happen two years later. The final bloodshed of the main claimants to the throne in the Wars of the Roses was the Battle of Bosworth in 1485. Richard III was killed, and Henry Tudor took the throne. Losing the Battle of Bosworth was seen as divine judgment for Richard's wrongs, and he has been seen in infamy ever since. We might think of Richard III very differently had he won that battle.

But who was Henry Tudor anyway? Henry V's widow, Catherine de Valois, married a Welshman, Owen Tudor. Catherine's sons with Owen Tudor were thus half-brothers to Henry VI. One of their sons, Edmund Tudor, then married a woman named Margaret Beaufort, who could trace her lineage in a direct line back to John of Gaunt, Duke of Lancaster, who was the third son of Edward III. Henry Tudor was the son of Edmund and Margaret Beaufort, and he claimed a right to the throne through both lines.

If Henry Tudor's claim sounds dubious, that's because it was. No contemporaries would have picked Henry Tudor as a strong claimant to the throne, but, thanks to the Wars of the Roses, by 1485, Henry Tudor and Richard III were the only real claimants left standing. (A pretender would be presented after Richard's death, with his defeat officially ending the wars.) With the defeat of Richard III at the Battle of Bosworth, Henry Tudor was effectively the only option. He became Henry VII. To further solidify his claim and put a final end to the bloodshed, Henry VII married Elizabeth of York, Edward IV's daughter. The Houses of Lancaster and York were united, and the war was finally over. England had entered a new era. The Middle Ages was over.

The End of the Middle Ages

Why exactly does this moment mark the end of the Middle Ages? After all, we have seen several dynasties come and go throughout the medieval period, and the Wars of the Roses was not the only civil war that plagued England during this time.

England in the Middle Ages had been formed and defined by warfare. The war with the Viking invaders had originally united the country under the Wessex dynasty, and throughout the next five centuries, warfare served as both the bane and boon of many English kings. Success in war solidified one's rule, but a lack of military prowess often led to rebellion. War was the sole force behind taxation rates, and law and order collapsed several times under the pressure of internal warfare. Although we often romanticize and exaggerate it, there can be no doubt that the medieval period was a violent time.

The end of the Wars of the Roses marked the beginning of a transition away from war being the government's primary purpose. Although Henry VII did deal with rebellions and could be quite ruthless to his political opponents, he strived to maintain the peace during his reign, passing the throne to his son, Henry VIII. This was the most stable the English throne had been in a long time. It was a throne based on the hereditary and sovereign right of the king to rule rather than on the right to rule through conquest. The personal authority of kings was a far more stable thing to rely on than their military authority (although the personal authority of kings would eventually come to be challenged in England during the English Civil War of the 17th century).

This does not mean that war had no place in England after the Middle Ages. Henry VIII would renew the conflict with France, and the defeat of the Spanish Armada by the English in 1588 would prove to have enormous effects on England's future. Over a century after the Wars of the Roses, another civil war would again strike England. Thus, wars would continue to be a shaping factor in English history, but it was no longer the axis around which the entire nation, particularly the government, turned. Industry and trade had been making steady progress, and as England moved into the Renaissance period, things like religion and art would become increasingly important definers of the English nation. England had begun as a nation bound together by conquest and the need for defense. It grew into a nation with a unique culture, systems, and people. We will examine these aspects more closely as we continue to look at medieval England in closer detail.

Chapter 4: The Anglo-Who?

As we already discussed in Chapter 1, the Anglo-Saxons were not the original inhabitants of Britain, but they were the ones who gave England (Angleland) its name. The first king of England was Anglo-Saxon, and the language of England (English) is derived from the Anglo-Saxon language. Clearly, the Anglo-Saxons are important to English history. They are the start of English history, but who exactly were the Anglo-Saxons, and what were they like?

The Dark Ages?

For a long time, the period between the Roman departure from Britain and the Norman Conquest, which was when the Anglo-Saxons held sway over England, had been known as the Dark Ages. This name comes from the idea that this period saw very little forward progress in anything like knowledge or culture. History from this perspective viewed the Anglo-Saxons as poor barbarians who were barely able to scrape up enough to get by.

Of course, this view of the Anglo-Saxon period has been proven wildly inaccurate. The belief that the period from around 400 to 1100 was a dark age bereft of culture and progress comes from an overly sentimental attachment to Rome and its culture. Rome referred to these people as barbarians, and historians for a long time followed the Roman perspective.

Still, it wouldn't be fair to act as though that's the only reason the Anglo-Saxon period has been dubbed the Dark Ages for so long. In some ways, it was the Dark Ages, at least in hindsight, because we know relatively little about this period. There are a handful of written sources such as St. Gildas's *The Ruin of Britain* (likely written sometime in the 6th century), the Venerable Bede's *Ecclesiastical History of the English People* (written in the 8th century), and the *Anglo-Saxon Chronicle* (first compiled during the reign of Alfred the Great in the 9th century). These few sources, which cover over five hundred years of history, are not much, especially when compared to the wealth of sources we have on ancient Rome.

Then there is also the fact that we must question the reliability of the sources. For example, both St. Gildas and Bede have clear biases and probable inaccuracies in their accounts. They display a devotion to the narrative, which, while it makes their accounts more interesting, also makes their accuracy questionable. For instance, Bede says that the Anglo-Saxon settlers (or invaders, depending on how you look at it) had two leaders, Hengist and Horsa, who were descended from the god Woden. Not only is the divine ancestor part highly questionable, but Hengist and Horsa also mean stallion and horse. These two were likely nothing more than mythical figures like Romulus and Remus from Roman mythology.

What all this means is that historians were likely making some assumptions about the Anglo-Saxons because they didn't have a lot of evidence to go on. So, how do we know that many of those assumptions were inaccurate? While the written sources may be few, we do have another way to gain insights about Anglo-Saxon England. There is a wealth of archaeological evidence, which has only been discovered in the past century, that has caused us to rethink the way we view the Anglo-Saxons.

Take, for example, the famous site of Sutton Hoo. Sutton Hoo was a burial site that was first excavated in the late 1930s. In it was found a variety of treasures: burial masks, buckles, weapons, jewelry, and more. These grave goods—items buried with the dead—showed us several things about the Anglo-Saxons. They did have wealth—enough even to bury quite a bit with their dead—and their society had structure and culture. The grave goods were an indication of status, showing the existence of a hierarchy, and the practice of burying the dead with such elaborate goods shows a belief system and rituals. The Anglo-Saxons were more than poor barbarians practicing only subsistence farming.

A replica of the Anglo-Saxon Helmet found at Sutton Hoo
British Museum, CC BY-SA 2.5 <https://creativecommons.org/licenses/by-sa/2.5>, via Wikimedia Commons
https://commons.wikimedia.org/wiki/File:Sutton_Hoo_helmet_reconstructed.jpg

Since the discovery of Sutton Hoo, there have been even more archaeological finds from the Anglo-Saxon period. Thus, our knowledge of this "Dark Age" is continuing to grow. However, the simple fact remains that we will never have as many exact facts about this period as we would like, but much the same could be said for many eras of history. Now, let's look at some specifics about the Anglo-Saxons.

Where Did They Come From?

The Anglo-Saxons were Germanic settlers that came to Britain after the Romans left. Specifically, according to the Venerable Bede, there were three main groups: the Angles, the Saxons, and the Jutes. Their movement to Britain has come to be known as the English settlement.

The written histories then go on to tell us that the Anglo-Saxons conquered the south and southeast of Britain in a reign of terror, annihilating the native Britons and pushing them into the west, which later became Wales. This version suggests that the English people are almost entirely descended from Scandinavian and Germanic peoples.

As we have already discussed, we have learned to be wary of taking everything these written histories say for granted. Archaeological and scientific evidence (such as from the field of paleobotany) suggest that the reality of the English settlement is more complicated than one group simply replacing another. It seems more likely that the native Britons assimilated into the Anglo-Saxon culture, much as they had become Romanized while they were a Roman province. The Anglo-Saxons may not have settled Britain in the enormous numbers that we once thought, but they did manage to form a society where they formed a higher level of the social hierarchy than the Britons. The Britons may then have gradually adopted the Anglo-Saxon language and culture to gain more social status in this new society. The Britons disappeared because they became Anglo-Saxon, not because they were massacred, so the Anglo-Saxons that lived in England may have included far more Britons than we originally thought. They were a combination of peoples that developed over time into a distinct English people.

Conversion to Christianity

When the Anglo-Saxons first came to England, they were undoubtedly pagan. Remember, Bede claims that their leaders were descended from Woden. However, by the time of Alfred the Great, many of the Anglo-Saxon kings were Christian. Alfred even required the Viking king Guthrum to convert to Christianity in 878. How did this religious change occur, and what did it mean for the Anglo-Saxons?

The story of how Christianity came to England is quite dramatic. Apparently, Pope Gregory I, before he was the pope, saw some beautiful slave boys in the market at Rome. When he asked who they were, he was told that they were the Anglii. He thought the name fitting since they looked like angels, and Gregory believed that they should be heirs of the angels in heaven. He made up his mind then and there to convert the English people to Christianity, but then he became pope and was no longer free to travel as a missionary. He thus sent Augustine in his stead in 597, and that was how Christianity came to England. Augustine would even become known as the "apostle to the English."

Whether this story is true or not, there are some problems with it. Firstly, Christianity had already reached Britain long before this while it was still a Roman province, and even the Anglo-Saxon kings of the time were aware of Christianity. King Æthelberht of Kent had a Christian wife before Augustine ever arrived. We should also be wary of the way this narrative suggests that Augustine's arrival simply brought Christianity to the Anglo-Saxons. For one, Augustine and the missionaries who came with him were not the only ones responsible for converting the Anglo-Saxons. Missionaries from Ireland may have had greater overall success. Also, the process was much more gradual than the story suggests. It took many decades, and it was made easier by the fact that the people were allowed to keep many of their practices and even temples. Pagan temples had their idols removed and were changed into churches. Pagan holidays became Christian feast days for saints. The Anglo-Saxons as a whole did not so much flip a switch to Christianity as much as they slowly slid into it.

Why is the conversion to Christianity an important thing to know about the Anglo-Saxons? While traditional historians, specifically Bede, may have placed too great an emphasis on how much this conversion affected Anglo-Saxon society, it did have a huge impact on the Anglo-Saxons, especially on their kings.

To put it simply, converting to Christianity proved to be a smart power move for Anglo-Saxon rulers for several reasons. The Roman Catholic Church was by now an established power to which many European kingdoms were connected. Converting to Christianity thus gave Anglo-Saxon kings connections and status they had not had previously. There were also the members of the clergy. Their presence gave the courts of Anglo-Saxon kings distinction, and they were useful because of their knowledge of writing. With writing, kings could issue demands that affected a much larger radius, which means they could expand the areas they controlled. The rituals of Christianity were also beneficial to Anglo-Saxon kings. Kings could place themselves in superior positions by acting as the godfather at baptisms. There was also the uniformity of Christian worship. All across their kingdom, churches could meet and pray for their king. Finally, the structure of the church proved useful. With the establishment of churches and monasteries, kings had the opportunity to see people loyal to them in institutions that would become the center of local life.

Thus, in many ways, Christianity truly did transform Anglo-Saxon England. Over the course of the 7th century, as Christianity spread, kings were able to use it to widen their control and increase their power. It was at this point that the many Anglo-Saxon tribes across England were consolidated into the seven kingdoms of the Heptarchy.

What Were They Like?

So far, we have talked about what the Anglo-Saxons were not, where they came from, and how Christianity changed them, but what were they really like? Although we are still limited by what information we have on this period, here are some things we know about Anglo-Saxon culture.

Let's start with the language, which is a key component of any culture. The Anglo-Saxons spoke Old English, which is not nearly as similar to modern English as the name suggests. Old English and modern English are two different languages, though modern English is certainly derived from Old English. For instance, contrary to what you might have heard, Shakespeare did not write in Old English. He used Early Modern English. Old English is a different beast altogether. For instance, Old English has gendered nouns and uses cases, and if you don't know what either of those are, that just shows you how different Old English really is.

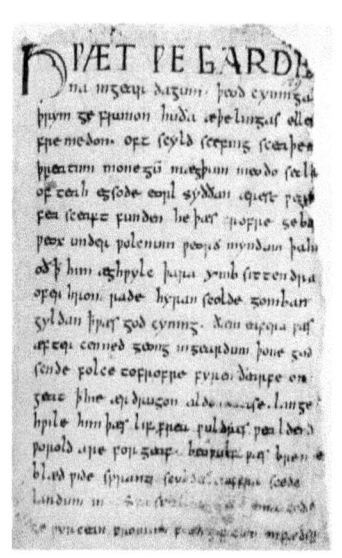

The first page of Beowulf in Old English
https://commons.wikimedia.org/wiki/File:Beowulf.firstpage.jpeg

As we mentioned in the first chapter, Britain is one of the only former Roman provinces whose modern language is not a Romance language (deriving from Latin). One reason for that may have been because of the importance the Anglo-Saxons placed on their language. Being able to speak Old English well, that is, without sounding like a Briton, was important for social status. The Anglo-Saxons were convinced that they were better than the native Britons, and speaking Old English was thus a mark of "superior" ethnicity. This hierarchy then encouraged native Britons to learn how to speak Old English just as the Anglo-Saxons did as a way to increase their social status, which helped to ensure the spread and dominance of the language.

Old English is also something that differentiated the Anglo-Saxons from the Germanic tribes on the continent. Although Old English is in the West Germanic group of languages, it emerged sometime around the 5th century on the isle of Britain, indicating that rather than simply being immigrants, the Anglo-Saxons were their own group of people fairly early on in the Middle Ages.

There was more than just their language that made the Anglo-Saxon culture unique. The Anglo-Saxons valued kin and family highly, and it had a great impact on their customs. For example, your family was responsible for avenging your death rather than the law. This practice got so out of hand that a system called the *wergild* had to be established. The *wergild* set a price on a person's life, which would then be the fine the guilty party had to pay if they killed or injured that person.

This system of using blood money to halt a constant cycle of revenge killings shows us a lot about the Anglo-Saxons. While they were a people who valued warfare and honor, the realities of how this played out were often complex. Anglo-Saxon values might make it important that you avenge your kin, but such practices were too chaotic to endure for long, so the *wergild* was established. Another example of the strain in Anglo-Saxon values and life can be found in their conversion to Christianity. The Anglo-Saxons clearly believed in the idea of revenge, but Christianity has a clear "turn the other cheek" doctrine. To get around this, some Anglo-Saxons would delay their conversion to Christianity until after they had dealt with a past grievance. After most of their society had converted, the Anglo-Saxons maintained a strange union between a society that valued kin and honor and a religion that valued humility. They were a society that produced poems about both religious piety and battles.

Although we may find it hard to understand, Anglo-Saxon society flourished despite these apparent contradictions. It simply shows that whatever we may know about the Anglo-Saxons on paper, the realities of their culture were far more nuanced and complex than we often give them credit for.

What Happened to the Anglo-Saxons?

The Anglo-Saxons were doing fairly well in England, but, as we already know, that didn't last. In 1066, the Normans conquered England. So, why is it that it's still England (the land of the Angles) today? What exactly happened to the Anglo-Saxons after the Norman Conquest?

The Norman Conquest did bring about large changes in Anglo-Saxon society. It was at this point that the language mutated into what we call Middle English, and even then, it did not have the same status as it once did, with French and Latin being the languages that signaled elite status. Speaking of the elite, the Anglo-Saxon nobles were almost entirely replaced by Normans, and the government systems and structures were also altered under Norman influence. England would never be the same after the conquest.

However, that is not to say that the Anglo-Saxon influence was completely wiped out. Although the elites may have turned to other languages, most people still spoke English, and that language has persisted in England and indeed has gained traction in many parts of the world thanks to British colonialism. Also, many of the modern towns and ports in England have their origin in the Anglo-Saxon period. There can be no doubt that the Anglo-Saxons are the people who first formed England, and in that respect, their influence continues to be felt to this day.

Chapter 5: Societal Structure

When you think about society in medieval England, you likely picture something resembling feudalism. A lord owned the land and had peasants that worked it and paid homage to him in exchange for small plots of their own where they could grow food for subsistence. This lord who ruled over the peasants was, in turn, under the king and had to supply knights and other things to the king when required. It was a basic social pyramid, with the king on top and the majority of the population sitting on the bottom.

While that is a fairly accurate picture of how feudalism worked in medieval England, the societal structure in this period was a bit more complicated than that. For around the first five hundred years of this time period (from 600 to 1066), England technically wasn't a feudal society, and even when they did become one, England did have some free peasants, which means not everyone fit as cleanly into that social pyramid as we might think. Also, as we have seen from the numerous revolts and internal fighting throughout this period, feudalism caused problems and needed to be reformed.

So, there is a bit more going on in medieval English society than just the King → Lord → Peasant structure. The eight-hundred-year period did not have a single stagnant society but a developing and changing one.

Before Feudalism

We often think of feudalism as a primitive form of society, and while that may be true in some ways, it also gives us the wrong idea about where feudalism comes from. Feudalism is not the default setting of society. Other social structures existed before it. In England specifically, it was not until the Norman Conquest that England adopted a fully feudal system, so what was society like under the Anglo-Saxons in the Early Middle Ages?

The Anglo-Saxons started as a tribal society. Instead of large kingdoms, they were divided into many smaller tribes that were constantly fighting since warfare was quite profitable. Conquering your neighbors gave you not only access to all their stuff but also to slaves, who could then be sold or used for free labor. Through this system, larger and more powerful tribes began to emerge. And the bigger a tribe got, the more defined the social hierarchy became.

How does that work? Imagine a king in charge of a group of one hundred people. He only gets tribute from those one hundred people, and he doesn't have a large enough force to win many battles. His wealth, therefore, probably does not differ too much from the people he rules over. Sure, he is still in charge, but his house, clothing, and other stuff look about the same as everyone else's. In other words, the gap between the top and bottom of society is very narrow. Now, picture a king ruling over five thousand people. Not only is he getting more tribute, but he also has a much bigger force to win battles with and acquire even more wealth. This king's clothing, living quarters, etc., will probably start to reflect the wealth he has gathered. The gap between the top rung and bottom rung of the social ladder is widening.

This change does not just affect the king. The wealth reaches other people too, and we begin to see the emergence of the elites. However, we are still a long way off from the feudal system. As social hierarchies became more defined in Anglo-Saxon society, the practice of paying tribute became much more organized. Manors, which were the estates of these elite, collected tribute from the peasants in the surrounding area. As kings and *thegns* (nobles) alike realized that staying put and collecting tribute might be more stable and profitable than constant warfare, the kingdoms of the Anglo-Saxon Heptarchy emerged. The development of these kingdoms with manors and nobles had already begun on the continent, so it did not take long for them to become established in England.

At this point, you might be thinking that this sounds an awful lot like feudalism. Why isn't this considered feudalism? The Kingdom of Mercia provides a good illustration of why this system of the Anglo-Saxons, though feudal-like, was not quite feudalism yet. Until the rise of Wessex, which came with the Viking raids, Mercia was the most dominant of the Anglo-Saxon kingdoms. In the 8th century, the Mercian kings controlled large swaths of territory, but their control was not of the sort that the Wessex dynasty established over England in the 10th century. Mercian kings conquered areas and turned them into client kingdoms. These kingdoms had to pay homage to Mercia in the form of tribute, but that was pretty much where the control stopped. The kingdoms kept their kings, laws, and customs. The Mercian kings were collecting tribute, but they were not "ruling" these territories. The feudal structure of the Normans would bring a lot more direct control.

Feudalism in Medieval England

It was the Norman Conquest in 1066 that fully introduced feudalism to England, but English feudalism was not exactly like that on the continent. As a conquering king, William I was in a position with a lot of power, and he used that power to strengthen the position of the king.

William created a chain through which the king owned all the land. The king gave the land to the lords, who then divided and subdivided it until it reached the bottom rung of the ladder with villeins, who were people that held small areas of land in exchange for their labor. The goal of this system was to ensure that everyone was ultimately loyal to the king.

This feudal chain was unique to England. In other feudal systems of the time, vassals only owed allegiance to their direct lord and not the king. William I's incredibly strong position after conquering England allowed him to partially invent this new system, which had the potential to give the monarchy substantially more power. The key word here is "potential" because this system essentially ensured loyalty to the king on paper. It would take a strong king to make that loyalty a reality.

These changes worked their way down to the peasantry as the new Norman barons reorganized their fiefs. Interestingly, this period saw a decrease in slavery in England, which, although it may have been in part due to efforts of the church, had a far less altruistic reason. The Norman barons were often absentee landlords. Many of them owned land on both sides of the Channel, and they preferred to receive their profits from the English holdings in the form of cash. It was, therefore, more beneficial for them to split their land among peasants who would work it and then pay them a tribute than to own slaves.

While slavery decreased, that did not mean that the lower classes were getting freer. The number of free peasants also decreased during this time, as land reorganization and the new feudal system increased the number of villeins. Villeins were not slaves, but they were classified as unfree. They rented land from a lord and, in exchange, worked part of the lord's land as well as their own. They also often had to pay their lord fees for various things, such as marrying one of their daughters off.

Men harvesting wheat
https://commons.wikimedia.org/wiki/File:Reeve_and_Serfs.jpg

Villeins had very few legal rights. They were unable to leave the land and unable to take legal action against their lord concerning the land. However, at this time, being a villein also brought with it a certain level of stability. Lords rarely kicked villeins off their land since they needed them for work, which offered some protection from the instability of farming. Also in this agricultural society, having access to land meant having access to food you could grow. If you didn't want to starve to death, it was better to be a villein than a free peasant with no land.

The People of Medieval England

Feudalism was the basic social structure of medieval England, but there was more to overall society than just the lords who owned the land and the peasants who worked it. There were, at its most basic, four types of people: peasants (the laborers), knights (the fighters), nobles (the administrators), and clergy (the prayers).

The peasants by far comprised the majority of the population. Although many of them worked as villeins or tenants on a lord's estate, there were also, though very few, peasants rich enough to own their own land. Many of them had holdings that were too small to feed their families and also offered their labor to nearby lords or better-off neighbors to earn the necessary income. Even if you did own your own land, if you were a peasant, there was a high chance that you spent some of your time working someone else's land. Still, farming was not the only occupation. Even though this was a primarily agricultural society, not everyone was a farmer. There were towns, which meant that there were craftsmen and traders. These skilled workers were a bit higher up the social chain than the peasants who worked the land, but they were still part of the working majority. Their labor just happened to not be farming.

As you can probably guess, these were the people that kept England running. The peasants were the ones growing the food and producing various goods, and their lives were centered around whatever job they performed. Villeins and rural peasants farmed their whole lives, and craftsmen became fully devoted to their trade from an early age. As this was the overwhelming majority of the population, your lot in life could vary wildly as a peasant. You might own enough land to feed your family comfortably. You might be barely scraping by and die of starvation during a bad year. You might be a blacksmith with a small shop in a town. You might find yourself under a lord who treated you horribly. You might work the land of a lord you would never see. There were a lot of possibilities, but wherever you were, you spent your whole life working, and most likely, you were working for someone else.

Besides a need for lots of labor, England in the Middle Ages also needed fighters. Enter the symbol of the medieval period: the knight. But were knights really what we picture them to be now? Heroes riding around in plate armor, defending damsels, fighting in crusades, and talking about chivalry? For the most part, no. In terms of social standing, knights were lesser nobles who held land under the more powerful magnates like barons. In exchange for the land, they provided military services for their lord and the king.

Thus, most knights were the medieval period's small-time landlords. Don't be too disappointed, though! They did do a lot of fighting. There was the Hundred Years' War with France and multiple crusades, which gave knights plenty of opportunities to make a name for themselves. But as for simply riding around the country doing chivalrous deeds? Knights didn't do that, and during the numerous internal conflicts that England suffered during this period, knights often ended up being the ones terrorizing rather than protecting the local population.

Now we have reached the top of the social hierarchy: the nobles. Technically, knights were nobles as well because they held a title, but we are focusing on the bigger nobles: the barons, earls, and even the king— the men who controlled England. These magnates controlled huge swaths of land. They divided this land among lesser nobles like the knights, who they could then command. They ran the judicial system and oversaw the protection of the realm. They granted positions and gave land to people under them. In other words, these were the administrators who ran England.

Based on the simple pyramid structure, you would think that the king would be the most powerful of these men. Although William the Conqueror designed the system so the king would wield the most power, this was not always the case. The First and Second Barons' Wars were clear proof that the magnates felt that they should and could keep the king in line. By the end of the Middle Ages, Parliament could refuse to grant the king funds for war, which was a major check on royal power. Even though nominally the king was at the very top of the hierarchy in medieval society, his ability to act as the top was often challenged by those immediately under him. The feudal system that William the Conqueror had created frequently did not work in practice as it did on paper.

The final class of people in England was the clergy. The clergy was definitely toward the top of the social hierarchy, but just how high depended on what position they held. The archbishops of Canterbury and York, as well as the bishop of London, were often amongst the most powerful men in the nation. Besides these individuals, the church as a whole played a significant role in English society. Monasteries and bishops often controlled land and employed peasants to work it just as nobles did. The bishops in any town were a huge part of the normal processes of life, playing a role in births, deaths, baptisms, and marriages.

We will discuss the role of the clergy more extensively in the chapters on faith and the church, but at this point, suffice it to say that the clergy was a vital and powerful group in the social make-up of England.

Changing Structure

The feudal system was a hallmark of the medieval period, but by 1485, things were evolving. The Black Death had killed so many people that it caused massive labor shortages, and for the first time, peasants could demand more for their labor. The Peasants' Revolt of 1381 is clear evidence of a world that was beginning to change, with the bottom of the social hierarchy pushing the top for the first time. The Renaissance era would see more and more growth in the urban population, and the social structure that relied so heavily on the peasants farming the lord's land would slowly disappear with the rise of industries and the middle class.

These changes took a long time, and some of England's early social structure survived. The monarchy would continue to be the effective head of the government until the very end of the 18th century. The nobility is still around in England today, though they do not hold the power they once did. England has undergone many eras of reform, but its social hierarchy still exists. Some things from the medieval era have proved to be longer lasting than others.

Chapter 6: Status of Women

You can probably already guess that women in the Middle Ages had fewer rights than their male counterparts. After all, women didn't even get equal voting rights in England until 1928, so it shouldn't come as a surprise that around a thousand years before that, there was some sexism present in the English system.

The better question then is what form did this take? Did women have absolutely no rights in the Middle Ages? What was their status under the law? What options did women have in the course of their life, if any? While it's accurate to say that women had fewer rights in the Middle Ages, there is a little more going on for the female half of the population than that for these eight hundred years of English history. Here's what it was like to be a woman in medieval England.

Eve vs. Mary

Perhaps the best way to capture the somewhat paradoxical view of women in this period is to look at two religious figures: Eve and Mary. Both of these women from the Bible had a large place in the religious understanding of the day, and that translated into how this society viewed women in general.

In the Christian account of the original sin, the serpent tempts Eve to eat the fruit from the forbidden tree. Eve eats it and convinces Adam to do likewise, causing the couple to be expelled from paradise and the overall fall of man. The medieval church saw Eve as the primary guilty party in this narrative. She was the one who had fallen first, and she dragged Adam down with her. Thus, women were not only more prone to sin, but they were also temptresses who would pull men into sin with them.

Whatever your personal religious views, you must remember that in the medieval period, the church was a powerful social institution. This view of Eve had a major impact on the way society viewed women. Because women were more likely to sin, they were regulated to an inferior position in society. Men needed to have authority over women because women could not be trusted.

This understanding of Eve goes a long way in explaining how the inferior status of women was justified in the Middle Ages. However, there was a bit more complexity to medieval attitudes toward women. Besides Eve, there was another female figure that was important to the medieval church, and this one had a much more positive reputation.

As the Middle Ages progressed, Mary, the mother of Christ, became increasingly important to the church. She was venerated as one of the most important saints. Eve had been the source of original sin, but Mary was the source of salvation since she gave birth to Jesus Christ. Women were paradoxically both responsible for the fall and the redemption of mankind.

The two contrasting characters of Eve and Mary pushed women into two extremes. Women were either temptresses or saints. Unfortunately, the result of these two opposing roles was that women couldn't win either way. They were condemned, either for being morally weak like Eve or when they failed to live up to the virginal perfection that Mary represented. Both the extremely high and extremely low standards placed women in a tough position, and it meant that throughout the Middle Ages, women were consistently seen as inferior.

The Role of Women in Society

Although women were viewed as inferior, this underlying assumption did not play out in medieval society the way we might expect. Due to the more recent practices of the 19th and 20th centuries, we tend to think of sexism as restricting women to the role of homemakers. Progress was when women were finally allowed to join the workforce and leave the home.

The idea that women should not work was not that prevalent in the Middle Ages. As we discussed in the last chapter, the majority of the English population at this time were laborers, and the women worked just as hard as the men. Wives and daughters worked alongside their husbands and fathers in the fields. Even as towns grew and more people turned to trades rather than farming, women continued to hold a fairly equal position in the type of work that they did. Women did the same jobs as men. The workforce did not have the gender segregation that we now see as a mark of sexual inequality.

That is not to say that there were not tasks that were more often given to women. Women at all levels of society were responsible for tending their households, and images of this time commonly depict a peasant woman with a distaff, which was a tool used for spinning wool. However, while there were duties that tended to fall to the women, there was not a strict restriction on what work women could do. Making a living and feeding your family was hard, and women were expected to contribute wherever they could.

Noblewomen also played a greater role in medieval society than you might initially think. They were responsible for their households just as peasant women were, and the larger size and political aspect of a noble household often meant that these duties were quite extensive. Noblewomen could be witnesses for legal documents, oversaw estates in their husband's absence, acted as patrons, and could even become involved in warfare, particularly during England's internal conflicts. While they legally had few rights and were officially labeled as lesser, women still did quite a bit in medieval society.

Marriage vs. Nunnery

While they might have been working alongside the men, women were still extremely limited in what they could do, and one way we see this is in the number of options a girl in medieval society had. There were basically two. If you were born a girl in the Middle Ages, you could either get married and work for your husband and family or become a nun.

Let's start with the second. What would being a nun mean for a woman in the Middle Ages? First of all, there were technically two religious paths a woman could take: nun or anchoress. Nuns lived in monasteries, while anchoresses lived on their own (kind of like female hermits) or in small groups. Both involved a life devoted to religious purposes and a vow of chastity.

Contrary to popular belief, being a nun did not necessarily mean being around only women for the rest of your life. There were double monasteries that housed both men and women. These double monasteries were run by an abbess and were thus one of the only places in medieval society where a woman could hold a position over a man. These double monasteries often played a significant role in culture and politics, so abbesses could wield a good deal of influence both within and outside their monasteries, especially in the Early Middle Ages. As the medieval period progressed, double monasteries became less common, and the church increasingly sought to isolate religious women for the sake of purity. Even so, completely separating nuns from men was never really possible. Priests had to tend to the nun's spiritual needs, nuns had to conduct business with their local communities, and workmen and servants had to occasionally enter the nunneries.

The life of a nun also wasn't truly open to everyone. Nuns typically came from families with at least a certain amount of wealth since girls had to pay dowries and often bring a few necessary items, such as bedding, when entering a nunnery. Although this was naturally exclusive, these payments and other gifts were what allowed nunneries to function. So, if your family had enough money, a life of religious devotion was the only alternative to marriage that women had at this time, and many chose this life out of a desire to avoid marriage.

The vast majority of women, however, went with the first option: marriage. As you might have guessed, marriage in this period was not based on love matches. Women rarely got to pick their partners (to be fair, men also didn't get much of a say). Marriages were arranged by parents, other kin, or even lords, and they were a business transaction as much as a personal agreement. Women in this period could own land, which meant that marriage was often deeply steeped in concerns about property. When a woman married, her legal identity became part of her husband's, so whatever land she had would belong to her husband. Even those in the lower classes, where there was little concern about property, could not marry freely. Tenants needed approval from their lord to marry. Almost any marriage in the medieval period had to be approved by those other than the couple involved. It wasn't until the 12th century and reforms were headed by the church that emphasis began to be placed on the consent of the couple.

What did marriage mean for a woman? Women were to obey their husbands. The work they did and the role they played were determined by their husbands. This subservient role and the fact that marriages were arranged often cause us to assume that many marriages were unhappy at best and abusive at worst, but that was often not the case. If for nothing more than practical reasons, a husband and wife greatly benefited from forming a working partnership. Trying to survive on your own was very difficult in this period, so a relationship of mutual trust and reliance was preferable. That's not to say that abuses of this system didn't happen because the system itself did little to protect women, but it would also be a mistake to think that every married woman was miserable. Marriage was a fact of life for virtually everyone, and most people likely chose to make the most of it.

Till Death Do Us Part

With marriage or religious devotion being the only option for women, there was a group that naturally did not fit well into this system: widows. Widows occupied a peculiar position in medieval society. Before marriage, a woman was under the control of her father. After getting married, she was under her husband, but as a widow, she was in her own power. Widows had the legal status of *femme sole*. Rather than being folded into a man's legal identity, a *femme sole* was a woman with her own legal identity. She could own land, run a business, and make her own decisions.

That did not mean that being a widow was the secret desire of every woman, for the position had a lot of complications. Upon the death of her husband, a new widow would need to secure her dower—her share of her husband's estate typically arranged at the time of marriage—and also make arrangements for the guardianship of her children. If there were any complications, the cases to sort these aspects out could become long and complicated. For much of the medieval period, though, a widow would often maintain control of a significant part of her husband's lands or business.

Even after settling these things, widows faced the looming prospect of remarriage. As a *femme sole*, a widow had the right to choose her next husband, but there was certainly pressure from family and, in some cases, the king himself depending on the property and titles that a widow held. It did happen that widows were sometimes forced to remarry. Kings used marriages to widows as a way to bestow lands and titles on their favorites. Ironically, if a woman was rich and did not need to remarry to secure herself financially, she would likely face pressure to remarry. If a woman was poor with many children and needed to remarry for security, it would often be more difficult to find a match. If a woman chose not to remarry, she was able to run her own property and finances. It was perhaps for this reason that many women remained widows for the majority of their lives.

The rights of widows decreased over time, as new laws and customs saw inheritance settled more and more often on solely the male heirs. By the Victorian period, widows held a lesser social position than they had in the Middle Ages.

Powerful Women of the Middle Ages

Because women were viewed as inferior, they rarely held real political power, but even so, history also tends to overlook the role that some women played in shaping the Middle Ages. Here are some of the women that left a mark on medieval England:

- **St. Hild of Whitby** - St. Hild, also called Hilda, was the founder and abbess of Whitby, a double monastery with both men and women. Hild was famous for the ordered way she ran the monastery. Under her leadership, Whitby produced several bishops and even a famous poet. She was well-respected and had considerable influence, as seen by Whitby hosting the Synod of Whitby, an important early church conference, in 664.

- **Æthelflæd** - Æthelflæd was the daughter of Alfred the Great, King of Wessex and later King of the Anglo-Saxons. She married the king of Mercia when she was sixteen, and while her husband was struggling with poor health, she led the Mercians in their efforts to drive back the Vikings. When her husband died in 911, Æthelflæd became the Lady of the Mercians. She ruled Mercia alone for seven years, during which time she allied with her brother, the king of the Anglo-Saxons, in continuing to push the Vikings out of England until she died in 918.

- **Empress Matilda** - The daughter of Henry I, Matilda fought her cousin Stephen of Blois for the English throne for eighteen years, causing the English civil war known as the Anarchy. Although she never successfully ousted her cousin, Matilda controlled large areas of England during the Anarchy, and she eventually left more because of a stalemate rather than defeat.

- **Eleanor of Aquitaine** - Eleanor was not only a powerful woman in England; she was perhaps the most powerful woman in 12th-century Europe. She was married to the king of France for fifteen years, and after that marriage was annulled, she married Henry Plantagenet, who became Henry II of England. As the queen of England, Eleanor played a large role in politics. She aided her sons in their rebellions against their father, and when her son Richard became king, she was one of the main people running England while the king was gone on his crusade. After Richard's death, she continued to aid her next son, John, as king, playing a role in several English military victories on the continent. Eleanor of Aquitaine was the wife of two kings, mother to two more, and she wielded significant influence and power with all of them.

- **Isabella of France** - Queen Isabella was married to King Edward II and earned the nickname the She-Wolf of France for her treatment of her husband. In 1326, she joined forces with her lover, Roger Mortimer, against her husband and helped to overthrow Edward II in 1327. Isabella and Roger Mortimer effectively ruled England for the next three years until her son Edward III had Mortimer killed. Isabella eventually retired to a nunnery.

- **Margaret of Anjou** - Margaret of Anjou was married to Henry VI and was one of the leaders of the Lancastrian forces in the Wars of the Roses. With Henry VI being a rather weak king at the best of times, Margaret was the main driver of royal interests during the conflict. She relentlessly tried to secure the kingship for her son but was ultimately defeated by Edward IV at the Battle of Tewkesbury.

These women are clear examples that men were not the only ones involved in the bloody power struggles of the Middle Ages. Queens did not always follow their kings. Still, although these women held great influence, they were connected to this influence through the men in their lives. Women in the Middle Ages worked alongside men, but they remained inferior in the eyes of both society and the law.

Chapter 7: Food, Clothes, Work, and Entertainment

Learning about the medieval period through major events like wars is fascinating, but it does leave us rather unclear on what daily life in the Middle Ages was actually like. What did they eat? What did they wear? What holidays did they celebrate? What was there to do in medieval England?

With around eight hundred years of history to cover, we cannot hope to tackle everything about daily life in the Middle Ages. That would take a whole book on its own! However, we will look at some of the more interesting tidbits about food, clothing, work, and entertainment in medieval England.

Food

Food is both something that we all need and something that can mark our differences. Not only is food an indicator of our culture, but it can also be an indicator of our social class, and in medieval England, this was especially true. The table of a lord and the table of a peasant looked very different.

Perhaps the most notable difference was meat. While lords would eat meat with almost every meal, meat was a luxury for peasants. Even though there were forests with deer, rabbits, and other animals for hunting, as well as rivers and other bodies of water with fish, peasants were not allowed to access this food source. Hunting was for the nobles. If a peasant was caught hunting in the lord's forest or fishing in the lord's pond, they would likely lose a hand. That was too high a price for a side of meat to go with your dinner.

Livestock was also not the abundant source of meat that you might think. Maintaining animals was expensive, and a cow was worth far more as a producer of milk than as a side of beef. Also, cheese and other dairy products made up a large portion of the peasant diet, so cows were more valued as dairy animals rather than sources of meat. The only animal that peasants regularly raised for meat were pigs. Pigs had little trouble taking care of themselves. They could find enough food to keep themselves alive with their foraging, so they were a food source that did not drain more resources than they were worth. Pork was thus the meat of choice for many peasants, but they were not able to enjoy it often. Those who lived close enough to the sea were also able to add more fish to their diet.

The freshness of meat was another marker of social class. Because the lords had regular access to it, they frequently enjoyed fresh game and fish. On the other hand, almost everything peasants ate was preserved. The meat they ate was typically salted or pickled.

There were other differences in what the poor and rich ate. While bread was a staple for everyone, the type of bread you ate depended on your wealth. White bread was made from wheat, which was much more difficult to grow and was thus typically only enjoyed by the upper classes. The majority of people ate darker bread made from rye and barley. When harvests were bad, peasants might also have to add other ingredients to make their bread, such as acorns.

Besides bread, another food that almost everyone in medieval England ate was pottage. Pottage is a thick stew that can contain a wide variety of different ingredients ranging from meat to vegetables and cereals. Like bread, the quality of the ingredients in a pottage varied between classes.

You might be thinking that with all of this bread and pottage, people were typically drinking water, but that was not the case. While sources of fresh water were fairly abundant, that water was also very dirty. Drinking water from your local river could easily make you sick. Although there was milk to drink if you had a cow, the drink of choice for most people was ale. Lords would have had access to wine as well.

So, if you were a peasant in the Middle Ages, you probably ate bread, cheese, and whatever vegetables you could manage to grow. If you did get to eat meat, it was probably pork or maybe mutton, and you likely drank ale that you made yourself. Lords had access to fresh meat and fish and higher quality bread, ale, and even wine. The wealthy also enjoyed access to various imported spices and dried fruits. However, it was at a banquet that the upper classes really showed off what their wealth meant in terms of food. A medieval banquet included normal dishes like stews and pies alongside exotic dishes like peacock and porpoise. There were also massive sculptures made out of sugar. These banquets were extravagant and showed just what the upper classes had access to in the Middle Ages, but even when they weren't hosting a banquet, the meals of the rich could still have ten courses. If you were poor or even just average, you had to rely mostly on the food you grew and preserved yourself, but if you were rich, your food would be fresh, covered in imported spices, and sometimes even sculpted.

Clothing

The differences in what people ate were a clear marker of social class, but what about what they wore? Even today, clothing choices can tell us a lot about someone's personality and place in society.

Surprisingly, the clothing style of nobles and peasants in medieval England did not differ drastically. Everyone wore the same basic styles and designs. What differentiated noble clothing was not the type of clothes but the materials used and the cut. While peasants' clothing was typically made out of wool, of which England had an abundance, nobles might also have had silk outfits. Nobles' clothing could also have furs and expensive decorative items like pearls and gems. In terms of cut, noble clothing tended to be overall better made with a finer and more fitting cut. In medieval times, it was likely that people were easily able to distinguish between the clothing of a noble and a peasant in the same way that we can tell the difference between a man's and a woman's running shoe today, even though their basic designs are the same. Clothing was still a sign of social class, but fashion did not differ as much across society as you might think.

Even more surprising than the similarities in clothing between peasants and nobles was the similarities between men and women. Although there were differences in style between the sexes, men and women wore the same basic garments. You could still tell the difference, but we are a long way off from the men wearing pants and women wearing dresses dynamic that came to dominate fashion for so long.

So, just what was everyone wearing? The main medieval garment was the tunic. Tunics were basically long shirts, often gathered at the waist with a belt. They tended to be a single color and had long sleeves. Men's tunics typically went to the knee, so they would wear hose or leggings underneath them. Women's tunics went all the way to the ankle. The exact style of tunics evolved over the medieval period. Tunics began as loose-fitting garments, but over time, they became much more close-fitting. The style of sleeves varied during the period as well, from close-fitting sleeves to sleeves with long cuffs, sleeves that were loose around the upper arm and then tightened, and more. Men's tunics also got progressively shorter over the Middle Ages.

Medieval clothing was all about layers, though. People typically wore a linen shirt under their tunics, or they might wear two tunics at once, with one acting like an undergarment. When they were outside, which was a good bit of the time for most people, a cloak or coat was added to the outfit. Cloaks were simply shaped pieces of cloth fastened at the shoulder with a brooch or chain. They could even be knotted. Like cloaks, coats were long, reaching well past a person's knees.

Besides tunics, another piece of medieval garb that everyone wore was hats. You did not walk around with a bare head in medieval England. Even indoors, both men and women wore hats. The basic headgear for women was called a wimple. It was a large piece of, usually white, cloth that wrapped over the head and under the chin, covering the hair and neck. A veil or hat might also be added to the wimple, especially when going out. Men wore close-fitting linen caps called coifs as their indoor head coverings. Like women, they would wear additional hats on top of this piece when going out or dressing up.

Portrait of a Woman by Robert Campin (shows a medieval woman in a wimple)
https://commons.wikimedia.org/wiki/File:RCampin.jpg

Speaking of dressing up, how fancy did medieval clothing get? Did they add decorations and embellishments to their outfits? Like us today, medieval people found ways to make their basic clothes more exciting, but overall, they kept things pretty simple. Embroidery might be used to decorate a tunic, but it was typically restricted to just around the cuffs, neckline, and maybe the hem. It would have been very rare to see a tunic covered from neck to hem in embroidery. Fur might also be used as a trimming for both warmth and decoration. That didn't mean that their tunics were boring, though! Bright colors, such as blue, red, green, and yellow, were standard, and there were elements like fringes, tassels, and even feathers added to give decoration. Belts, brooches, chains, and hats were also places where a person could add precious stones or metals to their outfit, adding style and, more importantly, displaying their wealth.

Although clothing did not differ greatly between the social classes, it was still seen as a very important way to demonstrate rank. There were laws that restricted who could wear what type of materials, and there were even limitations on the imports of fine materials like silk to limit the number of people who had access. The upper classes took steps to ensure that a peasant could not rise above his station with his clothing. The social classes were strictly divided, and there was no way for someone to pretend to be higher on the ladder than they really were.

Work

Now that we have a better idea of what people ate and what they wore, what did they do? In medieval England, the majority of people spent most of their time working.

There were two general types of jobs that a peasant could have: farmer or craftsman. Most people were farmers, and most of these farmers lived as tenants on lands owned by a lord. They were responsible not only for growing their own food but also for growing the lord's food as well. Some of the more well-off farmers owned their own land, and you could rent yourself out as a laborer to earn extra when times were hard.

Being a craftsman was the other option for a peasant, although they were a bit higher up the social ladder than the farmers. Craftsmen lived in towns or cities and produced particular goods. Examples of craftsmen would be a stonemason, blacksmith, baker, carpenter, miller, and goldsmith. Craftsmen relied on the upper classes of society since they were the ones who could buy what the craftsmen made. Craftsmen also often banded together in guilds. The guilds controlled entrance into the craft, which allowed them to control the labor supply and prices. It took a long period of study under a master before someone could hope to earn the approval of the guild and enter the craft in their own right.

When it came to exactly what type of job you ended up with in medieval England, there wasn't much choice. If you were a man, you likely ended up with whatever job you were born into (if your father was a farmer, you were probably going to be a farmer), and if you were a woman, you helped your husband. There was not an intense gender division of labor in the peasant classes, so women would work in the fields alongside their husbands and even help run their husbands' businesses in a town.

So, what if you weren't a peasant? Didn't nobles just sit around all day? While nobles certainly did not work nearly as hard as peasants, they did have a role to play in society. Lords were the organizational sector. Their estates produced surplus goods, their courts handled legal business, and their men defended the realm when it was needed. The lord himself likely did not do all of this, but his steward and other staff oversaw the bureaucratic and administrative tasks that were necessary for keeping England running as a whole.

So, when it came to work in medieval England, the bottom line is that everyone had a job to do. In fact, it was illegal to be jobless! In a society where most things, from growing food to making tables to keeping accounts and more, were done by hand, everyone had to work to ensure that society could maintain the necessities of life. This was a world where not having a job and a role would mean starving to death.

Entertainment

All of that talk about the necessity of work is making medieval life seem quite grim and hard. Did they ever have fun? Obviously, the noble classes had plenty of free time to amuse themselves, but let's start with the peasants. If you were a peasant in medieval England, would you ever get a day off or have time for entertainment?

In the Middle Ages, you didn't get vacations, and most people never traveled at all. However, they did celebrate frequent holidays, which they would have called feast days. The feast days in medieval England frequently had pagan origins, but they were tied to the Catholic Church. Besides the ones most of us still celebrate, like Easter, Christmas, and Valentine's Day, there were quite a few more, such as St. Crispin's Day, Michaelmas, All Saints' Day, Candlemas, St. John's Day, and around forty to sixty more. Yes, you read that right. There were as many as sixty holy days (that's where we get the word holiday) in a year.

While many of these feast days were more significant than others, the church insisted that people refrain from working on these holy days. Each day had its own traditions, such as exchanging gifts, and there might be plays and games to celebrate as well. Besides the numerous feast days, people also got Sundays off for the same reason. So, even though work was crucial, peasants in medieval England did not work 365 days a year.

Peasants found ways of entertaining themselves that were not tied to feast days as well. Traveling performers, called troubadours, were popular, especially for the music they provided. Telling stories, singing, and dancing were all ways to spend time. We might often picture the Middle Ages as grim, but the people, like all people, knew how to have a good time.

Of course, if you happened to be wealthy, you did have more opportunities to have a good time. What did the nobles do for entertainment? There was a large variety of options. Like the peasants, nobles celebrated the feast days and also enjoyed a performance by a good entertainer, though those who entertained nobles often held permanent positions at a castle. Minstrels provided music, and jesters were early comedians. These people would usually perform during or after meals, which for nobles could be a form of entertainment themselves with their extensive number of courses and extravagant dishes. Dancing might also follow meals.

When they weren't eating, nobles liked to get in a good bit of exercise. There were many popular outdoor activities, such as hunting, falconry, and tournaments. Hunting at this time was quite the affair. Forests were fiercely protected, and if a noble lacked one of his own, he could pay to hunt on someone else's estates. As we already mentioned, the price was high for peasants who hunted in a nobleman's forest. Falconry was immensely popular in this period, with even women participating in the sport. Tournaments were chances for knights to prove their valor and included jousting and the melee (a mock cavalry battle).

What did nobles do if it was raining then? Rain is not uncommon in England, but there were several ways to pass the time. Games from the East had made their way to England by this time. Chess was perhaps the most popular, but backgammon and dice were also well-loved. Gambling was frequent, but it did not have the negative reputation that it does today.

Knights Templar playing chess
https://commons.wikimedia.org/wiki/File:KnightsTemplarPlayingChess1283.jpg

Overall, there was more to do in the Middle Ages than you might think. They may not have had our modern entertainment options like TV, but they found plenty of ways to entertain themselves with sports, games, music, and more.

In medieval life, the split between the nobles and peasants showed itself in almost every aspect of daily life, from food to clothing and from work to entertainment. While this divide was sharp, we can still see a unified culture in the many shared aspects of daily life like similar clothing styles, feast days, bread, and more.

Chapter 8: Art and Architecture

When it comes to the medieval period, most of our attention is spent dwelling on the knights on horseback, castles, and kings, but medieval society, just like modern society, had many aspects. It may have been a more violent time in general, but the Middle Ages did find time to make a pretty hefty contribution to the world of English art.

It's pretty hard to make a living today as an artist, so how would it have been possible in the Middle Ages? Not only can you not sell records of your latest ballad or copies of your newest book to make ends meet, but it was also incredibly difficult to make art a serious side gig. Peasants were far too busy with the amount of work necessary to simply survive to be composing great epics in their spare time, yet somehow art still existed in the Middle Ages. How?

There are a few things you need to know about art in the medieval period to understand how this was possible. Perhaps most important was that art tended to have a practical purpose. The Anglo-Saxons made many beautiful things, but those things were also usually functional. Instead of using their sculpting skills to carve a statue, an Anglo-Saxon would probably use them to decorate a buckle, shield, or brooch. Even their function as status symbols was practical since it helped families to position themselves within the social hierarchy. As we progress through the Middle Ages, artistic objects get less obviously functional, but they often still have a practical purpose. For instance, much artistic skill was devoted to making religious items. The grandest architecture of the day is displayed in churches, which were buildings that served as both centers of local life and whose purpose made more elaborate designs appropriate. Even an item like the Bayeux Tapestry was politically functional, as it allowed the Normans to immortalize their version of the events surrounding the Norman Conquest. In all, art in this period rarely existed for art's sake. Whether religious or political or purely practical, art was mixed into many other aspects of medieval life. It was because of these other functions that art was able to flourish as much as it did during the Middle Ages.

Two other things in medieval life made art possible: monasteries and patrons. Monasteries were one of the only places a person could devote themselves to something other than manual labor. This did not mean that every monk or nun was a poet, but it did mean that the poets and historians that did exist, especially in early medieval England, often owed their careers to the support of a monastery. As the Middle Ages progressed and monasteries became less common and played less of a vital role in medieval life, patronage became another avenue through which an artist might find support. Patrons were wealthy benefactors, often aristocrats or clergy, who gave monetary and other support to an artist. Such support was the only way an artist could pursue their work and also not starve to death. The patronage system of supporting the arts gained increasing importance through the Renaissance and Victorian periods, but it had its start in the medieval era.

So, artists in the Middle Ages were not lone creators trying to convince the world of their genius. They had to have outside support, and their work often served several different roles in society. Let's look closer at various kinds of art in the Middle Ages.

Literature

In a time with high illiteracy and little leisure time, the written word did not have the same centrality that it does now, and what did exist differed greatly from what we now think of when we hear the word literature.

Perhaps the biggest difference between literature in medieval times and today was the lack of the novel. The first English novels did not appear until the 18th century. In the Middle Ages, poetry was far more popular than prose. Although prose was beginning to make headway by the end of the Middle Ages, it would be another few hundred years before the novel first appeared.

Why was poetry so much more popular? Remember that most of the population was illiterate. Books and stories were not written to be privately read but to be performed and read publicly. The earliest form of English literature was oral stories, like *Beowulf*, which were only written down at a later date. The cadence of poetry has two major advantages in such a setting. It sounds better, and the rhythm makes it easier to memorize.

What was all this poetry about, though? It may have all been in verse, but there were several different genres. Epics like *Beowulf* told stories about heroes facing monsters. Pieces like the *Battle of Maldon* took inspiration from real-life events, in this case, turning a military defeat into something heroic. Medieval romances contained tales of knights, chivalry, magic, damsels in distress, and love. The dream vision genre, like Chaucer's *Book of the Duchess*, had the narrator relating a dream that helped them to deal with a difficult event, such as the death of a loved one. There were also simply tales, such as Chaucer's *The Canterbury Tales*, most of which are written in verse with a few in prose. Fables told moral tales of anthropomorphic animals. Medieval England may not have had novels, but the people still had quite a bit of variety in their stories.

Drama also existed at this time, although it was nothing like what Shakespeare would write in the Elizabethan era. There were three types, and they were all religious. Mystery plays depicted important events from the Bible, such as creation. Miracle plays focused on the lives of saints, both real and fictitious. Morality plays were allegorical plays designed to teach a particular life lesson. The characters in morality plays were personifications of abstract concepts like death and charity. Together, all of these types of plays were designed to instruct the populace on proper godly living.

There was also nonfiction, which made up a large portion of medieval literature. Some of the surviving nonfiction works have become extremely important resources for what we know about the Middle Ages. Historians still quote and use books like the Domesday Book, the *Anglo-Saxon Chronicle*, and the *Ecclesiastical History of the English People*. Still, these historical pieces can also be quite frustrating because they sometimes seem to value telling a good story more than being accurate. Myths were often used to fill in the gaps in a historical account, with fact and fiction blending in a way that would make most writers today quite uncomfortable. For instance, Geoffrey of Monmouth's *The History of the Kings of Britain*, which contains the Arthurian legend, is written as though it was history even though it is mostly imagined.

Far more prominent than the historical writings were the religious works. Most of the people who were able to write were either monks or clergy, so theology was a very popular subject. For instance, Anselm, who was the archbishop of Canterbury from 1093 to 1109, wrote more than a dozen books on theology. Besides treatises, which were philosophical works examining and developing theology, there were also works written about the lives of saints and a large variety of hymns.

All in all, there was much variety in the literature of medieval England. There were romances, fables, epics, histories, allegories, philosophy, and more. Still, however much variety there was, the overwhelming majority of writing produced was religious in some way. While this may seem strange to us, we must remember that few people in the Middle Ages were educated, and the majority of those who were educated had received that education from the church. The amount of religious work, therefore, makes sense. When the majority of the writers are either monks or clergy, it is only natural that the majority of what they write would have a religious bent.

Architecture

Speaking of the church, medieval architecture in church buildings is one place where the full artistic capability of medieval England is on display. Medieval architecture may conjure up images of thatched roofs and blocky stone castles, but the buildings of this period could be truly magnificent. England saw the influence of several different architectural styles during the Middle Ages and also managed to develop some uniquely English styles. The evolution of architecture can most easily be traced in the churches of the medieval period, which was where elaborate techniques and designs were most often used.

The dominant architectural style of the Middle Ages was the Norman style. The Norman style was a type of Romanesque architecture that developed in areas controlled by the Normans. The key characteristic of Norman and Romanesque architecture is the semicircular arch. Such arches were used on windows and doors and also to connect columns. Columns, or cylindrical pillars, were another common feature of

Norman architecture. The Norman style created huge sweeping spaces filled with pillars and tiers of rounded arches.

The Norman style, with its focus on pillars and arches, left plenty of room for decoration. These large spaces often had plenty of wall space, which were often decorated with murals. Even the pillars and arches themselves were sometimes painted, adding a colorful and ornate feel to the style. Unfortunately, paint tends to not last nearly as long as the stone, so we have very few surviving examples of Norman architecture that was decorated in this way. We have far more of another kind of embellishment that took off around the 12th century. The rounded arches themselves were carved with geometric shapes or figures, and the pillars, too, were often carved at their head in patterns.

Many buildings constructed using the Norman style have since been destroyed or altered, which means little remains of the original architectural style. There are, however, some surviving examples. Durham Cathedral is one such surviving building. The cathedral was built sometime in the late 11th or 12th century. Not only does the cathedral use the characteristic round arches and pillars of Norman architecture, but it also has a stone vault ceiling. The stone vault ceiling of Durham Cathedral is an architectural milestone. Many buildings in England at this time continued to use wood roofs because of the difficulty of creating stone roofs that would support themselves. The large stone vaulted ceiling of Durham Cathedral was a sign of increased architectural know-how and foreshadowed the emergence of the medieval period's other famous architectural style: Gothic.

Gothic architecture began to emerge around the end of the 12th century. It also uses the grand sweeping style of Norman architecture, but the easiest way to spot the difference between the Norman and Gothic architecture styles is the shape of the arches. Norman architecture uses round arches, while Gothic architecture uses pointed arches. Gothic architecture was also a product of increased engineering ability. The style focuses on creating enormous open spaces. This goal created many of the Gothic style's other defining features, such as rib vaults, flying buttresses, and pointed arches, all of which helped to support those tall structures and large high ceilings.

A Gothic-style building
https://commons.wikimedia.org/wiki/File:An_introduction_to_the_study_of_Gothic_architecture_(1877)_(14576749870).jpg

While the Norman style began with painting and then adding carvings to embellish its buildings, the Gothic style is known for the tracery that embellishes its basic forms. Tracery uses bars and ribs of stone across openings, especially windows, or even overlaid on walls (known as blind tracery) to create a decorative effect. Tracery looks a bit like lace made of stone, and it is a large part of why the Gothic style feels so ornate.

With the rise of the Gothic style, many abbeys and churches originally built in the Norman style had Gothic elements added or used the new style when making additions or rebuilding. Although the Gothic style did not quite reach its peak in England as it did in France, there are many stunning examples of Gothic architecture left in England, such as the ruins of Whitby Abbey and the famous octagonal lantern of Ely Cathedral.

As it progressed, the Gothic style in many places got more ornate and flamboyant. England, however, had its own spin on things and developed the perpendicular style in the last two centuries of the Middle Ages. The perpendicular style was uniquely English, and, as the name suggests, it was characterized by an emphasis on vertical lines. Perpendicular churches were tall and filled with light. They included enormous windows that only used narrow tracery to allow in as much light as possible. Many of them also contained angel roofs. Angel roofs were a type of hammerbeam roof, which is where the beams that hold up the roof are stacked so that they support each other without the need for additional support. In angel roofs, these beams are then carved into the figures of angels. Angel roofs are intricately carved, but they sadly get little appreciation today because they are so hard to see. They are found in these tall perpendicular churches, which makes the rich detail and mastery behind them impossible to see with the naked eye.

The angel roofs and perpendicular churches that housed them were the height of English architecture in the Middle Ages. They were incredibly expensive to build and often overly lavish. Villages would build perpendicular churches larger than what the local population needed as a demonstration of piety. The construction of churches was not just about filling a practical need but also, maybe even more so, about displaying religious zeal and devotion. This helps to explain why so much of the medieval period's best architecture is found in religious establishments.

Visual Art

We have seen what the medieval period produced in both books and buildings, but what about what we usually think of when we hear the word art? What about paintings and sculptures and the type of stuff that gets hung in museums? The medieval period had these things but not in the way we picture when we hear the words fine art.

As we mentioned in the introduction to this chapter, art and function were closely tied. The angel roofs of English churches are a prime example of this. These angels are incredible sculptures carved by a master hand, but they are not sitting on a pedestal for everyone to admire. They are carved into the necessary supporting beams that hold the roof of the church. The same can be seen in the murals that decorated many Norman-style churches. These murals were undoubtedly fine pieces of art, but they were also completed with a specific purpose, decorating the empty spaces of the church. Medieval artists did create pieces of great beauty and skill but often with a specific purpose or commission in mind.

Take, for example, the Bayeux Tapestry, which is one of the most famous pieces of medieval English art that has been preserved to this day. The Bayeux Tapestry is a seventy-meter-long piece of embroidery that tells the story of the Norman Conquest. There are over seventy scenes depicting the events of the Conquest, as well as decorative borders showing fables. It was created sometime in the 11th century, and it is believed that it was commissioned by Bishop Odo, the half-brother of William the Conqueror. The Bayeux Tapestry is wonderful enough as a piece of art, but it is also more than that. It is a historical record. Since it has a clear bias toward the Norman version of events, it could also be a piece of political propaganda. Even something as decorative as a tapestry has a purpose that goes beyond simply looking pretty.

A section of the Bayeux Tapestry
https://commons.wikimedia.org/wiki/File:Bayeux_Tapestry_scene51_Battle_of_Hastings_Norman_knights_and_archers.jpg

The Bayeux Tapestry also shows us how the medium of visual art has changed over time. Wall hangings and tapestries were a major form of art in the medieval period, but they are practically unheard of today. Another form of art that was also widespread in the Middle Ages but has since declined is the illuminated manuscript. Illuminated manuscripts were originally created by monasteries. The name comes from the use of gold and silver to embellish the letters, which literally gives the pages an illuminated look. As the practice evolved, it came to refer to any manuscript that was decorated with bright colors and designs.

While illuminated manuscripts often included illustrations, their decorative features went beyond this. Illuminating a manuscript was not about adding pictures but about decorating the text itself. This included decorative borders, miniature pictures within the text itself, and highly ornate letters, especially capital letters at the beginning of a section. With the invention of the printing press in the 15th century, illuminated manuscripts fell out of style, but these hand-written and hand-decorated books were one of the main sources of visual art in the medieval period.

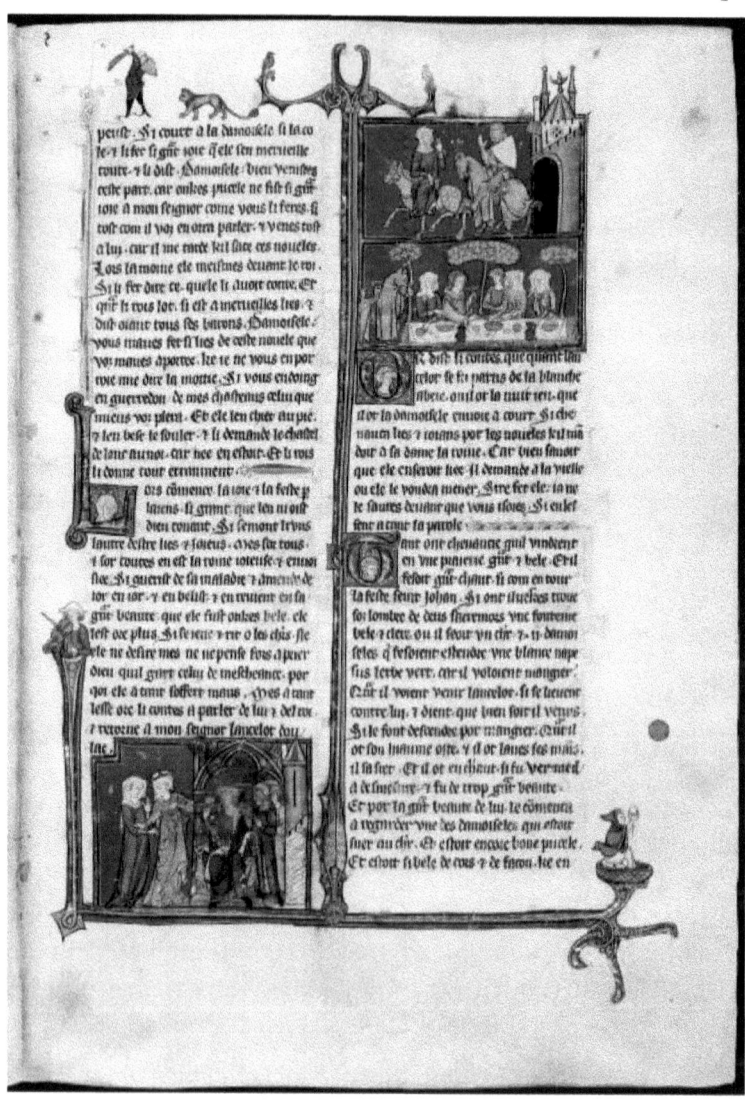

Page of an illuminated manuscript
https://commons.wikimedia.org/wiki/File:Page_from_the_Arthurian_Romances_illuminated_manuscript.jpg

For all their frills, illuminated manuscripts, like other medieval art, still maintain that connection to function. These were not isolated paintings but books. And based on what we have already learned about literature and architecture, you can probably guess that most illuminated manuscripts were religious books. Bibles and psalters (the Book of Psalms) were some of the most common and popular illuminated manuscripts. Like the building of expensive churches, creating ornate religious books was a way to show piety.

In the Anglo-Saxon period, art existed in the decorations used to embellish everyday objects like brooches and buckles. As we move through the Middle Ages to angel roofs and illuminated manuscripts, we begin to see art becoming less and less tied to practicality but still revolving around some kind of function, usually the display of religious devotion. In some ways, religion was responsible for much of the artistic growth of the medieval period because it provided a space in which pouring massive amounts of time and resources into making something beautiful was appropriate. It would have been a waste of time for a man to carve angels in his cottage, but to do it in his church was an act of faith.

Chapter 9: Royalty throughout the Middle Ages

Throughout this book, we have talked a lot about the various kings that held sway over England throughout the Middle Ages. While it is wrong to act as though these powerful men were the only ones steering the course of England during this time, it is equally wrong to underestimate the importance of the monarchy in the medieval period. These men wielded absolute power over the government of England, and their decisions, both the good and bad, made a large impact on the nation.

While today it is tempting to think of an absolute monarchy as a relatively simple and stagnant form of government, the place and power of royalty did undergo some changes throughout the Middle Ages.

In theory, the royalty works on a very simple hereditary system. The next king is the eldest son of the current king. However, in the Middle Ages, things often did not go this smoothly. Several of England's kings were kings by conquest rather than by blood, and in an era with shorter lifespans and higher mortality rates, England often found itself without a direct heir to claim the throne. Even when there was a direct heir, there were sometimes still problems with passing the scepter from one king to the next. In other words, who got to be king was often determined by factors other than lineage.

The Development of Kingship

Although we often picture a monarchy as being the default type of government, kings were something that had to develop in England. When the Anglo-Saxon tribes first arrived, they may have called their heads kings, but it would be a while before they resembled what we think of when we hear the word king.

The early Anglo-Saxon kings were essentially the chiefs of their tribes. The bigger their tribe was, the more power a king had, and to gain power, a king needed to excel at warfare. War was how a tribe could gain excess goods that would allow the royalty to amass their wealth and increase their status. A king could also gain wealth from his people directly through the use of tribute. To pay for the protection a powerful monarch offered, his subjects would pay tribute at an appointed place on a certain day. Royalty at this stage was tied closely to particular people rather than to an entire area.

As towns developed, the royalty began to see another and more efficient way for them to accumulate wealth. By taking control of towns and their trade centers and imposing fees, kings could amass far more riches and power without resorting to warfare. It was at this point that many kings started to set up around population centers.

Throughout the Early Middle Ages, the various Anglo-Saxon kings vied for power amongst themselves. More powerful kings forced their less powerful neighbors to pay them tribute, but they often stopped there instead of fully folding conquered territories into their own kingdoms. It wasn't until the coming of the Vikings that the Anglo-Saxons were forced to unify for the sake of defense, which allowed a king to control the entire English area.

The Wessex Dynasty

The Wessex kings were the first kings of all England. They rose to power when Æthelstan's grandfather, King Alfred the Great, beat the Vikings, causing Wessex to become the dominant Anglo-Saxon kingdom. Æthelstan was the first to officially have control over the entire English area. The House of Wessex ruled England uninterrupted from 927 to 1016 and then was restored from 1042 to 1066. Despite only ruling England for a total of 113 years, the Wessex dynasty included nine kings.

Of the nine Wessex kings, five ruled for less than a decade, and only two ruled for more than twenty years.

- Æthelstan (r. 927-939)
- Edmund I (r. 939-946)
- Eadred (r. 946-955)
- Eadwig (r. 955-959)
- Edgar (r. 959-975)
- Edward (r. 975-978)
- Æthelred the Unready (r. 978-1013; 1014-1016)
- Edmund Ironside (r. 1016-1016)
- Edward the Confessor (r. 1042-1066)

The relatively short rules of many of these kings are a prime example of why royalty could get messy in the Middle Ages. Life could be brutal, and many kings, just like many of their people, died fairly young. There are only two instances in the Wessex dynasty where the throne passed directly from father to son (Edgar to Edward and Æthelred to Edmund Ironside). In most cases, the throne went from brother to brother rather than from father to son. If you add Æthelred being deposed briefly in 1013 and the rule of the House of Denmark, which interrupted Wessex rule from 1016 to 1042, you can get a glimpse of how complex the royalty of this period was. If a family wanted to keep the throne, they needed two things: heirs and military prowess. Unfortunately, it was a lot harder to stay alive in the medieval period, so having and keeping heirs was often difficult. Even if you did have heirs, there was also the risk of someone seizing the throne by force.

The House of Denmark

The House of Denmark seized control of England briefly from 1016 to 1042. Their twenty-six years of rule saw three different kings rule England:

- Cnut (r. 1016-1035)
- Harold Harefoot (r. 1035-1040)
- Harthacnut (r. 1040-1042)

Although they did not hold control for long, the House of Denmark shows just how important military might was to the rulers of England. Although Cnut was a conquering king, his nineteen-year reign was a time of peace and prosperity for England. Ironically, kings by conquest are often remembered by English history as being good kings. Taking a kingdom through military conflict put kings in a powerful position, which allowed them to easily handle any opposition to their rule. This often resulted in an overall more stable government. Whether the populace liked the conquering king or not, the purges and crushing of opposition that came with seizing a throne by force typically caused a pause to infighting for several years.

The Norman Dynasty

Although the Wessex dynasty was restored with Edward the Confessor in 1042, it was not to last. William the Conqueror, Duke of Normandy, became king in 1066 after defeating Harold Godwinson at the Battle of Hastings.

As we discussed in earlier chapters, William I was able to make a lot of changes in the English system, including giving titles and lands to his Norman supporters and instituting the feudal system. Although it is certain that many of the Anglo-Saxons did not like William I, especially those who lost their lands and positions, his rule, like Cnut's, was relatively stable. Royalty was thus highly tied to military conflict. The rulers who proved their might on the battlefield held more secure positions than those who inherited their titles.

The Normans ruled England for sixty-nine years but only had three kings.

- William I (William the Conqueror) (r. 1066–1087)
- William II (r. 1087–1100)
- Henry I (r. 1100–1135)

As stable as the Norman dynasty was in its military strength, it fell after only three kings due to the other crucial aspect of maintaining power: heirs. Thanks to the tragic sinking of the *White Ship*, Henry I died without any male heirs.

The House of Blois

Throughout this chapter, you may have been wondering why we keep referring specifically to the kings of England. After all, we know that England had queens. Some of England's most famous and long-reigning monarchs have been queens (Queen Elizabeth I, Queen Victoria, and Queen Elizabeth II). While England may have been ruled successfully by queens in the Tudor period and beyond, this was not the case in the Middle Ages. As we saw in Chapter 6, women were not well-respected in the medieval period, and throughout the medieval age, England was never ruled by a queen. This did not mean that queens did not exist. The wife of the king was the queen, but no woman was the practical ruler of England in her own right, although several (Eleanor of Aquitaine, Isabella of France, and Margaret of Anjou) did wield a good deal of power.

Technically speaking, there was no law saying a woman couldn't rule England, unlike some other European countries at this time, but the overall sexism of the day meant it was not considered even if it was legally possible. The closest a woman ever came to being the monarch of England was after the death of Henry I. When his male heir died, Henry I named his daughter, Empress Matilda, as his heir. However, after Henry I's death, his nephew and Matilda's cousin, Stephen of Blois, took the throne.

Although Matilda fought Stephen for nearly twenty years in the civil war known as the Anarchy, she never successfully seized the throne of England. She did control areas of England at different times, but the fight between her and Stephen only resulted in a stalemate, so although Matilda came close, she was never technically the queen of England.

The Plantagenets

While Matilda never got to be queen, her son managed to make a deal with Stephen of Blois, and in 1154, Henry II became the first of the Plantagenet kings. Ruling from 1154 to 1485, the Plantagenets are by far the longest-lasting royal dynasty of the English Middle Ages. As such, their ranks contain some of the best and worst English kings. The fourteen kings of the Plantagenet dynasty are:

- Henry II (r. 1154–1189)

- Richard I (Richard the Lionheart) (r. 1189-1199)
- John (r. 1199-1216)
- Henry III (r. 1216-1272)
- Edward I (Edward Longshanks) (r. 1272-1307)
- Edward II (Edward the Leopard) (r. 1307-1327)
- Edward III (r. 1327-1377)
- Richard II (r. 1377-1399)
- Henry IV (r. 1399-1413)
- Henry V (r. 1413-1422)
- Henry VI (r. 1422-1461; 1470-1471)
- Edward IV (r. 1461-1470; 1471-1483)
- Edward V (r. 1483)
- Richard III (r. 1483-1485)

Compared to the other English royal dynasties of the Middle Ages, the Plantagenets were rather prolific when it came to heirs. Henry II and Eleanor of Aquitaine had eight children, five of whom were sons. From John to Edward III, the throne managed to pass in a direct line from father to son, which, as demonstrated by the Wessex dynasty, was not as common as one might have thought in the Middle Ages. Edward III also had five sons who survived into adulthood. Their ability to produce surviving male heirs may have been a large part of why the Plantagenet dynasty was able to hold the English throne for so much longer than their predecessors.

However, if not having children had proved to be a problem for English kings in the past, the Plantagenets proved that having too many children could also be a problem. Henry II had to deal with revolts led by some of his sons and his wife, but it was Edward III and his five sons who proved to be the downfall of the Plantagenets.

You might not recognize the names of Edward III's surviving sons (Edward the Black Prince, Lionel of Antwerp, John of Gaunt, Edmund of Langley, and Thomas of Woodstock), but you will recognize the two houses that descended from them: York and Lancaster. The House of Lancaster traces its lineage back to John of Gaunt, and the House of

York comes from both Lionel of Antwerp and Edmund of Langley. Thanks to Edward III's five sons, by the time you get to the reign of Henry VI, there were multiple people who could claim royal descent. The result was a very bloody and chaotic time known as the Wars of the Roses. That's not to say that Edward III's multiple children were the sole cause of the Wars of the Roses. There was a lot else that went wrong there, but the multiple claimants certainly contributed to how long and bloody the war became.

So, the Plantagenets had more than enough heirs to secure their royal dynasty, but they ended up killing each other off in a bloody civil war that made way for the Tudors. However, they still managed to keep the English throne for 330 years, and during that time, a lot changed in the way the English understood kingship. This was the time of the two Barons' Wars, the Magna Carta, and the Peasants' Revolt. If the Wessex, Dutch, and Norman dynasties had sought to establish the power of the king, the Plantagenet dynasty saw multiple challenges and a redefining of that power.

We often think of medieval kings as wielding absolute power, but it was during the medieval period that Parliament was established and met for the first time in 1215 in an effort to check the king's power. Parliament in these days was made up of nobles, so we are nowhere near a government controlled by the people. Still, it is important to recognize that Parliament did have some real power. Starting in 1362, Parliament had to approve any taxation the king wished to implement. This would prove to be a significant check on royal authority since kings could not wage war without gaining funds through taxation. By gaining control over the purse strings, Parliament had an effective check on the king's power. The king was still very much the one running the country, but he now needed the approval of England's most powerful men to do certain things.

The Problem with Royalty in the Middle Ages

Revolts against the king and the creation of the Magna Carta and Parliament show how mixed up our understanding of kingship can be today. Royalty in the Middle Ages did not command absolute power, nor were they necessarily respected as divinely appointed sovereigns. The idea that kings possessed a divine and sovereign right to rule absolutely, a theory known as the divine right of kings, was more prevalent in 17th-

century England than it was in the Middle Ages.

That probably sounds backward. How is it that kings came to have a higher status later? It has to do with the large underlying problem that many medieval English kings faced. They were just men.

Whether they were fighting rebels in their own country or foreign forces, English kings had to spend a lot of time demonstrating that they could hold the throne, and it seems like for every king that managed this, there was another one that didn't. Powerful kings conquered and ruled firmly only to have their son or grandson lose all they had gained, and there was no guaranteed way for a family to keep a secure grasp on the throne. In 1135, England faced the Anarchy as a result of King Henry I dying without an heir. In 1455, England again bled under massive internal conflict with the Wars of the Roses, but this conflict stemmed from too many claimants with royal blood. So, not having an heir and having too many heirs led to chaos in this period. Then there was also the fact that simply taking the throne by force was an option. Both Cnut and William the Conqueror were foreigners who seized the English throne. Richard I forced his father to name him heir, Edward II was deposed by his wife, Henry IV ousted his cousin Richard II, and Richard III did away with his nephews to seize the throne.

English royalty in the medieval period had a lot of power, but that power could be taken or at least conflicted if the king lacked the character to hold it. In many ways, medieval kings had to stand on their own merits if they wanted to keep the peace more than some later royalty would.

Overall, the English throne in the Middle Ages was never as stable as we might think, and as the monarchy moved into the era after the Middle Ages, more emphasis was placed on the ultimate sovereignty of the monarch. Throughout the Renaissance and beyond, English royalty came to be wrapped in more pageantry. To create a more secure throne and dynasty, kings could no longer be just men. They had to be seen as something more so that they would maintain a natural right to their position. It was one thing to overthrow a powerful man or family. It was another to overthrow a divinely appointed sovereign. Of course, this understanding of royalty also led to many issues, but that was a problem for the 17th century.

Chapter 10: Law and Order

Medieval England could be chaotic at times, but there was still a relatively stable system of law and order that kept the peace throughout the land. The medieval English law system is in some ways incredibly bizarre, and in other ways, it resembles what still exists today.

The Courts

Throughout the medieval period, the English law system saw a lot of changes, and one of the best ways to see that is in the number of different types of courts that were established.

The Anglo-Saxon period had two major types of courts: the hundred and the shire. The hundred was a division of the larger shire and heard minor cases, while the shire courts heard the larger cases. The Norman Conquest and the feudal system added another type of court: the manorial court. Manorial courts were held by landlords for their tenants. They dealt with things like buying and selling land and minor criminal offenses. The manorial courts were restricted to their particular lord's jurisdiction. The fines these courts collected were part of a lord's income.

If that's not complicated enough, there were also church courts. The jurisdiction between the secular (royal courts) and church courts was often a point of conflict. For a long time, clerics had the right to be tried by church courts exclusively, and when Henry II tried to change this rule, it resulted in the famous Becket controversy.

Henry II was responsible for some other major changes in the English law system. In 1166, in response to the extreme lawlessness that abounded after the Anarchy period, Henry II issued the Assize of Clarendon. This was a series of laws that reformed the judicial system, and one major change it instituted was to establish traveling judges. Judges appointed by the king were to travel circuits around England hearing cases. It was the duty of a grand jury, which consisted of twelve men, to report serious crimes to these judges. Under this system, those accused of serious crimes had to be tried before the king's men, consolidating the authority of the law under the central government (the king).

So, medieval England had both local courts that heard the majority of cases and higher courts that heard more serious offenses and appeals. The exact jurisdiction of the various courts overlapped and could be terribly unclear, but the basic structure of a multi-tiered court system was there. In other words, the judicial system had been complicated for a very long time.

Punishment

Before we talk about how medieval people determined if someone was guilty (they did that in some pretty bizarre ways), let's talk about what happened if you were found guilty. If you did happen to get caught breaking the law in the medieval period, what type of punishment could you expect?

Like today's crime and punishment, medieval punishment varied a lot depending on the crime. The medieval law system was harsh and even gruesome, but they didn't chop off the hand of anyone who broke any law. Medieval punishments ranged from paying a fine to being drawn, hanged, and quartered. Here are some of the punishments unique to the period:

- **Stocks and Pillory:** The stocks and pillory were both a form of shaming punishment. In stocks, the guilty person had their ankles trapped in a board, while in a pillory, the person's head and arms were trapped. The pillory was a bit worse than the stocks, but both punishments were for minor crimes like vagrancy and drunkenness. The trapped person could be taunted by crowds and have things like rotting vegetables thrown at them. However, sometimes people had flowers thrown at them if they were well-liked in the community. There were even rules against throwing hard things (so no rocks) at people in the stocks or pillory.

- **Flogging:** For more severe crimes, many villages and towns had more than just stocks and pillories. They also had a whipping post. Flogging is exactly what it sounds like, and like many other medieval punishments, it was done in public. This element of shame was added to many medieval punishments.

- **Mutilation:** Chopping off a hand was a punishment for stealing in the medieval period. The punishment did vary based on what was stolen. You probably wouldn't lose a hand for stealing an apple, but you could lose a hand depending on what you stole and whom you stole from. Losing a foot was another potential punishment.

- **Hanging:** Although they did have some far bloodier methods of execution, the primary method of execution in medieval England was hanging. However, the long drop method of hanging, which ensured that the person's neck snapped, was not put into practice until the 1800s. Hanging in the Middle Ages was a much slower death by strangulation. Depending on their crime, some criminals' bodies were left hanging on the gibbet as a public display. The body might also be mutilated after death. These practices served as a warning to others and were part of the medieval period's attempt at crime prevention.

- **Burning at the Stake:** Being burned at the stake is just as horrible as it sounds—probably even more so. It's impossible to imagine the agony of being burned alive. What crime would cause you to receive such a horrific punishment? Religious heresy, including witchcraft, was the crime that merited burning at the stake. The practice of burning those accused of heresy continued past the Middle Ages. Bloody Mary, who was the queen of England from 1553 to 1558, earned that nickname for her persecution of Protestants, which included burning over three hundred people. Burning at the stake was also used as a punishment for women guilty of treason and for a few other crimes as well.

- **Drawing, Hanging, and Quartering:** The medieval punishment reserved for the worst of the worst was drawing, hanging, and quartering. This punishment was for those guilty of high treason. Drawing involved dragging the criminal to the gallows. They were then hung, after which they were taken down and quartered. Quartered referred specifically to removing the limbs, but they were often mutilated in other ways as well, such as beheading and disemboweling. The various body parts were then displayed publicly. If that doesn't sound gruesome enough, the really horrible part is that the person was taken down from the gallows before they were quite dead, so they were still alive at the beginning of the next step. Often, their entrails were removed before their own eyes and then burned before they were quartered and sometimes beheaded. Drawing, hanging, and quartering remained the punishment for treason until the 19th century. The last time it was used was in 1867, and it was abolished in 1870.

What might be even more shocking than the punishments is the fact that many of these harsher punishments, such as burning at the stake and drawing, hanging, and quartering, developed in the later Middle Ages (around the 11th and 12th centuries) and persisted into the 18th and even 19th centuries. We may like to think that these punishments were the product of some sort of dark age, but the medieval period was not alone in dishing out gruesome punishments.

But why exactly were the punishments so harsh? Were medieval people just overly cruel? There was a logic behind these methods. Medieval law and order was a system based on prevention through fear. There were no police. There was no jail. Jails of the time were not for holding prisoners as punishment but rather for holding people until their trial. There was no system for stopping crimes as they happened, and there was no system for keeping criminals separate from the rest of society. The medieval system instead relied on these harsh punishments to dissuade people from committing crimes.

Compurgation

Now that we know what happened if you were found guilty of a crime in medieval England, let's talk about how your guilt was determined. Without forensic science or even police to investigate crimes, they had a very different system for conducting trials. One of the main ways of conducting a trial was through compurgation, which was also called the wager of law.

Compurgation was more of a method designed for proving one's innocence rather than for establishing guilt. Keep in mind that this was long before the doctrine of "innocent until proven guilty" came around. Those suspected of crimes in the Middle Ages had to prove themselves to be innocent, and compurgation was perhaps the most used method for doing that.

Compurgation was a system that centered on oath-taking. The accused would swear an oath declaring their innocence. Their oath would be believed if they could find enough people to also swear an oath to their innocence. This process typically required the accused to get twelve people to swear to their innocence. These people were not swearing that they knew that the accused had not performed the crime. Rather, they were swearing that they believed the accused's words. They functioned a bit like character witnesses.

Oaths were given precise monetary values, and the value of a person's oath also depended on their societal status. The word of a nobleman was worth more than that of a peasant. In some cases, to prove their innocence, the accused had to acquire oaths that added up to a total value.

Under this system, it seems like everyone should be able to prove their innocence to any crime, but that was hardly the case. Oath-making was a very serious business in the Middle Ages. It had religious and legal implications. Swearing an oath for someone with a bad reputation could get you into trouble, so people who appeared guilty or who had few friends would have a hard time meeting the requirements of compurgation.

Trial by Ordeal

One of the most puzzling aspects of medieval law to our modern understanding of law and order was the trial by ordeal. There were three larger types of trials by ordeal: trial by divination, trial by physical ordeal, and trial by combat. Of the three, trial by physical ordeal, which is usually simply called trial by ordeal, was the most common.

So, what was the trial by ordeal? It doesn't sound pleasant, and it definitely wasn't. Trial by ordeal was a way of determining a person's guilt that relied on God's judgment. A suspected person was subjected to a particular physical test with the belief that God would determine the outcome. If they passed, they were innocent. If they failed, they were guilty.

What were the actual physical tests, though? In medieval England, there were two versions of the trial by ordeal: the trial by cold water and the trial by hot iron. The trial of cold water involved tying the accused with ropes and tossing them into a body of water. If they sank, they were innocent. If they floated, they were guilty. This was based on water's connection with baptism. It was believed that the water would not accept a guilty person and thus would not sink. The trial by hot iron was perhaps even more unpleasant. A piece of iron was heated in a fire, and then the accused had to walk a certain distance holding it. Their guilt was not determined by whether they were burned at all but by how well the wound healed. Their hand was wrapped for a few days, and if it appeared unburned or if the wound did not appear diseased when it was unwrapped, they were innocent. Both trials were overseen by a priest, who would conduct the necessary rituals to prepare and conduct the trial.

When you first learn about the trial by ordeals, there are two understandable responses. Both "That's barbaric!" and "That's stupid!" may come to mind. Nearly drowning people and forcing them to hold hot metal seems both cruel and a terrible way to determine guilt, and that is true. It was both cruel and wildly inaccurate, yet for all that, there is more nuance to the trial by ordeal than there appears to be.

First of all, when was trial by ordeal used? Not everyone who was accused of a crime had to undergo one of these trials. Trial by ordeal was reserved for the king's court, which only heard serious crimes, so you wouldn't be facing trial by ordeal just for stealing an apple. Even in the cases that did go to the king's court, if you could satisfactorily prove your innocence, you did not have to face a trial by ordeal. The trial was meant to appeal to God's judgment when human judgment failed. We would expect it then to be used in cases where there was great uncertainty, but it was also used in cases where the accused was highly suspect. Trial by ordeal was frequently used on people who were considered untrustworthy or who could not find people to prove their innocence by compurgation. Trial by ordeal could be used both when there was uncertainty and also when a person appeared to be guilty.

The fact that the guilty were often subjected to trial by ordeal is evident from the cases where the person passed the trial. Even after passing the trial, some people were still ordered to leave England. God said you were innocent, yet you were still banished. This seems to suggest that in some cases, the people who underwent these trials were still believed to be guilty. So, what was the purpose of the trial?

To understand this, we have to realize something important about trials by ordeal. The fact was that most people passed the trials. The majority of people who underwent the trial of cold water sank, proving their innocence, and even more strangely, the majority of people who endured the trial of hot iron were also found innocent. This meant that if you were subjected to a trial by ordeal, chances were good that you would be proved innocent.

Think about what this means for guilty parties. Medieval punishment was harsh. If the crime was serious enough to warrant a trial by ordeal, then chances were the punishment if found guilty was far worse than the trial. You were probably facing death or mutilation. The trials were extremely unpleasant, but they were better than that. The trial by ordeal then could be a way for the guilty to escape much harsher punishment.

Of course, there was still a chance that you would fail the trial and then have to face the punishment for the crime on top of that, and there can be no doubt that innocent people were also forced to endure the trial at times. The practice did not make for a fair judicial system, but it may strangely have afforded mercy to more than we realize. Still, medieval society seemed to be aware of the faults with this. Trials by ordeal were outlawed by the church in 1215, and since priests were central to the trials, the trial by ordeal quickly disappeared after 1215.

Trials by combat were far less common, but they also existed in medieval times. These trials were usually only practiced by noblemen. Trials by combat also required that there be some sort of accuser for the suspect to face, so they were not practical in many cases. Like the trial by physical ordeal, the assumption was that God would be with the man in the right. If the accused lost the fight and survived, they would then have to face whatever punishment their crime dictated.

Trial by Jury

While many of the practices of medieval law and order seem either cruel and bizarre to us, this period also saw the start of something that has become central to many modern legal systems: trial by jury.

Trials by jury have a long history in England. They were not established by a single law but rather developed over time. The exact origins of the first jury trials are unclear. The Anglo-Saxon tribes may have already had the start of jury trials, but the practice might have been brought over by the Normans after the Conquest. The Assize of Clarendon in 1166 established the use of a grand jury to determine which cases came before the king's judges on their circuit. After the church abolished trials by ordeal in 1215, jury trials became more prominent since trials by ordeal were no longer an option.

Also, in 1215, the Magna Carta stated, "No free man shall be taken or imprisoned, or disseised, or outlawed, or exiled or anyways destroyed; nor will we go upon him, nor will we send upon him, unless by the lawful judgment of his peers, or by the law of the land." The "lawful judgment of his peers" shows clearly that trial by jury was a known concept at the time of the Magna Carta, and the fact that it was included in the Magna Carta shows that some importance was attached to the practice as well.

So, were medieval trials by jury the same as a jury trial today? In medieval practice, the jury was closer to what we would call witnesses. The jury was made up of men from the community who decided the case based on what they knew. There were no lawyers laying out evidence. The jury decided things based on whatever they happened to know about the case and the suspect.

The jury system was unique to medieval England. It spread to other areas with British colonialism and appeared in France after the French Revolution, but in the Middle Ages, juries were only found in England.

Medieval law often conjures up images of brutal executions and corruption, and while those things existed, there was more to the overall system than that. The period's introduction of trials by a jury has been one of the most lasting impacts of the English Middle Ages.

Chapter 11: Faith and Religious Identity

In the grand timeline of human history, atheism and even agnosticism are recent inventions. For most of the past, everyone at least professed to be religious or to believe in some deity. In medieval England, Christianity was the overwhelmingly dominant religion. It wouldn't be entirely inaccurate to say that at some point, everyone in medieval England was a Christian, at least in some sense. How is that possible?

Religion in the Middle Ages differed a lot from what we experience today. Remember that the American Bill of Rights with its freedom of religion amendment wasn't passed until 1791. Before that, religion was determined by the government. You were a Christian because your king had determined that you were a Christian. That didn't mean that everyone believed in the same things, but it did mean that officially everyone was of the same religion. And in the Middle Ages, that religion was Christianity.

Effects of Christianity

We have already discussed the conversion of the Anglo-Saxons in Chapter 4, so now let's look closer at what effect Christianity had on England and its people.

As we mentioned briefly when discussing the conversion of the Anglo-Saxons, one of the most important things that Christianity brought to

England was literacy. We are not talking about bringing literacy to the general population but simply the fact that monks and priests could read and write. Many of the enormously important historical sources we now have, such as the Venerable Bede's *Ecclesiastical History of the English People*, were written by monks and other members of the clergy. Having a group that could write things down also meant that it was much easier to create a more unified law system and to keep track of things like births, deaths, and marriages. Christianity was thus instrumental in creating larger, more organized Anglo-Saxon kingdoms, which eventually led to one English nation.

As you probably realized in the chapter on art and architecture, Christianity also had a large impact on the culture of the period. Most works of art, literature, and architecture had religious motivations. Besides Christian art, the laws and customs of the time were also deeply tied to the dominant religion. There were church courts and laws that prohibited things like usury because they were prohibited in the Bible. You could be arrested for being a heretic in the same way that you could be arrested for robbery or murder.

The truth is that the influence of Christianity was so widespread in the Middle Ages that it is difficult to describe. Christianity was in the culture and the laws. It permeated the very rhythm of medieval life. It seeped into the background and context so much that it makes it very difficult for us today to discern how seriously people took their faith and religious identity in this period. Everyone was a Christian, but how Christian were they? Perhaps the best way to answer this question is to look at the other religious beliefs in medieval England.

Remnants of Paganism

The first thing we want to remember here is that the truly native beliefs of the Britons had already taken a severe hit before the arrival of the Anglo-Saxons. The Romans did not like the Druids, so much of the original organized religion of the native Britons had already been lost when Britain became a Roman colony. When the Anglo-Saxons then converted to Christianity, the organized religion of England gradually and fully shifted to Christianity. What persisted for much longer was not organized pagan religions but rather the folk beliefs and practices that went along with those religions.

Peasants in medieval England called and believed themselves to be Christians. However, at the same time, they continued to believe in things like fairies and spirits. The same people who attended Mass every Sunday would also perform spells and wear charms to protect themselves from these supernatural beings. These folk beliefs not only existed alongside the Christian church but were also sometimes mixed with it. For example, one explanation for the existence of fairies was that they were fallen angels that had become trapped on Earth after God shut the gates to heaven and hell. Another example is the feast days. While the feast days were organized by the church and related to saints, many of them had pagan origins. Easter, for example, appears to have taken its name from the goddess of spring, Eostre. Dancing around the maypole in spring is a pagan tradition, and even things like decorating trees on Christmas have pagan roots. Even though these holidays were now celebrated for reasons tied to Christianity, the celebrations themselves often continued practices tied to pagan beliefs. Christianity was the dominant religion, but the traditional beliefs persisted in a strange mixture with Christianity.

How were people okay with believing in both fairies and God? You don't need to know much about the Bible to know that official Christian doctrine does not support this mixing of folk beliefs and Christianity. Does this mean that the peasants hadn't bought into Christianity?

Remember that the average person in this day was illiterate, so they couldn't read the Bible. Adding to that, Mass was said in Latin. So, while everyone was Christian, most people didn't know exactly what that entailed. They could easily believe in fairies and still be Christian because they didn't realize that those things were contradictory.

The church as an organization did try to stamp out these things to some degree, but the spread of information and enforcement of rules was much slower and more difficult in the Middle Ages. Whatever the pope might have thought about things had little effect on what a peasant in rural England did. The church was much more effective in establishing "orthodox" Christianity in cities and towns than in rural villages.

Besides the remnants of paganism, there were also those who more fully rejected Christianity. The most famous counter-religious movement in the Middle Ages was the Cathars. The Cathars were a group based in southern France that idolized Sophia, the goddess of wisdom. Cathars swore to serve Sophia much in the way that knights in courtly love poems swore to protect their ladies. The connection runs so deep that some people believe that the courtly love genre of this period was a product of the Cathars attempting to spread their beliefs.

The church did not look kindly on the Cathars or other religious heretics. The Cathars were wiped out in the Albigensian Crusade, and the church's inquisition dealt severely with anyone else they deemed to be heretical. So, even if you did not agree with the Christian faith in the Middle Ages, it was best not to advertise it.

Daily Life and the Church

So, does that mean that people weren't Christian but were just too scared of the church to act otherwise? Not exactly. As we already mentioned, Christianity had an enormous influence on everyone in medieval England, from the king to a tenant farmer. The people of medieval England were not just Christian in name. Christianity was a large part of everyone's lives.

We have already discussed the many feast days spread throughout the year, but to reiterate, there were a *lot* of feast days (between forty to sixty). Besides those days off, Sundays were also days dedicated to rest or rather dedicated to worship. Religion, therefore, determined the cycle of rest and work for everyone, and in such a labor-focused society, that was equivalent to determining the very rhythm of life.

Religion was an essential part of the greater cycle of life as well. Babies were baptized shortly after birth. The church was the authority that married you. It was also the institution that buried you. The church was there for all of life's most important events, which meant that its presence was constantly felt.

Besides setting the calendar and playing a key role in the important events of a person's life, Christianity also influenced people's lives through a practice that became incredibly widespread throughout the Middle Ages: pilgrimages.

Pilgrimages

The idea of a religious pilgrimage is far from unique to medieval Christianity. Before Christianity, Jews traveled to Jerusalem and the Temple for important religious events. Today, Muslims still perform the

Hajj, a pilgrimage to Mecca. However, in medieval England, the practice of pilgrimages was specifically linked with Christianity.

This itself is a bit strange because Christianity, unlike Judaism and Islam, does not specifically emphasize particular locations as holy. There is nothing in Christian doctrine that requires or even encourages taking a physical journey as an act of religious piety. If anything, the emphasis on Christian pilgrimages in the Middle Ages shows how tangled, or maybe rather influenced, medieval Christianity was by other beliefs and practices.

So, if Christian pilgrims weren't following some religious ordinance, why did they make pilgrimages? There were numerous reasons. Some people traveled to particular locations in hopes of finding miraculous healing. Other people made pilgrimages as a form of penance for their sins. There were also those whose pilgrimages were a mixture of faith and tourism. Early Christians traveled to the Holy Land to see the places where Christ and the apostles had walked. The resting places of saints became popular pilgrimage destinations as well. Many pilgrims would take pilgrimages tours, visiting several sites in a single trip. This desire to see things associated with their faith gave rise to the popularity of relics.

Relics are one of the more infamous things about religion in the Middle Ages. Sites claiming to have things like the bones of various saints, pieces of the cross, and even the Holy Grail (which was the cup Christ used at the Last Supper) attracted many visitors. Not only did people travel to see relics, but these religious objects also created quite the market. Pilgrims traveling to holy sites could purchase relics, both as a memento of their journey and for the powers these objects were said to possess. Visitors to Canterbury Cathedral, for instance, often bought vials of what was said to be Thomas Becket's blood diluted with water. The concoction was believed to have miraculous healing abilities.

When you learn about relics today, it's hard not to roll your eyes. It seems like an excellent system for tricking gullible travelers into buying random scraps of wood and animal bones. However, the people in the Middle Ages were aware of this downside to relics. Chaucer's *The Canterbury Tales*, which is a story about a group of people going on a pilgrimage to Canterbury, includes a character who sells fake relics. Relics were a big business in this period, but it's unclear how seriously people took it.

We might think of pilgrims as being a few isolated religious fanatics, but the practice was fairly widespread in this period. It was so prominent that there was a booming business surrounding pilgrimages. Inns cropped up along well-known travel routes to popular destinations, and pilgrims often bought distinctive badges, staves, and garments that marked them as pilgrims, not to mention the relics. To pay for these things, pilgrims had to carry all of their funds for the trip on their person, which made them an easy target for robbers. The Knights Templar were originally created to protect these pilgrims. Pilgrimages were so common that infrastructure rose around this activity.

Speaking of the Knights Templar, there was another type of pilgrimage that has become almost synonymous with the Middle Ages: the Crusades. Wait a second! The Crusades weren't pilgrimages. They were religious wars where European Christians attempted to retake the Holy Land from the Muslims and halt the spread of Islam. That's true, but the Crusades were, in a way, a type of pilgrimage. Like traveling to a particular holy site, participating in a crusade was an act of faith and was often viewed as a means of penance and redemption. Crusades were journeys with religious purposes, so they were pilgrimages, albeit violent ones.

Between crusaders and other pilgrims just wanting to see the sites, the Holy Land was a popular pilgrimage destination. Rome was another since it was the home of the church. England, however, was home to one of the most popular pilgrimage destinations: Canterbury. Canterbury was the site of the martyrdom of St. Thomas Becket in 1170, after which it became one of the most visited pilgrimage sites. Other pilgrimage sites included St. Albans, Westminster Abbey, York, Walsingham, and others. Most sites were visited largely by people within a local area, but the more venerated a site was, the farther people would travel to see it.

Other Religions of the Middle Ages

Although Christianity certainly dominated Europe, it was not the only major organized religion of this time. Judaism and Islam were the other two major faiths of the period.

As you can probably tell from the existence of the Crusades, Muslims and Christians did not get along in the Middle Ages. Remember, this was the period of history when the church was burning heretics at the stake, so the idea of religious tolerance was nonexistent. As Islam continued to expand in the Middle East, Christian Europe felt that it had to stop that advance and take back the Holy Land, hence the Crusades.

The exact history of the Crusades is messy. There were a lot of them, and they involved a lot of different groups. The Christian crusaders did not manage to drive the Muslims out of the Holy Land. With its position as an isolated island, England was not greatly affected by this religious conflict, although Richard the Lionheart did spend more time crusading than he did in England. England did, however, have a much more involved and rockier relationship with a different religious group: the Jews.

Since Rome had sacked Jerusalem and destroyed the Temple in 70 CE, the Jews had been without a homeland. They thus lived amongst various other nations, including England. Remember that religious tolerance was not a virtue in those days, so it can hardly be said that the Jews in England were well-liked. Antisemitism was rampant, yet somehow the presence of a small Jewish population was tolerated. Why?

It came down to money. In the Middle Ages, the church had laws against usury. While that would later come to mean lending money with exploitative interest rates, in the medieval period, it meant lending money with any interest. Christians were not allowed to lend money to make money, which made it very hard to acquire capital with which to fund larger projects and investments. Since the Jews were not members of the church, they did not have to follow such rules, so Jewish moneylenders were an important source of capital. Of course, that also meant that people often owed Jews money, which did not help antisemitic feelings.

While many wealthy English thus despised the Jews because they were indebted to them, the most powerful man in England had a very different relationship with the Jews. The king made quite a bit of money from his Jewish subjects. The Crown was allowed to confiscate all of the property of any usurer upon their death, although this privilege was not used as much as you might think. Instead, the Crown would allow the Jews to keep their wealth so that he might tax and fine them heavily.

In the 13th century, this forced partnership between the Jews and the Crown deteriorated. The Jews became increasingly poorer due to the heavy taxation from the Crown and were soon no longer a source of significant income for the king. Without the funds they provided, all pretense of tolerance ended. In 1290, Edward I issued the Edict of

Expulsion, expelling all the Jews from England. This decision stood for more than 360 years. Jews were not legally allowed back in England until 1657.

If you have been wondering why Christianity was so dominant in the Middle Ages, you have probably realized by now that it's largely because other religions were not tolerated. Heretics were burned, pagans were wiped out, and Jews were expelled. Still, like most things in the Middle Ages, there is more to medieval Christianity than that. Churches were the center of community life, and faith and piety were the motivation behind many of the period's greatest artistic achievements.

In the next chapter, we will take a closer look at the role of the church as an institution.

Chapter 12: Role of the Church: Church and State

It can be hard for us in the modern day to truly grasp just how central the church was in not only medieval England but all of Europe in the Middle Ages. The medieval Catholic Church was by far the most powerful institution in the Middle Ages. Kings sought the church's approval before invading other countries.

Organization of the Church

One of the things that made the church so effective in maintaining and growing its power was its organization. The church's hierarchical system allowed it to effectively wield power over an enormous area.

The organization of the medieval Catholic Church is very straightforward. At the highest level, you had the pope. Under him were the cardinals, who were the administrative heads of the church. Then come the archbishops and bishops, who exercised control over a particular cathedral and region. At the lowest level, you had priests who looked over smaller parishes and villages.

Looking at England specifically, the top of the church hierarchy was the two archbishops, the one for York and the one for Canterbury. The archbishop of Canterbury was actually above the archbishop of York on the church ladder, though, and was the head of the English church in the Middle Ages.

Besides the clear structure of the clergy, medieval England also had quite a few monastic institutions. These existed alongside the normal church order. They were run by abbots or abbesses. Since they were fairly self-contained and independent organizations, there weren't significant issues between the power and structure of the church and the monasteries.

Now, we said that one of the things that gave the church so much power in the Middle Ages was its organization, but how can that be? What was so special about this tiered structure? More than you might think. William the Conqueror tried to institute a very similar structure in the feudal system to strengthen the power of the king. The multiple levels, which all ultimately tie back to a central authority—in the church's case, that was the pope, who got his authority directly from God—both served to strictly unify and yet extend the reach of the church's power.

The lower levels of the hierarchy (the priests) ensured that the church had widespread influence. The higher levels of the hierarchy ensured that all of the different parts were on the same page. Instead of a world in where every church in every village was doing its own thing, everyone was doing the same thing

In medieval times, this level of bureaucracy was revolutionary. Remember that one of the reasons the Anglo-Saxon kings converted to Christianity was because they saw how such a system could extend the reach of their practical power. The church itself did this better than anyone. At its peak, the church was by far the most powerful institution in the Western world. Let's take a closer look at what powers the church had.

The Power of the Church

Perhaps the most extreme method that the church used to guide the medieval world was excommunication. Excommunication meant being kicked out of the church, but it was far more serious than it initially sounds. To be removed from the church would mean losing all fellowship with other church members, which in this time was everyone. The average person who was excommunicated would face severe social isolation, but that wasn't the worst of it. The church was God's authority on Earth. To be kicked out of the church also meant losing your place in God's kingdom. You would be condemning your eternal soul to hell, and that was something few people were willing to risk.

Excommunication was even used to keep kings in line. In 1208, King John was excommunicated for refusing to accept the pope's appointee to the office of archbishop of Canterbury. John held out for five years, but he gave in in 1213. Excommunication did not always push kings into doing what the church wanted, but it was one way that the church and state battled things out in this period.

The church's power also had a far more worldly source: money. Between both tithes and gifts that the church received, it was a very wealthy institution, and in the Middle Ages, just like today, money was power. Wealthy priests and bishops enjoyed lavish lifestyles and enormous influence, and the fact that they could excommunicate people meant it was practically impossible to call out even the most corrupt ones.

The church also had a level of jurisdiction in what we would now consider secular affairs. The legality of things like marriage and divorce was handled by the church rather than the state. Remember that it was priests who oversaw trials by ordeal, and those trials disappeared from use because the church outlawed them. So respected was the church's authority when it came to matters of law that people who committed major crimes, such as murder, could claim sanctuary in a church to escape punishment, at least temporarily. There were also church courts where you could bring disputes rather than going before a government court.

So, the power of the church in this day was very real, and the church also saw no problem with intervening in matters that we today would consider to be strictly secular. Such a situation naturally produced conflict.

The Becket Controversy

The church and state were quite entangled in this period. They both acted as governing authorities over the people of medieval England, and that was sure to lead to conflict. Kings often tried to fill church positions with their own men to reduce this conflict and strengthen their power. Perhaps nothing better illustrates the conflict between the state and church than the Becket controversy of the 12th century.

Thomas Becket began as a close friend of King Henry II. He was such a close friend that in 1155, Henry II appointed him to the highest position in England under the king: the chancellor of England. Then, seven years after that, in 1162, Henry II saw an opportunity to put his close friend in an even greater position. Thomas Becket was made the archbishop of Canterbury.

Becket's appointment as archbishop of Canterbury shows much of what had gone wrong in the medieval church. Becket was not a clergyman. He was a layman and a government official. The archbishop of Canterbury should have been elected, but instead, he had been appointed by the king. At the time of his appointment, Becket was also still the chancellor of England, so he now held both the most powerful church position and a powerful government position. It was clear that the king wanted those loyal to him in positions of power, regardless of whether those positions were ecclesiastical or political. The separation of church and state was nonexistent.

That is only the beginning of the story of Henry II and Thomas Becket, though. Henry II's plan of putting his close friend in a high church position backfired unexpectedly. Shortly after becoming the archbishop of Canterbury, Thomas Becket resigned his position as the chancellor of England. It was a clear sign that Becket was leaning toward the church's side of things rather than the king's, and it didn't stop there. Becket began to oppose Henry II, arguing that the king had overstepped his authority in interfering in ecclesiastical matters.

The irony of this situation is hard to miss. Thomas Becket, who had received his appointment as archbishop of Canterbury because the king interfered in church matters, was now telling his once close friend that the king needed to keep his nose out of the church's business. We can only imagine Henry II's outrage. As for why exactly Becket underwent such a dramatic change, we don't know. In a matter of such personal transformation, we lack any historical evidence to explain this matter. All we know is that Becket was very serious about his new stance.

The dispute that caused the great eruption between Henry II and Becket was criminous clerks. The clergy had the right to be tried exclusively by church courts rather than royal courts, regardless of the crime. A priest convicted of murder could essentially escape the king's justice by transferring his case to a church court, where he would receive a lesser punishment. Even if a man was convicted of something like rape or murder, church courts would likely only strip him of his office. Henry II saw this as a major problem, and it was more of a problem than we may first realize. Although there were not that many priests in England, there were a good many people who fell under the category of the clergy, even though they were not ordained—around one in six men, in fact. As part of his effort to establish stricter law and order after the Anarchy period (the civil war between Stephen and Matilda), Henry II wanted clergy convicted of serious crimes in church courts to be handed over to the royal courts for punishment.

To us today, this may seem reasonable, but not to the bishops of England and not to Thomas Becket. Turning over criminous clergy to the royal courts for punishment would destroy the base of clerical immunity from the secular courts. It would destabilize the church's freedom from the authority of the king. After much conflict, Henry II presented the bishops of England and Becket with the Constitutions of Clarendon, which included sixteen clauses that they would have to swear that the church would obey, among which was Henry II's idea for dealing with criminous clerks. Outright refusing to agree to it would have been bad enough, but Becket went a step further. Despite their reluctance, Becket convinced all of the other bishops to sign the Constitutions of Clarendon along with himself. Becket changed his mind a few days later and took back his oath.

Henry II was livid, but now instead of going after the entire church, he was after Thomas Becket. Henry II created charges to condemn Becket, but Becket refused to even hear the verdict of the king's council because he was a member of the clergy; they had no right to judge him. Becket then fled the country, seeking safety in France.

Becket lived in exile from 1165 to 1170, during which there were several attempts to get the archbishop of Canterbury and the king of England to reconcile. Ultimately, it was a matter of pride that brought Becket back to England. In 1170, Henry II had Becket's rival, the archbishop of York, crown his son Henry the Younger. It was a direct insult to Becket's office, and Becket finally agreed to return to England where he would re-crown Henry the Younger.

After returning from exile to a country where he was still fairly unpopular with the government, you might have expected Thomas Becket to lay low for a while, but Becket appeared to enjoy doing the unexpected. Immediately after returning to England, Becket excommunicated some of the members of the English clergy, including the archbishop of York. In a fit of anger at this news, Henry II said something that four of his knights took a bit too literally. The accounts of exactly what Henry said vary. Some say that the king asked, "Will no one rid me of this troublesome priest?" or "Will no one rid me of this turbulent priest?" Other accounts say that Henry II said, "What miserable drones and traitors have I nurtured and promoted in my household who let their lord be treated with such shameful contempt by a low-born clerk!"

Whatever he said, it was enough for four of the knights present. They rode to Canterbury Cathedral and attempted to arrest Becket. When he refused, things got out of hand. Becket was murdered in the cathedral. Murdering an archbishop in a church is not a good publicity move. Whatever people might have thought about Becket's actions in life, his death quickly turned him into a saint and a martyr. Canterbury Cathedral became one of the most popular pilgrimage destinations not just in England but in all of Europe, and Becket's remains, particularly his blood, were said to have miraculous healing properties. Henry II even visited the site of his old friend's murder and had to demonstrate penance for his involvement in it.

Depiction of Henry II and Thomas Becket
https://commons.wikimedia.org/wiki/File:Jindrich2_Beckett.jpg

The story of Thomas Becket and Henry II has quite a lot of drama and even some unexpected twists, but what we care about for our purposes is how this shows the strain between the church and state in the medieval period. The church was essentially a political entity, and having two political governing bodies acting within a single sphere is bound to cause problems. Questions of ecclesiastical versus royal authority would eventually cause England to leave the Catholic Church and establish the Church of England, wherein the head of state (the monarch) was also the head of the church.

Church Critics

Kings were not the only ones to have issues with the medieval Catholic Church. Even though the Protestant Reformation wouldn't get underway until the 1500s, there were already those who questioned how the church acted.

The king was upset because the church was interfering with his authority, but why did the average citizen have problems with the church? To put it simply, corruption was rampant. The power and wealth the church afforded made church positions very attractive. They were so attractive that people were willing to buy their way into them. This act, known as simony, was officially condemned but quite common. Another significant issue was nepotism, which was when church officials gave their kin prominent positions.

It doesn't stop there! The church was also heavily criticized for selling indulgences. Indulgences were payments a person could make to lessen their or a loved one's time in purgatory. It was a very lucrative business. People would pay quite a lot of money to get into heaven. Indulgences technically didn't start as a "pay your way" to heaven plan. The first indulgence appeared with the Crusades, as you could pay for your sins by participating in the holy war. Unfortunately, it didn't take long for corrupt church officials to see the dollar signs, and indulgences quickly became a money-making business.

England produced one of the medieval church's most famous critics before Martin Luther: John Wycliffe. Wycliffe, like many people, was opposed to the immense wealth the church controlled and continued to gain through practices like indulgences. He argued that the church should give up all its possessions. Wycliffe's ideas piqued the interest of some statesmen, particularly John of Gaunt, who was unhappy with the immense wealth and power of the church.

Wycliffe's opposition to the church became even more pronounced and vehement as time went on. He argued against the right of sanctuary, which, in his view, prevented justice from being served. He also heavily attacked the doctrine of transubstantiation, believed strongly in predestination, and was one of the first to promote an English translation of the Bible, all of which would later become key aspects of the Protestant Reformation. It is safe to say then that discontent with not only the church's power but also some of its doctrine did not begin with Luther. Many people in the medieval era were aware of the church's corruption. Kings like Henry II were not the only ones who thought that the power of the church had gone too far.

If this was the case, why did it take until the 1500s for all of this to boil over in the Reformation? We have to remember that there weren't any alternatives to the Catholic Church then. If you disagreed with the church, you couldn't just go down the street to a church you did agree with. And if you tried to break away, you would either be excommunicated or burned at the stake as a heretic. People took the idea of heaven and, even more so, hell very seriously. You weren't going to risk an eternity of punishment by disagreeing with the church. Even kings could be excommunicated. With this in mind, it's almost more surprising that people criticized the church at all.

By the end of the medieval period, the church's corruption had hit an all-time high, and it wouldn't be long before Martin Luther nailed his *Ninety-five Theses* to a door in 1517. It also wasn't long before the English government would have enough of the Catholic Church's interference. Henry VIII would break with Rome in 1534, creating the Church of England, with the English monarch as its head. This new system would attempt to solve the conflict between the church and state by more closely merging the two.

For all its problems, the medieval Catholic Church wielded enormous influence for a long time. Its organization and wealth made it a structure that even kings could not match. It could be argued that in medieval times, it was the church rather than the government that truly had the most influence on people's lives.

Chapter 13: Key Battles That Shaped Medieval History

As we have already seen, medieval history was full of plenty of violence and battles. We have made passing mention to many of these battles throughout this book, but which battles stand out as key moments in English history?

There are far more important battles that occurred in the English Middle Ages than we have time to cover, so we will take a look at just five battles that truly shaped medieval history. These are the engagements whose results would be felt down through the years in England. They are significant for their contribution to both English and military history.

The Battle of Edington (878)

You may be surprised to find that we are not starting with the Norman Conquest and the Battle of Hastings. While the Battle of Hastings does snag the second spot on our list of key battles, we couldn't forgive ourselves if we didn't include at least one battle from the Anglo-Saxon period. The Anglo-Saxons, after all, were pretty good at the whole warfare thing, and their success in this particular battle had huge repercussions for England.

The Battle of Edington took place in 878 between the forces of King Alfred of Wessex and the Vikings led by King Guthrum. The Vikings had invaded in large numbers in 865, and in the thirteen years between then and the Battle of Edington, they had managed to conquer almost all of England. Mercia and Wessex were the last Anglo-Saxon kingdoms to fall to the Vikings. As the story goes, King Alfred was driven out of his kingdom and took refuge in a swamp. Luckily for England, Alfred was about to make a major comeback.

After hiding in the marshes for several months, Alfred gathered a force to challenge the Vikings in the spring of 878. The two sides clashed sometime in May near the fortress of Chippenham, which was where Alfred had been defeated and forced to flee several months earlier. In the battle itself, the Anglo-Saxons used a shield wall formation against the Danes, and over a long day of fighting, they wore down the Vikings and routed them. The Anglo-Saxons had won a great and what proved to be a decisive victory.

The peace agreement that shortly followed the battle, called the Peace of Wedmore, had Guthrum converting to Christianity. The Danes agreed to retreat into the northeast and east of England, essentially leaving Wessex. This was the establishment of the Danelaw. While Alfred was not able to finish the job of driving the Vikings entirely out of England, the Battle of Edington was a reversal of the Viking takeover that had begun in 865 with the arrival of the *mycel hæþen here* (Great Heathen Army).

Without Alfred's victory at the Battle of Edington, England as a nation might have never come to be. Not only did this battle halt and lead to the eventual reversal of the Viking conquest, but it also gave the Wessex dynasty its start. Since Alfred was the only king able to drive back the Vikings, he paved the way for Wessex to dominate. His grandson, Æthelstan, became the first king of the English. That's more than enough to call the Battle of Edington a key battle in English history.

The Battle of Hastings (1066)

Sometimes the most significant battles in a nation's history are the losses. The Battle of Hastings in 1066 was a loss for the English, and it would end up being a huge turning point in the history of the Middle Ages.

To recap a bit from what we discussed in early chapters, in 1066, England's ruler, Edward the Confessor, died with no children, creating a succession crisis. Harold Godwinson took the throne, but he would have to fight for it, as multiple people saw Edward the Confessor's childlessness as an opportunity to claim the English throne.

Harold was successful in fending off his first rivals: his own brother Tostig and the king of Norway, Harald Hardrada. Harold's forces defeated them near York at the Battle of Stamford Bridge. We bring this up because the Battle of Stamford Bridge had a significant impact on the more famous Battle of Hastings. William of Normandy would land in England only three days after Harold's victory at Stamford Bridge, and the Battle of Hastings took place around nineteen days after Stamford Bridge. Furthermore, the Battle of Stamford Bridge took place near York in the north, while the Battle of Hastings took place in the far south near, big surprise, Hastings. Harold's forces had to march first from London to aid the northern earls in York with the Battle of Stamford Bridge. Then they had to turn around and march back south to engage William's forces. Thus, Harold's forces were far from fresh at the Battle of Hastings, and many historians consider Harold's decision to engage William's forces so soon as a fatal blunder.

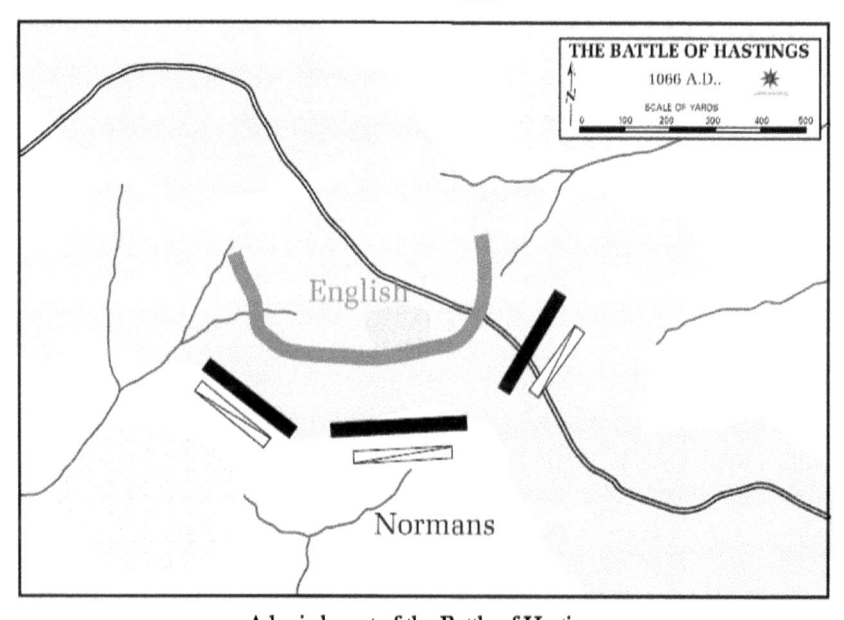

A basic layout of the Battle of Hastings
https://commons.wikimedia.org/wiki/File:Battle_of_Hastings,_1066.png

However, at the start of the actual engagement, it was not at all clear that the Normans would carry the day. Harold's forces held a position at the top of a ridge. For the Normans to win, they needed to charge and break the English line. For the English to win, they needed to hold the line until the Normans were exhausted and retreated. At first, the shield wall of the English was able to repulse the Norman cavalry, but their only real chance was if the Normans gave up. They didn't. Over time, the defensive position of the English was worn down by the repeated Norman assaults. At some point, Harold was killed, as were his two brothers. Leaderless, the English forces scattered as night fell.

After the Battle of Hastings, William faced no serious opposition to his invasion. He was crowned William I in London on December 25th. The story of the Battle of Hastings was told over and over again. The famous Bayeux Tapestry even has a pictorial depiction of this famous battle, showing things like the English axmen facing the Norman cavalry. Unfortunately, all of this retelling also means that there are several contradicting versions that historians are forced to sift through. We don't know all the details, like how exactly Harold died, but we do know that the Battle of Hastings was the key to the Norman Conquest, and there can be no doubt that Norman rule went on to cause some significant changes for England.

The Battle of Bannockburn (1314)

The kingdoms of Scotland and England were joined together under a single king in 1603 when James VI of Scotland became James I of England. The nations, however, remained two separate states with a single monarch until the Acts of Union of 1707, which officially united them. What does this have to do with medieval history? Well, Scotland and England might have been united a lot sooner were it not for the Battle of Bannockburn.

The Battle of Bannockburn was the final decisive battle in a conflict between Scotland and England known as the Wars of Scottish Independence. Edward I, known as the Hammer of the Scots, had begun the process of trying to take over Scotland in 1296, and he did a pretty good job. Although, largely because of the movie *Braveheart*, we remember William Wallace as the great figure who led the Scots to victory at the Battle of Stirling Bridge in 1297. Within a year, Edward I had defeated Wallace at the Battle of Falkirk. For the next six years, England and Scotland fought bitterly, but by 1304, due to diplomatic maneuvering rather than conflicts, Edward I had essentially triumphed. The English controlled Scotland.

The English might have kept their hold on Scotland were it not for the fact that Edward I died in 1307. After his death, the rebel Scots, led by Robert the Bruce, began making serious progress, winning battle after battle and taking back Scotland by force. Things came to a head in 1314 at Bannockburn.

Edward I's son, Edward II, could not simply sit by while Robert the Bruce took back Scotland. In 1314, he invaded Scotland and faced the Bruce's forces. The purpose of the invasion was to bring relief to Stirling Castle, which was the only remaining English stronghold in Scotland that had not surrendered to Robert the Bruce. When Edward II's forces arrived, though, the Scots were waiting for them.

The fighting lasted for two days, with both sides stopping for the night. As the English had a much larger force, the battle was a horrendous defeat for the English and a stunning victory for the Scots. The Scottish infantry had bested the English cavalry. The Battle of Bannockburn was the practical end to the Scottish Wars of Independence, although Scottish independence was not formally recognized by England until 1328.

Besides its importance in both Scottish and English history, the Battle of Bannockburn also has significance for its contribution to military history. The success of the infantry here helped to alter medieval warfare so that the infantry rather than the cavalry began to have more importance on the battlefield. This was the beginning of the end of the age of mounted knights, and our next battle, which occurred around one hundred years later, would only hasten that demise.

The Battle of Agincourt (1415)

Obviously, this chapter focuses on battles that shaped English medieval history, and while the Battle of Agincourt certainly fits the criteria, Agincourt also has a lot of significance in military history in general. The Battle of Bannockburn had shown the power of the infantry, but it was the events of this battle that sounded the death keel of the medieval knight in shining armor.

If you know anything about the Battle of Agincourt, you probably know that it was an astonishing victory for the English, so much so that it's almost taken on a mythical quality in English history. The Battle of Agincourt is the great climax to Shakespeare's play *Henry V*. During

World War II, that play and the Battle of Agincourt were depicted on film, with the famous actor Laurence Olivier in the lead role, as part of an effort to maintain British morale. Over five hundred years after it happened, Agincourt had remained a battle that swelled English pride. It was their great triumph. However, no one prior to the battle would have guessed that that would be the outcome.

The Battle of Agincourt took place in France during one of Henry V's campaigns of the Hundred Years' War. The campaign began when Henry V landed in Normandy in August of 1415. Henry V then laid siege to the city of Harfleur. Although he succeeded in capturing the city, the siege had taken longer and been far more costly than Henry V had hoped. In October, Henry V and his forces made for Calais, a port held by the English, where he could set sail back for England. Unfortunately for them, the English were unable to cross the River Somme and reach Calais before they were intercepted by the French forces. The odds were decidedly not in their favor. Although the exact numbers are up for debate, the French had a sure numerical advantage over the English at Agincourt. Henry V's army was around five thousand and six thousand men, and the French army was said to have been somewhere between twenty thousand and thirty thousand. While this may be an exaggeration, even the most skeptical scholars place the French army at around twelve thousand—twice the number of the English. Besides their numerical disadvantage, the English were also exhausted. They had fought a six-week siege at Harfleur and then marched hard to make it to Calais. Things did not look good.

To meet the French, Henry V placed his army on a field bounded on either side by forests. The archers were positioned in wedges on either side of the other soldiers. This formation was crucial since it worked to offset the French numerical advantage. The narrow front limited how many men the French could effectively throw at the English at a time and made it impossible for the French to surround them. The English were also helped by the weather. The rainy weather had turned the field to mud, which slowed the advance of the French knights, giving the English archers far more time to pick them off.

The first wave of French knights was unable to overwhelm and scatter the English archers as they needed to, partially because the English archers had come up with the idea of driving sharpened stakes at angles into the ground to protect themselves from the charge of the French knights. When the second wave of knights then arrived, they did more harm than good for the French effort. The French became too tightly packed to maneuver, and the battle began to highly favor the English. By the time the third wave of French arrived, between the corpses and churned mud, everything was too messy for them to charge at all or to escape the rain of English arrows. The English finished the battle quickly. Reports say that, in all, the Battle of Agincourt only lasted between half an hour to three hours.

Agincourt significantly weakened the French military position. Henry V was able to follow up on his victory with more successes, and by 1420, he was engaged to the French princess, Catherine, and had been named heir to the French throne.

Besides being an important English victory in the Hundred Years' War, Agincourt had also been a victory for the English archer over the mounted knight. Warfare tactics had already begun to evolve, as we saw with the Battle of Bannockburn, and Agincourt pushed them even further. The medieval knight would soon be a figure found in fairy tales and romances rather than on the battlefield.

The Battle of Bosworth (1485)

Speaking in terms of the monarchy and government of the Middle Ages, the Battle of Bosworth was the conflict that capped off the medieval period and started England down a new path.

The final engagement in the infamous Wars of the Roses, the Battle of Bosworth, was a battle between the forces of Richard III and Henry Tudor. The forces of Richard and Henry clashed on August 22nd, 1485. Like many of the battles on this list, it was the side that initially seemed to be at a disadvantage that ultimately carried the day. The forces of Henry Tudor were outnumbered and led by a young man inexperienced in battle. Richard III not only had superior numbers but was also a battle-hardened veteran of the Wars of the Roses. If the two monarchs were actually to meet on the battlefield, there was little doubt who would walk away from the encounter.

Fortunately for Henry Tudor, Richard III never reached him, so no hand-to-hand combat between the two took place. Despite his superior numbers, Richard III's army was defeated, and Richard himself was killed in battle. Henry's victory was at least in part thanks to the forces of the Stanley brothers. These two English lords had pledged their forces to both Henry and Richard. Thomas Stanley's forces remained neutral throughout the entire battle, but William Stanley finally threw his lot in with Henry at a key moment, swinging the battle in the future Tudor king's favor. While many see the actions of the Stanleys as evidence of Richard III's tyrannical nature, it also shows just how bloody and unstable the Wars of the Roses had made England. Men were reluctant to join either side in this clash of kings until a winner became clear because picking the wrong one was often a fatal mistake.

And the Battle of Bosworth truly was a clash between kings. Although they did not face each other directly, both Richard III and Henry Tudor had styled the battle as a sort of trial by combat. Whichever side came away the victor was the one that God favored. They would have the divine right to the throne. It was a battle that everyone seemed to understand would be decisive before it even began.

With these stakes, it is no wonder that after losing the Battle of Bosworth, Richard III has gone down in history as one of the most infamous kings in English history. Even so, history also records that Richard III fought bravely at Bosworth. In context, that famous line from Shakespeare, "My horse! My horse! My kingdom for a horse!" is not Richard seeking to run away but rather his desire to charge back into battle. Richard III had staked everything on the Battle of Bosworth, and when he lost, he lost not only his life but also his legacy.

Richard III was the last English monarch to be killed in battle, a fact that shows a lot about why this battle was so significant. The death of Richard III was the end of the Plantagenet dynasty, a line whose greatness had, in many ways, been tied to their martial abilities. The greats of the Plantagenets were mighty warriors: Richard the Lionheart, Edward the Hammer of the Scots, and Henry V, the hero of Agincourt. The bad Plantagenet kings were those who failed to win battles: King John, Edward II, and Henry VI.

When Richard III died at Bosworth, that legacy ended. The Tudor monarchs would not define themselves by warfare in the same way that the Plantagenets had. The Battle of Bosworth ironically would begin to push England down a less war-centered path. It was both a culmination of and an end to the warfare of the Middle Ages.

Chapter 14: Medieval Myth

When you hear the word myth, what do you think about? Do you picture the many Gods and Goddesses of the Greco-Roman world? Do you think about stories of heroes embarking on daring quests? Do you think about tales from folklore with their many versions and clear morals?

What is a myth? That is a harder question to answer than one might initially think. We associate a lot of different things with that little word. Is a myth a religious belief, or is it simply a story? Is it a way that people explain the world around them, or is it simply entertainment? How old does a story have to be to be considered a myth? There are a lot of questions that get in the way of our definition of a myth.

However, that is a debate for a more academically focused book. What we care about for this book is that myths can cover a wide range of things. So, we won't just be talking about gods in this chapter. We will be looking at the legends, epics, tales, and stories that made up the world of medieval English myth.

The Arthurian Legend

Before we look at some of the overarching themes and realities that influenced medieval myth, let's start with the most famous myth from medieval England: the Arthurian legend. If any medieval English myth has survived through the ages, it is the legend of King Arthur. Like most myths, there are a lot of different variations and stories surrounding King

Arthur. Besides King Arthur himself, the Arthurian legend also contains plenty of other famous mythic elements and characters like the wizard Merlin, the sword Excalibur, the Knights of the Round Table, the Lady of the Lake, and so much more. The Arthurian legend is the most famous surviving British myth, and it is one of the few legends that we associate specifically with Britain. However, this story, while it is British, isn't actually English.

King Arthur was originally a Celtic hero, and he may have been a real person. As we learned at the very beginning of this book, when the Romans left Britain, the Anglo-Saxons invaded. The Celtic inhabitants of the island were pushed out. However, historical records do tell of one incredible Celtic victory over the Anglo-Saxon invaders: the Battle of Badon. The earliest texts that mention Badon do not name Arthur, but in the 9th century, the *Historia Brittonum* by Nennius names Arthur as the Celtic leader and attributes the victory to him. This appears to be the earliest mention of Arthur, although another text from around this time, the *Annales Cambriae*, also mentions Arthur. The legend only grew from there, thanks largely to the writing of Geoffrey of Monmouth in the 12th century, who would come to be known as the father of the Arthurian tradition.

Arthur leading the charge at Mount Badon (an illustration for Tennyson's "Lancelot and Guinevere")
https://commons.wikimedia.org/wiki/File:Arthur_Leading_the_Charge_at_Mount_Badon.png

So, does that mean that Arthur existed? It's far from certain. Although both Nennius and Geoffrey of Monmouth claimed to be writing histories, both works clearly value the narrative more than historical accuracy. Also, the Battle of Badon took place sometime around 450, and Nennius, who was again the first to name Arthur, didn't write his account until around four centuries later. We aren't even certain that the battle itself took place. What we do know is that whether he began as a real person or not, King Arthur quickly moved beyond that.

Stories featuring Arthur abounded in oral traditions of the Middle Ages, and eventually, some medieval writers put the legend to paper. Chrétien de Troyes (a French writer) added tales of chivalry and romance to the legend, but the person we have to thank for most of our modern ideas of King Arthur is Sir Thomas Malory, who wrote *The Death of Arthur* (*Le Morte d'Arthur*), a book compiling many of the tales into a single story, in 1485.

The legend of King Arthur is thus a myth that is truly medieval in terms of its time of development. Even though the Battle of Badon took place slightly before the medieval period, stories about Arthur were first told and then written down in the Middle Ages, and the setting of the stories was altered to fit the period in which they were told rather than the period in which Arthur might have lived.

The fact that we think of Arthur as being so quintessentially British when he was originally celebrated for beating the Anglo-Saxons shows us something that made British and English myths in the Middle Ages unique. There was a lot of mixing. The small island of Britain had been conquered and settled by so many different people that it was host to Celtic, Christian, and Germanic myths all at the same time. Arthur is a Celtic myth. Now, let's turn our attention to the most famous Anglo-Saxon myth from this period.

Beowulf

Coming in just slightly behind Arthur in terms of notoriety is the epic Old English poem, *Beowulf*, which tells the tale of its titular hero. The story of Beowulf appears to take place around the 6th century. However, we are not sure when the poem was first written down. There is a surviving manuscript from around the year 1000, but some scholars believe it may have been put to paper as much as two hundred years earlier. Like other poetry and tales of its day, *Beowulf* likely existed in the oral tradition long before it was officially composed by an unknown author.

Beowulf is famous for being one of the earliest works of literature in Old English, and it also happens to be the earliest European epic that we know of. However, while it is famous for being written down for the first time in Old English, *Beowulf*, like the Arthurian legend, isn't exactly English. It is a Scandinavian tale. In the first half of the poem, Beowulf helps Hrothgar, the king of Denmark, by killing two monsters that have been terrorizing the Danes. In the second half, Beowulf becomes the king of Geatland, which was an area in what is now southern Sweden.

Beowulf is then part of a more Germanic culture that came to England with the Anglo-Saxons at the beginning of the Middle Ages. In the story, we can also see the influence of Christianity. Unlike the heroes of ancient epics like the *Odyssey*, *Iliad*, and *Aeneid*, Beowulf spends all of his time fighting monsters, pure incarnations of evil, rather than men. Even then, the tone of *Beowulf* feels far more somber. The story ends with an aged Beowulf becoming mortally wounded in his fight with a dragon. The classic warrior hero is there, but *Beowulf* also carries a sense of melancholy that is not present in other ancient epics. It reflects the tensions of a culture that glorified warfare while also valuing the doctrines of Christianity.

With both Celtic and Germanic influences, as well as the ever-present influence of Christianity, myth in medieval England came from a variety of sources. There are few stories from this period that are pure "English." However, there is a collection of tales that were written in the Late Middle Ages that do hold that title.

The Canterbury Tales

The Canterbury Tales was a book written by Geoffrey Chaucer near the end of the 14th century. It follows the journey of thirty pilgrims on their way to visit Thomas Becket's shrine at Canterbury Cathedral. On the way, they engage in a storytelling contest, and the book is mostly a collection of the various tales the pilgrims tell. There are twenty-four tales, but the book is uncompleted. Chaucer had plans for many more stories.

The *Canterbury Tales* may be closer to literature than a myth. Unlike the Arthurian legend and *Beowulf*, *The Canterbury Tales* was written first rather than starting as a popular story that was only later written down. However, many of the tales included are at least partially taken from other sources, so although Chaucer altered and wrote them in the 14th century, some of the stories were much older.

Another reason *The Canterbury Tales* is an important example of English myth is because of the sheer variety. The collection includes a large variety of stories, from crude humor to piety, tragedy, and fables. One reason it has so much variety is that Chaucer included so many different classes of people in his story. There is a knight, a nun, a monk, a miller, a physician, a sailor, and many more that make up the group of thirty pilgrims, and they all tell a tale that fits with their position. The book is thus an excellent example of many different types of medieval stories. You can read *The Canterbury Tales* and have a general idea of what types of stories people told in this period.

The Canterbury Tales is also important in the history of English culture. After the Norman Conquest, French became the preferred language of the powerful, and English (they were using Middle English at this time) was reduced to being seen as a lesser language used by peasants. Chaucer, however, wrote *The Canterbury Tales* in Middle English, not French, and it was one of the earliest works of truly English literature because of it. Between *Beowulf* and *The Canterbury Tales*, the medieval period is hugely important for how it turned English myths and stories into literature. This is the period when written stories first began gaining popularity, though it would be a long time yet before they surpassed the oral tradition.

Medieval Folklore

Speaking of the oral tradition, most people in the medieval period were illiterate, so telling stories aloud was how most myths and tales got passed around. Medieval folklore refers specifically to European stories that were popular between around 500 and 1500.

There is an immense variety of tales that fall under the category of medieval folklore, and there is a long history of scholars who have tried to sort through and categorize it. The main reason for the difficulty is the oral nature of folklore. While the Arthurian legend, Beowulf, and *The Canterbury Tales* all have famous pieces of literature associated with them, folk tales were not extensively written down until around the 19th century. Because they were purely oral, the tales varied from location to location and even from telling to telling. Telling a folk tale was not just a matter of recitation. It was a performance. Tellers would alter the basic formula for particular audiences and settings. All of that makes for a lot of different stories and different versions of the same story.

To try to make sense of all the variety, folklorists have developed different categories to describe some of the general types of tales from this period. Here are some of the kinds of stories you might have heard from the Middle Ages:

- Animal Tales - Remember Aesop's fables? Stories with animals acting like humans have been around for a long time, and these fables typically taught moral lessons.

- Anecdotes and Jokes - Just like today, medieval people enjoyed a good joke. There were lots of stories about cheating wives and stupid husbands.

- Tales of the Stupid Ogre - These were stories about supernatural beings that get outsmarted by the protagonist of the story.

- Religious and Realistic Tales - These tales often had contemporary settings and strong Christian morals.

- Magic Tales - As the name suggests, these tales have magic and include many popular fairy tales that have survived today, such as Cinderella and Rapunzel. The medieval version of most of these tales is much darker than the family-friendly versions that Disney made.

These varieties give you an idea of just how many different types of stories there were, and they still don't cover everything. *The Canterbury Tales* has good examples of many of the different kinds.

So far in this chapter, we have focused a lot on different stories that compromised medieval myth, but another aspect of medieval myths is the fantastical creatures that often appeared in the stories and which, for many people in the Middle Ages, might also be lurking around a corner in the real world.

Fairies and Monsters

We mentioned briefly in the chapter on religion that many people in England believed strongly in the existence of fairies and other spirits. However, these were not the cute tiny creatures that wear clothes made out of leaves and spread fairy dust. Medieval fairies were a different breed. They were malevolent beings that you needed to please, or they would play nasty tricks on you.

Take Puck or Robin Goodfellow, for example. In Shakespeare's *A Midsummer Night's Dream*, Puck is a mischievous and playful figure, but Shakespeare wrote it during the Renaissance. In the medieval era, though, "puck" could mean devil. A puck was not a fun-loving being but an evil spirit. Fairies were believed to be devils. After the spread of Christianity, one explanation said that fairies were said to be fallen angels that had become trapped on earth. They were eternally damned and malevolent creatures, and the people of medieval England took them very seriously. People didn't even like to say the word fairies and so often referred to them as the little people.

There were many different types of fairies. One type was a will-o'-the-wisp, which took the form of a glowing light that led people astray. They could get you lost or even lead you to your death in a marsh. Another type was brownies, which would do housework if you were nice to them. Banshees were foretellers of doom, and goblins were never good news. To the medieval mind, the English countryside was filled with magical beings.

The belief in the little people in England was so strong that it has not completely died out. There were reports of fairy sightings as late as the 20th century. In the British Isles, the little people are more than just stories. They are a part of the culture of the region.

Besides fairies and spirits, medieval stories and literature also had quite a lot of fantastic monsters. Bestiaries from the period were books filled with pictures of various animals, some real and some mythical. Even the real animals sometimes looked mythical since people in England tried to depict animals from far-away lands that they had never seen. Dolphins had human faces but with their mouths on their torso area. Here are some of the most well-known and also some of the most bizarre creatures of the period:

- Pegasus - The pegasus is a winged horse originally from Greek and Roman mythology.
- Dragon - The dragon is the ultimate beast. It is connected with serpents and thus also with the devil. Dragons in medieval mythology are purely evil.
- Manticore - A manticore is a beast with the body of a lion, the head of a man, and the tail of a scorpion. They were said to come from the area around India and Persia.
- Merknight - You have heard of mermaids, but the medieval period also had merknights and mermen, which are exactly what they sound like. Their bottom half is a fish, and the top half is an armored man.
- Sea Monk - These strange creatures were said to have the body of a fish and a head like a monk, with a shaved head and a ring of hair. This may have been describing seals.
- Onocentaur - A creature with the head of a donkey and the body of a man. It seems Shakespeare was not the one to make up that bizarre creation in *A Midsummer Night's Dream* after all.
- Blemmyae - A monster with the body of a man but with no head and its face on its chest.

These are just a few examples of the many varied beasts of medieval myth. They range from the classics that still appear in stories today to the downright bizarre. Since medieval people knew very little about the world beyond their local area, it was very easy for them to believe that these creatures existed somewhere. That may sound crazy, but when you think about it, a giraffe and an elephant can sound mythical to someone who has never seen one.

So, English myth in the Middle Ages was full of lots of creatures and magic, which is what we generally picture when we think of medieval tales. However, not every story saw Beowulf fighting a dragon or Arthur receiving the sword from the Lady in the Lake. There were fables, jokes, religious stories, and more. Also, medieval myths continue to have an impact today. While we may not be as concerned about offending the little people anymore, many of the fairy tales that we tell our children today are versions of stories that originated in the Middle Ages. A lot has changed, but we still enjoy many of the same stories that medieval people did.

Chapter 15: Medieval Medicine

Many people are guilty of over-romanticizing not just the Middle Ages but almost any past era in history. We probably do this because we are so aware of our problems in the present day. However, if there is one societal advancement that not even the most old-fashioned person wants to give up, it has to be modern medicine. Not dying is something that everyone can get behind, and thanks to things like vaccinations, anesthesia, the discovery of germs, antibiotics, and many more advancements, your chances of recovering from an illness today are significantly improved.

So, what was the world like before modern medicine? The first vaccine, which was for smallpox, wasn't developed until 1796. The first antibiotic was penicillin, and that wasn't discovered until 1928. We didn't even know that germs caused illness until 1861. A lot of the things that we consider to be hallmarks of medicine were still hundreds of years away in the Middle Ages, so what did they do instead? How did they understand health, and what did they do if someone got sick?

The Humors

A lot of medieval ideas about human health came from the ancient Greek and Roman societies. One of the big ideas from Greek medicine that had a large influence on medieval medicine was the four humors.

This was a theory developed by Hippocrates. It said that the human body consisted of four humors (fluids), which were yellow bile, phlegm, black bile, and blood. These four humors were controlled by the four elements: fire, water, earth, and air. Illness was believed to be the result of an imbalance of these four fluids. Having too much black bile made you melancholic, phlegm made you phlegmatic, yellow bile made you choleric, and blood made you sanguine.

Bloodletting was thus a common medicinal treatment because it was believed that purging the body of excess blood would restore balance. This procedure was often done through cuts, but blood could also be drained using leeches. If blood wasn't the problem, physicians might also suggest particular foods to restore the body's humor balance.

The humors went beyond just keeping you healthy. They were also believed to affect personality and were categorized based on heat and moisture.

- Black Bile: Cold and Dry
- Phlegm: Cold and Moist
- Yellow Bile: Hot and Dry
- Blood: Hot and Moist

The balance of humors in a person's body changed with their age, seasons of the year, and even their gender. For example, youths were considered to be hot and moist and thus had more blood, while older people were thought to be cold and dry, having more black bile. The balance of humors in a person could have a great impact on their temperament. It was believed that yellow bile made a person courageous, but too much phlegm made people cowardly.

Belief and reliance on the idea of the four humors persisted well past the Middle Ages. Emphasis on the humors' impact on a person's emotions and personalities became even more pronounced in the Renaissance. The theory of the humors did not fall out of favor until it was replaced by germ theory in the 19th century.

Diagnosis and Treatment

Medieval doctors may have been incorrect about the causes of illness, but they did take observing the symptoms of their patients very seriously. Medieval physicians were experts in diagnosis. They determined a person's ailment by listening to their patients, observing, feeling the pulse, and taking urine samples.

Urine samples were perhaps the most common method of diagnosis, so much so that the urine flask was the symbol of the medieval doctor. While medieval doctors could not run lab tests on urine like today, they did visually examine it to determine a diagnosis.

A medical practitioner examining a urine flask—painting from the 17th century
https://commons.wikimedia.org/wiki/File:A_medical_practitioner_examining_a_urine_flask._Oil_painting_Wellcome_V0017268.jpg

Once they had made a diagnosis, how did medieval doctors treat their patients? While some procedures like bloodletting were used, the main form of treatment was herbal medicine. You could get these medicines from a physician or monks at a monastery, but in rural areas, you often went to a local herbalist.

Like the theory of the four humors, much of what medieval people knew about medicinal plants came from the ancients. The *De materia medica,* written by Dioscorides, a Greek, was a highly influential book that described the use of hundreds of plants.

Medieval people did not solely rely on what they learned from the ancients, however. Monasteries housed gardens that grew important medicinal plants. Besides growing them, the monks would also experiment to learn more about the uses of these plants. However, while they were interested in what uses particular plants had, the monks were not as keen on discovering why exactly certain plants were able to cure particular ailments. They were content with the explanation that God had made it so.

Like many aspects of medieval life, there was a divide in the medical treatment of the rich and the poor. Only the rich had access to trained physicians. Peasants had to make do with whatever local wise woman or herbalist lived near them. These rural practitioners relied on their experience and folk knowledge that was passed down, which often included the uses of various herbs as well as other more surreptitious methods like charms.

That didn't mean that a peasant with a serious illness was completely out of luck, though. There were hospitals in the Middle Ages, thanks in large part to the church. Hospitals were often attached to large monasteries, and it was the monks and nuns who lived there who would treat the sick and dying. It is unclear exactly how much the average monk or nun knew about medicine, but monasteries were one of the largest sources of medicinal herbs, so it is safe to say that they probably knew more than the layperson.

Surgeries and Procedures

If medicinal herbs were not enough to deal with an illness, then other things could be used to treat a patient. As we have already mentioned, bloodletting was a common treatment, but there were also far more involved procedures. However, surgeries were not performed by doctors. In the Middle Ages, the doctor and surgeon professions were separate. Procedures were typically carried out not by doctors but by barber-surgeons.

The name of this profession may sound strange, but it is appropriate, for the barber-surgeons of the medieval era both cut hair and cut off limbs. A barber-surgeon did a variety of tasks, such as setting bones, bloodletting, pulling teeth, performing amputations, and, of course, cutting hair. They were especially valuable on the battlefield, where amputations and other emergency medical needs were quite frequent. However, overall, barber-surgeons were held in much lower esteem than physicians.

That lack of esteem might have been because no one wanted to undergo surgery if they could help it. Surgery was a horrific experience that might kill you rather than save you, and that was not because of a lack of skill on the part of medieval surgeons. The main problem was the lack of anesthesia. Imagine undergoing any type of surgery without being put to sleep first, and you'll have a pretty good understanding of why surgery was not the go-to solution for medical problems in the Middle Ages. Opiates, herbs, and alcohol were used to try to dull the pain, but it could only dull it. No matter what, surgery was sure to be an excruciating experience.

The pain was not the only problem. The other was infection. There is a reason that doctors today perform surgeries with masks on in a completely sterilized room. Even if the surgery is effective, if the wound from the procedure becomes infected, then the patient might end up in worse shape than when they started. In the Middle Ages, they lacked the disinfectants and sterilization techniques that we use now. To prevent infection, wounds were typically cauterized, which refers to the practice of burning a wound to stop the infection and halt the bleeding.

Because of these problems, surgeries in the Middle Ages tended to be on more external parts of the body. Without anesthesia, medieval surgeons could not reach a person's vital organs, like the heart, without a very high risk of killing them in the process. However, they were able to perform procedures like removing cataracts and even trepanning, which involved drilling a hole in the skull.

Perhaps the most shocking thing about medieval surgery, though, is how successful it often was. Thanks to the constant warfare, surgeons became quite skilled at setting bones and patching up traumatic wounds. They could not perform open-heart surgery, but they could mend broken skulls, amputate limbs, and more. Surgery was gory, painful, and quite dangerous, but it existed because it did get results.

Medieval Illnesses

What exactly were medieval doctors treating their patients for? We will talk extensively about the most famous illness of the period—the plague—in the next chapter, but that was far from the only disease that existed at the time. Here are some of the diseases other than the Black Death that plagued people in medieval England:

- Leprosy - While leprosy is a particular disease, in the Middle Ages, any skin condition that was disfiguring enough would have been referred to as leprosy. One of the main reasons for the prominence of leprosy was the lack of personal hygiene, which made it much easier for people to develop infections. The disease destroys the outside of the body, resulting not only in open sores but also in the loss of fingers, toes, and, in some cases, a person's nose. Leprosy was considered to be highly contagious, and lepers were typically isolated from society to protect others. They even had to ring a bell to warn people of their approach.

- St. Anthony's Fire - This disease is so named because it causes redness and burning in a person's hands and feet. Unfortunately, it doesn't stop there. The redness spreads, becoming gangrene that could cause the loss of entire limbs. St. Anthony's Fire was caused by ingesting rye that had been tainted by a particular fungus.

- Sweating Sickness - This was a fast-acting illness that appeared at the end of the Middle Ages. Symptoms progressed rapidly from a headache and prostration to severe sweating and delusions. A person was often dead within hours of the first sign of the disease, but if they managed to make it through the first day, then they often survived. Even today, we are not exactly sure what the sweating sickness was, but it virtually disappeared sometime after the last major outbreak in 1551.

- Smallpox - Until the vaccination was developed in 1796, smallpox was a devastating disease, especially for children. Those who survived often had scars from the pockmarks, but people were immune to a second infection.

- Tuberculosis - Another disease that was present in the Middle Ages that, like smallpox, lasted for a long time was tuberculosis. This illness causes masses in the lungs, which can cause people to cough up blood. Unlike almost all the other major diseases of the Middle Ages, tuberculosis is still a major disease. It spreads most rapidly in dense populations, so the impact of tuberculosis worsened after the Middle Ages when industrialization caused rapid city growth.

These illnesses were just some of the things that could afflict a person in medieval England. There were also issues like arthritis and, for women, the danger of childbirth. Infant mortality rates were especially high. It was not an easy time to stay healthy, no matter the person's class.

Religion and Medicine

Today, we may find it easy to sneer at the ignorance of medieval people, but without a knowledge of germs, the origins of various illnesses and ailments are quite mysterious. The four humors were one way that illness was explained, but like almost everything in this period, disease and medicine were also tied to religion.

In the Gospel of Luke in the Bible, there is a moment where Jesus and his disciples encounter a blind man. The disciples ask Jesus whose sin has caused the man's blindness, his own or his parents. This small moment is a perfect example of how the medieval church often thought of illness. All grief and destruction in the world were due to sin. Therefore, disease and illness must be the result of sin. This remains true in Christian doctrine today, but what Jesus's disciples implied with their question and how the medieval church viewed the relationship between sin and illness is different. It is not just that sin generally is the source of all bad things but that an individual's sin is the cause of their individual illness. If you fell ill, it was because you had sinned, and God was punishing you.

Now, if you keep reading that story in the Gospel of Luke, you will discover that Jesus specifically told his disciples that that was not the case. It was no individual sin that caused the man's blindness. However, the general population of medieval England could not read, nor did they even own a Bible. Everything they knew of their religious beliefs came from what the church told them, so the idea that illness was the result of a person's sin was blindly accepted. You can start to see why the translation of the Bible into English had such a large impact on the Protestant Reformation and the ultimate break with the Roman Catholic Church.

Understanding this view of disease and sickness being tied to sin is crucial for us to understand why so many people sought religious cures for physical ailments. Pilgrimages to shrines like Canterbury were common for those seeking healing, and particular shrines were appealed to for particular illnesses. Canterbury appears to have been especially important for people suffering from bleeding disorders. Besides traveling to particular holy sites, people could also pray to certain saints and seek blessings from their local clergy.

The tie between religion and treatments could get much more physical, though. For instance, one reason for trepanning, which was the practice of drilling a hole in a person's skull, might have been to relieve a person of an evil spirit. There was also a common belief called the doctrine of signatures, which said that plants that resembled certain body parts could be used in healing those body parts. This philosophy had its roots in antiquity, much like the humors, but in the medieval period, it was ascribed to God's will.

So, a lot of medieval medicine was influenced by religion, specifically Christianity. There was a general faith in providence that meant that people did not probe too deeply into the causes or the cures of various illnesses. We might declare such an attitude to be naive, but in a world without advanced medical technology, the attitude that things were so because God made them so may have been comforting. It gave reason to ailments that at the time seemed horrific and unreasonable.

Medieval Medical Blunders

Throughout this chapter, you have probably noticed several things that don't seem like the best idea for treating illnesses. Drilling holes in a person's skull is not a way to stop odd behavior, and the four humors are not the cause of disease. Considering what they had to work with, medieval medicine wasn't all bad, but they were very wrong about a lot of things.

Perhaps the most common blunder that medieval people made in terms of medical treatments was bloodletting. Because of the belief in the need for the balance of the four humors, bloodletting and leeches were very common treatments for a variety of ailments. However, in reality, you kind of need your blood. If you lost too much during the process, then the treatment would kill you faster than the disease. And even if it didn't kill you, the blood loss could leave you weakened, and the wound might become infected. Besides that, in most cases, bloodletting had no effect whatsoever on the diseases it was supposed to treat.

Why in most cases? Bloodletting may have been practiced so extensively because it did appear to help at times. A patient suffering from high blood pressure and other heart problems might experience a temporary recovery from bloodletting, but it did not fix the problem or cure the patient. It has also been suggested that bloodletting might have worked in some cases because it killed bacteria that needed the iron available in the blood to survive, but even if that's true, it's still a double-edged sword because the human body also needs iron. Even if bloodletting might have had some positive side effects, it was still dangerous and harmful and used widely for all sorts of illnesses.

The other serious health blunder of the Middle Ages went beyond medical treatments to medieval life in general, and that blunder was hygiene or rather a lack thereof. Smelling bad and being dirty are unpleasant enough, but it is the unseen things that make personal hygiene so important. Germs can easily spread like wildfire in a society where no one uses soap, and the chances of any type of infection are significantly higher.

The lack of self-cleaning wasn't the only problem, though. Society as a whole had some hygiene issues. Waste was not properly disposed of and could easily contaminate rivers and other sources of drinking water. Drinking water was so likely to make a person sick that most people in medieval England drank ale as their regular drink instead.

With no knowledge of germs, medieval people did not understand the need for sanitation. Although germ theory would not enter the scene until the 19th century, the people of medieval England started to clean up their act sooner thanks to one of the most infamous diseases to ever exist: the Black Death.

Chapter 16: The Black Death

As we come to the end of our walk through medieval England, we have to close with something that both helped to make the Middle Ages infamous and helped to end them. The Black Death swept through and ravaged Europe from 1347 to 1351. Since England was an island and thus more isolated, it did take longer for the plague to reach it, but by 1350, it had reached even the northern end of the British Isles.

The Black Death vs. Plague

Before we dive into the details of the spread, cause, and impact of the Black Death, we need to clarify some terms that can be quite confusing. What is the difference between the Black Death and the plague?

Plague does not refer to an outbreak of any deadly disease. The term plague refers specifically to the disease caused by the bacterium *Yersinia pestis*. It is a disease that exists primarily in rodents and is passed to humans through contact with fleas that have bitten infected rodents. Plague still exists today, especially in areas with large rodent populations that harbor the disease. There have been outbreaks of plague as late as the 20th century, but thanks to modern medicine, especially antibiotics, plague is no longer a serious threat to human life.

The Black Death, on the other hand, refers to a specific outbreak of plague in Europe from 1347 to 1351. This was not the only outbreak of the plague to occur. It is the second recorded pandemic of the plague, but it was by far the deadliest. Plague is the disease, while the Black

Death is a particular plague pandemic of the 14th century.

Spread

The Black Death came to Europe from Asia, and its spread is considered by many to be the first and also most devastating act of biological warfare. The Mongol army under Kipchak khan Janibeg laid siege to Kaffa (which is modern-day Feodosiya) in Crimea in 1346. Because the city of Kaffa (also spelled Caffa) had sea access, the Mongol army found it very difficult to force the city to surrender, although conditions in the city deteriorated quickly because of the siege.

The long siege kept the Mongol army in place for a long period, and the plague, which the army already carried, spread throughout the army. After around a year, the siege was far from the Mongols' biggest worry. The plague was wiping out the army, but Janibeg thought of one way to turn the situation to his advantage. The Mongol army used catapults to fling the corpses of those who had died from the plague into the city of Kaffa. In the cramped and dirty conditions of a besieged city, the result was inevitable. Kaffa, like the Mongol army on its doorstep, was brought to its knees by the disease. Tradition says that four boats attempted to flee Kaffa and sailed for Italy, and it was from these four boats that the plague spread to Europe.

This is a pretty dramatic version of events, but how accurate is it? This understanding of the plague's origins comes from a manuscript written by Gabriele de' Mussi of Piacenza. It was written only a year or two after the events it describes, and although de' Mussi may not have seen the events himself, he likely had access to eyewitnesses. Thus, it seems likely that we can trust his account.

However, there are a few things that may not be entirely accurate about this version of events, and it is surprisingly not the invention of biological warfare. That is entirely plausible. What we are less sure of is the idea that the plague spread to Europe entirely through the survivors of the siege of Kaffa. There were several other routes that probably had a hand in taking the disease from Asia to Europe as well. There were both overland and sea trade routes between the infected areas and Europe that likely also contributed to the spread.

What we do know is that the plague hit Italy first and then spread northward. England managed to escape infestation for around a year, but sometime in the summer of 1348, a ship carrying the disease landed at

Melcombe Regis in Dorset. It didn't take long to spread, and London was facing the pandemic before the end of the year. By 1350, the plague had reached even the northernmost part of Scotland.

This rapid spread is a large part of just what made the plague so destructive. It ran through the continent in an unstoppable march that left massive amounts of death in its wake. How exactly did it spread, though?

By now, the story of the rats and the fleas is almost legendary. Rats infected with the plague moved from location to location aboard ships. These infested rats were then bitten by fleas, and the fleas then bit people; thus, the Black Death swept through Europe.

That much is true, but the rats and fleas may not have been the only way the plague spread. Once humans became infected, it might have also passed more directly from person to person or from person to flea without the need for the rat hosts. The story of the catapulted corpses at Kaffa certainly confirms that the plague could be spread without the need for rats, but the rats did play a large role.

Cause

So, we know how the Black Death spread, but what caused it in the first place? At the time, there were a lot of theories. Some said that the plague was a punishment from God. Others believed that the plague was spread through bad smells. However, the most harmful belief for the cause of the plague was that the Jews were responsible.

Jews were thought to be less affected by the plague than Christians, and this might have been partially true because Jews often practiced better hygiene than medieval Christians due to their religious rituals. The idea spread that Jews had poisoned wells in major cities, making them the source of the plague. Jews were massacred, particularly in German-speaking areas. England did not participate in this antisemitic violence, but that was only because all the Jews had been expelled from England fifty years early with Edward I's Edict of Expulsion.

Needless to say, the plague was not caused by Jews, nor by bad smells, so what did cause it? Today, we know that the Black Death was caused by the bacterium *Yersinia pestis*, which can still cause plague today. *Yersinia pestis* is carried by resistant rats, which carry the plague but are not killed by it, and then passed to other species, including people, by fleas. The overall lack of hygiene in the Middle Ages meant that both rats and fleas were in abundance pretty much everywhere, so there was little they could do to halt the plague's spread.

Symptoms and Types of Plague

We have talked about how it started and what caused it, but what was the Black Death like? It's a very dramatic name, but did the sickness live up to it? In truth, the name does not even begin to cover how horrible the plague was.

You may have heard the plague also referred to as the bubonic plague, and that is because there are three forms that the plague could take, depending on the strain of *Y. pestis* that caused it. Bubonic plague was by far the most common, but all three were present during the Black Death, and they caused different symptoms.

- Bubonic Plague - This was the most common form of plague. It caused massive swelling of the lymph nodes. The swellings were known as buboes, and they occurred around the neck, groin, and armpits. They were around the size of eggs, oozed pus, and were incredibly painful. The buboes were not the only symptom of the plague. There was also a high fever, nausea, aching joints, and just generally feeling awful. Most people who contracted bubonic plague were dead within a week, and it is believed to have had around a 70 percent mortality rate. What makes matters worse is that bubonic plague was the least deadly form the plague took.

Image of people with bubonic plague
https://commons.wikimedia.org/wiki/File:Peste_bubonique_-_enluminure.jpg

- Pneumatic Plague - At some point, another strain of the disease appeared, and this version was airborne. It attacked the lungs first, and the survival rate was virtually nonexistent. The more positive estimates place the mortality rate of pneumatic plague at around 90 percent to 95 percent. Today, the pneumatic plague is considered to be the most dangerous because it can be spread easily from person to person.

- Septicaemic Plague - You might have thought things couldn't get worse, but the plague had one final form that was even more deadly in the Middle Ages. Septicaemic plague infects the bloodstream and is spread through the bite of an infected insect. It can occur on its own or develop due to bubonic plague. Because it is in the blood, it spreads the plague throughout the entire body, causing skin and other tissue to die and turn black. Some believe that this may be where the name Black Death originated, but we don't know for sure. Body parts like fingers and toes could even fall off. It was essentially blood poisoning, and in the Middle Ages, it killed everyone who got it. The mortality rate was 100 percent, maybe 99 percent if you want to be positive. Luckily, this was the rarest form of plague.

Whatever form of plague you got, your chances of survival ranged from practically nonexistent to extremely low. Your only real hope was to avoid contracting the disease.

The plague was an indiscriminate killer. It didn't care if you were rich or poor. Even royalty was not safe. In 1348, Joan, the daughter of Edward III, contracted the plague and died at the age of thirteen. Still, those who could afford to were able to lock themselves away in rural estates where they did have a better chance of avoiding the disease.

Treatment

So, was there anything that could be done for those suffering from the plague? Doctors did attempt to treat patients, but there was simply no cure, and it was highly dangerous for the doctors themselves. The gear doctors wore to protect themselves has since become an easily recognizable costume. Plague doctors wore a mask with a long beak that resembled a bird and glass holes for their eyes. The beak held things like flowers and herbs because it was believed that the disease spread through smell. Doctors also wore long coats and gloves and used a cane to examine patients to protect themselves. The outfit was completed with a brimmed hat that was the sign of their profession. Plague doctors got their start during the Black Death, but the iconic outfit as we know it today probably wasn't completely developed until later outbreaks of the plague.

Plague doctor
https://commons.wikimedia.org/wiki/File:Paul_F%C3%BCrst,_Der_Doctor_Schnabel_von_Rom_(Holl%C3%A4nder_version).png

The lack of an actual cure did not stop people from trying several bizarre things. One method was to pluck a live chicken and place the chicken against the buboes of the infected person. The idea was that the chicken would draw the sickness out of the person and into itself. Another method was eating or drinking crushed emeralds. There were several different potions and mixtures that claimed to cure the plague, and people even drank urine. Some sought more spiritual cures. There was the standard prayer and fasting, but people also practiced public flagellation (whipping themselves) because they believed that the plague was the result of God's wrath.

The only treatments that might have been somewhat successful were running away and quarantine. Those who fled the town and cities stood a chance of avoiding the plague altogether, but they also often succeeded in spreading it. Quarantine might have put a halt to the plague's rapid spread, but it was impossible to enforce. People did not understand what was causing the plague, so their attempts to treat it were focused on incorrect assumptions and information.

Death Toll

We know that the Black Death was horrible, but just how bad was it? Over four years, the plague killed twenty-five million people in Europe, which was around 40 percent of the entire population (although some estimates go as low as 30 and as high as 60 percent). England itself faced a similar death rate, with between 30 to 40 percent of people dying. That's just looking at Europe, though. The plague started in Asia and also spread to Africa, where the death rates were similar.

To put things in perspective, let's look at some more recent tragedies in human history. World War II was the deadliest military conflict in history, with anywhere from thirty million to sixty million deaths caused by the war worldwide. The Black Death killed about twenty-five million in Europe alone, which is close to the lower estimate for World War II. Still, comparing the numbers directly like this doesn't offer a full comparison of how deadly the two events were. Remember that the total population in the 1940s was far greater than it was in the 14th century. Percentages tell a clearer story. In World War II, the countries hit the hardest lost around 20 percent of their population, with most countries losing far less than that. The Black Death's impact was double that at around 40 percent and spread far more evenly across all of Europe.

Another way to understand just how bad the Black Death was is to compare it to other epidemics. The Spanish influenza pandemic of 1918 killed around fifty million people across the globe. If we include Asia and Africa, the Black Death may have had a similar or higher death count. However, again, percentages paint a clearer picture. Spanish influenza killed close to 3 percent of the world population. The Black Death killed 40 percent; even the lower estimate of 5 percent (which seems unlikely) is higher. In terms of deadliness, almost nothing else comes close.

If you want to understand the deadliness of the plague, you also need to remember that the Black Death refers to only a single outbreak of the plague from around 1347 to 1351. That single outbreak killed between a third and a half of the population of an entire continent. It's hard to find a catastrophe that even comes close to the Black Death.

Impact

Death on such a massive scale has far-reaching consequences, and the Black Death's impact was subsequently enormous.

The first impact was on medical knowledge. Medieval doctors had relied on ancient knowledge with ideas about the humors and the importance of the positions of the planets, but the Black Death shattered many of those conceptions. The plague refused to retreat with any of the treatments that medieval physicians tried, and the need for more medical knowledge became clear. The Black Death was thus a push to begin expanding medical knowledge, which was a big change in mindset from the traditionally medieval "people are sick because God wills it" approach.

The Black Death impacted religious attitudes beyond that as well. The plague was understandably viewed by many as possibly heralding the end of the world. Half of the people living in some cities and even entire villages were wiped out. Under such circumstances, an increase in religious piety and interest is only natural. At the same time, the Catholic Church was weakened by the loss of so many of its clergy. People were more interested in religion, while the church in Rome had less of a death grip. More colleges and universities sprang up but with stronger national rather than papal ties. This was the beginning of a process that would eventually lead to the Reformation. The absolute power and unity of the medieval church were at an end.

The Black Death also had an impact on the societal structure. With almost half the population suddenly gone, there were no longer enough workers. Large areas of previously cultivated lands fell into disuse, which was a serious blow to the wealthy landowners who owned them. The labor shortage gave the peasants who had not died leverage they had never had before. The demand for workers was higher than the supply, and for the first time, landowners were offering better wages and conditions to try to entice workers. The feudal system was seriously shaken.

The feudal system and overall social hierarchy of medieval England were also struck by the plague in another way. Since the plague killed both the elites and peasants alike, everyone was suddenly on a more equal footing. If the Black Death was God's wrath, then His wrath had descended on everyone. Peasants began to have a new awareness of their rights and dignity.

Peasants who survived the plague also began to experience better living. Not only were they being paid more, but taxes also went down. The destruction of 40 percent of the population also created a surplus of goods, which drove down the prices of everything. So, peasants had more money, and everything was cheaper. People were able to buy things that they had never been able to afford before and enjoy a new standard of living.

The changes in the lives of the lower classes are hard to overstate. It was only around thirty years after the Black Death that England experienced its first popular uprising: the Peasants' Revolt of 1381. The Black Death effectively broke the iconic feudal system of the Middle Ages, and for that reason, many people consider it to be the event that ended the medieval period.

Conclusion

That's the basic story of medieval England. The Black Death was the event that started the ball rolling toward the end by destroying the basic structure of medieval life, and we use the Battle of Bosworth and the end of the Plantagenet dynasty as a more distinct line in the sand for the end of medieval England. However, placing history into eras like this, while it certainly makes studying them more convenient, does create a sense of separation that doesn't exist in reality. The medieval period is not strictly confined between the borders of 600 and 1485. While it may feel like ancient history, things that happened in medieval England were crucial in shaping the world as we know it today.

We think of the Middle Ages and feudalism as a highly oppressive time, where the rich exploited the poor and where human rights were virtually nonexistent. This is, to a large degree, true, but medieval England was also the place where much of our understanding of human rights got started. The Magna Carta of 1212 is one of the most important documents in the history of democracy, for it was there for the first time that rules were set out to protect people from their own government. Around 150 years after the Magna Carta, England saw its first popular uprising in the Peasants' Revolt of 1381. What the barons had realized in their fights against the king, the general population now understood. They could make demands. They were human beings with dignity that should not be ignored by those above them. It was thus *during* the Middle Ages that people first began to get a real sense of their basic rights and to fight for them. The Renaissance often gets credit for developing the ideas that became central to our modern world, but it was in the Middle Ages that the necessary shifts in attitude began. Who knows where human rights and democracy would be today if not for the changes in mindset that took place in the medieval period?

That is far from the only way in which the medieval period has shaped our world. The wars and battles of the Middle Ages formed nations and governments. The Viking invasions pushed England into a unified nation. The Scottish Wars of Independence assured the independence of Scotland for another four hundred years, which would prove to have an enormous impact on English and Scottish history. King John's losses put an end to England's claim to lands that would become France. The map of England and Europe that we know today was in many ways drawn in the blood spilled in the Middle Ages.

Perhaps the most subtle impact of the Middle Ages has been in culture. Stories from the Middle Ages like the Arthurian legend, Beowulf, and a myriad of fairy tales continue to be told and retold in the present day. Buildings, especially churches, from the period still stand and are even used today. Games like chess and backgammon were introduced to the West in this era.

Finally, we cannot end the book without looking at how the medieval church has shaped our modern world. Whether you are a Christian or not, if you live in the Western world, you have been greatly affected by Christianity. It's hard to talk about almost any aspect of the Middle Ages without mentioning the church. It influenced everything from art, architecture, and literature to philosophy, law, and the very rhythm of life. The holidays we celebrate, the fact that we tend not to work on Sunday, hospitals, schools, and so many more aspects of daily life got started by the medieval church. The medieval church produced scholars and poets, started universities, and preserved manuscripts from the ancient world. Love it or hate it, Western civilization owes much of what it is to the medieval church.

There's a lot that people get wrong about medieval England. As we said at the very beginning of this journey, medieval England was neither as glamorous nor as horrendous as we often paint it. However, perhaps the thing we get most wrong is the idea that it was an entirely separate time. The modern world would not exist without the changes and developments that took place in the Middle Ages. The people who lived then may not have been as different from us as we think.

Part 3: The House of Tudor

An Enthralling Overview of the History of the Tudors

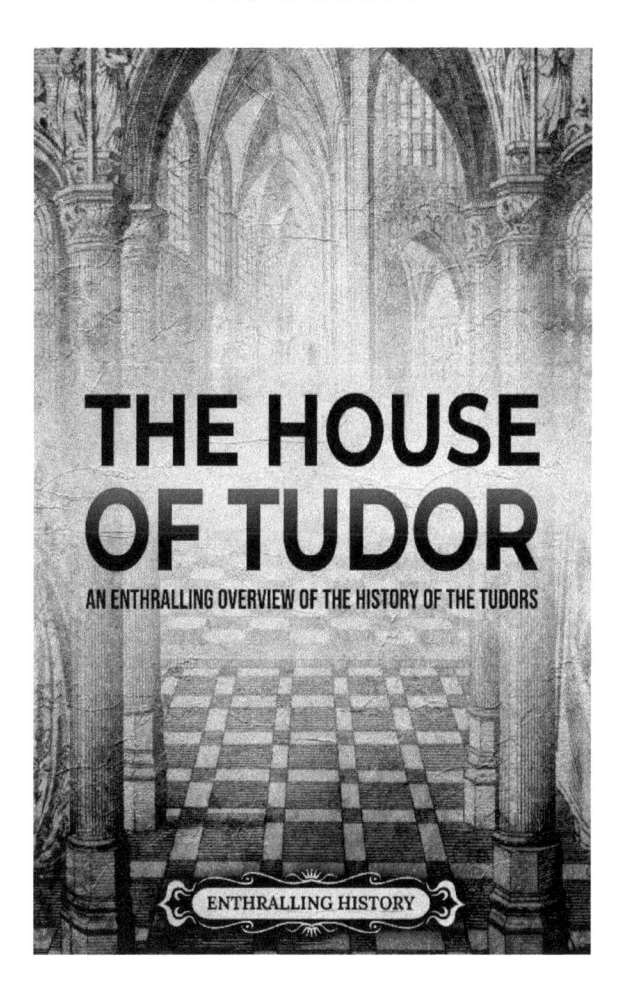

Introduction

The House of Tudor is arguably England's most famous ruling dynasty. In the wake of the Wars of the Roses, the country was divided and wartorn since its leaders had been fighting against each other for control. For decades, the most prominent families in England vied for the throne and found themselves split between the House of York and the House of Lancaster. The mighty Plantagenet dynasty had come to a nasty end, and someone needed to take control. With legitimate heirs to the throne on both sides of the war, England was ravaged by ambitious and powerful individuals.

Finally, at the Battle of Bosworth Field, a victor emerged and claimed his crown on the battlefield. Henry Tudor became Henry VII, and England would never be the same again. Along with his tight-knit council, he ruled England and navigated his country through the aftermath of one of the bloodiest civil wars in its history. While Henry's rule ushered in a new period of peace, his dynasty became the center of intrigue and political plotting that lasted for generations until the Tudor line ended with his granddaughter, Elizabeth I.

This comprehensive guide to the fascinating Tudor family discusses the origins of the royal house, whose roots were founded in Wales and France. The first part of the book delves into what events led to Henry VII being crowned on the battlefield. It will explore interesting topics such as the fall of the Plantagenet dynasty and the origin of the Tudor line. After establishing the foundation of the House of Tudor, an explanation of the Tudors' rise to power will be provided.

Once the Tudors secured the throne, four more Tudors would take the throne in less than fifty years, with the family line ending with Elizabeth I. The second part of the book is dedicated to discovering more about the Tudor rulers. Each chapter outlines the lives and influences of those monarchs. The Tudor family was deeply divided, and each member of the family had their own agenda. Henry VII had two male heirs, but when his firstborn son, Arthur, died, a new heir had to be primed for the throne. Henry VIII wasn't born to be king, but he found himself as the heir to the English throne when he was only a boy. He was trained under his father and received the best education in the world, but by the end of his reign, he was seen as a tyrant with a murderous reputation. While three of the Tudor monarchs were siblings, they had wildly different policies and ideals.

The Tudor dynasty was built on war and sacrifice, which means that Tudor history features some of the most famous English battles. Starting with the Wars of the Roses and ending with "Elizabeth Gloriana," the third part of the book will discuss the battles that helped to define the Tudor line. Besides discussing famous battles, there are chapters dedicated to discussing the Tudors' military and weapons that helped them win vital battles, as well as the failures that contributed to some catastrophic losses.

Finally, life during the Tudor dynasty wasn't always easy. Henry VII inherited a throne that was weakened by wars and a treasury that reflected the devastation of those wars. Henry VIII was a changeable king who led his people through religious and political turmoil, most of which he personally caused. His children were religiously divided, and his male heir was little more than a child who was used to promoting the ideals of his advisors. When he died, his half-sister, Mary I, seized the throne and decided to reform the country. She earned the title "Bloody Mary" and caused more religious turmoil. Finally, Elizabeth I took the throne, and while she was a more popular leader, her rule wasn't always peaceful. While the Tudor monarchs and their courts are a continuous source of fascination, the common people were intensely impacted by the whims of these monarchs. The final section of this book reveals what life was like for the subjects of the Tudor dynasty and discusses social factors such as religion, education, and art.

The Tudor dynasty was marked by some of the most significant periods in English history, and this book organizes those events in a simple format. It features accurate information that explains the religious, political, and social factors that made the House of Tudor unique. Discover personal profiles about some of the most famous rulers in history, and get to know the dynamic individuals who built and ended the Tudor dynasty.

The Tudors were one of the most intriguing ruling families in history, and this book brings their struggles and triumphs to life.

Section One:
England before the House of Tudor

Chapter 1: England before the Tudors

The Tudor family had a lasting effect on English history and ushered in a new era. However, before they came to the throne, Britain was ruled by a powerful family known as the Plantagenets. The Plantagenets were a fascinating family that ruled England for about three hundred years and produced fourteen kings. Their triumphs and struggles shaped the country and would have a lasting impact that the Tudors had to deal with when they took the throne.

The Plantagenet kings were bold, dynamic, and powerful. They also fought viciously amongst themselves for control of the country. Some of the Plantagenet kings were legendary and greatly beloved by their citizens, while some of them were so brutal or ineffective that they caused widespread revolts. Understanding the effect that the Plantagenets had on England will help modern readers understand why the Tudors made certain decisions and what challenges they faced when they established a new dynasty.

The Plantagenets

The Plantagenet family was founded in Anjou, France. The name Plantagenet began as a nickname for Geoffrey, Count of Anjou, in the 12th century. The Plantagenets became viable contenders for the English throne during a violent time in English history known as the Anarchy. The Anarchy was a vicious civil war that nearly tore England apart. In

1120, Henry I's only son died when his ship sank. King Henry I decided that he would make his daughter, Matilda, his heir, but this was a difficult process. She became known as Empress Matilda, but much of the nobility opposed her succession. When Henry I died in 1135, his nephew, Stephen Blois, claimed the crown. This would eventually lead to the Anarchy, which lasted from 1138 to 1153. Empress Matilda and Stephen fought bitterly while the country descended into chaos. At that time, the country was controlled by barons who fought each other and grabbed power while Matilda and Stephen were otherwise occupied. Many people died, and packs of mercenaries bullied farmers and villagers.

Before the war, Empress Matilda married Geoffrey Plantagenet, Count of Anjou, and the two had a son, Henry. King Stephen also had a son named Eustace. Both sides fought to gain the throne for their sons. While Stephen fought against rebellious barons, the Welsh, and the Scots, he also had to deal with Matilda's multiple invasions. In time, Stephen controlled the southeast of England, Matilda controlled the southwest, and wealthy barons fought each other for the rest of England.

In 1143, Geoffrey conquered Normandy for Matilda. The war continued, and by 1150, even the power-hungry barons were tired of war. By that time, Matilda's son, who became known as Henry FitzEmpress, had invaded England. Stephen's son, Eustace, had died, and Stephen didn't have an heir. The church stepped in and negotiated the Treaty of Wallingford, which allowed Stephen to keep his throne but made Henry his successor. Both parties agreed to the truce, but Stephen didn't live long enough to enjoy the peace that the truce created. He died in 1154, which made Henry the king of England.

Henry II

Henry was born in 1133, and although his mother's claim to the throne was dismissed, he was still raised to become the next king of England. He married Eleanor of Aquitaine, who had been married to King Louis VII of France. She was a beautiful woman who would help him rule his territories effectively, and they made a formidable couple. When his father died in 1151, he became the duke of Normandy and the count of Anjou. He proceeded to invade England to claim his birthright and defeated the barons who refused to support him or give up their power. Thanks to the Treaty of Wallingford, he became King Stephen's heir, and in 1154, he inherited England and other territories,

including Wales and Scotland.
1. Henry II

https://commons.wikimedia.org/wiki/File:King_Henry_II_England.jpg

Henry was a natural leader who inspired men to fight for him, but he could be merciless when it was necessary. As soon as he was king, he began improving England and led the country as it recovered from the brutal years of the Anarchy. For years, the country had been terrorized by war, and it needed serious reformation. Henry quickly put administrative systems in place and reformed the judicial system. He increased England's borders through warfare as well as through diplomacy. He arranged suitable marriages for his children, and he gained territory in Castile, Sicily, Germany, and Normandy. While Henry II was a great king who led his country through difficult times, he was also a controlling and often insensitive man. This led to serious personal problems that led to serious consequences for his reign.

The first personal fight involved one of his closest advisors. Thomas Becket was Henry's trusted friend, and he proved to be a capable leader. Henry sought to control the church in England but needed someone who would be on his side to accomplish that goal. Thomas had already proved his worth several times before, so Henry helped Thomas become the archbishop of Canterbury in May 1162. Unfortunately, Thomas and Henry disagreed on several matters, and this led to a fight between the two. Thomas chose to be exiled, which was a serious inconvenience for Henry. Their feud ended tragically on December 29th, 1170, when Thomas Becket was murdered in Canterbury Cathedral by four knights. Henry was blamed for the murder, and he faced backlash from the church and his subjects.

During his reign, he had eight children with Eleanor: William, Henry, Geoffrey, Richard, John, Matilda, Eleanor, and Joan. Unfortunately, Henry, William, and Geoffrey died while they were still quite young. Thomas Becket's murder was exacerbated when Henry's own sons rebelled against him. The rebellion was backed by Eleanor of Aquitaine, King Louis VII of France, and King William, the Lion of Scotland. Henry managed to suppress the rebellion in 1174 and pardoned his sons. However, Eleanor wasn't pardoned; she was kept in custody until her husband died. His troubles were far from over, as another rebellion broke out in 1181 between his sons Richard and John. Richard later allied himself with the king of France against Henry II in 1189. This rebellion broke Henry, and he stepped aside so his son could take the throne. Henry II died in 1189 with the knowledge that his sons were united against him and his wife was still in custody.

While his personal life was a mess, Henry II was a good king who managed to reform an almost broken country. Today, he is seen as a capable ruler.

Richard the Lionheart

Richard was Henry II's and Eleanor of Aquitaine's third son, and he was born in September 1157. He was known for being an impressive knight and politician. Due to his military successes during the Third Crusade, he inspired several myths and became known as a romantic hero. His early life was marked by rebellion, as he and his brothers repeatedly rebelled against their father. He ruled Gascony and Poitou from a young age, and he was known for being a brutal leader. The Gascons tried to expel Richard from the duchy, but the rebellion failed when Richard's brother, Henry, died in 1183.

2. Richard I (Richard the Lionheart)

https://commons.wikimedia.org/wiki/File:Merry-Joseph_Blondel_-_Richard_I_the_Lionheart.jpg

As Henry II's heir, Richard stood to inherit England, Normandy, and Anjou. For much of his reign, Henry II struggled to assign his sons' inheritances, and his decisions were often met with rebellion. When Richard became Henry's heir, Henry asked Richard to give Aquitaine to John. Richard refused and made an alliance with King Philip II of France. In 1189, they led another force against Henry. The rebellion was successful, and Richard was named Henry's heir.

Although Richard had fought to become the king of England, he showed no real interest in ruling his kingdom and instead set his sights on joining the Third Crusade. As soon as he became king, he began selling government positions, land, and other assets to raise an army. In 1190, he set sail for the Holy Land. While en route to the Crusade, he stopped in Sicily and helped to negotiate the Treaty of Messina, which made Tancred of Lecce the king of Sicily. However, this offended the Germans. Richard also married Berengaria of Navarre, but their relationship was a formal one. They had no children together.

While Richard experienced great victories in the Holy Land, he was unable to capture Jerusalem. He also fought with other European leaders, including Leopold V, Duke of Austria, and Philip II. After securing a truce with Saladin in the Holy Land in 1192, Richard decided to go home. Unfortunately, the offenses that he caused in the Holy Land had disastrous results when his ship was driven off course. He found himself in Vienna. Duke Leopold captured him and eventually handed him over to Henry VI, the Holy Roman emperor. Henry VI imposed a heavy ransom on Richard of 150,000 marks. England was prospering at the time, so Richard was able to pay most of the ransom and return to his kingdom.

He returned to England on April 17th, 1194, and was crowned again. This was likely due to the fact that his brother, John, had been slowly usurping the throne in his absence. However, Richard didn't remain in England for very long and left for Normandy the next month. He wouldn't return from Normandy, though; he died due to a battle wound in 1199. Richard died without an heir, and his younger brother, John, succeeded him.

The Magna Carta

For years before Richard I died, John had tried to usurp the throne. As Henry I's youngest son, John was likely used to being overlooked when it came to receiving a fair inheritance. When Richard died without any heirs, John was able to seize the throne, but he was in a precarious position. Unlike his older brother, he wasn't an accomplished warrior, and his people were unhappy because of the taxes that had been imposed on them during Richard's reign.

John also failed to provide his barons and clergy with a general charter of their rights when he ascended to the throne. Starting with William the Conqueror, the kings of England always gave their barons and clergy promises of goodwill and granted them certain rights. This ensured that the nobility and the church stayed on the king's side. Since John neglected this serious duty, the barons began revolting early on in his reign. He faced another disaster when he lost Normandy in 1204. John began taxing his people more harshly to make up for the loss. This outraged his people, and he went further by taxing the church relentlessly. His mistreatment of the church was so serious that he was excommunicated in 1209.

Facing widespread rebellion, John was forced to negotiate a charter with the nobility. The fact that the nobility was willing to meet with the king was incredible because most of them wanted to fight for their rights, but William Marshal, Earl of Pembroke, managed to gather the most important members of the nobility. In 1215, John signed the Articles of the Barons, which met most of the barons' demands and curbed some of his power. By agreeing to their demands, John effectively avoided another civil war. While this document helped avoid an immediate civil war, further discussions were needed to satisfy the barons. Later that year, John signed the Charter of Liberties, which became known as the Magna Carta.

The Magna Carta had to be reissued three more times in 1216, 1217, and 1225. It was refined, and sections were added over the years, but the main purpose of the charter was to establish feudal law. The Magna Carta was also a symbolic document because it gave people hope and power to fight against oppression. It had a lasting effect on English history, and some of its clauses were later used to govern English colonies.

England vs. France

When Henry II ascended the English throne, he brought a lot of French territory with him, including the Duchy of Normandy and the Aquitaine lands. This land was passed on to his successors, but it was also a source of contention between England and France. While Henry II's sons were able to hold onto that land for a while, much of it was eventually lost when Philip II of France and Richard I fought for control. Richard I was able to keep his inherited lands, but his successor wasn't able to hold onto the lands for very long. In 1202, John lost Normandy and its surroundings to Philip II.

John didn't give up that easily, though. In 1213, he went to war against France. In 1214, Pope Innocent III formed an anti-France alliance, which John quickly joined. The English forces and their allies met Philip

II at the Battle of Bouvines, where England was defeated. From there, France conquered Flanders, and much of England's continental lands were lost. It was a devastating blow, one that John wouldn't recover from, and he stopped trying to regain the lands his predecessors had used to make England rich.

It did not, however, end the conflict between England and France, as the House of Plantagenet would not give up on their Angevin lands that easily. The two countries had a long and contentious history, and the Battle of Bouvines wouldn't be the last time that England and France met on the battlefield. The wars between the two countries had a disastrous impact on ordinary people, as they had to give up sons to become soldiers, were taxed mercilessly, and had to deal with armies marching through their lands and farms. The residents who lived in Angevin lands had to deal with upheaval since they were usually caught in the middle of the conflicts.

Edward I

While the Magna Carta was supposed to establish feudal law, John mostly ignored the charter. He was a widely unpopular king. When he died, his son, Henry, inherited a country that was on the brink of civil war. He was largely considered to be an ineffectual king, and his reign was riddled with problems. King John treated his barons terribly, which led to the Barons' Wars, which Henry was able to resolve, but he also suffered many losses on the battlefield. His military failures caused him to impose harsh taxes on his people, but they rebelled against him. He was taken prisoner by Simon de Montfort in 1264. In 1265, Henry III was rescued by his son, Edward. Once Henry III was freed, he took an interest in architecture and allowed his son to take over many of his duties.

As a young man, Edward I gained a reputation for being a harsh ruler and was known for having a violent temper. However, he was born to be a king and displayed many noble qualities. He was so tall that he gained the nickname "Longshanks," and he proved to be a capable warrior when he strengthened his father's rule and defeated Wales. Unlike King John, he upheld the Magna Carta and spent a lot of time securing his rule in England. He built several magnificent castles and joined the Crusades for some time. While he was a prince, he married Eleanor of Castile. The couple had four sons and eleven daughters together. When she died, he built twelve monuments in her honor.

3. Edward I

https://commons.wikimedia.org/wiki/File:Edward_I_-_Westminster_Abbey_Sedilia.jpg

While he was a good English king, he was also an ambitious man and set his sights on Scotland. Unfortunately for him, the Scots proved difficult to subdue, and his actions caused friction between the two countries that would endure long after he had died. His attacks on Scotland earned him the nickname "Hammer of the Scots." He died on July 7th, 1307, while en route to Scotland and was succeeded by his son, Edward II.

Edward I left England in a relatively strong position, but his heir proved to be a spectacular failure. He seemed more interested in spending time with his friends than ruling his country. He essentially allowed his kingdom to fall into chaos. In 1314, Edward II was defeated by Robert the Bruce at the Battle of Bannockburn, effectively shattering Edward I's hope of conquering Scotland. In 1327, his wife, Isabella of France, forced him to abdicate. Edward II was imprisoned by his wife and her lover, Roger Mortimer. The king was later murdered, and historians suspect that Isabella and Roger were guilty of regicide.

King Arthur and the Impact of Chivalry

By the 12th century, the legend of King Arthur had a massive impact on England's overall culture. The literature of the period created the idea of a chivalrous knight who was a hero and only used his weapons to defend the helpless. The ideal knight was also a poet and a musician. The literature also included the concept of courtly love, which was an intricate social practice that was emphasized by chivalry. A hero could only win over his lady love if he was a man of exceptional courtesy, sportsmanship, generosity, and poetry.

The legend of Lancelot, one of King Arthur's knights, exemplified chivalry. Lancelot was known for being the greatest knight, with all other knights seeking to imitate him. He was a kind man who never lost control, except when it came to his true love, Queen Guinevere. Their relationship is also an example of how popular tragedies were during this period. Lancelot and Guinevere were doomed lovers, and this fact made their story incredibly popular.

Medieval knights were an important part of the social hierarchy. Knights were sworn to lords and were sworn to uphold the Knights Code of Chivalry. The code was supposed to ensure that knights would always protect the helpless, but many knights simply ignored the code. Knights would fight for their lords in battles and took part in tournaments. Tournaments were essentially war games that included jousts and group combat. Sometimes, the fighting became so fierce that men died. In time, tournaments became fairs that included entertainment such as dancing and feasting.

Medieval England was a dangerous place. While knights were supposed to protect the general population, they often took advantage of times of chaos and anarchy to bully the local countryside. While chivalry was a popular concept, many people died brutally and were subject to the violent tempers of the Plantagenet kings. In time, the Plantagenet dynasty would come to an end but not before the Hundred Years' War with France and the brutal Wars of the Roses. The Tudors were nearly extinguished during those chaotic years, but due to the actions of a few shrewd individuals, the Wars of the Roses would end with a Tudor on the throne.

Chapter 2: The Origins of the House of Tudor

The House of Tudor was a noble house with ties to the Welsh, French, and English royal families. It was uniquely situated to take hold of the English crown, but several things needed to happen before its claim could be considered legitimate. When the family was founded, no one could have imagined the heights that would be achieved by their descendants. The Tudor dynasty began in Wales in a village named Penmynydd. From the beginning, the family was involved in politics, but they were mostly involved in local matters and Welsh state of affairs. While the family eventually split into different branches, the most prominent branch descended from a Welsh courtier named Owen Tudor, who captured the heart of a queen.

To fully understand how the Tudors rose to power, it is important to understand how the mighty House of Plantagenet fell apart. While the Plantagenets had risen to dizzying heights under Henry II, their lineage weakened through the rule of weak and ineffectual kings. The Plantagenets were famous for their stubborn and violent tempers. The great kings either overcame their tempers or used their passion to motivate them. However, weaker kings indulged in petty vices and brought the kingdom to the brink of destruction. While matters looked bleak for the Plantagenets after the disastrous reign of Edward II, another great king was on the horizon. Edward III would usher in another age of prosperity for the Plantagenets, but his death would effectively rip the dynasty apart, paving the way for the Tudors to take the English throne.

Edward III

Edward III inherited a country that had slipped into chaos. After all, his mother had become his father's greatest enemy (and possible murderer). He didn't have the easiest upbringing or succession, but Edward III went on to accomplish great things. Edward was able to unify the barons and strengthen the country. However, his rule was also beset by problems, such as the Hundred Years' War with France, the Black Plague, and a corrupt government influenced by his thieving mistress, Alice Perrers.

4. King Edward III

https://commons.wikimedia.org/wiki/File:King_Edward_III_from_NPG.jpg

Edward III was born in 1312 in Windsor Castle, but he spent most of his childhood in France with his mother since his parents had a strained relationship. While in France, Isabella took to wearing black, declaring that her marriage with her husband was dead. She took a lover named Roger Mortimer. Together, they plotted to take the throne from Edward II, who was extremely unpopular in England. In October 1326, Isabella and Roger invaded England, and Edward II was forced to abdicate early the next year. Edward III was crowned at fourteen years of age, but his mother and Roger Mortimer acted as his regents.

The couple planned on ruling England through the boy and began enriching themselves as soon as he was coronated. However, Edward III had different plans. In 1330, he had Roger Mortimer imprisoned in the Tower of London, where he was later executed for treason. Isabella was imprisoned in Norfolk. Edward III began ruling in earnest with his wife, Philippa of Hainault, and the pair had thirteen children. Their oldest son, Edward, became a famous knight who won many victories in France. Together, father and son gained incredible glory for their kingdom. England's future seemed bright, especially since the two established a new era of chivalry.

Edward III proved to be a good warrior and revived the military aspirations of previous English kings. He fought against David II of Scotland, but in 1336, he turned his attention to France. In the 1330s, Edward III boldly claimed the right to inherit the French throne. Since his mother belonged to the French royal family, he had the right to inherit the throne through her, but the French didn't recognize his claim since they preferred to recognize the patrilineal lineage. So, while Edward was Charles IV's closest living male relative, the French chose to recognize Philip VI as the new king of France. Edward III's claim to the throne led to violent wars between the French and English that lasted for over a century.

Unfortunately, that war led to the death of Edward III's heir, Edward the Black Prince. Edward III ruled for half a century, and his reign led to a golden era that enriched his country. Unfortunately, as he got older, he lost the keen senses that helped him become a great king. Toward the end of his reign, he took a mistress named Alice Perrers. While his health declined, the government began to slip into corruption, which caused Edward to become unpopular among his subjects. The English Parliament decided to clean up the government and identified the main culprits behind the spread of corruption. This decision would lead to serious consequences for Edward III's successors.

However, Edward III wouldn't feel those consequences, as he had a stroke in 1376 and died the following year. He was succeeded by Richard II, who had to fight against his uncle, John of Gaunt, Duke of Lancaster.

The Hundred Years' War

The Hundred Years' War was a brutal and costly war. During it, several English and French kings fought for dominance of the Angevin lands. The war started out relatively simple, pitting Edward III against Philip VI of France. Instead of declaring war outright, Edward III claimed his right to the French throne, which would have prevented the intervention of the church since he had the right to inherit through his mother, Isabella. Philip VI didn't take the claim lightly. In 1340, he sent a fleet of ships to attack England, but he lost most of his ships at Sluys in the Scheldt estuary.

When the two kings met on land, Edward III offered to solve the matter with a duel, which reflected the culture of military chivalry that Edward III upheld. Over the next few years, Edward III gained an advantage in the war. In 1345, English forces captured Gascony, and in 1347, Edward III gained the port of Calais. Philip VI tried to strike back by persuading the Scottish to invade the north of England, which would force Edward III to invade and make him fight on two fronts. The Scottish obliged, but their king, David II, was captured in battle. Later, in the midst of the devastation of the Black Plague, Philip VI's successor, John II, fought against the English but was captured by the Black Prince in battle.

In 1359, Edward III marched to France with the intention of becoming the French king, but his troops were laid low by harsh weather conditions. So, he changed tactics and began negotiating a treaty. The Treaty of Brétigny recognized Edward III's claims to land in France, and Edward III withdrew his claim to the French throne. However, things were far from over. Edward III soon learned that he couldn't hold onto his French lands. His rule was beset by the Black Plague, and John II's successor, Charles V, proved to be a wily enemy who slowly claimed Edward III's lands in France.

Edward III started a war that he wouldn't be able to finish, which eventually drained the English treasury and cost hundreds of thousands of lives. When Edward III died, his successors would continue their father's fight, and it would leave a lasting mark on English history.

The Black Death

The war in France had to be halted when a more serious threat arrived on European shores. The bubonic plague was brought to Europe when ships from the Black Sea docked at Messina in Sicily. Most of the sailors aboard the ships were dead, and the port authorities had no idea what had just hit them. From there, the Black Plague spread like wildfire and killed up to 30 to 50 percent of Europe's population. England wasn't immune, and in 1348, the Black Death struck. Edward III's ambitions had to be put on hold as the plague ripped through his ranks and destroyed his workforce.

The effects were disastrous. Entire families, skilled laborers, and craftsmen all succumbed to the disease. The European economy took a massive dip, and kings had to stop fighting each other to try and save their people. Edward III wasn't immune to the effects of the plague, as his daughter, Joan, died from it. While dealing with personal tragedy, he had to find ways to revive the economy and guide his people through the deadliest pandemic in history. Unfortunately, the Black Death would have lasting consequences on Edward III's efforts to hold onto the lands granted to him in the Treaty of Brétigny. People died quickly due to the plague, and the greatly reduced population meant that it was harder to get soldiers and workers who could advance English interests in France.

It also meant that there were fewer Englishmen to occupy the lands in France and protect themselves from invading French forces. While Edward III and his son, Edward the Black Prince, won massive victories at the beginning of the Hundred Years' War, they were laid low by the sheer devastation of the Black Plague. Europe would never be the same after the Black Death. Millions of people died, and it left destruction in its wake. The impact of the war and the plague were so severe that Edward III was forced to declare bankruptcy in the 1340s. England was able to recover in time, but a new era in Plantagenet history was about to arrive shortly after the death of Edward the Black Prince and Edward III. The mighty House of Plantagenet found itself divided into the House of Lancaster and the House of York, which would eventually spell disaster for the Plantagenet line.

House of Lancaster

The House of Lancaster was founded when Henry III (r. 1216-1272) made his youngest son, Edmund, the earl of Lancaster. Unfortunately, both of Edmund's sons died, which meant that the lands passed to his granddaughters, Maud and Blanche. Maud died soon after her father, and Blanche married John of Gaunt, who was Edward III's son. John had been involved in the corruption scandal that erupted toward the end of Edward III's reign, but he still held a lot of power at court when his nephew became king.

5. House of Lancaster insignia

Sodacan, CC BY-SA 3.0 <https://creativecommons.org/licenses/by-sa/3.0>, via Wikimedia Commons https://commons.wikimedia.org/wiki/File:Red_Rose_Badge_of_Lancaster.svg

When Edward III died, his grandson, Richard II, took the throne. He was only ten years old at the time, and he inherited a crown that was deeply in debt. The government's response was to impose a heavy tax on the people, which led to the Peasants' Revolt a few years after Richard's coronation. Despite his young age, he successfully ended the revolt, but this was likely due to the efforts of his advisors. As Richard's reign continued, he slowly alienated himself from his high-ranking nobles. Meanwhile, the House of Lancaster under John Gaunt, Edward III's son, began gaining power. Richard II eventually became a harsh tyrant who was determined to enhance his own prestige as king.

In 1399, John of Gaunt died, and his son, Henry, deposed Richard II and became King Henry IV. The king merged his Lancastrian inheritance with the throne, and for the next sixty years, England was ruled by the Lancastrians. Henry IV was succeeded by his son, Henry V, who experienced great success in the Hundred Years' War. In 1415, he won the historic Battle of Agincourt, which made him one of the most popular kings in English history. In 1420, he signed the Treaty of Troyes, which named Henry as Charles VI's heir. He married Catherine of Valois, who later went on to marry Owen Tudor.

Henry V's success in the Hundred Years' War locked him and his descendants into further conflicts, especially against the Dauphin Charles, who was Charles VI's original heir. The war in France heated up, and Henry V was forced to join the fighting again in 1422, which was the year he died. Unfortunately for England, Henry V died young. His son, Henry VI, was little more than a baby. Henry VI wasn't as successful as his father, and the French soon gained strong leaders, such as Joan of Arc, which turned the tide against England.

Unlike his father, Henry VI wasn't interested in continuing the war against France, and in 1445, he married Margaret of Anjou. In time, Henry VI became unfit to rule, as he was seized by a mysterious illness that left him unresponsive for over a year. It was during this time that the House of York seized the opportunity to take the throne.

The House of York

The House of York was founded by Edward III's son, Edmund Langley. The first two dukes of York didn't do much but rule their duchy. When Edmund's son, Edward, died without an heir, his assets and title were passed to his nephew, Richard. The new duke of York was related to Edward III's son, Lionel, which gave him a prestigious lineage. Richard set his sights on further glory when Henry VI slipped into madness. During that time, the throne was controlled by Margaret of Anjou.

6. House of York insignia

Sodacan, CC BY-SA 3.0 <https://creativecommons.org/licenses/by-sa/3.0>, via Wikimedia Commons https://commons.wikimedia.org/wiki/File:White_Rose_Badge_of_York.svg

Margaret's rule was largely unpopular, and Richard was a direct descendant of Edward III, which made his claim legitimate. Both the House of Lancaster and the House of York could claim rights to the throne since they could trace their lineage back to Edward III. The House of York had ties to Lionel, Duke of Clarence, who was John of Gaunt's older brother. Meanwhile, the House of Lancaster was directly descended from John of Gaunt. The crown was in a precarious position since the Lancaster king, Henry VI, was weakened by his mysterious illness, and Margaret of Anjou was proving to be an ineffectual regent.

For years, Richard, the 3rd Duke of York, tried to work with Henry VI's government, but he eventually decided to claim the throne. Parliament arranged a compromise in which Henry would remain king, but Richard would inherit the throne when Henry died. Both parties were appeased, and Henry VI accepted the act. However, Margaret of Anjou didn't accept the treaty since it would disinherit her own son. These factors would eventually lead to the Wars of the Roses, which would destabilize the country and lead to a new dynasty.

While the Lancastrians and Yorkists were heading to war, the Lancastrians found themselves at a disadvantage due to a distinct lack of male heirs. They found a solution to this problem through the marriage of Margaret Beaufort and Edmund Tudor. Margaret Beaufort was a descendant of John of Gaunt, while Edmund Tudor was Henry VI's half-brother and a descendant of the House of Valois, the French royal house.

Owen Tudor

Owen Tudor was a descendant of the Welsh Tudor family, which was heavily involved in the Welsh government. The family first rose to prominence in Wales under Ednyfed Fychan, who worked under Llywelyn the Great. His loyal service to the monarch earned him vast lands in northern Wales, which included Penmynydd. This became the family's seat of power. The Tudors allied themselves with Edward I and remained loyal supporters of the English royal house. However, in time, the family joined Owain Glyndwr, who rebelled against the English in the early 1400s. They were soundly defeated, and the Tudors lost much of their land. Many members of the family were executed for treason. Thankfully, Owen Tudor was able to rise above this failure and went on to work for Henry V.

7. House of Tudor genealogy chart

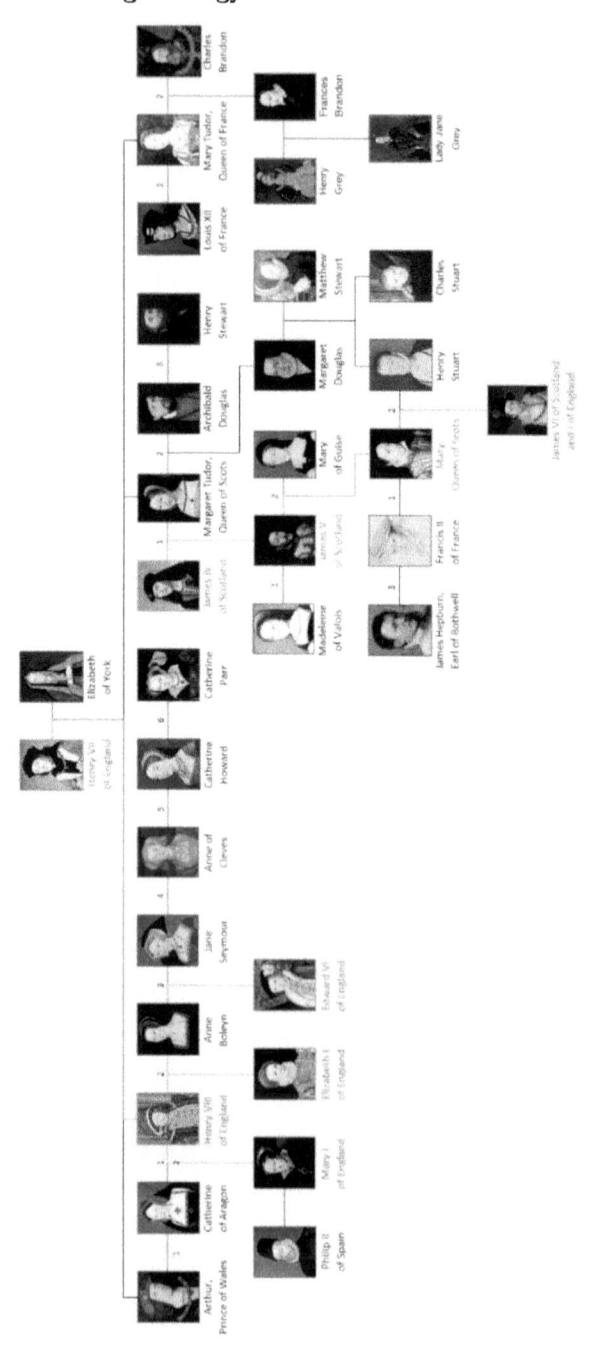

Wdcf, CC BY-SA 3.0 <https://creativecommons.org/licenses/by-sa/3.0>, via Wikimedia Commons https://commons.wikimedia.org/wiki/File:House_of_Tudor.png

His background is famously obscure, but historians know that he was born around 1400, and he was the son of Maredudd Tudor. In time, Owen became the keeper of the queen of England's wardrobe. When Henry V died, his wife, Catherine of Valois, was still a beautiful young woman who faced early retirement. Catherine and Owen fell in love and married without permission. They were able to keep their marriage secret for a few years, during which time they had five children: three sons and two daughters.

Unfortunately, when their secret was discovered, Catherine was exiled to a nunnery, and Owen was imprisoned in Newgate Prison. However, he managed to escape and returned to Wales. Catherine died in the nunnery around 1437, while Owen returned to Wales in 1438. When Henry VI was threatened by Yorkist forces in 1461, Owen took an army to support the king. Owen was captured by the Yorkists and was executed in Hereford. Although he was beheaded as a prisoner of war, the Tudor dynasty had already begun. Owen and Catherine's sons, Edmund and Jasper, would help raise the House of Tudor to glory, and their descendants would usher in another golden age in England's history.

Jasper and Edmund Tudor

Catherine of Valois was only twenty years old when her husband died, and ambitious nobles immediately set their sights on the dowager queen. In response, English Parliament forbade her from marrying without a special license and express permission from the king. However, Catherine and Owen Tudor fell in love and ignored this law. They had several children, but the two most influential were Edmund and Jasper. After their mother died, they were placed in the care of Katherine de la Pole, and they were eventually called to court by their half-brother, Henry VI.

Henry VI declared Edmund and Jasper legitimate and made Edmund the earl of Richmond, while Jasper became the earl of Pembroke. In 1453, they were officially recognized as the king's brothers. They both received large portions of land, and in 1454, they were made Lady Margaret Beaufort's wards. She was the sole heiress of her father's immense fortune. Edmund married her in 1455 when he was twenty-nine years old, and she was only twelve. At that time, the Yorkists were already gaining power, and the War of the Roses was looming.

8. Margaret Beaufort

https://commons.wikimedia.org/wiki/File:Meynnart_Wewyck_Lady_Margaret_Beaufort.jpg

During that time period, it wasn't unusual for girls to be married off at a young age, but to protect her, their husbands were ordered to wait until the girl was at least fourteen years old before they began trying for an heir. Edmund ignored this rule, and Margaret became pregnant soon after their marriage.

Once the Wars of the Roses began, Edmund and Jasper fought for King Henry VI, but Edmund was captured in 1456 by Yorkists and taken to Carmarthen Castle in Wales. He died from the plague later that year. Jasper took Margaret to Pembroke Castle, where she gave birth to a son. She was still only twelve years old, and the process was extremely traumatic. Margaret was never able to have children again, despite the fact that she got married two more times after. Despite her difficult early years, Margaret became a formidable figure in the War of the Roses and was instrumental in helping her son gain the English throne.

The War of the Roses had begun, and while the Yorkists had the advantage at first, the future king of England, Henry VII, had just been born. Through his mother and father, Henry Tudor had connections to the royal houses of France, Wales, and England, and he already had two formidable supporters in the form of Margaret Beaufort and Jasper Tudor.

Chapter 3: The Tudors' Rise to Power

The Wars of the Roses began in 1455, and by that time, the days of Plantagenet glory were long gone. The mighty ruling house had been divided into the Houses of York and Lancaster, which were about to rip into each other and cause one of the bloodiest civil wars in history. By the end of the civil war, about half of England's noble houses were gone. The House of Plantagenet came to a brutal end when the last Plantagenet heir, Edward, 17th Earl of Warwick, was executed in the Tower of London.

9. Battle of Towton, Wars of the Roses

https://commons.wikimedia.org/wiki/File:Battle_Near_Towton_bw.jpg

During the decades-long war, several influential individuals rose to power and influenced the course of history. People like the Kingmaker, Richard Neville, were able to become major players. While some of the central figures of the war were at the forefront of the action, some players, like Margaret Beaufort, kept to the shadows and manipulated events to their advantage. Many noble families were decimated, but others gained incredible fortunes, such as the infamous Woodvilles. It was a time of intense upheaval, brutal battles, and terrible losses, but it led to the foundation of the Tudor dynasty.

The Beginning of the Wars of the Roses

The Wars of the Roses were named after the white rose that represented the House of York and the red rose that represented the House of Lancaster. Before the catastrophic civil wars, the House of Lancaster ruled England through Henry VI. He was the son of the great king, Henry V, and due to his father's untimely death, he became the king of England while he was still an infant. There were high hopes for his rule, but unlike his father, Henry VI wasn't a natural leader and didn't seem too interested in his kingly duties. In time, his nobles decided to take matters into their own hands.

As Henry VI's rule progressed, he lost many hard-won lands in France, which enraged his nobles, many of whom had fought alongside Henry V to gain them. In 1450, his people rebelled against him as a result of heavy taxes. The rebellion was led by Jack Cade, who demanded that the king allow Richard of York to return to England. Richard of York was also a descendant of Richard III and could make a claim to the throne.

Henry VI refused, and he eventually defeated the rebellion. For much of his reign, Henry VI and his wife, Margaret of Anjou, were influenced by the duke of Somerset, Edmund Beaufort. This blatant favoritism caused friction within the court. When Richard of York returned to England in 1452, he urged Henry VI to fire Edmund Beaufort. Unfortunately for Richard, Margaret gave birth to Edward of Lancaster in 1453, which put Richard one step further away from the throne. By then, tensions were running high in England, and the Yorkists and Lancastrians were already beginning to fight with each other.

10. Richard of York

https://commons.wikimedia.org/wiki/File:Richard_Plantagenet,_3rd_Duke_of_York_2.jpg

In 1454, disaster struck the House of Lancaster when Henry VI slipped into a state of catatonic madness. Richard was appointed as the Lord Protector of England. Richard wasted little time and quickly began putting his own allies into positions of power within the government. During this time, Margaret of Anjou and Richard of York became clear enemies.

Henry VI managed to recover by 1455, but the damage was done. The stage was set for the Wars of the Roses. A few months after Henry VI recovered, he was forced to meet Richard of York and Richard Neville, Earl of Warwick, in battle at St. Albans. The Lancastrians were soundly defeated. Somerset was killed, and Henry was taken prisoner. Richard became the Lord Protector of England again while Margaret and her son fled into exile.

It was the first battle in a long civil war, but important alliances had already been created. Richard of York and Richard Neville were a force to be reckoned with, and Richard Neville's efforts on behalf of the

House of York earned him the nickname "Kingmaker."

The Kingmaker

Richard Neville was born in 1428 and became the earl of Warwick in 1449. In 1453, he made an alliance with Richard of York and became one of his most important allies. Although the Yorkists scored a crucial victory at the Battle of St. Albans, their problems were far from over. Henry VI was a weak king who wasn't suited to rule or strengthen his throne through war, but his wife was ambitious and wanted to secure the throne for her son. When her most trusted ally, Edmund Beaufort, was killed, she took matters into her own hands. For the next few years, she raised armies to fight against the House of York.

11. Richard Neville, Earl of Warwick

https://commons.wikimedia.org/wiki/File:Warwick_the_Kingmaker.gif

In 1459, the House of Lancaster defeated the House of York, and Richard of York was forced to return to Ireland. However, things were far from over. Richard returned in 1460, and the Yorkists were able to capture Henry. In an effort to avoid more fighting, Parliament passed the

Act of Accord, which named Richard Henry VI's successor. Henry VI would be allowed to keep the crown until he died, but then the throne would pass to the House of York. This seemed like a fair compromise to most of the involved parties, but Margaret of Anjou didn't accept the Act of Accord.

This led to one of the most brutal battles in the entire civil war. Margaret led an army against the House of York, and the two armies met at Wakefield Green. For years, Margaret had been forced to run for her life and fight for her son's inheritance. The Battle of Wakefield was supposed to cement the York inheritance, but Richard was defeated by Margaret's army. Margaret showed no mercy and had Richard beheaded. However, she wasn't satisfied with Richard's execution. She took it one step further by having his head (wearing a paper crown) mounted on Micklegate Bar. This brutality shocked the country and mobilized her enemies against her.

Richard of York's sons joined the fight, and his oldest son, Edward, became a new contender for the throne. Backed by Richard Neville, Earl of Warwick, Edward fought against Margaret's forces a few more times but was defeated at the Battle of Mortimer's Cross and the Second Battle of St. Albans. In 1461, both sides met at Towton and engaged in one of the bloodiest battles in English history. Once the fighting was done, Margaret was on the run again. Edward IV was crowned the king of England.

Warwick had been Edward's strongest supporter, and his tireless efforts helped earn Edward his crown. He was given great honor and wealth in Edward's new government, and Warwick began negotiating with European powers to get Edward a bride with the hopes of building a powerful alliance. However, Edward had other ideas, and his choice of a wife would cause catastrophic consequences. In time, Warwick set his sights on putting the Lancastrians back in power, and he helped Henry VI return to the throne in 1470. Warwick was an ambitious and manipulative individual who put two men on the throne to further his own causes.

Edward IV

Edward IV wasn't born to be king, but he was crowned in 1461 following the Battle of Towton. The Wars of the Roses had been raging for about six years at that point, and he had lost his father to the fighting.

For the first few years of his reign, he remained in London while Warwick fought against the Lancastrians. It was clear that Warwick was the most powerful man in the realm. Things were about to change, though, as Edward was growing tired of submitting to Warwick and began looking for ways to distance himself from his advisor.

Warwick was determined to keep his power and began negotiations with the French to find Edward a French princess who would become his bride. Instead, Edward married Elizabeth Woodville in 1464. Elizabeth was extremely beautiful, but she was the widow of a defeated Lancastrian noble and already had two sons. Her own mother, Jacquetta, had served Margaret of Anjou at court. This marriage caused a massive rift between Edward and Warwick. Edward quickly began giving Woodvilles positions in power, which helped build his own power. Warwick quickly lost power and favor, which incensed him. In 1469, he sought to regain his power by capturing Edward IV in battle. He kept the king prisoner, but Edward IV escaped. Warwick was forced to flee to France, where he set up an alliance with Margaret of Anjou.

Warwick and his allies fought against Edward in 1471, and Edward had to retreat. In 1471, the two met in battle again, and Warwick was killed. Margaret of Anjou arrived in England just as Warwick was defeated. The two armies met at Tewkesbury, and Margaret was confident that her side would win. Finally, her son, Edward, Prince of Wales, would be crowned king. Edward IV defeated the Lancastrians, and Margaret's son was killed, much to her horror. When Edward returned to London, he "learned" that Henry VI had died in the Tower of London soon before his arrival. (The Yorkists claimed that the old king died of sadness, but it is more likely that he was murdered on Edward's orders.)

For the rest of his reign, Edward IV concentrated on enriching his kingdom and improving law enforcement. The country had been ravaged by wars, and his efforts helped stabilize the country again. His reign was extremely successful, and he had seven children with Elizabeth Woodville. They had two sons, Edward and Richard, as well as five daughters. The oldest daughter, Elizabeth of York, would become an important component in the unification of the Houses of York and Lancaster. During Edward IV's reign, the kingdom enjoyed peace and prosperity, but unfortunately, the Wars of the Roses were far from over.

The Boys in the Tower

Richard of York had three sons: Edward, George, and Richard. When Edward became king, he made George the duke of Clarence, and Richard became the duke of Gloucester. During the early years of Edward's reign, he enjoyed the support of his brothers. However, during his ongoing struggle against Warwick, George changed sides and joined Warwick. Although George betrayed Edward, he was eventually pardoned. Unfortunately, George didn't learn his lesson and betrayed Edward again. In 1478, Edward was forced to execute his brother.

Richard remained loyal to his brother and king, and before Edward died in 1483, he appointed Richard as the Lord Protector of England. As soon as Edward died, his son, Edward V, was appointed king immediately. Edward V was only twelve years old, and Richard was supposed to rule as protector until Edward was old enough to rule. However, Edward's mother, Elizabeth Woodville, had him crowned immediately, likely to inhibit Richard's power.

12. The princes in the Tower

https://commons.wikimedia.org/wiki/File:Princes.jpg

This would have allowed the Woodvilles to rule England through Edward V. Richard was far too ambitious to allow that to happen. In

1483, he met the Earl of Rivers at Stony Stratford and placed the earl in prison before taking Edward with him. Once in London, he was declared the Lord Protector and placed Edward in the Tower of London. Elizabeth and her children sought shelter in Westminster Abbey with her remaining children, but on June 16th, Richard had Edward's younger brother also taken to the Tower. It was becoming increasingly apparent that Richard wasn't going to give up his power.

On June 26th, he made a claim to the throne by declaring that Edward IV's sons were illegitimate. Richard became Richard III, and he was crowned the king of England in early July. However, his rule was far from secure since Edward IV's sons were still alive in the Tower of London. Most people were shocked by Richard's actions. The situation worsened when both boys simply disappeared. Richard was now undisputedly the king of England. No one knows what happened to his nephews. Edward V was never heard from again, but several pretenders claimed to be his younger brother, Richard. Richard III was now the most powerful man in England, but his nephews' disappearance made him wildly unpopular.

Richard III

Richard III was Edward IV's youngest brother. While he was born into wealth and was well connected, he didn't stand to inherit much, and his future didn't look very bright. However, when the Wars of the Roses began, he and his brothers were supposed to become Henry VI's heirs. When their father died and Edward became king, Richard became a prince and was made the duke of Gloucester. Richard and George were placed in Warwick's care until they were old enough to take over their estates.

When he entered adulthood, the Wars of the Roses had resumed when Warwick fought against Edward IV. While George and Warwick turned against Edward, Richard remained loyal to his brother. When Edward IV defeated George and Warwick, he rewarded Richard's loyalty by appointing him as the king's representative in Wales. Throughout Edward's reign, Richard remained loyal and fought on Edward's side during several key battles against the Lancastrians. As a result, Edward lavished lands on his brother, mostly giving him lands in the north of England, which strengthened Richard's power considerably. Later, Richard married Warwick's youngest daughter, Anne Neville, and received most of Warwick's lands.

Richard was very popular in the north, but his growing power worried several nobles, including the queen, Elizabeth Woodville. When Edward IV died, there were fears that Richard would use his position as Lord Protector to essentially rule the country, so the queen had her son, Edward V, declared the king of England. Unfortunately, Richard usurped the throne, and his nephews mysteriously vanished. Since Richard had the most to gain from their disappearance, people suspected that he had his nephews murdered.

During his reign, Richard tried to be a good king and abolished some of Edward IV's unpopular edicts, such as forced gifts from nobles. However, he faced unrest in the south of England, the threat of invasion from France, and economic hardship. He found that ruling England was much harder than ruling his own lands in the north. Disaster struck in 1483 when many Yorkists deserted him, and the south of England rebelled against him. He managed to stop the rebellion, but many nobles, including the Woodvilles, went to Brittany, where they supported Henry Tudor's claim to the throne. In 1484, his son (and only child) died, leaving him without an heir. The next year, his wife also died.

In the midst of these tragedies, Richard found a seemingly perfect solution. He planned to marry his niece, Elizabeth of York, Edward IV's oldest daughter. Elizabeth was young and beautiful, which would provide Richard with a chance to have another heir and would strengthen his claim to the throne. While his plan was perfect on paper, it was very unpopular, and his supporters quickly dwindled. While his supporters could stomach the disappearance of Richard's nephews, they drew the line at allowing the king to marry his niece. Richard never ended up marrying Elizabeth.

While Richard III desperately looked for ways to keep ruling England, Henry Tudor was gathering support for his own claim to the throne. The Yorkists had successfully kept their power for most of the Wars of the Roses, but they had turned on each other and fought amongst themselves until they made their cause unpopular. The Lancastrians had been forced to bide their time, and as Richard III struggled to keep his throne, they saw their chance.

Margaret Beaufort

While the Wars of the Roses raged on, Margaret Beaufort went from a child to an influential player in some of the most dramatic events during the bloody civil war. When she was just twelve or thirteen years old, she gave birth to Henry Tudor. From then on, she was committed to securing her son's inheritance. Unlike Margaret of Anjou, Margaret Beaufort used subtle tactics to further her cause.

When her husband, Edmund Tudor, died, she was betrothed to Sir Henry Stafford, who was the duke of Buckingham. Margaret was forced to leave her son with Jasper Tudor for his own safety since he was a Lancastrian heir with ties to the throne during a time when the Yorkists were quickly gaining power. As the only child of John Beaufort, Margaret was an extremely wealthy heiress, but when Edward IV became king, he took her lands and gave them to his brother, George. She campaigned to have her lands returned to her, but she wasn't successful. When Henry VI was defeated at the Battle of Barnet, Margaret helped Jasper and Henry Tudor flee from England when Henry was only thirteen years old.

In 1472, Margaret married Lord Thomas Stanley after Lord Stafford died a year earlier at the Battle of Barnet. She was allowed to join Edward IV's court, where she sought the king's permission to allow her son to return to England. She became close to Elizabeth Woodville during this time. When Edward IV died and Richard III became king, she served in Queen Anne's court but secretly worked with Elizabeth Woodville to make her son, Henry, king.

Elizabeth Woodville had lost both of her sons but didn't allow her loss to force her into a quiet retirement. In 1483, she played a prominent role in Buckingham's rebellion, and Henry was set to invade England to help Buckingham. Unfortunately, the plan failed, and Margaret was almost executed. Richard III ordered her husband, Lord Stanley, to make sure that Margaret was isolated at one of his estates and cut off communication between her and her son. Margaret outwitted the king and managed to continue corresponding with her son. Lord Stanley was secretly on Margaret's side, and together, they arranged a new rebellion, which led to the Battle of Bosworth.

Margaret Beaufort managed to survive England's bloodiest civil war and founded a dynasty during times of incredible political upheaval. Not only did she survive when most of England's nobility went extinct, but she also managed to secure the English throne for her son.

The Unification of the York and Lancaster Dynasties

On August 22nd, 1485, Henry Tudor met Richard III at Bosworth. It would be the last battle of the Wars of the Roses, and everyone involved seemed to sense that things were coming to a head. Henry was supported by France and many English nobles, who had deserted Richard III. For thirty long years, England had been subjected to a series of battles that uprooted their way of life. The throne changed hands often, kings had been imprisoned, and heirs had been declared illegitimate as old scandals were dug up and exposed for political reasons. Finally, the Wars of the Roses were about to end. Henry Tudor won the battle, and Richard III was brutally killed. The battle inspired legendary stories, and apparently, the crown was taken from Richard's head and placed on Henry's.

Henry became Henry VII, but his troubles were far from over. The country was deeply divided after the civil war. In an effort to reunite the country, he married Edward IV's daughter, Elizabeth of York. The House of Tudor had taken the throne of England, but Henry VII would have to face financial difficulties, rebellions, and personal tragedy during his reign. He faced an uphill battle from the start, but with some powerful allies, he was able to secure the Tudor dynasty and leave the throne in a stable position for his heirs.

Section Two:
Monarchs and Royalty (1485–1603)

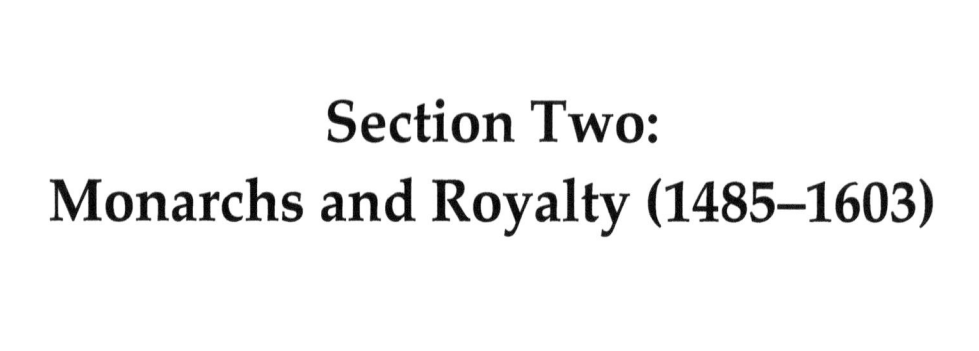

Chapter 4: Henry VII (r. 1485–1509)

When Henry VII was born, his future looked bleak. His mother was barely a teenager, and his father was dead. Due to the Wars of the Roses, his inheritance had been seized and distributed to other nobles. Things didn't look good for the Lancastrians; their king was mad, and their queen was brutal and ambitious. It was a miracle that Henry and his family survived at all, as power changed hands often. For most of the civil war, it looked as though they were on the losing side. However, his mother's shrewd politics and a series of vital alliances meant that the Tudors rose steadily in the background of the Wars of the Roses.

13. Henry VII

https://commons.wikimedia.org/wiki/File:Enrique_VII_de_Inglaterra,_por_un_artista_an%C3%B3nimo.jpg

Finally, Henry Tudor returned from exile and won the crown of England. He faced many challenges to get the throne, and he would face even more hardships to keep the crown in his possession, especially since new kings had appeared seemingly overnight during the civil war. Thankfully, he had powerful allies and learned to be a good king. Thanks to his efforts, the Houses of York and Lancaster were reunited, and he led his country through the aftermath of the bloody civil war. Margaret Beaufort and others helped him get the throne, but it was up to him to prove himself worthy of their efforts.

Early Life

Henry Tudor was the son of Edmund Tudor and Margaret Beaufort. Through his parents, he had a rich and varied lineage. On his father's side, he was the grandson of a Welsh nobleman and a French princess and former queen of England. On his mother's side, he was the great-great-grandson of John of Gaunt, the son of Edward III. When he was born, he was a distant Lancastrian heir behind Henry VI, Henry VI's son, and older male Beauforts. At first, it didn't appear as though he had a particularly bright future, but then the Wars of the Roses began in earnest. In one fell swoop, the Lancastrian line was jeopardized when Henry VI, his son, and the Beaufort line fell in battle. Suddenly, Henry Tudor's distant claim to the throne was the best that the Lancastrians could hope for.

While the deaths of the other Lancastrian heirs meant that Henry could hope for a chance to become the king of England, it also meant that he would be in grave danger during the Wars of the Roses. Soon after he was born, his mother, Margaret, married Sir Henry Stafford. Henry was left in the care of his uncle, Jasper Tudor, Earl of Pembroke. Jasper Tudor was a loyal Lancastrian who was devoted to his nephew's cause. Unfortunately for the Lancastrians, they were soundly defeated at the Battle of Tewkesbury in 1471, and the Yorkist line was firmly established when Edward IV took the throne. Henry and Jasper Tudor were forced to flee to Brittany, where it seemed that Henry would die in obscurity. However, the Wars of the Roses were far from over.

When Edward IV died, Richard III began plans to usurp the throne. The House of York was divided, and Henry's fortunes changed again. In an effort to build a strong alliance against Richard III, Henry was betrothed to Edward IV's oldest daughter, Elizabeth of York. This was an ingenious plan since it would reunite the Houses of York and

Lancaster after nearly thirty years of civil war. Richard III had great plans for his reign, and he made plans to invade France, which motivated the French to support Henry's claim to the English throne. Henry Tudor had fled into exile when he was a young teenager, but in 1485, at the age of twenty-eight, he arrived on English soil with an army.

The Battle of Bosworth

When Richard III claimed the throne and his nephews went missing in the Tower of London, the Yorkist party was split in two. Many of the nobles were alarmed by Richard III's usurpation and were hesitant to support his rule. Meanwhile, Henry Tudor had grown into a strong young man with a good reputation. When his betrothal to Elizabeth of York was finalized, it seemed to many that he would be the better king. Richard III's people began to rebel against him, and Henry Tudor could finally fight back against the Yorkists.

In 1483, the duke of Buckingham, Henry Stafford, led a rebellion against Richard III and asked for Henry Tudor's support. The rebellion was crushed before Henry Tudor could aid the duke's efforts, but it wouldn't be Henry's last chance. In the meantime, the Lancastrians formed an alliance with Yorkists who had abandoned Richard III's court. Richard III dealt with a great loss in 1484 when his heir died, but that only helped the Lancastrian cause and strengthened Henry's claim. In 1485, Henry landed in Wales with a small army and marched into England. As he marched, more people joined his army, but he was still outnumbered when he met Richard's forces in Leicestershire at Bosworth Field.

Unfortunately for Richard, many nobles were tired of war. One of his most important allies, Henry Percy, Earl of Northumberland, refused to join the battle until he knew who was going to win. During the battle, a few more of Richard's allies left him to join Henry's side. When Richard realized that Henry Percy wasn't going to help him, he allegedly broke off from the main army with his knights and decided to kill Henry Tudor himself. Lord Stanley, Margaret Beaufort's husband and Henry's stepfather, had been waiting to see how the battle would pan out. When he saw that Richard had broken away from his main forces, he decided to intervene on Henry's behalf. Richard was surrounded by enemies and quickly killed.

According to legends about the battle, Richard III had worn a crown into battle, which was knocked off his head when he was killed. That same crown was then used to crown Henry VII on the battlefield. After spending his life fighting the Yorkists and years in exile, Henry established the Tudor dynasty. He was now the king of England.

Family Life

Henry's ascent to the throne had been difficult, but he faced even more serious challenges trying to secure his crown. The country had been ripped apart by civil war, and his most pressing task was uniting the Houses of York and Lancaster. This was achieved by marrying Elizabeth of York in 1486. Many powerful Yorkists were angry about the loss at the Battle of Bosworth and would later go on to launch rebellions against Henry VII, but by marrying Elizabeth of York, he strengthened his claim to the throne and won more allies.

14. Elizabeth of York

https://commons.wikimedia.org/wiki/File:Elizabeth_of_York.jpg

After their marriage, Henry VII used the Tudor rose as an emblem of unification. The Tudor rose was a mixture of the white and red roses that represented the Houses of York and Lancaster. When Richard III took the throne, he enacted the Titulus Regius, an act that declared the marriage of Edward IV and Elizabeth Woodville invalid. This made their children illegitimate and made Richard III the legal heir. As soon as he was able, Henry reversed that act, making Elizabeth of York and her siblings legitimate again. This move strengthened Henry's hold on the throne since he had married one of Edward IV's heirs.

15. Tudor rose

Sodacan, CC BY-SA 3.0 <https://creativecommons.org/licenses/by-sa/3.0>, via Wikimedia Commons https://commons.wikimedia.org/wiki/File:Tudor_Rose.svg

Elizabeth of York also helped her husband at court. Since Henry VII had spent most of his life in exile, he was largely unfamiliar with the English nobles. Elizabeth, on the other hand, had grown up among them as a princess. She was used to courtly life, and her father had been a good king, which probably helped her to be a good queen. The couple had seven children together, but only four survived to adulthood. They had two sons, Arthur and Henry, and two daughters, Margaret and Mary. Margaret went on to become the queen of Scotland, and Mary became the queen of France.

Thanks to Henry VII's marriage to Elizabeth of York, his family was secure, and his children could claim a noble heritage and wouldn't have to spend their childhoods in exile. However, his throne was far from secure, and more effort was required to bring peace to his war-torn country.

Policies and Economy

The Wars of the Roses had been expensive, and the royal treasury was often used to fund the wars of whichever king was in power at the time. When Henry came to the throne, he found that he was in a court that was foreign to him after a life of exile. He was aware that the nobles in England were used to changing regimes and that many Yorkists were looking for an opportunity to advance their cause. As a result, he felt that there weren't many people he could trust. He built up a close-knit council of allies who had proven that they were trustworthy. He used lawyers and clerics in specialized councils, which he personally oversaw. This allowed him to keep a tight hold on his kingdom's affairs.

Henry also saw the need to impress his reign on his people through extravagant tournaments. He began renovating major castles, such as Windsor Castle, Richmond Castle, Greenwich Palace, the Tower of London, and Westminster Abbey. These were expensive endeavors, and Henry didn't want to rely on money from Parliament and allies. He also needed a way to keep the nobles in line and decided to solve both problems through a series of financial policies that would both enrich the monarchy and prevent the nobles from becoming too powerful. Henry and his council set up a series of taxes, fines, and rents, which proved to be very useful. Misdemeanors were punished through fines, and large taxes were placed on nobles. He also encouraged exports and helped increase the health of the English economy.

Henry paid close attention to his relationships with other European powers and signed trade treaties with Spain, Portugal, Florence, Denmark, and the Netherlands. In 1489, he sent an army to help his allies in Brittany when France threatened to invade, but he received money from Charles VIII of France to stay out of his affairs. As Henry's reign progressed, he proved that he was a capable king and did wonders for the English economy. He was adept at making money, which helped to keep the throne and country stable. Instead of punishing nobles with violence and battles, he imposed massive fines on them, which was lucrative and effective.

While Henry's reign was mostly focused on peace, he still faced times of trouble. Several Yorkists hoped to return a York heir to the throne, and while it was a good move to legitimize Edward IV's children, it also meant that Edward IV's sons were the true heirs. And not everyone believed that the princes in the Tower were actually dead.

Edward of Warwick and Perkin Warbeck

Henry VII has been credited with bringing an end to the Wars of the Roses, but the aftermath of the civil wars haunted him for much of his reign. On top of that, he had been forced to spend most of his childhood in exile, and during that time, his family wasn't in power. This meant they couldn't spend that time gathering connections for his rule. When Henry finally ascended to the throne, he found himself in charge of a court that was basically foreign, and even though the Yorkists had been defeated, they had not given up. The problem was that there were still a few legitimate Yorkist heirs with good claims to the throne, and many were happy to believe that one of the York princes had survived their ordeal in the Tower of London. These factors led to a few serious rebellions during Henry VII's reign, some of which were led by pretenders who imitated the legitimate Yorkist heirs.

The first Yorkist heir with a legitimate claim to the throne was Edward of Warwick, Edward IV's nephew through his brother George, Duke of Clarence. As a boy, Edward, Earl of Warwick, was locked up in the Tower of London soon after Henry VII ascended to the throne. However, enterprising Yorkists spread a rumor that the child had escaped and built an uprising around him. Edward was still safely in the Tower while the rebellion gained popularity. It turned out that the rebellion was led by a boy, Lambert Simnel, who looked like Edward. The Yorkist force was defeated at the Battle of East Stoke in 1487. Henry VII pardoned Simnel and gave him a job in the royal kitchens.

Unfortunately, the next rebellion wasn't defeated so easily. A man pretending to be Richard, Duke of York, the son of Edward IV, appeared in Europe. He won the support of European kings who were eager to stir up rebellion in England. Many nobles defected to the man's cause, and Henry VII faced the threat of invasion. In 1497, the two opposing armies met in Cornwall, where the rebellion was defeated. The "duke" turned out to be a lowborn man named Perkin Warbeck. He was executed two years later.

Throughout Henry's reign, he faced minor and major rebellions, but he managed to defeat the rebels and keep a firm hold on his throne. He managed to end the Wars of the Roses at the beginning of his reign, but he lived under the shadow of the civil war for the rest of his life.

My Lady, the King's Mother

During the Wars of the Roses, Margaret Beaufort fought for her son's cause. When people forgot about his claim to the throne and discounted his significance, she quietly plotted and furthered his cause. She became a masterful politician out of necessity and helped her son become the most powerful man in the kingdom. He never forgot her help, and when he became king, he made her one of his advisors. Margaret received extraordinary precedence at Henry's court, and reports indicate that he relied heavily on her advice. When Henry married Elizabeth of York, Margaret's influence wasn't diminished. In fact, she was allowed to wear the same quality clothes as the queen. She also adopted the new title, "My Lady, the King's Mother."

Margaret didn't waste her influence on ordering new clothes and making her daughter-in-law's life difficult. She also enacted new legal acts. During the civil war, the victorious kings were allowed to take land from defeated nobles. Margaret had been a victim of this practice, so when her son was king, she made it illegal for the nobles and royals to steal land from each other. She also made it possible for her to take control of her own lands even though she was still married.

As Margaret grew older, she also invented new protocols that involved family life, mainly childbirth. While many resented the power that she held in the royal court, there was no doubt that she used her influence to stabilize the Tudor dynasty. While Edward IV owed much of his success to the Kingmaker, Richard Neville, Henry VII owed his kingship to his mother, who also earned the title "Kingmaker." Margaret and Elizabeth Woodville had a notoriously strained relationship, but they were able to work together to arrange Prince Arthur's marriage to the Spanish Infanta, Catherine of Aragon.

Unfortunately, Elizabeth of York died in 1503 due to complications of childbirth when she gave birth to her youngest daughter, Catherine, who also died. With the queen gone, Margaret became the most important woman in the Tudor court, and she would go on to outlive her only son and play an important role during the beginning of Henry VIII's reign.

Personality

Throughout his life, Henry VII received a lot of help that allowed him to take the English throne, but his own efforts and personality helped him to endure exile and the challenges of ruling. He had a fascinating life as the first Tudor monarch, and his efforts stabilized England after thirty years of war. According to his contemporaries, he had a good memory, which helped him with affairs of state, and he was an intelligent man with a great head for business. His approach to fines and financial punishments was a stark contrast to his predecessors' practice of battles and land grabs.

Henry's years in exile also had a lasting effect on him, as he was a cautious man who wouldn't let anyone else get too powerful during his reign. Francis Bacon praised him for being a wise man who was determined to be an independent ruler. During his lifetime, Henry VII saw rulers who suffered betrayal from their closest companions, and he was careful not to make the same mistakes. While he was known for being extremely cautious with money, he also knew the value of entertaining like a king. He threw lavish tournaments and feasts. When his son Arthur married Catherine of Aragon, he arranged a massive wedding ceremony that impressed the monarchs of Europe. As a king, he kept up appearances but didn't bankrupt himself in doing so.

Henry also took good care of his family and had a special bond with his mother. He never forgot her loyal years of service and treated her very well. As one of his trusted advisors, Margaret was allowed to propose laws and protocols that he took very seriously. He didn't view her position as his advisor as symbolic; he actively sought out her advice. While Henry was a busy king, he also took good care of his children and made time for his family. His marriage to Elizabeth of York started off as political, but he genuinely grew to love her. According to reports, he was inconsolable when she died.

Henry VII was a good king and a cautious man who didn't forget the lessons he had learned during the difficult times in his life.

Legacy

Henry VII wasn't a very popular king, as his financial policies earned him many enemies, but he managed to navigate the country through extremely difficult times and left a stable throne behind for his son. He outlived his oldest son, Arthur, but died suddenly in 1509. His son, Henry VIII, was coronated on June 24th, 1509. While Henry VII wasn't known as the greatest king in English history, he still did his best during extremely difficult times. He was buried alongside his wife at

Westminster Abbey, and his building efforts at Westminster Abbey were immortalized when a chapel was named after him.

16. Henry VII Chapel at Westminster Abbey

https://commons.wikimedia.org/wiki/File:View_of_Henry_VII%27s_Chapel,_Westminster_Abbey_from_Old_Palace_Yard,_1780s.jpg

Henry VII was born during difficult times and had an uncertain future, but he rose to incredible heights and ushered in a new dynasty that would become one of England's most famous royal families.

Chapter 5: Henry VIII (r. 1509–1547)

Henry VIII was arguably the most infamous Tudor. He started off as the second son of a king and was expected to become nothing greater than a duke. The generation before him had been subjected to a war that wiped out many noble families and who knew the danger of ambitious men who were allowed to get too close to the throne. Henry VII settled the country down after the civil war and left a stable throne for his family. His lineage was secure, and his son, Arthur, was being primed for the throne. Unfortunately, Arthur died, and Henry VII's second son was thrust into the spotlight.

17. Henry VIII

https://commons.wikimedia.org/wiki/File:After_Hans_Holbein_the_Younger_-_Portrait_of_Henry_VIII_-_Google_Art_Project.jpg

During his lifetime, Henry VIII achieved many great things. He won wars and passed successful policies, but his triumphs were overshadowed by his personal drama. When he failed to produce a legitimate heir, he went to great lengths to secure the future of the Tudor lineage, which led to several dramatic and failed marriages. Henry left the Catholic Church and set the stage for decades of religious upheaval that turned England from a Catholic to a Protestant country. He left behind a fascinating legacy that still captures the imagination of the general public.

Life as the Second Son

Henry was born in 1491 and was given several appointments while he was still a toddler, such as the Lord Warden of the Cinque Ports, Lord

Lieutenant of Ireland, and Duke of York. It's likely that these positions were given to him at such a young age so that his father could keep control of the positions until his son was old enough to assume the responsibilities that were given to him. He was raised well and given the best tutors. He became fluent in French and Latin, which was expected of royal children at the time. Few records exist of his childhood since no one expected that such records would be important.

According to contemporary reports, he was an athletic youth who enjoyed participating in the tournaments that his father arranged, which he often won. He also enjoyed hunting and dancing and was reportedly an excellent student. Henry VIII took a keen interest in theology and built up an impressive knowledge about religious matters, which would become useful later in his life when he researched how to get out of his marriage to Catherine of Aragon. Historians have found that he enjoyed knightly pursuits, such as horse riding, tennis, and archery. While his brother was sickly and spent most of his time learning how to be king, Henry was allowed to pursue his own interests.

When he was a young man, he was tall and had an athletic figure, which was quite different from his later portraits that show how his excessive lifestyle had taken its toll. The intelligent young prince charmed nobles and foreign dignitaries alike, and the future of the Tudor dynasty looked bright with a studious crown prince and an enthusiastic duke of York. Unfortunately, things were about to change for the entire family, and Henry would be required to step up and learn the business of ruling a kingdom.

Prince Arthur

When Henry VII and Elizabeth of York got married, they unified the warring Houses of York and Lancaster. Their son would be the ultimate symbol of that unification, a prince who would become king and belong to both sides of the war. They likely hoped that he would have an easier time ascending the throne than Henry VII did. Arthur was born in September 1486 and was given the titles prince of Wales and earl of Chester. His parents and their advisors immediately began scouring Europe to find the perfect marriage alliance. When Arthur was eleven years old, he was betrothed to Catherine of Aragon, the daughter of the Spanish monarchs. The alliance represented the hopes that the two royal houses would become powerful allies, which would help secure both dynasties.

18. Prince Arthur Tudor

*https://commons.wikimedia.org/wiki/File:Anglo-
Flemish_School,_Arthur,_Prince_of_Wales_(Granard_portrait)_-004.jpg*

A popular belief exists that Arthur was a sickly child, but there isn't a lot of evidence to support that theory. By many accounts, Arthur was a gentle person who did well in his studies as he trained to become king. While he was still a teenager, he was sent to Wales to secure authority in the country on behalf of his father. At fifteen years old, he was married to Catherine of Aragon. His family spared no expense for the wedding ceremony that took place in September 1501, and it was apparently one of the most lavish events in English history. The wedding was a clear demonstration of the Tudors' prosperity and signified the great hopes that were invested in the marriage.

Once the royal couple was married, they were sent to Ludlow Castle. However, Arthur was growing sicker as time went on, and there are theories that he was suffering from the mysterious sweating sickness. The illness arrived on English shores when Henry VII became king, and it was a serious concern during the beginning of his reign. The sweating sickness struck quickly, and people reportedly died within hours of developing symptoms. In March 1502, Arthur and Catherine became ill during an outbreak of the sweating sickness. Catherine survived, but Arthur didn't. The Tudor dynasty was shocked by the tragedy. As news of Arthur's death spread, Henry was thrust into the spotlight, and Catherine's own future was in danger.

Political Life

When Arthur died, Henry became the heir, and his father's last years were spent training Henry to become the next king. In 1509, Henry VII died, and his son became King Henry VIII. He was eighteen years old. There were high hopes for Henry VIII's reign. He was young, handsome, charming, and athletic. His father had been unpopular because of his strict financial policies, but Henry VIII had a much different personality. Almost as soon as Henry VIII became king, he dismissed some of his father's unpopular financial policies, which endeared him to the public. Unfortunately, he soon found that it was necessary to reintroduce several of those policies since he had ambitious military plans.

Henry's court was famous for allowing men of lower birth to gain power. One such example was Thomas Wolsey. He was the son of a butcher but became the cardinal archbishop of York and one of Henry's closest advisors for some time. Another famous advisor was Thomas Cromwell, whose father was a blacksmith. For much of his reign, Henry was influenced by powerful advisors who could rise from nothing to become some of the most powerful men in the kingdom. The fortunes of these men, Cromwell and Wolsey in particular, were dependent on Henry's favor, which could prove to be fickle if he didn't get what he wanted. When Cromwell and Wolsey fell out of favor, Henry elected a Privy Council that was made up of multiple advisors instead of just one favorite.

19. Thomas Wolsey

https://foundation.wikimedia.org/wiki/File:Cardinal_Thomas_Wolsey.jpg

Henry also worked with English Parliament and was intent on creating a united kingdom by becoming king of Wales and Ireland. In 1536, Wales was included in the state of England. Henry also created the Council of the North, which helped him rule the north of England more effectively. Welsh was banned, and in 1543, the country was divided into manageable counties. In 1541, Henry named himself the king of Ireland, which indicated his determination to bring Ireland more firmly under his rule.

Besides taking more control over Britain and Ireland, Henry also had dreams of foreign conquests and was eager to go to war for the glory of England.

Foreign Conquests

In 1512, Henry got his chance at military glory when he joined an alliance with Ferdinand II of Aragon against France. His advisors were unhappy about the alliance, but Henry was ready to go to war. The campaign was arranged by Wolsey, and Wolsey's support proved to cement his friendship with the king. When Henry VIII declared war on France in 1513, Scotland responded by declaring war on England. Henry set sail to invade France, while Scotland invaded England in an effort to distract Henry from his war. James IV of Scotland was eager to win independence from England, and he was France's loyal ally. James was defeated by the earl of Surrey at the Battle of Flodden, where he was killed along with many of his nobles.

In 1513, Henry had his first taste of glory when he won the Battle of the Spurs, after which he captured Thérouanne and Tournai. However, Henry was unable to keep up the invasion of France, and in 1514, his sister Mary married the French king to form an alliance between the two nations. Henry never got his glorious war with France and was forced to make a series of peace treaties with the French. During his reign, he spent a lot of time and effort creating a navy, which included massive warships.

There's no doubt that Henry VIII wanted to be a heroic warrior, but his dreams of glory on the battlefield were pushed into the background as his personal life took center stage. As king, he was required to produce a male heir who would succeed him, and his failures to do so would eventually rip England away from the Catholic Church and lead to the English Reformation. The road to reformation began with the "Great Matter" of his marriage to Catherine of Aragon.

Catherine of Aragon

Catherine of Aragon was the daughter of King Ferdinand and Queen Isabella of Spain. Her marriage to Prince Arthur was meant to secure a powerful ally for England, but when her young husband died just months after their wedding, she was left in a difficult position. The problem was seemingly solved when it was decided that Catherine would marry Henry. Unfortunately, this plan was problematic since Catherine was Arthur's widow, and such a pairing was considered incestuous. As a result, they needed papal dispensation to be allowed to marry. It took a few years, but soon after Henry was crowned, he married Catherine.

20. Catherine of Aragon

https://commons.wikimedia.org/wiki/File:Catherine_of_Aragon.jpg

It would appear as though Henry truly loved Catherine, and the two had a very happy marriage at first. They were married for twenty-three years, and Henry trusted Catherine implicitly. When he left to invade France in 1513, he entrusted the care of the country to Catherine. However, Henry needed an heir. Although Catherine became pregnant and gave birth a few times, only one child, Mary, survived to adulthood. As time went on, Henry became increasingly desperate for an heir. Matters worsened for Catherine in 1519 when Henry's mistress, Elizabeth Blount, gave birth to a boy who was recognized as Henry's son. He was given the title of duke of Richmond.

For years, Henry viewed Catherine as a model wife and always praised her as such, but when she failed to give him an heir, he decided to take drastic measures.

The English Reformation

When Catherine of Aragon became forty, her chances of providing Henry with a legitimate heir dwindled to nothing. The king began to think of ways to get a different wife. In the 1520s, one of the queen's ladies-in-waiting, Anne Boleyn, caught the king's eye, and he fell madly in love. He decided that she would be the perfect second wife, but the problem was that he needed to get rid of Catherine of Aragon first. Anne Boleyn was an ambitious woman, and she wasn't prepared to settle for being the king's mistress. She refused to start a family with him before marriage. King Henry VIII was stuck in a very difficult situation, which he referred to as the "Great Matter." The Catholic Church didn't permit divorce, and he didn't want to wait until Catherine died.

21. Henry VIII meets Anne Boleyn

https://commons.wikimedia.org/wiki/File:Daniel_Maclise_Henry_VIIIs_first_interview_with_Anne_Boleyn.jpg

Henry VIII had an avid interest in theology and discerned that the only way out of his marriage barring death was an annulment granted by the pope. He used the principle of the Prohibition of Leviticus to argue that his marriage to Catherine was never valid. According to Leviticus, a man was forbidden from marrying his brother's widow. Unfortunately for Henry VIII, Charles V was the emperor of the Holy Roman Empire, and he was Catherine's nephew. The pope at the time was Clement VII, and he wasn't going to risk Charles V's displeasure by granting Henry an annulment.

Faced with opposition from the papal office and most of the rulers in Europe, Henry had to get creative. In 1529, Cardinal Lorenzo Campeggio was sent to investigate the "Great Matter," but nothing was decided. Henry separated from Catherine. In the meantime, he lived with Anne Boleyn, who refused to sleep with him. However, in 1532, Anne Boleyn changed her mind, and she soon became pregnant. This increased Henry's desperation to get his marriage annulled.

Together with Wolsey, Henry concocted a creative plan to separate the church in England from the church in Rome, which would make Henry the head of the Church of England. This would give him total control of the church. Unfortunately, Wolsey wasn't able to achieve this. In 1530, Wolsey was accused of treason, which indicates how far he had fallen from the king's favor. He died while en route to his trial, but he probably would have been executed had he not died of natural causes. He was replaced by Thomas More, who refused to take the Oath of Supremacy and was promptly accused of treason and executed soon afterward. Thomas More was replaced by Thomas Cromwell.

Henry VIII's marriage was annulled by Thomas Cranmer, Archbishop of Canterbury, in 1533, and the Act of Succession was passed, which made Henry's daughter, Mary, illegitimate. Henry was excommunicated from the Catholic Church, but in 1534, the Act of Supremacy was passed. This act made Henry the highest authority in the Church of England, which meant that he, not the pope, was allowed to settle all legal matters. And finally, the Treason Act was passed in 1534, which made it treasonous to criticize the king. The Treason Act meant that Henry was allowed to execute anyone who spoke against the monarch. These people were seen as traitors, which would have violent consequences as the English Reformation progressed.

At first, Henry only wanted control of the church, but eventually, the Church of England faced serious reforms that led to England becoming a predominantly Protestant country. However, the English Reformation only started with Henry, as it would be continued by his heirs. In the meantime, Henry had a new wife and was eager to finally get a legitimate male heir. In fact, his enthusiasm for an heir was so great that Anne Boleyn's entire life was dependent on her giving birth to a boy.

Meanwhile, Catherine of Aragon never agreed to the annulment and was shocked by Henry's actions. In 1536, she died at Kimbolton Castle with the knowledge that her daughter had been disinherited.

Anne Boleyn

Anne Boleyn was the woman who sparked the English Reformation, and she finally became queen in 1533. She had spent some of her childhood in the French court, where she learned the ways of the royal court. Her sister, Mary, had become Henry's mistress sometime in the 1520s but was eventually married off. Anne inspired a deeper sense of commitment in Henry and fought for years to be made his queen. When she became pregnant in 1533, there were high hopes that she would finally provide Henry with a male heir, but she gave birth to the future Queen Elizabeth I instead.

22. Anne Boleyn

https://commons.wikimedia.org/wiki/File:AnneBoleynHever.jpg

As their relationship progressed, Henry became increasingly disillusioned with her, especially as she failed to give birth to a boy. Their relationship dissolved as the couple slipped into despair, and Henry took another mistress. Finally, Henry had Anne arrested on counts of treason and adultery. Their marriage was annulled in 1536, just two days before Anne was beheaded. While Anne didn't provide Henry VIII with an heir, she had inadvertently helped him find a way to do whatever he wanted.

Jane Seymour

As soon as Anne was dead, Henry moved on to a new wife. He married his mistress, Jane Seymour, who had served both Anne and Catherine. According to historical reports, Anne and Jane had fought on multiple occasions before Anne's death. Henry and Jane married soon after Anne was beheaded, and in 1537, Jane gave birth to Henry's heir, Edward. Jane managed to do something that neither of Henry's previous wives had done, but she didn't live long enough to enjoy her triumph.

Jane Seymour died a few weeks after giving birth to her son, and at the king's request, she was laid to rest at St. George's Chapel, where he would eventually be buried next to her.

Anne of Cleves, Catherine Howard, and Catherine Parr

Once Henry had his son, he married three more times, but he was now relieved of the burden of worrying about his heir. He married Anne of Cleves two years after Jane died in order to secure an alliance with the German duke of Cleves. Unfortunately, he was distressed by Anne's looks and divorced her in 1540, about six months after their marriage. She lived off her generous divorce settlement for the rest of her life.

23. Anne of Cleves

https://commons.wikimedia.org/wiki/File:Portrait_Anne_of_Cleves_by_Hans_Holbein_the_Younger_(Louvre).jpg

By 1540, Henry was no longer the young athletic king who had ruled England energetically. He was overweight and unable to walk properly due to an injury in his leg, but that didn't stop him from marrying the young and beautiful Catherine Howard. The king was infatuated with his new bride and gave her many gifts, but their differences proved to be too great. Rumors soon emerged that Catherine had been unfaithful. In 1542, Catherine Howard was executed on charges of treason and adultery.

A few months later, Henry married his final wife, Catherine Parr. Catherine was a very intelligent woman who influenced culture, education, and religion. She was reportedly a kind woman who took good care of Henry's children and stabilized Henry's personal life. Henry VIII's last wife provided him with a few years of peace as his energy dwindled and his life came to an end.

Legacy and Reputation

In his youth, Henry was an avid athlete who was crowned the victor at many of his father's tournaments. He was a handsome young man who charmed the royal court and bravely rose to the task of ruling England when his older brother died. However, in his later years, he was so overweight and sick that he had to be wheeled around. His leg was so ulcerated that it reportedly festered and stank. He died in January 1547, leaving his hard-won heir, Edward VI, to be crowned as king at only nine years old.

When Henry VIII became king at seventeen, there were high hopes for his reign. While he achieved great things, there aren't many arguments in favor of his policies and character. Henry VIII began his rule as a hopeful youth who dreamed of glory, but he would be remembered mostly for his climatic split with the Catholic Church and his melodramatic love life.

Chapter 6: Edward VI (r. 1547–1553)

Henry VIII spent most of his life agonizing about the fact that he needed an heir to continue the Tudor dynasty. He split England from the Roman Catholic Church so that he could annul his first marriage. However, he had to marry twice more before he finally fathered a legitimate son who would inherit the throne. Unfortunately, Henry VIII also led a life of excess that led to his premature death. This prevented him from helping to guide his heir. Edward VI was a young boy when he took the throne, and he was left in the care of advisors who used his power for their own gain.

24. Edward VI

https://commons.wikimedia.org/wiki/File:Edward_VI_of_England_c._1546.jpg

While Henry VII was a relatively unpopular king, he left behind a secure throne with a decent-sized treasury. Henry VIII, on the other hand, grew to be unpopular in his later years and left behind a country that was on the brink of political instability. Thanks to his efforts, the English Reformation had begun, which opened the doors to conflict between Protestants and Catholics. That religious conflict would stir up serious issues for his heirs. Edward VI was still a child when he claimed a throne that desperately required a strong king.

Early Life

When Henry VIII turned his attention to Jane Seymour, he was still married to Anne Boleyn. He had become disillusioned with his marriage since he had expected his second wife to give birth to a son, but after a few years, their relationship deteriorated. Jane Seymour served Anne as a lady-in-waiting, and her relationship with the king often made her a target for Anne's anger. However, the king stuck by Jane's side and married her as soon as he could. Soon after they were married, Jane gave birth to Edward VI on October 12th, 1537. The birth was difficult, and Jane died a few days afterward.

His birth caused several rumors, and later on, people would claim that he had to be cut from his mother's body. When he was born, Henry arranged massive celebrations, and the whole country was delighted with the birth of the young boy. The general public also preferred Jane Seymour over Anne Boleyn, as Anne had a terrible reputation and was widely hated.

Edward grew up to be a vibrant young boy who shared his father's love of sports and music. His father made sure to provide him with good tutors, and he proved to be a good student. He learned subjects such as theology, Greek, Latin, French, military engineering, and geography. As soon as he became king, he began making records of important events, which later helped historians gain an accurate picture of his reign.

In time, Edward VI would lay the foundations that led to England turning from Catholicism to Protestantism. His efforts on behalf of the Protestant Church meant that he was widely revered by Protestants, who embellished details of his life, but the truth was that he was a bright boy who benefited from the privileges of a royal upbringing. Soon after his mother's death, his father remarried again, but Henry VIII's fourth and fifth marriages didn't last long. However, Henry VIII's final marriage provided his children with a conscientious stepmother who would have a lasting impact on the young king.

Catherine Parr

Catherine Parr had been married twice before the king met her. She had a good reputation and displayed a natural talent for avoiding the king's anger. After she married the king in 1543, she took a keen interest in her stepchildren and took care of their education. She developed a friendship with each of his children, which was likely a refreshing change of pace for the children of a king who kept changing wives.

25. Catherine Parr

https://commons.wikimedia.org/wiki/File:Queen_Catherine_Parr_v2.jpg

During this time, the church was quickly undergoing various reforms, and some people were turning to Protestantism, which angered the Catholic clergy and led to conflict. Even the queen of England wasn't immune to this anger. When she showed an interest in Protestantism, she made powerful enemies, such as Stephen Gardiner. She was nearly imprisoned in 1546, but the king intervened on her behalf, and she was spared the humiliation.

Catherine was an intelligent woman with an excellent education. She loved learning, and she was also the first woman to publish an original English book in her own name in England. The king trusted her greatly, so when he went on a military campaign in France, he appointed Catherine as regent while he was away. And if he died, she would have been responsible for Edward until he was old enough to rule. While acting as regent, she signed royal proclamations and took care of financial matters. She didn't sit back and wait for the king to return but rather took her duties very seriously. Some historians theorize that Catherine Parr had a lasting effect on her stepdaughter, Elizabeth.

Henry deeply respected Catherine and made provisions for her before he died. He ordered that she receive the respect of a queen for the rest of her life. Soon after he died, Catherine married Thomas Seymour, the brother of Edward Seymour, who became the Lord Protector of England when Edward VI became king. She took care of Lady Elizabeth, Henry VIII's second daughter, for a short time and published another book. Edward VI held Catherine in high regard, and the two exchanged many letters. Unfortunately, Catherine Parr died in 1548 after giving birth to her first child. She was the first person to have a Protestant funeral of a royal in England. Catherine Parr was a unique woman who left a lasting impression on the Tudor heirs.

The Young King

Edward VI was crowned in January 1547, and he wasn't governed by a regent. While he was officially ruling, the Privy Council held a lot of power. They elected Edward Seymour, Edward VI's maternal uncle, as Lord Protector. Edward Seymour's position gave him unrestricted access to the king, and he became Edward VI's principal advisor. Seymour held immense power and ruled England through his young nephew. The two shared a love of military strategy and spent time studying military and naval battles. Unfortunately for Seymour, he lost favor in 1549 and was replaced by John Dudley. Edward had to deal with ambitious nobles who wanted to rule his country for him, as well as war with Scotland and strained relations with France. To make matters worse, the royal treasury was in danger, as officials had embezzled funds from the crown. The country slipped into economic instability.

The young king was also a staunch Protestant, and while the true extent of his involvement in Protestant reforms is unknown, he must have, at the very least, supported the efforts of Thomas Cranmer, who led the English Reformation in Edward VI's name. These reforms were controversial and caused real conflict that would have violent consequences. While the king faced many problems during his reign, he also had a few triumphs. In 1549, the *Book of Common Prayer* was authorized, and it became a highly influential literary work that is seen as one of the king's greatest achievements. In 1551, Edward was allowed to join the French chivalric Order of St. Michael, which reflected improved relations with France.

Despite his youth, Edward knew the importance of keeping up appearances, and his luxurious lifestyle at the royal court impressed foreign ambassadors. He was an energetic young man who enjoyed sports, hunting, and masques. The young king was also a compassionate person who showed genuine concern for his subjects by commissioning grain surveys and encouraging the cloth trade. While only a young teenager, Edward VI faced serious problems during his reign, but he did the best he could.

Edward Seymour and John Dudley

When Jane Seymour became queen, her family quickly gained political power. Her brother, Edward, became the earl of Hertford and led English forces against the Scottish and French, which earned him the king's favor. When Henry VIII died, Edward Seymour was given the post of Lord Protector by the Privy Council and became the duke of Somerset. While Seymour won military glory, he wasn't a very good politician. He tried to secure a marriage alliance for Edward VI with the Scottish princess, Mary. Unfortunately, the Scots weren't in favor of the alliance, and Seymour invaded Scotland in 1547, which further antagonized the Scots. He tried to smooth over religious tensions with the first *Book of Common Prayer*, which aimed to provide a compromise between Catholic and Protestant beliefs. He also revoked the heresy laws passed by Henry VIII.

26. Edward Seymour, Duke of Somerset

https://commons.wikimedia.org/wiki/File:Edward_Seymour,_Earl_of_Hertford,_Attributed_to_Hans_Eworth_(1515_-_1574).jpg

Finally, Seymour decided to get rid of enclosures. This was the practice of using fertile land for grazing, and Seymour's decision to forbid the practice led to serious backlash from landowners. With many landowners allied against him, the final blow to his power came when the poorer classes rebelled in Norfolk. Seymour was imprisoned in 1549 and released the next year. Unfortunately, his main rival, John Dudley, had gained more power during Seymour's absence. Seymour was executed on charges of supposed treason in 1551.

With his main rival executed for treason, John Dudley could grasp royal power. He was an ambitious man who rose to the rank of duke of Northumberland. As the most powerful man on the Privy Council, he took wealth from the church and continued the English Reformation. While he mainly tried to gain more power for himself, he tried to help the English economy by expanding trade and fighting inflation. Unfortunately, he is mainly remembered for being an unscrupulous politician who only cared about his own power. His power was tied to Edward VI, and once the young king died, Dudley would try to use the Devise for the Succession to his own advantage, which had disastrous consequences.

The Reformation Continued

Edward VI was responsible for more drastic departures from Catholicism than his father. Under the archbishop of Canterbury, Thomas Cranmer, the Church of England saw serious changes during Edward VI's reign. While Henry VIII was king, the Protestant Reformation had gained massive popularity at the expense of the Catholic Church. To many, the Catholic Church had been abusing its power for too long, and it had gained too much wealth. In 1539, the state began to close down monasteries and directed the money from the monasteries to the royal treasury. This had a serious impact on English citizens since monasteries were community centers that provided medicine, financial aid, and employment.

When Edward VI became king, more drastic changes were implemented. Cranmer issued sermons that had to be used in services, and the *Book of Common Prayer* was made compulsory. Catholic teachings, such as transubstantiation and purgatory, were no longer allowed. These reforms had a real impact on the way people worshiped and were popular with some people but were viewed as heresy by others. The Bible was translated into English and widely distributed, while icons, stained glass, and murals were removed from churches. While the religious reforms were supposed to purify worship, it was also a lucrative undertaking that enriched the nobility and the royal family.

These reforms weren't implemented easily, and many Catholics protested. When the monasteries were abolished, any dissenters were executed. In an act that shocked Christendom, the abbots of Reading, Woburn, Colchester, and Glastonbury were hanged for resisting when their monasteries were shut down. The general public also revolted when their monasteries were abolished. Edward VI faced more revolts when England's economy faced problems. The decline in prosperity and changes to centuries-old traditions were too much for the people, who longed for stability. In 1549, a serious rebellion was led by Robert Kett in Norfolk but was viciously defeated by a mercenary force. The English Reformation led to unprecedented changes in the church, but it also led to terrible acts of brutality to enforce the reforms.

Instability in England

Although there was no regency when Henry VIII died, with his son becoming the king in his own right, it was apparent that the young king was ruled through his Privy Council. Edward VI was too young to know any better, and he was utterly devoted to his religion. While he had some good ideas about ruling, he was still only a child who was a few years away from reigning on his own. As a result, he was content with the reforms that were being carried out in his name since they conformed with his own religious beliefs. Unfortunately, these reforms had a serious impact on his kingdom's stability.

Meanwhile, his advisors did their best to gain as much power before the king reached an age where he felt he didn't need them anymore. The Privy Council was split under men such as Edward Seymour and John Dudley, who didn't mind causing further instability as long as it furthered their own interests. For example, John Dudley was happy to join a coalition of landowners and Catholics who conspired against Edward Seymour, but as soon as Seymour was displaced, Dudley continued the English Reformation and secured a lucrative title for himself.

While the nobility and royal family benefited from the Protestant reforms that directed the wealth of the church into the royal treasury, the country was suffering economically. The English coin was debased, which meant the value of the English currency was quickly lowered. This had a serious effect on aspects like trade. The nobility and political officials also had no qualms about embezzling funds from the state and royal family. The royal coffers had also been dried up by Henry VIII's lavish lifestyle. The country was suffering, and as peasants became poorer and more desperate, they received little help from their political leaders and were driven to rebel. These revolts were worsened by the reformation. For centuries, the people had worshiped in the same way, and they had come to accept monasteries and Catholic practices as cornerstones of their existence.

While Edward VI's Privy Council fought each other for dominance and his people suffered through times of unprecedented changes, the king also had to deal with difficult foreign affairs.

War with Scotland

The Tudor dynasty clashed with Scotland on multiple occasions. Henry VII's daughter, Margaret, became the queen of Scotland in an effort to forge an alliance between England and Scotland. Unfortunately, peace was abandoned when Henry VIII invaded France during the early years of his reign, as Scotland invaded England in retaliation. As Henry VIII struggled to secure an heir, it looked as though his nephew, James V, would inherit the English throne. However, those hopes ended when Edward VI was born. James V died in 1542, leaving his baby daughter, Mary, to become the queen of the Scots. In 1543, the Treaty of Greenwich was signed, which ensured peace between England and Scotland and secured a marriage alliance between Mary and Edward VI.

27. Battle of Pinkie

LORD GREY OF WILTON'S CHARGE AT PINKIE (see page 137).

https://commons.wikimedia.org/wiki/File:Lord_Grey_of_Wilton%27s_charge_at_Pinkie.jpg

In an effort to implement the Treaty of Greenwich, Edward VI's advisor, Edward Seymour, invaded Scotland. In 1547, the two countries fought at the Battle of Pinkie. The English forces won the battle, and the day came to be known as "Black Saturday" to the Scots. Meanwhile, the young queen was smuggled out of the country to France, where she was betrothed to the French Dauphin, Francis. She married Francis in 1558 and became the queen of France when Francis ascended the throne the next year. The war against Scotland was expensive, and it was considered a failure, as Scotland and France developed a strong alliance as a result of Mary's betrothal. Unfortunately, Edward VI couldn't do much to strengthen his relationship with Scotland since he had too many problems in his own country. In time, he developed an illness that would lead to his untimely death.

Devise for the Succession

Edward VI's reign was marked by political and religious changes. He was a devout Protestant who approved of massive reforms in the church and went through a lot of effort to spread his Protestant ideals throughout his country. Unfortunately, in 1553, he caught a fever that led to a serious illness. He was only fifteen years old when he realized that he was dying. This left him with a serious problem. The young king hadn't fathered a son to continue his line, and his official heir was his half-sister, Mary. The only problem was that Mary was a staunch Catholic who was horrified by the English Reformation. As the daughter of Catherine of Aragon, she was allied with some of the most powerful Catholic monarchs in Europe and would certainly reverse all the Protestant reforms that had taken place during Edward VI's reign. At only fifteen years old, he was facing death and the reversal of his life's work. His advisors were also in trouble since their power and fortunes rested on the young king.

Instead of allowing Mary to take the throne, Edward VI began looking for ways to prevent Mary from taking the throne. Unfortunately, they couldn't exclude Mary from the line of succession since Henry VIII had recognized Mary and Elizabeth as being eligible to sit on the throne in 1544 with the Act of Succession. Besides that, if they excluded Mary, they would also have to exclude Elizabeth, who was a Protestant. Instead, Edward VI and the duke of Northumberland focused on Lady Jane Grey, the granddaughter of Edward VI's aunt. Lady Jane Grey was connected to the throne, and she was a Protestant. The duke of Northumberland quickly betrothed his son, Guildford Dudley, to Lady Jane Grey and brought his proposal before the sickly king.

Edward VI signed the Devise for the Succession, and it was quickly passed by Parliament. As the king's health declined, he invited his sister, Mary, to come to him. However, Mary had grown up in a dangerous court, and she knew better than to go to the king. Instead, she traveled to East Anglia and waited for the king to die. Finally, the young king died in July 1553, and Lady Jane Grey became the queen of England.

Legacy

For most of his life, Henry VIII went to extraordinary efforts to get a male heir to continue the Tudor line. His efforts resulted in a religiously divided country and a nine-year-old boy on the throne of England. Edward VI faced immense troubles during his short reign, but he might have been able to grow into a great king if he had lived. Instead, he died at fifteen years of age, and one of his last acts was to disinherit his older sister and put a young girl on the throne in an effort the preserve the Protestant reforms.

While Henry VIII went to great pains to secure a son, his son was ruled by ambitious men who allowed England to slip into instability to secure their own wealth. Edward VI's reign was marked by monumental changes, but the truth is that he was little more than a puppet in the hands of unscrupulous advisors. Unfortunately, the Devise of Succession would ultimately fail, and the throne would pass on to a woman who was willing to use brutality to undo the English Reformation.

Chapter 7: Mary I (r. 1553–1558)

Catherine of Aragon suffered several miscarriages, and some of her children died soon after they were born. At the time, childbirth was a difficult process; many children died before their first birthday. But as the queen of England, Catherine's losses meant national disappointment. While she never gave birth to a prince, she was able to have a daughter who would outlive her. Princess Mary had a bright future ahead of her, but when her father had his first marriage annulled, the young princess was disinherited. Her fortunes changed drastically as a result.

28. Mary I

https://commons.wikimedia.org/wiki/File:Maria_Tudor1.jpg

For years, Mary had to live in obscurity since her royal birthright was denied. She was the granddaughter of some of the most powerful monarchs in Europe, but she had to watch as her mother was set aside for Anne Boleyn. Worse yet, her beloved religion was replaced by Protestantism since her younger brother was a devout Protestant. When Edward VI's health declined, Mary began making plans to take the throne of England, but once again, she was denied her birthright when Edward VI named Lady Jane Grey as his successor. However, Mary wasn't going to passively allow someone else to take her throne. In time, Mary I finally ascended to the throne, and she began putting Catholicism back in place. Unfortunately, royal life was full of more disappointments, as Mary I had to deal with the same fertility problems as her mother and faced a court full of enemies who wanted to put her younger Protestant sister on the throne.

Princess Mary

Mary was born in 1516 and was Catherine's fifth child; however, she was the only child who survived infancy. Despite Henry VIII's desire to have a son, he loved Mary deeply and often boasted about her beauty and temperament. When she was only two years old, she was betrothed to the Dauphin of France, Francis, but the marriage never took place, as their betrothal was broken a few years later. At six years old, she was betrothed to Charles V, the Holy Roman emperor, but that contract also fell through. During that time, another marriage contract was negotiated with the French, but an alliance was secured without the need for marriage, leaving the young princess once again single. Finally, it was suggested that Mary should marry James V of Scotland, but the two were never betrothed. The subject of Mary's marriage would be discussed throughout her life, but the contracts somehow always fell through. Unfortunately for the young princess, she would only marry once she was queen and far past her prime years.

While the royal court was trying to find a suitable marriage alliance for the princess, she grew up to be a well-mannered and accomplished child. She studied Latin, music, dance, French, and Spanish. When she was nine years old, she was sent to the border of Wales and given her own court at Ludlow Castle. She was called the "Princess of Wales," but there is no evidence that she was ever invested with the title, likely because the privileges were usually reserved for the crown prince, and Henry still held out hope that he could get a son.

The young princess lived a charmed life and enjoyed all the privileges of her station. She was close to her mother and shared many of Catherine of Aragon's traits. Those traits, such as her pride and stubbornness, would affect the rest of Mary's life.

The Act of Succession

Unfortunately, Catherine's barrenness would have serious effects on the young princess's life. As Mary grew from a child to a young woman, it became common knowledge that her father was dissatisfied with her mother and that he frequently took mistresses. This wasn't uncommon for the time period, and such news wasn't particularly distressing, even though it was stressful for the queen. However, everything changed when the king became obsessed with Anne Boleyn. Suddenly, Catherine had become part of the "Great Matter" that Henry wanted to solve. Catherine Aragon went from being the queen of England to an irritation that prevented Henry from getting what he wanted.

During her teen years, Mary was forced to watch from the sidelines as her father sought permission to annul his marriage to her mother, a move that would disinherit her. Pope Clement VII was stuck in a difficult position, as Charles V had surrounded Rome during the War of the League of Cognac. If he indulged Henry VIII's request, he would risk angering Charles V, who was Catherine of Aragon's nephew. The pope had enough to deal with and chose to reject Henry VIII's request for an annulment. While this may have been a relief to Catherine and Mary, it only served to push Henry VIII to take drastic action.

In time, Henry separated from the church in Rome and made himself the head of the Church of England. This was a shocking decision, which Catherine and Mary viewed as heresy. In 1533, Catherine's marriage to Henry was annulled, and in 1534, the Act of Succession was passed. This act declared that the king's marriage to Anne was "undoubted, true, sincere and perfect" and made Mary illegitimate. Catherine refused to acknowledge that her marriage was illegitimate, and for years, Mary followed her mother's example until she was finally pressured to accept the Act of Succession.

Adolescence

As Mary's parents' marriage fell apart and various marriage alliances failed to become a reality, Mary was reportedly frequently sick. To make matters worse, her mother was forced to move to obscure palaces while

Henry continued life at court with Anne by his side. Mary wasn't allowed to see her mother, and the two were forced to correspond secretly. This would have added to Mary's stress since she and her mother were very close. The young princess suffered from irregular menstruation and depression, but the exact causes of her sickness aren't known.

When Henry VIII married Anne and the Act of Succession was passed, Mary's household was dismissed, and she was forced to serve as her baby sister's lady-in-waiting at Hatfield. In addition, her titles were revoked, and she was called Lady Mary. Despite all the problems she faced, Mary followed her mother's example and refused to acknowledge the Act of Succession, which incensed Henry and Anne. In retaliation, her freedom was restricted, and she was often threatened. Mary got sick often and had a difficult time, especially since she still wasn't allowed to see her mother. She had few allies since her position was greatly diminished, and she had to rely on the imperial ambassador, Eustace Chapuys, to plead her case before the king.

In 1536, Catherine became ill, and Mary asked permission to travel to see her mother, but her request was denied. Catherine died shortly after, and Mary slipped into despair. During her childhood, Mary had been at the center of court life and was beloved by her father. Unfortunately, life became very difficult for her after she was stripped of her inheritance. Her relationship with her father deteriorated, and they didn't speak to each other for three years. Mary's refusal to accept the Act of Succession contributed to her troubles since the king was used to getting what he wanted. By denying Anne as the queen of England, Mary was breaking the laws that her own father had enacted.

Adulthood

In time, Anne Boleyn was executed, and a new queen took the throne. Any hope that Mary would be restored to her birthright was shattered when Edward VI was born. Jane Seymour tried to make life better for Mary and interceded with Henry on her behalf. Henry agreed to make peace with his daughter if she agreed to recognize his authority as the head of the church. Mary was pressured into accepting his demands before she was allowed to return to court. This made her life somewhat easier, as she was allowed to have a household of her own again. There were attempts to return Mary's inheritance during the English Reformation. The Pilgrimage of Grave was a rebellion led by Lord Hussey. He demanded that Mary's birthright be restored to her.

Unfortunately, the rebellion was destroyed, and Hussey was executed.

Meanwhile, Mary was allowed to be her young brother's godmother, and several more marriage alliances were negotiated but fell through. At one point, she almost married the duke of Bavaria and the duke of Cleves, and there were even rumors that Thomas Cromwell tried to marry Mary. This rumor led to Cromwell's execution once the minister fell out of power. While queens came and went, Mary was allowed to live in relative peace. Following the execution of Catherine Howard in 1542, Mary was allowed to act as the hostess of the courtly Christmas Festivities, an honor that was usually reserved for the queen. Finally, Henry married Catherine Parr, who brought peace and happiness to the royal court. Henry's final queen made a real effort to be friends with the royal children. Thanks to her efforts, Mary and Elizabeth were returned to the line of succession when an updated Act of Succession was enacted in 1544. Mary was now the heir to the throne behind her younger brother, but she was legally illegitimate, which restricted her movements and privileges.

When Edward VI became ill, and it was apparent that he would die, he attempted to keep Mary from the throne since she was sure to reverse the Protestant reforms. However, Mary had spent a lifetime in one of the most dangerous courts in Europe. She wasn't going to let anyone keep her from her birthright again. Unfortunately, due to the actions of Edward VI and his Privy Council, an innocent young woman was caught in the crossfire.

Lady Jane Grey

Lady Jane Grey has become one of the most tragic figures in English history. She is known as the Nine Days' Queen and had the shortest reign in British history. Lady Jane was a young noblewoman and the daughter of the duke of Suffolk. While she was supposed to be fifth in line to the throne, Edward VI gave her precedence since she was a Protestant. John Dudley quickly identified her as the perfect heir and betrothed her to his son, Guildford Dudley. The ambitious plot was quickly approved by the dying king and his council. Lady Jane was married without delay, and on July 10th, 1553, she was crowned the queen of England. According to reports of the time, she was a beautiful young woman who had studied French, Latin, Greek, Hebrew, and Italian.

While Edward VI's Protestant reforms pervaded England, Mary refused to give up her faith and traditions. She was used to defying the orders of a king, and in 1550, she realized that her life was in danger. She almost left for mainland Europe. Edward VI's council members, John Dudley in particular, had made life very difficult for Mary. They knew that once she took the throne, she would retaliate. Efforts were made to entrap Mary in the Tower of London before Edward VI died, but Mary proved to be too shrewd for her enemies. While the Devise for the Succession was passed by Parliament, it was an unpopular plan that most of the nobility were reluctant to enforce. These two factors led to the downfall of John Dudley and Lady Jane Grey.

Mary quickly gained supporters, and on July 19th, 1553, she declared herself queen. She marched on London with a force of thirty thousand men who quickly captured Dudley, who led his own force of two thousand men. The unscrupulous duke was executed on August 22nd, 1553.

To her credit, Mary was reluctant to execute the young woman. Lady Jane Grey hadn't wanted to be queen and was pressured into the coup by her father and father-in-law. Mary was able to take the throne with little trouble, and crowds of people cheered for her in London. Unfortunately, a rebellion was raised by Sir Thomas Wyatt in 1554, and it became apparent that as long as Lady Jane Grey was alive, she would be the focus of rebellions against Mary. On February 12th, 1554, Lady Jane Grey and her husband were executed.

29. The execution of Lady Jane Grey

https://commons.wikimedia.org/wiki/File:PAUL_DELAROCHE_-_Ejecuci%C3%B3n_de_Lady_Jane_Grey_(National_Gallery_de_Londres,_1834).jpg

Philip II of Spain

When Mary became queen, crowds of people cheered for her, and most of the nobility joined her army against John Dudley's coup. Unfortunately, she wouldn't remain popular. Her determination to return England to the church in Rome would lead to disastrous consequences. Mary was crowned in 1553 and immediately began reversing the Protestant reforms, which made her unpopular among the noble classes, as they had benefited greatly from them. Most of the populace was indifferent to the reforms, but the return to Catholicism meant more instability for the country.

Mary's popularity was further damaged when she announced her betrothal to Philip II of Spain. This was an immensely unpopular decision since Spain was seen as England's enemy. Her decisions made her people suspicious, as they feared that Spain would invade England. In 1554, Sir Thomas Wyatt led a rebellious force to London, where he planned to replace Mary with her sister, Elizabeth. The rebellion was quickly defeated, and Elizabeth was placed in the Tower of London. Mary swore to her people that her loyalty would always remain with England. Parliament took its time accepting Mary's betrothal and set limits on Philip's power. He would only be allowed to act as the queen's consort, and no foreigners would be allowed to gain political positions in the country.

30. Philip II of Spain

https://commons.wikimedia.org/wiki/File:Philip_II_portrait_by_Titian.jpg

Mary was finally married on July 25th, 1554, at thirty-seven years old. Unfortunately, Philip was nearly eleven years younger than Mary, and the couple spent most of their time apart. Mary announced two pregnancies, one in 1554 and one in 1557. Both turned out to be false pregnancies, and it was clear that Mary was past her childbearing years. In 1556, Philip became the king of Spain, which made Mary the queen consort of the

Spanish king. Together, they waged war on the Protestant Reformation, an action that would earn Mary the title of "Bloody Mary."

Religious and Foreign Policies

Along with her husband, Mary waged war against France in 1557. At first, the couple won a victory at Saint-Quentin, but their lack of funds led them to begin losing the war they had started. In 1558, Mary lost Calais, which had been held by England for centuries. While the war was a disaster, Mary managed to help stabilize the economy in England. Her marriage to Philip brought Spanish money to the English economy, and she governed the country well. Like her successful predecessors, Mary created specialized councils that took care of various aspects of the government. This allowed her to control the way her country was governed. Mary had spent years on the fringes of her father's court and had time to study how to do her job correctly.

Mary's main ambition was to return England to the papacy, and she enacted several Acts of Repeals to undo the English Reformation. The Second Act of Repeal in 1555 made the pope the head of the Church of England. Mary was finally able to repeal the acts that had ruined her life and allowed her religion to be reformed. Unfortunately, the queen wasn't content with merely enacting repeals; she zealously enforced her acts and began persecuting Protestants. During the next four years, she burned around 287 Protestants at the stake. These numbers included prominent men, such as Hugh Latimer, Nicholas Ridley, and Thomas Cranmer. The queen was already becoming unpopular before these acts, so the public burnings only turned the tide of public opinion against her.

However, it should be noted that Mary's acts were exaggerated to ruin her reputation. The infamous burnings were rare, and she only used the tactic as a last resort against rebellions and resistance. In fact, Mary preferred to educate the general public about religious matters and took a keen interest in how the clergy was educated. Training schools were established, and the priesthood had detailed outlines of what was expected of them. While she did persecute Protestants, many atrocities committed against Protestants were perpetrated by angry mobs and Catholic parishioners. While Mary's actions were unsavory, it would be unfair to dismiss her completely.

Mary's time as queen was extremely stressful, as she had to deal with personal and political turmoil. She frequently had to fight with

Parliament and the House of Commons, and her enemies made her job very difficult. In time, her health began to fail, and England prepared itself for a new queen.

Legacy

In 1558, Mary died from stomach cancer at the age of forty-two. At that point, she was so unpopular that the date of her death was celebrated as a public holiday for years after she died. People were relieved that the religious turmoil was over. Mary's younger sister, Elizabeth, became queen. She would face threats from Spain and her own council. Like Mary, Elizabeth had grown up in the dangerous Tudor court and had learned how to take care of herself. Elizabeth would usher in a golden age in English history, which included the English Renaissance that saw famous playwrights and poets flourish.

When Mary was born, she had a bright future as the daughter of Henry VIII and Catherine of Aragon. She led a charmed life as the princess of England, and her early proposed marriage alliances represented great hopes for her future. Unfortunately, Henry VIII betrayed his daughter in his quest for a son, and Mary was forced to live on the outskirts of a court that had once doted on her. She was forced to live through extremely difficult times but maintained her poise and dignity. Her pride and devotion to her religion moved her to defy kings and fight for what she thought was right. Mary faced threats of execution and was forced to deny her own convictions, which took a toll on her. Due to her father's actions, she remained lonely and unmarried for most of her life. The crisis of succession meant that her country was divided and unstable when she took the throne. During her time as queen, she was forced to fight for what she believed in, and in time, she died of a terrible disease, with her people celebrating her death.

Chapter 8: Elizabeth I (r. 1558–1603)

Elizabeth I is one of the most famous queens in history. She wasn't supposed to become queen; in fact, her father had disinherited her when she was still a young child. For most of her life, she was branded as the illegitimate daughter of Henry VIII and his most notorious wife, Anne Boleyn. Elizabeth's early life was tumultuous, but she survived her siblings and became the most powerful woman in England.

31. Elizabeth I

https://commons.wikimedia.org/wiki/File:Elizabeth_I_by_Nicholas_Hilliard.jpg

Once she became queen, the foremost issue on everyone's mind was that of her marriage. Mary I had proven that the wrong marriage could cause serious problems for the whole country, and if Elizabeth I married a foreign man, then that man could claim the right to become the king of England. However, Elizabeth I was a shrewd and forward-thinking woman who knew that the only way to keep control of her throne was by remaining single.

Elizabeth I had seen how Edward VI had been ruled by his advisors and how Mary I had to defend her throne when she married a Spanish prince. She survived the scandal of remaining unmarried and brought political, religious, and economic stability to her country. During her long reign, the arts flourished. By remaining unmarried, Elizabeth I brought an end to the Tudor dynasty. But after spending her formative years at the hands of the Tudor court, Elizabeth I was well aware of the consequences of her decision and became the "Virgin Queen."

Early Life

Anne Boleyn gave birth to Elizabeth in 1533 and named her daughter after Henry VIII's mother, Elizabeth of York. Unfortunately, Elizabeth was still a toddler when Henry VIII had his marriage to Anne annulled and branded Elizabeth as illegitimate. While Mary I spent most of her childhood as the princess of England, Elizabeth spent most of her childhood as Henry VIII's illegitimate daughter. When she was born, Henry VIII was sorely disappointed since he had pinned all his hopes on Anne giving him a son. Their marriage began to fall apart shortly after.

Henry VIII married Jane Seymour just a few days after Anne was executed, and Elizabeth faded into the background. Her early education included studying French, Dutch, Spanish, and Italian. Elizabeth showed a natural gift for learning languages, and by the time she was twelve years old, she had translated Catherine Parr's book, *Prayers or Meditations*, into Italian, French, and Latin from English, which she then gave to her father as a New Year's gift. She made a habit of translating classical works and seemed to have enjoyed the practice. Later, she studied Scottish, the Irish languages, Cornish, and Welsh. Elizabeth was a gifted student, and her final stepmother, Catherine Parr, took a keen interest in Elizabeth's education. As a result, Elizabeth studied subjects such as history, music, philosophy, rhetoric, and theology, which would later help her during her reign.

32. A portrait of Elizabeth Tudor (far right) with her father, his court jester, and her siblings

https://commons.wikimedia.org/wiki/File:Henry_8_with_children.jpg

When her father died, Elizabeth lived with Catherine Parr and Thomas Seymour at their estate in Chelsea. Unfortunately, this period in her life would lead to a scandal involving Thomas Seymour. According to reports, Thomas Seymour enjoyed entering Elizabeth's rooms while he was in his nightgown and engaged in horseplay with the young teenager that involved tickling. Elizabeth didn't seem to invite these visits and went through pains to make sure that she was never alone with him. In 1548, Elizabeth left her stepmother's house after Catherine Parr allegedly discovered her husband and stepdaughter in an embrace. When Catherine Parr died a few months later, Thomas Seymour expressed a desire to marry Elizabeth. In 1549, Seymour was arrested after conspiring to marry Elizabeth after deposing his brother as Lord Protector. Elizabeth was interrogated during this time, but she never admitted to being involved in the plot. Thomas Seymour was executed on March 20th, 1549.

Thomas Wyatt's Rebellion

In 1554, a massive rebellion led by Sir Thomas Wyatt the Younger took place in opposition to Mary I's marriage to Philip II of Spain. In all fairness, the causes of the rebellion were much more intricate than the matter of the queen's marriage to a foreign prince. The English economy had been stalling ever since Henry VIII's reign, and it had been worsened by the greedy nobles who ruled through Edward VI. Several nobles also took part in the rebellion, but this was likely to increase their own wealth. When Mary I took the throne, she immediately began reversing the Protestant reforms put in place by her predecessor. However, many Protestants wanted England to become a Protestant country. All of these causes contributed to the rebellion, and when Queen Mary I announced her betrothal to Prince Philip, the rebels found a golden opportunity.

Spain was becoming rich from the loot that came from the New World, and it was a staunchly Catholic country. Rumors flourished, as nationalistic English citizens feared that the foreign prince would one day become the king of England and rob the country of its resources to build his own empire. Suddenly, the same people who had cheered for Mary I when she took the throne were murmuring against her and remembering the fact that her mother had also been Spanish. It also seemed that a few of the rebels wanted to replace Mary I with her younger sister, Elizabeth. This would have prevented the country's return to Catholicism, which would have allowed many nobles to keep the riches that they had taken from the church during the English Reformation.

The rebels planned to march in November of 1553 and planned four other uprisings that would be supported by the French, who would send their fleet to England. Word got out about the rebellion, and three of the uprisings couldn't take place. In January 1554, Wyatt led his rebel force from Kent to London in an attempt to stop the queen's marriage. At first, the rebels gained the upper hand, as they forced the royal army to retreat, and some royal soldiers joined Wyatt's cause. The rebels marched forward, and it seemed that nothing would be able to stop them. Matters looked so desperate for Mary that she was forced to destroy the bridges that crossed the River Thames.

Eventually, Thomas Wyatt reached London, where he crossed the Thames and rebuilt the bridges so that his army could enter the city. The two armies fought within London, and Wyatt was eventually surrounded. Once the rebellion was destroyed, Mary executed Wyatt and two hundred of his men. Mary was forced to execute Lady Jane Grey since she knew that the young noblewoman would be the figurehead for future rebellions. Parliament was allowed to reduce her husband's future privileges, and Elizabeth was imprisoned. Unfortunately, the rebellion served to make Mary I more paranoid, and she began persecuting the Protestants relentlessly.

The Virgin Queen

After the Wyatt rebellion was defeated in 1554, Elizabeth was imprisoned in the Tower of London, even though she had never said anything against her sister or spoken publicly about Mary's policies. After two months, Elizabeth was put under house arrest in Oxfordshire. Finally, Elizabeth made peace with her sister after a year of imprisonment and was allowed to live freely again. In 1558, Mary I died of stomach cancer, and Elizabeth was crowned at twenty-five years of age at Westminster Abbey. While her coronation was a magnificent affair, the truth was that England was in a delicate state. There were no more lands in France, and foreign alliances were far and few between. To make matters worse, the state was in serious financial straits. It was clear that everyone expected Elizabeth to marry someone as quickly as possible, and she became the most sought-after woman in the world. England needed a strong leader, and everyone expected Elizabeth's husband to be the leader they needed.

33. Elizabeth I in her coronation robes

https://commons.wikimedia.org/wiki/File:Elizabeth_I_in_coronation_robes.jpg

However, instead of looking for a husband, Elizabeth began looking for capable advisors. She appointed William Cecil as her secretary, Sir Francis Walsingham as the secretary of state, and Robert Dudley the earl of Leicester. These men became Elizabeth's favorites and aided her through much of her reign. She put herself in charge of policymaking, and nobles had to approach her directly to push their ideas. The queen proved to be an independent woman who carefully took care of the royal treasury and didn't waste time on expensive foreign conquests. She took time to tour her country, and whenever anyone brought up the subject of her marriage, she claimed to be married to England. When Elizabeth I took the throne, she was courted by many nobles and received offers of marriage from Philip II of Spain, the king of Sweden, two Habsburg dukes, and a French prince.

Elizabeth used symbols that were associated with the Virgin Mary to enhance her own image as the Virgin Queen, but there were several friendships with young men that may have been intimate in nature. These friends included Sir Walter Raleigh, Sir Christopher Hatton, and Robert Devereux, although no one held as much sway over the young queen as Robert Dudley.

Robert Dudley

Robert Dudley was born in 1532. He was the son of the duke of Northumberland, John Dudley. Unfortunately, John's father had been involved in the plot to place Lady Jane Grey on the throne and had been executed by Mary I. Robert himself had also been part of that plot and was imprisoned in the Tower of London, but Mary eventually released him. The Dudleys had been an unlucky family in regards to treason, as Robert's grandfather had also been executed for treason in 1510. Unlike Robert's family members, he was able to survive his charge of treason and became an important political figure in Elizabeth I's royal court.

34. Robert Dudley

https://commons.wikimedia.org/wiki/File:Robert_Dudley,_1st_Earl_of_Leicester,_Collection_of_Waddesdon_Manor.jpg

Robert married Amy Robsart in 1550 and was appointed as the Master of the Horse. This allowed him to take care of the royal stables and transportation. He was also invited to join the highly prestigious Order of the Garter. There were reports that he and Elizabeth became friends before she ascended the throne, but there's no doubt that the two shared a close relationship by the time she became queen. Robert was given apartments close to Elizabeth's own royal rooms, and there were rumors that Robert would become Elizabeth's husband. Unfortunately for Robert, he was already married to a sickly wife. In 1560, Robert's wife fell down the stairs in the couple's home, breaking her neck and dying. Rumors began to swirl that Robert was responsible. The scandal surrounding his wife's death counted against him in the race for Elizabeth's hand. She might have sensed that she would lose the public's respect if she married Robert due to the accusations of murder and the fact that his family name had been disgraced by the charges of treason.

While Robert never became Elizabeth's husband, he was appointed as part of her Privy Council, and he became the earl of Leicester. When Mary, Queen of Scots, became a problem, Elizabeth suggested that Robert Dudley marry her, but he wisely refused. Robert was clearly the queen's favorite and hosted her frequently at his many estates, which led to her giving him more honors and lands. In time, Robert Dudley slowly fell out of favor, as the queen was distracted by other favorites. In 1578, she found out that he had married Lettice Knollys in secret, and she banished him from her court. He was allowed to return eventually and lead a force of men to support a rebellion in the Netherlands against Philip II of Spain, although his force ultimately failed. In 1588, Queen Elizabeth faced the Spanish Armada, but Robert was too sick to help his beloved queen and died that year.

Religious Policies

When Mary I took the throne, she immediately reversed many of her brother's Protestant reforms, but when it became apparent that she was going to die without an heir, the whole country braced itself for a return to Protestantism. Elizabeth I reinstated the Protestant reforms and brought the Act of Supremacy back, which made her the head of the Church of England. She also brought back the *Book of Common Prayer*. However, unlike her predecessors, Elizabeth wasn't interested in imposing her beliefs on the general public and allowed people to worship as they wished. Her policy of religious tolerance catered to the common populace, who were indifferent to royal protocols but were impacted by the religious back and forth.

Elizabeth I allowed Catholics to worship in peace, but she was excommunicated by the pope in 1570. She actively supported Protestantism and sent support to the Huguenots in France and the Protestants in the Netherlands. When she tried to impose Protestantism in Ireland, she was met with fierce backlash and multiple rebellions, which were supported by Philip II of Spain. Her policy of religious tolerance brought peace to a country that had seen many religious conflicts, but there were many who were unsatisfied with her approach and wanted to further their own agendas. The Catholics viewed Elizabeth as illegitimate since Henry VIII never received papal approval to annul his marriage to Catherine of Aragon. As a result, the Catholics began looking for a different queen.

They soon found the perfect candidate in Mary, Queen of Scots. Mary was firmly Catholic and had been brought up in France. She also had a claim to the English throne. As a result, she became the figurehead of treasonous Catholic plots against Elizabeth I.

Mary, Queen of Scots

Mary was born in 1542 and made the queen of Scotland just days after her birth when her father, James V, died. Unfortunately, she wasn't able to spend much time in her native Scotland, as the war against England forced her to flee to France, where she was betrothed to the Dauphin of France, Francis. The war against England was a result of the efforts of Henry VIII to betroth his son, Edward VI, to Mary. As the granddaughter of Margaret Tudor, Mary had a connection to the English throne, and Henry VIII hoped to unite the two countries through marriage, but the Scottish Parliament refused the betrothal.

In France, Mary was treated like a queen and given an excellent education. She was popular in the French court and known for being a lively young woman who enjoyed dancing. During her time in France, she became a Catholic, which would eventually cause serious consequences. She married Prince Francis in 1558 and became the queen of France the next year. Mary also made her claim to the English throne known, and when she returned to Scotland after Francis's death in 1560, she continued her claim. This caused problems between her and Elizabeth I. When Mary returned to Scotland, she wasn't given safe passage back home by Elizabeth. Mary refused to recognize the Treaty of Edinburgh, which accepted Elizabeth's absolute claim to the English throne.

When Mary returned to Scotland, she found that most of the country was Protestant. Many of her nobles didn't want a Catholic woman on the throne. Mary married Lord Darnley in 1565, who eventually murdered her Italian secretary, David Rizzio. Lord Darnley was murdered in 1567 but not before Mary and Darnley had a son, James Stuart. Soon after Darnley's murder, Mary married Lord Bothwell, which proved to be too much for the Scottish lords. Mary was defeated on the battlefield and imprisoned soon after. She was forced to abdicate the throne in 1567, and her son became James VI of Scotland. James VI was ruled by his lords and became a Protestant.

Mary escaped Scotland in 1568 and fled to England. Elizabeth found herself in a difficult position, and she decided to imprison Mary in different castles. In the end, Mary was imprisoned for twenty years and never saw Scotland or her son again. During the next two decades, Mary was the figurehead for several plots against Elizabeth, and in 1586, Lord Walsingham found undeniable proof of treason against Mary. Elizabeth didn't want to sign Mary's death warrant, but in 1587, Elizabeth relented. Mary was executed soon after.

Legacy

Later, Elizabeth would be accredited with fostering the best part of the English Renaissance and defeating the Spanish Armada. These were impressive feats, and Elizabeth's reign was known for being peaceful and bringing stability to England. When she became queen, she inherited a kingdom that had been drained of money and had experienced severe religious conflict. However, she soon nursed the country back to health and allowed her subjects to worship as they wished. Her triumph against the Spanish Armada would prove to be one of the most glorious Tudor victories and earn her the title Elizabeth Gloriana.

Elizabeth's decision to remain unmarried took remarkable strength of character, and it proved to be a clever choice since she never had to share her throne with anyone. Her fierce independence led to one of the most peaceful periods in English history. Despite her religious tolerance and shrewd ruling style, she still had many enemies. During her long reign, she faced treasonous plots and threats from powerful foreign kings but managed to hold her own and keep her crown. She never had any children, and when she died, the Tudor line ended with her.

While Elizabeth's reign was mostly successful, the last years of her life were defined by high taxes, inflation, and failing crops. She passed many laws and policies to help the poor, but times were tough, and there were a few food riots. Queen Elizabeth I died in 1603, and the throne passed to her closest living male relative, James VI of Scotland, who became James I of England. James I was England's first Stuart king, and the Stuarts would rule England until 1714.

The Tudor dynasty was defined by times of momentous change that saw the country split from the Church of England, as well as some of the most interesting battles of the time. Under the Tudor reign, military and warfare in England were forever changed.

Section Three:
Military and Warfare

Chapter 9: Wars and Battles

The Tudor era saw some of the most important battles and wars in European history. During this time, many European countries were locked in a battle of wills that saw mighty dynasties rise and fall. The Tudors' own rise to power was aided by a bloody civil war that pitted families against each other. When Henry Tudor became king, England's army wielded medieval weapons, and men were called to arms whenever their lords summoned them. Over the next few decades, the army would be refined into a deadly force supported by superior weapons, warships, and gun forts. After all, England faced threats from France, Spain, and Scotland.

The evolution of the Tudor army can be seen through some of the most significant battles of their time. In the beginning years of the Tudors' reign, the Tudor army was armed with traditional weapons. The guns were owned and used by mercenaries. However, by the time Henry VIII went to war against France, he had powerful weapons at his disposal. Under the Tudor rule, English warfare and weapons would never be the same.

The First Battle of St. Albans, 1455

The first battle of the Wars of the Roses was far from the glorious battles that were romanticized by medieval chivalric literature. At that time, the Hundred Years' War had come to an end, and many soldiers who had fought in France were finally back home and could be called upon by their lords. The First Battle of St. Albans was fought in the streets and lanes of the town, which meant that soldiers had to fight on foot and try to get at their enemies over street barricades. It was a messy affair that would set the tone for the rest of the war.

Soldiers were armed with swords and shields, and while artillery and firearms were available, they were still difficult and unreliable. Besides that, those types of weapons were completely unsuited for the close-quarter combat that took place during the First Battle of St. Albans. The battle began on May 22nd, 1455, when Richard, Duke of York, met Henry VI. The duke of York was supported by the earl of Salisbury and the earl of Warwick, while Henry VI fought alongside the dukes of Somerset and Buckingham.

Unfortunately for Henry VI, he was outnumbered when the Yorkist alliance mustered three thousand men; he only had two thousand men at his command. To make matters worse, the Yorkist army had a force of experienced longbowmen who were led by Sir Robert Ogle, who had fought in France. The king's forces were ultimately defeated, and he was imprisoned by the Yorkists.

Battle of Bosworth, 1485

After three decades of near-constant war, England was on the brink of the final major battle of the Wars of the Roses. By that time, many noble families had become extinct, as men were executed for treason or died in battle. As various forces amassed at Bosworth Field, the stage was set for the dramatic showdown between Richard III and Henry Tudor.

On August 7th, 1485, Henry Tudor landed in Wales. As he marched, he began gathering support, and Richard was forced to meet Henry's army. Lord Thomas Stanley, Margaret Beaufort's husband, and William Stanley arrived at the battlefield with significant forces but refused to join the war until they knew who would win. Henry's army was outnumbered, but Henry had experienced allies on his side, such as the earl of Oxford. Richard commanded the duke of Norfolk to make up the vanguard, which steadily began losing against the earl of Oxford. Richard desperately commanded the duke of Northumberland to assist his army, but Northumberland didn't respond. Richard felt the need to charge at Henry himself, at which point the Stanleys joined the fray and attacked Richard III.

It was a decisive battle that saw the birth of the House of Tudor. The Yorkist forces may have numbered up to twelve thousand men and had a force of archers and a cannon. Meanwhile, Henry had about eight thousand men, with mercenaries and exiles in his ranks that had been joined by Englishmen as his army marched. The nobles and commanders in both armies fought on top of horses and wielded swords, shields, and lances, while common soldiers fought on foot. The soldiers fought with pole weapons, such as halberds, pikes, and swords.

Battle of Stoke Field, 1487

While the Battle of Bosworth Field determined that Henry VII would be the king of England, there were still many Yorkist enemies who wanted to take the throne from him. The Battle of Stoke Field took place on June 16th, 1487. In an effort to take the throne from Henry VII, the earl of Lincoln hired an army of mercenaries from Switzerland, Germany, and Ireland. Lincoln claimed to have Edward of Warwick in his possession and crowned the boy King Edward VI of England. The Yorkist army had about eight thousand men and decided that they had the advantage. They marched on England.

King Henry VII's army, once again led by the earl of Oxford, met the Yorkist army at Stoke Field. This time, Henry was in the majority with about twelve thousand men. With the River Trent behind them, the Yorkist army had no option but to fight for their lives since retreat simply wasn't possible. Despite their sincere efforts, the royal army broke their ranks and chased the mercenaries down the ravine, which became known as the Bloody Gutter. The fleeing mercenaries were cut down, and the king's army was victorious. It was soon discovered that the supposed King Edward VI was no more than a pretender, a lowborn boy known as Lambert Simnel, who was later sent to work in the king's kitchens.

Instead of executing all the traitors, Henry VII chose to impose fines on some of the leading nobles and had the Irish clergy who supported Lincoln excommunicated from the church. Lincoln chose to hire many Irish kerns, who were soldiers who could travel quickly because they were lightly armed. This may have led to Lincoln's downfall since Henry VII made sure that his army was well equipped when he marched to defeat the pretender.

Battle of Flodden, 1513

The next significant battle in the Tudor era involved Henry VIII and the king of Scotland, James IV. In 1511, Henry VII joined the Holy

League alongside Spain, the pope, Venice, and the Holy Roman Empire against France. Since Scotland and France were allies, James IV was forced to negotiate with England. He offered peace on the condition that Henry VIII refrain from fighting against France, but Henry VIII rejected the offer.

35. The Battle of Flodden

THE BATTLE OF FLODDEN (*see page* 125).

https://commons.wikimedia.org/wiki/File:The_Battle_of_Flodden.jpg

In 1513, Henry VIII invaded France with a massive army, and James IV invaded England, taking many of his nobles with him. James IV expected that no one would be left to defend England in Henry VIII's absence and amassed a large and well-equipped army. Unfortunately for James IV, Henry had left England under the watchful care of the earl of Surrey.

Both sides were equipped with cannons, but they were difficult to transport and very slow. The Scots were mostly armed with swords, but before the battle, they had been equipped with long pikes that had been brought over by French dignitaries. This proved to be a mistake, as the Scots weren't trained to use the weapon, which was about five yards long. The long pikes were very effective when soldiers used them in unison, but the Scots hadn't had time to learn to do that yet. Thus, the weapons, which had lethal potential, were worse than useless to the Scots.

Meanwhile, the English brought many longbowmen, who fired on the Scots with deadly accuracy. Finally, the Scots were defeated, and King James IV was killed in battle along with many of his nobles, which threw Scotland into a massive crisis.

Battle of the Spurs, 1513

When Henry VIII became king, he was young and energetic with dreams of military glory. He had the royal treasury at his disposal and was surrounded by young and ambitious men who wanted their shot at battle. Finally, the perfect opportunity presented itself when Henry joined the Holy League. Not only was Henry VIII going to fight against the hated French, but he also had the backing of the papacy, which made it a holy war. Unfortunately, the war in France proved to be a difficult and expensive endeavor. In 1512, Thomas Grey failed to win Aquitaine and was forced to go back home empty-handed. In May 1513, English forces landed in Calais and immediately began marching toward Thérouanne. Henry VIII landed in Calais in June of that same year with a significant force. The army was comprised of cavalry, artillery, infantry, and longbowmen, all ready for war. They were also accompanied by hundreds of hired mercenaries.

The English army set siege to Thérouanne, while Henry VIII set up camp at a distance. In August, Holy Roman Emperor Maximilian traveled with a light force to meet Henry VIII, but Henry VIII refused to be distracted from his main goal. The French tried to break the siege but were unsuccessful, and Henry was forced to move to Guinegate. The two armies met later in August in battle, where the French hoped to engage the army and then retreat as a diversion so that supplies could be delivered to Thérouanne. Unfortunately, the plan was a disaster, as the French were attacked while retreating. They were completely defeated. Finally, Henry VIII experienced his long-awaited military glory. In time, the battle came to be known as the Battle of the Spurs, owing to how quickly the French left the battlefield on horseback.

Battle of Solway Moss, 1542

While Henry VIII hoped to bring military glory to England, he was mostly known for his infamous break with the church in Rome. When he split from the church, he advised his nephew, James V, the king of Scotland, to do the same. James V ignored his uncle's advice, and in

1542, Henry VIII sent an army to raid Scotland in retaliation. Unfortunately, the Scottish army was small and relatively unorganized.

James V responded to the English raid by sending about eighteen thousand Scots into England under Lord Maxwell. Unfortunately, the chain of command wasn't very clear, as Oliver Sinclair, one of James V's favorites, announced that he was supposed to lead the attack. The Scottish lords fought amongst themselves, which may have led to their disastrous defeat. The two armies met at Solway Moss. The English force of about three thousand men was led by Lord Wharton and Sir William Musgrave.

The battle took place near a river and marshy lands, which made it difficult to fight back or flee. According to reports, the fighting was intense, and the Scots fought with all their might but were eventually forced to retreat. Hundreds of Scottish soldiers were said to have drowned in the river. When news of the defeat reached James V, he became sick with fever and retreated to Falkland Palace, where he died at thirty years of age.

Sieges of Boulogne, 1544

In 1541, King Henry VIII was shocked to discover that his fifth wife, Catherine Howard, had been unfaithful to him. He threatened to kill her himself but was held back by his courtiers. In an effort to distract the world from his public humiliation, Henry VIII decided to declare war on France, as France was fighting with Spain over control of parts of Italy. The war would force France to renew pension payments to Henry.

Henry VIII surprisingly decided to lead the army himself, and he was joined by the duke of Norfolk and the duke of Suffolk. In 1544, Holy Roman Emperor Charles V and Henry became allies against France. The two rulers planned to lead a major force against France and capture Paris. The duke of Norfolk landed in Calais first and besieged the town of Montreuil. The siege was beset by food shortages, bad weather, and bad planning.

Henry finally left England in July 1544 with great fanfare. Instead of going to help Norfolk at Montreuil, Henry marched for Boulogne. The English forces were supported by archers, pikemen, gunners, and horsemen. Henry's siege guns were impressive and caused serious damage to Boulogne's walls. Henry was confident that he would soon defeat Boulogne. Unfortunately for Henry, he was soon bogged down by bad weather, which destroyed valuable gunpowder. Henry was only able to continue the assault on Boulogne's walls in August. In September, Boulogne surrendered, while things went badly at Montreuil.

Unfortunately, Charles V made peace with France soon after, and Henry VIII decided to go home. The battle also prompted retaliation from France, which tried to invade England through the English Channel. Henry VIII was forced to go on the defensive. In 1546, Henry VIII made peace with France and died shortly thereafter.

Battle of the Solent, 1545

In May 1545, the French brought their fleet to England in an attempt to invade the country through Portsmouth, which happened to be Henry VIII's naval base. King Henry VIII was forced to go to Portsmouth with his Privy Council to prevent the invasion. In July, the French entered the Solent with 150 warships and galleys and about 30,000 troops. The English fleet was outnumbered since they only had about eighty ships, led by the warships the *Mary Rose* and *Great Harry*. Thankfully, the English row barges were able to force the French to retreat.

Once the French were beaten back by the English navy, they decided to invade the Isle of Wight, which had a small population of well-trained civilians. They had learned to defend themselves during the Hundred Years' War. The battle dragged on, and the great warship *Mary Rose* sank during the battle. Despite this, the French were forced to retreat back to France on July 28th.

Battle of Ancrum Moor, 1545

After the Battle of Flodden, Scotland was unable to fight any wars against the English, as the country had been seriously destabilized by the resounding loss. However, the country recovered just in time to fight against England at the Battle of Solway Moss, which resulted in another major loss and the eventual death of Scotland's young king, James V. Unfortunately, James V hadn't had a male heir yet, so he left the kingdom to his infant daughter, Mary.

Henry VIII seized the chance to enforce a peace treaty with Scotland and tried to force Scotland to agree to the betrothal of Mary, Queen of Scots, to his young son, Edward. The Sots refused, which led to a series of military engagements that came to be known as the "Rough Wooing."

In 1545, an English force of about five thousand men entered Scotland, where they plundered Melrose. The Scots raised a small army in response, which was led by the earl of Angus. The Scots drew the English into a trap at sunset, which caused the English army to fall into chaos, as they were caught off guard and blinded by the bright sun. The Scots also used long pikes, which helped them win the fight, unlike at the Battle of Flodden. The English were defeated and forced to retreat.

Battle of Pinkie, 1547

Unfortunately, the Battle of Ancrum Moor wasn't the end of the Rough Wooing. When Henry VIII died, the duke of Somerset was left in charge of the young King Edward. In 1547, he planned an invasion into Scotland to conquer large portions of land. Somerset planned to use the English army and navy to his advantage, but he was met by the earl of Arran. The Scottish forces were largely outgunned and outnumbered, but their pikemen were able to inflict serious damage before the army came under fire from the English ships, artillerymen, and archers.

The Scots were forced to retreat while under heavy fire, and many drowned while trying to cross the Roman Bridge over the Esk River. While they fought bravely, the Scots were soundly defeated in the disastrous battle but were able to smuggle Queen Mary out of the country to France. Without a marriage alliance, the cost of war against Scotland was too much to justify, and England was forced to abandon the endeavor.

Loss of Calais, 1558

For hundreds of years, England and France had been enemies, as they both fought over the lands that had once been occupied by Henry II and Eleanor of Aquitaine. While most of those lands had been lost to the English, they managed to keep a strong grip on Calais. Unfortunately, in 1558, Mary I waged war on France at the urging of her husband, Philip II of Spain.

The French were provoked to engage in the fight, and the famous port town was captured by François de Lorraine in only six days. This was a tremendous loss, as Calais was a wool production center and opened up trade for staples such as lace, wool, and lead. The loss of Calais was the final straw for Mary I in her short and unsuccessful reign, and she died a few months after.

The Spanish Armada, 1588

One of the biggest challenges Elizabeth I faced during her reign came during the latter half of her rule when she was forced to face the formidable Spanish Armada. In July 1588, the Spanish Armada sailed toward England to remove its Protestant queen from the throne. For decades, the Spanish had become rich by sending ships to the New World and plundering its wealth, which allowed them to build massive warships. Elizabeth I had been a thorn in the Spanish fleet's side, as she allowed her privateers to attack and plunder Spanish ships. Finally, things deteriorated between England and Spain when Elizabeth provided aid to Protestants in the Netherlands when they rebelled against Spain.

36. The Spanish Armada

https://commons.wikimedia.org/wiki/File:The_Spanish_Armada.jpg

Philip II gained papal approval for his invasion and declared that his daughter, Isabella, would be the next queen of England. The Spanish soon sailed for England in their trademark crescent shape, with massive warships in the middle surrounded by smaller fighting ships. Along the way, Philip appointed the duke of Medina Sidonia to command the Spanish Armada, which turned out to be a bad decision. The duke had no seafaring experience and was frequently seasick.

Elizabeth I made Lord Howard of Effingham the commander of her fleet, and the two fleets met and began to attack each other. Drake fired on the ships from a distance, which caused the Spanish to fire back and waste their ammunition. They were forced to dock at Calais and wait for supplies. In response, the English released old ships loaded with materials that would burn up easily among the Spanish Armada. The Spanish knew that these ships could take down their whole fleet, and some ships fled to the sea.

With their formation broken, the Spanish were blocked off and forced to retreat amid terrible weather conditions. The Spanish Armada was soundly defeated, and England reveled in its victory.

In a few short decades, warfare went from medieval skirmishes to sophisticated naval battles. The Tudor era was marked by significant battles that changed the fortunes of Tudor monarchs and led to serious advancements in their weapons and military. As the Tudors went from battle to battle, they were forced to rethink the way their army was structured, and this helped them to win some of their most significant battles.

Chapter 10: The Military and the Royal Navy

Medieval warfare was as interesting as it was brutal and barbaric. The medieval times included periods of immense changes and wars that ravaged Europe. During this time, great advancements were made in warfare and military tactics. When the Wars of the Roses began, England was stuck in an internal struggle that saw local nobles fight bitterly against one another. The age of English military glory under strong Plantagenet kings was long gone. As a result of the stagnation caused by the civil war, when the Tudors came to power, the English army used the same types of weapons and military tactics as they had during the Hundred Years' War against France.

However, under the ever-enthusiastic and ambitious Henry VIII, things began to change rapidly, as the king built up a mighty fleet spearheaded by impressive warships. A study of the military and army during the Tudor era provides invaluable insight into the rapidly changing times that the Tudors oversaw and the mindset of a continent that was slowly advancing from the Dark Ages toward the Enlightenment.

Medieval English Military Tactics

There are three specific periods of warfare during medieval England that helped advance the army and its military tactics. These periods were the Norman Conquest, the Hundred Years' War, and the Wars of the Roses. The Norman Conquest introduced castles and mounted armored knights to English warfare. English footmen were woefully outmatched by mounted Norman knights at the Battle of Hastings. While the English fought bravely, they were overrun by the Norman cavalry, which used spears to their advantage. Knights who were seated on horses had impressive capabilities, as they had the higher ground and were firmly anchored on their mounts. From their lofty position, they were able to strike precisely at their enemies.

The first English castles were simple structures protected by wooden blockades. These were built by the Normans. These buildings allowed the army to keep supplies and were easily defensible positions. Soon, wooden blockades were replaced with stone, and English kings recognized the usefulness of castles and began building them and keeps throughout the country. Unfortunately, it soon became apparent that these early rectangular castles were vulnerable to siege warfare, which led to the necessity of different shapes, such as polygonal and cylindrical castles.

37. Totnes Castle, Devon

kitmasterbloke, CC BY 2.0 <https://creativecommons.org/licenses/by/2.0>, via Wikimedia Commons https://commons.wikimedia.org/wiki/File:Totnes_Castle,_Devon.jpg

As England engaged in more wars, its mounted knights received more sophisticated weapons, such as the longbows. These weapons gave England a distinct advantage, which could be seen at the Battle of Agincourt. However, while many nobles used horses to go to war, most of these battles were fought on foot. In time, cannons and firearms were used in warfare, but these early guns were difficult to transport and load, which often proved to be disastrous during battle. Thanks to the efforts of the Norman conquerors and the Plantagenet kings, England was well equipped and ready to go to war with its enemies. However, toward the end of the Plantagenet dynasty, the fighting in England turned inward once the nobility ripped itself apart.

Military Recruitment

In the medieval era, the king could call his nobles to battle, and his nobles had to respond to the summons by raising an army of fighting men from their lands. However, this meant that nobles often had fighting forces at the ready to further their own causes. It also meant that the majority of the king's fighting forces were made up of men who weren't trained for war; rather, they were farmers and other ordinary men. Many nobles responded to this problem by keeping a highly skilled force of knights and household troops. Sometimes, mercenaries had to be hired to make up numbers or provide a skilled fighting force.

From the time of the Norman Conquest, it became apparent that knights were an invaluable asset in an army, so kings rewarded a knight's loyal service with gifts of land. These gifts came with strings, though; a knight was duty bound to heed a call to arms. For some time, there was a law in England that required every man to fight for forty days, but that wasn't enough time to complete a military campaign. This eventually gave way to the scutage arrangement, where a man could pay to be let out of his military obligation and allowed England to keep a standing army. All of this still wasn't enough, and from the 12th century onward, there was a massive mercenary market in Europe. Kings could pay to have a highly skilled fighting force that didn't require continuous maintenance.

These mercenaries often organized themselves into highly skilled bands, which allowed anyone with enough money to temporarily own a small, top-notch army. Unfortunately, these mercenaries were loyal to the highest paying bidder, and they weren't above robbing and looting any towns they came across. Often, mercenaries were foreign men who terrorized the unfortunate countryside where they were let loose.

Henry VII's Army

Henry VII didn't have access to royal funds when he fought the most crucial battle of his life at Bosworth Field. Instead, he had to rely on money from his allies and a force of foreign mercenaries who were only loyal to money. As he marched through England, he managed to amass a larger army than he arrived with, but he was still outnumbered. It was only thanks to the efforts of more experienced commanders and the last-minute assistance from powerful nobles that allowed him to win his crown. Henry VII was aware of this fact and knew that he had taken possession of a country where nobles were used to raising armies on a whim.

Henry declared himself king by right of conquest, which meant that anyone who fought with Richard III was guilty of treason. Henry VII could also take hold of all of Richard III's properties and resources. He then made all the nobles swear fealty to him under the threat of losing their lands. Due to the constant threat of rebellion, Henry VII had his own personal security force to protect him from any kind of danger and restrict access to the royal family.

In an effort to bring peace to his troubled country, Henry VII appointed many justices of the peace, which were men who served a shire for a year and were then replaced. They were in charge of overseeing law enforcement in their area and were instrumental in bringing justice after the lawlessness of the civil war. However, Henry VII wisely curbed their power. Since the justices of the peace had a lot of influence, minor nobles were eager to join their ranks, which gave Henry VII more control over them.

Unlike other European leaders at the time, Henry VII did little to advance his army, and men were called up as they were needed. Henry VII faced the unenviable task of building up royal funds after the Wars of the Roses, and he didn't have enough money to spare on a permanent army. Besides, a large royal army could fall into the wrong hands, and Henry VII was well aware of the many threats that surrounded his kingship.

The Ban on Private Armies

While Henry VII had to deal with many problems when he became king, the problem of retaining was one that most of his predecessors had also faced. This practice allowed nobles to use lower-born men to advance their interests in the area, which often included taking up arms. Nobles were allowed to give out livery or uniforms and badges to their followers. Another facet of retaining was that of maintenance, as nobles were allowed to keep numerous male servants who could also act as soldiers if necessary.

In the past, kings were forced to accept retaining since nobles felt they needed to keep their lands through force and were responsible for keeping peace on their properties. Kings could also rely on retainers to support their military campaigns, although as time progressed, it became clear that powerful nobles could use their power to influence the outcome of key battles. This was clearly evidenced during the Wars of the Roses. While Henry VII had benefited from strong nobles, he wasn't willing to allow the practice to continue.

As soon as he became king, he made his thoughts about retaining clear when he condemned the practice. While he couldn't directly outlaw it, he went through a lot of effort to restrict it. Nobles were allowed to participate in "lawful retaining," which included keeping a retainer for the purpose of serving the king. If a noble wanted to participate, he had to get a license from the Privy Council that only lasted until the king died. Henry also set laws on livery and maintenance, which restricted the nobles' power.

Henry VII is also accredited with strengthening the English navy. He commissioned the dry dock at Portsmouth, which would become the home of the Royal Navy. While Henry VII had many problems to deal with, in many ways, he set the stage for much of Henry VIII's triumphs.

Henry VIII's Royal Army

When Henry VIII inherited the throne, England's army was slightly behind the times. The soldiers still used outdated weapons, such as cavalry lances and bows. Henry VII wasn't particularly military-minded and preferred to focus on saving money for the royal treasury, but young Henry VIII was determined to advance the English military. He began by encouraging the production of arms and armor on English soil and went out of his way to bring more advanced weapons into the country.

38. Guards during the reign of Henry VIII

https://commons.wikimedia.org/wiki/File:P609e_Guards_of_the_Reign_of_Henry_VIII.jpg

His soldiers became familiar with the pike and hand firearms, which had traditionally been reserved for foreign mercenaries. While Henry VIII had high hopes for his army and put a lot of effort into reforming it, he still needed to hire large numbers of foreign mercenaries when he went to France in 1544. Unfortunately for the king, who dreamed of advancing England's military, scholars have paid little attention to Henry VIII's military exploits since his army fought mostly with outdated weapons and tactics. During this same time, the Italian Wars were being fought. These wars helped enhance warfare in Europe and saw great innovations, while Henry VIII's wars were smaller and less influential by comparison.

While the English still used tactics that helped them win the Battle of Agincourt, France's and Burgundy's cavalries used pikes and guns, which gave them the advantage on the field. However, it has been theorized that Henry VIII had probably been wise not to suddenly abandon traditional English fighting methods since Europe was still experimenting with new technology. During that time, firearms were still being developed and were cumbersome, inaccurate weapons that failed against experienced archers. In time, firearms would become deadlier and more accurate, but for the time being, the English probably didn't see the need to reproduce clumsy firearms when their archers were more capable of winning battles.

Gun Forts

Medieval castles helped fend off a variety of enemies, but they were essentially homes with heavy fortifications. The Tudor era saw the rise of gun forts, which were military buildings that were constructed with the sole purpose of assisting in battles. The forts that were built during the Tudor era would stand for centuries and be useful in future wars. Henry VIII saw their potential and built over thirty forts along the English coast between the years 1539 and 1547. It would prove to be the first project of its kind since the Romans. When Henry VIII caused the dramatic split between the Church of England and the Roman Church, he faced the wrath of Catholic powers in Europe, which threatened to invade England with the divine approval of the papacy. As a result, Henry VIII needed to defend his shores, and the gun forts helped him to do that.

39. Pendennis Castle

Nilfanion, CC BY-SA 3.0 <https://creativecommons.org/licenses/by-sa/3.0>, via Wikimedia Commons https://commons.wikimedia.org/wiki/File:Pendennis_Castle_keep.jpg

These gun forts were simple round structures that would withstand fire from enemy ships and provide a place for English gunners to fire on foreign fleets. If an enemy armada tried to invade England, the ships would find themselves under heavy fire as soon as they approached the coast. The forts were fitted with "ship-killing" guns that would deter any potential enemies. Henry VIII built gun forts all along England' Nil fanion, southern and eastern coasts. It was surely one of the highlights of his reign, and the king kept his forts well stocked at all times. The forts proved to be so useful that Elizabeth I used them when she faced the Spanish Armada. Over the years, the structures were renovated with more advanced weapons, and more sophisticated architecture was added. In fact, the gun forts were so effective that some of them were used in the Second World War.

Henry VIII's Royal Navy

Despite the fact that Henry VII didn't show much military ambition, he still began the project of building warships before he died. When Henry VIII took the throne, he had five warships at his disposal. He began building up a formidable Navy so that by the time he died, the navy was made up of more than forty ships. He began building dockyards in 1512 in Deptford and Woolwich, which were located near his own palace at Greenwich, likely so that he could keep a close eye on his pet project. He also built the dockyard at Portsmouth, which would prove useful when facing future threats of invasion.

Almost as soon as Henry VIII began building up the navy, he realized that more was needed than dockyards and ships. Along with his new naval bases, he also had to build massive storehouses, and he began looking for top-notch supplies for his navy. The king also founded the Navy Board, which would deal with the daily duties of caring for the navy. The first warships were made out of wood, but they were powerful vessels that could inflict a lot of damage in battle.

Unlike past ships, Henry VIII's ships had to transport dozens of massive cannons, which were situated all along one side of the ship and could be fired at the same time, causing devastating damage to enemy ships. While these cannons were a game changer, they also presented a unique problem. How could they stick out of the ship without allowing water through the holes they were aimed through? As a result, gunports were invented. Cannons were pointed through these holes during battle, but they were each fitted with watertight flaps on hinges that could be closed while the ship was sailing. This allowed more guns to be fitted to ships, and cannons were taken further down the ship so that the vessel didn't become unbalanced. Henry VIII's warships were massive ships that were fitted with twenty heavy cannons and sixty light cannons. The ships carried hundreds of people into war. While the navy was a source of immense pride to the vain king, his flagship, the *Mary Rose*, was the crown jewel of his naval achievements.

The *Mary Rose*

Before Henry VIII, kings had to hire merchant ships if they needed to go to war. This had the advantage of being cheaper than keeping a navy, but it was a time-consuming practice that could cost valuable time when facing the threat of invasion. Henry VIII knew that it was only a matter of time before an enemy country showed up on English shores with a more advanced fleet. As a result, he began building up his navy with enthusiasm, and he soon had dozens of ships. However, none were as special to him as his flagship, the *Mary Rose*.

40. The *Mary Rose*

Mary Rose Trust, CC BY-SA 3.0 <https://creativecommons.org/licenses/by-sa/3.0>, via Wikimedia Commons https://commons.wikimedia.org/wiki/File:MaryRose-ship_hall.jpg

The *Mary Rose* may have been built as early as 1510, along with *Peter Pomegranate*, in Portsmouth. While there are claims that the ship was named after Henry VIII's favorite sister, Mary, it's more likely that the ship was named after the Virgin Mary, who was known as the "Mystic Rose" in those times. The ship was fitted with powerful cannons and gun ports, which made it one of the most technically advanced ships of its time. By the time Henry VIII declared war on France in 1512, his flagship was completed and ready to carry the king toward military glory.

The ship was used at the Battle of Saint-Mathieu in 1512 and as a transport ship during the Battle of Flodden in 1513. By 1514, the war in France was winding down, and the ship was decommissioned and left at Portsmouth. However, when Henry VIII went to France in 1520 for the meeting of the Field of the Cloth of Gold, Henry VIII chose to take his favorite ship with him to display his wealth and glory to his old enemy. For the next few years, the *Mary Rose* took part in the skirmishes against France, but it was mostly inactive until 1539, when Henry VIII faced serious threats of invasion from Catholic European powers.

In 1544, Henry VIII went to war against France and won Boulogne, which led to the Battle of the Solent. This battle would have tragic consequences for his beloved flagship. While engaged in the battle, the ship turned suddenly. The wind pressed the ship down, and her starboard side was pushed into the water. Unfortunately, the gunports were all open, and the ship took on massive amounts of water and sank in a little over half an hour. Hundreds of men died while the battle raged on. Henry VIII was forced to watch as his beloved ship disappeared under the waves.

Attempts were made to raise the ship from the depths, but the *Mary Rose* would remain below the water until 1982.

Elizabeth I's Fleet

When Elizabeth I took the throne, piracy was a massive problem, as pirates roamed the seas virtually unchecked. As a result, they plundered merchant ships, which caused heavy losses for England. Elizabeth I countered this problem by commissioning privateers. These men were private merchants who were authorized to attack and loot pirate ships, although they were mostly used to plunder Spanish ships returning with riches from the New World. The Spanish Armada was growing at a rapid rate, and instead of engaging with the fleet directly, Elizabeth I's privateers, or "Sea Dogs," would pick off individual ships and rob them, which helped reduce Spain's wealth and power.

Some of her most notable Sea Dogs were Sir Walter Raleigh and Sir Francis Drake. These men were known as adventurers and for being competent naval officers. Sir Francis Drake helped the queen against the Spanish Armada. While the Spaniards condemned the Sea Dogs, Elizabeth I used her privateers to great advantage along with her official navy.

While the Tudor era was defined by dramatic social changes and climatic religious reforms, it was also a time of advancement for the national military and the foundation of the Royal Navy. As the military advanced, the need arose for new and more sophisticated weapons.

Chapter 11: Tudor Weapons

When the Tudor era began, Europe was in the midst of a time of great change and upheaval. Various wars led to the development of modern weapons and the rejection of medieval military tactics. By the time England emerged from the Wars of the Roses, its military had stagnated, and it was vastly behind its peers. While it managed to successfully wage wars against countries like Ireland and Scotland, it was only able to win the majority of those battles since those countries were on the same footing. While Europe was fighting massive wars, such as the Italian Wars, England's days of large-scale foreign conquests seemed to be over.

However, when Henry VIII was an energetic young man who didn't have the same haunted and wary tendencies as Henry VII, who narrowly won the Battle of Bosworth Field. Henry VIII quickly began reforming his military and investigating the new weapons that were making their debut in Europe. The Tudor era saw a rapid change in England's military, going from conventional weapons to gunpowder weapons. The English army used a mixture of both types of weapons until gunpowder weapons became more sophisticated and prevalent.

Traditional Tudor Weapons

Although the Tudor period was a time of change for the English military, the traditional medieval weapons had seen great success at legendary battles, such as Agincourt. The change from traditional weapons to modern weapons was gradual. English soldiers and weapons manufacturers weren't unaware of modern weapons. After all, they were exposed to foreign mercenaries who brought their weapons with them. However, it's likely that they weren't impressed by what they saw. In the beginning, gunpowder weapons were inconvenient and took time to load, which may have made the traditional bow and pike weapons seem vastly superior in the hands of experienced soldiers.

- Longbow

The English longbow was a popular weapon during medieval times for hunting and warfare. It stood at about six feet tall and is thought to have had a range of about four hundred yards. This would have allowed experienced archers to stay well away from the battlefield and rain deadly arrows upon their enemies with accuracy. The arrows would have used steel points that could easily penetrate mail armor.

Longbows were used during the Hundred Years' War against France, and the Tudors adopted the weapon into their arsenal. This is evidenced by the fact that thousands of arrows and over a hundred longbows were found aboard the *Mary Rose* when it was salvaged.

- Ballock Dagger

The ballock (or bollock) dagger was popular in Europe from the 13th century to the late 18th century. It was a simple weapon with a hilt that had two oval shapes near the guard that was supposed to aid with grip. These oval shapes looked like male testes, thus leading to the distinctive name. The weapon served as a last resort when a soldier's lance and/or sword failed. Most soldiers carried this type of dagger, and hundreds were found aboard the *Mary Rose*.

- Battle-ax

Battle-axes have a long history that predates the Tudor era by several centuries. The earliest battle-axes were little more than normal axes that were used to smash enemies to pieces. In time, battle-axes became more specialized. During the Tudor era, battle-axes were about thirty centimeters (one foot) in length and varied in weight according to what had been added to the weapon. Many horsemen used an ax while charging since it was unwieldy to use in close combat. Battle-axes had sharp pikes attached to the top and back of the blade to give the weapon extra penetrating power.

- Caltrop

A caltrop was an ingenious weapon that consisted of a long pole with a sharp spike at the top. They were traditionally used by knights at a long distance, but caltrops also caused devastating damage to cavalrymen when they were planted with their spikes facing up. The horses would charge into the field of caltrops and get seriously injured. These types of tactics proved to be fatal on the battlefield, but the caltrops needed to be supplemented by other weapons. A soldier couldn't rely on caltrops alone.

42. Caltrops

https://commons.wikimedia.org/wiki/File:Drevnosti_RG_v3_ill130c_-_Caltrop.jpg

- Billhooks

A bill or billhook was a tool that could be used to trim trees or inflict damage on enemy soldiers. They were especially popular during the times when a noble called on his men to march into war since they could be used by soldiers or farmers. Billhooks could be adapted for whatever purpose they needed to accomplish. Some variations had spikes or sharp points that accompanied the hooks. They were often used in conjunction with longbows and were notably used at the Battle of Flodden. Billhooks were used through most of the Tudor era and were a traditional medieval weapon that survived the test of time due to their simplicity and usefulness.

43. Medieval Billhook

https://commons.wikimedia.org/wiki/File:Antique_billhooks_at_Ludlow_market.JPG

- Lances

Lances were popularly used by knights in jousts, but they could also be used in battle. They were long weapons with a sharp point that could be used to charge at an enemy. During a joust, two knights would charge at each other on horseback, aiming to break the other's lance or pierce the other knight's armor. While the knights weren't trying to hurt each other, these jousts were extremely dangerous. Henry VII nearly died on two separate occasions while jousting. Medieval knights were known to carry lances into war with them, but they could prove to be cumbersome if used incorrectly.

- Halberd

Halberds were pole weapons that were essentially ax blades with a sharp spike on top of a long pole. They were popular from medieval times to well into the Tudor era. In the hands of experienced halberdiers, they were devastating weapons that could be used at long range to kill enemy soldiers. It's possible that either a halberd or a billhook was used to kill Richard III at the Battle of Bosworth. Halberds were effective when used to attack other pikemen, but they were ineffective in the hands of foot soldiers when it came to a cavalry charge or gunpowder weapons.

- Spears

Spears were used by some of the earliest warriors, but they weren't used much during the Tudor era. They were rarely taken to war since they were more useful for close combat. By the Tudor era, battles were increasingly being fought with longer-range weapons. Spears are simple weapons, and there were much more sophisticated weapons that were widely available to common soldiers. That doesn't mean that no one used spears, as there is some evidence that at least some soldiers still preferred them.

Gunpowder Weapons

As the Tudor era progressed, gunpowder weapons became increasingly popular. While they were cumbersome and inconvenient at first, their potential was explosive. As they became more common, they slowly replaced the English longbow, which had long been a favorite for English soldiers. The use of gunpowder led to other innovations, as it became necessary to protect gunpowder from the elements. Cannons were fitted to warships, and gun forts were used to protect England from Catholic invasions. The Tudor forces also found that gunpowder weapons were useful in siege warfare, and slowly, the English army fully embraced these sophisticated weapons.

- Muskets

Muskets arrived in Europe in the 1520s, and the immediate response was armor becoming thicker. Unfortunately, thicker armor was very heavy and expensive. As armor became thicker, larger guns that released more powerful bullets were used, making armor ineffective. Muskets were heavy, but they could be used during sieges or to fight off invaders from a longer distance. As muskets became more sophisticated and powerful, they outmatched longbows. Tudor era soldiers were forced to keep up with the times or face armies with guns while only wielding arrows and bows. Eventually, the choice was clear.

- Cannons

For most of medieval history, castles were effectively forts that could withstand sieges and remain standing while wars and battles raged around them. However, the onset of cannons saw the popularity of castles decline, as cannons could destroy castle walls and make sieges much shorter. Enemy forces could fire continuously at castle walls, and within a few weeks or even days, the castle would be overrun by enemy forces. Henry VIII appreciated the potential of cannons and used them at Boulogne, in his navy, and in his gun forts. Cannons varied according to their purpose and could be larger or smaller as was needed. They were essentially large guns that shot massive cannonballs and became an important part of Tudor warfare.

44. Tudor era cannon

https://commons.wikimedia.org/wiki/File:Cannon_in_the_Garden_of_Tudor_House,_Southampton.jpg

- Arquebus

The arquebus was an early form of the gunpowder weapons that are prevalent in modern times. It first appeared in the Ottoman Empire and in Europe in the 1500s. It was essentially a handgun with a hook-like mechanism that allowed it to be attached to walls or armaments. The advent of the matchlock mechanism allowed muskets to become smaller and more like handguns. As the use of the arquebus became more widespread, armies began to support arquebusiers, who were infantrymen armed with the weapon. The large arquebus became known as the musket, which eventually became the term that was used to refer to all long guns.

45. Soldier with an arquebus

https://commons.wikimedia.org/wiki/File:Musket_and_Arquebus_Gheyn.jpg

- Matchlock Mechanism

The matchlock mechanism allowed arquebusiers to use shorter weapons that were easier to wield in battle. It also allowed the gunpowder weapons to be equipped with a trigger that made it easier to fire. A matchlock mechanism was essentially a device that ignited gunpowder by burning a small piece of rope when an arquebusier pulled the trigger. Unfortunately, they were difficult to load, which slowed their popularity. It seems that the matchlock firearms originated in the Ottoman Empire before being transported to Europe.

- Flintlock Mechanism

Before triggers, people had to use one arm to steady the arquebus and the other to light the gunpowder, which was a difficult and inconvenient process. However, the matchlock mechanism changed the way guns were used since it introduced the trigger. In time, the matchlock was replaced by the flintlock. The matchlock was inconvenient, as it required the shooter to light a match to ignite the mechanism. The flintlock used flint to ignite the gunpowder and was much easier to use. Unfortunately, it was only developed in the 17th century.

Swords

Many different swords were used during the Tudor era. Swords had been used during many periods in history and were still immensely popular during Tudor times. There were many different types of swords, and they were used for different occasions. Swords could be personalized, which meant that they could be passed on through the generations. During the Tudor period, there were three types of swords that were especially popular. Many experienced soldiers who could afford swords chose to use the weapon, even though gunpowder weapons were becoming increasingly popular. Although other weapons became outdated during the Tudor era, the use of swords remained widespread throughout the period.

- Cutting Sword

By the time the Tudor era began, the cutting sword was already declining in popularity. Throughout most of the medieval period, cutting swords proved to be useful on the battlefield. Swords are ancient weapons that went through many changes over the years. Norman conquerors began to develop cross-guards in the 11th century, which helped to stabilize the weapon. As the Tudor era progressed, armor became more advanced and sophisticated, which made it more difficult for swords to inflict wounds. The swords had to be modified to cut specifically at weaknesses in the armor. The cutting swords of the past had to be exchanged for sleeker, thinner weapons.

- Broadsword

In medieval times, people had different swords for different occasions. Traditionally, broadswords had basket hilts that protected a warrior's hand. They were heavy instruments that were better for cutting at enemies. A broadsword was a lethal weapon that could take down many enemies depending on the soldier's strength and skill level. However, it was too heavy to use for duels, fencing, or ceremonies. A broadsword usually had a longer hilt so that it could be used with both hands.

- Rapier

Fencing was a popular sport among noblemen in the Tudor era, and the advent of the rapier made the sport much more enjoyable. Unlike the heavy cutting swords used by the military, rapiers were sleek and light, which made them perfect for thrusting and lunging at enemies. Rapiers became so popular that noblemen took their rapiers wherever they went, and they became an accessory to complement any nobleman's wardrobe. The rapier originated in continental Europe and allowed a person to move quickly and strike at a distance.

46. Different rapiers

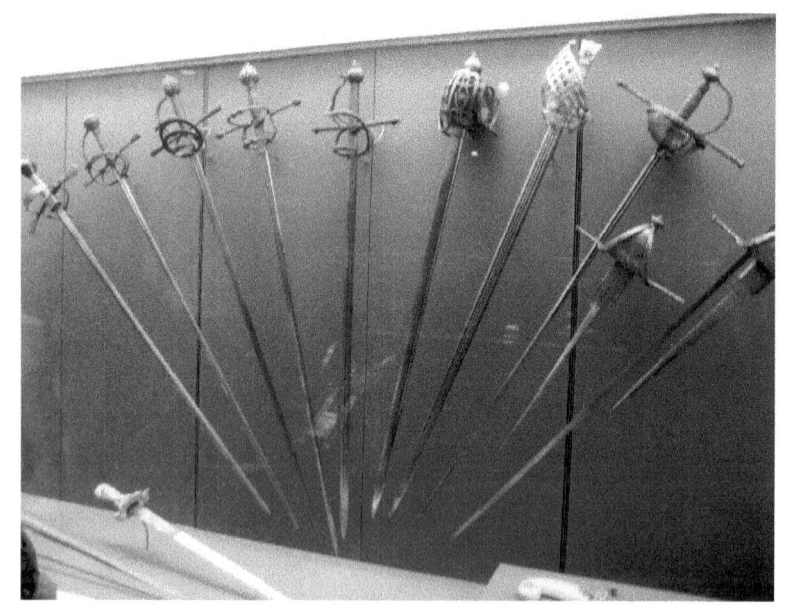

Claire H., CC BY-SA 2.0 <https://creativecommons.org/licenses/by-sa/2.0>, via Wikimedia Commons https://commons.wikimedia.org/wiki/File:Different_Rapiers.jpg

Tudor Soldiers

As the army evolved in the Tudor era, it became necessary to change the way that the army was structured. This restructuring happened gradually, as ordinary soldiers changed their traditional weapons for more sophisticated instruments of war. While some traditional posts were kept, many conventional institutions changed. Henry VII saw the need to employ a permanent force of guards, and when Henry VIII took the throne, he found a way to renew the nobility's interest in the military. By the time the Elizabethan era began, a lot of things had changed in the army from Henry VII's day.

- The Yeomen of the Guard

The Yeomen of the Guard was founded by Henry VII in 1485. These men traditionally wear the Tudor costume. Although the Tower of London had Yeomen Warders, the two companies weren't related. The Yeomen of the Guard was tasked with protecting the monarch in all aspects of his life. They traveled with the monarch and even tasted their food to make sure it hadn't been poisoned. Many former English monarchs hadn't felt the need to create such a force, but Henry VII had every right to be wary after spending most of his life fighting off potential usurpers. Due to the guards' duties, they were the only standing military force in the country.

- The Gentlemen Pensioners

Henry VIII saw a way to involve the nobility in his own protection by creating the Troop of Gentlemen, which was made up of the sons of noble families. This gave the younger sons of noble families who didn't stand to inherit a way to interact with the monarchy and a chance to rise above their stations. The Troop was a mounted force armed with spears and lances. The men rode with the king and ensured his safety. By protecting the king, they also enhanced their own prestige and impressed their importance on everyone around them.

- Infantry

As the army was revitalized, so were the weapons of infantrymen. Henry VIII's infantry force was made up of pikemen, billmen, and archers. In time, archers were replaced with capable gunmen. While Henry VIII admired and imported the newer weapons, most of his forces still carried traditional weapons when he went to war in 1544. It wasn't until the Elizabethan period that gunpowder weapons began to outnumber conventional weapons. Infantry forces were usually divided into smaller companies that were comprised of pikemen in the middle and archers on the flanks.

- Cavalry

In the past, knights had been one of the most important components of any army, but as soldiers were being trained with more sophisticated weapons, it became apparent that the days of knights were numbered. For one thing, their armor wasn't strong enough to withstand the increasing power of gunpowder weapons, and the use of lances and swords failed when faced with weapons that could be shot from a distance. However, the cavalry was a valuable part of the Tudor army. It was usually made up of mounted nobles who paid for their own armor and weapons. As older weapons became obsolete, the mounted forces would use pistols when they went to war.

Foreign Mercenaries

Henry VIII had great dreams for his army, but like his contemporaries and predecessors, he was forced to rely on foreign mercenaries to boost his numbers when he went to war. Mercenaries were highly skilled soldiers who sometimes formed large bands that could be hired for a military campaign. Since it was very expensive to keep a standing army made up of skilled warriors, mercenaries seemed like a necessary evil. Since foreign mercenaries fought alongside English soldiers, the English had a chance to learn about the weapons and tactics that were being used in Europe.

- Landsknechte

The Landsknechte were German pikemen. They were some of the most effective soldiers of their time. They were highly trained individuals who spent most of their time fighting for the highest bidder. These mercenaries used pikes and halberds with ease and were used to moving quickly. Their shock tactics caught their enemies off-guard, and they could even hold their own against a cavalry charge. It is no wonder that Henry VIII used them in his army. They were brutal warriors who fought without mercy and were among the most feared mercenaries in Europe. At first, Henry VIII had access to the Landsknechte since they were created by Maximilian I, the Holy Roman emperor, who loaned several companies to Henry VIII during his war with France. After all, Catherine of Aragon was related to the emperor.

- Stradioti

The Stradioti were mercenaries hired from the Balkans who used Byzantine and Balkan war tactics. They were experienced cavalrymen, which made them attractive to many military leaders since cavalrymen were always in short supply. The Stradioti were able to pioneer many cavalry tactics, which put them ahead of their competition and made them deadly on the battlefield. They were highly skilled men who used complicated tactics that caught their enemies by surprise and were especially adept at traps and ambushes.

• Spanish and Italian Arquebusiers

As gunpowder weapons became more popular in Europe, soldiers who fought in the Italian Wars and other conflicts in Europe had a lot of experience with the new weapons. Once those wars ended, highly skilled soldiers became mercenaries who offered their expertise to anyone who would have them. Henry VIII used these men when he went to war against France, especially in 1544, as his own men had to be trained to use the new weapons since they were mostly archers and pikemen. In time, the English army had its own skilled arquebusiers, leaving behind their traditional bows.

The Tudor era was marked by periods of climatic change, and their army reflected those changes. As newer, more sophisticated weapons were invented, the Tudor forces used a mix of conventional and new weapons to their advantage and held their own against Europe.

Section Four:
Life in Tudor England

Chapter 12: Politics and Economy

The Tudor era was a remarkable time that featured some of the most influential monarchs in English history. These rulers lived lavishly and spent extraordinary amounts of money on their projects. This leads to a question; where did they get all that money? The answer lies in England's economy. The rulers had to be careful to stimulate the economy so they could keep up their lifestyles. However, when the economy declined, not only did they have to curb their spending habits, but they also faced serious riots and rebellions that threatened their way of life.

Furthermore, the Tudor court was a dangerous place filled with manipulative schemers who would do anything to get ahead and make a name for themselves. Many individuals within the Tudor government managed to take advantage of the social, political, and religious changes that took place. As Henry VIII proved, the fortunes of entire lineages rested on the whims of a monarch. In an effort to solve his "Great Matter," Henry VIII was willing to forever change the Church of England and put his people through incredible religious reforms. This change had far-reaching consequences that impacted both politics and the economy. In time, England left the medieval era and entered the Renaissance. Elizabeth I found new and creative ways to stimulate the economy, as well as a unique approach to politics.

Agriculture

In Tudor England, many farmers didn't own the land that they worked; instead, they rented land from rich landowners who were usually part of the nobility. Sometimes, the land the farmers rented didn't produce enough to feed them and their families, which meant they had to spend some of their time working as laborers on larger farms. If a person couldn't afford to rent a piece of land, they would work exclusively as laborers. However, most villages had common lands that provided small game for hunting. Farmers who owned animals could let their animals graze on that land.

Agriculture formed a large part of England's economy, and farmers helped landowners become rich, which, in turn, enriched the monarchy. When there were good harvests, there was more than enough to sell and eat, which benefited everyone. However, when the harvests failed, people relied on common lands or handouts from the rich. If a harvest failed, a monarch would have to arrange relief efforts and find ways to stimulate the economy.

Common lands were an important part of a peasant's lifestyle, as they often depended on hunting rabbits for food when times were tough. However, when the cloth trade began to increase, sheep became a valuable commodity due to their wool, and more land was needed for the animals to graze. Large landowners realized they could profit more from raising sheep than renting out their land, so they began charging exorbitant rents. This forced their tenants to abandon the land that they previously farmed. In many communities, rich landowners began closing off large pieces of common land for their sheep. This caused serious problems since peasants weren't allowed to use the land that had sustained them for centuries. As a result, there was a massive outcry, and many peasants revolted. In 1549, there was a huge rebellion led by Robert Kett, who encouraged peasants to destroy fences that closed off common land.

These rebellions were often defeated since peasants had little to no military expertise and very few weapons. In the case of the Kett rebellion, Edward VI's government sent a force made up of mostly foreign mercenaries who outmatched the peasant army in every way. They brutally put down the rebellion. In time, Parliament tried to fix the matter by imposing laws against enclosures, but since landowners were often in charge of enforcing those laws, they would simply keep the enclosures where they were.

English Wool Trade

The most important commodity that England produced during the Tudor era was wool. English wool was widely considered to be vastly superior to other types of wool. It was often exported in its raw form to Europe, where it was turned into woolen cloth and sold for a massive profit, which benefited England greatly.

The Tudor monarchy, especially under Henry VII, found ways to profit off the wool trade by placing taxes on wool exports, which earned a lot of money. In time, English farmers began to include sheep rearing in their other work. However, the wool industry was seasonally based, which meant that farmers often had other projects too. At first, individuals owned flocks of sheep, but as the Tudor era progressed, rich landowners began amassing larger flocks. Many individuals couldn't afford to keep sheep anymore. The government tried to limit the number of sheep that one person could own, but once again, these laws were largely ignored.

Sheep rearing was a lot of work and provided jobs for peasants. Merchants would fund a lot of the wool trade process, which included shearing sheep, dyeing, and cleaning. The wool trade made up the largest part of England's foreign trade market, and places such as Calais were valuable ports in the trading system. It's estimated that the wool trade made up 90 percent of England's overseas trade during Henry VII's reign.

However, rearing sheep could be difficult, and the wool trade could be impacted by a number of different factors. Europe was prone to outbreaks of war, which could put a complete halt on the wool trade. Even if England didn't participate in the war, its economy was still affected. Another factor was the plague. The plague spread quickly through merchant ships, which meant that if there was an outbreak, trade ground to a halt.

Sheep are also delicate creatures that don't deal well with too much rain. They could also pick up diseases or parasites that would affect their wool production. The wool trade was incredibly profitable, but it could be extremely delicate, which made it risky to base the country's economy on it. Besides wool, England also exported lead, tin, and coal.

The Privy Council

During the Tudor era, the Privy Council was one of the most important parts of the government. The council was involved in the administration of the country, policymaking, and justice. It was also the source of a lot of the political conflicts that affected the Tudor period. It was essential to the Tudor monarchs and was usually made up of experienced men, trusted allies, or the monarch's favorites. Unlike the privy councils in other European countries, the Tudors' Privy Council had a lot of authority, and sometimes, they didn't need the monarch to sign off on their decisions.

The duties of a monarch were numerous and seriously impacted the country, which meant that they needed councilors who could give advice and help make good decisions. The nobility was made up of the monarchs' peers and often provided a useful pool from which to choose advisors and favorites. During medieval times, monarchs made up their own councils or chose their own advisors. While Parliament was a formal institution that met at times, the monarch's advisors met whenever they required assistance. While the advisors handled serious matters, they were somewhat less formal than the proceedings that took place in Parliament.

Henry VII had hundreds of councilors who were charged with a variety of different duties, but he didn't have a privy council and chose to be involved in the intimate details of ruling his country. However, everything changed with Henry VIII. When he took the throne, he relied on a small number of his father's trusted advisors. In 1515, Thomas Wolsey became the Lord Chancellor and began organizing the council more effectively. For the next few years, Henry VIII was advised by an "inner ring" of councilors. Wolsey fell out of favor when he failed to resolve the king's "Great Matter." In 1530, Thomas Cromwell joined the inner ring, and the king's annulment soon became a reality.

It was only around 1536 that the "inner ring" was identified as the Privy Council. The Privy Council was incredibly important, and Henry VIII chose his son's council before he died. When Mary and Elizabeth took the throne, they each chose their own councilors.

Local Government

England was divided into counties or shires, which made it easier to dispense justice and handle administrative affairs. The most important offices of local government were those of the sheriff and the Lord Lieutenant. The sheriff was appointed to a term of one year, and all appointments were made through the Privy Council. He would be responsible for choosing under-sheriffs and bailiffs who would assist him in dispensing justice. His duties included presiding over a monthly court that took care of any criminal cases, enforcing judgments, and running the jail.

The office of Lord Lieutenant was created by Henry VIII. The men appointed to this office were responsible for representing the king in each county. They were tasked with dealing with the local nobility and arranging the local military. This impressed the king's authority throughout the country and took care of the intricacies of mobilizing a local military force when the king called them to arms. A Lord Lieutenant also had the important task of trying to keep the local gentry happy when the army mobilized, as there was a culture of petty infighting when the king called his men to arms, as everyone wanted the honor of leading the force. The Lord Lieutenant had an enviable measure of power, and it was a potentially risky office for the king, but Henry VIII made sure to curb their power and set up a chain of command that prevented any ambitious rebellions.

While military and judicial matters were taken care of by sheriffs and Lord Lieutenants, there were also justices of the peace. These men were responsible for administrative tasks. Constables, mayors, aldermen, and churchwardens were other facets of the local government during the Tudor era. Unfortunately, many of these positions were filled by the nobility, who chose their friends or favorites to occupy other important roles within the local government. This system didn't offer much representation for peasants or the lower classes, which meant that their complaints often went unheard. In many cases, laws were ignored if they didn't benefit the nobility, such as the laws about enclosures and the size of sheep herds. During times of trouble, peasants often felt they had no other option but to rebel since it was clear that the justice system had failed them.

The Reformation Parliament

When King Henry VIII broke away from the Catholic Church, the split had serious political consequences. In the past, the church had been under the jurisdiction of the papacy, but in solving the "Great Matter," Henry VIII allowed Parliament to be involved in religious matters. This meant that the government had authority over every aspect of national life. It also allowed Henry VIII to change religious doctrine and institute the religious reform that would allow him to get divorced from Catherine of Aragon. Parliament was extremely busy during this time, as it had to pass laws that stripped the pope's authority in England.

Soon, the church was stripped of many of its privileges. The clergy were allowed to be tried like any other subjects in England and wouldn't be given preferential treatment in the eyes of the law. Parliament passed a law that prevented people from involving foreign powers in matters of English justice, which effectively allowed Henry VIII to persecute any Catholics who asked the pope for help. Soon, Parliament stepped up its tactics and threatened to deprive the pope of taxes and levies from Catholics in England. This was a massive chunk of income and was usually paid in return for papal authorization of bishop nominations and other church taxes.

Moreover, Parliament was used to pass the Act of Succession and the Act of Supremacy, which made Henry VIII the head of the Church of England and allowed him to divorce Catherine of Aragon. Thomas Cromwell was responsible for many of the acts, and Parliament was mainly responsible for dealing with religious legislation. The "Great Matter" had to be solved at all costs, but the split from Rome meant that there were many administrative matters that had to be put in place before it was possible. After the split from Rome, Henry VIII and his successors used Parliament to pass other laws and statutes during their reigns. Laws were usually more effective when Parliament agreed to enforce them. However, the monarchy and Parliament had to work together closely to keep up this arrangement.

The Economic Consequences of the Reformation

The Catholic Church exerted an enormous amount of influence over Europe during the medieval ages, and during that time, it became incredibly rich. However, as the Protestant Reformation began to spread through the continent, the Catholic Church often reacted violently, which led to many religious conflicts. Despite its efforts, Protestants made a lot of progress, and England eventually split from the church in Rome and began adopting Protestant ideals. In time, the English monarchy and nobility took many resources from the church and put money into their own pockets. This increased the wealth of many people, and it may have helped to popularize the English Reformation.

For decades, the Catholic Church held the monopoly on religious offices and enriched itself by holding the keys to heaven and imposing spiritual laws on ordinary people. Catholic universities focused on theology, and many graduates became members of the clergy. Protestantism removed much of the mystery surrounding religion, and many people chose to enter secular positions once they left university since the clergy had declined in prominence. This led to economic secularization, which is a theory that suggests prosperity lessens the need for religion and leads to the eventual decline of religion's role in a country.

While England became richer from plundering the church's wealth, the split from Rome also led to some trading restrictions. Catholic countries tried to please the pope by limiting contact with England. This didn't change Henry VIII's mind, though. As the church declined, there wasn't much of a need to build religious buildings in Protestant areas, and people were increasingly employed by secular authorities.

In the past, people used their money to fund the church by paying for levies, taxes, nominations, and indulgences. However, as the national religion changed and such things were condemned, people felt comfortable using their money to stimulate the national economy instead. There were some economic repercussions in terms of trade, but these didn't last long. However, the Reformation led to religious conflict and the threat of invasion, which forced Henry VIII to spend more money on national defense. While there were several unfortunate consequences, the English Reformation also caused a shift in the people's thinking, which eventually benefited the economy. It also served to increase Henry VIII's treasury and enrich several noble families, which made them reluctant to return to Catholicism.

Exploration

As Europe left the medieval era, several European countries began to build ships to explore the seas. Spain became immensely rich after its conquest of the New World. The Spanish brought shiploads of gold back to the continent, which motivated other European countries to begin their own exploratory efforts. Elizabeth I was quick to follow Spain's example. Thanks to her father's efforts, she had a whole fleet of ships at her disposal. She began looking for ways to increase her country's wealth and sent explorers to Asia, the Americas, and Africa, where they would find resources that could be used to enrich England.

These explorers were sometimes referred to as Elizabeth I's Sea Dogs, and they were a major threat to the Spanish. As the Spanish ferried gold between the Americas and Europe, they were sometimes attacked by pirates who would sink their ships and steal their gold. Somehow, that gold managed to make its way back to England, and the queen profited greatly. Tudor explorers took to the seas to look for new trading routes, while some carried religious refugees who were looking for a new land where they could practice their religion in peace. In time, these explorers managed to colonize pieces of territory for England, which served to boost England's economy in incredible ways.

The Tudor period marked a shift from the medieval era to the sophisticated Renaissance era, which had a definite impact on politics and the economy. It also affected English society and education.

Chapter 13: Society and Education in Tudor England

It would be easy to focus on the fascinating lives of the Tudor monarchs and forget about the people they were supposed to take care of, but that would be a mistake. Many interesting factors of Tudor life can be gleaned from taking a look at Tudor society. Since the Tudor era was marked by distinctive times of change, it is worth looking at what society and education were like during these times, as the people who lived through the period had to deal with the trials of living as well as political, economic, and religious changes.

This chapter will delve into the four social classes that made up Tudor society and explain how the different classes lived. It will start at the very top with the nobility who lived in luxury and go down to the bottom classes, which could be executed for refusing an honest day's work. There will also be a quick glance into what education was like in England.

The Nobility

The highest social class in Tudor times was the nobility. The nobles won the "birth lottery," as they were the most powerful class besides the royal family. Some of the most important families and individuals in the Tudor era were from the nobility, and they wielded incredible influence in Tudor society. These were the people who were the closest to the monarchs and, as a result, were able to benefit from a royal's favor.

However, if they angered the monarch, they could just as easily lose everything. The nobility was an extremely closed-off class since they didn't want to share their power. The more people who rose up, the less power there was to go around. The people in the nobility were either born into powerful families or were appointed to their positions.

- Food

The nobility had a large and varied diet since they had more access to expensive food. They also usually dined with the king or other nobles, which meant that rich feasts and banquets were typical. At royal banquets, exotic dishes such as conger eel and porpoise were served, along with sweet dishes. Typical banquets had game, meat pies, lambs, swans, and venison. The nobles also had access to the finest wines and beverages, and these dinner parties were usually lively affairs accompanied by entertainment.

- Clothing

Nobles wore flamboyant and high-quality clothes. They often had massive wardrobes filled with expensive clothing. Women wore linen shifts that were changed daily but had intricate outer layers and headdresses. Fashion changed frequently, and the queen or king's mistresses usually influenced courtly fashion.

Headdresses were often heavy and elaborate, and they required women to wear linen caps or hoods underneath. Men wore silk shirts with frills at the wrists and neck. They also wore doublets, which were richly embroidered jackets with striped pants. While men didn't wear headdresses, they often wore ruffs that were starched and pleated garments that fit around their necks.

- Professions

The nobility often didn't have to work. They owned a lot of land and collected rents from their tenants. However, male members of the nobility who were close to the monarch often had high positions within the government. They received favors and responsibilities from the monarch and had a chance to rise higher within the government.

Tudor Sumptuary Laws

Prestige was an important part of being a monarch. Henry VIII put a lot of effort into asserting his glory and prosperity through his portraits, attire, and entertainment. When he entertained foreign ministers, he always made sure to put on a good show so his guests would take reports of his strength and glory back to their own monarchs. He also viewed sumptuary laws as important and revised the Acts of Apparel multiple times during his reign. The nobility was an extension of his own authority, and he wanted to keep the newly rich or common-born people from imitating his court or family.

The sumptuary laws restricted the clothes that people wore so that a strict social hierarchy could be maintained. For example, anyone outside of the family was forbidden to wear the color purple. By restricting the types of clothes that people wore, Henry VIII could impress his own authority and maintain the strict boundaries between social classes. The sumptuary laws had the added benefit of encouraging people to support local textile markets.

During Elizabeth I's era, the sumptuary laws were loosened once the import market grew.

47. Robert Dudley in Garter robes

Yale Center for British Art, CC0, via Wikimedia Commons
https://commons.wikimedia.org/wiki/File:Robert_Dudley_in_Garter_Robes_ca._1587.png

Besides clothing, the sumptuary laws also limited the amount of money that people could spend on their food and furniture. In Tudor England, status was everything, and a person's clothes told everyone which social class they belonged to. The rich were allowed to wear silk and certain colors, but only the royal family was allowed to wear what they wanted. Royal clothing, particularly ceremonial robes, was trimmed with ermine to represent the royals' advanced status. Below the royalty was the nobility, who were allowed to wear different clothes based on their titles. Those who were above viscounts and barons could wear gold, silver, tinseled satin, cloth with silver or gold, or silk. The viscounts, barons, members of the Privy Council, and the Knights of the Garter were allowed to wear furs, velvet, crimson, gold, silver, or pearls.

The Gentry

The next social class was the gentry. This social class was made up of rich landowners, knights, squires, and gentlemen. If a person didn't have to work with their hands, they were part of the gentry. The gentry exploded during the Elizabethan era and became the most important class of the time. Usually, a person became part of the gentry when they became a knight. From there, they could use their position to build up their fortunes, and in time, they could receive a title that would make them part of the nobility. One could also enter the gentry through marriage, although the gentry often didn't marry below their class.

- Food

Depending on their status, the gentry didn't often eat at court but still had luxurious diets. They would often have swans, peafowl, geese, boars, or deer, as these animals often lived on the lands they owned. Hunting was seen as a gentleman's sport and was a favorite pastime among the rich. They also used herbs, such as rosemary, thyme, sage, and mint, to season their food. The rich also ate manchet, which was a soft bread made out of expensive white flour.

- Clothing

Like the nobility, the gentry spent a lot of time and money on their clothes. Depending on their wealth, women could wear fine floor-length gowns, and men could wear silk shirts and doublets over their trousers. The sumptuary laws were very strict for the gentry, and those who earned over £100 a year were allowed to wear damask, silk, camlet, satin, or taffeta. After that, the sumptuary laws became stricter according to a person's title.

48. Mayor, alderman, and liveryman, 1574

https://commons.wikimedia.org/wiki/File:Mayor,_Alderman,_Liveryman_1574.jpg

Since many people weren't part of the nobility, they had to pay careful attention to the sumptuary laws, or else they would be fined or face serious repercussions.

• Professions

Like the nobility, many members of the gentry didn't have to work. They owned land and/or businesses or occupied positions within the local government. The gentry often became justices of the peace, Lord Lieutenants, or sheriffs. They were mostly preoccupied with running their estates and taking care of their investments. However, the gentry often had to heed the monarch's call to arms and lead men into battle at their ruler's command. They were often well equipped for battle and had some measure of military training. As the merchant class rose in England, some of them were able to buy their way into the gentry and eventually into the nobility.

The Yeomanry

The "middle class" in Tudor England was known as the yeomanry. They had better jobs than the poor and usually became apprentices when they were young. As a result, they could usually afford to save some money or look for ways to improve their lives. The life of a yeoman consisted of hard work, but their lives were generally better than the poor. However, the people in this class could lose their status very easily in times of plague, famine, or war. Many of the people in this class were servants, tradesmen, or merchants.

- Food

Depending on their profession, the middle class was usually able to get their hands on vegetables, such as cabbages and onions. Eventually, tomatoes, peppers, and potatoes were imported from the New World, but those vegetables were expensive at first. The yeomen usually ate whatever meat they could afford, which was commonly rabbits, hens, pheasants, partridges, ducks, fish, and pigeons. They also ate yeoman's bread or ravel, which was made out of wholemeal.

- Clothing

Under the sumptuary laws, ordinary people couldn't wear silk, jewels, or gold. This was unfortunate for those of the yeoman class, like merchants, who could afford to wear such items. Instead, women usually wore kirtles, which were ankle-length dresses made from wool that had square necks. Wealthier women usually wore a gown over their kirtles. All women had to cover their heads, and they wore linen caps under bonnets or veils. They usually had girdles that were attached to their waist and helped them carry their possessions.

Men usually wore simple leather doublets over their pants and hung their purses or daggers from their belts.

- Professions

Yeomen usually started out as apprentices at the age of fourteen and would work with experienced tradesmen for about seven years until they were able to strike out on their own. During that time, they would live with their master and weren't allowed to get married until they were done with their apprenticeship. Typical professions were cordwainers, weavers, tailors, smiths, masons, and barbers. The yeomanry was also made up of farmers, servants, and merchants. This class usually rose above their station if they made enough money, but this required a lot of money and effort.

The Poor

Unfortunately, this was the largest class during the Tudor era. Many people lost their possessions due to war, illness, or famine. Weather during the Tudor period could be unpredictable, which could lead to bad harvests. This could have disastrous consequences on the whole economy. Furthermore, as enclosures became more common, people who used to have profitable farms suddenly found themselves without a job or home and were forced into a life of extreme poverty. There were some efforts to help the poor (although the poor laws were often meant to punish beggars), but these didn't do much to alleviate the suffering of the lowest class.

- Food

All classes had bread with their meals in Tudor England since it was easy to make, but the quality varied between the classes. The poor usually ate Carter's bread, which was very cheap but made from low-quality ingredients. This bread was made from rye and wheat and was usually quite tough to eat. Ale was a popular beverage since the water was usually dirty or polluted and could cause illnesses. The poor had to rely on whatever meat they could catch, and they often caught rabbits, birds, or fish on common land.

- Clothing

Sumptuary laws didn't really apply to the lower classes since they usually couldn't afford the restricted items. Women wore simple kirtles and linen dresses made from cheap fabric or wool. The poor wore clothing that wasn't very different from the clothing yeomen wore, but they were usually made from cheaper material. The poorer class had fewer clothes as well. Nightgowns were only worn by rich people, and the lower classes simply wore their shifts or smocks when they went to bed.

Poor Laws

For much of English history, monasteries were responsible for supplying aid to the poor and needy. However, once the monasteries closed down, a new system of relief was needed, which led to the poor laws. At first, these laws didn't help the poor and were unforgiving. Anyone who was termed a beggar or vagrant had to be placed in the stocks for a few days before being sent out of town. Later, justices of the peace were allowed to assign begging areas, and anyone who was caught begging would be whipped for laziness instead of being put in the stocks. Eventually, the situation became so dire that collections were taken for the poor in churches.

During Edward VI's reign, the poor laws became harsher. Anyone who was named a vagrant would be branded as a first warning and executed on their second offense. Along with this brutal law, the king also created the position of Collector of Alms in each parish, which would serve to help the poor. Houses of correction were also established to help the poor; these were places of refuge that provided work for the needy.

Mary I also enacted brutal laws, calling for punishments, such as burning through the ear or hanging, for anyone who was a professional beggar. When Elizabeth I took the throne, she ordered everyone who earned money to donate money to the poor and had towns collect resources to help their poor populations.

Tudor Education

Education was an important part of the Tudor era, but there was no state system of schooling. Education was mostly reserved for the rich and powerful. Most of the yeomanry sent their boys into apprenticeships at young ages so that they could learn a trade and look after themselves as they grew older. This meant that a large portion of the population were skilled laborers. Girls weren't usually educated, but they were taught to run households and look after their families. However, the rich classes required their women to run estates, and they sometimes had serious responsibilities that required education. These girls were educated at home by private tutors. Henry VIII's daughters received a top-notch education, which was somewhat unusual at the time.

Rich boys went to leading schools such as St. Anthony's and St. Paul's, where they were taught Latin, mathematics, literature, and geography. In time, schools were opened for orphaned boys and girls. They were funded by rich merchants and taught basic subjects such as writing, reading, and arithmetic. Children usually went to school from early in the morning until the early evening and worked six days a week. They used hornbooks and wrote with feather quills that often had to be sharpened with knives. Discipline was an important part of Tudor education, and students were punished with beatings.

After they left grammar school, some rich boys attended universities, while others were included in the family estate or found some other profession.

Society and education played an important role in the Tudor era, but perhaps one of the most fascinating subjects of the era was that of the church and religion. The Tudor monarchs changed the course of history according to their faiths and beliefs, which meant that England's religion went through incredible changes in just a few short years.

Chapter 14: Religion and the Church

Religion played a major part in daily life in medieval England. Churches were a stable source of comfort and relief, places where people could turn to in times of need. The people's traditions and beliefs gave them hope during difficult times and helped to keep order in the realm. The poor could turn to monasteries when everyone else refused to help them. However, the church also took a lot of money from its people and endorsed various conflicts. While it did help the poor, much of the clergy lived in relative luxury, and a lot of the church's money was sent to the pope in distant Rome.

When the Tudors took the throne, the old religion was dutifully observed by Henry VII and his family, but his focus was on stabilizing the country. In contrast, Henry VIII was a religious man who was well versed in theology. He became obsessed with the notion that his first marriage was cursed and took matters into his own hands. At first, the English Reformation began as a way to solve Henry VIII's "Great Matter," but it led to England becoming a Protestant nation. The sequence of events that led to that monumental shift is fascinating and worth studying.

Religion during Henry VII's Reign

England was a Catholic country when Henry VII was king. His mother, Margaret Beaufort, was an extremely pious woman who had great influence in the early Tudor court. She wouldn't have allowed any hint of religious reforms while she was alive. There were small groups who questioned the Roman Catholic Church, but they were persecuted relentlessly and branded as heretics, a charge that carried some of the heaviest penalties at the time. The royal court faithfully observed the old religious practices, including religious plays, saints' days, and pilgrimages.

Henry VII wasn't particularly interested in religion and focused on other matters during his reign. He had inherited a volatile country and spent much of his reign chasing down pretenders and protecting his family from treason. Margaret Beaufort, by contrast, was fanatically devoted to her religion. She was a powerful patron of the church, regularly gave to the poor, and supported religious studies. Later in life, she made a public vow of chastity and enrolled as a "sister" in several monastic houses. Although she was still married when she took her vow, she was allowed to move away from her husband and live in her own home to fulfill her vow. Margaret's piety was well known throughout Europe, and she was often complimented for being so zealous. She was never missing from Mass, which was recited in Latin at the time, and she helped to translate some religious works into English. During that time, religion was shrouded in mystery since most texts and all services were conducted in Latin. This made it somewhat inaccessible to the common people, who only spoke English.

Henry VIII and Religion

Despite what Henry VIII did in his later years, he enthusiastically observed the traditional Catholic religion during the beginning of his reign. It's also important to note that Catherine of Aragon was a devout Catholic woman who was related to some of the most powerful Catholic rulers in Europe. Margaret Beaufort also guided Henry VIII through the beginning weeks of his reign, and it was obvious that she left a powerful mark on her young grandson. Henry VIII took a keen interest in theology and was known for being a benefactor of the church. His support for the church was so powerful and energetic that Pope Leo X gave Henry the title of Defender of the Faith in 1521. Unfortunately, his support wouldn't survive the "Great Matter."

49. The Divorce of Catherine of Aragon

https://commons.wikimedia.org/wiki/File:Catherine_Aragon_Henri_VIII_by_Henry_Nelson_O Neil.jpg

When England first split from the Roman Church, it retained many of the traditional beliefs and practices. However, the Protestant Reformation had begun to take hold in Europe, and those ideas began to filter into England. At first, Henry was dismissive of Protestant beliefs since he didn't put much stock into them, but his mind began to change. While he didn't enthusiastically embrace the new beliefs, he was happy to dissolve the monasteries in 1535. Meanwhile, some of his ministers began the Reformation in earnest. Thomas Cromwell took the lead and was appointed as the king's vice regent in church affairs. He quickly began overturning old traditions and instituted guidelines for the new priests he recruited.

The new clergy aimed to educate their congregations about the seven deadly sins and the Ten Commandments. Cromwell was heavily influenced by the writings of Martin Luther, who rejected many Catholic teachings. What had started as a way to get the king a divorce had become a full-blown Reformation that stunned the Catholic Church.

The Protestant Reformation in Europe

The winds of change began blowing against the Catholic Church in 1517 when a German monk named Martin Luther began challenging the church's teachings. It all started when Martin Luther published his *Ninety-five Theses*, which was a list of topics about Christianity that directly opposed the teachings of the church. One of his biggest grievances was indulgences. At the time, the church sold a certificate that pardoned sins and could be bought in advance. Martin Luther argued that forgiveness was a gift of faith and obedience, not something that could be put up for sale.

50. Martin Luther

https://commons.wikimedia.org/wiki/File:Martin_Luther,_1529.jpg

He paved the way for splinter groups that broke away from the Catholic Church; they became known as Protestants. Soon, the church was faced with a wave of opposition, as learned men such as John Calvin and Ulrich Zwingli challenged fundamental church practices, such as the Holy Communion. A group called the Anabaptists emerged and argued that baptism should be performed on consenting adults instead of on uncomprehending infants.

In essence, the Catholic Church had presented itself as the intermediary between humans and God for centuries. The only way to get to God was through the church and his chosen representative, the pope. Most of the reforms were aimed at making people less dependent on the church, as Protestants wanted people to be responsible for their own spirituality. This led to radical practices such as distributing the Holy Bible in common languages and the rejection of fundamental Catholic practices.

The New Beliefs

After Martin Luther wrote his *Ninety-five Theses*, he pinned it to the door of his local church. Before long, it spread like wildfire. His ideas about religion were revolutionary and sparked fierce debate throughout the continent. As soon as his *Theses* was published, he began translating the Bible from Latin to German, which enraged the church. For centuries, the clergy was tasked with helping the ordinary people to understand the Bible, which made congregations reliant on the preacher. If people wanted to know anything about religion, God, or the Bible, they had to approach priests, who would then recite church doctrine back at them.

Luther's ideas spread, and before long, the Reformation had begun. The Catholic Church had a serious problem on its hands. While Protestants and Catholics shared the same God, their approach to religion was vastly different. Their vastly differing ideas would lead to vicious conflicts. Protestants believed that saints, pilgrimages, relics, and images were unnecessary and that everyone had a personal responsibility to maintain their faith. This was in direct contrast to the Catholic faith; the things Protestants rejected were fundamental aspects of the Catholic religion. Catholics believed that they needed the church to connect them to God, while the Protestants believed that the Catholic Church was corrupt and keeping people from God.

Relics, in particular, were important to Catholics. They believed that relics were the physical remains of a saint. Anything that was touched or left behind by a saint had holy significance. These artifacts were so important that Catholics would undertake long journeys to pray to relics during times of distress. These journeys were known as pilgrimages. Another key difference between Protestants and Catholics was their ideas about Mass. The Catholics believed in transubstantiation, a process during which the bread and wine became the body and blood of Christ when consumed. Many Protestants rejected the belief in transubstantiation.

Edward VI's Protestant Reforms

Henry VIII may have started the English Reformation, but England only became a Protestant country during Edward VI's reign. The young king had been heavily influenced by his stepmother, Catherine Parr, and his main advisors, Edward Seymour, John Dudley, and Thomas Cranmer. Edward VI was only a boy, but he enthusiastically endorsed Protestantism. While he may not have personally enacted many of the reforms, they were all carried out in his name. During this time, radical reforms had become a reality, as icons, stained glass scenes, and murals were taken out of churches. Church services were conducted in English, priests were allowed to marry, and the saints faded into obscurity.

There were some rebellions against these new reforms, but they were brutally defeated. People were concerned about the sudden and radical changes that were taking place. The English Reformation had moved from debates to drastic actions, which caused instability for the general population. Edward VI's reign saw the destruction of old traditions that had been observed by the people for hundreds of years. Catholic altars were replaced with communion tables, and Catholic icons were removed or destroyed. While the Reformation had been around for a few years already, it had mostly occurred in small pockets in Europe or had been a matter of theoretical debate. However, when Edward VI took the throne, those reforms touched almost every church in the country.

While the young king was greatly influenced by powerful advisors, it was clear that he was a devout Protestant. After all, he made great efforts to keep his Catholic sister, Mary, from the throne.

Thomas Cranmer

Thomas Cranmer was responsible for most of the reforms that took place during Edward VI's reign, and he was the first Protestant archbishop of Canterbury. As the youngest son of a gentleman, it was traditionally accepted that Thomas would join the clergy. However, while studying at Cambridge University, he became a part of the "White Horse" group, which was interested in the Protestant Reformation. Cranmer came into contact with the royal family when he served as

Thomas Boleyn's (Anne Boleyn's father) chaplain. Cranmer was instrumental in solving the king's "Great Matter," which launched him to prominence in the Tudor court.

In fact, it was Cranmer who may have planted the idea that Henry VIII should split from the Roman Church. He proposed the idea that the matter of the king's divorce wasn't a legal matter but rather a moral one and that the pope should have no say in the king's divine judgment. Cranmer was eventually made the king's chaplain, and in time, he became the archbishop of Canterbury. For the next few years, Cranmer would be instrumental in obtaining the king's divorce and presided over the king's next marriages.

Cranmer also took the lead in the dissolution of the monasteries and other reforms during Henry VIII's reign, but he would go on to implement more radical changes during Edward VI's reign. In 1547, he released the *First Book of Homilies*, which set the guidelines for how priests should conduct their services. However, his greatest accomplishment was the *Book of Common Prayer*.

The *Book of Common Prayer*

The *Book of Common Prayer* was written by Thomas Cranmer in 1549. It was used during church services and outlined reforms that the church was forced to observe, as the Act of Uniformity made it mandatory for the whole country. The first edition of the book was meant to serve as a bridge between new and old religious ideas. It was supposed to help make the English Reformation more palatable and easier to understand, but it was still a departure from the traditional beliefs. It was purposefully vague on some matters, but it still stirred up opposition since it was too radical for the supporters of the traditional religion and not radical enough for staunch Protestants. Finally, a second edition was released in 1552, which was even more radical than the first and made some clarifications.

For example, the second edition completely rejected the teaching of transubstantiation and angered Catholics. It was the radical changes that the Protestants had wanted, but it also led to opposition and rebellions. The book was an important part of the English Reformation and helped to spread Protestant beliefs. It was a way to impose the Reformation in every church in the country. While the *Book of Common Prayer* was likely one of Cranmer's proudest achievements, it made him even more unpopular with the Catholics. The book also included offensive prayers against the pope, which didn't help its popularity with the Catholics. Unfortunately for Cranmer, his efforts during the English Reformation made him some dangerous enemies, including the next queen of England, Mary I.

Mary I's Return to Rome

While Edward VI and his Protestant advisors tried desperately to keep Mary I from the throne, they vastly underestimated how many people would fight for her. While Lady Jane Grey was a Protestant and would ensure that England remained a Protestant country, Mary I was the legitimate Tudor heir. There were many nobles and commoners who disapproved of the way she had been disinherited, and they were eager to support her rise to the throne. Unfortunately for the Protestants, she immediately began undoing the Reformation and dutifully returned England back to the pope. She was a staunch Catholic, and she had been horrified by what had happened.

In 1553, she removed the *Book of Common Prayer* and returned the old Latin prayer books to the churches. She quickly removed all the reforms that had taken place during her predecessors' reigns. However, the country's return to Catholicism wasn't as popular as she had hoped. For one thing, the nobles weren't eager to return their new lands and relinquish money to the church. Her marriage to a Spanish prince angered the populace. Some people had also become attached to Protestantism, which was a difficult fact for Mary to accept. She wasn't willing to compromise, and after Wyatt's rebellion, she began taking more extreme steps. In 1554, she began burning prominent Protestants. Thomas Cranmer was arrested in 1555.

Cranmer had helped to enact the law that made it treasonous to observe different religious beliefs than the monarch, and he was forced to recant his Protestantism. It was a heavy blow against the Reformation. However, when Cranmer was led to the stake in 1556, he stuck his hand in the fire and claimed that he was burning off the hand that signed his recantation. This action became legendary and turned Cranmer into a Protestant martyr. Unfortunately for Mary I, the English Reformation was far from over.

Elizabeth I and Protestant England

When Elizabeth I became queen in 1558, the country would once again switch religions. However, this time, the transition would be permanent. Elizabeth I was a practical woman and chose not to impose radical reforms on her people. When she became queen, she restored the *Book of Common Prayer* but took out some of the more radical or offensive aspects. She also maintained a strict hierarchy within the church and appointed bishops. Elizabeth had seen what misplaced religious zeal could do to a monarch, so she was much more careful in instituting her reforms. While some people were frustrated by her approach, it was a success. English Protestantism became known as Anglicism.

Chapter 15: Culture and Art

The Tudor dynasty brought about some of the most climatic changes in English history. The Tudor court was filled with dangerous, ambitious individuals who didn't flinch when the country descended into chaos for their own gain. It was an interesting time filled with fascinating characters and deadly conflicts. However, it was also a time of great cultural and artistic changes. Toward the end of the Tudor period, the arts flourished, and the English Renaissance began.

The Tudor court also housed some of the most interesting and famous artists of the time. The royal family's portraits were painted by highly talented individuals, while London was the home of some of the most influential writers of all time. Elizabeth I, in particular, was a great patron of the arts, and under her care, the Renaissance took root in England. Moreover, renowned literary and architectural works were developed during the period, and some of those elements can still be seen in modern society. While the Tudors were gripped in personal, political, and religious turmoil, art became an important and defining feature of the period.

English Renaissance

The English Renaissance began in the latter half of the 15th century and was a result of the Renaissance that had begun earlier in Europe, most notably in Italy. The Wars of the Roses kept England isolated from developments in Europe, especially in regard to its military, but the civil war also restricted cultural innovations. When the Tudors took over, these artistic and cultural aspects were allowed to arrive in England from Europe, but the Renaissance gained the most momentum during Elizabeth I's reign.

While the Italian Renaissance saw great advancements in paintings and sculptures, the English Renaissance was more focused on music and literary works. The English Renaissance mainly took place during the Tudor era, but English literature had been ahead of its time for decades. Writers such as Chaucer popularized writing their works in French while most of Europe still used Latin. However, England was far behind the visual styles that were being used in mainland Europe, and many of their most famous artists had been imported from there. The most notable examples of foreign artists in the Tudor court were Hans Holbein and Levina Teerlinc.

As the Reformation ripped through the country, it also impacted the artists of the time. Icons were banned in England, and as a result, the visual arts of England were focused on portraits and landscapes. A particularly popular form of art was the portrait miniature, which was invented and developed in England. Skilled artists created miniature portraits that could be kept in lockets. This art style became very popular in Europe over time. As time went on, portraits became more intricate, as artists painted symbolic objects meant to convey certain messages to viewers. The *Armada Portrait* painted during Elizabeth I's reign is a prime example of that trend.

51. *Armada Portrait*

https://commons.wikimedia.org/wiki/File:Elizabeth_I_(Armada_Portrait).jpg

Many of Elizabeth I's portraits were filled with symbolic objects. These portraits were usually painted to emphasize the queen's virginity and purity.

Tudor Literature

English authors had built up a reputation for writing their works in the common English language for decades before the English Renaissance began. This would have provided a firm foundation for writers who worked during the Renaissance. The Reformation also helped to popularize the practice of writing in English instead of Latin. For centuries, Latin had been seen as the learned language and was used for many literary works, but the English Renaissance helped to change that trend somewhat. The practice of writing in English also helped to develop the language in terms of structure and grammar. As the Bible was being translated from Latin to English, there were fierce debates about how to capture the essence of the holy writings in a comparatively limited language. In 1526, William Tyndale published his translation of the Bible, which helped develop the English language.

The Tudor princesses, Mary and Elizabeth, received some of the finest education in Europe, which likely influenced Elizabeth's love of theater and literature. One of Elizabeth's tutors, Roger Ascham, was known as the "Father of English Prose." As London's population grew and people began making a lot of money, they found that they wanted entertainment. London's theaters filled that need, which led to the emergence of remarkable plays and playwrights.

Tudor Architecture

One of the most famous Tudor building projects was that of Hampton Palace, which was started in 1515 and built for Thomas Wolsey. However, when Wolsey fell from grace, he gave the palace to Henry VIII to try and appease the king's anger. Wolsey had spent a large amount of money on it with the aim of creating the most beautiful palace in England. This ambition likely contributed to his downfall. The architectural style of this time is known as the Tudor style, and it featured a blend of Gothic and Renaissance styles. Buildings constructed in the Tudor style usually featured intricate decorative brickwork.

52. Hampton Court Palace

During Elizabeth I's reign, the wool trade declined in profitability, which led to a resurgence in farming that helped to enrich many of her subjects. However, this new money didn't motivate the queen to build new palaces or castles. Instead, her nobles built luxurious houses and were required to host the queen during her travels. Country manors were modernized, and government buildings were updated, which led to the emergence of the distinctive Elizabethan style that featured a lot of glass.

Influential Tudor Artists

For much of the Tudor dynasty, foreign artists were employed by the royal court with the express purpose of painting portraits of the royal family and high-ranking nobility. These artists lived in luxury but had the responsibility of painting flattering portraits of their patrons. This kind of lifestyle would have been stressful, and it wouldn't have allowed for a lot of creative freedom. However, several notable people managed to keep royal favor for most of their lives. In some cases, these artists were sent overseas to paint portraits of prospective brides or grooms. This was an important job since there could be dire consequences if it was not done right, as was demonstrated in the case of Henry VIII and Anne of Cleves.

- **Hans Holbein the Younger**

Hans Holbein came from a long line of artists who gained fame and renown in Europe, especially in Germany. Holbein studied under his father and began working by himself in 1515 in Switzerland. During his younger years, he traveled through Europe and developed a distinctive style that helped his career develop. In 1523, he painted a portrait of the famed Dutch scholar Desiderius Erasmus. By 1537, he was officially employed by Henry VIII. He painted portraits of Henry VIII, Jane Seymour, and Anne of Cleves. Holbein was famous for his precise and realistic drawings and paintings, which likely helped to launch him to fame.

- **Levina Teerlinc**

Levina Teerlinc was born around 1520 in Flanders and became one of the most famous miniature portrait painters of her time. It's likely that Levina learned her craft from her father and gained a level of popularity in Flanders before she was invited to work at Henry VIII's court in 1546. She worked hard and rose to prominence within the English royal court and worked for all of Henry VIII's heirs. The fact that she was a favorite in the royal court was evidenced by the fact that she received many expensive gifts from the Tudor monarchs.

- Nicholas Hilliard

Nicholas Hilliard was born in 1547 and became one of the most famous English painters during the English Renaissance. He was a particular favorite of Queen Elizabeth I and brought the art of miniature portrait painting to new heights. Hilliard was sent to Geneva as a child to escape the persecution of Protestants but returned by 1559. By 1570, he was working in Queen Elizabeth I's court. Hilliard also had considerable skill as a goldsmith and jeweler. The queen admired his skills so much that she appointed him to design her second great seal.

Tudor Writers

In modern times, English is a complex language with precise rules and thousands of words. However, that wasn't always true, and in the medieval era, English was a simple vernacular language. There weren't many established rules for the language. While there were dedicated schools that taught Latin grammar, English didn't receive the same treatment, as it wasn't seen as the language of learned scholars. In time, this would change. English writers began to develop the language and invented new words. These writers originally came to prominence to satisfy London's growing need for dramatic entertainment, but they ended up creating some of the most influential works in English history.

- William Shakespeare

William Shakespeare was one of the most famous and influential writers of his time. He was born in 1564 in Stratford-upon-Avon. Shakespeare came from a humble background and married a local girl named Anne Hathaway when he was eighteen years old. He couldn't stay in the little town forever and went to London in 1592. Shakespeare began to rise quickly and was invited to join Lord Chamberlain's Men, a theater company. Shakespeare's plays were performed at the Globe and featured the relatively famous actor, Richard Burbage. Almost as soon as he began his career as a writer, he began accumulating wealthy friends and patrons who greatly appreciated his writing. By the end of his career, he had written 154 sonnets and about 37 plays.

Shakespeare is famous for the universality and relatability of his works. His works show great wit and perceptiveness that gave them lasting power.

- **Edmund Spenser**

Edmund Spenser was one of the most famous and influential poets in English history. He was born around 1553 to a noble family that didn't have much money. When he was a teenager, his poems were featured in an anti-Catholic tract commissioned by a rich Flemish man named Jan Baptista van der Noot. When Spenser graduated from grammar school, he attended the University of Cambridge, where he studied literature in various languages.

He learned from epic poets, such as Virgil and others. In time, he wrote the epic poem, *The Faerie Queene*, which later inspired writers like Shakespeare. He lived through some of the most interesting times of the Reformation, and much of his work was influenced by the religious turmoil. Spenser gained a lot of fame for *The Faerie Queene*, which celebrated Elizabeth I's reign, but he was famous in his own right before penning the epic.

- **Sir Thomas Wyatt**

Sir Thomas Wyatt was born in 1503 and gained attention for his questionable alliances and, more importantly, his highly individualistic poetry. He had been accredited with introducing elements from French and Italian poetry to English literature. Wyatt was known for being an attractive man who gained a lot of attention at Henry VIII's court, where the ideals of medieval chivalry were celebrated. The young nobleman fit the picture of the romantic medieval knight since he was skilled in tournament games, poetry, and music. However, his popularity with women nearly got him executed in 1536 when he was arrested for allegedly having an affair with Anne Boleyn.

Wyatt wrote several poems and sonnets during his lifetime, as well as songs that increased his fame. Unfortunately, he wasn't as gifted at politics and was arrested after his friend Thomas Cromwell was executed. His son would lead the Wyatt rebellion, which got Elizabeth I arrested.

- **Henry Howard**

Henry Howard was born in 1517 and received a fine education as the son of Lord Thomas Howard. Henry eventually became the duke of

Norfolk. He had a prominent position in Henry VIII's court, which may have influenced some of his poetry. He was accredited with creating the foundation for the age of English poetry. During his youth, he was nearly betrothed to Princess Mary, but that betrothal (like so many of her betrothals) fell through. Later, he served in Henry's army in Scotland and France. Unfortunately, his fortune fell when the Seymours took over once Edward VI was appointed as king.

Henry Howard was charged with treason when it was discovered that he was closely allied with Roman Catholics. He was executed at thirty years old but left behind numerous poems that were only published after his death.

- **Sir Philip Sidney**

Sir Philip Sidney was born in 1554 and is considered to be the ideal gentleman of the Elizabethan era. He also had the distinction of writing one of the best sonnets of the period. Sidney was responsible for introducing many European Renaissance ideas to English literary circles and worked as a statesman in Elizabeth I's court. He studied at Shrewsbury School as a child and later attended Oxford. He spent some time during his younger years traveling around Europe, where he was likely introduced to the themes and ideas that pervaded his works.

Sidney spoke Latin, Italian, and French perfectly, which helped to increase his knowledge and appreciation of European poetry. By his early twenties, Sidney was working in Queen Elizabeth I's court and given serious responsibilities. He had many interests and was friends with some of the most important artists of his time, including Edmund Spenser.

- **Roger Ascham**

Roger Ascham was born around 1515 and became a renowned scholar who had revolutionary theories about education. He was also one of the biggest promoters of the vernacular English language and was known for being a humanist. Humanism focuses on the individual and social potential of all people. It is a philosophy that believes people have the responsibility of conducting moral and philosophical inquiries.

Ascham studied at Cambridge University, where he learned to appreciate the classical Greek writers. He tutored Princess Elizabeth in Greek and Latin while also holding several positions within the Tudor court. He later served as Mary I's Latin secretary. When Elizabeth took the throne, he became her secretary and helped her study Greek. His most famous work, the *Scholemaster*, was published after his death.

Famous Tudor Portraits

Unlike the Italian Renaissance, the English Renaissance wasn't focused on the visual arts. This might be partly due to the fact that during the Reformation, icons were destroyed and discouraged. Icons were associated with the Roman Catholic religion, and many artists didn't want to find themselves on the wrong side of the law, especially since there were other places in Europe where the visual arts were being developed. However, portraits and landscapes were favorites in England. The Tudor era saw the development of portrait painting as an art, and artists eventually focused on symbolism. Some of the most famous portraits during the time were of various members of the royal family.

- **The *Portrait of Henry VIII***

While Henry VIII had many portraits of himself commissioned during his reign, one of the most notable portraits is the *Portrait of Henry VIII* by Hans Holbein the Younger. It was painted when Henry was in his forties. The portrait depicts Henry as a younger and healthier version of himself when he was, in reality, old, obese, and grossly afflicted by an ulcerated leg. Holbein's portrait gave Henry the powerful presence that he had long since lost, which enchanted the king. He spread the portrait throughout the kingdom. His nobles had the portrait recreated to please the king. The original was lost in a fire, but since there were so many recreations, we are able to know what it looked like.

53. Portrait of Henry VIII

https://commons.wikimedia.org/wiki/File:After_Hans_Holbein_the_Younger_-_Portrait_of_Henry_VIII_-_Google_Art_Project.jpg

- **The Portrait of Jane Seymour**

An unfinished portrait of Jane Seymour has been the subject of scholarly curiosity since it depicts the deceased queen and was likely painted soon after her death in 1537. There are various elements in the painting that were never finished, and while it showed distinctive painting styles of the time, it was never completed. It's possible that it was commissioned by the Seymour family but abandoned when they fell from prominence.

- The *Rainbow Portrait* of Queen Elizabeth I

One of the most famous portraits of Elizabeth I is the *Rainbow Portrait*, in which she holds a rainbow, a symbol of peace. No one is sure who painted the portrait, and several artists, including Isaac Oliver, Marcus Gheeraerts the Younger, and Taddeo Zuccari, have been accredited with the painting. While the rainbow symbolizes peace, the queen's dress is embroidered with wildflowers and pearls, which are images associated with the Virgin Mary. The eyes and ears that were painted on her skirt are supposed to remind the viewer that the queen was keenly aware of the needs of her people. Other symbols include a snake, which symbolizes wisdom. The painting hints that her power is as important as the sun to her people.

54. The *Rainbow Portrait*

https://commons.wikimedia.org/wiki/File:Elizabeth_I_Rainbow_Portrait.jpg

There's no doubt that the Tudor era ushered in a period of literary and artistic innovation that left its mark on English history and the English language.

Chapter 16: Daily Life in Tudor England

Since the Tudor era was filled with climactic changes, it would be easy to imagine that daily life in the period would be filled with exciting events and strange customs. However, most of the population wasn't affected by the scandalous lives of the royals and nobles. Sometimes, they would have to answer a call to arms or march off to a foreign country to fight in a war, but other than that, life was relatively restful for those who had nothing to do with the noble houses.

Daily life in Tudor England depended greatly on a person's status. There were different rules for the social classes, and a person's rank was displayed through their clothes and food. However, that didn't mean that life was always better for the rich. Many nobles had to live at the royal court, which was a boring and extremely expensive way of life. The poor didn't have things easy either. They had to navigate a biased justice system to eke out a living. While most people weren't directly affected by the changes that occurred in the Tudor era, in time, their ways of life were subtly impacted. This could be seen in church life, entertainment, and the observance of public holidays.

Family Life

Families in Tudor England tended to be larger than most modern families. Parents were encouraged to have as many children as possible. Besides the parents and children, family units usually consisted of grandparents, cousins, servants, and apprentices. If something happened to a person's parents or spouse, they could usually expect to move in with their extended family. Family was an important part of life in Tudor England.

Unfortunately, illness was common, and babies often didn't survive infancy. Living conditions were usually dirty, damp, and overcrowded, which proved to be fatal for young children. There was no distinction between the poor and rich in this regard, and most parents lost at least one child.

The prevalent belief during the time period was that children were born with a natural badness in them. It was the parents' responsibility to discipline the children, which involved beating them. Despite the harsh disciplinary rules of the time, parents cared deeply for their children and often bought or built toys for their little ones.

55. Toy horse constructed sometime after the medieval era

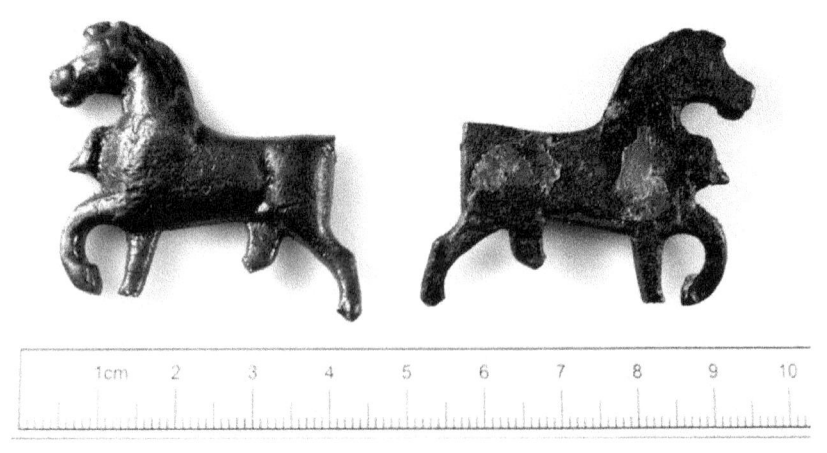

The Portable Antiquities Scheme/ The Trustees of the British Museum, CC BY-SA 2.0 <https://creativecommons.org/licenses/by-sa/2.0>, via Wikimedia Commons https://commons.wikimedia.org/wiki/File:Post-medieval_,_Toy_(FindID_220719).jpg

Rich families spent much less time together. As soon as a child in a wealthy family was born, they were handed over to a wetnurse who fed them. The children grew up with tutors or sometimes in other noble houses. Royal children were taken from their parents while they were still babies and received a household to care for their needs. Most princes and princesses never lived with their parents and weren't part of a traditional family unit.

Marriage

There is a common misconception that everyone married young during the Tudor era, but this is untrue. Marriage was commonly viewed as an economical affair rather than having anything to do with love. Rich families usually arranged marriages for their children when they were still young, perhaps even babies. Their primary concern was the economic or social viability of a match. While rich children knew who they would marry by the time they reached puberty, they didn't actually get married until the bride was in her late teens, often until she was about sixteen. This practice was enforced by Margaret Beaufort when she set several acts about marriage and childbirth; this was likely due to her own traumatic experience. For most of English history, this had been an unspoken rule, but she saw the need to make it a spoken one.

Marriage among the lower classes was a much simpler affair. Women usually got married in their mid-twenties, while men waited a little longer. Since life expectancy was shorter during this period, it wasn't uncommon for people to be married a few times during their life. If a man was widowed, he would usually marry as quickly as possible so that his family would be taken care of while he worked. The same was true of widowed women who could still expect to have children. A common practice during the time was for the widow of a tradesman to marry one of her deceased husband's apprentices so that they could keep the business going. In certain cases, a widow past her childbearing years would marry if it was a good economic match, as was the case of Margaret Beaufort's marriage to Lord Thomas Stanley.

Death

Death was a common and unfortunate feature of the Tudor era that usually affected daily life. The beginning of the Tudor era saw the world emerging from the horrors of the Black Death, which had left a definite mark on the common people. They were suddenly tormented by the religious teachings of purgatory and hell since many of them had lost at least one family member to the plague.

The religious teaching of hell stated that people who were judged as sinners would be burned and tortured for the rest of eternity. The teaching of purgatory stated that some people weren't bad enough to warrant hell but weren't good enough to reach heaven either. This meant that they languished until they were cleansed of their sins and allowed to reach heaven. As a result of these teachings, people paid massive sums to have the clergy pray for their family members who might have been trapped in purgatory. It also led to the practice of chantries, where rich people could be buried and prayed for together. Some wealthy families even donated to chapels or built family burial sites on holy ground.

56. Tomb in Beauchamp Chapel

https://commons.wikimedia.org/wiki/File:Beauchamp_Chapel_-_geograph.org.uk_-_2838141.jpg

Of course, the church made a lot of money off of death rites, but all that changed during the Reformation. From then on, death rites became more private and were conducted according to a person's conscience.

Holidays

The Tudor era saw the rise of public holidays, which were observed by both the rich and the poor. These were days when people could take a break from normality and let loose. Drinking and merrymaking were common on feast days, and some fun traditions were born. For example, a "king of the feast" would be chosen and paraded around for all to see. Apprentices could roam around the streets and "discipline" their elders by setting ridiculous rules and laws. These traditions were a source of great entertainment. The rich would also impress their social status in their communities by paying for such revelries and giving money to the poor.

Holy days were favorites among the people because they could expect feasts, music, and games, which gave them a well-deserved rest from their daily work. New Years, Christmas, Twelfth Day, Ash Wednesday, Lady Day, Easter, May Day, and Accession Day were all public holidays, but there were many more that had their own customs and traditions.

May Day and Whitsunday were particular favorites since these were summer festivals during which feasts, dancing, and plays were common. While these holidays were a source of joy, they also required a lot of work. Usually, people would begin making food and preparing for the feast the night before the holiday. Sometimes, they would also fast before a holy day, which usually meant they avoided meat. Most people didn't mind, however, as they knew they could look forward to a massive meal the next day.

Life in the Royal Court

The nobility certainly led an easier life than the lower classes, but that didn't mean they enjoyed constant glamor or entertainment. Often, they were called to serve the monarch at court and couldn't leave without express permission from their ruler. They received rooms at court according to their rank and were expected to furnish these rooms and keep their own servants. This was massively expensive since they were expected to display their wealth and only have the finest furniture. Moreover, they were expected to keep up with courtly fashion, which could cost a fortune. Life at court was a constant drain on resources, and many noble families ended up bankrupt after living there.

The royal court was the heart of the nation, especially in regard to politics. Nobles could gain a lot of lands and money if they made their monarch happy, but it could be a boring way of life, as they had to wait for the monarch to make an appearance. Some nobles had important positions, such as on the Privy Council or as the monarch's advisors, while others just lived at court. When the monarch moved to a different palace, the courtiers were expected to pack up and follow them.

Nobles dined together, and there were different spaces for different ranks of nobles. The king's dining rooms were always filled with roasted meat and luxurious dishes. And the Tudor monarchs' palaces were designed like mazes, with the royal family's rooms in the middle. They were surrounded by their favorites, while lower-ranking nobles lived on the outer edges of the maze and rarely saw the monarch.

Entertainment

Entertainment was an important part of Tudor society. There were many different activities to keep people busy, but they usually depended on a person's social standing. Common activities included going to the theater or going to a bear baiting. The latter was a brutal pastime in which a bear was chained to a pole by its neck or leg. Dogs would be released into the arena, and the crowds would watch the ensuing fight with interest.

Music was a popular feature of the era, and people usually gathered together to hear or play music together. Dancing events allowed people to get together to dance and socialize. These events ranged from local dances to noble balls where alliances were created. There were also more casual pastimes, such as board games, gambling, and card games.

The rich had more time than the other classes and were constantly looking to provide the most lavish entertainment for their friends. They would host great feasts and balls with exotic menus. They also used the time to show off their belongings and hired acrobats, jesters, musicians, or jugglers to keep their friends entertained. If they weren't entertaining guests or attending court, they usually kept busy in their gardens or pursued hobbies like painting or music.

The poorer classes usually had Sunday afternoons to themselves or looked forward to public holidays.

Sports

Sports were a popular pastime during the Tudor era. People used to take part in tennis, archery, fencing, bowls (this game is played on a bowling green and involves rolling a large ball toward a stationary object), football (soccer), and hockey. While these games are still played, the Tudor versions were much less refined and could lead to injuries. The richer classes enjoyed pursuits such as hunting or hawking. They kept large lands stocked with deer and other game, which could provide hours of entertainment. Trained hawks were also used in hunting expeditions. Unfortunately, nobles often closed off large pieces of land for their hunting and restricted their access to the common people. They also persecuted poachers harshly.

Fishing was enjoyed by all classes, but it was mostly pursued by the rich as a hobby. Some poorer people relied on fishing as an extra source of food. Lawn games became especially popular during the Elizabethan era, and nobles were often seen playing bowls or lawn tennis. These games were usually reserved for the rich since they required a lot of time and expensive equipment.

More leisurely pastimes included reading and needlework, the latter of which was always reserved for women. Meanwhile, men would engage in more rowdy games, such as hot cockles or blind man's bluff. The first game, hot cockles, involved one player putting his head in the lap of another player. Then, the other players would take turns slapping his rear end. The first player could only leave the lap if he correctly guessed who hit him last.

Chess, draughts, and checkers were also popular at the time, as was gambling, which led to a lot of fighting.

Tournaments and Masques

Tournaments and jousts remained a popular pastime for the aristocracy. While the Tudor era progressed, armor and knights became obsolete, as wars were fought with guns, warships, and cannons instead. Still, the practice of jousting was still a fun activity for the rich. These tournaments were usually accompanied by other entertainment, such as performers, musicians, and feasts. Tournaments also featured many militaristic elements to delight the crowd. Soldiers, such as pikemen and archers, usually showed off their skills to the public, which served as military propaganda and entertainment. Archery and knife throwing were popular games during festivals and tournaments, and the people could usually take part in some of the games.

57. Jousting

https://commons.wikimedia.org/wiki/File:Medieval-Jousting-Tournaments.jpg

In time, fencing became more popular than jousting, as it was a safer and more sophisticated sport. While tournaments and festivals were usually public affairs, and common people could sometimes enjoy these pastimes, masques were part of the entertainment hosted only by the royal court. Masques were pageants where nobles could show off their singing, dancing, and acting skills. These events usually had themes, storylines, or recreations that involved different characters dressed in rich costumes. They were meant to emphasize the luxury and sophistication of the royal court. The monarch was usually featured in a prominent role.

Henry VIII, in particular, enjoyed participating in masques and presenting himself as a knight from medieval romantic literature. Masques were popular in European royal courts and were an important part of courtly life, especially during Henry VIII's reign. Sometimes, these masques featured allegorical content and were very dramatic, which delighted everyone involved.

A Trip to the Theater

The theater industry boomed during Elizabeth I's reign. Her reign signified the height of the English Renaissance, and she was the patron of several influential playwrights. During this time, actors became famous, and dramatic plays were developed to please the crowds. The theater entertained people of all classes, and everyone was welcome, although some theaters were exclusively for the rich. The Globe was one of the most famous theaters of its time and featured many of Shakespeare's plays.

At first, actors were part of traveling troupes who went from village to village all throughout the kingdom, but as the troupes made more money, they were able to stay in one place. This allowed them to put more money into their costumes and sets, which heightened the quality of their performances. Some theaters put on daily plays. In the past, plays were mostly recreations of religious events, but in the Tudor era, plays were about history, revenge, murder, romance, comedy, and tragedy. This new form of art thrilled the poor and rich alike, and they eagerly lined up to watch this exciting form of entertainment.

All-purpose theaters were built in London and were simple buildings with a stage and seats for the poor and rich. Nobles sponsored actors and playwrights alike, which meant that a lot of money was pouring into the industry. This allowed more people to become actors and playwrights. As the Elizabethan era progressed, incredible talent was revealed and nurtured. One thing was for sure; going to the theater was a treat for all classes during the closing years of the Tudor era.

Conclusion

The Tudor era is one of the most fascinating periods in English history. It featured scandalous monarchs and ambitious individuals who changed their country forever. While the Tudors made powerful enemies in the Catholic Church, they held out against invasion and helped England out of the dark ages that were the Wars of the Roses. Since their antics are the source of much study and debate, it is clear that the Tudors deserve their place in history.

While the Tudors inherited a country that had been ravaged by civil war, by the end of the Tudor era, England had experienced a cultural renaissance and had an advanced fleet at its disposal. Henry VII produced two male heirs and left behind an economically stable country, but his heir would struggle in his own search for an heir and cause incredible instability that saw the total reformation of the church. In the end, the Tudor line died out with a woman who chose to remain single so that she could keep her power intact. It wasn't an easy choice, and she was pressured to find a husband, but she remained firm and became one of the greatest monarchs in English history.

This compelling book took a thorough tour of the era, beginning with an overview of what England was like before the Tudors took power. England was ruled by the Plantagenet dynasty, which was marked by either great or completely ineffectual kings. The country saw glory under kings such as Henry V, but in just a few short years, it was plunged into chaos under a weak king, Henry VI. The Wars of the Roses began during this period and led to vicious fighting that wiped out most of the noble families in the country. These years weren't an easy time for anybody, and the country stalled in terms of innovation and development. Greedy, ambitious nobles ripped their country apart for whatever power they could find, while crafty politicians used their wits to thrive. Out of this chaos, Margaret Beaufort emerged as a victor. She started off as a traumatized young girl with a boy whose life was in constant danger, but she elevated her son to the throne of England. This period also produced tragic stories, such as the princes who were lost in the Tower of London. The Wars of the Roses were brutal, and many people died in the effort to find a true king.

The second section discussed the Tudor monarchs. Henry VII was the first Tudor king, and he was dramatically crowned on the battlefield after defeating the Lancastrian king, Richard III. He united the warring Houses of York and Lancaster and brought peace to the country. Unfortunately, his years in exile left a mark on him, and he suffered a difficult reign marked by treason and rebellion. He faced tragedy when his firstborn died. The throne was then thrust on the young Henry VIII. Despite the promising early years of his reign, Henry VIII became an obese, sickly man who disinherited his daughters and killed or divorced his wives when they made him unhappy. He plunged his country into the English Reformation that was continued by his son, Edward VI.

The Boy King inherited the throne at only nine years old, but he was ruled by ambitious men who were willing to use a child for their own gains. As a devout Protestant, Edward supported the Reformation, but an early death saw the undoing of all his hard work when his Catholic half-sister took the throne. Mary I had been the apple of her father's eye but was cast off when her mother didn't produce a son. Ever since then, she had lived in obscurity and humiliation as everything was stripped away from her. When her time on the throne finally came, she gleefully undid the Reformation but faced backlash from her own people and died alone from a painful disease. Finally, Elizabeth I took the throne. She restarted the Reformation, led her country into the English Renaissance, and fought off the Spanish Armada.

The third section discussed the military and wars that took place during the Tudor era. Henry VII wasn't very interested in war after spending his life fighting to take the throne, but Henry VIII enthusiastically brought his army out of the dark ages with the help of foreign mercenaries. He also built up the navy, which his daughter used to great success against the Spanish.

Finally, the last section dealt with daily life in the Tudor era. Aspects such as politics, religion, society, and culture were discussed in great detail. Life in Tudor England wasn't always peaceful, and society was biased against the poor, but there were also fun occasions that people could look forward to.

The Tudor era was filled with highs and lows, as well as immense changes. The Tudors led their people through foreign wars, a religious reformation, and a cultural renaissance. They truly left behind a unique and enduring legacy.

Part 4: Early Modern England

An Enthralling Overview of the Tudors, Stuarts, Renaissance, Reformation, and Other Events That Shaped Early Modern England

Introduction

Early modern England.

The name itself suggests some sort of progress. The word "modern" makes us think of this period as the first step in the process of development that would eventually transform England into the modern society of today. But how true is that?

The idea that there is some sort of sharp divide between the Middle Ages and the early modern era is fiction. The Battle of Bosworth in 1485 saw the end of the Plantagenet dynasty and the start of the Tudors, but the change in ruling dynasties did not automatically end medieval society. The transformation of a nation is a much slower process than that.

Instead of seeing early modern England as the absolute end of medieval society and the hard beginning of modern society, it can be helpful to view this entire period as a time of transition. This was a connecting period that led England from the Middle Ages into the modern era, but it took over two hundred years to do that.

In this book, you'll learn about the gradual changes that took place in English society from 1485 to 1714 and how those changes led to the modern England we know today. Everything from economics to religion to government was changing during this time, but those changes took decades, and the journey was not the strictly uphill climb that we like to picture. Real history is far more complicated than that.

For instance, did you know that witch trials took place in this era but not in the Middle Ages? So much for the idea that it was just medieval law that could be ignorant and cruel. Also, Shakespeare, that pretentious guy that everyone had to read in school, was not particularly sophisticated. His plays entertained the public and were considered by some to be scandalous. This was indeed the age of the Renaissance, but it wasn't all enlightened thinking and high-class art.

Then there is the matter of England's empire. England would begin to build its colonial empire in this period, greatly increasing its wealth and influence. The colonization of the New World connected the world to a previously unimagined extent, but there were also a lot of dark sides to this expansion. Natives, African slaves, and even indentured servants from England were treated horribly and lost their lives for the sake of the empire's progress.

Another example of complicated changes is religion. The Reformation saw the introduction of many new denominations of Christianity, which we put under one label of Protestantism. Over time, so many different religious opinions forced religious tolerance, but it took quite a long time to get there. In the immediate aftermath (and by immediate, we mean for the next two hundred years or so) of the Reformation, religious tolerance was seen as a bad thing. Many people were killed, discriminatory laws were passed, and even full-scale revolutions occurred because of an extreme lack of religious tolerance.

So, if you think that early modern England was a time when England was walking into the light and out of the "darkness" of the Middle Ages, think again. History of any time and any place involves change, but that change is rarely just good or bad. As you read about this era, remember that this is not the story of inevitable human progress. This is the story of a real nation and real people. England made some advancements during this period, but there are also some low points and other things that are neither good nor bad.

Is early modern England a fitting name, or is it a deceptive title designed to make us think that this period was more progressive than it really was? It depends. What do you consider to be a mark of modern society? Is it more personal freedom, a bureaucratic government, a more economically connected world, a less agricultural-based society, or something else? As you read about various events and trends in this era, consider what you think modernity is and whether you can see the roots of that in early modern England. Either way, you are bound to discover something you didn't know about the period from 1485 to 1714 in English history.

Chapter 1: Who Were the Tudors?

Dividing history into eras is both beneficial and tricky. Looking at a particular era, like early modern England, gives us a much more manageable chunk of information to explore, but it immediately raises the question of boundaries. If we want to talk about early modern England, where do we start, and where do we end? We'll save the second question for much later in the book, but we have to figure out where we should start before we can even begin to explore this unique and interesting time.

Roughly, early modern England encompassed the 15th to the 18th century. However, "roughly" isn't quite good enough. If we are just using rough dates, then events taking place in the transition between periods become hard to define. Are the Wars of the Roses part of early modern England just because they took place in the 15th century? Most people tend to consider this a medieval event. To avoid this type of confusion, historians tend to draw lines in the sand when they divide history into different periods. A particular event is used to mark the end of one age and the beginning of another.

In many ways, setting these strict dates is misleading. The transition between these periods is often the result of gradual change rather than a singular event. However, singular events give us clear boundaries to organize our history and watershed moments that vividly illustrate the changing times. In a monarchy like England, there is an almost built-in system for defining different eras. The reigns of various monarchs have often been used to define periods in English history, such as the

Elizabethan era and the Victorian era, and it is this system that we typically use to define the early modern era. Medieval England fell with the Plantagenet dynasty, and early modern England rose with the Tudors.

Who Were the Tudors?

For us and early modern England, the watershed moment was 1485. The place was Bosworth. After decades of internal fighting in the Wars of the Roses, England was under the control of Richard III, who was rumored to have murdered his nephews to secure the throne for himself. The Houses of Lancaster and York had almost annihilated each other in their rivalry for the throne, and it seemed that Richard III, who was of the House of York, was simply the last man standing. However, there was one remaining claimant on the Lancastrian side: Henry Tudor.

If you are wondering just who Henry Tudor is, you aren't far off from what many people of the day might have thought. Henry Tudor had a dubious claim to the English throne at best. He was the son of Edmund Tudor and Margaret Beaufort. Margaret Beaufort was the great-granddaughter of John of Gaunt, who started the House of Lancaster and was Edward III's son. Edmund Tudor was the son of Catherine of Valois, Henry V's widow, and a Welshman by the name of Owen Tudor. Edmund Tudor was the half-brother of Henry VI, the last true Lancastrian king. Thus, Henry Tudor could claim the throne through both his mother's and his father's side.

If it sounds confusing, don't worry; it is. No one believed Henry Tudor had a strong claim to the throne, but by 1485, it didn't really matter that much. Everyone with a better claim was dead. Henry Tudor was the sole surviving member of the Lancastrian side, and he decided to try to take the throne from Richard III. In 1485, the two forces met at Bosworth. Richard III was a veteran hardened by the Wars of the Roses, and Henry Tudor was a young man with little experience. Had it been a one-on-one duel, there is no doubt who would have walked away, but luckily for Henry, it wasn't. Henry's forces were victorious, and Richard III died during the battle. Henry Tudor was soon crowned Henry VII.

Richard III at the Battle of Bosworth by James William Edmund Doyle.
https://commons.wikimedia.org/wiki/File:A_Chronicle_of_England_-_Page_453_-_Richard_III_at_Bosworth.jpg)

With Henry's victory at Bosworth and Richard III's death, England saw not just a change of kings but also a change of dynasties. Richard III was the last of the Plantagenets, a line that had ruled England for over three hundred years. Henry Tudor began a new line that would lead England through the Reformation and the Renaissance. The Tudors may have been a relatively unknown Welsh family at first, but they would become one of England's most successful and famous ruling families.

The Tudor Myth

Beginning with Henry VII in 1485 and ending with the death of Elizabeth I in 1603, the Tudors ruled England for 118 years. They began their reign at the end of the Wars of the Roses when England was emerging from the Middle Ages, and the Tudors used the timing of their reign to their advantage.

If you think that modern political figures are the only ones who worry about image, think again. Even back in 1485, rulers were constantly concerned with the overall myth that surrounded them. Propaganda was not a tool invented in the 20th century, but it did look a bit different during the time of the Tudors. To be the monarch was to be more than a person. It was to be a symbol, and the Tudors understood that perhaps better than any dynasty that ruled before them.

So, what exactly did the Tudors do? During the Tudor era, the Middle Ages was consistently painted as the Dark Ages. The medieval period was seen as a time of ignorance, violence, and stagnation. Portraying the period that came before their rule in such a horrible light made it easy for the Tudors to portray their own rule as a golden age. They were the rulers who saved England from the muck of the Dark Ages and ushered it into a time of prosperity.

The fact that many people still think of the Middle Ages as the Dark Ages shows just how effective the Tudors were at perpetuating this myth. But how exactly did they manage it?

The symbol that Henry VII took after he became king is a prime example of how this worked. Henry VII took the Tudor rose as his symbol, which is a white and red rose.

Tudor rose.
Sodacan This W3C-unspecified vector image was created with Inkscape., CC BY-SA 3.0 <https://creativecommons.org/licenses/by-sa/3.0>, via Wikimedia Commons: https://commons.wikimedia.org/wiki/File:Tudor_Rose.svg

This two-hued rose served as a symbol for the union of the Houses of York and Lancaster, whose conflict had caused the very bloody Wars of the Roses. By picking the white and red rose as his symbol, Henry VII constantly reminded everyone that he was the one who had brought an end to the civil war and restored peace to England. It was a brilliant political move, but how accurate was this symbolism?

The short answer is not nearly as much as we want it to be. The red and white Tudor rose works because it combines the red rose of the Lancasters and the white rose of the Yorks. The only problem is that the two houses didn't use the rose symbols prominently. Both sides had multiple families and multiple standards and heralds. During the Wars of the Roses, the two opposing sides were not facing off under different colored rose banners.

So, why is it called the Wars of the Roses then? Simply put, the Tudors were incredibly successful at rewriting history. Henry VII's Tudor rose, even with its dubious origins, was a powerful symbol. When people in the Tudor era looked back at the chaotic civil war of the 15th century, they applied the symbol they knew to it, and the conflict soon became the Wars of the Roses. Thanks to Shakespeare immortalizing this idea in his play *Henry VI, Part 1*, the idea that each side was represented by a different colored rose has become so prevalent that most people think it's real history.

The Tudor rose is just one small aspect of the Tudor myth. The Tudor era also saw the great vilification of Richard III. Henry VII was technically a conquering king. He won his throne on the field of battle, so to make the Tudor claim more legitimate and avoid being styled as a usurper, it was important that the king from whom Henry VII had taken the throne was seen in the worst possible light.

Again, we know that the Tudors were very successful here because history does not remember Richard III kindly. Shakespeare portrayed him as a hunchbacked tyrant who was so power-hungry that he murdered his own nephews for the crown. Who wouldn't prefer the golden rule of the Tudors to someone like that? By painting Richard III as the worst possible villain (being dead, he couldn't do much to defend himself), Henry VII and his successors furthered the idea that they were the saviors of England.

So, that's the Tudor myth. It's the idea that the Middle Ages was a truly dark time and that the Tudors were the ones who brought England out of this darkness and into the light. But why is the Tudor myth important? For one, it was so effective that it has greatly influenced the way we understand both Tudor England and medieval England to this day. We still call it the Wars of the Roses, Richard III is still considered one of England's worst kings, the medieval period is still called the Dark Ages, and Tudor England is still a golden age in English history.

Knowing about the Tudor myth is important as we dive deeper into this era of English history. Some of your preconceptions about this time may be challenged. While England did see a lot of progress and growth during the Tudor era, it was not a completely golden age any more than the medieval period was a total dark age.

What Was Tudor England Really Like?

Now that we have taken a look at why the Tudor age tends to be a bit overly glorified in English history, let's consider what the period from 1485 to 1603 was really like. Is there any truth to the idea that this was England's golden age?

Like most effective myths, the Tudor myth works because there is some truth to it. The Tudor era saw a lot of changes for England, and many of those changes allowed England to transform into a world power that, by 1922, had an empire that spread across a quarter of the globe.

The event that captures this change the most succinctly is the defeat of the Spanish Armada by the English in 1588 during Elizabeth I's reign. When the Spanish fleet tried to cross the English Channel to invade England, they were defeated by the English navy, with the Spanish fleet returning home in shambles. We will discuss the details of this immense English victory in Chapter 12, but for now, let's consider why this event was so important and what it tells us about England under the Tudors.

Defeating the Spanish Armada was the moment at which the English took command of the seas. The naval dominance that England won in 1588 would be maintained for the next several centuries and is one of the biggest factors that allowed Britain to become a world power. During the coming times of colonization and trade, England's control of the waves gave them a distinct advantage. If the English had not destroyed the Spanish fleet in 1588, Britain likely would not have become the world's leading colonizing power in the next few centuries.

So, the defeat of the Spanish Armada was crucial for establishing Britain's naval preeminence, but how much does it tell us about Tudor England? This important victory against a foreign power hints at something perhaps even more important about the Tudors. They maintained internal stability.

Although history has exaggerated things to some degree, medieval England was indeed a violent and sometimes chaotic place. There were two civil wars (the Anarchy and the Wars of the Roses), which resulted in the breakdown of basic law and order, and many other smaller internal conflicts. Fighting amongst themselves to such an extent left the English with little time to make an impact on a global scale in the Middle Ages. However, under the Tudors, the monarchy stabilized.

Although religious tensions ran high during the Tudor era, they never erupted into a full-scale war. In some ways, the Tudor era was a golden age simply because England didn't have any major internal conflicts. One hundred eighteen years under a single ruling family without a major internal dispute created a more united England, one that could stand strong against other foreign powers. The defeat of the Spanish Armada is thus not only significant for its impact on England's future but also in showing how much England had healed under the Tudors. The war-ravaged land of 1485 would never have been able to defeat Europe's leading power, but one hundred years of relative stability under the Tudors had created a far more powerful nation.

Wait. Does that mean the Tudor era was a golden age? Not quite. One major misunderstanding that the Tudor myth has caused about this era is the assumption that it was far more progressive than the Middle Ages. The Tudor era was the time of Shakespeare and the Renaissance. It was a time when trade was expanding, and England was getting richer. However, that is only telling part of the story. In many areas, there is not as much of a sharp divide between medieval and early modern England as the Tudor myth has taught us to believe.

For example, one of the main reasons that Tudor England did not see a major internal conflict was because of how harshly the germs of rebellions were stifled. Revolts like the Pilgrimage of Grace, the Prayer Book Rebellion, and Kett's Rebellion were crushed swiftly and thoroughly. Although trade expanded and feudalism ended, Tudor England saw an increase in poverty, and the strict divide between the social classes remained. This era saw the expansion of schools and education, but it also saw a sudden spike in trying women for witchcraft. There were great discoveries made thanks to exploration, but there was also the rise of piracy and the slave trade.

So, while Tudor England did see many advancements, it was not a purely golden age. No era in history is. It was a time of change, but it was not a time of pure progress. The Tudor myth is just that, a myth.

The Legacy of Tudor England

Even so, the Tudors did forever change England. The period from 1485 to 1603 was crucial in transforming England into a nation in the modern sense of the word.

In the medieval period, the country's structure was based on the feudal system. This hierarchal structure had each noble ruling over his land and answering to the king only when necessary, usually in times of war. It was a pyramid in which the king, and hence the central government, was at the top. This meant the central government had direct control over relatively little.

During the Tudor era, the central government's power grew. Instead of every noble being the king of his own small kingdom on his country estate, the country's ruling elite spent more time in London in government positions. Parliament passed more acts, and the government was far more involved in the economy. The English government was transforming from a pyramid structure to a tree where the trunk of the central government branched out to various sub-sections.

This transformation of governing styles was essential if England was to thrive in the early modern world. The nation had to be able to act with a unified sense of identity and interest in the competitive economic realities of the 16th century. The Tudors helped make this possible by expanding the monarchy to represent more than just them. The monarch was no longer just a person. They were the embodiment of England. The reality behind that ideal was an ever-growing bureaucratic system that served the nation's increasingly complex governmental needs.

However, this expansion of the central government would not come without its challenges. What would happen when the monarch and the governing class disagreed? England's next ruling dynasty would have to answer that question.

Chapter 2: Who Were the Stuarts?

Elizabeth I is one of England's most well-remembered monarchs. She ruled long enough to have an entire era named after her, and the nation prospered under her. She was a well-liked monarch, but she did have one rather annoying flaw. She refused to name an heir.

We will talk more about Elizabeth I, but if you don't already know, Elizabeth I was famous for being the Virgin Queen. She never married, ruling England as the sole monarch for close to forty-five years. Obviously, that meant she did not have any direct heirs because she had no children. Perhaps that would not have been such a problem, but Elizabeth I also seemed to think she was going to live forever. No matter how her advisers prodded her, Elizabeth I would not name her successor.

Was Elizabeth I just being unreasonably stubborn? To a degree, yes, but she did have a reason. The English court was a solar system, and everyone orbited around the monarch. The closer you were to the queen or king, the more power you had. When Elizabeth I named an heir, she would essentially be creating a secondary solar system. People, especially those who were unhappy with Elizabeth, would begin flocking to the future monarch to try to gain favor in anticipation of Elizabeth's death. If Elizabeth named a successor, she might very well be pushing her opponents and maybe even supporters into the arms of a powerful rival.

Thus, Elizabeth I refused to name an heir. However, she was mortal, and the day came when the queen died.

The Stuarts

In 1603, Elizabeth I died, and while she may have put off the matter during her lifetime, the throne had to pass to someone. Unclear succession was a dangerous thing in a monarchy. In England's past, it had led to a long and bloody civil war. No one wanted to see that happen again, which is why when Elizabeth I died, her advisers already had the next man picked: James Stuart, or rather James VI of Scotland.

James I by John de Critz.
https://commons.wikimedia.org/wiki/File:James_I,_VI_by_John_de_Critz,_c.1606.png

In some ways, James Stuart was the obvious pick because he was Elizabeth I's closest relative of royal blood. To understand just who James was, we have to go back to the first Tudor king: Henry VII. Henry VII had four children: Arthur, Henry, Margaret, and Mary. Arthur died young before he had any children. While Henry VIII was famous for having many wives, he only had three children, all of whom died without children to take the throne. Since family names were only passed through the male line, the Tudor line died with the last of Henry VIII's children, Elizabeth I.

However, while the Tudors were gone, that did not mean there was no one left who carried Henry VII's blood. His daughter and third child, Margaret, married James IV of Scotland. Their granddaughter was Mary, Queen of Scots (there were several important figures named Mary at this time, so to avoid confusion, this Mary is always referred to as Mary, Queen of Scots). Mary, Queen of Scots was Elizabeth I's cousin and closest blood relative before her death in 1587. After Mary, Queen of Scots died, her son, James Stuart, became the English queen's closest relative.

James Stuart had the best blood claim to the throne, but his succession was by no means certain. Elizabeth and James's mother had not gotten along. In fact, Elizabeth I had Mary, Queen of Scots executed for her involvement in a plot against the Crown. It was unclear if James's mother's treason would prohibit him from inheriting the throne.

There was also the matter of James being Scottish. James Stuart was better known as James VI of Scotland. He had been the king of Scotland since his mother was forced to abdicate in 1567. Scotland and England had a less than friendly history as well as different churches by this point (Scotland was Presbyterian, and England was Anglican). Would the English accept a Scottish king?

To much surprise and relief, James Stuart's ascension to the throne of England went smoothly. It may be that his previous experience as a monarch made the English more willing to accept him, or perhaps they simply preferred any king that ascended peacefully over the chaos of having several people vie for the crown. Either way, in 1603, James VI of Scotland became James I of England, and the line of Stuart monarchs began. The Stuarts would rule England for the next 111 years, with a significant eleven-year gap in the middle of that period.

You might think that with James Stuart being both James VI of Scotland and James I of England that Scotland would be united with England and Wales to form the country of Great Britain. Surprisingly, that union was still one hundred years away. Although they shared a monarch, Scotland and England still had separate parliaments and separate governments. James Stuart was James VI of Scotland and James I of England at the same time.

England under the Stuarts

England under the Tudors is seen as a golden age in English history, but no one says the same thing about England under the Stuarts.

Royal arms of the Stuarts.
Sodacan This W3C-unspecified vector image was created with Inkscape., CC BY-SA 3.0 < https://creativecommons.org/licenses/by-sa/3.0>, via Wikimedia Commons: https://commons.wikimedia.org/wiki/File:Royal_Arms_of_England_(1603-1707).svg

The Stuart dynasty ruled England for 111 years, from 1603 to 1714. During that time, two Stuart monarchs were ousted. One was executed, and the other fled the country. There was a nine-year civil war. The capital city nearly burned to the ground in the Great Fire of 1666, and England was involved in many costly wars with foreign powers. What went wrong? What happened to the growth of the Tudor era?

The first thing we should clarify is that the Stuart era was not a dark age any more than the Tudor era was a golden one. There were a lot of noticeable problems in this era, but by the end of it, England was well on its way to becoming one of the world's most powerful nations. The growth of the Tudor era did continue, especially in the economy. What the Tudor era had that the Stuart era lacked was internal peace.

What went wrong with the Stuarts was in part a result of the governmental growth that occurred under the Tudors. When James I became the first Stuart monarch of England, the English government was long past the stage where the monarch could effectively rule without Parliament's consent, but this system of cooperation between monarch and Parliament was at odds with the Stuarts' understanding of the monarchy. Monarchs like James I and Charles I believed strongly in the king's sovereignty. They would not play the game of negotiating with Parliament, and the tensions this caused eventually erupted into the English Civil War.

This does not mean that the Tudors ran England as a constitutional monarchy or that the early Stuarts were tyrants. Tudor monarchs were absolute monarchs, but where Henry VIII and Elizabeth I succeeded and James I and Charles I failed was public relations. The Tudors knew how to sell themselves. In Elizabeth's addresses to Parliament, she was sure of her own power but also tactful.

For example, in a speech shortly after she ascended the throne, Elizabeth I said, "The burden that is fallen upon me maketh me amazed, and yet considering I am God's creature, ordained to obey his appointment, I will thereto yield." Calling the throne a "burden" was Elizabeth leaning into the perceived limitations of her sex, but she quickly flips this by saying that she has been appointed by God and therefore must yield to the appointment. She is claiming that she has divine approval but in a disarmingly humble way.

Charles I was not as tactful with his dealings with Parliament. In a speech in 1641, shortly before tensions between the king and Parliament erupted into civil war, Charles I said, "Nay, I have given way to every thing that you have asked of me, and therefore me thinkes you should not wonder if in some thing I begin to refuse, but I hope it shall not hinder your Progresse in your great Affaires. And I will not stick upon trivial matters to give you Content. I hope you are sensible of these beneficial favors bestowed upon you at this time."

Here, Charles I is informing an already greatly disgruntled Parliament that they ought to be grateful for what he has done for them. You can almost hear the sarcasm behind phrases like "I hope it shall not hinder *your* progress in *your* great affairs" and "I hope *you* are sensible of these beneficial favors bestowed upon you at this time." This was not the way to deal with Parliament. They had had too much real power for far too long to take such an overbearing attitude from the monarch.

Charles I was the only monarch to lose his head, but he wasn't the only Stuart monarch to lose the throne. Charles I's son, James II, had to flee the country after his own people invited William of Orange to invade. What did James II do that was so horrible? He committed the ultimate sin in the eyes of the English people in the 17th century. He was Roman Catholic.

The overthrow of Charles I and James II shows us the paradoxical nature of England in the Stuart era. On the one hand, this was a time when notions like the divine right of kings were being challenged. Even the monarchy itself was ultimately questioned. On the other hand, this was also a time of intense religious persecution and superstition. The Stuart era is proof that human progress is not a strictly linear development.

Becoming a World Power

While the Stuart era had its fair share of difficulties, at the end of it, England was positioned to become the dominant world power over the course of the next century. How is that possible?

Although England had internal disagreements during the Stuart era, that did not prevent it from getting involved in what was going on in the world at large. The 17th century was a time of colonization and foreign conflict. Europe's leading powers like Spain, France, the Netherlands, and England were busily trying to expand their empires and gain more control over lucrative trade. Wars like the Anglo-Dutch Wars and the War of the Spanish Succession were part of this vie for power.

While we often think of the Elizabethan era as the grand time of exploration, England's colonial empire did not start to gain traction until the Stuart era. After all, the first American settlement of Jamestown was named after the first Stuart king, James I. It was during this era that most of the thirteen American colonies were founded, as well as settlements in Canada and the Caribbean (which proved to be the most lucrative thanks to the sugar trade). If the Elizabethan era was about exploration, the Stuart era was about colonization, and that practice proved to be far more permanently beneficial for England's economy and power.

England arrived somewhat late to the colonization game compared to other European powers. The American and Canadian settlements were largely all that was left for England since Spain had already seized most of the southern New World. However, by the ending years of the Stuart era, England (or rather Britain) had carved out an empire for itself. Successes in the War of the Spanish Succession at the beginning of the 18th century gave England access to more colonies, which helped to build its trading empire. The wealth these colonies provided then gave England the resources it needed to continue expanding and fend off its rivals.

Despite events like the English Civil War and the Glorious Revolution, England came out of the Stuart era in a very strong position globally. England's main rivals (the Netherlands, France, and Spain) were war-torn and weary. England had a firm grasp on the New World and several profitable trade routes. English power would only continue to grow over the next two centuries.

So, while the Stuart era saw major internal conflicts, England did manage to come out on top against its foreign rivals by the end of the period.

The Legacy of the Stuarts

Centuries after the end of both dynasties, it's fairly obvious that the Stuarts will never have the personal magnetism that the Tudors managed to craft. However, in terms of national success, England was not much worse off under the Stuarts than it was under the Tudors. The monarch was just gradually becoming less essential to the country's overall state.

The last Stuart monarch, Queen Anne, is a prime example of how far this separation between the monarch and the government had gotten by the end of the Stuart era. Queen Anne, although she did desire to personally rule, was often sick and unable to manage the daily running of the country. The major events of her reign, such as the War of the Spanish Succession and the union with Scotland, were largely devised and carried out by her government. She still had the ultimate say, but she was strongly influenced by those closest to her. The government under Anne was a battle between the two major parties in Parliament, the Whigs and the Tories, rather than a battle between the monarch and Parliament.

We are still a long way off from the monarch becoming a figurehead, but in the Stuart era, it was becoming clearer that the monarch could not rule alone. Parliament held the real power, and no monarch could rule without its consent. If the Tudors turned the English monarchy into a grand myth where the monarch was the embodiment of the nation itself, then the Stuarts were the reality check. The nation had grown to be bigger than its ruler.

Chapter 3: The Monarchy in Early Modern England

The early modern period of English history saw the rise and fall of two royal lines and the reigns of twelve monarchs. During this time, the monarch wielded absolute power, so these kings and queens truly steered the English nation's course. Some of them were beloved, and others were vehemently disliked. Some of them were successful, while others can only be described as failures.

For better or worse, this was the last grand age of royal power in England since the next period would see the monarch's power wane. Let's take a closer look at these twelve men and women.

Henry VII (r. 1485–1509)

Henry VII.
https://commons.wikimedia.org/wiki/File:Henry_Tudor_of_England.jpg

The early modern period began with Henry VII's victory at Bosworth and the founding of the Tudor dynasty. Henry VII's victory put an end to the bloodshed of the Wars of the Roses. To further solidify the peace, Henry VII married Elizabeth of York, the daughter of Edward IV. With this marriage, the opposing sides of Lancaster and York were united, and the chaos was finally over.

Henry's marriage shows just how aware he was of the nation's state. The Wars of the Roses had created so much chaos that it also drastically destabilized the English monarchy. When Henry VII took the throne in 1485, he needed to restrengthen the king's position, which wasn't easy. Throughout his reign, Henry VII had to deal with multiple Yorkist uprisings and plots. While Edward V and his brother Richard had been pronounced dead by their uncle Richard III, their bodies had never been found. Imposters claiming to be either Edward or Richard or even other members of the House of York popped up at the head of uprisings and were backed by Henry VII's powerful opponents.

Despite the odds, Henry managed to quell the uprisings and undermine the plots against him. Unfortunately, taking over an unstable throne and having to constantly deal with these issues made Henry VII distrustful and hard. By the time he died in 1509, his suspicious nature had made him hated or at least not well-liked. However, Henry VII was a hard-working and efficient king who succeeded in bringing stability back to the English throne after such a long period of chaos. He passed a much different throne to his son than what he had started with in 1485.

Henry VIII (r. 1509–1547)

Henry VIII by Hans Holbein.
https://commons.wikimedia.org/wiki/File:Henry_VIII_Chatsworth.jpg

Henry VIII is one of the most famous English kings, and there's a good reason for that. His marital troubles have become the source of songs and plays, as well as being the catalyst that separated England from the Catholic Church. This part of Henry VIII's reign is so interesting that we have an entire chapter on it later, which is why we are not going to dive into that here. So, aside from marrying six different women and breaking up with the pope, what else did Henry VIII do?

In some ways, Henry VIII was the opposite of his father. While Henry VII had created policies, overseen the Crown's funds, and, in general, ran the kingdom with his own two hands, Henry VIII relied more on his councilors. Men like Thomas Wolsey, Thomas More, Thomas Cranmer, and Thomas Cromwell (Thomas was a very popular name with Henry VIII) were the ones running the show. That might make Henry VIII sound like a pushover, but that is far from the truth. Henry VIII had no problem interfering with the business that he mostly left to his councilors. These men only lasted as long as they did what Henry VIII wanted, and for all of them, like Henry VIII's wives, there came a time when the king no longer had a use for them. Henry VIII's reliance on his councilors, therefore, had more to do with the fact that he would rather be doing something else.

It could also be argued that Henry VIII's less hands-on style of kingship was better for the nation because when he did decide to take things into his own hands, they didn't go very well. He involved England in costly foreign wars and worsened its relationship with Scotland. His reign also saw the rise of growing religious tensions, but the fault for that cannot be laid entirely at the king's door. This was the era of the Reformation. Growing religious tensions were everywhere in Europe at this time.

In terms of pure ruling effectiveness, Henry VII was likely a better king than his son, but Henry VIII was more well-liked. He was a vibrant and young man when he took the throne, and he breathed life back into Henry VII's suspicious court. While Henry VIII may not have understood how to make effective policies, he did understand how to look like a king. He brought a charm and grandeur that has made him a lasting symbol of the monarchy.

Edward VI (r. 1547-1553)

Edward VI by William Scrots.
https://commons.wikimedia.org/wiki/File:Edward_VI_of_England_c._1546.jpg

Although Henry VIII was married six times, when he died in 1547, he had only one male heir, the child of his third wife, Jane Seymour. Nine-year-old Edward became king after his father's death, and he died only six years later at the age of fifteen. History remembers Edward VI as the "Boy King."

Since Edward VI came to the throne at such a young age, he was simply a symbol through, with other men ruling through him. The first man was Edward Seymour, the Duke of Somerset and the king's uncle. Somerset was overthrown and replaced by John Dudley, the Duke of Northumberland. Both Seymour and Dudley took steps while in control to confirm the Reformation, which was in keeping with Edward VI's own religious zeal and strong devotion to Protestantism.

Edward VI's early death naturally meant there were no direct heirs. Edward VI planned to pass the throne not to one of his half-sisters (Mary and Elizabeth) but to Lady Jane Grey, who was John Dudley's daughter-in-law. This was not carried out after Edward VI's death. Jane Grey lasted all of nine days before she was replaced by Henry VIII's eldest daughter Mary.

Mary I (r. 1553–1558) and Philip (r. 1554–1558)

Queen Mary Tudor by Antonis Mor.
https://commons.wikimedia.org/wiki/File:Maria_Tudor1.jpg

Mary I was the first woman to ever rule England in her own right, but she is not remembered fondly, largely because of one fatal flaw. She was Roman Catholic.

Mary I was the daughter of Henry VIII and Catherine of Aragon. Soon after ascending to the throne in 1553, she married Spanish Prince Philip (who soon became the Spanish king, Philip II), despite the warnings of her advisers. This marriage to a Catholic was part of Mary I's attempts to bring her nation back into the Roman Church. However, by this time, the "damage" of the Reformation had impacted England. The country did not look kindly on her marriage to Philip, but Mary I had her father's stubborn streak. Despite a Protestant revolt, she married

Philip anyway, who, as part of the conditions for their marriage, became co-monarch rather than simply her husband.

After her marriage, Mary I tried her hardest to turn England back to Catholicism. She persecuted the Protestants, whom she saw as heretics, burning around three hundred people at the stake. This campaign had the opposite effect of what Mary had hoped for. It earned her the nickname Bloody Mary and caused the people to hate her. It is unclear just how deep the resentment toward Mary I went during her lifetime. Since England stayed Protestant, Mary I has been viewed as a villain, but we must also remember that England's break with Rome had happened only twenty years prior to her reign. There were probably many Catholics remaining in England while Mary I was alive. However, as time passed and England became more Protestant, Mary I's posthumous reputation only deteriorated.

Elizabeth I (r. 1558–1603)

Elizabeth I, "The Pelican Portrait," by Nicholas Hilliard.
https://commons.wikimedia.org/wiki/File:Nicholas_Hilliard_Elizabeth_I_The_Pelican_Portrait.jpg

Henry VIII had only one remaining child. Elizabeth I was the last of the Tudors and arguably the best of them. Even now, she remains one of England's most well-remembered and beloved rulers, and she is the only monarch of the early modern period to have an era named after her (the Elizabethan Age). So, what made Elizabeth I such a good leader?

Elizabeth I had an interesting and, at times, incredibly dangerous upbringing before her ascension to the throne. At the age of three, her mother was beheaded, and she was declared illegitimate. She had to survive through the reigns of both her half-siblings, where she was seen as a potentially volatile spark for any rebellions or discontent, especially under the reign of Mary I. To survive in these circumstances, Elizabeth I learned from an early age an enormous amount of self-control. She was able to show people exactly what they wanted to see, carefully controlling her actions and reputation to best suit her needs.

This quality continued to serve Elizabeth I well once she took the throne. She was an expert at putting on a show and crafting herself into a symbol of both the monarchy and the nation itself. Instead of allowing her sex to be used against her (there was pervading sexism at this time), she painted herself as the mother of the nation, creating a sense of love and devotion. This strict attention to how she presented herself also meant that she was fairly unreadable. Elizabeth I could be generous when it benefited her and wrathful when pushed. There was a sense that no one knew what Queen Elizabeth thought, and she used that air of mystery to play rival factions against each other in her court, maintaining firm if not absolute control of her government.

To put it simply, Elizabeth I was one of England's most politically savvy monarchs. She could work both a crowd and individuals to her advantage. There can be no doubt that England prospered under her rule. To this day, the Elizabethan Age is viewed as a golden era of English history.

James I (r. 1603–1625)

James I by John De Critz.
https://commons.wikimedia.org/wiki/File:James_VI_and_I.jpg

We discussed how the throne went from the Tudors to the Stuarts in Chapter 2, so here we will focus more on James I as a monarch.

When James I became king of England, he had already ruled Scotland for around thirty-seven years. It was true that he was only one year old when he took the throne, but nevertheless, thirty-seven years was a long time. This gave him an advantage few other monarchs had when they ascended the throne: experience. In many ways, James I's experience as king of Scotland served him well in England. His policies were often reasonable and effective, but there were ways in which James I's experience hurt him in England.

Having already been a king for so long, James I had a very clear idea of what kingship ought to be. He believed in the absolute authority of the king, which brought him into conflict with a uniquely English institution: Parliament. Parliament had been around in England since the 13th century and had grown in authority and its willingness to question the English monarch. It was Parliament that held the right to levy taxes, which made raising funds for the government practically impossible without Parliament's approval.

James I had dealt with assemblies in Scotland, but he had no idea how to deal with the English Parliament. James I came into frequent conflict with Parliament, and in 1611, he dissolved it. Parliament would not meet again for ten years (except for a brief meeting in 1614). During this time, James I had to find other ways to raise money since he could not create taxes without Parliament. These other means, such as the sale of monopolies, were often unpopular and did not improve the king's image. James I's lack of respect for the Parliament did not have drastic consequences in his lifetime, but it did set the stage for the civil war that would break out during his son's reign.

However, what James I is most famous for is something that had little effect on his reign: the King James Bible. James I authorized this translation of the Bible in 1604 and approved the list of scholars assigned to the project. The translation was completed and published in 1611 and remains one of the most popular English translations of the Bible to this day. The King James Bible has proved to be the most lasting legacy of the first Stuart monarch.

Charles I (r. 1625–1649)

Charles I by Anthony van Dyck.
https://commons.wikimedia.org/wiki/File:Van_Dyck,_Sir_Anthony_-_Charles_I_-_Google_Art_Project.jpg

The monarchs of early modern England have their share of successes and failures, but Charles I might just be the biggest failure of them all. Charles I's reign saw the outbreak of a civil war, which ended with his execution and resulted in an eleven-year span during which England had no king or queen.

We will cover the details of the English Civil War in Chapter 10, but for now, let's talk about what the problem was with Charles I. What was so bad about this king that caused England to decide they didn't want any king?

Like his father, James I, Charles I was a proponent of royal absolutism and the divine right of kings, which meant that kings get their right to rule from God and thus are subject to no earthly authority. The Catholic Church could have still presented a check to the king's power, but during the Stuart era, England was no longer Catholic. The king was the head of the church and the government, and based on the divine right of kings, this gave him absolute and supreme power.

You can begin to see just what kind of king this doctrine made. Charles I did not believe that anyone had the right to question or challenge him. He refused to listen to Parliament and the complaints of his kingdom's magnates. This eventually led to a civil war, but it caused an even greater problem when the war was over. Although Charles I had been defeated, he refused to negotiate with the victors. He would make no concessions. He wouldn't even talk to his captors. Finding the king so intractable, Parliament eventually convicted him of treason. Charles I was beheaded on January 30th, 1649.

Not only did Charles I's reign get him beheaded, but it also caused England to abandon the monarchy for a while. After Charles I's death, England entered an eleven-year period known as the Interregnum (between kings). After these eleven years, England decided the problem may not have been monarchs in general but Charles I specifically. They decided to restore the monarchy and invited Charles I's son to return and take the throne.

Charles II (r. 1660–1685)

Charles II by John Michael Wright.
https://commons.wikimedia.org/wiki/File:John_Michael_Wright_(1617-94)_-_Charles_II_(1630-1685)_-_RCIN_404951_-_Royal_Collection_-_1.jpg

Charles II's ascension to the English throne could have been a very messy affair. After all, Charles II was returning from the continent after having to flee England in fear of his life. Even though the people of England had decided they wanted a king again, there was much anxiety in inviting Charles II to take the throne. Wouldn't he want to seek revenge against those who had murdered his father? The members of Parliament were understandably worried.

As messy as it might have been, the restoration of the monarchy went surprisingly smoothly, thanks in large part to the council of Edward Hyde, the Earl of Clarendon. Under Hyde's guidance, Charles II issued a general pardon for crimes committed during the English Civil War and the Interregnum. This meant that Charles II wouldn't be taking revenge on his father's enemies. The leaders of England were so relieved to hear they wouldn't be losing their heads that they welcomed Charles II back with open arms.

As a ruler, Charles II was neither the worst nor the best English monarch. He was known as a man who enjoyed his pleasures, and he was very good at letting his advisers take the fall for his bad policies. During his reign, he faced a lot of religious discontentment. Charles II's attempts to allow more religious tolerance were firmly shut down by Parliament, and fear of the throne passing to his Catholic brother, James, was rampant in the late years of his rule.

However, Charles II managed to delicately balance these tensions and kept the peace until he died in 1685. He was a king with enough political skills to secure his own position, but he lacked the inspiration necessary to truly solve the problem. When he died without a legitimate heir, his brother James was left facing the issues that Charles II had only delayed.

James II (r. 1685–1688)

James II by Godfrey Kneller.
https://commons.wikimedia.org/wiki/File:King_James_II.jpg

If the Stuarts' luck had appeared to be improving with the restoration of Charles II, it took a downward turn with his brother, James II. James II only ruled for three years before his reign ended in the Glorious Revolution and the installment of Mary II and William III. James II was the only English monarch in the entire early modern period to be forced to leave the throne while he was still alive. What was so bad about James II? The answer is similar to the problem with Mary I. James II was Roman Catholic.

Thanks to the Reformation, religious tensions in Europe were at an all-time high. In England, the fear and hatred of Roman Catholics had reached levels of almost paranoia. We will discuss more of why exactly this was in later chapters, but suffice it to say, it was not good for James II, who was a member of the Catholic Church.

To be fair to James II, from an objective viewpoint, it doesn't seem like his religion affected his ability to rule an Anglican nation all that much. James II was a capable military commander who served his brother Charles II well, and his daughters, Mary and Anne, were raised Protestant. Unlike Mary I, it didn't seem like James II was planning to bring the English nation back under Rome's guiding hand, but by the time of his reign, the mistrust of Catholics was much greater than it had been when Mary I held the throne.

So, when James II took the throne in 1685, the nation simply did not trust him. He had to deal with two rebellions almost immediately, which soured the new king's opinion of his subjects. James II became mistrustful and began favoring Roman Catholics, seeking to overturn the laws against them. Unfortunately, in 17th-century England, religious tolerance was not a popular move. Three short years after James II's reign had begun, he found himself facing a usurper, William of Orange, who had been invited there by his own people. When James II's largely Protestant army refused to stand with him, he was forced to abdicate and flee the country. His Protestant daughter Mary, along with her husband William, took the throne with relatively little bloodshed, which earned this event the name of the Glorious Revolution.

Mary II (r. 1689–1694) and William III (r. 1689–1702)

Mary II by Peter Lely.
https://commons.wikimedia.org/wiki/File:1662_Mary_II.jpg

William III technically seized the English throne through force when his arrival with an army forced James II to abdicate. However, he also invaded at the request of English leaders, so William III has the strange claim of being a welcomed conquering king.

Because William outlived his wife by eight years, history tends to remember William of Orange or William III more than his wife, Mary II. However, it was through Mary that William had a claim to the English throne. Mary II was the daughter of James II and the next in line after her father abdicated. She was offered the throne, and she insisted that her husband reign as co-monarch. While Mary II was still alive, she technically shared power with William III, but she simply followed his lead and direction in almost everything, making William III the ruler.

As king of England, William III was extremely interested in foreign affairs and spent a good deal of his reign campaigning in Europe. He was particularly concerned about preventing the French from expanding their control but was often frustrated by the English Parliament's lack of enthusiasm for his cause. Time proved William III right, as England would join the War of the Spanish Succession against the French shortly after William III's death.

The matter of the war with France summarizes William III's reign. He was a relatively effective king who was still disliked by the English court for being a foreigner. Still, he was well-liked by the general people because of his Protestantism, and his time as the king saw the English Crown stabilize.

Anne (r. 1702–1714)

Queen Anne by Edmond Lilly.
https://commons.wikimedia.org/wiki/File:Queen_Anne_Lilly.jpg

The final Stuart monarch and the final monarch in the early modern period was the second daughter of James II, Anne. Although their father was ferociously disliked by the English people, both Mary and Anne escaped his legacy because they did not share their father's fatal flaw. They were not Catholic; they were Protestant.

As queen, Anne never gained the independence that she wanted. She was often ill, leaving the government largely in the hands of her advisers. The major policies of this government were centered around the war that her predecessor, William III, had predicted, the War of the Spanish Succession, which lasted the entirety of Anne's twelve-year reign.

Although Anne was pregnant many times, she had no surviving children, which meant her death was viewed with some anxiety. English leaders were afraid that James the Old Pretender, the son of James II, would make a move for the throne. To prevent the English throne from passing into Catholic hands, the Hanovers, who were descended from James I, were selected to succeed the Stuart dynasty.

The Stuart dynasty ended very similarly to the Tudors, with the death of a childless queen, and like with the passing of the throne from the Tudors to the Stuarts, the transition from the Stuarts to the Hanovers was surprisingly smooth. Despite low points with Charles I and James II, the English monarchy in the early modern period was a relatively stable institution at the height of its power. English monarchs would soon never again wield the power they did in this age. By the end of the 18th century, the monarch would be little more than a figurehead.

Chapter 4: Key English Figures from 1485 to 1714

When talking about important people in the early modern era, it's easy to get caught up with the royalty. After all, royalty in this period did wield real power, and so every English king and queen, whether they were good or bad, had an enormous impact on the nation.

However, that does not mean that England did not produce other figures that steered the course of history and whose impact we continue to feel today. Some of the key English figures from this period have had a far wider and longer-lasting impact than the monarchs. The following figures are listed in chronological order based on their births.

Mary, Queen of Scots

There are quite a few famous Marys from this period, but for pure drama, Mary, Queen of Scots has to be the most interesting. Born in 1542, Mary was the only child of James V of Scotland. When her father died six days after her birth, she became queen of Scotland.

No one actually expects a six-day-old to rule, so Mary's mother became regent. Mary was sent off to France, where she was raised in Henry II's court. Although Mary received a thorough education in France, her French upbringing would ultimately prove to be far more harmful than helpful. She was pampered and raised as a Roman Catholic, and at the age of eighteen, when she returned to rule Scotland in her own right, she found herself at the head of a tempestuous Protestant nation.

Mary was not well equipped for the role in which she found herself, but she still might have made a tolerable queen had she made wiser decisions in love. Her marriage to Lord Darnley was a love match, but it proved disastrous. Darnley was not well-liked, and by marrying him, Mary managed to agitate many of the Scottish nobles, including her half-brother, who had been of great help to Mary up until that point.

Mary soon realized her mistake. A year after their marriage, Darnley murdered Mary's secretary in front of her, and Mary began to realize just what sort of man she had married. It is unclear if Mary played a part in what happened next, but the intolerable Darnley soon met his end. In 1567, the house where Darnley was staying blew up, killing him.

This might have been a chance for Mary to turn things around, but after three short months, she married again. And she again chose poorly. This husband, Lord Bothwell, was the chief suspect in the murder of Mary's previous husband, and he was not any more liked by the Scottish nobility than Darnley had been. Before the end of the year, Bothwell had been exiled, and Mary was forced to step down. The crown of Scotland passed to her one-year-old son, James.

Like a real-life soap opera, losing the throne of Scotland was not the end of Mary's troubles. After all of this, Mary fled to England, seeking sanctuary with her cousin, Queen Elizabeth. That was a mistake. As Elizabeth's cousin, Mary was the next in line to the throne of England and, thus, in Elizabeth's eyes, her rival. After Mary arrived in England, Queen Elizabeth kept her imprisoned for the next eighteen years.

Unfortunately, Mary's tale was not meant to end happily. As a Roman Catholic and the next in line to the English throne, Mary was the natural core around which English Catholics gathered. They wished to return England to Catholicism. When a conspiracy was discovered in 1586 to assassinate Queen Elizabeth and replace her with the Catholic Mary, Elizabeth I had had enough. She decided that her cousin was too big of a threat. Mary, Queen of Scots was executed in 1587.

To this day, historians argue about how much Mary was to blame for the woes that befell her. She has been seen as both a tragic figure and a scheming murderer. Whatever she was, her life is certainly proof that fact can be just as dramatic as fiction.

William Shakespeare

William Shakespeare.
https://commons.wikimedia.org/wiki/File:Shakespeare.jpg

If there is a competition for the most well-remembered and idolized figure from early modern England, then William Shakespeare is the undisputed winner. He was born around 1564 and died in 1616. During his lifetime, Shakespeare wrote 38 plays and over 150 poems. In the four hundred years since his death, he has come to be widely regarded as one of the best, if not the best, English writers of all time. The Bard is so praised and widespread that you practically cannot get a high school education in English without reading Shakespeare.

Because he is so adored by scholars and teachers, many people today associate Shakespeare with elitism and pretentiousness. However, to be fair to the Bard, it pays to put him in the context of his own time. When he was alive, Shakespeare was less of what we would today call an artist and more of an entertainer. Standing room in one of the period's outdoor theaters was cheap enough that pretty much anyone could afford it, and live theater, in general, was seen as entertainment for the unwashed masses.

Live theater was so far from being considered a high-end pursuit that many people believed it to be a terrible influence. Theaters were not allowed in the city of London itself, so they were instead built on the other side of the Thames River in Southwark, an area that was home to other institutions not wanted in the city proper, such as brothels and bear-baiting arenas. The Globe Theatre was even located next to a bear-baiting arena, and the theater used the blood from the arena for performances.

So, Shakespeare is not as fancy as you might think. His language may feel incredibly sophisticated today, but that has more to do with the fact that it was written four hundred years ago and less to do with Shakespeare trying to be pretentious. If you take the time to dissect some of Shakespeare's plays, you'll find them full of bawdy jokes and witty lines.

Does this mean that Shakespeare isn't as great as people make him out to be? If anything, it should make him better. Shakespeare was so good with words that even though he was writing for entertainment and didn't even make up most of his own stories, he is still the gold standard in English literature four hundred years later.

Guy Fawkes

If you're not from the United Kingdom, you probably see nothing special about the 5th of November, but in the UK, it's Guy Fawkes Day. You might be thinking that Guy Fawkes must have done something pretty great to earn an entire holiday, but that's not the reason this figure from early modern England has his own holiday.

Guy Fawkes is famous for being one of the conspirators behind the Gunpowder Plot, which was an attempt by Roman Catholics to blow up Parliament on November 5th, 1605. The conspirators hoped that by killing the king and other English leaders, there would be enough confusion for Catholics to seize control of the country. When the plot was discovered, it had the opposite effect of what the plotters had intended. News of a Catholic plot to kill the king only increased the fear and hatred of Catholics in England, and even stricter laws were enacted to restrict Catholics as a result.

Ironically, Guy Fawkes was not the leader of the plot. The conspiracy was headed by Robert Catesby. However, Fawkes was the one caught guarding the barrels of gunpowder and was arrested, tortured, and executed.

That wasn't enough, though. November 5th became a national holiday, and effigies of Guy Fawkes are still burned on this day. Guy Fawkes was not the leader of the conspirators, nor did he succeed in killing the king, but he remains perhaps the most infamous person from early modern England.

Oliver Cromwell

Although his name might not be as familiar as Shakespeare or Guy Fawkes, Oliver Cromwell is easily one of the most influential figures in English history. When England found itself without a monarch during the Interregnum, Oliver Cromwell ruled the nation as Lord Protector.

Who was Cromwell, and how did he land such a high position? Kings and queens are afforded the right to rule by virtue of their birth, but what virtue placed Oliver Cromwell at the head of England from 1653 to 1658?

Born in 1599, Oliver Cromwell lived a fairly uneventful life for his first thirty years. Just before he turned thirty, though, Cromwell converted to Christianity, which would have a profound impact on him. With the awakening of his religious zeal, Cromwell became far more active in politics. He was a Puritan and spoke out against the authority of the bishops, believing that congregations should be able to pick their own ministers instead of having them appointed by the king. Because of his religious views, Cromwell began to oppose Charles I's government.

If Cromwell had been nothing more than a deeply religious man, history likely would not have remembered him, but when the English Civil War broke out, Cromwell proved himself to be a soldier as well. As Parliament faced the king in open warfare, Oliver Cromwell rose through the ranks as a practical and effective leader. Cromwell's success as a soldier made him the head of the army, making him the most powerful man in England after the death of Charles I.

Still, Cromwell did not exactly leap into Charles I's place. It took four years after the king's execution before Cromwell became Lord Protector. For those four years, Parliament attempted to govern, but there was much distrust between Parliament and the army, which made an effective government difficult. Cromwell himself disliked the radical republicanism promoted by some members of Parliament, believing that a more moderate course was necessary to reestablish stability and prosperity in England. He eventually accepted the position as Lord Protector, conceding that providence (God) seemed to will that it be so.

That might sound like a thin cover-up of his ambitions, but whether you agree with him or not, it does appear that Cromwell took his religion seriously. He believed that he was following God's wishes in becoming the most powerful man in England.

Despite having been one of the men to sign the king's death warrant, Cromwell was rather conservative as Lord Protector. He did want reform, especially in increasing religious tolerance, but he butted heads with the more radical members of Parliament, who were far more interested in redoing the constitution. Cromwell feared that dissolving England's traditional government would only result in anarchy. His desire to maintain stability resulted in a government that resembled a constitutional monarchy rather than a republic. This resemblance to a monarchy was confirmed when Cromwell named his son Richard as his successor shortly before his death in 1658.

To this day, people's opinion of Oliver Cromwell is divided. He has been seen as a dictator who used his military power to seize control of the nation. He has been viewed as a religious fanatic who used his belief in divine providence to justify his actions. He has also been criticized for halting the radical reinvention of the English government, and he has been praised for restoring and maintaining order in England with his more moderate reform approach. Whatever your opinion of him, it is clear that Oliver Cromwell was a highly capable man. For good or ill, he seized and maintained effective control of the English government for five years, making him the only self-made English ruler from this period.

Edward Hyde (Earl of Clarendon)

Edward Hyde by Peter Lely.
https://commons.wikimedia.org/wiki/File:Peter_Lely_(1618-1680)_(after)_-_Sir_Edward_Hyde_(1609%E2%80%931674),_1st_Earl_of_Clarendon_-_1257076_-_National_Trust.jpg

Speaking of English rulers, you likely got the impression from the last chapter that some monarchs were better than others. Since the monarchs had control over the government, what happened when the king or queen was lazy or incompetent? Who ran the country when the monarch didn't feel like it?

Although history tends not to remember their names nearly as well, most of England's monarchs had close advisers. These people often helped steer the course of England as much as the monarch. People like Robert Cecil under Queen Elizabeth I, Sarah Churchill under Queen Anne, John Dudley under Edward VI, and Thomas Wolsey and Thomas Cromwell under Henry VIII all wielded enormous influence because the monarch turned to them for advice and, in many cases, gave them powerful positions.

There were so many people that stood behind the monarchs of this period that we can't possibly begin to discuss them all, but as an example, we will look at one man who stood behind two kings and greatly impacted English history—Edward Hyde.

Edward Hyde is more commonly known by his title as the Earl of Clarendon or simply Clarendon. He was born in 1609 and served as an adviser to both Charles I and Charles II. Under Charles I, Hyde attempted to advise the king to take a more moderate approach in his conflict with Parliament but to little avail. The situation erupted into the English Civil War, and Hyde was sent to the continent as the young prince's guardian.

Hyde's service to Charles II proved just how capable he truly was. The Declaration of Breda of 1660 was Hyde's handiwork and allowed for Charles II's peaceful restoration to his father's throne. Once restored to his throne, Charles II relied heavily on Hyde, who became the first earl of Clarendon a year later in 1661. Clarendon (Hyde) was a competent administrator, but he eventually learned, like many close royal advisers, the dangers of being so close to the Crown.

In a monarchy, the king can do no wrong. You cannot impeach a king, so the king's close advisers are often forced to take the fall for government failures. By 1667, Clarendon's age (he was fifty-eight) and strict sense of morality did not sit well with the court of a man known as the Merry Monarch. In the aftermath of the Second Anglo-Dutch War, which was a disaster for the English, Clarendon was made a scapegoat. Charles II allowed the blame to lay on his oldest adviser rather than on himself, and Clarendon had to flee, living the rest of his days in exile in France.

Clarendon is an example of what many royal advisers and key political figures in this period were unable to overcome—the changing whims of the monarch. Political careers rose and fell based on who the monarch favored, and even those who proved themselves capable were not protected from fickle human nature. Politics and government at this time were deeply personal, and it showed in how quickly many rose and then fell from power.

John Churchill (Duke of Marlborough)

John Churchill (left) with General Armstrong (right).
https://commons.wikimedia.org/wiki/File:Major_General_John_Armstrong_with_John_Churchill_1st_Duke_of_Marlborough.jpg)

Known as England's greatest soldier, John Churchill is a figure from the later part of the early modern era. His military prowess was key in cementing England's position as a world power.

John Churchill was born in 1650. He began his military career at the age of seventeen and advanced steadily. By 1685, with the ascension of James II to the throne, John Churchill was the practical commander of the English military. It was at this point in his career that Churchill showed his capabilities extended to the political sphere as well. With William of Orange's invasion in 1688, Churchill saw the writing on the wall and switched sides. He abandoned the Roman Catholic James II and gave his allegiance to William. As the leader of England's army, Churchill's decision meant that James II had no army with which to oppose William. The result was a relatively bloodless transfer of power that has come to be known as the Glorious Revolution.

Even though John Churchill's decision to side with William of Orange was a major factor in what allowed William to take the throne from James II, Churchill's career did not advance as one might expect. William was distrustful of a man who would abandon his sovereign and suspected Churchill of plotting to restore James II. Churchill's military career was thus cut short for a few years until William III needed him for a more pressing issue—stopping Louis XIV.

In 1701, it became clear that King Louis XIV of France had set his sights on the Spanish throne, and William III was determined to halt his ambitions. In such a conflict, a military mind like John Churchill was essential. Although William III would end up dying in 1702, his successor, Queen Anne, confirmed Churchill's appointment to command the forces opposing Louis XIV's bid on Spain.

It was during the War of the Spanish Succession (1701-1714) that Churchill's reputation as a soldier was truly established. He won impressive victories at Blenheim (1704), Ramillies (1706), and Oudenaarde (1708). It appeared that Churchill simply could not be beaten in battle, yet the war dragged on. Unfortunately, wars are expensive even when you are winning them. Despite Churchill's victories, support for the war in England eventually wavered, and support for Churchill went too. In 1711, Churchill was dismissed from his military command. He died eleven years later in 1722.

That was life for many key political figures of this era. There were many who shone brilliantly for a moment, but very few managed to die with their star undiminished. The early modern era was a turbulent and changing time, not just for England but also for the world. Many were able to achieve greatness, but precious few were able to maintain it.

Chapter 5: The Renaissance

The Renaissance. The word brings to mind images of marble statues, finely detailed oil paintings, and ornate clothing. It makes us think of poetry, music, and philosophy. The Renaissance is the era that started the modern age. It brought Western civilization out of the Dark Ages and ushered in a new era of enlightenment and reason.

Or did it?

We think of the Renaissance as being an era that rescued humanity from ignorance, resurrecting our interest in science and the arts. But just how true is this? And what impact did it have specifically on England?

What Was the Renaissance?

When you hear the phrase Renaissance, you likely think of art. Paintings like Leonardo da Vinci's *Mona Lisa*, sculptures like Michelangelo's *David*, and large frescoes like Raphael's *The School of Athens* are visual embodiments of the Renaissance. However, to confine the Renaissance to an artistic movement is to greatly misunderstand what it was. The Renaissance was far more than a particular artistic style.

Perhaps the easiest way to approach what the Renaissance was is to consider what the word itself means. Renaissance is French for rebirth. The Renaissance was given this name because it saw a revival of interest in the classical period (Greek and Roman civilization). The Middle Ages had largely been characterized by the domination of the Roman Catholic Church and theological thinkers, but thanks to events like the Black

Death, the increasingly obvious corruption of the church, and a growing sense of nationalism, the systems of the Middle Ages were destabilizing. As their world began to transform irrevocably, people turned to other places to make sense of what was happening, which eventually led to a renewed interest in classical culture, sparking the Renaissance.

For a long time, this understanding of the Renaissance was taken to a more extreme level. The Middle Ages was seen as a dark time of ignorance, where religious dogma prevented any real sense of philosophical, artistic, or scientific progress. The reality is far more complex. Humanity did not completely stagnate during the medieval period. We now know that the Middle Ages was far richer in culture and thought than the Renaissance era would have us believe.

The phrase Middle Ages (which implies this period was somehow a pause between classical times and the Renaissance) was not used until the Renaissance. What all this means is that when Renaissance thinkers act as though they were saving humanity from a dark age, we need to take it with a grain of salt. The Renaissance was a crucial moment in European history, but it was not an absolute paradigm shift that saved Western civilization from decay.

Still, the Renaissance was a reaction to the gradual breakdown of medieval society and a time of great transformation. The movement that characterized the direction of this transformation was humanism.

Humanism, as the name implies, takes humanity as its subject. Instead of the heavy focus on God and theology that had been the drive of intellectual projects in the Middle Ages, humanists began to take a keener interest in things related to humans. That included areas of study like philosophy, history, art, drama, and more. They are the subjects that we today call the humanities because they involve the study of humans at some level.

This interest in humanity affected not only what people were thinking and studying but also led to deeper shifts in the culture. The medieval period's interest in God had placed humanity in a less than dignified position. There was a great emphasis on the value of penance in the Middle Ages. Humanism, in contrast, asserted the dignity of man. Life was not about penance but about striving to achieve creative greatness. It was this belief that provided the push for the scientific, philosophical, and artistic achievements of the Renaissance.

Knowing all that, how do we answer the question of what was the Renaissance? The Renaissance was a shift in intellectual focus from God to humanity in response to the failures of medieval society. It saw a greatly renewed interest in classical culture and thought and resulted in many achievements in the areas of art and science.

Where Did It Start and How Did It Spread?

Now that we have a better idea of what the Renaissance was, let's turn to the matter of geography and timing. Much like a disease, intellectual movements like the Renaissance often have a point of origin and a method through which they are transmitted.

The time is the late 13th century, and the place is Italy. The Renaissance itself had not yet gotten underway, but it is here that we find the seeds that would sprout into the Renaissance. By this time, the problems with medieval society were becoming more and more apparent. By the early 14th century, men like Dante (the author of the *Divine Comedy*), Giotto (an artist), and Petrarch (a poet and scholar) were showing humanist interests and styles in their work. This was the proto-Renaissance, and it seemed like a fully-fledged Renaissance would soon develop. However, thanks to the outbreak of plague known as the Black Death and several internal conflicts, the 14th century proved to be a rough time for Italians, and the movement that we can see beginning with Dante, Giotto, and Petrarch nearly disappeared.

In the 15th century, a level of stability returned, and the Renaissance truly emerged in Italy. In cities like Florence, the arts flourished, and when these artists studied and imitated classical styles, they revived interest in Greco-Roman culture. The Renaissance had arrived.

The Renaissance clearly got its start in Italy, but how did it spread throughout Europe and all the way to England? In the present day, we often take for granted our ability to find information quickly. Thanks to the internet, the world is more connected than ever, but back in the medieval and early modern era, this was clearly not the case. New ideas took time to spread. Had it not been for one very important invention, the Renaissance would likely not have had the impact it did outside of Italy. That invention was the printing press.

The earliest printing press to appear in Europe was Johannes Gutenberg's. Gutenberg's press appeared around the middle of the 15th

century and could print around 250 sheets per hour. While that may not sound impressive today, before the invention of the mechanized printing press, the only way to copy books was by hand, which meant there were no mass-produced books. Without the ability to produce many copies of a book, there was no way to spread and share information.

The importance of the printing press in both the Renaissance and later in the Reformation cannot be overstated. With the ability to mass-produce books, both education and religion were forever changed. Students could now study classical writers, and everyone (and by everyone, we mean everyone who could read, which was still a small portion of the population) could read the Bible. This access to knowledge, in large part, made the Renaissance possible. Without the printing press, the renewed interest in classical thought and culture would never have been able to reach as many people as it did.

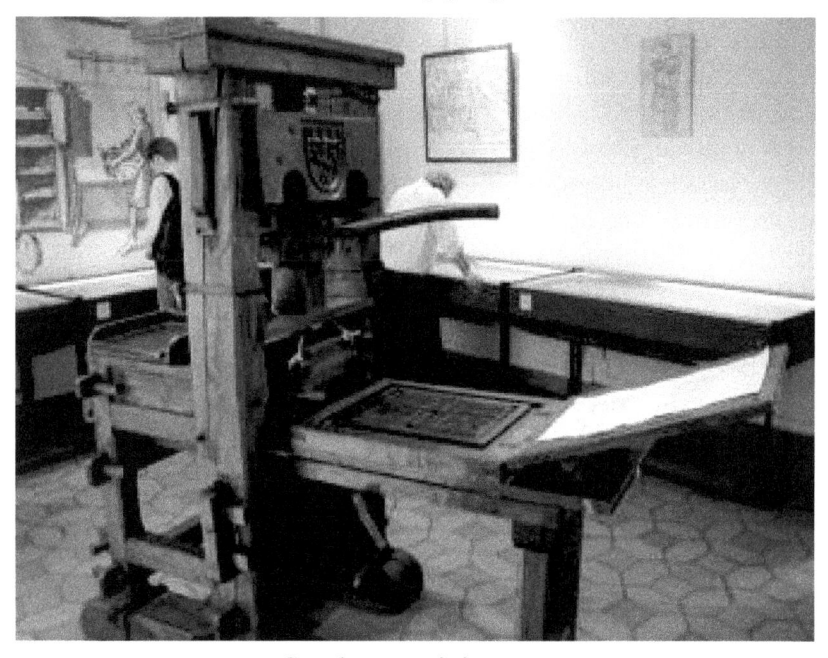

Gutenberg era printing press.
https://commons.wikimedia.org/wiki/File:Gutenberg.press.jpg

The printing press was not the only reason the Renaissance took off the way it did, though. In 1492, Christopher Columbus landed in the Bahamas, discovering two entire continents of which Europeans had no knowledge. In later chapters, we will discuss this exploration in more detail, but in terms of understanding the Renaissance, this Age of

Exploration was a vital contributing factor. Europeans at this time were contending with the fact that the world was much larger than they had realized. This new awareness brought greater levels of scientific inquiry and simple curiosity that helped to drive the desire for knowledge that characterized much of the Renaissance at a fundamental level.

That's a basic overview of how the Renaissance started and spread, but how did it end? In one sense, the Renaissance didn't end, as the ideas that it sparked continued to develop and create the modern world. However, in terms of the artistic style and intense interest in classical culture, the Renaissance did end, and the event that is typically used to mark that end is the Sack of Rome by the Holy Roman Empire's forces in 1527.

The Sack of Rome is used to mark the end of the Renaissance largely because it disrupted and ended the Renaissance in its place of origin, Italy. However, looking at the Renaissance on a more European-wide scale, the end was far more gradual. Ultimately, the Reformation brought an end to much of the Renaissance. The Renaissance era's reverence for classical culture created much tension with the Christian faith. As religious issues exploded with the Reformation, this tension became more and more unbearable, eventually causing the decline of humanism, which had defined the Renaissance era.

What Did the Renaissance Look Like?

We have mentioned several times that the Renaissance saw great achievements in art, but what exactly does that include? What made Renaissance art so different?

The Renaissance produced many talented artists, but there are three who stand out as the quintessential Renaissance man: Leonardo da Vinci, Michelangelo, and Raphael. By taking a glance at these three men, we can better understand both the art of the Renaissance and the Renaissance itself.

Leonardo da Vinci was truly a Renaissance man in that his interests and skills covered a wide array of subjects. The Renaissance was not an era of specialization but a time when all knowledge and truth were believed to be intimately connected. You may know Leonardo da Vinci as the artist who painted the *Mona Lisa*, but did you know he was also an engineer, an architect, and a scientist who studied things ranging from anatomy to flight? Leonardo was a busy man, and what he captures about the period is an underlying desire for knowledge. The Renaissance was about far more than painting. Humanism sought greater knowledge of humanity, and that desire for knowledge found expression in many ways.

Mona Lisa by Leonardo da Vinci.
https://commons.wikimedia.org/wiki/File:Mona_Lisa,_by_Leonardo_da_Vinci,_from_C2RMF_retouched.jpg

If the Renaissance was about the knowledge of humanity, why was art such a key part of it? Those two ideas may seem disconnected, but in this period, art was highly valued as a type of knowledge. Our understanding of the world comes largely through our sight, and the visual arts were, therefore, a means to record these observations. At the time, art was almost mathematical in nature. For instance, Raphael's work shows a great adherence to balance and harmony. Art allowed man to order what he saw of the world, and in doing so, it was believed that man could come to understand himself and his place in the world better.

The School of Athens by Raphael.
https://commons.wikimedia.org/wiki/File:%22The_School_of_Athens%22_by_Raffaello_Sanzio_da_Urbino.jpg

Michelangelo's work, in particular, displays an interest in understanding humanity. Michelangelo considered himself a sculptor before all else, and his sculptures, such as the *David* and the *Pieta*, show admiration for the human form. His paintings, such as his work on the Sistine Chapel, display the human form boldly. This is what made art so important in the Renaissance. Artists like Michelangelo argued for the dignity of man in the way in which they visually represented people. Their art declares the beauty of the human form in a way that art in the Middle Ages had never done.

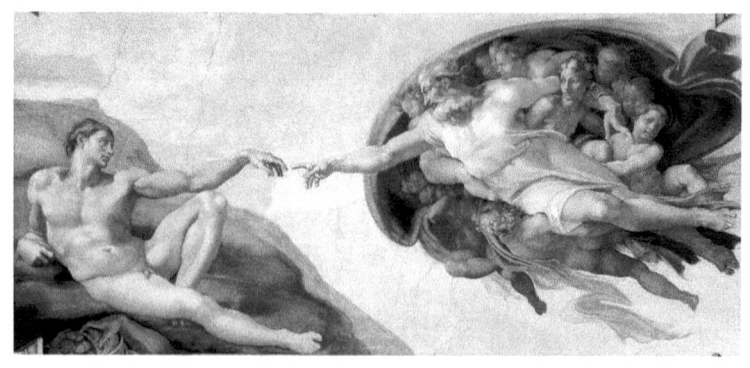

The Creation of Adam from the Sistine Chapel by Michelangelo.
https://commons.wikimedia.org/wiki/File:Creation_of_Adam_Michelangelo_(1475%E2%80%93 1564),_circa_1511.jpg

In Italy, the Renaissance clearly found expression in the visual arts, but in other places, other aspects of culture flourished. The Renaissance in England looked quite different from its Italian muse.

The Renaissance and England

Despite the greatly increased printing speed of Gutenberg's printing press, the people were nowhere near the speed at which information spreads around the globe today. Intellectual movements moved slower than the plague in the early modern era. It was not until the 16th century that the Renaissance reached the shores of England.

The Wars of the Roses had ended the medieval period in England and left the country in shambles. While the Renaissance was taking off in the late 15th century in Italy, in England, the first Tudor king, Henry VII, was performing the monumental task of restoring order and stability. It was not until Henry VII's son, Henry VIII, took the throne that England could focus on culture.

In several ways, Henry VIII was a Renaissance king. He could write poetry and play music. He was aware of and interested in the humanist movement, and his court included many great humanist thinkers, such as Thomas More. However, Henry VIII was also a passionate man. While he surrounded himself with many of England's brilliant men, he also grew dissatisfied with all of them at some point, often to the great misfortune of those men. His court was one where the values and interests of the Renaissance were present but where they also took a backseat to larger political aspirations and ambitions.

Ultimately, the cultural renaissance that appeared briefly in Henry VIII's court was lost by Henry VIII's marriage troubles and the Reformation. These circumstances will be discussed in great detail in the next chapter, but what you need to know now is that these religious changes greatly disrupted the government and nation for many decades. Under Henry VIII, England broke with the Roman Church. Under his son, Edward VI, England became more Protestant, and under Queen Mary, England was briefly pushed back toward Catholicism. Cultural exploration and progress slowed in the face of these pressing religious issues. It was not until the reign of Elizabeth I that England settled down enough to experience its own national renaissance.

Unlike the Italian Renaissance, which was focused largely on the visual arts, England's cultural renaissance of the late 16th and early 17th centuries was far more literary. This was the era of Shakespeare, and although Shakespeare is the most well-remembered English writer from this period, he was far from the only one. John Donne, Christopher Marlowe, Ben Jonson, Edmund Spenser, and more all wrote exceptional plays and poems in this period.

What made the Elizabethan Age such a grand era for English writers, though? The English literary renaissance was, in many ways, a direct result of the Italian Renaissance. Humanism's devotion to studying humans led to the creation of more schools, and the invention of the printing press made it possible for those schools to have access to more teaching materials, such as classical texts, which before had only been accessible by an elite few. Men like Shakespeare and Marlowe were educated in these "grammar schools."

Thus, because of the impact of humanism and the Renaissance, these great English writers received a classical education that was focused largely on language. The influence this had on Shakespeare and other writers is extremely evident in the many references to classical literature in their works and their highly advanced command of the English language.

What do we mean by advanced command of the English language? The writers of that age achieved literary greatness not necessarily because of the stories they told but because of their ability to use words precisely and shape sentences eloquently. Shakespeare has not remained the most famous English writer because he came up with the story about a man who finds out his uncle murdered his father. Shakespeare didn't come up with many of his stories. He is the most famous English writer because he wrote things like "To be or not to be, that is the question." It was how Shakespeare used words that made him great, and the same can be said for many of his contemporaries. If the Italian Renaissance saw new heights of skill and expression with the paintbrush, then the English Renaissance saw the same happen with the pen.

In this discussion about the English writers' great skills during this period, it can be easy to fall into a common misconception, which is that the English Renaissance was a snobbish affair confined to the upper class. Today, we think of Shakespeare and poetry as the height of sophistication, but that was far from the case at the time. Plays were attended by all classes of society and were even viewed as scandalous and immoral by some. The writers of this time wrote about things like God and questions of morality, but they also wrote about pretty women and told dirty jokes.

The culture that these writers represented was not something confined to museums and galleries but rather something experienced by a large portion of society, which is what makes the Renaissance as a whole so important. Yes, we can spend a long time naming particular men and discussing their work, but the Renaissance was not confined to just these men. Its impact was felt directly by many through the changes it brought to education and culture, and we can still see the impact of those changes in our modern world today.

Chapter 6: The Reformation and Henry VIII

There can be no question that one of the most important events to happen in England between 1485 and 1714 was its break with the pope and the Roman Catholic Church in 1534. This event had drastic consequences at the time, and its impact shaped England for centuries to come. So, who was responsible for this momentous decision, and how exactly did it happen?

As you probably guessed from the chapter title, Henry VIII was the monarch who broke with Rome, but his reasons for doing so were far from a sense of religious conviction. It all started with Henry VIII's unfruitful marriage to Catherine of Aragon in an affair that was known as the King's Great Matter.

The King's Great Matter

The King's Great Matter was how the people of the time referred to Henry VIII's attempt to annul his marriage with Catherine of Aragon.

Catherine of Aragon by Joannes Corvus.
https://commons.wikimedia.org/wiki/File:Catalina_de_Arag%C3%B3n,_por_un_artista_an%C3%B3nimo.jpg

Catherine of Aragon was originally married to Henry's older brother, Arthur, but he died a few months after their marriage. Catherine then married Henry when he ascended to the throne in 1509. The couple appeared well matched enough until the late 1520s brought trouble in the form of Anne Boleyn.

The fact that Henry VIII simply took a liking to Anne Boleyn was not a problem for his marriage by itself. Henry VIII had already had other extramarital affairs by this point, including one with Anne's sister, Mary Boleyn. Anne, however, refused to become the king's mistress. She would not go to bed with him unless they were married.

Anne's motivation here was likely more ambition than virtue, but her stance proved to be effective. As a good Roman Catholic, Henry VIII turned to the pope to annul his marriage to Catherine so that he could marry Anne.

Anne Boleyn.
https://commons.wikimedia.org/wiki/File:AnneBoleynHever.jpg

Unfortunately for Henry VIII, the pope was not too keen on the idea. In 1527, Rome was sacked by Holy Roman Emperor Charles V. The pope was essentially Charles V's prisoner, and Charles V happened to be the nephew of Catherine of Aragon. Charles didn't like the idea of Henry VIII throwing his aunt to the side, and with his army surrounding Rome, the pope was inclined to listen to Charles V's opinion on the matter.

This dilemma went on for some time. Anne Boleyn refused to be the king's mistress. Catherine of Aragon refused to step aside. The pope refused to annul the marriage, and Henry VIII refused to give up. It went on for years, and the frustrated Henry VIII eventually began taking steps without the pope's approval. In 1531, Catherine of Aragon was kicked out of court. A year later, Henry VIII and Anne Boleyn exchanged secret vows.

However, secret vows were not enough to make Anne queen. In 1533, the highest church official in England, Thomas Cranmer, the Archbishop of Canterbury, declared Henry's marriage to Catherine of

Aragon illegitimate and pronounced his marriage to Anne valid. The pope was greatly displeased, as it was clear that the English king had turned his back on Rome. In another year, the Act of Supremacy was passed by Parliament, making the king the head of the Church of England and making the break with Rome official.

Let's pause here in this real-life drama to consider a few things. First off, is it true that Henry VIII tried to get rid of his first wife and ultimately broke with Rome all because he wanted to have sex with Anne Boleyn? Anne's refusal to be the king's mistress played a role in everything that unfolded, but there was another factor that likely had a bigger influence on the king.

Catherine of Aragon was in her forties by this time, which was past childbearing years for a woman in this era. The queen had only one living child, and that child was a girl, Princess Mary. When Anne Boleyn came on the scene in the 1520s, Henry VIII had probably concluded that his current wife was not going to give him the male heir he desired. His aim in marrying Anne Boleyn was not just to fulfill his lust but also in the hopes of producing a son.

Before we judge Henry VIII too harshly, we must recognize that the lack of a male heir at this time was a very real and serious concern. At this point, England had never been ruled by a woman, and the last time a woman had been the intended heir to the throne, the country had fallen into a horrible fifteen-year civil war known as the Anarchy. None of this is to say that Henry VIII was justified in casting off his wife after almost two decades of marriage, but it does help to explain why Henry VIII was so desperate.

The next interesting thing to notice in this situation is that Henry VIII was not seeking a divorce. Although many people mistakenly say today that Henry VIII divorced three of his wives, that was not the case. Divorce back then was pretty much never allowed. Henry VIII was trying to get an annulment.

What's the difference? An annulment declares a marriage null and void. It not only ends the marriage but also renders the entire marriage invalid. If Henry VIII succeeded in gaining an annulment from Catherine of Aragon, it would be as though they were never married. Catherine would lose her title as queen, and their daughter, Princess Mary, would be considered illegitimate.

So, an annulment was serious business. Why did Henry VIII ever think the pope would grant him one? Henry VIII did have a case for his annulment, and that case rested in the Old Testament Book of Leviticus, specifically Leviticus 18:16 ("Thou shalt not uncover the nakedness of thy brother's wife: it is thy brother's nakedness") and Leviticus 20:21 ("If a man shall take his brother's wife, it is an unclean thing ... they shall be childless"). According to these verses, it appears that a man is not to marry his brother's wife. Catherine of Aragon had previously been married to Henry's brother Arthur before his death.

This issue of marrying his brother's wife had already come up. When Henry and Catherine were originally married in 1509, they had to have the pope's approval. Their marriage was only allowed because Catherine insisted that she had never consummated her marriage with Arthur, which meant that she and Arthur were never truly married. Henry VIII was hoping that the new pope would overturn that initial ruling and declare his marriage to Catherine invalid, which would allow him to marry Anne and produce a male heir.

What all this means is that the idea that Henry VIII was simply a spoiled man who changed his entire country's religion just because he had the hots for a woman isn't completely true (though it isn't completely wrong either). Henry VIII was a king without a son in a time when such circumstances often spelled disaster. He became convinced that Anne Boleyn was the key to fixing that problem.

That's how Henry VIII's marital troubles led to the establishment of the Church of England. However, none of this would have been possible had Europe not been in the midst of great religious changes in the first place. Had Henry VIII wanted to annul his marriage one hundred years prior, and the pope refused, it would have been tough luck. To truly understand why Henry VIII was able to even create the Church of England, we need to take a closer look at the religious changes that were taking place at this time.

The Reformation

The Reformation is one of the few historical movements for which we have a clear start date: October 31st, 1517. On this day, Martin Luther nailed his *Ninety-five Theses*, which were a collection of points of debate against the Catholic Church, to the door of a church in Wittenberg and launched a movement that would lead to a schism in the church and a long period of religious tension and even wars in Europe.

Martin Luther by Lucas Cranach the Elder.
https://commons.wikimedia.org/wiki/File:Martin_Luther,_1529.jpg

By 1517, the fact that the Catholic Church had problems with corruption was no secret. Indulgences, which was a practice that allowed people to pay off their sins, were the hot topic of the day. Luther was not the only one to take issue with indulgences. Paying off sins was a matter of utmost importance to the people who believed strongly in hell, which was practically everyone. Many of the clergy abused this fear to profit from indulgences. Luther also attacked other issues in his *Ninety-five Theses*, including church doctrine.

Luther's attack on doctrine made him different from others who had complained about the church's rampant corruption. For a long time, many had complained about corrupt clergy abusing their positions. Luther, however, went past attacking the individual clergy to debate the teachings of the church.

Still, it is unlikely that Luther could have predicted the effect his *Ninety-five Theses* would have. Such publications are normally only of interest to other theologians, but thanks to the recent invention of printing, Luther's theses spread rapidly throughout Germany, and his ideas then moved throughout Europe. The genie was out of the bottle, and the Catholic Church soon discovered that there was no putting it back.

As the name suggests, Luther's original intention was to reform the Catholic Church. He did not set out to cause a split, but the pope and other leaders in the Roman Church wanted nothing to do with Luther's suggestions. As time went on, Luther came to disagree with the Roman Church more, and the Reformation gave birth to a new sect of Christianity: Protestantism.

Luther was the spark, but many others took up the mantle of Reformation after Luther. These included men like John Knox, John Calvin, and others who would go on to found various sects of Protestantism.

It was in the backdrop of this religious upheaval that Henry VIII found himself at odds with Pope Clement VII. Many kings before Henry VIII had been frustrated by the pope's power, but Henry was the first king who was in a position to do something about it. Seventeen years after Luther published his *Ninety-five Theses*, Henry VIII started the English Reformation by breaking with the Roman Catholic Church.

The Reformation in England

Because England left the Catholic Church for political rather than religious reasons, the English Reformation was a top-down transformation. It was not the result of a change in the people's religious sentiments but rather the result of people in power making system-wide changes that trickled down to the masses. But what were these changes?

Henry VIII's Church of England was far from a radical departure from the Roman Church. Other than his denial of the pope's authority, Henry VIII appeared to hold to Catholic beliefs until his death. As such, in the new Church of England, much of the Catholic doctrine was retained, as was the general church structure with bishops and archbishops. The biggest changes were that the monarch was now head of the church instead of the pope, the monastery system was systematically extinguished, and the Bible was made available in English for the first time.

As relatively minor as these changes were, there was still resistance. Many were executed for treason in the years following the split with Rome for refusing to accept the king's supremacy over the church, including prominent men like John Fisher and Thomas More. There was also a popular uprising, the Pilgrimage of Grace, that Henry VIII thoroughly crushed. Still, for the common people, life under Henry VIII's Church of England probably did not feel that different from life under the Roman Catholic Church. Henry VIII seemed content with the few changes he had made.

Thus, the Henrician Reformation was a rather slow process whose interests were more political (the supremacy of the king) than doctrinal. Those who were executed due to Henry VIII's religious policies were often accused of treason rather than heresy. However, the English Reformation would take on a new flavor with Henry's death and the ascension of his son, Edward VI.

While Henry VIII can best be described as a Catholic who did not like the pope, Edward VI was a Protestant in name and belief. He was far more interested than his father had been in changing the people's actual beliefs, and his short six-year reign saw a much larger push toward Protestantism.

One example of this push was the Act of Uniformity passed in 1549. This act required churches to use the new English *Book of Common Prayer* written by Archbishop Cranmer. This had enormous implications for the religious lives of the English people. The *Book of Common Prayer* was used to conduct services, so the Act of Uniformity forced a great change in the weekly religious services of the common people. It was a much more substantial religious change than anything that Henry VIII had done, and it created a backlash. The Prayer Book Rebellion started in response to the Act of Uniformity and was put down by John Dudley.

Since Edward was only nine years old when he took the throne in 1547, it was men like Dudley who effectively ruled the kingdom. Dudley's success with the Prayer Book Rebellion made him essentially the most powerful man in the kingdom. He was made duke of Northumberland, and in the hopes of keeping his new power, Northumberland (Dudley) wanted to please the adolescent king.

It was this desire to stay on Edward VI's good side that likely prompted Northumberland's following actions. He greatly promoted the *Book of Common Prayer*, even getting Cranmer to write a more Protestant version in 1552. He encouraged image breaking and even the whitewashing of many ornate church walls. Under his influence, a new statement of church doctrine, the Forty-two Articles of Faith of 1553, established a more Protestant system of beliefs for the Church of England.

This was the nature of the Edwardian Reformation in England. While the Henrician Reformation had changed the church's structure, the Edwardian Reformation set out to make England Protestant in both name and belief. Catholicism was being swept away from the shores of England under the firm hand of men like Northumberland.

Unforeseen circumstances, however, soon produced a serious obstacle to this sweeping tide of Protestantism. Northumberland had bet on the wrong horse. While his radical religious stance was appreciated by Edward VI, it was heresy to others. Henry VIII's Catholic daughter Mary was next in line for the throne, and when Edward VI died in 1553, despite a brief attempt to put Lady Jane Grey on the throne, Mary became queen. Although England had been rushing toward Protestantism under Edward VI, it would soon experience religious whiplash. Queen Mary was determined to bring her country back to the Roman Catholic Church.

Unfortunately for Queen Mary, by this time, the English Reformation had effectively trickled down to the masses. Her attempts to stamp out the heresy that was Protestantism only earned her the nickname Bloody Mary. Although the English Reformation had started because of the whims of a monarch, only twenty years later, it was far too embedded in English society for anyone to turn back the tide.

Mary's attempt to make England Catholic again was brief. She died in 1558 and was replaced by her Protestant half-sister, Elizabeth. Elizabeth I's forty-four-year reign finally allowed a sense of religious stability to be established. Henry VIII had made overarching changes to the system, Edward VI had pushed drastic changes to everyday religious life, and Mary had tried to roll back these changes. Elizabeth I chose a more moderate path.

While Elizabeth restored Protestantism to England, she also firmly resisted leaning too radically into Protestantism. Despite the push for the growing sect of Puritans, the Church of England still had many resemblances to the Catholic Church. It was a church that was Protestant enough for the people of England but not Protestant enough to prompt crusades against England by Catholic nations. In this moderation, England found relative religious peace despite the religious turmoil of this period. While Henry VIII, Edward VI, and Mary had all stirred the nation, Elizabeth I allowed the nation to settle, and in doing so, she cemented the Reformation's impact on England. By the end of Elizabeth I's reign, England was Protestant, and there was no going back.

Chapter 7: Exploration and Trade

As the familiar rhyme tells us, "Columbus sailed the ocean blue in fourteen hundred ninety-two." In doing so, he inadvertently discovered a new world. The consequences of this discovery would have enormous repercussions for England and the rest of the world.

You probably already know that Columbus's discovery of the Americas was a pivotal event in world history, but there's more to this event than just its consequences. If we want to understand the nature of trade and exploration in the early modern era, we must also address the question of why Columbus was sailing the ocean blue in the first place. Columbus did not set off to find a new world. He was looking for a westward route to Asia, and the reason he was looking for such a route was quite simple: trade.

Trade in the Early Modern Era

Trade was not an invention of the early modern period. It had long been an essential part of the wealth of any city or nation. For a village to move beyond a mere subsistence existence, trade must be established to make use of surplus goods and to bring in goods only obtainable elsewhere. Trade is the very lifeblood of cities, and in the early modern period, national governments seemed to become more aware of this. Trade was how a nation could obtain great wealth—wealth that was necessary for fighting wars and maintaining defense.

The early modern era doesn't necessarily make us think of grand battles and tumultuous times in the same way the Middle Ages does, but it was a violent time nonetheless. Thanks to the Reformation, Europe was rocked by religious tensions that frequently led to armed conflicts. Dynastic conflicts also arose, as well as trade disputes. Some nations rose into world powers. Others scrambled to try to be one of those nations, and trade was their ticket.

Nations wanted power for both safety and in the hopes of dominating other nations, but power could not be had without money. And trade was where the money was. When everyone wants a piece of the action, though, there is never enough to go around. Under these circumstances, governments like Spain sent off explorers like Columbus to find new trade routes. The exploration of this period was primarily the result of the increasing importance of trade.

England and Trade

Now that we understand a bit more about trade in general in this period, let's take a closer look at English trade. As we have already mentioned, trade occurs when there is a surplus of goods that can be exchanged for something else. But how do cities and nations get enough surplus to start trading?

Specialization is the name of the game. Trade is beneficial because there are some things that a nation can easily create and other things that it can only get from other nations. For England, wool was the undisputed export king. England did not have the climate nor the landscape to make wine, silk, or grow different spices, but it did have plenty of sheep. These sheep produced wool that was then spun and made into cloth. The export of this cloth made up over three-quarters of England's exports by the start of the Elizabethan era.

Who exactly was England trading this cloth with? Their trading partners were close to home. English cloth went to cities in France and Spain, but most of all, it went to Antwerp. During the 16th century, as trade with Asia increased in importance, Antwerp became the trading hub of Europe. The majority of English cloth went there, where it was then sold and traded throughout the rest of Europe.

While England's export business was focused heavily on a single commodity, their imports were much more varied. England imported flax, wine, salt, woad (a plant used to make blue dye), spices, timber, alum, and many other goods from different countries. Surprisingly, much of what England imported came from Europe rather than from more exotic and distant locations like China. While Columbus and other explorers might make us think this period was rampant with long trade routes, at the beginning of the 16th century, much of English trade was focused within the English Channel.

Things did change over time. England's trading system took two severe hits as the early modern period progressed. The first was the lack of growth in the wool trade. Wool and the heavy cloth made from wool were close to being England's only export, and it was needed primarily by northern Europe. Eventually, there was less demand for this heavy woolen cloth. Instead of growing, English trade stagnated, and while there were attempts to fix this by developing a lighter cloth (which was called new draperies), wool prices continued to fall at the beginning of the 17th century.

The problem with the wool industry was only exacerbated by the other problem: Antwerp. Antwerp was where England sent most of its wool, but due to numerous wars, by the late 16th century, Antwerp was effectively closed to English trade. Although merchants attempted to find other locations to trade their wool, it was simply not the lucrative material it had been a century prior.

The decline of this industry was disastrous not only for the merchants but also for the government. The English government needed the money that trade brought in and was willing to intervene in the market to stop the collapse of the trade industry. The Crown's method of averting the crisis was by granting royal charters to certain companies. These charters created royal monopolies, where only those approved by the government had the right to trade in a particular area. Examples of companies created by a royal charter include the East India Company, the Virginia Company, the Massachusetts Bay Company, the Muscovy Company, the Levant Company, and the Royal Africa Company.

Originally, these companies were formed in the hopes of finding new places to trade English wool, but many of them went on to specialize in different products. The Virginia Company was focused on tobacco. The East India Company specialized in tea, and the Royal Africa Company traded slaves. While several of these companies would go on to be enormously successful, things didn't start that way. Since we know with the benefit of hindsight that England would eventually acquire a massive empire, it can be easy to overestimate England's position in world trade in the latter half of the 16th century and into the beginning of the 17th century.

With the wool trade declining, England needed to establish alternate avenues of trade, but they were late to the party. Much of the trade with Asia was already dominated by the French and the Dutch, and Spain had already claimed huge swaths of the New World. England's late arrival forced it to begin looking for new trade routes and new lands to colonize.

Exploration

You might be thinking that because England is on an island that it has easy access to great trade routes, but that was not the case at the very beginning of the 17th century. England wasn't in the best geographical position to dive into the trade and exploration that was making countries like Spain filthy rich.

The problem was how far north England is. Attempts by the English to find northeastern or even northwestern routes to Asia ended in the ice of the North Pole. Traveling due west led English ships not to the Bahamas like Columbus but to the icy shores of Newfoundland. Despite easy access to the sea, England did not have any exclusive trade routes. Instead, England was forced to try to find a place along routes already dominated by other countries.

That is not to say the English made no contributions to the great exploratory expeditions that were going on at this time. Sir Francis Drake successfully circumnavigated the globe on a voyage from 1577 to 1580. However, Drake also used the voyage as an opportunity to harass the Spanish, making quite a bit of money with his successful pirating. Despite his piracy, Drake was welcomed back by Queen Elizabeth herself and knighted when he arrived back in England.

Drake's circumnavigation of the globe is a telling example of what most explorations boiled down to in this era: money. While circumnavigating the globe was a grand feat of human perseverance and an indication of just how much more Europeans knew about the world, it was also a money-making expedition. Drake raided the Spanish and then used the loot to purchase exotic goods, such as spices, as he traveled. We may want to believe that the spirit of adventure motivated the explorers of the early modern era, but from Columbus to Sir Francis Drake, their motivations were often more pecuniary in nature.

Trade Wars

Economics in the early modern era was more than ledger books and trade routes. There was a lot of money and power to be made and lost in international trade, and countries were willing to go to war to protect their interests.

Establishing trade routes and posts was one thing, but defending them was of equal importance. Piracy was rampant, and in India, disputes with the Dutch and French over the right to trade would escalate until the English East India Company had amassed a large army to fight its rivals. That was how intense economics was at this time. Companies had their own armies. Monopolies (which means only a single company was allowed to do business in a certain region or with a certain group) were the rule at this time, so the only way to steal business from the competition was to use force.

England was far from being a mere victim in all this. In the late 16th century, many English privateers (pirates) received implicit support from Queen Elizabeth in their raids on Spanish vessels and trading settlements. Sir Francis Drake, the famous English admiral, was among those who greatly benefited from the spoils he took from the Spanish. The English privateers harried the Spanish so much that they were a major reason for open hostilities between Spain and England from 1585 to 1604.

Sometimes, England's conflict with other nations over trade interests went beyond piracy. England fought three wars in the latter half of the 17th century with the Dutch. Both the conflict with Spain and the conflict with the Netherlands were largely about establishing naval supremacy. The country that controlled the seas controlled trade, and as the English navy dominated the waters, England's position as a world power was secured.

However, England's success in naval warfare was not the only component in making England a dominant power. Beating its rivals in warfare was not enough to make England rich. England needed steadier and more reliable income, and it soon realized that could only be obtained with permanent settlements. Colonizing the New World was England's path to riches and power, and we will discuss how exactly that worked in Chapter 15.

The Impact of Trade and Exploration on the English People

We have discussed just how important trade and exploration were to governments in this era, but how far did this importance extend down the social ladder? Nations were becoming wealthier, but did this increase the standard of living of the average person?

The answer is not really. Trade with other nations allowed England to import new goods, but these goods were often luxury items. Silk, taffeta, and wines were brought into England in large numbers for the elite, but these luxury products were reserved for only a select few. They did little to help bolster the nation's economy as a whole.

Even the English government was aware of the problem of importing too many luxury goods instead of necessities. The Crown tried to set restrictions on the import of the elite's frivolous items, but it had little effect other than to increase smuggling. So, while trade brought money into England, that money tended to circulate amongst the upper class instead of bolstering the nation as a whole.

At this point, you may have decided that trade and exploration were nothing more than a scheme to make the rich richer and to fund wars with rival nations. However, there were some benefits beyond having cash in the treasury, and some of those benefits did impact the English people.

During the medieval period, natural disasters caused destruction on a scale that is difficult for us to fully grasp today. The Great Famine of the 14th century killed between 10 to 15 percent of the English population. In the Middle Ages, if something went wrong with the crops, there was simply nowhere else for an English peasant to get food. There was no security against the fickleness of nature.

In the early modern era, thanks to growing trade networks, there were finally alternatives to starvation when crops failed. During years of bad harvest, England was able to import grain from the Baltic, which greatly lessened the impact of crop failures. Trade did little to put more money in the pocket of the average English person, but it did help to ensure there was food at the market to buy.

Trade also brought new elements into English culture. As the early modern era went on and exploration continued, both tobacco and tea were discovered, becoming staples of English society. Sugar from the Caribbean was a prominent moneymaker for England, as well as a product that would eventually work its way into English homes everywhere. There are innumerable resources and products that came into England because of trade and forever changed the country.

By expanding what resources the country had access to, trade and exploration changed England on many levels. From necessities to interesting new products, the world was becoming increasingly interconnected, as people in different places came to rely on goods they could only obtain elsewhere. Explorations soon led to colonization as a more permanent means of securing goods. The world was changing. People were growing accustomed to what trade provided, and there was no going back.

Chapter 8: Protestantism and Its Growth

In Chapter 6, we discussed how the Reformation came to England, and we learned that the English Reformation was unique in that it was a top-down transformation where systematic changes enacted by those in power altered the country's religion. In this chapter, we look to address a slightly different question: how did Protestantism come to England?

While the Reformation and Protestantism might seem like the same thing, there is a difference. The Reformation was a reactionary movement to the people's problems with the Catholic Church. It began as an attempt to reform the Catholic Church but instead led to the establishment of Protestantism.

Protestantism is the belief system (or rather belief systems because there are many different sects) that arose as a direct result of the Reformation. It moved beyond criticizing Catholicism to having a different and opposing set of doctrinal beliefs. What this means in England particularly is that the Reformation was a series of systematic changes to religious forms and practices, but Protestantism was a change to doctrine and belief itself.

The Reformation and Protestantism are closely tied together, and in many cases, discussing them as if they were practically the same causes no harm. However, England is a unique case. Although Henry VIII did undoubtedly bring the Reformation to England, he did not make great efforts to bring Protestantism along with it. Henry VIII was a Catholic who denied the pope's authority. He was not a true Protestant in any sense of the word. However, in bringing the Reformation to England, Henry VIII had opened a door, and Protestantism would soon follow.

Catholicism vs. Protestantism

To understand how Protestantism came to and impacted England, we first need to understand what the difference between Catholicism and Protestantism was. If denying the pope's authority didn't make Henry VIII a full Protestant, what did?

The main difference between Catholicism and Protestantism at this time lay in where they found the truth. Catholics saw divine revelation in the Bible, church tradition, and church authority. Although the Bible was considered to be God's Word, for Catholics, the average person could not be trusted to interpret it. The clergy was responsible for telling the people what the Bible said, and in doing so, they became sources of truth. Protestantism, however, saw the Bible alone as the source of truth. The clergy and church tradition should only be followed when they agreed with scripture.

Because Protestants believed in the authority of scripture alone, they thought it was important for everyone to be able to read the Bible. This led to the first English translation of the Good Book. The denial of the clergy as sources of truth also meant that the Protestants viewed priests differently. Priests were not sacred to Protestants, so their role became less about performing sacraments and more about preaching. Protestants even rejected the idea that the Eucharist was transformed into the literal body and blood of Christ because that had the priest performing a supernatural miracle.

What these differences culminated in and what made the debate between Catholics and Protestants so momentous was ultimately a different path to heaven. Catholicism believed that salvation was the product of both faith and good works. To get to heaven, one not only needed to believe, but one also needed to do what the church said by engaging in the sacraments. Protestantism saw faith alone as the way to salvation. The path to heaven was a matter of personal belief, and a priest or the church could do nothing to put someone on that path.

These differences between Catholicism and Protestantism quickly created a chasm. To Catholics, Protestantism was heresy. It denied the authority of God's church and God's spokesman on Earth, the pope. To Protestants, Catholicism was blasphemous in suggesting that Christ's redemptive work on the cross needed assistance from humans in the form of good works. There was no reconciling the two, and the tension between them led to many conflicts, both on an individual and national scale.

Sliding into Protestantism

Now that we have a better idea of just what everyone was so upset about, let's return to the question of Protestantism in England. When Henry VIII broke with Rome, he denied the authority of the pope. As we have seen from the differences between Catholicism and Protestantism, rejecting the clergy's authority, particularly the pope, was to deny the source of truth itself. Henry VIII had led England down a slippery slope, and now it was just a matter of how fast the country would slide down it.

One of the big questions we must stop and ask at this point is just what everyone else was thinking at this time. Sure, Henry VIII had marital troubles, and he didn't like the pope telling him what to do, but he had to get Parliament to agree to break with Rome and create the Church of England.

The fact that Henry VIII does not appear to have had much trouble getting his nobles to agree to leave the Catholic Church indicates that Protestantism had at least some roots in England before the break with Rome. These Protestant sympathies among the ruling classes became more obvious after the break. People like Thomas Cromwell, Thomas Cranmer, and even Anne Boleyn tried to push Henry VIII toward more Protestant ideas. However, the king still considered himself a good Catholic, and other powerful people wanted him to stay that way. In some ways, the English court after the break with Rome was a microcosm of the religious tensions in Europe, as those with Catholic and Protestant sympathies sought to influence the king.

However, the debate between Catholicism and Protestantism would not be solved in Henry VIII's lifetime. Henry VIII never really leaned into Protestant doctrine, but as long as he denied the pope's authority, Catholicism wasn't truly an option either. The English court would continue to oscillate between Protestantism and Catholicism for the next several decades until Elizabeth I.

The Dissolution of the Monasteries

The English elite were made up of both Catholic and Protestant sympathizers, all of whom were trying to ensure that the king or queen was on their side. But how did the common people feel about all of this? Perhaps the best place to illustrate the difference between the move toward Protestantism in the upper and lower classes is with the dissolution of the monasteries.

Monasteries were a unique institution in the medieval and early modern era. They often served a critical role in the local area, acting as schools and hospitals, but as religious institutions, they were independent (not under the control of the government). When Henry VIII became the head of the Church of England, effectively combining the government and church, something had to be done with the eight hundred or so religious houses in England.

The natural solution seemed to be to fold the monasteries into the new religious system. This meant the monasteries had to accept the king's supremacy. In making himself head of all the monasteries, Henry VIII also made himself the owner of all monastic properties in England, which was no small amount. At this time, monasteries owned around a fourth of all the worked land in England. It was a very tempting acquisition for Henry VIII.

Still, it was not immediately obvious that the government intended to dissolve the monasteries. Things began with Henry VIII sending out commissioners, overseen by Thomas Cromwell, to visit and value the various monasteries. The information-gathering expeditions proved to be quite the ordeal. The government lacked the infrastructure to perform such a task satisfactorily, and the previously independent monasteries did not react well to the government sticking its nose in their business. However, Cromwell was a determined man, and despite setbacks, the commissioners completed several circuits of the kingdom's monasteries in the years following the break with Rome.

For a time, it appeared that the government's great interest in the monasteries would lead to reform. However, in 1536, the first Act of Suppression was passed, and the writing was on the wall. All monasteries whose income amounted to less than two hundred pounds a year were to be dissolved. Their possessions and land were to be taken by the Crown.

As you can imagine, many monasteries did not react well to this. There were widespread attempts to destroy monastic property and thus rob the Crown of its gain. Some monasteries were aided in this attempt by the local populace, while others found the locals took the opportunity to help themselves to monastic property. The reaction against the dissolution of the monasteries was so strong that it resulted in an uprising in the north.

The Pilgrimage of Grace, as it came to be known, was thoroughly and swiftly crushed by Henry VIII, but it did show there was an adverse reaction to the reforms amongst the general population. Monasteries played vital roles in communities. They were a place for the sick to seek treatment, for boys to receive some education, and even for the poor to seek shelter. Dissolving them was a noticeable disruption to local life, which caused some to protest against the top-down reformation that Henry VIII's government had imposed on England. It was clear that whatever Henry VIII's government had decided, the people of England were still attached to their old religious institutions.

However, the Pilgrimage of Grace did nothing to halt the changing tides. In 1539, the Second Act of Suppression was passed, which allowed for the dissolution of larger monasteries. By 1541, all of the monasteries in England had been dissolved.

The nobles of English society showed far less discontent than the working class had at this decision, and that was most likely because they benefited from it. Henry VIII gifted monastic lands to his supporters, which was a very simple and effective way to ensure that more of the upper class were at least outwardly embracing the religious changes. With the dissolution of the monasteries, England was sliding closer and closer to Protestantism, and the lower classes were being pulled along for the ride.

Habit and Belief

With moves like the dissolution of monasteries, the common people found their lives irrevocably changed, and there was unrest. The Pilgrimage of Grace in 1536 is one such example, as is the Prayer Book Rebellion of 1549. It is clear from these examples that England was not wholly Protestant in belief, but at some point, that attitude changed. By the time James II took the throne in 1685, the English people could not stomach the thought of a Catholic king. What changed? How did the English go from having Protestantism forced on them by Henry VIII and Edward VI to despising James II for being Catholic?

One reason may simply be nothing more than the nature of religion in this period. Today, we view religion as a choice, not only in whether you want to be religious or not but also in the myriad of different religious options available. In early modern England, religion was not a choice. Everyone was religious, and all of the churches were essentially the same. There was no going down the street to a different church if you didn't like the way your church conducted worship. Religion was a national affair, and everyone across the country was pretty much part of the same church.

This meant that whatever your personal beliefs, thanks to Henry VIII and the Reformation, you were now worshiping in a Protestant service. And as they say, habit builds character. Changing how the English people worshiped and even what they were taught in services were bound to eventually change their beliefs as well.

Since most people had little access to religious information outside of what their local priest told them, this transition likely occurred faster and smoother than we might anticipate since people simply followed the guidance of their local priest. Centuries of medieval Catholicism had trained the majority of people to follow the clergy, and ironically, that might have made England's transition to Protestantism easier. The top-down style of the English Reformation was effective partially because the old Catholic religious system already had a hierarchical structure in place. Protestantism was spread simply by changing the people at the top of this structure.

Fear of Popery

Of course, the problem with discussing the spread of Protestantism is that we are dealing with a matter of personal belief. We know that the English people were forced to act more Protestant through the changes instilled by their government, but it's very difficult to track what exactly this did to the average person's beliefs.

However, we can get a sense of just how Protestant England was becoming through external events. We know that England was truly becoming Protestant because of the rising fear of popery.

Until the 1534 break with Rome, England was Roman Catholic. After that, England's relationship with the Roman Catholic Church began to deteriorate. When Queen Mary took the throne and tried to push the nation back toward Catholicism, it only worsened the English people's opinion of Catholics. Mary burned around three hundred Protestants at the stake, and many more fled the country during her reign. Propaganda after Mary's death only served to worsen Mary's image and the overall view of Catholics.

The next major strike against Catholics in the English mind was the Gunpowder Plot of 1605. The Gunpowder Plot was a conspiracy hatched by some English Roman Catholics to blow up Parliament and kill the new king, James I.

Nothing makes paranoia worse than a real conspiracy. The Gunpowder Plot made Catholics the worst sort of villains in the eyes of the English people. To this day, people in England burn effigies of Guy Fawkes on November 5th every year. With the Gunpowder Plot, mistrust and fear of popery (Catholicism) were beginning to become part of the English culture.

England's Protestant government saw no reason to check this growing paranoia, and by 1678, it had reached its peak. In that year, a man named Titus Oates created a story that Jesuits were planning to assassinate Charles II and put his Catholic brother James on the throne. The conspiracy was entirely made up, but it resulted in dozens of arrests and even executions. It took years before the government was able to see through Oates's story, despite the fact that Titus Oates was an incredibly untrustworthy character with a bad reputation.

The success of the fabricated Popish Plot in stirring up England against Catholics demonstrates just how much the country was steeped in Protestantism. Distrust of Catholics was almost part of being English. The hostility against a common enemy united the English people and even helped contribute to a growing sense of nationalism. When James II, who was a known Catholic, took the throne, he never stood a chance.

In 1553, Mary was able to hold the throne until her death, despite being Catholic and even ordering the deaths of Protestants. By 1665, James II was king for only three years before being forced to flee. In the century between these two Catholic rulers, England had changed. While we may not be able to tell exactly at what point many English people accepted Protestantism, we can tell from the rising dislike of popery that it had become widely accepted. Catholicism was out, and Protestantism was there to stay.

The Puritans

To close this chapter on Protestantism in England, we should take a moment to ask ourselves just how Protestant England was. You might be thinking, based on their hatred of Catholics, that England was strictly Protestant, but that was far from the case. The Anglican Church or the Church of England was in many ways similar to the Catholic Church.

Understanding just where England fell on the Protestant spectrum may be most easily understood by looking at a smaller group within England's religious scene: the Puritans. Their name comes from the fact that they wanted to purify the Church of England by removing all Roman Catholic practices. The fact that such a group existed in the first place tells you already that the Church of England was not at the extreme end of Protestantism.

The Puritans were a rather outspoken group throughout the 16th and 17th centuries, and because of this, they were a source of frustration to the monarch. Puritans wanted the Church of England to be far more reformed, and there were enough of them in Parliament that Elizabeth I had to hear about it constantly. However, Elizabeth I was determined to stick with her moderate religious settlement, and the Puritans were repressed though not eliminated.

They continued to be an outspoken group in England, reaching the height of their influence during the Interregnum when Oliver Cromwell, who was a Puritan, ruled England as Lord Protector. After the English Restoration, though, England's patience with the Puritans sharply declined. Many Puritans, realizing they would never be able to create the pure religious state that they wanted in England, moved to try their experiment in the American colonies.

What this extremely brief history of the Puritans demonstrates is that England never fully embraced the more radical versions of Protestantism that were taking hold in places like Geneva and Germany. Starting with the break with Rome in 1534, England slipped further from Catholicism into Protestantism, but where they ultimately landed was fairly close to the middle.

Chapter 9: Law(s) and Order

Some things never change. No matter the time or the place, crime and disorder are something that every society has to find ways of dealing with. However, the way in which different societies at different times deal with issues of law and order varies greatly.

In the 16th and 17th centuries, law and order in England looked very different than it does now. If someone broke into your house, there were no police to call. If a riot broke out in the city of London, there was no standing army to put it down. If you were arrested, there was no jail to send you to as punishment. Maintaining peace and punishing offenders had to be achieved through different means than what we rely on today. Some of those means may seem strange or even brutal, while others may appear quite close to our modern procedures.

Common Law vs. Statutory Law

Before getting into specific laws and procedures for dealing with crime, we first need to discuss the basic breakdown of English law in this period. By the early modern era, English law was made up of both common law and statutory law.

Common law has been around since the Early Middle Ages and refers to law based on custom. Common law uses previous cases and decisions to decide the proper course of action in new cases. Before the existence of a written legal code, common law was the only thing keeping the English judicial system coherent and consistent.

Statutory law refers to written laws, such as acts of Parliament. In England, statutory law did not come into existence until Edward I's reign in the late 13th century. This was the first time that legislation was written down that both amended and clarified common law.

While we often think of the law as being a set of written rules (which would be statutory law), both English and American law to this day rely heavily on common law. Following common law means that we expect the court to refer back to previous cases and to act consistently in the way in which the law is interpreted. Then, when a court decides on a particular case, they are adding to common law. Courts do not create new laws, but how they rule sets a precedent, and that precedent is part of common law.

The early modern era was crucial for both common and statutory law. For common law, this period saw a much greater emphasis on documentation. Although common law is based on custom rather than statutes, the lack of a written record leaves far too much room for abuses. There is little that cannot be claimed when referring to an abstract body of legal tradition.

Writing down the already existing common law was of vast importance, and a man named Sir Edward Coke did much of this. In his four-volume *Institutes of the Lawes of England*, Coke examined what common law said about various legal matters, creating a much-needed and concise documentation of common law. Coke also aided common law in his eleven-volume *Reports*, which was a collection of court cases with Coke's commentary.

These books became important references for others since they were a valuable resource for clarifying just what the common law's customs were. Since common law is based on precedent, having records of those precedents is crucial.

Acts of Parliament

Of course, the early modern period also saw changes to statutory law, meaning it saw the creation of entirely new laws. While judges and courts are the ones who create common law through their interpretations and precedents, legislators are the ones who create statutory law.

Parliament was certainly busy during the 229 years of the early modern period, and we can't even begin to discuss all of the laws it passed. However, we will look at four particular acts of Parliament to get a better idea of what statutory law includes and how it was used in England at this time.

- **Poor Law:** The Poor Law refers to numerous laws passed in the Elizabethan era that were designed to address the growing problem of poverty. These laws gave responsibility for the poor to parishes. Parishes were to provide aid to the sick, infants, disabled, and elderly and provide work for the able-bodied poor, resulting in the creation of workhouses. We will learn more about why England faced a poverty problem and just how effective these relief efforts were in Chapter 11.

- **Book of Sports:** The Book of Sports was a declaration made by James I in 1618, which permitted recreational activities on Sunday. The Puritan reaction against this order was so strong that James I was forced to withdraw it. Charles I reinstated it, despite the still vocal opposition, in 1633, but it was overturned during the Interregnum and not made legal again until the English Restoration in 1660.

- **Clarendon Code:** The Clarendon Code, so-called because it was passed during the ministry of Edward Hyde (the Earl of Clarendon), was a series of four acts passed from 1661 to 1665 that attacked the Nonconformists or Dissenters. Nonconformists were Protestants who did not adhere to the beliefs and practices of the Church of England. The Corporation Act, the Act of Uniformity, the Conventicle Act, and the Five Mile Act did everything from excluding Nonconformists from holding church offices to making it illegal for them to worship. Essentially, the code was designed to make it impossible to be a Nonconformist in England.

- **Toleration Act:** The Clarendon Code proved to be ineffective in wiping out Nonconformists. Twenty-four years later, the Toleration Act was passed. This act granted freedom of worship to Nonconformists. They still faced legal discrimination in other areas, such as being unable to hold political office, but they could now have their own churches and preachers.

- These four acts of Parliament give a brief glimpse of what the lawmakers of the early modern period were interested in regulating. Many of the major acts of this time were focused on religion, which was a product of both the English government's new jurisdiction over religious matters following the break with Rome and the high religious tensions of the day. Creating the Church of England had combined the state and church, and the state was trying to figure out what aspects of religion they could control.

What stands out about statutory law in the early modern era was its readiness to regulate morality. In the phrase "law and order," we reveal our own modern mindset that the purpose of the law is to maintain order. However, in early modern England, there was more of a willingness to go beyond that purpose. Laws like the Book of Sports and the Clarendon Code are not necessarily about keeping order but more about guiding the people toward certain values and a particular religion. In the cases of both of these laws, though, the government soon learned that policing the people's morals and beliefs is practically impossible.

The Toleration Act is a clear sign that England was beginning to accept that trying to force a perfectly uniform religion on its people would never lead to lasting peace. Using the law to control people's personal beliefs simply does not work. The Toleration Act was still a long way off from religious freedom, but we can see a slight shift from laws regulating beliefs to a law that makes concessions to maintain order. This shift would continue over time, but even today, it is far from fully settled. Governments still struggle with finding the line in what laws can and cannot regulate about citizens' behavior.

Crime in Early Modern England

We have talked at length about the law, but that's only half the picture. To understand the state of overall order in early modern England, we also have to look at crime.

One assumption that many people make unwittingly is that violent crimes were rampant. After all, this was a time when dueling and fistfights were acceptable ways to settle a conflict. It was also a time when most people went around armed in some fashion. It seems like a recipe for a society to be torn apart by violence.

Surprisingly, this was not the case. Records from the day show that premeditated murder was rare. The majority of violent crimes were spontaneous, erupting as drunken brawls or in the heat of a dispute. However, even these spontaneous acts of violence were far from being the majority of criminal activity. That honor goes to a different class of crime.

Property offenses were by far the dominant crime in early modern England. Property-based crimes made up well over half of the court cases. Your stuff getting stolen was far more likely than you getting stabbed.

To some degree, the large degree of theft makes perfect sense. As we discussed in Chapter 7 on trade and exploration, the rich were getting richer, but this was not trickling down to the lower classes. The gap was only made more visible by population spikes that led to an ever-growing number of impoverished people. It should not come as a surprise that in a society where poverty was increasing, theft was common.

However, we should be careful in using this explanation of class warfare to account for all property offenses. Not all property offenses involved a poor person taking from a rich person. The lower classes also stole from each other, and neighbors of the same class were willing to take each other to court over these crimes, indicating that stealing was viewed as a punishable offense by virtually everyone. Even though it is likely that the economic realities did have an impact on the prevalence of theft, this was not a society embroiled in secret class warfare where the poor cheered each other on as they took from the rich.

Speaking of class warfare, some crimes did point to the struggle between the classes far more clearly. Rioting was fairly common and used by the lower classes to express their displeasure with a particular issue, such as an increase in food prices.

What is strange about rioting in this period is that it seems to have been a generally accepted safety valve through which the lower classes were allowed to vent their frustrations. While the government tended to react harshly against rebellions, which were organized political revolts, its reaction to riots was relatively lax. The hierarchical feudal system of the Middle Ages was disappearing, but there was still a paternalistic sense of duty that existed between the upper and lower classes. Lords were supposed to care for those under them, and the lower classes saw riots, despite their illegality, as a legitimate way of reminding the elite of their duty.

Another way in which crime often showed a difference between the upper and lower classes was in the area of moral offenses. Things like adultery and drunkenness were not only frowned upon but illegal. The punishments for such offenses typically involved public humiliation, such as being paraded through the streets or whipped in the square, to discourage such behavior.

In general, the lower classes were far less likely to drag someone to court over these types of offenses. For example, the elite attempted to outlaw unregulated alehouses because they viewed them as dens that bred immorality. However, the lower classes had no problem with their neighbors drinking wherever they chose, so the law against unregulated alehouses was virtually unenforceable.

Therefore, in certain moral offenses, we can see a sharp divide between the attitudes of the classes. What the wealthy viewed as criminal, the poor might view as a mere nuisance or entirely harmless. The lack of agreement on these types of offenses made enforcing them extremely difficult. The elite's attempt to police the lower class's morality was often a fruitless endeavor that showed just how necessary consistency is to the power of the law.

Enforcing the Law

We have talked about how people broke the law, but what happened after someone broke it? As we mentioned earlier in this chapter, jail time was not a common form of punishment. Jails in this period were simply used to hold those awaiting trial. They were not a way to punish offenders.

The biggest detriment of how the law was enforced in early modern England was the victim. As long as there were no deaths, the victim was the one who chose whether to get the law involved. Since punishments were harsh, there were instances of people working out their issues without resorting to a court decision.

If the victim decided to report the matter, they would inform the constable, whose responsibility was to investigate and make the arrest. However, the constable was a part-time position, so there was a real possibility that while the constable was trying to do this, the accused could catch wind of everything and flee.

If the accused were arrested, they were brought before the judge. At this point, if the victim wanted to prosecute the accused, they had to pay prosecuting costs. If the judge and victim agreed on the charge, an indictment would be created. A grand jury would then meet and decide whether the case went to court or if the indictment would be thrown out. If it went to court, the case would be tried before a jury, which determined innocence or guilt. The judge was the one who passed the sentence.

What this perhaps tedious explanation of the justice system shows us is two things. One, the early modern justice system has a lot in common with many justice systems today. Trial by jury was the standard, although it would be a while before that jury included anyone other than landowning white men.

Two, there were a lot of steps in the process, and all of those steps left the accused with many places to get out of trouble. Punishments were harsh. Stealing goods valued at over one shilling was a hangable offense, but we should not assume that meant early modern people were hanging everyone who stole a piece of bread. Even for those who made it all the way through the process and were found guilty by the jury, less than half were sentenced to death by the judge. Justice in early modern England was not that sadistic.

Then, why were the punishments so harsh? Remember, there were no police. There was no system for crime prevention. Enforcing the law was strictly regulated to punishing criminals. Punishments were harsh because this was seen as the only viable way to deter crime. The only way to stop someone from stealing was to make sure they were more afraid of what would happen if they were caught.

Accusations of Witchcraft

We have so far explored an overview of crime, law, and order in early modern England, but before we end the chapter, let's take the time to look at one of the most bizarre aspects of law and order in this period: witchcraft.

Despite what the movie *Monty Python and the Holy Grail* implies, accusations against witches were not common in the Middle Ages. In the

Middle Ages, they didn't even have any laws outlawing witchcraft. Parliament passed the first law making witchcraft a crime punishable by death in 1542, but the law was repealed just five years later. It was not until 1562 that it was restored. Things soon started to get out of hand.

For around eighty years in England, starting in the 1560s, accusations and prosecutions of alleged witches skyrocketed. One instance in Pendle in 1612 saw twelve people from two families accused of witchcraft. Of the twelve, one died while awaiting trial, and ten were found guilty and executed. Only one of the accused escaped with their life.

There has been a myriad of attempts to explain this sudden and unprecedented rise in the accusation and prosecution of witches. Some historians have connected it to the religious changes brought on by the Reformation, but that does not necessarily explain why the accused tended to fit the witch stereotype, typically being old, poor, single, and female. Feminists argue that it was the result of patriarchal society's attempts to exercise power and control over women, but this explanation does not seem to explain why women often accused other women or why this phenomenon occurred at this particular time. English society had been sexist (at least by our standards) for a long time.

In the case of the Pendle witches, there appear to have been multiple factors at play. Some of the accused did confess to believing in their own powers, and there was a rivalry between two families that likely fueled the accusations. Prior illnesses and deaths in the village were used as evidence, and a nine-year-old child was allowed to act as a key witness (something that was not allowed in English courts back then for any crime other than witchcraft). If the Pendle witch trial is anything to go on, it is hard and likely incorrect to point to a single reason as the definitive explanation for this strange phenomenon.

The eighty years in which witchcraft trials exploded serves as a grim reminder that while the early modern period was the time of the Renaissance and many advancements, superstition still abounded. The narrative that this period left behind the dark ignorance of the Middle Ages does not tell the whole story. We should be wary of any historical explanation that acts as those a country makes nothing but uphill progress. Accusing people of witchcraft was not a problem in the Middle Ages. It was a uniquely early modern phenomenon.

Chapter 10: Revolution and Rebellion

Early modern England was nothing if not a time of change. The Reformation produced religious changes that rippled outward, impacting all levels of society. Exploration introduced new products and brought in new wealth. The Renaissance widened the scope of education and caused innovation in the arts and sciences. The overall population was growing, and the importance of urban areas was increasing as England slowly began to move from an agrarian to an industrial society.

All of those changes created the England we know today, but if there's one thing we all know about change, it is that's it hard. England was a pot that was constantly being stirred, which created quite a bit of agitation. A time rife with change was also rife with revolutions and rebellions. Here are some of the most interesting and most important ones from the early modern era.

The Cornish Rebellion (1497)

Cornwall has always had a strong sense of identity and autonomy, and the Cornish Rebellion of 1497 is a potent example of that.

It was twelve years after the Wars of the Roses. Henry VII's grip on the throne was relatively secure, but there were those who were not ready to completely give up the Yorkist claim. The problem was a man named Perkin Warbeck. Warbeck claimed to be Richard, Duke of York, one of the princes who had been imprisoned in the Tower of London by their uncle, Richard III, and then presumably killed. Warbeck's story wasn't convincing, but he managed to gain the support of James IV of Scotland, who supported Warbeck as the rightful claimant to the English throne, likely because he wanted to cause trouble for Henry VII and England.

With James IV's support, Warbeck became a real threat, and Henry VII had to deal with him. However, this was happening in Scotland in the north. What does it have to do with Cornwall? Fighting wars takes money, and as one of the measures to raise money, Henry VII raised taxes in Cornwall.

As much as we don't like the government raising taxes today, in 1497, it was even worse. A centralized government was still a relatively new concept. The idea that the government could take money from people in one region to deal with a problem in a separate region was strange, and the Cornish people didn't like it.

Still, that might not have pushed them over the edge if Henry VII hadn't added another insult: dissolving the Stannary Parliament. Tin mining was so big in Cornwall that it had its own law and government institution: the Stannary Parliament. Although the Stannary Parliament was not technically a national assembly (it only controlled tin mining), so many people in Cornwall were involved in tin mining that it was a powerful institution and gave Cornwall a sense of autonomy. Thus, Henry VII dissolving it was a slap in the face to the Cornish. Adding that to the new taxes was enough to push the region over the edge.

The angry Cornish rebels soon amassed around fifteen thousand people. They were enough of a threat for Henry VII to leave his conflict with Scotland and bring his forces south to deal with the uprising. The two sides faced off outside London at the Battle of Blackheath on June 17th, 1497.

The outcome was almost inevitable. The rebels were outnumbered and had no military experience or leadership. The king's forces crushed them. However, despite losing the battle, the Cornish got what they wanted. Henry VII brought back the Stannary Parliament, and he never tried to tax Cornwall so highly again.

Because the rebellion was fairly successful in its aims, the Cornish Rebellion of 1497 is seen as a high point for Cornwall. To this day, the region continues to maintain a sense of independence and identity.

The Prayer Book Rebellion and Kett's Rebellion (1549)

The Prayer Book Rebellion and Kett's Rebellion are two popular uprisings that occurred in different regions of England around the same time in 1549.

The Prayer Book Rebellion, as the name implies, started because of the *Book of Common Prayer*. Parliament had passed the Act of Uniformity, which required the new English prayer book to be used. In the west of England, the common people did not take kindly to this and began to demand that the services be returned to Latin.

The unrest caused by the changes to religious services was only made worse by the economic problems. The population was growing faster than the economy could adjust. There were too many people and not enough jobs and resources. These economic problems caused another rebellion to break out in the north of Norfolk.

Kett's Rebellion began as a riot when Robert Kett enclosed his land. Enclosure was when the English gentry seized control of common land, which was available for use by everyone. You can imagine why enclosing land made so many people angry, especially during times of economic hardship. Common land was often the only land those further down the social ladder had access to.

Enclosure riots were extremely common in this period, but what was remarkable about the one in Norfolk in 1549 was that Robert Kett listened. He agreed with the rioters. He joined them and ended up leading a mass of rebels. The rebels were even able to capture the city of Norwich and sent a list of demands to the government, which included moderate requests like reducing rent and radical ones like ending private land ownership.

While one rebellion was more religious in nature and one more economic, the fact that both the Prayer Book Rebellion and Kett's Rebellion broke out around the same time shows just how tense this time was. Religious changes and economic problems were putting a strain on the English people, and the pot was starting to boil over.

Ultimately, the pot did not boil completely because both rebellions were put down similarly: they were put down brutally. John Dudley used the rebellions as a chance to seize power. He dealt with both Kett's Rebellion in the north and the Prayer Book Rebellion in the west by raising an army and swiftly crushing the rebels. By doing this, he proved his ability to maintain order and became the de facto leader of the country until Edward VI's death.

Such effective crushing of popular uprisings was typical of the Tudor era. While the people's grievances were often reasonable, the dissolution of order could not be allowed. This strict attitude may have kept England from dissolving into something more chaotic during the chaos of the Reformation.

The English Civil War (1642–1651)

The English Civil War had some drastic consequences. It ended with the execution of a king and led to eleven years where England was without a king (the Interregnum). But what started it in the first place?

As we discussed in Chapter 3, Charles I was a king who believed greatly in his power. However, by the 1600s, Parliament had been around for over four hundred years, and its members were used to having the monarchs heed their advice.

The sticking point, as usual, was war and money. Monarchs wage wars, but wars cost money, and under the English governing system, taxes could only be raised with Parliament's consent. By the late 1620s, Parliament had had enough of war (at least enough of Charles I's wars because he kept losing). There were several disagreements between Charles I and Parliament at this time, but it culminated in a dramatic ending of Parliament in 1629.

Parliament and Charles I were in open disagreement. Charles I again wanted money to fight wars, but Parliament did not want to give it to him. Seeing that he was getting nowhere, Charles I decided to dissolve Parliament, but this time, the assembly refused to go quietly. Parliament was adjourned when the speaker of the House of Commons announced the adjournment and rose from his chair. When the speaker tried to rise and adjourn the House on March 2nd, 1629, several members of Parliament forcibly held him down so that the House could pass three further resolutions, all of which condemned Charles I's actions. It was an open and clear statement that Parliament did not believe it existed to do the king's bidding. Charles I was furious. He would not call another meeting of Parliament during the next eleven years.

The eleven-year period in which Charles I tried to rule without Parliament is known as the Personal Rule, and it required Charles I to get quite creative. Running a country takes money. The typical way governments get that money is through taxation, and only Parliament could approve taxes. To meet his financial needs without the ability to levy taxes, Charles I relied on a combination of stricter budgeting and several other creative methods, such as selling monopolies, collecting fines, and leveraging taxes from laws that were long forgotten but still technically on the books.

This was not enough. Scotland rebelled, and Charles I had to have money to raise an army. In the spring of 1640, Charles I called Parliament again. Parliament, however, was not about to give Charles I the money he wanted to raise an army. After eleven years of Personal Rule, Parliament did not trust Charles I. When it became clear that Parliament was not going to give Charles I what he wanted, he dissolved the assembly after only three short weeks, giving this event the nickname of the Short Parliament.

Dismissing Parliament did not solve Charles I's problems, though. Scotland was still in rebellion and making advances in the north of England. Without money, Charles I could not raise a royal army to stop the Scottish invasion. London itself was wide open, so later that same year (1640), Charles I was forced to call Parliament yet again. This time, the meeting would be much longer.

When the Long Parliament first met, the vast majority of the assembly was in agreement that Charles I had gone too far. A man named John Pym emerged as the leader of this huge majority, and Parliament began passing bills to reform the king's policies. With the threat of Scotland hanging over him, Charles I was forced to agree. As time went on, though, the bills became more and more radical. Parliament began to lose its unified front against the king as conservatives and then moderates began to think that Pym and his party were going too far. While they might have disagreed with the king's policies, many still did not question his right to rule, and the attacks on royal power were losing support.

By the end of 1641, Parliament, which had been firmly united at the beginning of 1640, was split in two. When Pym introduced the Grand Remonstrance, which was a list of grievances with the king, Pym's radical group barely won the vote, with the final count being 158 to 149. Parliament and the country were split into two groups: Royalists and Parliamentarians. Royalists believed the king should still be the practical ruler, while Parliamentarians wanted to push the government toward a constitutional monarchy.

At this time, with the country now split down the middle, Ireland rebelled. With both Scotland and Ireland up in arms, England needed an army, but for either Parliament or the king to raise one would be seen as a threat by the other side. Trust between the Royalist side and the Parliamentarian side had deteriorated to such a degree that there was no longer a path forward. Each side armed itself, and when Charles I raised his banner on August 22nd, 1642, the English Civil War began.

We do not have the space here to dive into the military details of this conflict, but the hostilities lasted for around nine years. The main conflict between the forces of Charles I (nicknamed the Cavaliers) and the Parliamentarians (nicknamed the Roundheads due to their short-cropped hair) lasted for around four years, from 1642 to 1646. While the Cavaliers did well at the beginning of the conflict, they were unable to capture London, without which it was impossible to bring a true end to the conflict. During this time, Oliver Cromwell rose as a competent military leader of the Roundheads.

Cromwell at the Battle of Naseby by Charles Landseer.
https://commons.wikimedia.org/wiki/File:Charles_Landseer_Cromwell_Battle_of_Naseby.JPG

The turning point was the Battle of Naseby (June 14th, 1645). Here, the Roundheads won a decisive victory, and fortune turned against the

Cavaliers. Royalist forces continued to lose battles, and with the help of the Scottish, Parliament defeated the king's forces by 1646.

Now, what should happen at this point was clear to everyone involved. This was not the first time disagreements between the monarch and the ruling elite had come to blows. Barons and kings had fought against each other in the medieval period, and when the king lost such conflicts, the normal procedure was for the king to make concessions. Beating the king in a war meant he had to agree to the winners' demands. It did not mean that he stopped being king.

In 1646, this is what everyone expected to happen. Charles I had lost, and he would have to do at least some of what the Parliamentarians wanted. However, Charles I decided that he would make no concessions. Despite having lost the war and being under house arrest, Charles I believed so strongly in his own sovereignty that he refused to negotiate with the victors. Efforts to speak to the king and reach an agreement lasted for three years. Finally, in 1649, Parliament turned to drastic measures. Charles I was tried for treason and executed. England had killed its king.

The fighting dragged on after the execution of Charles I, lasting until around 1652. Both Ireland and Scotland chose to support Charles II, Charles I's son, but Cromwell and his army were able to defeat all opponents. When Charles II fled to France in 1651, the hostilities ended. The English Civil War was over, and England had overthrown its king.

We know with the benefit of hindsight that this situation did not last. England was without a king for eleven years, during which time Oliver Cromwell ruled as Lord Protector. Once Cromwell died, England found itself unsure how to proceed, and Charles II was invited back. The monarchy was restored in 1660.

Because the monarchy was restored, many people today overlook the English Civil War when considering the end of the monarchy and the beginning of democracy in Europe. We often look to the American and French Revolutions as the beginning of the end of monarchy, but a century before those revolutions, England had proven there was indeed a limit to how far a king could exercise his power.

The fact that England restored its monarchy after this tumultuous period simply shows that there was still relatively little understanding or thought put into what an alternate government would look like. Under Cromwell, England's government was far closer to a constitutional monarchy than a republic. Nevertheless, the English Civil War is important. It would spark a century of thinking and political philosophy that would provide the foundation for the later American and French Revolutions.

The Glorious Revolution (1688–1689)

What makes a revolution glorious? Is it the fight for a noble cause? Is it a bloody overthrow of a tyrannical government? Is it the upending of an old system to be replaced by something new? In the case of the Glorious Revolution, it was quite the opposite. The Glorious Revolution was almost bloodless, and it was a revolution against change rather than for change. It all started with England's greatest fear: a Catholic monarch.

If you are interested in what James II was really like, you should read the profile on him in Chapter 3, but to understand why the Glorious Revolution occurred, there are a few key things to know.

1. James II was Roman Catholic. This made him instantly distrustful in the eyes of pretty much every proper English person.

2. James II reacted to the distrust of his people poorly. Feeling that he could not trust Anglicans, he began to fill his court full of Catholics and Dissenters, two unpopular groups.

3. James II made the mistake of trying to push more religious tolerance on the English people. He wanted to repeal the discriminatory laws against Catholics and Dissenters. While today, we can hopefully see that discrimination based on religion is bad, in 17th-century England, religious tolerance was a very unpopular move.

4. James II's final sin was being a father. While he had two Protestant daughters, in 1688, James's new Catholic wife gave birth to a son. The nation was appalled. A Catholic king was one thing, but a Catholic heir was unbearable.

Thanks to a combination of these four things, James II was a very unpopular king. In fact, he was so unpopular that in the summer his son was born, a group of England's most powerful men took a drastic step. They invited William of Orange to invade England.

But who was William of Orange? William of Orange was the husband of James's eldest daughter Mary. She was, thus, excluding James II's new son, next in line for the throne, and she was a good Protestant. What's more, her husband, William, was a capable military commander. He was deeply involved in a conflict with the Catholic nation of France, and he saw helping rid England of its Catholic monarch as a way to secure English help. He was the Protestant savior who would rescue England from the Catholics.

William of Orange landing in England by Hoynck van Papendrecht.
https://commons.wikimedia.org/wiki/File:William_of_Orange_III_and_his_Dutch_army_land_in_Brixham,_1688.jpg

On November 5th, 1688, William of Orange landed in England with an invading force. While landing had proven easy due to fortuitous winds, James II still had a large army. It was very likely that he would succeed in driving the would-be invader back into the sea.

At least, it should have been very likely, but this was an invader who had been invited by James II's own people, and those frayed loyalties soon began to show. James II's advisers and commanders abandoned him, defecting to William's side. James saw the writing on the wall and made his escape, fleeing to the continent.

After James II had made his escape, William of Orange marched into London at the head of an invading army that he hadn't even had to use.

While there was a debate in Parliament over whether to give the crown to William, it was ultimately decided that in fleeing, James II had abdicated the throne. William and Mary were made the king and queen of England.

The Glorious Revolution got its name because it was a bloodless and extremely smooth transition of power. This smooth transition also caused people to think that it was divinely ordained, adding to the idea of it being "glorious."

The Glorious Revolution was proof that not every revolution had to be as bloody as the English Civil War. Ironically though, the Glorious Revolution was not too revolutionary. It was a revolution started over the fear of Catholicism and a distaste for religious tolerance.

Chapter 11: Societal Structure

So far in this book, we have spent the majority of our focus on the larger trends and events of the period. We have talked about revolutions, monarchs, religion, and trade. These are all the broad strokes that make up history.

But what about the small strokes of history? What was life like in England in the 16th and 17th centuries? What was the difference in the daily lives of the elite and the poor? In this chapter, we will take a look at early modern English society. From the hierarchical structure to the differences between genders and more, we will learn what one could expect out of life in early modern England.

The Great Chain of Being

The fact that society tends to break into different classes is a universal fact of humanity. When you put enough people together for a long enough period, eventually there emerges the "haves" and the "have nots." The fundamental economic problem of scarcity means that as long as we have limited resources, there will always be the rich and the poor.

However, while the existence of disparity in economics means that a class divide is almost inevitable, social classes are far from universal in how they appear in each society. The de facto divides of economics are often only the beginning. They become permanent or are added to by divides based on things like race, bloodlines, religion, etc. The picture of the "haves" and the "have nots" becomes far more complex when we add in these other social considerations. At its most basic, societal structures may be very similar across time and space, but the individual context makes that structure unique. So, our question then is not whether early modern England had social classes but what defined this period and made its social classes unique.

In early modern England, the governing principle that supported the social hierarchy was a philosophical concept known as the Great Chain of Being. The Great Chain of Being was first introduced by the Neoplatonists and saw a revival of interest in Europe during the Renaissance. It consists of three major points: plenitude, continuity, and gradation.

Plenitude is the idea that the universe is "full." Everything possible exists. Continuity is the idea that while the universe is infinitely diverse (as established in the point of plentitude), everything in the universe shares an attribute with something else. Nothing is totally unique. The final point, gradation, then says that the commonalities between the different components of the universe are not random but exist in a linear hierarchy. The top of this hierarchy is perfection itself, which was commonly understood to be God, and the hierarchy then goes down, with each component becoming less "perfect" until it covers everything in existence.

You may be wondering what such a philosophical concept has to do with social structure, and the answer lies in large part with the concept of hierarchy. The Great Chain of Being sees the universe as being ordered through a hierarchy. If the universe is a hierarchy, then the natural social hierarchy that emerges through economics and other factors is a part of the order of the universe. It is not just that a noble has more money and therefore is in a higher position than a yeoman. It is that this disparity is integral to the very nature of existence. The Great Chain of Being provides an explanation for and justification of social classes. To attempt to break out of one's social class would be to overturn the very order of the universe. To uphold stability, the social hierarchy must be maintained.

Before you immediately dismiss this understanding of the world as nothing more than a trick to keep the lower classes down, you should remember that people in this time were more afraid of anarchy. They were emerging from the Middle Ages, which was a time full of bloody internal conflicts. For the people of early modern England, especially the elite, it was more important to maintain order than it was to ensure that people had personal freedom. This is not to say they were correct about the Great Chain of Being, but we should remember that different values cause society to be structured differently. If society values order more than freedom, it tends to be stricter about social hierarchies.

The Social Classes

So, what were the social classes in early modern England? Today, we might use terms like the upper, middle, and lower class, but in early modern England, things were a bit more specific. The social classes in order were the nobility, the gentry, the yeomanry, and the poor.

The nobility and the gentry were the elite of society. Nobles were those who held aristocratic titles. Besides royalty, the nobility includes (in order of rank) dukes, marquesses, earls, viscounts, and barons. These are the members of English society who sat in the House of Lords and who surrounded the monarch. The early modern period saw an increase in the number of noble families. After the bloody Wars of the Roses, the number of noble families left in England was less than fifty. That number steadily grew throughout the 16th and 17th centuries, but even so, the nobility made up a very small portion of society, with the total number of noble families in the early modern period reaching less than two hundred.

By contrast, the gentry grew much more rapidly, and part of the reason for that was that the understanding of who exactly qualified as a gentleman was expanding. Traditionally, gentlemen were those who owned land but were not part of the nobility. This included knights, esquires, and baronets, a title added by James I. Gentlemen could also include those without any title who owned an estate. This understanding of a gentleman began to expand once professionals with an education could be considered members of the gentry.

In short, the definition of a gentleman was a bit vague. The main thing for all of the elite was that they did not work. This did not mean that the nobility and gentry sat around doing nothing all the time (although that was part of it). The definition of work in those days meant manual labor. The elite did not work with their hands, but they did work in the government and ran their estates.

The next group on the social ladder was the yeomen, who were the closest to the middle class. Yeomen either owned land or were freeholders (people who technically rented land but who could not be evicted and who could do with the land what they wanted). Yeomen generally worked their own land but were well off enough to have farmhands and servants as well. Their sons (and daughters on occasion) often received at least some education.

These top three groups were the ones who owned all the land in England, but they only made up around 10 percent of the population. The other 90 percent of people in England were considered poor.

The poor class is a very broad term that encompasses a wide spectrum. Those just below the yeomen were cottagers and husbandmen. Husbandmen were tenants who rented land that they worked for food and income. The terms of their leases were often harsh, and they could be thrown out at any time. Cottagers rented cottages from landlords but typically had little to no land, leaving them to earn wages to support themselves.

After the husbandmen and cottagers were the homeless, those who migrated for work or who had become destitute to the point of losing their homes. Society had no place for these people. They did not fit into the established social order of landlords and tenants, thus violating the Great Chain of Being. Because of this violation of the natural order, this group was widely mistrusted, yet their numbers continued to grow.

There was a significant gap between husbandmen and the migratory poor without a home, but they were all included in a single social class because of how easy it was to move between them. Social classes back then had fairly rigid boundaries. It was not easy (or often even realistically possible) to move between social classes, but when hard times came, it was very easy for a cottager or husbandman to become completely impoverished and lose their homes.

The Growing Poor

Poverty and the growing number of migratory poor increased in early modern England.

The biggest reason for the increase in the number of poor was a simple matter of arithmetic. The population in early modern England was increasing drastically, more than doubling in seventy-five years (from 1525 to 1600).

Unfortunately, agricultural technology did not advance as rapidly. Food production did not increase at the same rate as the population. This caused food prices to increase while wages remained the same. The result was inevitable for many people. They could not buy food and pay their rent. Eventually, they lost their homes and had to resort to begging or wandering in search of work.

The increasing number of poor became an even bigger issue after the Reformation and dissolution of monasteries. Catholicism's emphasis on good works made taking care of the poor a duty. With the Protestant emphasis on faith alone, the amount of private charity gradually declined.

Worse than this was the dissolution of the monasteries. Monasteries had been places where the poor could seek medical attention and other basic needs. With them gone, England had lost its biggest charitable institutions at a time when poverty was on the rise.

Because of these issues, England's first Poor Law was passed during Elizabeth I's reign. For the first time, the poor were considered to be the responsibility of the state rather than the church. The new laws made each local parish responsible for caring for their poor, and the money for this was raised through local taxes.

How did the government help the poor, though? The able-bodied poor were sent to workhouses, where they performed some sort of work, such as spinning wool, and were, in theory, cared for in exchange. Workhouses were not nice places. Families were separated, and the inhabitants were often treated harshly.

The miserable state of workhouses demonstrates the overall hostile view many people in this era had of the poor. Able-bodied people who did not work were seen as lazy and criminals. There was little understanding of the idea that there might be more people than jobs. This had never been the case before, so society viewed this growing class of vagrants as purposefully deviant. Stories about groups of hardened criminal bands wandering the countryside abounded while being completely unfounded.

The mistrust and harsh treatment caused many of the poor to seek a better life somewhere else. Many chose to travel to the colonies as indentured servants. Some colonies were even designed to provide a place for England's growing number of debtors and other undesirables.

This poverty problem was one way in which we see England straining to grow. This period was the beginning of modernization, but that development did not come without challenges.

Private Life

Those are the groups that made up the societal structure in early modern England, but what was life like for the different classes? As you can probably guess, life was quite different for the elite than it was for the lower classes.

During the Middle Ages, the upper classes were the fighters of society. Feudalism was a system based on the idea that the lower classes worked the land and provided the necessities of life while the upper classes protected the land. In the early modern era, the ruling elite's role began to shift from focusing on warfare to service. The nobility were the administrators who ran the government and, through it, the economy, the justice system, and more.

These types of roles meant that upper-class life was a public affair. When noblewomen gave birth, their babies were typically handed over to a wet nurse so that the mother could return to running the household as quickly as possible. Marriage was an economic and strategic exchange that required planning and impacted far more than just the couple. As time went on, nobles started spending more time in London instead of at their secluded country estates, as they wanted to be close to the seat of government and the positions they either held or wanted. The medieval era had seen local lords exercising control over a particular region. The early modern era saw the power of the upper classes become more nationalized in the central government.

The increasing public role of the upper classes put a strain on their private lives. Married couples might spend most of their lives apart, as wives stayed in the country running the estates while their husbands worked in London. Children were separated from their parents almost as soon as they were born. Even when at home, the elite were expected to frequently act as hosts.

We can see the effect this had on the psyche of the upper classes in the layout of their homes. The homes of the wealthy tended to be in the shape of an E or an H, which allowed for distinct wings. One side of the house would be for public life, such as lavish dinners and greeting guests. The other side was the family's private chambers, where they could retreat from the public eye. This period even saw the inclusion of a withdrawing room (this term was eventually shortened to drawing room) where the family could relax in private.

So, being a part of the upper class was not all banquets and balls. There was a duty that came with it. You were expected to serve, and that meant that it was difficult to have a rich personal life. However, that does not mean that being wealthy was a burden. The elite still had it pretty easy. They prided themselves on never having to do manual labor and on being idle. They had a privileged position, even if it did come with a string or two.

In some ways, the experience of the lower classes was the exact opposite of that. While in the nobility, a husband and wife might spend most of the year living in separate parts of the country, spouses with less money and lower positions usually worked alongside each other. Children were nursed and raised by their actual mothers instead of by wet nurses and tutors. Family units also tended to be much smaller since homes were not big enough to house multiple generations. The lower life expectancy meant that multiple generations also rarely occurred.

Marriage was not nearly as business-like for the poor, but there were still economic considerations. A man had to be able to support his wife, and it often took years for a man to get to the point where he could do that. Because of this, the poor tended to marry far later in life than the rich, which also meant they often had fewer children because the women had fewer childbearing years left by the time they married.

So, the poor had more opportunities to choose their spouses, spend time with their children, and generally be with their families more, but it was still hard to be a poor person. Your economic position was insecure. A few years of bad harvests could turn a husbandman into a vagrant, or your landlord could kick you off his land without warning. Food prices were rising, wages were not increasing at the same rate, and the wool industry, which was England's biggest industry, stagnated in the late 16th and early 17th centuries. Early modern England was a place where the poor were getting poorer while the rich got richer, and the tensions this placed on society erupted in the form of riots and popular rebellions.

Still, a poor person in early modern England had it better than a poor person in the medieval era. The houses of even the poor were sturdier and larger. While food prices were a problem, access to food was less of one thanks to the expansion of trade. You were far less likely to sleep on a dirt floor or die of starvation. For these reasons, we must acknowledge that England was making progress. The social classes remained distinct, but what life was like at the bottom of the hierarchy was slowly improving.

Chapter 12: Battles and Wars Abroad

When examining the history of a particular country, there is a danger of developing tunnel vision. England was not isolated from the rest of the world at this time. In fact, it was interacting more than ever with other countries, and not all of those interactions were friendly.

The early modern era saw the rise of world powers. Empires were beginning, and countries were pushing to dominate. How England handled itself in these conflicts against foreign nations would determine if it could rise to the status of superpower.

The Conflict with Spain (1585–1604)

During the first half of the 16th century, England had a relatively good relationship with Spain. However, that began to change when Elizabeth I took the throne in 1558.

Philip II of Spain had been married to Elizabeth's half-sister, Queen Mary. When the Protestant Elizabeth took the throne, there was apprehension about whether Philip II would make a move to push England back to Catholicism. Although nothing happened at the time, and Philip appeared to have no problem with his sister-in-law taking the throne, it was the beginning of a mistrustful relationship that would eventually explode into open hostilities.

Surprisingly, religion did not ultimately cause the split between Spain and England. It was Spain's success. During the first half of Elizabeth I's reign, Spain's empire continued to grow and, with it, its wealth and power. England grew increasingly uncomfortable with the might of this Catholic kingdom and increasingly desirous of a piece of what Spain had.

When the Spanish attacked an English slave fleet in 1568, Elizabeth I had the excuse she needed to start taking a bite out of Spain. English privateers soon began raiding Spanish settlements and ships, stealing both goods and bullion. Elizabeth I officially denounced these acts, but unofficially, she authorized and even encouraged them. But Spain had a way to indirectly fire back at England.

Elizabeth I was unmarried and thus without an heir. Her closest royal relative was Mary, Queen of Scots. Mary had been kicked out of Scotland and was currently residing in England. She had one quality that made her useful to the Spanish. Mary, Queen of Scots was Roman Catholic.

There were still many Roman Catholics in England who found the idea of a Roman Catholic on the throne appealing. Thus, Mary, Queen of Scots was the center of plots and conspiracies, and it is almost certain that the Spanish were involved in a number of these. A Roman Catholic would be far more sympathetic to the Spanish than the piracy-approving Protestant Queen Elizabeth I.

Piracy and plots caused tensions between Spain and England to rise, but the two countries might have managed to keep the peace were it not for another problem: the Netherlands. The Netherlands had become a Spanish possession in 1556 when Philip II inherited the crown, and the Dutch were not thrilled about it. In the late 1560s, a revolt against Spanish rule broke out in the north of the Netherlands, which was a Calvinist-dominated area that was unhappy with the rule of Catholic Spain.

Elizabeth I had to make a decision. Would she support her fellow monarch Philip II, or would she support the Dutch Protestants? While Elizabeth I was notorious for delaying such momentous decisions, her hand was forced by circumstances. A Spanish ship carrying quite a lot of gold was forced to shelter in an English port. The Spanish assumed the English would seize the ship and arrested English merchants in the Netherlands, seizing these English goods in retaliation for something

Elizabeth I had not done yet. Her response was to do exactly what they expected. She seized the Spanish ship and began supporting the Dutch rebels with money.

England and Spain had once been allies, but by 1568, the trust between them had completely disappeared. Still, neither country was eager for war, and it would take another seventeen years for open hostilities to erupt. In 1585, Elizabeth I sent English troops to the Netherlands to support the rebellion. For Philip II, it was an act of war. The Spanish king soon began making plans to invade England.

Philip II had every intention of thoroughly crushing the English. Over the next 3 years, he amassed an invasion fleet of 130 ships. The fleet was to carry over thirty thousand troops for a full-scale invasion of England.

Elizabeth I did not have an army that could hope to compete with such a force. The English army was made up of poorly trained or completely untrained troops. Spain's army was well trained and well paid. If the Spanish landed their army, England would be in trouble. Their only real chance was to stop the fleet at sea.

England's Royal Navy was not in as terrible of a position as you might think. The Spanish fleet was large, but it was also slower and lacked a significant number of heavy cannons, which would have allowed them to engage the English at a distance.

As the Spanish fleet proceeded through the Channel, it was harried by the more maneuverable English ships. When the fleet docked at Calais, the English sent fire ships into the harbor, forcing the fleet to scatter. Once they were out of formation, they were easy targets for the Royal Navy.

Hopes of invasion were now over. The Spanish fleet retreated, but the ships were unable to make the passage through the Channel because it was controlled by the English. Instead, they sailed around Scotland and Ireland, but unfavorable winds kept the ships floundering. By the time the armada limped back to Spain, half of it was gone.

The *Defeat of the Spanish Armada* by Philip James de Loutherbourg.
https://commons.wikimedia.org/wiki/File:Defeat_of_the_Spanish_Armada,_8_August_1588_RMG_BHC0264.tiff)

The defeat of the Spanish Armada was a major moment for England. They had proven themselves able to stand against Europe's mightiest power, which did a lot for English confidence. England's command of the seas would go on to be a major reason for why it was able to dominate the empire game in the coming centuries.

While the defeat of the Spanish Armada in 1588 was a triumph for England, it was not the end of the conflict with Spain. The two superpowers continued to clash. England continued to support the Dutch rebels, and English privateers raided Spanish settlements in the New World with waning success. Spain, in turn, supported an Irish rebellion against England that turned into a very costly war.

The conflict with Spain was never declared war, but the expense of being in constant open hostilities with another nation put a strain on the English government. Parliament gained more power since Queen Elizabeth I needed more and more funds for military expeditions. This planted the seeds of the dispute between Parliament and the monarch, which would lead to the English Civil War decades later.

The Anglo-Dutch Wars

Spain was not the only country that England found itself competing with for command of the seas and trade. The Netherlands was also one of England's main rivals. England fought three wars against the Dutch between 1652 and 1672.

England's wars with the Dutch were mostly naval, as the two countries vied for control of the seas. The First Anglo-Dutch War erupted in 1652 due to high tensions over the control of trade. The English were dominant in this first conflict, and hostilities ended in 1654.

In the Second Anglo-Dutch War, the English were not as successful. The war began in 1665. In the same year, a plague epidemic broke out, and the following year, the Great Fire of London raged. By 1667, Charles II's government was broke, strained, and eager to win the war, but the Dutch wanted to press their advantage.

In 1667, the Dutch raided the dockyards in the Medway. The ships docked there had only skeleton crews, making them essentially defenseless. The Dutch were able to capture and burn several ships and even sailed off with the ship named *Royal Charles*. It was a great embarrassment to the English. They had been completely unable to defend themselves. Peace was made shortly after this.

After the embarrassment of the Raid on the Medway, England was eager to take revenge on the Dutch. War again broke out in 1672 but this time as part of a larger European conflict. In this war, England allied with France against the Netherlands. The Netherlands was able to hold off invasion attempts for two years. England dropped out of the alliance, making peace with the Netherlands in 1674. Soon after this, the Glorious Revolution saw the two countries sharing a ruler for a time. With a shared ruler came shared goals, namely stopping the French, and there would be around a century of peace between the Netherlands and England.

The conflict between the Netherlands and England demonstrates how economic rivalries led to bloodshed in this period. Both countries wanted to control trade, and they were willing to fight each other for that control.

War of the Grand Alliance (1688–1697)

When William of Orange invaded England in 1688 and became William III of England, it was largely with one goal in mind. He wanted England's aid in putting a halt to France's expansion efforts.

To William of Orange, France was a growing tyrant that was conquering Protestant Europe. France was making moves to absorb both the Dutch and the Spanish into its empire. Stopping France's expansion was William III's goal in life, and while he saw the English as being central to that goal, the English did not necessarily agree. They were part of a small country separated from the continent by the Channel. They did not see themselves as a superpower, and they did not see William's war against the French as affecting them. After fighting both the Spanish and the Dutch themselves in the last century, it would be a hard sell to convince the English that they should commit to an expensive war on the continent.

However, whether they meant to or not, the English had already committed themselves to a side in the conflict. They had invited William of Orange to depose James II. After the Glorious Revolution, France supported James II in his hopes of reclaiming the throne, supporting him directly when he landed in Ireland in the hopes of winning his kingdom back. If England was against James II, then they were against France.

So, in choosing William III over James II, England found that it had agreed to an alliance against France. Although the English never showed great enthusiasm for the war, they were a part of the Grand Alliance, which included England, the United Provinces of the Netherlands, Austria, Spain, and other smaller states.

For a war that lasted nine years, the War of the Grand Alliance achieved relatively little. The war was mostly a matter of long sieges and stalemates. Neither side could win a decisive victory, and in 1697, peace was established by the Treaty of Rijswijk. The only problem was that the treaty did not fix anything. France still had hopes of expanding its empire, and the rest of Europe still did not want that to happen. The same issues would turn into another war only four years later.

The War of the Spanish Succession (1701–1714)

The War of the Spanish Succession was a continuation of the problems from the War of the Grand Alliance. The general issue was France's expansionist drive, but the specific problem was the Spanish succession.

Charles II was the childless king of Spain and the last of the Spanish Habsburgs. When he died, there would be no male heir to take the Spanish throne. Thanks to the constant marriage alliances of European royalty, both the Bourbon dynasty of France and the Austrian branch of the Habsburgs had fairly equal claims to the Spanish throne.

As Charles II's death drew closer, it became clearer that war was inevitable. Attempts were made to create a treaty that would divide the Spanish Empire rather than allow one person to inherit the entire thing, but no solution could be found that was satisfactory to everyone. The Spanish Empire was vast, and neither the Habsburgs nor the Bourbons were willing to give it up without a fight. Charles II died in 1700. King Louis XIV of France named his grandson, Philip, king of Spain, and war soon followed.

Technically, this had nothing to do with England directly, and England might have stayed out of the fight had Louis XIV not acknowledged James II's son as James III, the rightful king of England. If France was going to ally itself with England's enemies, then France could not be allowed to gain the Spanish Empire's power and wealth.

The military history of this thirteen-year war is complex. There were multiple fronts, many countries involved, and different stages to the conflict. There were several attempts at peace negotiations, but the war continued to drag on and on. England and its allies had many successes, thanks in large part to the military mind of John Churchill, but they could never gain enough ground or win a victory that would devastate France into ending the war.

In some ways, the war was simply too big. It covered too much ground for one side to seize complete control, and the military strategies of the time would not commit enough men to a bold offensive maneuver that would end the war in one stroke. The only way the war was going to end was through negotiations.

By 1711, Queen Anne and the majority of Parliament had had enough of the war, despite John Churchill's victories. The war was expensive, and those victories were not getting them closer to completely overwhelming France and forcing a surrender. It would take over two years to finalize the agreement that became the Treaty of Utrecht.

The Treaty of Utrecht was a true master play for Britain, although, on the surface, it did not appear that way to Britain's allies. Britain acknowledged Philip V as the king of Spain, which was the issue that had started the war in the first place, but France had to promise that Philip and his descendants were exempt from the French line of succession. The Crowns of France and Spain could never be united.

Britain also gained territories in the treaty, such as Gibraltar, Minorca, Nova Scotia, Newfoundland, Hudson's Bay, and St. Kitts. Another part of the treaty was the Asiento, which gave British slave traders a thirty-year monopoly on selling slaves to the Spanish Empire. King Louis XIV also had to promise to stop supporting James III's aims on the English crown.

For many, the territories Britain gained in the treaty and the promises the treaty required of France were nowhere near enough after thirteen years' worth of blood and money poured into the war. However, the Treaty of Utrecht placed Britain in a position that would allow it to become the dominant world power over the next century.

The territories Britain gained allowed it to expand its trading empire, and the Asiento was a further boon to Britain's trading power. Britain was setting itself up to prosper, while France had been broken economically by the war. Including the War of the Grand Alliance, France had been fighting for over twenty years. The country was spent, so while the Treaty of Utrecht might not have been harsh enough on France for some, there was no need for it to be. While France tried to recover from its scheme of making a grand empire, Britain continued to amass more wealth from its new colonies and trading deals.

This wealth would place Britain in a superior position as it continued to clash with France over the next century, allowing it to come out on top the vast majority of the time. The War of the Spanish Succession initially had very little to do with England, but thanks to its involvement in the war and the gains made in the Treaty of Utrecht, England was able to position itself to dominate and become the world's largest empire.

Chapter 13: Scotland and Wales

Although they share an island and are now part of the same nation, for most of their history, England, Wales, and Scotland have been three distinct countries.

The union of the island began in the medieval era with Edward I. Edward I conquered Wales in the 13th century. He nearly conquered Scotland as well, but the Scottish were able to maintain their sovereignty after a long conflict. From this point on, the heir of the English throne was given the title Prince of Wales as a sign of England's control over this territory.

However, Wales was not politically united with England at this time. While English kings ruled Wales by right of conquest, their governments remained separate. The justice system was different, and the Welsh had no members in the English Parliament. It was only in the early modern era that Wales officially joined England. Under Henry VIII, the Act of Union, which was passed in 1536, united Wales and England. English law would be used in Welsh courts, and Wales was divided up into local districts (shires and boroughs), which meant they could now elect members to English Parliament. Essentially, Wales and England were both operating under the same rule book, whereas before, they had the same king but different laws.

Scotland's union with England would eventually follow a similar pattern. When Elizabeth I died in 1604, her closest heir was James VI of Scotland. From that point on, England and Scotland had the same monarch. However, the two countries were not officially united until about one hundred years later with the 1707 Acts of Union during Queen Anne's reign. This act created the country of Great Britain.

Union Jack. (Source: Original code by Stefan-Xp with modifications to ratio by Yaddah. *https://commons.wikimedia.org/wiki/File:Flag_of_the_United_Kingdom_(3-5).svg*

Of course, the history of England, Scotland, and Wales in the early modern period involves a lot more than acts of union. While these three places made up the country of Great Britain, they were (and still are) three distinct places with complex and changing relationships. Here's a bit of what those relationships were like during the early modern period.

Scotland in the Tudor Era

Relations between England and Scotland had always been, for lack of a better word, tense. England repeatedly tried to conquer Scotland in the Middle Ages, and the northern country repeatedly tried to make life difficult for the English. Scottish raids over the Anglo-Scottish border were common, and one of Scotland's biggest allies was also one of England's biggest enemies: France. France and Scotland had been allies for so long that the relationship had come to be known as simply the Auld Alliance.

So, at the start of the early modern era, Scotland and England were not exactly best friends, and having an enemy as your nearest neighbor is enough to make anyone nervous. It is no wonder that the first Tudor king, Henry VII, married his daughter Margaret to James IV of Scotland in 1503. This marriage secured peace for a time, but by 1513, Scotland

and England were at blows again when Henry VIII invaded France, triggering Scotland to respond due to the Auld Alliance.

As the 16th century wore on, however, Scotland soon found itself infected by the same disease that was infecting all of Europe: the Reformation. Unlike England, which experienced a top-down Reformation, Scotland's monarchs remained Catholic for much longer. Scotland also had a weaker central government that exercised less control over the country. Scottish nobles wielded considerable political power, and as the Reformation spread throughout Scotland, many of these nobles (called lairds in Scotland), particularly those in the Lowlands, turned to Protestantism.

This was partially due to the preaching of men like John Knox, but it also was because of an increasing Scottish desire to break away from French influence. The last Scottish king, James V, died in 1542, leaving an infant daughter as queen and Scotland in the hands of her mother, Mary of Guise, who acted as regent. Mary of Guise was French and Catholic, and many Scottish lairds thought that she was turning Scotland into a French auxiliary. These suspicions were only exacerbated by Mary sending her daughter, who was technically the queen of Scotland, to be raised and educated in France. Mary of Guise also arranged for her daughter to marry the future French king, Francis II, making James V's daughter the queen of France and Scotland. With these acts, Mary of Guise was clearly tying Scotland more closely to the French, and embracing the new religion was a way to buck against the French and declare Scottish autonomy.

This bucking turned into a full rebellion in 1559, and the French sent troops to help Mary of Guise seize control again. The Scottish rebels then turned to England and Elizabeth I for assistance. This put Elizabeth I in a dilemma. She could support the Protestant rebels, declaring her sympathy with Protestantism, or she could support Mary of Guise, showing her support for a fellow monarch. It was always a risky suggestion for one monarch to help those rebelling against the authority of another monarch.

Ultimately, though, this was an opportunity for England to break up the Auld Alliance. If the French succeeded in putting Mary of Guise back in control of Scotland, England would have a Catholic enemy on its northern border, and what's worse, a Catholic enemy whose monarch (Mary, Queen of Scots) was also Elizabeth's cousin and the next in line for the English throne. England sided with the Scottish rebels. The conflict ended shortly after it began, thanks to the death of Mary of Guise in 1560. The Treaty of Edinburgh, which officially ended the hostilities, established religious tolerance in Scotland and set up a ruling council that was half Protestant and half Catholic.

Elizabeth I's decision to support the rebels proved to be a good move for England. Tensions between the two countries lessened considerably after this, and there was peace on the Anglo-Scottish border. The two countries were destined to grow even closer when the Scottish king became the next English monarch.

Same Monarch, Different Kingdoms

In 1603, James VI of Scotland became James I of England. We have talked in greater detail about how this came, so now let's look at what having the same monarch did to the relations between Scotland and England.

If you are thinking that one king trying to rule two different kingdoms with different governments and laws sounds like a bad idea, you wouldn't be the only one. James I thought the same thing, and when he first took the crown of England, he did his best to remedy the situation by promoting a union. Unfortunately for James I, England was having none of it. The English Parliament resolutely rejected the idea of a union with Scotland, revealing their deeply held prejudices. The English viewed their northern neighbors as poor and backward. They felt that to unite with Scotland would be to take on a burden.

So, where did this leave Scotland? Their king had headed off to London, where the Stuart monarchs would remain, ruling Scotland from afar. A king could not keep in touch with his people over such a long distance, and this became glaringly evident when Charles I tried to impose the English *Book of Common Prayer* on the Presbyterian Scots.

One should never underestimate what people are willing to do for their religious convictions. The Scottish didn't just riot or protest. In 1638, the Scottish created a document entitled the New Covenant, which was essentially a new constitution organizing the church and state. Rearranging the government without the king's consent can only be seen as an open rebellion. The Scottish rebels were known as the Covenanters after the document they had created. Charles I had to get Scotland in line. This was the start of the First Bishops' War.

The First Bishops' War didn't last very long. Charles I found that his English army was unenthusiastic about his cause, and he was broke. A truce was established in 1639, but it was only temporary. In England, things were falling apart. Charles I hadn't called Parliament to meet in eleven years, but he desperately needed funds to face the Scottish rebellion. The Scots pushed their advantage, starting the Second Bishops' War in 1640. They were quickly able to invade the north of England, forcing Charles I to turn to the English Parliament for assistance. This was the parliament that would come to be known as the Long Parliament and led to the English Civil War.

So, to some degree, the Scots caused the English Civil War, and their involvement in the conflict did not stop there. The English Civil War is perhaps more accurately called the War of the Three Kingdoms. Charles I was king of Scotland, England, and Ireland, so the war against him came to involve all three nations.

At first, Scotland was against Charles I. After all, it had technically been the first to rebel, but after Charles I was captured and the unfruitful negotiations began, Scotland entered its own negotiations with Charles I and agreed to restore him. This led to the outbreak of the Second English Civil War, but Oliver Cromwell's armies were able to stop the Scottish with ease. Charles I was soon executed, and Scotland found itself without a king for the next eleven years.

While the two countries were still politically separate entities, having the same king meant that Scotland found itself dragged along by what was happening in England, often whether it wanted to or not. This was again the case after the Glorious Revolution deposed James II. Jacobitism, which was the belief that James II and his male heirs were the rightful rulers of England, Scotland, and Ireland, had the strongest following in Scotland.

How is that possible though? Weren't the Scots Presbyterians? Why would they support a Catholic king? The history of Scotland during this period deserves an entire book of its own, but in short, things were more complex than just the idea that Scotland was full of Presbyterians after the Reformation. Before the Glorious Revolution, Scotland had seen a revival of Catholic power and persecution of Presbyterians. When the Glorious Revolution occurred, it returned the Presbyterians to power, but they returned to power full of resentment for the previous decade of bad treatment. The result was a less glorious and more bloody revolution in Scotland.

This bad blood only served to isolate certain groups: Episcopalians in the Lowlands and Catholics in the Highlands. These two groups would form the core of the staunch Jacobite movement that developed in Scotland over the next several decades.

With events like the English Civil War (the War of the Three Kingdoms) and the Glorious Revolution, it was obvious that Scotland and England were irretrievably intertwined, but it was unclear if that would continue. The Scottish were becoming increasingly annoyed at being ruled by London. In the early 18th century, the Scottish Parliament began passing laws that were anti-English, including one that said that after Queen Anne's death, Scotland would choose its next monarch.

This was very alarming to the English. It was likely that Scotland would pick Prince James, the son of James II. This would put a Catholic pro-French monarch on England's northern border. It would be a return to the Auld Alliance and most likely a return to the constant feuding that had shaped most of Scotland's and England's history.

When James I tried to unite England and Scotland in 1603, the English had been opposed to the idea, but now they had the motivation to make the union happen. The only question was how they could convince the Scots, who were currently very unhappy with their southern neighbors.

In the end, it came down to economics. Scotland was a poor nation, and a union with England offered wealth. As part of the union agreement, Scotland would be able to trade freely with England and its colonies. England was a trading giant, and Scotland would become part of that system. If that was not convincing enough for the Scots, the English also paid them a lump sum called the Equivalent. This was out-and-out bribery, but it got the job done. The Scottish Parliament voted to end their own government.

Scotland was now part of England. It still retained its individuality in things like its church and laws, but there was no parliament in Edinburgh. The Scots sat in the Parliament in London. Great Britain was born.

Wales: Same Kingdom, Different Language

Welsh flag.
https://commons.wikimedia.org/wiki/File:Flag_of_Wales.svg

We have examined England's relationship with its northern neighbor, but what about its western neighbor? As we mentioned in the introduction to this chapter, England conquered Wales back in the 13th century, but it was not until Henry VIII's reign that the two were officially united.

Why did Henry VIII suddenly decide to officially make Wales part of England? Was there some sort of pressure like with Scottish unification?

Not really. Unification with Wales was largely because Henry VIII realized that it would make governing a lot easier. As we mentioned in Chapter 1, the Tudor era saw the strengthening and centralization of the national government. To effectively rule his entire realm from London, Henry VIII needed Wales to use the same judicial system and districts. It was unification for the sake of bureaucracy.

But unification did not mean total assimilation. Wales remained its own place with its own culture, and we can see this best in its language. Although Wales had been conquered by England for over three centuries, in the early modern era, Welsh remained the main language. Most Welsh people did not know English.

The language difference was so pronounced that part of the unification treaty stipulated that all Welshmen who held government positions had to be able to speak English. This created a situation in which the Welsh elite were bilingual. The majority of people still only knew Welsh and had to rely on the bilingual elite for information from England.

The dominance of Welsh created an interesting situation in Wales with the arrival of the Reformation. The Reformation emphasized the importance of scripture, and as part of this, the Bible was translated into English so that the average person could read it. After the Reformation, church services were conducted in English instead of Latin. However, for the average person in Wales, religious services in English were little better than religious services in Latin.

Some leading Welsh scholars became convinced that Welsh translations of the Bible were necessary, both for the sake of religion and the Welsh culture. They succeeded in getting Parliament to pass an act requiring the Bible to be translated into Welsh. The New Testament and the *Book of Common Prayer* were translated by 1567, and by 1588, the entire Bible had been translated into Welsh.

The translation of the Bible into Welsh was a huge achievement for the Welsh people and also a smart move politically for England. The translation of the Bible into Welsh connected the Protestant movement with Welsh culture. Instead of forcing an English Reformation down the throats of the Welsh, it became the Welsh Reformation. In other places in the British Isles where a different language was spoken, namely Ireland and the Scottish Highlands, the Bible was translated much later. Catholicism had a much stronger grip on these areas.

Wales was far more closely aligned with England than Scotland, but it was still a distinct place. Another time where we see this is in the English Civil War. There was much royalist support in Wales in the dispute between Charles I and Parliament, but in the end, it didn't do Charles I much good. Like Scotland, Wales was poorer and less populated than England. They were not in a position to threaten its larger and wealthier neighbor.

It would be some time before Wales began to catch up to England in terms of wealth. In the early modern era, Wales remained an agricultural society. Progress was essentially a matter of enclosing and cultivating more land so that less was wasted. The rich were getting richer since they gained control of even more land, and the poor only continued to get poorer.

Eventually, the economy of Wales would change with the discovery of coal and its importance to the Industrial Revolution, but in the early modern era, Wales remained an agricultural-based society.

Overall, Wales experienced far less tension with England than Scotland did at this time, which makes sense considering that Scotland was still a separate country until 1707. Still, it is a mistake to lump Wales and England together too much. Even in the 16th century, the Welsh were proud enough of their cultural differences to want the Bible in their language. Wales was politically and governmentally united with England while maintaining a distinct culture that has carried on to this day.

While non-Britons may confuse the three regions of Great Britain, Wales, England, and Scotland are united but unique. The early modern era was when the union known as Great Britain started, and it is a union that has lasted to this day.

Chapter 14: The Irish Question

Scotland, Wales, and England don't have this small region of the world entirely to themselves. There was a fourth kingdom in the British Isles, and its relationship with England was messy.

Ireland, like Wales, was initially conquered by England in the Middle Ages during the time of Henry II, but unlike Wales, English control of Ireland was far from total. The English only managed to subdue part of Ireland. In the area controlled by the English, which came to be called the Pale, the Anglo-Irish nobles held power. Outside of the Pale, Ireland was controlled by the Gaelic Irish, and the land was split among various sects and chieftains.

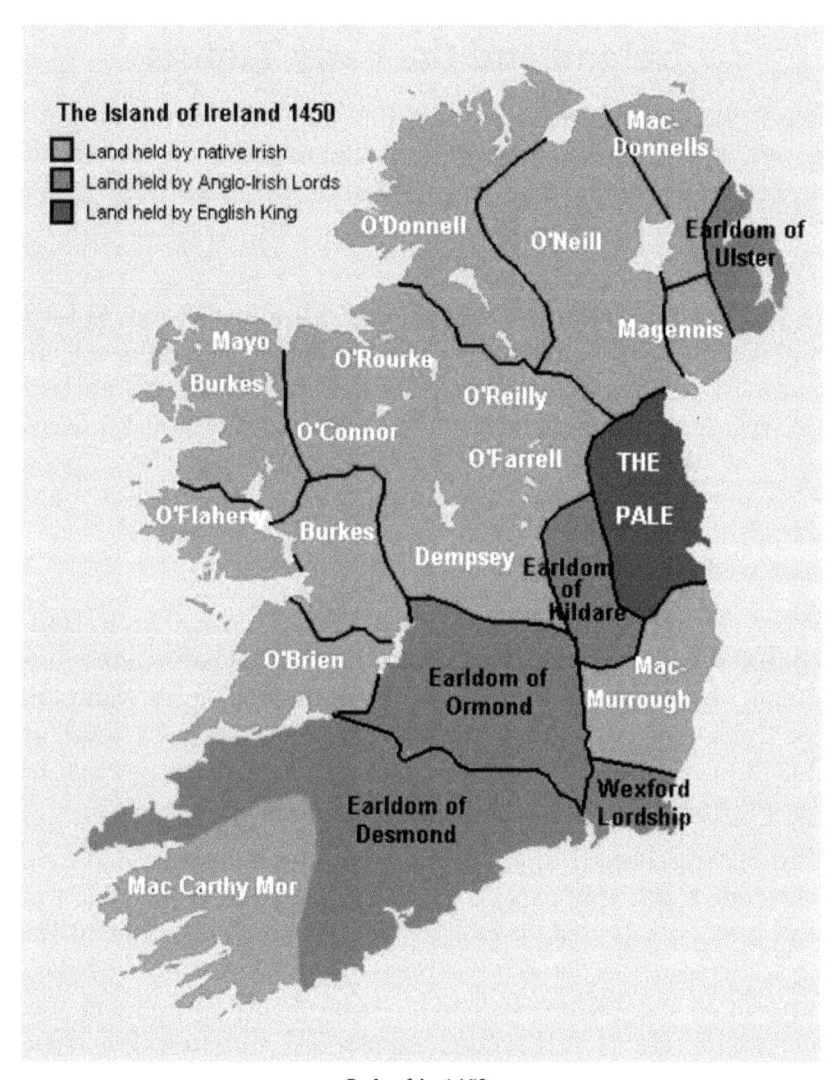

Ireland in 1450.
https://commons.wikimedia.org/wiki/File:Ireland_1450.png

But who exactly were the Anglo-Irish and the Gaelic Irish? The Gaelic Irish were the Gaelic-speaking Irish who had inhabited the island before Henry II's invasion. The Anglo-Irish were the English settlers who settled in Ireland after England conquered it in the Middle Ages. Over time, the Anglo-Irish came to accept many Gaelic customs and intermarried with the Gaelic Irish until they were far more Irish than English.

Ireland and the Early Tudors

This was the general situation when the Tudors took the throne. The Pale was under English control, but the majority of the island was controlled by the Gaelic Irish. Even within the Pale, the Anglo-Irish lords were often unruly, and their loyalty to the English Crown was questionable.

In fact, at the start of the Tudor era, Irish influence was particularly strong since there was a resurgence of Irish culture and influence around this time. The Irish Renaissance was heavily focused on poetry, and many Irish lords showed their power and sophistication by becoming patrons of these poets. The English rightly saw these poets as problematic because they encouraged a growing sense of Irish nationalism. The Tudors would soon find that maintaining control of Ireland would be problematic.

When Henry VII became the first Tudor monarch, Ireland was practically ruled by Gerald FitzGerald, Earl of Kildare. Kildare was an Irishman, and he maintained his power through alliances with both the Gaelic Irish and Anglo-Irish. Kildare was not especially loyal to the Tudor monarchy, so Henry VII replaced him, naming an Englishman, Edward Poynings, as the new lord deputy of Ireland.

Poynings discovered what almost every Englishman trying to control Ireland did. It was very expensive. Although Poynings was able to seize control and even passed several laws in an attempt to solidify English control, including the famous Poynings' Law, which subjected the Irish Parliament to the English monarch's control, his government was too expensive for Henry VII's taste. Henry VII withdrew Poynings and restored Kildare to control Ireland. Thanks to Kildare's complex series of alliances, he was the only man able to maintain effective control in Ireland.

When Kildare died, Henry VIII appointed his son to take his place as deputy. While such a move made sense to the English king, it demonstrated a misunderstanding of Irish politics. The Irish did not necessarily pass powerful positions from father to son, which means the younger Kildare did not gain immediate respect from the Irish simply because of his birth. The elder Kildare also ruled effectively because he understood the various allegiances and feuds that made up the Irish political landscape. His son had been raised in England and had none of this essential firsthand knowledge.

Thus, things in Ireland did not go as smoothly as Henry VIII expected. English control gradually slipped during the first half of Henry VIII's reign. The Gaelic lords simply felt no allegiance or fear of the English Crown outside the Pale, and even within it, the Anglo-Irish were too fond of their autonomy to be easily led. Relations between England and Ireland would only worsen with the Reformation.

Ireland and the Reformation

Throughout Europe, the Protestant Reformation proved the same thing over and over. The ruler of a nation and its people could not be of different religions. Either the people would force the ruler to change or leave, or the ruler would impose their will on the people. England saw how true this was from both directions when Henry VIII brought the Reformation to England due to his political goals and when the English people forced James II to leave for being Catholic. Presbyterian Scotland had rebelled against the Catholic Mary of Guise. A nation could not thrive if its rulers and people were of different religions.

Ireland was the only European country to learn this truth the long way. When Henry VIII broke with Rome and started the process that would turn England Protestant, the Reformation was inevitably going to make its way to the shores of Ireland. In 1536, another Act of Supremacy made Henry the head of the Irish Church, and in 1541, Henry VIII took the title "King of Ireland" (before this, English kings had simply been the "Lord of Ireland").

Henry VIII was on a mission to consolidate his control over Ireland, and as part of this mission, he began the "surrender and regrant" method. This was a policy where the Irish surrendered their lands only to have them regranted along with titles by the English Crown. While no specific mentions were made of religion in this policy, to surrender and accept titles from the English king, who had made himself head of the Irish Church, had clear implications. It would be an acceptance of England's authority and an acceptance of the Anglican Church. The Irish Catholics were not having it, and Protestantism made virtually no headway in Ireland. Practically all of the Gaelic Irish and most of the Anglo-Irish remained Catholic.

It's unclear why the Reformation completely failed in Ireland. Henry VIII likely expected some support from at least the Anglo-Irish within the Pale, but the Reformation only pushed this group closer to the Gaelic Irish and further from England. Some have speculated that if the Bible and the *Book of Common Prayer* had been translated into Gaelic, it would have had a greater impact on the religious sentiments of the Irish, much as the Welsh translation aided the Reformation in Wales. As it was, to the Irish, the Reformation was an English movement designed to grant the English king greater control over them.

Because of the stiff Irish resistance to the Reformation, little changed in Ireland during the reigns of Edward VI and Mary. The Reformation had made little to no progress to begin with, so Ireland did not experience the religious whiplash that England did under these monarchs. The rule of Elizabeth I, however, would not be as uneventful.

Elizabeth I and Irish Rebellions

Elizabeth I is a monarch often known for her political tact and skill, but little can be said that is positive about her policy regarding Ireland. After both her father and two half-siblings had gotten nowhere with the Irish, Elizabeth I seemed strangely determined to bring them in line.

Compared to Edward VI and Mary, Elizabeth's religious settlement was moderate. It was designed to please as many people as possible and keep the peace, but it was still not acceptable to the Irish. They remained strictly Catholic, and there were frequent rebellions against English rule and Protestantism. Unable to convert the Irish, Elizabeth I turned to a different method for subduing the island: plantations.

Plantations were lands taken from the Irish (usually Catholics) and redistributed to English settlers, who were Protestant. This usually occurred after a rebellion, such as after the Shane O'Neill Rebellion and the Desmond Rebellion. England confiscated the rebels' lands and then redistributed them to loyal English subjects. It was a crude method of peace-making that relied on replacing the rebellious Irish population with a more obedient English one. This Protestant English population was known as the New English.

However, this method of replacing the rebellious population with a loyal population was not thorough enough to really work. The populations of the plantations were not as purely New English as they needed to be for England to truly dominate. The Anglo-Irish (also called the Old English) and the Gaelic Irish remained in large numbers, and they were still Catholic and opposed to English rule. Perhaps the worst of these rebellions was Tyrone Rebellion, also known as the Nine Years' War, which lasted from 1594 to 1603.

The Tyrone Rebellion took place in Ulster, the northernmost region of Ireland. Thanks to the plantations, Ulster was the only region of Ireland not heavily infected by the English. The earl of Tyrone, Hugh O'Neill, was the most powerful man in this region. It is unclear what precisely sparked the rebellion. O'Neill likely felt isolated and threatened by increasing English power and decided to strike first in 1594.

Going up against the far more organized and wealthy English was a risky move for O'Neill, but he did have a good sense of timing with his rebellion. The English were embroiled in other conflicts on the continent, which made it difficult for them to spare the resources to deal with the Irish rebellion. Furthermore, Spain, as a Catholic country and England's enemy, was willing to lend its support to O'Neill, though, in the end, this amounted to more moral support than the actual troops O'Neill needed.

The Tyrone Rebellion dragged on for nine years. At first, the English lacked the manpower to respond at all, but when English settlers began to be slaughtered, Elizabeth I had to respond. The first military commander she sent over was the earl of Essex, and he proved to be utterly incompetent. He was replaced in 1600 by Lord Mountjoy, who managed to force O'Neill to surrender in 1603.

The Tyrone Rebellion was a bitter and bloody war that only served to further sour Anglo-Irish relations. The warfare involved lots of guerrilla tactics, causing the deaths of many civilians and the destruction of much land and property, especially in Ulster but also in the southern regions of Ireland as well. The English showed no mercy in subduing the region, and while they were successful in the short term, this only deepened the Irish people's resentment of English rule.

Shortly after the Tyrone Rebellion, in 1607, many of the Irish nobility fled to Europe. Their goal was to garner Catholic support for their cause and return to reclaim their lands and power. However, they never returned. This event, known as the Flight of the Earls, left the Irish laypeople to be subjected to the whims of the English. The English government confiscated the lands of the earls who had fled and redistributed them to the New English settlers (including many Scots).

With these new settlements, Ulster suddenly had a large population of both English Protestants and Scottish Presbyterians, which has remained to the present day. This was the origin of what is now Northern Ireland, the only part of Ireland that is united with England in the United Kingdom.

New Dynasty, More Rebellions

After their experience under Elizabeth I, the Irish were relieved when James I took the throne, but their joy was short-lived. The new king made it clear almost immediately that he did not intend to relieve the persecution of Catholics, and he continued the expansion of the plantations, settling Ireland with English Protestants. These Protestants became the landlords, and the Irish, who used to own the lands, were either forced to move to infertile and hostile areas or become tenants, paying outrageous prices and being exploited.

So, once again, the Irish rebelled. Similar to the Tyrone Rebellion, they again waited for the perfect opportunity. It was the autumn of 1641. Charles I had been forced to call Parliament to deal with the Scottish rebellion in the north, and England was fracturing along Royalist and Parliamentary lines. The king was in an extremely weak position, which would hopefully make him willing to concede to demands. The time was ripe, and the Catholics of Ulster rose.

The uprising spread throughout the island, and after decades of building resentment, it quickly became bloody. While the stories of slaughter were likely exaggerated by the time they reached England, the Gaelic Irish did kill the New English settlers by the thousands. Despite this bloodshed, the Old English joined the Gaelic Irish in the rebellion in 1642, forming the Confederation of Kilkenny as a provisional government. The ties of religion had proved stronger than the ties of ancestry.

The Irish rebellion thoroughly frightened the English people. They were convinced that the evil Catholics were going to invade and kill all the Protestants. England needed to respond, but to do so, it needed to raise another army. It was at this point that Charles I and Parliament began taking separate military actions, and the English Civil War began.

The Irish rebellion was the final push that forced the king and Parliament into warfare.

What happened to the Irish rebellion since the king and Parliament had turned on each other? For the next seven years, England was too busy with its own situation to send an army to pacify Ireland. The Irish were involved in the English Civil War during this time, siding with the king in the hopes of negotiating religious tolerance for Catholics (something the Puritan-led Parliament was not likely to grant).

But then, in 1649, Charles I was executed, and the new English Commonwealth turned its attention to Ireland. Cromwell and his army arrived within the year and proceeded to win back the island in a brutal fashion. The memory of the 1641 rebellion and slaughter of English settlers was still fresh. The English army killed Catholic priests and civilians. The soldiers burned and destroyed almost everything they came across. The destruction was so bad that over 200,000 died either directly through violence or by starvation.

After the island was officially reconquered, the English government returned to the plantation method, again confiscating land from Catholics and redistributing it to English Protestants. Persecution of Catholics in this period (when Puritans controlled the English government) reached a new high. So much land was confiscated that by the time of the English Restoration, Catholics owned less than 10 percent of the land in Ireland; they had owned 60 percent of the land in 1641.

As you can imagine, all of this further intensified the deep resentment and bitterness between the Irish and English. Anglo-Irish relations were nothing more than a series of rebellions and harsh reprisals. The English failed again and again to understand the situation in Ireland and only succeeded in maintaining control through military force. Unfortunately, this pattern was not destined to change anytime soon.

Jacobite Ireland

With the restoration of the monarchy and the ascension of Charles II, things in Ireland did look up briefly. Charles II restored some of the lands that had been taken during the Cromwellian era to the Catholics. Charles II was the first monarch in quite a while who was sympathetic to the Irish Catholics, but his sympathy only extended to not bothering them. He needed the support of the Irish Protestants, who were now the landowning class in Ireland and thus the ones who controlled the purse strings.

When James II became king in 1685, the Catholics finally had a king on their side. During the three short years of his reign, the Irish army saw an influx of Catholics, and Protestants were removed from many local government positions. The New English began to leave the country. It seemed like the tide might finally be turning to the Catholics, but then the Glorious Revolution happened.

In the Glorious Revolution, Ireland was the only one of James II's three kingdoms to stay loyal. After fleeing England, James II devised a plan, with the support of the French, where he would seize control of the Irish throne and use Ireland as a base from which to retake England. In 1689, James II landed at Kinsale and set out to do just that.

James II's takeover of Ireland initially went rather well. He had the support of the Irish Catholics, so he had control of the south and west of Ireland. Ulster in the north was the Protestant holdout, and James II's forces had them under siege. It looked like James II might be able to move on to invade England, but then King William III arrived to personally take command of the situation.

William III at the Battle of the Boyne by Jan Wyck.
https://commons.wikimedia.org/wiki/File:King_William_III_at_the_battle_of_the_Boyne,_1690.jpg

William's forces began pushing back James II's troops, and at the Battle of the Boyne on July 1ˢᵗ, 1690, the two sides clashed. It was the largest battle to occur in the British Isles, and James II's side was forced to retreat. Although his army was still intact, the defeat caused James II to flee back to France. He would never again set foot in the British Isles. Despite James II's flight, his army held out for another year before being defeated in 1691.

Once again, the Irish Catholics had fought in the hopes of retaking control of Ireland, and once again, they had failed. The Protestant landowners' retribution in the wake of the Battle of the Boyne and the defeat of the Irish Catholics was, to put it mildly, harsh. Over the next few decades, the Irish Parliament, which was controlled by the Protestants, passed the Penal Code, which forbade Catholics from doing practically anything, from voting to carrying a sword to buying land worth more than a certain amount.

So, as the early modern era came to a close, Ireland was in a pretty miserable position. The majority of the population were Catholic, and they had virtually no rights. The country was controlled by London, but London had no understanding of the Irish people and acted only in the interest of the English Protestant ruling class. The numerous rebellions show that the Irish question was indeed a problem for England during the early modern era, but by the end of the era, England had come no closer to solving it. If anything, it was worse than before.

Chapter 15: Conquest and Colonization

In 1919, the British Empire reached its height with territories on every continent. It took three hundred years for this small island to reach the point where it controlled an area that spanned the entire globe, and it all got started in the early modern era.

The First British Colony

So, where did it all start? What was the first settlement that began what would become the largest empire in history? Was it Plymouth? Jamestown? What about the lost colony of Roanoke or the fisheries in Newfoundland?

We tend to focus on the colonies across the Atlantic when considering the start of the British Empire, but the first colony was a lot closer to home. Remember that England conquered both Wales and Ireland in the Middle Ages. Now conquest does not necessarily equal colonization. Colonization involves creating settlements, and while England did not do that in the Middle Ages, the English did begin to colonize Ireland in the early modern period.

Although we don't often think of Ireland as being an English colony, the plantations discussed in the last chapter, where land was confiscated and redistributed to new English settlers, are a textbook example of colonization. The land was conquered and then settled to establish the dominance of the English over the original Irish population.

Although the plantations were a core part of Elizabeth I's policy, they began during Queen Mary's reign. Mary approved the creation of English plantations in Ireland during her short reign from 1553 to 1558. This makes Ireland the first English colony, and as you likely noticed from the previous chapter, it was not exactly a successful colony. Ireland constantly rebelled, costing the English lots of blood and money. The plantations themselves were not extremely successful monetarily either. If England's other colonies followed the pattern of Ireland, colonization would prove to be more difficult than it was worth.

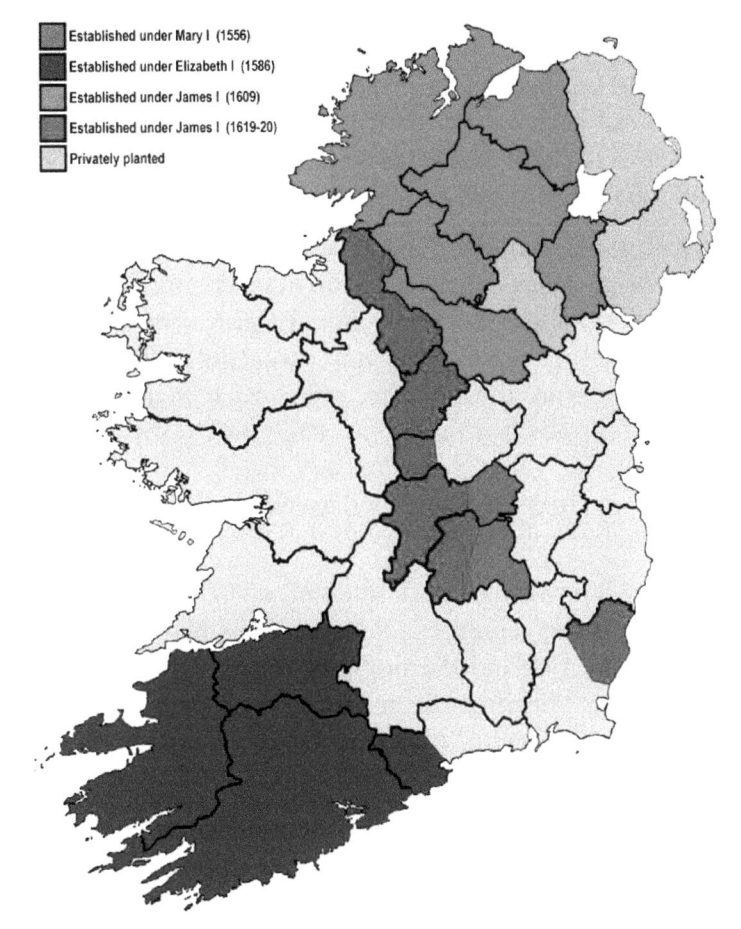

Establishment of Irish plantations.
User: Asarlaí, CC BY-SA 4.0 <https://creativecommons.org/licenses/by-sa/4.0>, via Wikimedia Commons: https://commons.wikimedia.org/wiki/File:Plantations_in_Ireland.png

Early Attempts at Colonization

Since we know what happened later, we often think of Britain as being the king of colonization, but as we mentioned in Chapter 7, England was late to the party. Spain was the first to jump on the colonization train, establishing its first settlement in 1493. The New World brought Spain vast wealth, and by the Elizabethan era, England was aware that it had missed out.

England's first attempts at colonization did not go as planned. The first area English explorers discovered was Newfoundland in 1497. Newfoundland proved to have an abundance of one particular resource: fish. Fish, however, did not require a permanent colony. English fishermen would sail over to the Newfoundland area, fill their ships with fish, and then sail back to sell the fish. Newfoundland would eventually become a colony in 1610, but for around a century, it remained a fishing outpost and not a settlement.

The next colonization attempt was an actual settlement. In 1587, Sir Walter Raleigh approved the settling of Roanoke. Had Roanoke been successful, it would have been the first English settlement across the Atlantic. However, Roanoke was not successful. The first year was difficult, so the mayor, John White, sailed back to England for more supplies. When he returned three years later, the colony was abandoned. It has been speculated that the colonists moved to a nearby island and joined the natives there, but to this day, we don't know for sure what happened to the lost colony of Roanoke.

This was the Elizabethan era's attempt at colonization. Despite the exploration and daring ventures of famous sailors like Francis Drake and Sir Walter Raleigh, England did not achieve any permanent settlements across the Atlantic. This might seem strange because we tend to connect exploration and colonization together. Explorers find new places, and then those places get colonized.

That is technically how it works, but saying it like that greatly condenses how long that takes, especially back then. Traveling across the Atlantic took weeks, and you could not set up a settlement on your first trip. Explorers like Walter Raleigh made several voyages to determine where the best place for a settlement would be. You needed to be at least somewhat familiar with the area before bringing over colonists. There were many decades between discovering the New World and settling it.

So, the wealth England gained in the grand Age of Exploration was mostly due to piracy and participation in the slave trade rather than from its settlements. The Spanish had discovered gold in the New World. So far, the English had found fish.

The Age of Colonization

In the Stuart era, colonization really kicked off for the English. The first permanent colony of Jamestown was founded in 1607, and other colonies soon followed. St. Kitts, Barbados, and Nevis (all islands in the Caribbean) were settled by the English in the 1620s. The English established trading posts in Bengal in 1636 and gained control of Bombay in 1661. In 1655, the British took Jamaica from the Spanish and then seized control of the New Netherlands (which became New York) from the Dutch in 1664. The Bahamas was colonized in 1666, and the 1713 Treaty of Utrecht (the treaty that ended the War of the Spanish Succession) gave Britain control of Hudson Bay, Newfoundland, and more.

What all those dates and place names illustrate is the gradual and steady expansion of British colonial power in the Stuart era. While the Stuarts saw a lot of internal conflict in things like the English Civil War and the Glorious Revolution, Britain's foreign power was growing. In fact, in some ways, the internal conflicts might have helped to fuel the drive for colonization.

The chaos of the English Civil War sparked the growth of several religious sects, some of which, like the Quakers, would seek religious freedom in the colonies. After the Restoration especially, England was far less friendly to the Puritans and other Dissenters (Protestants outside of the Church of England), prompting many to try their luck across the Atlantic. Colonies, such as Plymouth, Massachusetts Bay, and Pennsylvania, were founded by people seeking the freedom to practice their religion in peace.

However, saying that a lot of the British colonies were founded for freedom of religion can be potentially misleading. Ironically, the groups that traveled to the New World for religious reasons tended not to be for religious freedom in general. For instance, the Massachusetts Bay Colony (which was founded by Puritans) banished those who disagreed with their beliefs. They could do this because the governments of these colonies were often theocracies, meaning church leaders were also the government leaders. So, the idea that America has always been about religious freedom and the separation of church and state is far from the truth. Several of the first American colonies were religiously strict and theocratic.

Religion was not the only reason people moved to the colonies. The other leading factor was of a more earthly nature: economics. As we discussed in Chapter 11, poverty was a growing problem in England, and the colonies offered an opportunity for those who were down on their luck. Poor people often traveled to the colonies as indentured servants.

In theory, indentured servants had someone else pay for their passage to the colonies and then worked for that person for a certain amount of time until the debt was paid. Sometimes it did work this way, but other times, the employer of an indentured servant would add items, such as room and board, to a person's debt to ensure the person would never be able to work it off. In these circumstances, indentured servants could become virtual slaves, with their children even being forced to continue in servitude to pay off a parent's debt.

During the initial colonization of places like Virginia, indentured servants did most of the work, but this practice eventually became less popular when the colonists discovered an even cheaper source of labor: slaves. The Royal African Company was founded in 1660, and the slave trade became an integral part of American economics, particularly in the more agricultural-focused southern colonies. It would take two centuries and a very bloody war to put a stop to this horrific practice.

Indentured servants and the slave trade are a dark side of the era of colonization, and it shows just how economics-oriented colonization was. When we are young, we learn about the brave men and women who set off to lands unknown for religious freedom, adventure, and opportunity, but the fact is that most colonizers wanted to make money. The New World had resources like tobacco and sugar, and there were vast amounts of money to be made by trading those resources. Many people were abused horribly in the pursuit of that wealth.

Speaking of people who were abused in the pursuit of economic gain, there were native populations in the places the British colonized. What happened to them? The British may not have followed the practice of the Spanish conquistadors of razing native cities, but there were other ways to devastate the native populations. Smallpox was deadlier than European guns.

It is estimated that around 90 percent of the indigenous population of the Americas died from diseases brought over by the Europeans. This apocalyptic level of destruction was why the British and other Europeans were able to colonize the New World so easily. When the British colonies began to expand, they would show no hesitation about pushing the remaining natives out.

Colonization was like a fire. It provided Britain with wealth and resources, but it was destructive to many groups. Colonization is a controversial subject. There can be no doubt that the world would not exist as we know it today without the British Empire, but whether that was ultimately for the best is a question that continues to be debated.

How Did Colonization Work?

We have talked a lot about the overall shape and impact of English colonization, but now is the time to stop and consider if we know how colonization works. Is colonization just about landing somewhere, planting an English flag in the soil, and claiming the land for England? How did a place become colonized? In the following chapter, we will cover the specifics of what was happening in different English colonies in the early modern period, but let's consider the basics of the colonization process.

Although we are discussing English colonization in general, colonization was not carried out by the English government in most cases (Ireland is an exception). Instead, colonization was the work of companies.

Yes, companies. The English Crown granted charters to companies, giving them the right to colonize and trade in certain areas. These charters gave companies a monopoly, meaning that no one else was allowed to start a settlement or trade there.

So why would a company want to start a colony? At first, they didn't. Before the founding of Jamestown in 1607, companies like the Levant Company and the East India Company were founded to trade with the Ottoman Empire and India, respectively. The Virginia Company was the first to establish a permanent settlement (Jamestown).

Founding a settlement gave a company far more control over the acquisition of resources. Without a settlement, if companies wanted to gather resources to trade, they would need to either find natives to make a deal with or only gather resources periodically, such as with fish in Newfoundland. In the case of agricultural products like tobacco and sugar, it was crucial to have settlements to farm and harvest products.

So, a company wanted to establish a colony so that it could take advantage of the resources in an area. How did it go about that? A company usually consisted of a group of wealthy individuals. Once they had the monarch's approval, which included a charter that gave them the exclusive right to trade and settle that area, this group would fund the colony. They paid for the ships and resources to send the colonists over and start the settlement. In exchange, the company had control over the resources the colony produced, as well as control over trade with the colony.

Religious colonies started in an almost identical manner. Though their goal might have been less economical, religious colonies had to request a charter from the monarch, and the owners of that charter were responsible for funding the colony. They also had control over trade in that area. Some religious groups partnered with a group of wealthy individuals to get the resources to start the settlement and agreed to give the owners so many years of the colony's profits to pay for the initial backing.

However, religious colonies made the idea of charters and companies more political by transferring the company's ownership to the colony itself. Once it had paid back its owners, the colony essentially bought back control of itself. This was what happened in Massachusetts.

That might seem like a small difference, but it was highly significant. It made the colony an almost self-contained legal entity capable of governing itself and having only a vague connection to England. This type of independent attitude may help to explain why the American colonies were the first to rebel against British rule. New England was where many of these religious colonies were founded, and from the beginning, many of them had more of a separatist attitude toward England.

In contrast, the Caribbean colonies were almost purely economic. The sugar plantations were often owned by absentee landlords who continued to live in England, so the chances of an independence movement that stretched across class lines were virtually none. Economics was a bond that both started and strengthened colonization.

The problem with a general discussion of colonization is that it obscures the uniqueness of each situation. England colonized a lot of places. Colonization efforts in Ireland, India, the American colonies, and the Caribbean were all different. In the next chapter, we will dive deeper into the individual colonies to gain an understanding of what the British Empire looked like around the world in the early modern era.

Chapter 16: The Continuation of the Empire

In the last chapter, we looked at English colonization from a wider viewpoint. Now let's zoom in on the individual colonies for a deeper understanding of the specifics of colonization in early modern England.

The American Colonies

We are starting with the American colonies for the simple reason that England's first permanent settlement was Jamestown, Virginia, in 1607. Twelve more colonies were then founded to make the thirteen American colonies that would later become the start of the United States. Of the Thirteen Colonies, twelve were founded in the Stuart era, with the only exception being Georgia, which was founded in 1732.

Because we know that the Thirteen Colonies would later become a single nation, we often discuss them as if they were a single entity, but that was not the case. The Thirteen Colonies were thirteen separate settlements that were founded at different times and for different reasons.

Virginia was an economic venture. It was England's attempt to get a foothold in the New World. While the Jamestown settlement got off to a very rough start, it managed to survive. And when the cultivation of tobacco was introduced, it moved from surviving to thriving. By 1619, Virginia even had its own local government.

The colonies that immediately followed Virginia were less economically focused. The Pilgrims who founded Massachusetts in 1620 were Separatists (Puritans who wanted to fully separate from the Church of England). They came to the New World seeking religious freedom. Other colonies that began for religious reasons include Rhode Island (which was founded by people banished from the Massachusetts Bay Colony), Maryland (founded for Roman Catholics), and Pennsylvania (founded by the Quakers).

But economics and religion were not the only reasons colonies formed. New York and Delaware were originally founded by the Netherlands and Sweden and became English colonies when England gained control. Other later colonies were the result of population expansion and movement from the original colonies. For example, North and South Carolina were started by settlers from Virginia. The final colony, Georgia, was founded as a debtor's colony, providing a home for many of the debtors in England's prisons.

Though they may have become united later, at the start, the Thirteen Colonies were a variety pack of different groups. These were the colonies that welcomed settlers who felt uncomfortable in England for one reason or another. The colonists sought economic opportunities, religious freedom, or simply a fresh start. The fact that so many of the American colonists were looking to get away from Britain may help to explain why they were the first to rebel against British rule in 1776.

So, the American colonies were a land of opportunity for many, but just how important were they to Britain as a nation? The Thirteen Colonies were not very important economically for England. Virginia made money trading tobacco, and the southern colonies participated in the slave trade, but these colonies were not gold mines. The American colonies became almost a dumping ground for groups that Britain didn't know what to do with rather than a jewel in its colonial crown. When Britain lost the Thirteen Colonies after the American Revolutionary War, it did not put much of a dent in the British Empire's wealth. There were other colonial holdings that Britain was far more eager to hold onto.

Canada

In Canada, it was colder, which you might think meant that it was a far less profitable area, but Canada had a lot of one high-end commodity:

furs.

The fur trade in the Canadian area was a lucrative business, so much so that Britain was not the only one in this area. The French had more of a presence in Canada than the British in the early modern era. It was not until Britain's victory in the Seven Years' War (1756-1763) that the French ceded control of Canada to Britain.

However, that does not mean the British were not doing anything in Canada during this time. As we mentioned in the last chapter, Newfoundland was one of the first areas that English explorers discovered in the New World in 1497. Fishermen began regularly fishing off the Canadian coast.

The first permanent English settlement in Canada was the settlement of Cupids Bay in Newfoundland in 1610. This was rather early in the history of English colonialism, coming only three years after the founding of Jamestown, but the settlement only lasted until 1628. Still, the founding of Cupids Bay shows that England was aware of and interested in Canada early on.

Canadian colonialism in the 17th century was dominated by the French. The only other major development for the English was the founding of the Hudson's Bay Company in 1670. The Hudson's Bay Company was primarily interested in the fur trade, and unlike tobacco in Virginia and sugar in the Caribbean, the easiest way to engage in the fur trade was to trade with the natives, who were far better at navigating the Canadian wilderness and trapping animals.

This meant that the Hudson's Bay Company was not nearly as interested in creating the type of permanent settlements that existed in the southern American colonies. Instead, they built trading posts from which they conducted trade with the natives. Most of these posts were seized by the French, but the British were able to regain control as part of the Treaty of Utrecht, which ended the War of the Spanish Succession.

The Treaty of Utrecht's effect on fur trading posts in Canada shows just how connected the British Empire was. Successes in a war that largely took place on the European continent were instrumental in helping the British maintain control of Hudson's Bay. While they may have been geographically distinct from England, it is impossible to understand the history of England without considering its colonies.

The Caribbean

Speaking of colonies that had a profound impact on England, the Caribbean, or the West Indies as it was referred to at the time, were the money-making colonies. It was through sugar plantations in the West Indies that many British fortunes were made.

The West Indies, however, did not begin in British hands. By the time the English arrived on the scene, the Spanish had already seized control of most of the West Indies. The English, however, were not willing to let the wealth this tropical paradise had to offer slip through their fingers. At first, English privateers simply tried to turn a profit by selling slaves from Africa to the Spanish colonies in the Caribbean. However, the Spanish government did not want their monopoly on trade disrupted and destroyed the English vessels attempting to trade. This led to a more aggressive form of English piracy. Instead of trading with Spain, the English would simply take the bullion directly from the ships.

In the Elizabethan era, English pirates were a constant threat not only in the Spanish-controlled Caribbean but also in the Pacific Ocean. When Francis Drake circumnavigated the globe, he did so at the expense of many Spanish vessels. You may be wondering why English vessels attacking Spanish ships and stealing gold did not immediately lead to war. After all, if that happened today, Spain and England would be at war almost immediately.

During this time, there was a saying that went, "No peace beyond the line." What this meant was that past a certain point in the Atlantic Ocean, the diplomacy and peace agreements of Europe no longer held sway. There is debate as to whether there was a specific line at which this occurred, but the sentiment is correct. The New World was a frontier, and the normal rules of engagement did not apply. Even if Spain and England were at peace in Europe, they regularly crashed into each other in the Caribbean. While it may have technically been the work of English pirates, it was clear to everyone that Elizabeth I supported the privateers. Francis Drake was knighted by the queen after returning from his circumnavigation of the globe, during which he plundered quite a few Spanish ships.

Elizabeth I knighting Francis Drake from the Tavistock Monument.
Joseph Boehm, CC0, via Wikimedia Commons
https://commons.wikimedia.org/wiki/File:DrakeKnightedTavistockMonument.jpg

This was the Tudor presence in the West Indies. It was pirates taking bites out of Spanish power, but Spanish power was destined to decline. In the Stuart era, England began by setting up colonies on islands that were yet unclaimed, such as St. Kitts (1623), Nevis (1628), and Barbados (1627).

These Caribbean settlements were excellent for crops like tobacco and sugar, but they were not as hospitable for the settlers. Tropical diseases killed a huge portion, and many settlers who were interested in starting a new life in the New World ended up moving north to the American colonies. The high mortality rate also meant that the West Indies needed a constant influx of workers to keep the plantations running, which arrived in the form of indentured servants and then slaves. The Caribbean kept the slave trade running for close to two centuries until it was banned in 1807.

So, England had a few settlements in the Caribbean by the mid-1650s, but these colonies, like the thirteen American colonies, had all been set up as private ventures. The next question was how the English government itself could profit from these colonies, and that question was answered not by a monarch but by Oliver Cromwell. During the Interregnum, Oliver Cromwell came up with two ideas to try to take advantage of the opportunities of the New World.

The first idea was the Navigation Acts. These acts prohibited English colonies from trading with foreign powers. This was based on the idea that any trade with other countries was a loss for England. The Navigation Acts were continued after the English Restoration and remained British colonial policy for around two centuries.

Oliver Cromwell's other colonial plan was more specific to the Caribbean and more ambitious. Cromwell's Western Design was a plan to seize control of Spanish colonies in the Caribbean. This marked a huge shift in the understanding of colonialism. It was the English government, not private companies, that was doing the colonizing, and instead of settling unclaimed lands, they were taking them directly from the Spanish. For the first time, the English government was directly seeking to expand its empire.

As far as how successful the Western Design was, it could have gone much better. The English failed to capture the main Spanish colony of Hispaniola. They managed to seize Jamaica in 1655, but it would cost a good deal of trouble to maintain control of it. England actually encouraged the presence of buccaneers (pirates) to help defend Jamaica from the Spanish, but when the Spanish finally backed off, the pirates were still there. England had to spend the next several decades getting piracy in the Caribbean under control.

In the Stuart era, English control in the Caribbean gradually expanded, and these colonies became crucial to the mercantilism on which colonization was based. Mercantilism is an economic system in which the government exercises strict control over the economics of its colonies. It came from the idea that a nation must have precious metals (gold and silver). If a nation did not have mines to get those metals, then they must trade for them. For a country like England to trade for gold and silver, it relied on the raw resources it gathered from its colonies. The colonies were a source of trading materials that the mother country could use to trade for precious metals.

To ensure that the motherland always had access to these raw resources, colonies were forbidden from trading with other nations and from producing manufactured goods. They were to remain reliant on the old country so that the established trade routes would remain open and profitable.

Those established trade routes can be simplified into the triangular trade system, which connected West Africa, the Caribbean and other colonies, and Europe. Slaves from West Africa were sent to the colonies, and the colonies then sent raw resources back to Europe. It was a system that greatly benefited Europe.

What all this means is that while the Caribbean was a key component of England's trade empire, the settlements mostly churned out raw goods, particularly sugar. Many of the Caribbean plantations were owned by absentee landlords who remained in England, where they enjoyed the profits of their plantations and slave labor. Someone else oversaw the daily running of the plantation. The Caribbean was a place where the English went for a few years to make their fortunes and then returned home. It was not a place where settlers moved to start a new life. The Caribbean was disease-ridden, full of pirates, and home to a cruel slave system, but all of that was overlooked for one simple reason: it made money.

Slaves cutting sugarcane.
William Clark, CC0, via Wikimedia Commons
https://commons.wikimedia.org/wiki/File:Slaves_cutting_the_sugar_cane_-_Ten_Views_in_the_Island_of_Antigua_(1823),_plate_IV_-_BL.jpg

India

We have been focusing pretty heavily on the colonies across the Atlantic, but England did not confine its colonial endeavors to the New World. There was still much wealth and power to be had in the Old World.

In the early modern era, India was not directly colonized by Britain. Direct British control would not occur until 1858 with the establishment of the British Raj. In the early modern era, the British presence in India was largely confined to trade and was the work of a single company—the English East India Company.

The English East India Company was formed in 1600. The royal charter that created the company gave it a monopoly on trade in India, as well as Southeast and East Asia.

The English East India Company began with the spice trade. At first, each trading voyage was treated as a separate investment. Each voyage was planned and funded as its own expedition. It was not until 1657 that a permanent joint stock was created. The creation of a joint stock meant the company could make money as a whole instead of having individuals invest separately and profit separately. In other words, the company was more of a single entity.

The English East India Company may have started relatively small, but it soon grew ambitious. Trade expanded from just spices to cotton and silk. While the company attempted to trade in the area that is now Indonesia, they were pushed out by the Dutch. However, the company was able to defeat the Portuguese in India in 1612 and gain trading rights with the Mughal Empire. This development turned the company's focus from East Asia to India.

In India, with the agreement of the Mughal Empire, the English East India Company set up trading posts (known as factories). They then began to turn a nice profit, which caused other merchants in England to resent the company's monopoly. There were several attempts by other companies to seize part of the business, but none of the East India Company's competitors were able to break its monopoly. However, by the end of the early modern era, the English government insisted that the East India Company merge with its competitors to create the United Company of Merchants of England. That's a mouthful of a name, but it was basically the same company, only larger.

At this point, the English East India Company may sound like nothing more than a group of merchants peacefully trading with the natives, but there's more going on here. To ensure that their monopolies were not encroached on by other nations, many countries used force to keep the natives trading with them exclusively. In the late 17th century, the English East India Company tried to do that but found that the Mughal Empire was too strong to be coerced. Instead of securing its trading rights, the company harmed its relations with the empire and was forced to build its own trading port in Calcutta in 1690. The factories also had to be turned into forts.

This new, more violent relationship with India would eventually transform the English East India Company from a group of merchants interested in trade into an entity on par with a government. The company had its own army. It could make treaties, ally itself with different groups, and levy taxes. The English East India Company was private colonization at its most extreme, but this colonization was purely economic. The English were not interested in settling in India. Like the Caribbean, the main purpose of England's presence in India was to make money.

By 1714 and the end of the early modern era, the British Empire was steadily growing. Most of Britain's colonies were for economic gain, and the wealth these colonies provided would allow Britain to defend and expand its empire over the next two hundred years. England had come out of the medieval age war-torn and chaotic after the Wars of the Roses. It ended the early modern age with a growing empire. Britain was a world power.

Conclusion

A lot happened in early modern England. Wars (both internal and external), religious changes, the Renaissance, new discoveries, and changing economics all contributed to transforming England during this time.

Looking at each of these aspects separately has allowed us to gain a broad view of what happened in early modern England, but we should also remember that these events did not happen in isolation. In a book, it is easy to separate discussions of religious changes, colonization, and social structure, but in reality, all of these things are deeply intertwined.

Take the execution of Mary, Queen of Scots, for example. This one event was impacted by many of the larger trends going on. Mary was kicked out of Scotland and took shelter in England. Although she was politically Elizabeth I's enemy, refusing shelter to a fellow monarch would have upset the idea of the Great Chain of Being, at least in Elizabeth's eyes. Monarchs had to stick together, or else they jeopardized the very idea of monarchy.

However, this put Elizabeth I in a dilemma. Mary, Queen of Scots was a Catholic and the next in line for the English throne. That made her a natural rallying point for the Catholics in England, who were still hoping to reverse the Reformation. Then there was also the problem of the Spanish. England and Spain were in conflict over English piracy and the Netherlands, and Mary, Queen of Scots was an easy way for the Spanish to sow plots and hopefully destabilize the English court.

Thus, when Elizabeth I decided to execute her cousin, it was fueled by several factors. Mary was a problem for both England's foreign affairs and internal religious peace. However, Elizabeth I still needed to demonstrate a belief in the Great Chain of Being. Chopping off a fellow monarch's head disrupted the idea that monarchs were divinely appointed. So, what did Elizabeth I do?

Elizabeth I signed Mary's death warrant but did not order the warrant to be sent to the Tower to be carried out. Her secretary, William Davison, sent the warrant without her explicit orders. Mary, who had been a thorn in Elizabeth I's side, was out of the way, but Elizabeth was able to claim that she had not ordered her death. Davison took the fall and was arrested and imprisoned. However, he was soon released quietly, leading most people to assume that it was all part of Elizabeth's plan.

This event shows us a glimpse of how all the different areas of early modern England combined to shape the country in this era. The decision to execute Mary arose out of religious tensions, foreign conflict, and also plain politics.

The execution of Mary, Queen of Scots is far from the only event to be so multi-faceted. The Glorious Revolution was the final rejection of Catholicism and also demonstrated how the ideology of the Great Chain of Being was collapsing. The break with the Roman Catholic Church was only made possible by the wider religious changes in Europe, but it was brought about largely for political reasons, namely Henry VIII's desperation for a male heir. We place these events in categories, but the reality is more often a mixture of factors.

The larger trends that create these events are intertwined as well. Trade not only boosted the national economy overall but also brought more relative stability to an economy that was previously solely agricultural and, therefore, subject to the mood of the weather. The importance of trade pushed England to want a piece of the colonization pie, especially when England's main export, wool, began to stagnate. England's empire-building led to conflicts with foreign nations, and England's success in those conflicts is what allowed it to continue building its empire.

The Reformation is another movement whose impact went beyond religion. The dissolution of the monasteries forced England to come up with another way to care for the poor, and the growing poor prompted many people to move to the New World. The failure to convert Ireland to the new religion would lead to increasing tensions between England and Ireland. The conflict with Ireland pushed England over the final edge into civil war. The Reformation also sparked a growing fear of popery, which eventually led to the Glorious Revolution.

The point is that it is all connected. We can study early modern England from the perspective of religion, politics, social structure, foreign affairs, and more, but we should never lose sight of the fact that all of these aspects are part of a single story. Early modern England was a time of great change. It saw religious transformation, the beginning of an empire, the centralization of government, the growth of Parliament's power, the decline of the monarchy, the increasing wealth of the rich alongside a growing poor class, the rise in education and professional careers, and much more.

All of those changes combined to transform England from a medieval society to the beginnings of the modern society we know today. The period from 1485 to 1714 was the start of a new direction for England and the world, so, in many ways, it does deserve the name of *early modern* England.

If you enjoyed this book, a review on Amazon would be greatly appreciated because it would mean a lot to hear from you.

To leave a review:
1. Open your camera app.
2. Point your mobile device at the QR code.
3. The review page will appear in your web browser.

Thanks for your support!

Here's another book by Enthralling History that you might like

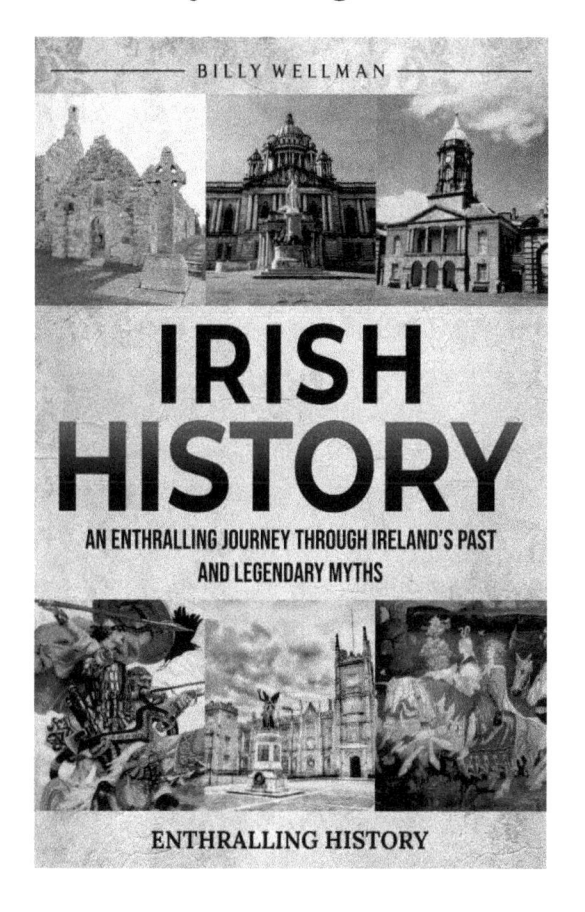

Free limited time bonus

> **We forget 90% of everything that we've read in 7 days...**
>
> Get the free printable pdf summary of the book you've read AND much, much more... shhhh...
>
> Enter Your Most Frequently Used Email to Get Started
>
> **DOWNLOAD FREE PDF SUMMARY**
>
> © Enthralling History

Stop for a moment. We have a free bonus set up for you. The problem is this: we forget 90% of everything that we read after 7 days. Crazy fact, right? Here's the solution: we've created a printable, 1-page pdf summary for this book that you're reading now. All you have to do to get your free pdf summary is to go to the following website: https://livetolearn.lpages.co/enthrallinghistory/

Or, Scan the QR code!

Once you do, it will be intuitive. Enjoy, and thank you!

Bibliography

Part 1

Adams, S. "Battle of Edington." Encyclopedia Britannica, April 29, 2023. https://www.britannica.com/topic/Battle-of-Edington.

"An Introduction to Prehistoric England." English Heritage. Accessed June 24, 2022. https://www.english-heritage.org.uk/learn/story-of-england/prehistory/.

Badian, E. "Narcissus." Encyclopedia Britannica, January 1, 2022. https://www.britannica.com/biography/Narcissus-Roman-official.

Blake, R. Norman William and Blake, Baron. "David Lloyd George." Encyclopedia Britannica, August 29, 2023. https://www.britannica.com/biography/David-Lloyd-George.

Brain, Jessica. "King Eadwig." Historic UK, August 27, 2022. https://www.historic-uk.com/HistoryUK/HistoryofEngland/King-Eadwig/.

Brain, Jessica. "The History of the Coronation." Historic UK, May 3, 2023. https://www.historic-uk.com/HistoryUK/HistoryofBritain/History-Of-The-Coronation/.

Breeze, D. J. "Hadrian's Wall.' Encyclopedia Britannica, September 1, 2021. https://www.britannica.com/topic/Hadrians-Wall.

Britannica, T. Editors of Encyclopaedia. "Boudicca.' Encyclopedia Britannica, December 10, 2020. https://www.britannica.com/biography/Boudicca.

Britannica, T. Editors of Encyclopaedia. "" Encyclopedia Britannica, June 12, 2023. https://www.britannica.com/event/Carnatic-Wars.

Britannica, T. Editors of Encyclopaedia. "Celt." Encyclopedia Britannica, April 25, 2022. https://www.britannica.com/topic/Celt-people.

Britannica, T. Editors of Encyclopaedia. 'Declaration of Breda." Encyclopedia Britannica, June 24, 2019. https://www.britannica.com/topic/Declaration-of-Breda.

Britannica, T. Editors of Encyclopaedia. "Decline of the British Empire.' Encyclopedia Britannica, October 12, 2020. https://www.britannica.com/summary/Decline-of-the-British-Empire.

Britannica, T. Editors of Encyclopaedia. 'East India Company.' Encyclopedia Britannica, August 13, 2023. https://www.britannica.com/money/topic/East-India-Company.

Britannica, T. Editors of Encyclopaedia. "Edmund I.' Encyclopedia Britannica, May 22, 2023. https://www.britannica.com/biography/Edmund-I.

Britannica, T. Editors of Encyclopaedia. "First Battle of the Somme." Encyclopedia Britannica, October 9, 2023. https://www.britannica.com/event/First-Battle-of-the-Somme.

Britannica, T. Editors of Encyclopaedia. "Industrial Revolution." Encyclopedia Britannica, August 17, 2023. https://www.britannica.com/money/topic/Industrial-Revolution.

Britannica, The Editors of Encyclopaedia. "Irish Rebellion". Encyclopedia Britannica, 16 May. 2023, https://www.britannica.com/event/Irish-Rebellion-Irish-history-1798. Accessed 18 September 2023.

Britannica, The Editors of Encyclopaedia. "Orange Order". Encyclopedia Britannica, 28 Jul. 2023, https://www.britannica.com/topic/Orange-Order. Accessed 18 September 2023.

Britannica, T. Editors of Encyclopaedia. "Pytheas." Encyclopedia Britannica, December 16, 2009. https://www.britannica.com/biography/Pytheas.

Britannica, T. Editors of Encyclopaedia. "Roman Britain." Encyclopedia Britannica, February 19, 2022. https://www.britannica.com/place/Roman-Britain.

Britannica, T. Editors of Encyclopaedia. "Seven Years' War." Encyclopedia Britannica, August 18, 2023. https://www.britannica.com/event/Seven-Years-War.

Britannica, T. Editors of Encyclopaedia. "Treaty of Aix-la-Chapelle." Encyclopedia Britannica, October 11, 2022. https://www.britannica.com/event/Treaty-of-Aix-la-Chapelle.

Britannica, T. Editors of Encyclopaedia. "Treaty of Versailles." Encyclopedia Britannica, September 5, 2023. https://www.britannica.com/event/Treaty-of-Versailles-1919.

Britannica, T. Editors of Encyclopaedia. "War of Jenkins' Ear." Encyclopedia Britannica, August 1, 2014. https://www.britannica.com/event/War-of-Jenkins-Ear.

"Bog Body: British Museum." The British Museum. Accessed June 24, 2022. https://www.britishmuseum.org/collection/object/H_1984-1002-2.

Bucholz, Robert, and Newton Key. Early Modern England 1485-1714: A Narrative History. 2nd ed. Chichester, West Sussex: Wiley-Blackwell, 2009.

Butser Ancient Farm. Accessed June 24, 2022. https://www.butserancientfarm.co.uk/.

Cartwright, Mark. "Ancient Celtic Torcs." World History Encyclopedia. https://www.worldhistory.org#organization, June 22, 2022. https://www.worldhistory.org/article/1687/ancient-celtic-torcs/.

Cartwright, Mark. "Ancient Celts." World History Encyclopedia. https://www.worldhistory.org#organization, April 1, 2021. https://www.worldhistory.org/celt/.

"Celt (n.)." Etymology. Accessed June 24, 2022. https://www.etymonline.com/word/celt.

Farley, Julia. "Who Were the Celts?" British Museum Blog - Explore stories from the Museum, February 22, 2022. https://blog.britishmuseum.org/who-were-the-celts/.

Harrison, Julian. "Who Were the Anglo-Saxons?" British Library

Heyck, Thomas William and Meredith Veldman. The Peoples of the British Isles: A New History: From 1688 to the Present. 4th ed. New York: Oxford University Press, 2016.

Hingley, Richard. "Julius Caesar in Britain." World History Encyclopedia. https://www.worldhistory.org#organization, July 11, 2022. https://www.worldhistory.org/article/1926/julius-caesar-in-britain/.

Holt, J. "John." Encyclopedia Britannica, March 29, 2023. https://www.britannica.com/biography/John-king-of-England.

Johnson, Ben. "Prehistoric Britain." Historic UK. Accessed June 24, 2022. https://www.historic-uk.com/HistoryUK/HistoryofEngland/Prehistoric-Britain/.

Johnson, Ben. "Roman England, the Roman in Britain 43 - 410 AD." Historic UK. Accessed July 15, 2022. https://www.historic-uk.com/HistoryUK/HistoryofEngland/The-Romans-in-England/.

Jones, Dan. The Wars of the Roses. New York: Penguin, 2014.

"Julius Caesar Invades Britain - 55BCE and 54BCE." mytimemachine.co.uk, May 5, 2016. http://www.mytimemachine.co.uk/?p=5.

"Julius Caesar on Britain - 55BCE and 54BCE." mytimemachine.co.uk, May 5, 2016. http://www.mytimemachine.co.uk/?p=7.

"Julius Caesar on Britain II - 55BCE and 54BCE." mytimemachine.co.uk, May 5, 2016. http://www.mytimemachine.co.uk/?p=9.

Knowles, M. David. "Henry II." Encyclopedia Britannica, July 2, 2023. https://www.britannica.com/biography/Henry-II-king-of-England.

Law, C. M. "The Growth of Urban Population in England and Wales, 1801-1911." Transactions of the Institute of British Geographers, no. 41 (1967): 125-43. https://doi.org/10.2307/621331.

Meigs, Samantha A. and Stanford E. Lehmberg. The Peoples of the British Isles: A New History: From Prehistoric Times to 1688. 4th ed. New York: Oxford University Press, 2016.

Morrill, J. S. and Myers, Alexander Reginald. "Henry VII." Encyclopedia Britannica, July 4, 2023. https://www.britannica.com/biography/Henry-VII-king-of-England.

Myers, A. Reginald. "Edward IV." Encyclopedia Britannica, April 24, 2023. https://www.britannica.com/biography/Edward-IV-king-of-England.

Nicholas, H. G. "Winston Churchill." Encyclopedia Britannica, October 21, 2023. https://www.britannica.com/biography/Winston-Churchill.

Pearson, M. Parker. "Stonehenge." Encyclopedia Britannica, March 2, 2021. https://www.britannica.com/topic/Stonehenge.

Ross, C. "Henry V." Encyclopedia Britannica, November 8, 2022. https://www.britannica.com/biography/Henry-V-king-of-England.

Small, Andrew. "Why Is Britain Called Britain?" These Islands, December 23, 2017. https://www.these-islands.co.uk/publications/i281/why_is_britain_called_britain.aspx.

Steinbach, S. "Victorian era." Encyclopedia Britannica, October 3, 2023. https://www.britannica.com/event/Victorian-era.

"The Celtic Tribes." The Celtic Tribes - history of Celtic people. Accessed June 29, 2022. https://www.englishmonarchs.co.uk/celts_6.html.

"The Celts of England." Celtic Life International - Celebrating the Celtic Life for over 30 years. Accessed June 24, 2022. https://celticlifeintl.com/the-celts-of-england/.

"The Roman Occupation of Britain." The Roman occupation of Britain. Accessed July 15, 2022. https://sites.psu.edu/romanoccupationofbritain/roman-conquest-of-britain-ad-43/.

"Visit Resource - Prehistoric Britain." British Museum. Accessed June 24, 2022. https://www.britishmuseum.org/sites/default/files/2019-09/visit-resource_prehistoric-britain-KS2.pdf.

Wallace, W. M. "American Revolution." Encyclopedia Britannica, August 27, 2023. https://www.britannica.com/event/American-Revolution.

Watson, J. Steven. "George III." Encyclopedia Britannica, July 3, 2023. https://www.britannica.com/biography/George-III.

Whitelock, D. "Alfred." Encyclopedia Britannica, May 16, 2023. https://www.britannica.com/biography/Alfred-king-of-Wessex.

United States Holocaust Memorial Museum. "The British Policy of Appeasement toward Hitler and Nazi Germany." Holocaust Encyclopedia. https://encyclopedia.ushmm.org/content/en/article/introduction-to-the-holocaust.

"Viking Place Names." JORVIK Viking Centre, March 13, 2023. https://www.jorvikvikingcentre.co.uk/the-vikings/viking-place-names/.

Part 2

"A Brief History of Capital Punishment in Britain." HistoryExtra, December 15, 2021. https://www.historyextra.com/period/modern/a-brief-history-of-capital-punishment-in-britain

"An Introduction to Early Medieval England." English Heritage. Accessed December 6, 2021.

https://www.english-heritage.org.uk/learn/story-of-england/early-medieval

"Anglo-Saxons: A Brief History." The Historical Association. Accessed December 6, 2021

. https://www.history.org.uk/primary/resource/3865/anglo-saxons-a-brief-history

"Athelstan." Encyclopedia Britannica. Encyclopedia Britannica, inc. Accessed December 6, 2021. https://www.britannica.com/biography/Athelstan

"Battle of Agincourt." Encyclopedia Britannica. Encyclopedia Britannica, inc. Accessed

December 10, 2021. https://www.britannica.com/event/Battle-of-Agincourt

"Battle of Bannockburn." Encyclopedia Britannica. Encyclopedia Britannica, inc. Accessed

December 10, 2021. https://www.britannica.com/event/Battle-of-Bannockburn

"Battle of Bosworth Field." Encyclopedia Britannica. Encyclopedia Britannica, inc. Accessed

December 10, 2021. https://www.britannica.com/event/Battle-of-Bosworth-Field

"Battle of Edington." Encyclopedia Britannica. Encyclopedia Britannica, inc. Accessed December 10, 2021. https://www.britannica.com/topic/Battle-of-Edington

"Battle of Hastings." Encyclopedia Britannica. Encyclopedia Britannica, inc. Accessed December

6, 2021. https://www.britannica.com/event/Battle-of-Hastings

"Beowulf." British Library. Accessed January 25, 2022.

https://www.bl.uk/collection-items/beowulf

"Bria 16 1 b the Murder of an Archbishop." Constitutional Rights Foundation. Accessed January 17,2022.

https://www.crf-usa.org/bill-of-rights-in-action/bria-16-1-b-the-murder-of-an-archbishop

"Crime and Medieval Punishment." History, December 2, 2021.

https://www.historyonthenet.com/medieval-life-crime-and-medieval-punishment

"Danelaw." Encyclopedia Britannica. Encyclopedia Britannica, inc. Accessed December 6, 2021. https://www.britannica.com/place/Danelaw

"Divine Right of Kings." Divine Right of Kings - New World Encyclopedia. Accessed December 29, 2021.

https://www.newworldencyclopedia.org/entry/Divine_Right_of_Kings

"Durham Cathedral - an Overview." Durham Cathedral Durham World Heritage Site. Accessed

December 29, 2021.

https://www.durhamworldheritagesite.com/learn/architecture/cathedral

"Four Humors - and There's the Humor of It: Shakespeare and the Four Humors." U.S. National

Library of Medicine. National Institutes of Health, September 19, 2013

. https://www.nlm.nih.gov/exhibition/shakespeare/fourhumors.html

"Gothic Architecture." Encyclopedia Britannica. Encyclopedia Britannica, inc. Accessed December 29, 2021. https://www.britannica.com/art/Gothic-architecture

"Harthacnut." Hardicanute, or Harthacnut, King of England and Denmark. Accessed December 6, 2021. https://www.englishmonarchs.co.uk/vikings_4.htm

"King Athelstan." Athelstan Museum, February 27, 2020.

https://www.athelstanmuseum.org.uk/malmesbury-history/people/king-athelstan

"King Canute." Canute or Cnut the Great, son of Sweyn Forkbeard. Accessed December 6, 2021. https://www.englishmonarchs.co.uk/vikings_2.htm

"King Edward I of England." BBC Bitesize. BBC, December 6, 2019.

https://www.bbc.co.uk/bitesize/topics/z8g86sg/articles/z77dbdm

"List of 5 Most Significant Battles of the Hundred Years' War." List of 5 Most Significant Battles of the Hundred Years' War - History Lists. Accessed December 6, 2021.

https://historylists.org/events/list-of-5-most-significant-battles-of-the-hundred-years-war.html

"List of English Monarchs." Wikipedia. Wikimedia Foundation, December 5, 2021.

https://en.wikipedia.org/wiki/List_of_English_monarchs

"Magna Carta (1215) to Henry IV (1399) - UK Parliament." parliament.uk. Accessed December 29, 2021.

https://www.parliament.uk/about/living-heritage/evolutionofparliament/originsofparliament/birthofparliament/keydates/1215to1399

"Medieval Architecture." English Heritage. Accessed December 29, 2021.

https://www.english-heritage.org.uk/learn/story-of-england/medieval/architecture

"Medieval Religion." English Heritage. Accessed January 17, 2022.
https://www.english-heritage.org.uk/learn/story-of-england/medieval/religion

"Monsters, Marvels, and Mythical Beasts: Medieval Monsters." Research Guides. Accessed January 25, 2022.
https://guides.library.uab.edu/c.php?g=1014328&p=7346799

"Old English Language." Encyclopedia Britannica. Encyclopedia Britannica, inc. Accessed December 6, 2021. https://www.britannica.com/topic/Old-English-language

"Plague - Symptoms." Centers for Disease Control and Prevention. Centers for Disease Control and Prevention, November 15, 2021. https://www.cdc.gov/plague/symptoms/index.html

"Robert the Bruce." BBC Bitesize. BBC, December 6, 2019.

https://www.bbc.co.uk/bitesize/topics/z8g86sg/articles/zm2747h

"The Anglo-Saxon Tribal Kingdoms." The Anglo-Saxon Tribal Kingdoms - The Heptarchy.

Accessed December 6, 2021. https://www.englishmonarchs.co.uk/saxon_25.html

"The Battle of Edington." The Battle of Edington. Accessed December 10, 2021.

https://www.englishmonarchs.co.uk/vikings_16.html

"The Canterbury Tales by Geoffrey Chaucer." British Library. Accessed January 25, 2022.

https://www.bl.uk/collection-items/the-canterbury-tales-by-geoffrey-chaucer

"The Celts of England." Celtic Life International - Celebrating the Celtic Life for over 30 years.

Accessed December 6, 2021. https://celticlifeintl.com/the-celts-of-england

"The English Invasion of Wales." Historic UK. Accessed December 6, 2021. https://www.historic-uk.com/HistoryUK/HistoryofWales/The-English-conquest-of-Wales

"The First Battle of St Albans." Historic UK. Accessed December 6, 2021. https://www.historic-uk.com/HistoryMagazine/DestinationsUK/The-First-Battle-of-St-Albans

"The Great Famine." The great famine. Accessed December 6, 2021.

http://www.halinaking.co.uk/Location/Yorkshire/Frames/History/1315%20Great%20Famine/Great%20Famine.htm

"The History of the English Longbow." Historic UK. Accessed December 10, 2021.

https://www.historic-uk.com/HistoryUK/HistoryofEngland/The-Longbow

"The Medieval Marvel Few People Know." BBC Travel. BBC. Accessed December 29, 2021. https://www.bbc.com/travel/article/20170427-the-extraordinary-angel-roofs-of-england

"The Period of the Scandinavian Invasions." Encyclopedia Britannica. Encyclopedia Britannica, inc. Accessed December 6, 2021. https://www.britannica.com/place/United-Kingdom/The-period-of-the-Scandinavian-invasions#ref482644

"The Plague, 1331-1770." The Black Death. Accessed January 27, 2022.

http://hosted.lib.uiowa.edu/histmed/plague

"Trial by Ordeal." *Oxford Reference.* Accessed 1 Jan. 2022.

https://www.oxfordreference.com/view/10.1093/oi/authority.20110803105644353

"Romanesque Architecture." Encyclopedia Britannica. Encyclopedia Britannica, inc. Accessed December 29, 2021. https://www.britannica.com/art/Romanesque-architecture

"Scotland's History - the Wars of Independence." BBC. BBC. Accessed December 10, 2021. https://www.bbc.co.uk/scotland/history/articles/the_wars_of_independence

"St Hild of Whitby." English Heritage. Accessed December 29, 2021. https://www.english-heritage.org.uk/visit/places/whitby-abbey/history-and-stories/st-hild

"Viking Ships." Royal Museums Greenwich. Accessed December 6, 2021.

https://www.rmg.co.uk/stories/topics/viking-ships

"Wars of the Roses." Historic UK. Accessed December 6, 2021.

https://www.historic-uk.com/HistoryUK/HistoryofEngland/The-Wars-of-the-Roses

"Wat Tyler and the Peasants Revolt." Historic UK. Accessed December 6, 2021. https://www.historic-uk.com/HistoryUK/HistoryofEngland/Wat-Tyler-the-Peasants-Revolt

"What Happened to Britain after the Romans Left?" The Great Courses Daily, July 29, 2020.

https://www.thegreatcoursesdaily.com/britain-after-the-romans-left

"Women Get the Vote." UK Parliament. Accessed December 13, 2021.

https://www.parliament.uk/about/living-heritage/transformingsociety/electionsvoting/womenvote/overview/thevote

Abbott, G. "Burning at the Stake." Encyclopedia Britannica, July 5, 2019.

https://www.britannica.com/topic/burning-at-the-stake.

Barker, Juliet. *1381: The Year of the Peasants' Revolt.* Cambridge: The Belknap Press of Harvard University Press, 2014.

Barlow, Frank. *The Feudal Kingdom of England 1042-1216.* 5th ed. London: Longman, 1999.

Bell, Bethan. "A Ghoulish Tour of Medieval Punishments." BBC News. BBC, July 2, 2016.

https://www.bbc.com/news/uk-england-36641921

Bovey, Alixe. "The Medieval Church: from Dedication to Dissent." British Library, April 30,

2015. https://www.bl.uk/the-middle-ages/articles/church-in-the-middle-ages-from-dedication-to-dissent

Bovey, Alixe. "The Medieval Diet." British Library. Accessed January 4, 2022.

https://www.bl.uk/the-middle-ages/articles/the-medieval-diet

Bovey, Alixe. "Medieval Monsters." British Library, April 30, 2015. https://www.bl.uk/the-middle-ages/articles/medieval-monsters-from-the-mystical-to-the-demonic

Bovey, Alixe. "Women in Medieval Society." British Library, April 30, 2015.

https://www.bl.uk/the-middle-ages/articles/women-in-medieval-society

Boyer, Sam. "The Battle of Mount Badon." The Battle of Mount Badon | Robbins Library Digital

Projects, 2004. https://d.lib.rochester.edu/camelot/text/boyer-battle-of-mt-badon-overview

Bremner, Ian. "History - British History in Depth: Wales: English Conquest of Wales C.1200 –

1415." BBC. BBC, February 17, 2011.

https://www.bbc.co.uk/history/british/middle_ages/wales_conquest_01.shtml

Britannica, T. Editors of Encyclopedia. "Arthurian legend." Encyclopedia Britannica, May 27,

2021. https://www.britannica.com/topic/Arthurian-legend.

Britannica, T. Editors of Encyclopedia. "Assize of Clarendon." Encyclopedia Britannica,

September 6, 2007. https://www.britannica.com/event/Assize-of-Clarendon.

Britannica, T. Editors of Encyclopedia. "Bayeux Tapestry." Encyclopedia Britannica, May 30,

2021. https://www.britannica.com/topic/Bayeux-Tapestry.

Britannica, T. Editors of Encyclopedia. "Beowulf." Encyclopedia Britannica, August 20, 2021. https://www.britannica.com/topic/Beowulf.

Britannica, T. Editors of Encyclopedia. "Black Death." Encyclopedia Britannica, August 27, 2021.

https://www.britannica.com/event/Black-Death.

Britannica, T. Editors of Encyclopedia. "Compurgation." Encyclopedia Britannica, November 22,

2011. https://www.britannica.com/topic/compurgation.

Britannica, T. Editors of Encyclopedia. "Drawing and Quartering." Encyclopedia Britannica, July

5, 2019. https://www.britannica.com/topic/drawing-and-quartering.

Britannica, T. Editors of Encyclopedia. "Illuminated Manuscript." Encyclopedia Britannica, July

15, 2021. https://www.britannica.com/art/illuminated-manuscript.

Britannica, T. Editors of Encyclopedia. "Manorial Court." Encyclopedia Britannica, February 15,

2007. https://www.britannica.com/topic/manorial-court.

Britannica, T. Editors of Encyclopedia. "Miracle Play." Encyclopedia Britannica, February 6,

2019. https://www.britannica.com/art/miracle-play.

Britannica, T. Editors of Encyclopedia. "Morality Play." Encyclopedia Britannica, January 16,

2014. https://www.britannica.com/art/morality-play-dramatic-genre.

Britannica, T. Editors of Encyclopedia. "Ordeal." Encyclopedia Britannica, April 13, 2018.

https://www.britannica.com/topic/ordeal.

Britannica, T. Editors of Encyclopedia. "Plague." Encyclopedia Britannica, August 6, 2020.

https://www.britannica.com/science/plague.

Britannica, T. Editors of Encyclopedia. "Templar." Encyclopedia Britannica, April 28, 2020.

https://www.britannica.com/topic/Templars.

Britannica, T. Editors of Encyclopedia. "The Canterbury Tales." Encyclopedia Britannica, May

14, 2020. https://www.britannica.com/topic/The-Canterbury-Tales.

Britannica, T. Editors of Encyclopedia. "Tuberculosis." Encyclopedia Britannica, July 29, 2021.

https://www.britannica.com/science/tuberculosis.

Britannica, T. Editors of Encyclopedia. "Sweating Sickness." Encyclopedia Britannica, February

15, 2019. https://www.britannica.com/science/sweating-sickness.

Brooke, John. "The Black Death and Its Aftermath." Origins, June 2020.

https://origins.osu.edu/connecting-history/covid-black-death-plague-lessons?language_content_entity=en

Buis, Alena. "The Romanesque in Normandy and England." Art and Visual Culture Prehistory to

Renaissance. Accessed December 29, 2021.

https://pressbooks.bccampus.ca/cavestocathedrals/chapter/the-romanesque-in-normandy-and-england

Carpenter, David. *The Struggle for Mastery: Britain 1066-1284*. Oxford: Oxford University Press,

2003.

Cartwright, Mark. "Clothes in Medieval England." World History Encyclopedia. World History

Encyclopedia, June 28, 2018. https://www.worldhistory.org/article/1248/clothes-in-medieval-england

Cartwright, Mark. "Leisure in an English Medieval Castle." World History Encyclopedia. World

History Encyclopedia, May 31, 2018.
https://www.worldhistory.org/article/1232/leisure-in-an-english-medieval-castle

Castelow, Ellen. "The Origins and History of Fairies." Historic UK. Accessed January 25, 2022

. https://www.historic-uk.com/CultureUK/The-Origins-of-Fairies

Cybulskie, Danièle. "Medieval Pilgrimages: It's All about the Journey." Medievalists.net, August

4, 2017. https://www.medievalists.net/2015/08/medieval-pilgrimages-its-all-about-the-journey

Daileader, Philip. "Henry II vs. the Church: The Murder of Thomas Becket." The Great Courses

Daily, November 4, 2020. https://www.thegreatcoursesdaily.com/henry-ii-vs-the-church-the-murder-of-thomas-becket

de Beer, Lloyd, and Naomi Speakman. "Thomas Becket: The Murder That Shook the Middle Ages - British Museum Blog." British Museum Blog - Explore stories from the Museum, May 27, 2021. https://blog.britishmuseum.org/thomas-becket-the-murder-that-shook-the-middle-ages

Duggan, L. G. "Indulgence." Encyclopedia Britannica, November 25, 2015.

https://www.britannica.com/topic/indulgence.

Fee, Christopher R. *Gods, Heroes, and Kings: The Battle for Mythic Britain.* Cary: Oxford

University Press, Incorporated, 2004. Accessed January 25, 2022. ProQuest eBook Central.

Flantzer, Susan. "Royal Deaths from Plague." Unofficial Royalty, January 9, 2022.

https://www.unofficialroyalty.com/royal-deaths-from-plague-4-23/.

Fleming, Robin. Britain After Rome: The Fall and Rise: 400 to 1070. New York: Penguin, 2011.

Goldiner, Sigrid. "Medicine in the Middle Ages." Metmuseum.org, January 1, 2012.

https://www.metmuseum.org/toah/hd/medm/hd_medm.htm.

Hajar, Rachel. "The Air of History (Part II) Medicine in the Middle Ages." Heart views: The

official journal of the Gulf Heart Association. Medknow Publications & Media Pvt Ltd, October

2012. https://www.ncbi.nlm.nih.gov/pmc/articles/PMC3573364/.

Harrison, Julian. "Who Were the Anglo-Saxons?" British Library. Accessed December 6, 2021.

https://www.bl.uk/anglo-saxons/articles/who-were-the-anglo-saxons.

Hannan, M. T. and Kranzberg, Melvin. "History of the Organization of Work." Encyclopedia

Britannica, November 1, 2021. https://www.britannica.com/topic/history-of-work-organization-648000.

Highman, Nicholas J., and Martin J. Ryan. *The Anglo-Saxon World.* New Haven: Yale University

Press, 2013.

Hitti, Miranda. "Bloodletting's Benefits." WebMD. WebMD, September 10, 2004.

https://www.webmd.com/men/news/20040910/bloodlettings-benefits

Hudson, Alison. "The Battle of Hastings: Fact and Fiction." British Library. Accessed December

6, 2021. https://www.bl.uk/anglo-saxons/articles/the-battle-of-hastings-fact-and-fiction

Ibeji, Mike. "Becket, the Church and Henry II." BBC. BBC, February 17, 2011.

https://www.bbc.co.uk/history/british/middle_ages/becket_01.shtml

Johnson, Ben. "Æthelflæd (Aethelflaed), Lady of the Mercians." Historic UK. Accessed December

29, 2021. https://www.historic-uk.com/HistoryUK/HistoryofEngland/Aethelflaed-Lady-of-the-Mercians

Johnson, Ben. "Norman and Medieval Fashion and Clothing." Historic UK. Accessed January 5,

2022. https://www.historic-uk.com/CultureUK/Medieval-Fashion

Jones, Dan. *The Wars of the Roses.* New York: Penguin, 2014.

Kemp, J. Arthur. "St. Anselm of Canterbury." *Encyclopedia Britannica,* September 20, 2021.

https://www.britannica.com/biography/Saint-Anselm-of-Canterbury

Kerr, Margaret H., Richard D. Forsyth, and Michael J. Plyley. "Cold Water and Hot Iron: Trial by

Ordeal in England." *The Journal of Interdisciplinary History* 22, no. 4 (1992): 573–95.

https://doi.org/10.2307/205237

Leyser, Henrietta. *The Anglo-Saxons.* London: I.B Tauris & Co., 2017.

Mark, Joshua J. "Medieval Cures for the Black Death." World History Encyclopedia. World

History Encyclopedia, April 15, 2020. https://www.worldhistory.org/article/1540/medieval-cures-for-the-black-death

Mark, Joshua J. "Medieval Folklore." World History Encyclopedia. World History Encyclopedia,

February 19, 2019. https://www.worldhistory.org/Medieval_Folklore

Mark, Joshua J. "Medieval Literature." World History Encyclopedia. World History

Encyclopedia, December 26, 2021. https://www.worldhistory.org/Medieval_Literature

Mark, Joshua J. "Religion in the Middle Ages." World History Encyclopedia. World History

Encyclopedia, June 28, 2019. https://www.worldhistory.org/article/1411/religion-in-the-middle-ages

Mark, Joshua J. "The Medieval Church." World History Encyclopedia. World History

Encyclopedia, June 17, 2019. https://www.worldhistory.org/Medieval_Church

Mark, Joshua J. "Women in the Middle Ages." World History Encyclopedia. World History

Encyclopedia, March 18, 2019. https://www.worldhistory.org/article/1345/women-in-the-middle-ages

Masson, Victoria. "The Black Death." Historic UK. Accessed January 27, 2022.

https://www.historic-uk.com/HistoryUK/HistoryofEngland/The-Black-Death

Palmer, Bill. "Our 1918 Pandemic – the Numbers Then and Now." marshallindependent.com, March 27, 2021. https://www.marshallindependent.com/opinion/local-columns/2021/03/our-1918-pandemic-the-numbers-then-and-now

Pernoud, R. "Eleanor of Aquitaine." *Encyclopedia Britannica*, May 31, 2021.

https://www.britannica.com/biography/Eleanor-of-Aquitaine

Rhodes, P. and Bryant, John H. "Public Health." Encyclopedia Britannica, April 22, 2021.

https://www.britannica.com/topic/public-health.

Ross, David. "Anglo-Saxon England - Culture and Society." Britain Express. Accessed December

9, 2021. https://www.britainexpress.com/History/anglo-saxon_life-kinship_and_lordship.htm

Ruben, Miri. The Hollow Crown: A History of Britain in the Late Middle Ages. New York:

Penguin, 2005.

Shipman, Pat Lee. "The Bright Side of the Black Death." American Scientist, May 2, 2018

. https://www.americanscientist.org/article/the-bright-side-of-the-black-death

Simons, E. Norman. "Mary I." Encyclopedia Britannica, November 13, 2021.

https://www.britannica.com/biography/Mary-I.

Singer, Sholom A. "The Expulsion of the Jews from England in 1290." *The Jewish Quarterly*

Review 55, no. 2 (1964): 117–36. https://doi.org/10.2307/1453793

Sorabella, Jean. "Pilgrimage in Medieval England." Metmuseum.org, April 1, 2011.

https://www.metmuseum.org/toah/hd/pilg/hd_pilg.htm

Stacey, J. "John Wycliffe." Encyclopedia Britannica, December 27, 2021.

https://www.britannica.com/biography/John-Wycliffe.

Stephens, J.E.R. "The Growth of Trial by Jury in England." jstor.org. The Harvard Law Review

Association. Accessed January 3, 2022.
https://www.jstor.org/stable/pdf/1321755.pdf

Trueman, C N. "Food and Drink in Medieval England." History Learning Site. The History

Learning Site, March 5, 2015. https://www.historylearningsite.co.uk/medieval-england/food-and-drink-in-medieval-england

Ward, Jennifer. *Women in England in the Middle Ages*. London: Hambledon Continuum, 2006.

Webb, Diana. "Pilgrimage Destinations in England." The Becket Story. Accessed January 17, 2022. https://thebecketstory.org.uk/pilgrimage/destinations-england

Wheelis, Mark. "Biological Warfare at the 1346 Siege of Caffa." Emerging infectious diseases.

Centers for Disease Control and Prevention, September 2002.

https://www.ncbi.nlm.nih.gov/pmc/articles/PMC2732530

Zeisel, H. and Kalven, Harry. "Jury." Encyclopedia Britannica, March 29, 2019.

https://www.britannica.com/topic/jury.

Part 3

- Link: https://www.britannica.com/topic/house-of-Plantagenet Date Accessed: 7/2/22 Title: House of Plantagenet

- Link: https://www.englishmonarchs.co.uk/plantagenet_18.htm Date Accessed: 7/2/22 Title: Plantagenet Kings and Queens

Link: https://www.britannica.com/biography/Henry-II-king-of-England Date Accessed: 7/2/22 Title: Henry II

- Link: https://www.historic-uk.com/HistoryUK/HistoryofEngland/King-Henry-II-of-England/

Date Accessed: 7/2/22

Title: King Henry II

Link: https://www.britannica.com/biography/Richard-I-king-of-England Date Accessed: 7/2/22 Title: Richard I

- Link: https://www.english-heritage.org.uk/learn/story-of-england/medieval/

Date Accessed: 7/2/22

Title: An Introduction to Medieval England (1066-1485)

- Link: https://www.worldhistory.org/article/1504/the-wars-of-the-roses-consequences--effects/

Date Accessed: 7/2/22

Title: The Wars of the Roses: Consequences & Effects

Link: https://www.britainexpress.com/History/Knights_and_Fights.htm
Date Accessed: 7/2/22 Title: Medieval Knights and Warfare

- Link: https://www.bl.uk/medieval-literature/articles/love-and-chivalry-in-the-middle-ages

Date Accessed: 7/2/22

Title: Love and Chivalry in the Middle Ages

Link: https://www.britannica.com/topic/Magna-Carta Date Accessed: 7/2/22 Title: Magna Carta

- Link: https://dbpedia.org/page/Anglo-French_War_(1213%E2%80%931214)

Date Accessed: 8/2/22

Title: Anglo-French War (1213-1214)

Link: https://www.worldhistory.org/Henry_III_of_England/ Date Accessed: 8/2/22 Title: Henry III of England

Link: https://www.worldhistory.org/Edward_I_of_England/ Date Accessed: 8/2/22 Title: Edward I of England

Link: https://www.worldhistory.org/Edward_II_of_England/ Date Accessed: 8/2/22 Title: Edward II of England

- Link: https://englishhistory.net/tudor/genealogy-chart-family-tree/

Date Accessed: 8/2/22

Title: House of Tudor Genealogy Chart & Family Tree

Link: https://www.worldhistory.org/Edward_III_of_England/ Date Accessed: 8/2/22 Title: Edward III of England

Link: https://www.britannica.com/biography/Edward-III-king-of-England Date Accessed: 8/2/22 Title: Edward III

Link: https://www.worldhistory.org/Hundred_Years'_War/ Date Accessed: 8/2/22 Title: Hundred Years' War

Link: https://www.britannica.com/topic/house-of-York Date Accessed: 8/2/22 Title: House of York

Link: https://www.britannica.com/topic/house-of-Lancaster Date Accessed: 8/2/22 Title: house of Lancaster

Link: https://www.britannica.com/topic/Valois-dynasty Date Accessed: 8/2/22 Title: Valois Dynasty

Link: https://www.worldhistory.org/Owen_Tudor/ Date Accessed: 8/2/22 Title: Owen Tudor

Link: https://www.britannica.com/biography/Catherine-of-Valois Date Accessed: 8/2/22 Title: Catherine of Valois

Link: https://www.britannica.com/biography/Jasper-Tudor-duke-of-Bedford Date Accessed: 8/2/22 Title: Jasper Tudor, duke of Bedford

Link: https://www.tudorsociety.com/edmund-tudor-1st-earl-of-richmond/ Date Accessed: 8/2/22 Title: Edmund Tudor, 1st Earl of Richmond

Link: https://www.anglesey-history.co.uk/places/penmynydd/index.html Date Accessed: 10/2/22 Title: Penmynydd-birthplace of royalty

Link: https://www.history.com/topics/european-history/wars-of-the-roses Date Accessed: 10/2/22 Title: Wars of the Roses

Link: https://www.britannica.com/biography/Richard-Neville-16th-earl-of-Warwick Date Accessed: 10/2/22 Title: Richard Neville, 16th earl of Warwick

Link: https://www.britannica.com/biography/Edward-IV-king-of-England Date Accessed: 10/2/22 Title: Edward IV

Link: https://www.britannica.com/biography/Richard-III-king-of-England Date Accessed: 10/2/22 Title: Richard III

- Link: https://soundideas.pugetsound.edu/cgi/viewcontent.cgi?article=1015&context=summer_research

Date Accessed: 10/2/22

Title: The Queens' Blood: A Study of Family Ties during the Wars of the Roses

- Link: https://www.history.co.uk/articles/margaret-beaufort-the-kingmaker-and-mother-of-the-tudor-dynasty

Date Accessed: 10/2/22

Title: The Kingmaker Margaret Beaufort: Mother of the Tudor Dynasty

- Link: https://www.historic-uk.com/HistoryUK/HistoryofEngland/The-Princes-in-the-Tower/

Date Accessed: 10/2/22

Title: The Princes in the Tower

Link: https://www.history.com/this-day-in-history/battle-of-bosworth-field Date Accessed: 10/2/22 Title: Battle of Bosworth Field

Link: https://www.worldhistory.org/Henry_VII_of_England/ Date Accessed: 16/2/22 Title: Henry VII of England

Link: https://www.britannica.com/biography/Henry-VII-king-of-England Date Accessed: 16/2/22 Title: Henry VII

- Link: https://www.historylearningsite.co.uk/tudor-england/henry-vii-the-man/#:~:text=His%20spirit%20was%20distinguished%2C%20wise,was%20not%20devoid%20of%20scholarship.

Date Accessed: 20/2/22

Title: Henry VII- the man

Link: https://www.britannica.com/biography/Henry-VIII-king-of-England Date Accessed: 21/2/22 Title: Henry VIII

Link: https://www.worldhistory.org/Henry_VIII_of_England/ Date Accessed: 21/2/22 Title: Henry VIII of England

Link: https://www.history.com/news/henry-viii-wives Date Accessed: 21/2/22 Title: Who Were the Six Wives of Henry VIII

- Link: https://www.historyextra.com/period/tudor/henry-six-wives-guide-who-were-they-how-many-spouse-catherine-aragon-anne-boleyn-jane-seymour-anne-cleves-howard-parr-facts/

Date Accessed: 21/2/22

Title: Henry VIII's six wives: your guide to the Tudor king's queen consorts

- Link: https://www.historyextra.com/period/tudor/prince-arthur-catherine-katherine-aragon-king-henry-viii-marriage-death-brother/

Date Accessed: 21/2/22

Title: Prince Arthur, Catherine of Aragon, and Henry VIII: a story of early Tudor triumph and tragedy

Link: https://www.worldhistory.org/English_Reformation/ Date Accessed: 21/2/22 Title: English Reformation

- Link: https://www.britannica.com/topic/Protestantism/The-Reformation-in-England-and-Scotland

Date Accessed: 21/2/22

Title: The Reformation in England and Scotland

Link: https://www.britannica.com/biography/Edward-VI Date Accessed: 21/2/22 Title: Edward VI

- Link: https://www.encyclopedia.com/people/history/british-and-irish-history-biographies/edward-vi

Date Accessed: 21/2/22

Title: Edward VI (England) (1537-1553; Ruled 1547-1553)

Link: https://www.thehistorypress.co.uk/articles/catherine-parr-henry-viii-s-last-love/ Date Accessed: 21/2/22 Title: Catherine Parr: Henry VIII's Last Love

Link: https://www.britannica.com/biography/Edward-Seymour-1st-Duke-of-Somerset Date Accessed: 21/2/22 Title: Edward Seymour, 1st duke of Somerset

Link: https://www.britannica.com/biography/John-Dudley-duke-of-Northumberland Date Accessed: 21/2/22 Title: John Dudley, duke of Northumberland

Link: https://www.britannica.com/biography/Catherine-Parr Date Accessed: 22/2/22 Title: Catherine Parr

Link: http://www.luminarium.org/encyclopedia/edwardtoparr1548.htm Date Accessed: 22/2/22 Title: King Edward VI to Queen Katharine Parr 1547

Link: https://www.britannica.com/biography/Mary-I Date Accessed: 22/2/22 Title: Mary I

- Link:https://www.worldhistory.org/Mary_I_of_England/#:~:text=Mary%20I%20of%20England%20reigned,her%20nickname%20'Bloody%20Mary'.

Date Accessed: 22/2/22

Title: Mary I of England

Link: https://www.englishmonarchs.co.uk/tudor_23.html Date Accessed: 22/2/22 Title: Philip II of Spain

Link: https://www.historic-uk.com/HistoryUK/HistoryofEngland/Lady-Jane-Grey/ Date Accessed: 22/2/22 Title: Lady Jane Grey

Link: https://www.britannica.com/biography/Elizabeth-I Date Accessed: 24/2/22 Title: Elizabeth I

Link: https://www.worldhistory.org/Elizabeth_I_of_England/ Date Accessed: 24/2/22 Title: Elizabeth I of England

Link: https://courses.lumenlearning.com/britlit1/chapter/english-renaissance/ Date Accessed: 24/2/22 Title: English Renaissance

Link: https://www.worldhistory.org/Wyatt_Rebellion/ Date Accessed: 24/2/22 Title: Wyatt Rebellion

Link: https://www.worldhistory.org/Robert_Dudley_1st_Earl_of_Leicester/ Date Accessed: 24/2/22 Title: Robert Dudley, 1st Earl of Leicester

- Link: https://www.worldhistory.org/Mary_Queen_of_Scots/#:~:text=She%20was%20the%20daughter%20of,country%20in%20her%20own%20right.

Date Accessed: 25/2/22

Title: Mary, Queen of Scots

Link: https://www.britishbattles.com/wars-of-the-roses/first-battle-of-st-albans/ Date Accessed: 25/2/22 Title: First Battle of St. Albans

- Link: https://www.historic-uk.com/HistoryMagazine/DestinationsUK/The-Battle-of-Stoke-Field/

Date Accessed: 25/2/22

Title: Battle of Stoke Field

Link: https://www.britishbattles.com/anglo-scottish-war/battle-of-flodden/ Date Accessed: 25/2/22 Title: Battle of Flodden

Link: https://www.henryviiithereign.co.uk/1513-battle-of-spurs.html Date Accessed: 25/2/22 Title: The Battle of the Spurs

- Link: https://warfarehistorynetwork.com/2016/06/17/king-henry-viii-england-siege-of-boulogne-his-last-war/

Date Accessed: 25/2/22

Title: King Henry VIII of England and the Siege of Boulogne: His Last War

- Link: https://www.historic-uk.com/HistoryUK/HistoryofEngland/The-Great-French-Armada-of-1545-The-Battle-of-The-Solent/

Date Accessed: 25/2/22

Title: The Great French Armada of 1545 & the Battle of the Solent

- Link: https://www.battlefieldstrust.com/resource-centre/medieval/battleview.asp?BattleFieldId=40

Date Accessed: 25/2/22

Title: Battle of Solway Moss

- Link: https://www.battlefieldstrust.com/resource-centre/medieval/battleview.asp?BattleFieldId=72

Date Accessed: 25/2/22

Title: Battle of Ancrum Moor

- Link: https://www.battlefieldstrust.com/resource-centre/medieval/battleview.asp?BattleFieldId=68

Date Accessed: 25/2/22

Title: Battle of Pinkie

- Link: http://historicaltriumphsanddisasters.blogspot.com/2015/12/england-loses-calais1558.html

Date Accessed: 25/2/22

Title: England loses Calais, 1558

Link: https://www.historic-uk.com/HistoryUK/HistoryofEngland/Spanish-Armada/ Date Accessed: 25/2/22 Title: The Spanish Armada

Link: https://www.english-heritage.org.uk/learn/story-of-england/medieval/war/ Date Accessed: 26/2/22 Title: Medieval: Warfare

- Link: https://www.historic-uk.com/HistoryUK/HistoryofEngland/The-Wars-of-the-Roses/

Date Accessed: 26/2/22

Title: The Wars of the Roses

Link: https://www.britishbattles.com/wars-of-the-roses/battle-of-bosworth-field/ Date Accessed: 26/2/22 Title: Battle of Bosworth Field

- Link: https://www.jstor.org/stable/3816474

Date Accessed: 26/2/22

Title: Notes on the Organization and Supply of the Tudor Military under Henry VII

Link: https://www.jstor.org/stable/44230050 Date Accessed: 26/2/22 Title: The Army of Henry VIII: A Reassessment

• Link: https://core.ac.uk/download/pdf/30695522.pdf

Date Accessed: 26/2/22

Title: The military obligations of the English people 1511-1558

Link: https://www.english-heritage.org.uk/about-us/our-places/forts-and-defences/ Date Accessed: 26/2/22 Title: Forts and Defenses

Link: https://www.rmg.co.uk/stories/topics/henry-viii-his-navy Date Accessed: 26/2/22 Title: Henry VIII and his navy

Link: https://maryrose.org/the-history-of-the-mary-rose/ Date Accessed: 26/2/22 Title: The History of the Mary Rose- 1510-1545

Link: https://www.thehistorypress.co.uk/articles/queen-elizabeth-i-s-sea-dogs/ Date Accessed: 26/2/22 Title: Queen Elizabeth I's Sea Dogs

• Link: https://www.medievalchronicles.com/medieval-weapons/tudor-weapons/#:~:text=The%20conventional%20weapons%20used%20during,%2C%20matchlock%2C%20flintlock%20and%20canons.

Date Accessed: 28/2/22

Title: Tudor Weapons

• Link: https://www.medievalchronicles.com/medieval-history/medieval-history-periods/tudor-england/tudor-weapons-list/

Date Accessed: 28/2/22

Title: Tudor Weapons List

• Link: http://myarmoury.com/feature_armies_eng.html

Date Accessed: 28/2/22

Title: Renaissance Armies: The English- Henry VIII to Elizabeth

• Link: https://www.warhistoryonline.com/history/military-reforms-of-king-henry.html?chrome=1

Date Accessed: 28/2/22

Title: Military Reforms of King Henry the Eighth- He Built Up a Modern Fighting Force in Medieval England

Link: https://www.medievalchronicles.com/medieval-armour/tudor-armour/ Date Accessed: 28/2/22 Title: Tudor Armour

Link: https://www.britannica.com/topic/Landsknechte Date Accessed: 28/2/22 Title: Landsknecht

Link: https://www.britannica.com/topic/Yeomen-of-the-Guard Date Accessed: 28/2/22 Title: Yeomen of the Guard

- Link: https://hsu.edu/uploads/pages/2003-4afthedeathof_the_knight.pdf

Date Accessed: 28/2/22

Title: The Death of the Knight: Changes in Military Weaponry during the Tudor Period

Link: http://home.mysoul.com.au/graemecook/Renaissance/06_English.htm
Date Accessed: 28/2/22 Title: Part 6: Henry VIII's Army

- Link: https://www.jstor.org/stable/2639241

Date Accessed: 28/2/22

Title: Review: Politics and Government in Tudor England

- Link: https://www.gale.com/intl/essays/david-j-crankshaw-tudor-privy-council-c-1540%E2%80%931603

Date Accessed: 28/2/22

Title: The Tudor Privy Council, c. 1540-1603

- Link: https://www.hoddereducation.co.uk/media/Documents/History/AQA_A-level_History_My_Revision_Notes_The_Tudors_sample_pages.pdf

Date Accessed: 28/2/22

Title: The Tudors, England, 1485-1603

- Link: https://www.jstor.org/stable/2594614

Date Accessed: 28/2/22

Title: Population Change, Enclosure, and the Early Tudor Economy

Link: https://spartacus-educational.com/TUDagriculture.htm Date Accessed: 1/3/22 Title: Agriculture and Enclosures

- Link: https://tudortimes.co.uk/politics-economy/the-english-wool-trade/economics-of-sheep-farming

Date Accessed: 1/3/22

Title: The English Wool Trade

Link: https://www.historylearningsite.co.uk/tudor-england/henry-vii-and-trade/ Date Accessed: 1/3/22 Title: Henry VII and Trade

- Link: https://www.parliament.uk/about/living-heritage/evolutionofparliament/originsofparliament/birthofparliament/overview/reformation/#:~:text=Henry%20VIII's%20Reformation%20Parliament%2C%20which,Papacy%20in%20Rome%20was%20blocking.

Date Accessed: 1/3/22

Title: Reformation Parliament

- Link: https://www.jstor.org/stable/10.1086/339721

Date Accessed: 1/3/22

Title: An Economic Analysis of the Protestant Reformation

- Link: http://elizabethanenglandlife.com/thetudorsfacts/tudor-times-exploration-of-the-world.html

Date Accessed: 1/3/22

Title: Tudor Times Exploration of the World

- Link: https://www.history.org.uk/student/module/4536/overview-of-elizabeth-i/4543/social-structure#:~:text=Elizabethan%20England%20had%20four%20main,and%20their%20children%20could%20get.

Date Accessed: 1/3/22

Title: Social Structure

- Link: https://www.museumoflondon.org.uk/Resources/learning/targettudors/education/theme.html

Date Accessed: 1/3/22

Title: Education: hard work and little play!

- Link: https://www.mylearning.org/stories/the-painted-lady--tudor-portraits-at-the-ferens/254#:~:text=the%20Sumptuary%20Law.-,Sumptuary%20Law,%2C%20food%2C%20furniture%2C%20etc.

Date Accessed: 1/3/22

Title: A Passion for Fashion

656

Link: https://tudortimes.co.uk/people/nobility Date Accessed: 1/3/22
Title: Nobility

- Link: https://www.rmg.co.uk/stories/topics/tudor-fashion#:~:text=Rich%20men%20wore%20white%20silk,were%20fashionable%20throughout%20the%20period.

Date Accessed: 1/3/22

Title: Tudor Fashion

- Link: https://www.hrp.org.uk/hampton-court-palace/history-and-stories/tudor-food-and-eating/#:~:text=Food%20for%20a%20King&text=Dishes%20included%20game%2C%20roasted%20or,which%20he%20ate%20sweet%20preserves.

Date Accessed: 1/3/22

Title: Tudor Food and Eating

Link: https://www.historic-uk.com/CultureUK/Tudor-Guide-To-Getting-Dressed/ Date Accessed: 1/3/22 Title: A Tudor Guide to Getting Dressed

Link: http://www.durhamrecordoffice.org.uk/article/10861/Tudor-Jobs Date Accessed: 1/3/22 Title: Tudor Jobs

- Link: https://www.hrp.org.uk/hampton-court-palace/history-and-stories/life-at-the-tudor-court/#:~:text=In%20the%201500s%2C%20a%20monarch's,pleasure%20palace%20and%20a%20hotel.

Date Accessed: 1/3/22

Title: Life at the Tudor Court

- Link: https://www.nationalgeographic.org/article/protestant-reformation/#:~:text=The%20Protestant%20Reformation%20began%20in,people%20to%20debate%20with%20him.

Date Accessed: 3/3/22

Title: The Protestant Reformation

- Link: https://www.english-heritage.org.uk/learn/story-of-england/tudors/religion/#:~:text=But%20although%20Henry%20had%20rejected,radically%20Protestant%20Edward%20VI%20(r.

Date Accessed: 3/3/22

Title: Tudors: Religion

Link: https://www.worldhistory.org/Thomas_Cranmer/ Date Accessed: 3/3/22 Title: Thomas Cranmer

Link: https://www.britannica.com/topic/Book-of-Common-Prayer Date Accessed: 3/3/22 Title: *Book of Common Prayer*

Link: https://www.newadvent.org/cathen/02376a.htm Date Accessed: 3/3/22 Title: Lady Margaret Beaufort

- Link: https://www.mylearning.org/stories/tudor-clothing--dress-to-impress/406?

Date Accessed: 3/3/22

Title: What to Look for in Tudor Paintings

- Link: https://www.infoplease.com/encyclopedia/arts/english-lit/20th-century-plus/english-literature/the-tudors-and-the-elizabethan-age#:~:text=A%20myriad%20of%20new%20genres,of%20Surrey%2C%20a%20seminal%20influence.

Date Accessed: 3/3/22

Title: English literature: The Tudors and the Elizabethan Age

Link: https://courses.lumenlearning.com/britlit1/chapter/english-renaissance/ Date Accessed: 3/3/22 Title: English Renaissance

Link: https://www.thespruce.com/tudor-architecture-4788228 Date Accessed: 3/3/22 Title: What is Tudor Architecture

Link: https://www.britannica.com/biography/Hans-Holbein-the-Younger Date Accessed: 3/3/22 Title: Hans Holbein the Younger

- Link: https://www.encyclopedia.com/women/encyclopedias-almanacs-transcripts-and-maps/teerlinc-levina-c-1520-1576

Date Accessed: 3/3/22

Title: Teerlinc, Levina (c. 1520-1576)

Link: https://www.britannica.com/biography/Nicholas-Hilliard Date Accessed: 3/3/22 Title: Nicholas Hilliard

Link: https://www.britannica.com/biography/William-Shakespeare Date Accessed: 3/3/22 Title: William Shakespeare

Link: https://www.britannica.com/biography/Edmund-Spenser Date Accessed: 3/3/22 Title: Edmund Spenser

Link: https://www.britannica.com/biography/Thomas-Wyatt Date Accessed: 3/3/22 Title: Sir Thomas Wyatt

Link: https://www.britannica.com/biography/Henry-Howard-Earl-of-Surrey Date Accessed: 3/3/22 Title: Henry Howard, Earl of Surrey

Link: https://www.britannica.com/biography/Philip-Sidney Date Accessed: 3/3/22 Title: Sir Philip Sidney

Link: https://www.britannica.com/biography/Roger-Ascham Date Accessed: 3/3/22 Title: Roger Ascham

- Link: https://joyofmuseums.com/museums/europe/spain-museums/madrid-museums/thyssen-bornemisza-museum/portrait-of-henry-viii-of-england-by-hans-holbein-the-younger-2/

Date Accessed: 3/3/22

Title: "Portrait of Henry VIII of England" by Hans Holbein the Younger

- Link: https://thetudortravelguide.com/2019/10/19/jane-seymour/

Date Accessed: 3/3/22

Title: Jane Seymour: The Unfinished Portrait of a Tudor Queen

Link: https://www.worldhistory.org/image/12314/elizabeth-i-rainbow-portrait/ Date Accessed: 3/3/22 Title: Elizabeth I Rainbow Portrait

Link: https://www.worldhistory.org/article/1581/holidays-in-the-elizabethan-era/ Date Accessed: 4/3/22 Title: Holidays in the Elizabethan Era

- Link: https://www.worldhistory.org/article/1579/sports-games--entertainment-in-the-elizabethan-era/

Date Accessed: 4/3/22

Title: Sports, Games & Entertainment in the Elizabethan Era

Link: https://www.worldhistory.org/article/1583/education-in-the-elizabethan-era/ Date Accessed: 4/3/22 Title: Education in the Elizabethan Era

Link: https://www.worldhistory.org/Elizabethan_Theatre/ Date Accessed: 4/3/22 Title: Elizabethan Theatre

- Link: https://www.hrp.org.uk/hampton-court-palace/history-and-stories/life-at-the-tudor-court/

Date Accessed: 4/3/22

Title: Life at the Tudor Court

Link: https://tudortimes.co.uk/daily-life/family-life Date Accessed: 4/3/22 Title: Family Life

Link: https://tudortimes.co.uk/daily-life/death-rites Date Accessed: 4/3/22 Title: Death Rites

Link: https://tudortimes.co.uk/daily-life/pastimes Date Accessed: 4/3/22 Title: Pastimes

Link: https://tudortimes.co.uk/daily-life/daily-life-objects Date Accessed: 4/3/22 Title: Objects in Daily Life

- Link: https://www.museumoflondon.org.uk/Resources/learning/targettudors/family/theme.html#:~:text=Tudor%20families%20were%20generally%20larger,as%20part%20of%20the%20family.

Date Accessed: 4/3/22

Title: Family Life: the more the merrier!

- Link: https://www.penguin.co.uk/articles/2017/a-day-in-the-life-of-a-tudor-courtier.html

Date Accessed: 4/3/22

Title: A day in the life of a Tudor Courtier by Simon Thurley

Part 4

"13 Colonies: Facts, Information, Colonies & History." Revolutionary War, March 4, 2020. https://www.revolutionary-war.net/13-colonies/.

Admin. "Shakespeare's Works." Shakespeare's Works. Folger Shakespeare Library, April 3, 2020. https://www.folger.edu/shakespeares-works.

Ashley, M. and Morrill, John S. "Oliver Cromwell." Encyclopedia Britannica, August 30, 2021. https://www.britannica.com/biography/Oliver-Cromwell.

Bowen, Lloyd. "Information, Language and Political Culture in Early Modern Wales." Past & Present, no. 228 (August 1, 2015): 125–58. https://search.ebscohost.com/login.aspx?direct=true&AuthType=ip,shib&db=edsjsr&AN=edsjsr.24544897&site=eds-live&scope=site.

Bradford, E. and Fernández-Armesto, Felipe. "Sir Francis Drake." Encyclopedia Britannica, January 24, 2022. https://www.britannica.com/biography/Francis-Drake.

Brain, Jessica. "Timeline of the British Empire." Historic UK, February 8, 2019. https://www.historic-uk.com/HistoryUK/HistoryofBritain/Timeline-Of-The-British-Empire/.

Brain, Jessica. "Titus Oates and the Popish Plot." Historic UK. Accessed May 25, 2022. https://www.historic-uk.com/HistoryUK/HistoryofEngland/Titus-Oates-Popish-Plot/.

Britannica, T. Editors of Encyclopedia. "American Colonies." Encyclopedia Britannica, October 19, 2021. https://www.britannica.com/topic/American-colonies.

Britannica, T. Editors of Encyclopedia. "Anglo-Dutch Wars." Encyclopedia Britannica, December 13, 2021. https://www.britannica.com/event/Anglo-Dutch-Wars.

Britannica, T. Editors of Encyclopedia. "Anne." Encyclopedia Britannica, February 2, 2022. https://www.britannica.com/biography/Anne-queen-of-Great-Britain-and-Ireland.

Britannica, T. Editors of Encyclopedia. "Book of Sports." Encyclopedia Britannica, February 14, 2022. https://www.britannica.com/topic/Book-of-Sports.

Britannica, T. Editors of Encyclopedia. "British Empire." Encyclopedia Britannica, March 13, 2022. https://www.britannica.com/place/British-Empire.

Britannica, T. Editors of Encyclopedia. "Clarendon Code." Encyclopedia Britannica, March 3, 2021. https://www.britannica.com/event/Clarendon-Code.

Britannica, T. Editors of Encyclopedia. "East India Company." Encyclopedia Britannica, February 12, 2021. https://www.britannica.com/topic/East-India-Company.

Britannica, T. Editors of Encyclopedia. "Great Chain of Being." Encyclopedia Britannica, December 10, 2021. https://www.britannica.com/topic/Great-Chain-of-Being.

Britannica, T. Editors of Encyclopedia. "Gunpowder Plot." Encyclopedia Britannica, December 13, 2021. https://www.britannica.com/event/Gunpowder-Plot.

Britannica, T. Editors of Encyclopedia. "Hudson's Bay Company." Encyclopedia Britannica, May 7, 2020. https://www.britannica.com/topic/Hudsons-Bay-Company.

Britannica, T. Editors of Encyclopedia. "King James Version." Encyclopedia Britannica, February 2, 2021. https://www.britannica.com/topic/King-James-Version.

Britannica, T. Editors of Encyclopedia. "Mary II." Encyclopedia Britannica, December 24, 2021. https://www.britannica.com/biography/Mary-II.

Britannica, T. Editors of Encyclopedia. "Massachusetts Bay Colony." Encyclopedia Britannica, June 6, 2021. https://www.britannica.com/place/Massachusetts-Bay-Colony.

Britannica, T. Editors of Encyclopedia. "Mercantilism." Encyclopedia Britannica, May 13, 2020. https://www.britannica.com/topic/mercantilism.

Britannica, T. Editors of Encyclopedia. "Peerage." Encyclopedia Britannica, September 6, 2019. https://www.britannica.com/topic/peerage.

Britannica, T. Editors of Encyclopedia. "Poor Law." Encyclopedia Britannica, May 19, 2020. https://www.britannica.com/event/Poor-Law.

Britannica, T. Editors of Encyclopedia. "Printing Press." Encyclopedia Britannica, October 1, 2021. https://www.britannica.com/technology/printing-press.

Britannica, T. Editors of Encyclopedia. "Puritanism." Encyclopedia Britannica, May 15, 2020. https://www.britannica.com/topic/Puritanism.

Britannica, T. Editors of Encyclopedia. "Renaissance." Encyclopedia Britannica, March 30, 2022. https://www.britannica.com/event/Renaissance.

Britannica, T. Editors of Encyclopedia. "Short Parliament." I, June 23, 2019. https://www.britannica.com/topic/Short-Parliament.

Britannica, T. Editors of Encyclopedia. "Southwark." Encyclopedia Britannica, April 10, 2014. https://www.britannica.com/place/Southwark-London.

Britannica, T. Editors of Encyclopedia. "Spanish Armada." Encyclopedia Britannica, February 5, 2021. https://www.britannica.com/topic/Armada-Spanish-naval-fleet.

Britannica, T. Editors of Encyclopedia. "Toleration Act." Encyclopedia Britannica, May 17, 2022. https://www.britannica.com/event/Toleration-Act-Great-Britain-1689.

Britannica, T. Editors of Encyclopedia. "War of the Grand Alliance." Encyclopedia Britannica, December 13, 2016. https://www.britannica.com/event/War-of-the-Grand-Alliance.

Britannica, T. Editors of Encyclopedia. "War of the Spanish Succession." Encyclopedia Britannica, February 26, 2021. https://www.britannica.com/event/War-of-the-Spanish-Succession.

Bucholz, Robert, and Newton Key. Early Modern England 1485-1714: A Narrative History. 2nd ed. Chichester, West Sussex: Wiley-Blackwell, 2009.

Burton, I. F. "John Churchill, 1st Duke of Marlborough." Encyclopedia Britannica, June 14, 2021. https://www.britannica.com/biography/John-Churchill-1st-duke-of-Marlborough.

Carter, H., Gruffudd Pyrs, and Smith, Beverley. "Wales." Encyclopedia Britannica, November 30, 2021. https://www.britannica.com/place/Wales.

Castelow, Ellen. "The Pendle Witches." Historic UK. Accessed May 26, 2022. https://www.historic-uk.com/CultureUK/The-Pendle-Witches/.

Clark, James. The Dissolution of the Monasteries: A New History. New Haven: Yale University Press, 2021. https://search.ebscohost.com/login.aspx?direct=true&AuthType=ip,shib&db=nlebk&AN=3047017&site=eds-live&scope=site.

Clarke, C. Graham and Brereton, Bridget M. "West Indies." Encyclopedia Britannica, May 26, 2022. https://www.britannica.com/place/West-Indies-island-group-Atlantic-Ocean.

"Colonization." The Canadian Encyclopedia. Accessed June 14, 2022. https://www.thecanadianencyclopedia.ca/en/timeline/colonization-and-immigration.

Coops, Oliver. "Cornish Rebellion of 1497." Historic UK. Accessed May 31, 2022. https://www.historic-uk.com/HistoryUK/HistoryofEngland/Cornish-Rebellion-1497/.

Crowther, David. "Robert Kett's Petition, 1549." The History of England, May 27, 2020. https://thehistoryofengland.co.uk/resource/robert-ketts-petition-1549/.

Dickson, Andrew. "Key Features of Renaissance Culture." British Library, March 30, 2017. https://www.bl.uk/shakespeare/articles/key-features-of-renaissance-culture.

Dikshit, K., Schwartzberg, Joseph E., Srivastava, A. L., Spear, T. G. Percival, Wolpert, Stanley A., Thapar, Romila, Calkins, Philip B., Alam, Muzaffar, Subrahmanyam, Sanjay, Champakalakshmi, R., and Allchin, Frank Raymond. "India." Encyclopedia Britannica, June 8, 2022. https://www.britannica.com/place/India.

"Divine Right of Kings." Divine Right of Kings - New World Encyclopedia. Accessed February 15, 2022. https://www.newworldencyclopedia.org/entry/Divine_Right_of_Kings.

Edwards, R. Walter Dudley, Boland, Frederick Henry, Kay, Sean, Fanning, Ronan and Ranelagh, John O'Beirne. "Ireland." Encyclopedia Britannica, June 8, 2022. https://www.britannica.com/place/Ireland.

Elton, G. R., and Morrill, John S. "Henry VIII." Encyclopedia Britannica, January 24, 2022. https://www.britannica.com/biography/Henry-VIII-king-of-England

Fraser, A. "Mary." Encyclopedia Britannica, February 4, 2022. https://www.britannica.com/biography/Mary-queen-of-Scotland.

Grant, R. "Raid on the Medway." Encyclopedia Britannica, June 5, 2021. https://www.britannica.com/event/Raid-on-the-Medway.

Harris, L. and Hiller, James. "Newfoundland and Labrador." Encyclopedia Britannica, April 6, 2021. https://www.britannica.com/place/Newfoundland-and-Labrador.

Heisch, Allison. "Queen Elizabeth I: Parliamentary Rhetoric and the Exercise of Power." Signs 1, no. 1 (1975): 31–55. http://www.jstor.org/stable/3172965.

Heydenreich, L. Heinrich. "Leonardo da Vinci." Encyclopedia Britannica, April 28, 2022. https://www.britannica.com/biography/Leonardo-da-Vinci.

Hiller, J. and Harris, Leslie. "Newfoundland and Labrador." Encyclopedia Britannica, April 6, 2021. https://www.britannica.com/place/Newfoundland-and-Labrador.

Hogeback, J. "The Lost Colony of Roanoke." Encyclopedia Britannica, June 13, 2022. https://www.britannica.com/story/the-lost-colony-of-roanoke.

Johnson, Ben. "Dissolution of the Monasteries." Historic UK. Accessed May 24, 2022. https://www.historic-uk.com/HistoryUK/HistoryofEngland/Dissolution-of-the-Monasteries/.

Kenyon, J. P. "James II." Encyclopedia Britannica, October 10, 2021. https://www.britannica.com/biography/James-II-king-of-England-Scotland-and-Ireland.

Lewis, A. D. E., Glendon, Mary Ann and Kiralfy, Albert Roland. "Common Law." Encyclopedia Britannica, October 30, 2020. https://www.britannica.com/topic/common-law.

Macleod, I. C., Cameron, Ewen A., Brown, Alice and Moulton, Matthew James. "Scotland." Encyclopedia Britannica, October 6, 2021. https://www.britannica.com/place/Scotland.

Marty, M. E., Bainton, Roland H., Spalding, James C., Nelson, E. Clifford and Chadwick, W. Owen. "Protestantism." Encyclopedia Britannica, March 7, 2022. https://www.britannica.com/topic/Protestantism.

Mattingly, Garrett. "No Peace Beyond What Line?" Transactions of the Royal Historical Society 13 (1963): 145–62. https://doi.org/10.2307/3678733.

Mathew, D. "James I." Encyclopedia Britannica, June 15, 2021. https://www.britannica.com/biography/James-I-king-of-England-and-Scotland.

McMullan, John L. "CRIME, LAW AND ORDER IN EARLY MODERN ENGLAND." The British Journal of Criminology 27, no. 3 (1987): 252–74. http://www.jstor.org/stable/23637302.

Meigs, Samantha A., and Stanford E. Lehmberg. The Peoples of the British Isles: A New History: From Prehistoric Times to 1688. 4th ed. New York: Oxford University Press, 2016.

Mills, G. E.M. and Momsen, Janet D. "Saint Kitts and Nevis." Encyclopedia Britannica, March 10, 2021. https://www.britannica.com/place/Saint-Kitts-and-Nevis.

Morrill, J. S. "Edward Hyde, 1st Earl of Clarendon." Encyclopedia Britannica, February 14, 2022. https://www.britannica.com/biography/Edward-Hyde-1st-Earl-of-Clarendon.

Morrill, J. S. "Edward VI." Encyclopedia Britannica, October 8, 2021. https://www.britannica.com/biography/Edward-VI.

Morrill, J. S. and Greenblatt, Stephen J. "Elizabeth I." Encyclopedia Britannica, March 20, 2022. https://www.britannica.com/biography/Elizabeth-I.

Myers, A. Reginald and Morrill, John S. "Henry VII." Encyclopedia Britannica, January 24, 2022. https://www.britannica.com/biography/Henry-VII-king-of-England.

Ohlmeyer, J. H. "English Civil Wars." Encyclopedia Britannica, November 30, 2021. https://www.britannica.com/event/English-Civil-Wars.

Ravenhill, W., Barr, Nicholas A., Colley, Linda J., Gilbert, Bentley Brinkerhoff, Frere, Sheppard Sunderland, Chaney, William A., Spencer, Ulric M., Josephson, Paul R., Kellner, Peter, Hastings, Margaret, Kishlansky, Mark A., Joyce, Patrick, Briggs, Asa, Whitelock, Dorothy, Smith, Lacey Baldwin, Prestwich, Michael Charles, Morrill, John S. and Atkins, Ralph Charles. "United Kingdom." Encyclopedia Britannica, June 7, 2022. https://www.britannica.com/place/United-Kingdom.

Roseveare, H. Godfrey. "Charles II." Encyclopedia Britannica, February 2, 2022. https://www.britannica.com/biography/Charles-II-king-of-Great-Britain-and-Ireland.

Simons, E. Norman. "Mary I." Encyclopedia Britannica, February 14, 2022. https://www.britannica.com/biography/Mary-I.

Spencer, T. John Bew, Brown, John Russell and Bevington, David. "William Shakespeare." Encyclopedia Britannica, December 17, 2021. https://www.britannica.com/biography/William-Shakespeare.

Stone, Lawrence. 1949. "Elizabethan Overseas Trade." The Economic History Review 2 (1): 30-58. doi:10.2307/2590080.

Stuart, Charles I. THE KINGS SPEECH To both Houses of Parliament, the fifth of Iuly, 1641; Ann Arbor: Text Creation Partnership, 2022. https://quod.lib.umich.edu/e/eebo/A32124.0001.001/1:2?rgn=div1;view=fulltext

"The British West Indies." The British Empire in The Caribbean: The British West Indies. Accessed June 14, 2022. https://www.britishempire.co.uk/maproom/caribbean.htm.

"The Thirteen American Colonies." We the People. Accessed June 13, 2022. https://wethepeople.scholastic.com/grade-4-6/thirteen-american-colonies.html.

"Witchcraft - UK Parliament." UK Parliament. Accessed May 26, 2022. https://www.parliament.uk/about/living-heritage/transformingsociety/private-lives/religion/overview/witchcraft/.

Wolfe, Brendan. "Roanoke Colonies, The." Encyclopedia Virginia, May 24, 2022. https://encyclopediavirginia.org/entries/roanoke-colonies-the/.